MAYWOOD PUBLIC LIBRARY
3 12 0 98 714
9-09
W9-BUB-965
Maywood Public Library
121 S. 5th Ave.
Maywood, IL 60153

# The Complete Book of Pasta

The Complete Book of

# Pasta

The definitive guide to choosing, making and cooking your own pasta, with over 350 step-by-step recipes and over 1500 fabulous photographs

Editor **Jeni Wright**

This edition is published by Hermes House

Hermes House is an imprint of Anness Publishing Ltd
Hermes House, 88–89 Blackfriars Road, London SE1 8HA
tel. 020 7401 2077; fax 020 7633 9499; info@anness.com

© Anness Publishing Ltd 1999, 2005

All rights reserved. No part of this publication may be reproduced, stored in a retrieval system, or transmitted in any way or by any means, electronic, mechanical, photocopying, recording or otherwise, without the prior written permission of the copyright holder.

A CIP catalogue record for this book is available from the British Library.

Publisher: Joanna Lorenz
Executive Editor: Linda Fraser
Senior Editor: Toria Leitch
Copy Editor: Madeline Weston
Indexer: Dawn Butcher
Production Controller: Ben Worley
Designer: Carole Perks

Additional Recipes: Catherine Atkinson, Carla Capalbo, Maxine Clark, Roz Denny, Christine France, Sarah Gates, Shirley Gill, Norma MacMillan, Sue Maggs, Elizabeth Martin, Annie Nichols, Jenny Stacy, Liz Trigg, Laura Washburn, Steven Wheeler

Photography: William Lingwood (recipes) and Janine Hosegood (techniques and cut-outs), also Karl Adamson, Edward Allwright, David Armstrong, Steve Baxter, Jo Brewer, James Duncan, Michelle Garrett, Amanda Heywood, Patrick McLeavey, Michael Michaels

Food for Photography: Lucy McKelvie and Kate Jay (recipes) and Annabel Ford (techniques), also Nichola Fowler, Wendy Lee, Jane Stevenson, Elizabeth Wolf-Cohen

Illustrator: Anna Koska

Previously published as *Pasta Cooking*

10 9 8 7 6 5 4 3 2 1

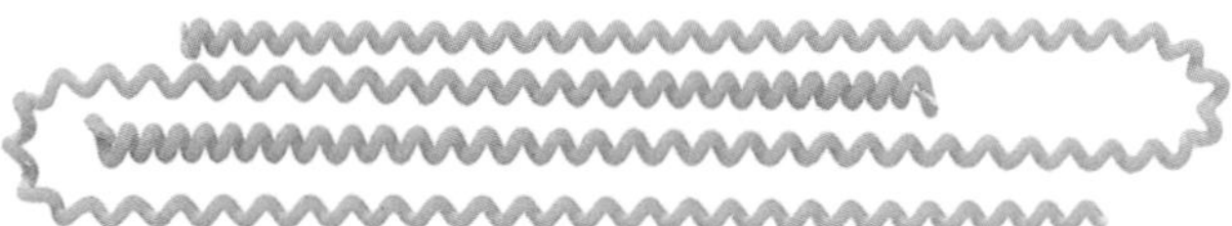

NOTES

For all recipes, quantities are given in both metric and imperial measures and, where appropriate, measures are also given in standard cups and spoons. Follow one set, but not a mixture because they are not interchangeable.

Standard spoon and cup measures are level.
1 tsp = 5ml, 1 tbsp = 15ml, 1 cup = 250ml/8fl oz

Australian standard tablespoons are 20ml. Australian readers should use 3 tsp in place of 1 tbsp for measuring small quantities of salt etc.

Medium eggs are used unless otherwise stated.

# CONTENTS

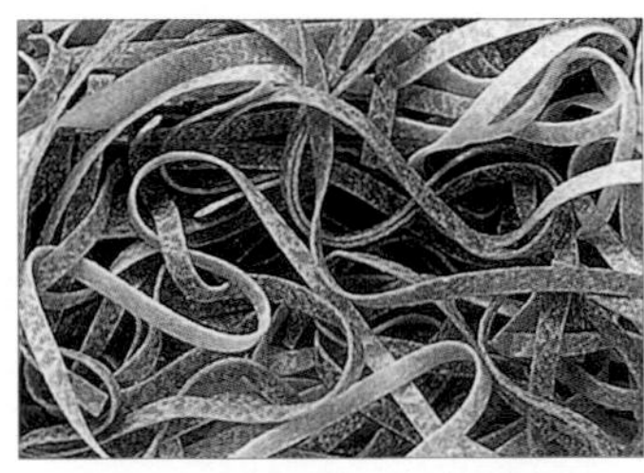

# Introduction

Pasta is one of the most popular foods in the world today. Available in an amazing range of shapes and flavors, it is incredibly versatile, and can be served in scores of different ways. Students love it for the energy it gives them at low cost, chefs delight in introducing light and healthy sauces for modern palates, families favor bakes that can be cooked ahead and which will stretch to serve extra guests. Simple or sophisticated, quick and easy to cook, it is the perfect choice for everyday and spur-of-the-moment meals.

# Introduction

## The origin of pasta

There is a great deal of controversy surrounding the origin of pasta. Who invented it? Was it the Chinese, the Italians, or even the Arabs? There is absolutely no doubt that Marco Polo brought noodles back to Italy from China in 1295, but most food historians agree that a kind of pasta was well known in Italy long before this time. Wall paintings in an Etruscan tomb show utensils—a pastry board, rolling pin and wheel—that are remarkably similar to those used today for making pasta. There is also evidence that the Romans made an unleavened dough of flour and water which they fried, cut into pasta-like strips and ate with a sauce. Apicius, the famous Roman gastronome of the 1st century AD, described baked dishes in which a pasta-like dough was layered with other ingredients. A kind of Roman lasagne?

Wherever or whenever pasta was first "invented," it seems to have been the Sicilians who were the first to boil it in water. They learnt irrigation and cultivation from the Arabs who conquered the island in the 9th century, and by the 12th century there is evidence they were eating a long thin type of pasta like spaghetti. Meanwhile, the Calabrians had mastered the art of twisting pasta strips to make tubes that resembled modern-day macaroni.

In a 13th-century Italian cook book published just before Marco Polo's return from China, there are recipes for making different pasta shapes, including ravioli, vermicelli and tortelli. So one way or another, pasta did exist in Italy before Marco Polo, and the pasta museum in Rome has many writings, paintings and etchings to substantiate this.

By the time of the Renaissance, pasta featured frequently on Italian menus. The rich Florentines teamed it with costly sugar and spices, but the less well-off had to content themselves with eating pasta plain or with humble ingredients, such as garlic, vegetables and cheese.

In those early days, pasta was simple, fresh and hand-made, a far cry from the many different commercially produced dried shapes and flavors that we know today. The credit for inventing these must go to the Neapolitans.

The fertile soil in the region around Naples was found to be ideal for growing durum wheat, which makes the best flour for commercial pasta, and the unique combination of sun and wind in this part of southern Italy was just right for drying out the shapes. Once the Neapolitans discovered this, the pasta-making industry burgeoned around the city of Naples, and by the late 18th century the consumption of pasta in Italy had really taken off. Maccheroni, spaghetti and tagliatelle were among the first shapes to be produced commercially, made with flour and water only.

At this time pasta was regarded as food for the poor, and tended to be served with tomato sauces. Tomatoes loved the growing conditions in the south as much as the durum wheat, and once the Italians fell in love with the tomato there was no going back.

The egg-enriched pasta that northern Italians favored was not produced commercially at this time. *Pasta all'uovo* was freshly

*There is no doubt that Marco Polo brought back noodles to Italy from China in the late 13th century. However, an Italian cook book, which was published just before his return, includes recipes for making pasta. His departure from Venice is depicted in this early 14th-century painting, Romance of Alexander.*

*Workers in the fields at Pitti Palace, Florence, in the late 19th century tending the hard durum wheat, which Italians call grano duro. This type of wheat produces the ideal flour for pasta.*

made, often with a meat filling or sauce, and was served to the rich. It was not until the 20th century that improvements in industrial equipment made the manufacture of egg pasta a viable commercial proposition.

## Pasta today

Wherever Italians went, they took their pasta with them. Those that emigrated to America and Great Britain adapted pasta shapes and sauces to suit local tastes and ingredients, a tradition which happily continues to this day.

Pasta is becoming more and more popular as a healthy, quick-cooking and versatile food, and Italian manufacturers have quickly responded to the demand, constantly developing new flavors and using the latest technology to create original shapes.

Commercially produced dried pasta has always been highly regarded in Italy. It is in no way inferior to fresh home-made pasta, but is simply a different form of this fabulous food. Italian cooks always keep a few packages of dried pasta in their store cupboards and use it on a daily basis—even in the north of Italy, where the tradition of making fresh pasta at home endured for a lot longer than it did in the south of the country.

## The right kind of wheat

The ideal variety of wheat for the flour used in commercial pasta making is durum (Triticum durum), which Italians call *grano duro*. This hard summer wheat produces a flour that is high in gluten. Dough made from durum wheat flour is pliable and easy to knead and shape. The majority of durum wheat for the Italian pasta-making industry is grown in Italy or imported from North America. The flour from durum wheat, called *semola* in Italian, makes a high quality pasta that holds its shape well. Cooked properly until *al dente*; it should be just tender, with a pleasant nutty bite. When you are buying pasta in packages, always check that it is made from 100 per cent durum wheat. The Italian phrase to look out for is *pasta di semola di grano duro*. This type of pasta may be more expensive than one made with a mixture of durum wheat and soft wheat, but you will get a much better result. Inexpensive pasta made with soft wheat flour tends to stick together during cooking and its texture is often soft and flabby. Generally speaking, the Italian makes are the best. Ask the staff at your local delicatessen or Italian specialty store which brands they recommend, and spend as much as you can afford. There is a big difference in texture and taste between the higher priced Italian brands and the cheaper types of pasta, and you will quickly find that it pays to buy the best.

## The northern preference for egg pasta

In southern Italy the majority of pasta is made with durum wheat and water only, and literally hundreds—if not thousands—of different shapes are manufactured. In northern Italy, the preference is for pasta with added egg, *pasta all'uovo*. The tradition for using this type of pasta began in Emilia, where filled and stuffed pasta shapes originated. Home cooks found that adding a little egg to the dough strengthened it, and helped to keep the filling in during cooking. As Italian housewives began

*Above: Healthy ingredients, such as olive oil, tomatoes, garlic and peppers, combine wonderfully well with pasta and are used over and over again by Italian cooks. This may be one of the reasons that the incidence of heart disease in Italy is one of the lowest in the world.*

*Below: The various sizes and shapes of holes in these commercial pasta dies allow for the production of a wide range of long and short pasta shapes.*

*Above right: In modern pasta factories sophisticated machines are used to weigh and pack the finished product.*

to make less and less fresh pasta at home and turned to buying it from the stores, small factories started making dried egg pasta to meet the demand. Now it is fast becoming a huge industry, although there are fewer fancy shapes made with egg than there are with plain pasta. This is because egg pasta is more difficult to work with. It is not used for making long thin shapes like spaghetti because they would break too easily. Commercially manufactured pasta all'uovo may contain as many as 7 eggs to 2 1/4 pounds flour, so it has a richer taste than plain pasta and absorbs more water.

If you buy Italian egg pasta, the packet should state that it is 100 per cent durum wheat and egg *(semola di grano duro e uova)*. *Pasta all'uovo* complements the cream and butter sauces that are popular in the north. The tomato and olive oil sauces of the south have always been traditionally served with plain pasta, although *pasta all'uovo* is now catching on in the south, too.

### The nutritional value of pasta

Rich in protein, vitamins and minerals, pasta is a complex carbohydrate food. It provides as much energy as a pure protein like steak, but with little or no fat. Of the eight amino acids essential to make up a complete protein, pasta contains six, so it only needs a small quantity of cheese, meat, fish, pulses or eggs—the traditional ingredients for serving with pasta—to make it complete. If you are using *pasta all'uovo*, you need even less additional protein.

The key to healthy eating lies in eating pasta as the Italians do, with only a small amount of extra ingredients. In Italy, it is traditional for pasta to be served as a first course, before the main course of fish or meat. Eaten with a small spoonful of sauce and a light sprinkling of grated cheese, nothing could be more well-balanced and nutritionally sound.

The incidence of heart disease in Italy is one of the lowest in the civilized world, and doctors, nutritionists and scientists agree that the Italian diet plays a large and important role in this. In Italian cooking, healthy ingredients, such as extra virgin olive oil, fresh and canned tomatoes, garlic, onions, olives, red bell peppers and fresh parsley are used all the time, plus lots of fresh fish, vegetables and salad greens, fruit, pulses and lemon juice. Most of these ingredients combine wonderfully well with pasta, and they are used over and over again in the recipes in this book.

Pasta is a completely natural food that contains no additives. Pasta with egg contains the most nutrients, while wholewheat pasta has the highest percentage of vitamins and fiber. Always check the label when buying colored pasta, because some varieties include artificial colorings.

Pasta is inexpensive, quick and easy to cook, and incredibly versatile. It is the perfect convenience food: in the time it takes to boil the water and cook the pasta, most sauces are ready to serve. *Pasta all'uovo* is especially nutritious and good for children who don't like eggs in a more recognizable form. Another plus point, which athletes and other sportspeople appreciate, is that as a high-energy food, pasta is easy to digest and yet immensely satisfying.

It makes sense, therefore, to include pasta in our diets as often as possible, if not every day. Since everybody loves it, this should be very easy to do. People watching their weight may be surprised to know that a 3 ounce portion of cooked pasta yields only about 100 calories and can therefore be eaten as part of a calorie-controlled diet, as long as it is only lightly sauced.

### Pasta as an everyday meal

In Italy pasta is generally eaten as a first course (*primo piatto* or just *primo*) as part of the main meal of the day. This may be at lunchtime or in the evening, depending on family circumstances and whether the meal is served during the week or at the weekend. The meal usually begins with antipasto, which is followed with a *primo piatto* of either soup, pasta, rice or gnocchi. Pasta used to be served as a lunchtime first course when lunch was traditionally the main meal of the day, but now that more and more Italian women are working outside the home, these customs are changing and there are fewer hard-and-fast rules about lunch and dinner. After the *primo piatto*, the second course, *secondo piatto*, is served. This is either fish or meat followed by vegetables or salad, then cheese, fresh fruit and coffee. Desserts are normally reserved for special occasions.

When pasta is served as a first course, the usual amount is 2½–3½ ounces uncooked weight per person. Sauce is added sparingly; this is usually tossed with the freshly drained hot pasta in the kitchen, and the mixture is then brought to the table in one large bowl.

*Colored pasta looks and tastes very good, but always check the label before buying, because some varieties include artificial colorings.*

By the time the pasta reaches the dining room it has mingled with the sauce and taken on some of its flavor. In some homes the bowl is passed around the table and everyone helps themselves, while in others one person does the serving. When you are serving pasta directly from the bowl, it looks most attractive if you retain a small ladleful of the sauce to put on top of the pasta after tossing, then sprinkle this with cheese or herbs at the last moment.

If it suits your lifestyle best to serve pasta as a main course for lunch or supper, simply increase the weight of uncooked pasta to 4–6 ounces per person and make more sauce. For convenience, you may prefer to serve pasta in shallow soup plates or bowls or on dinner plates. Warm these beforehand and serve and eat the pasta as soon as possible so that it can be enjoyed at its best. If you accompany your main course with a fresh leafy green salad and follow with some fresh fruit, you will have a tasty, nutritious and supremely satisfying meal. *Buon Appetito!*

*Although traditionally served from one large bowl that is passed around the table, you may prefer to serve pasta in shallow soup plates or bowls.*

# Dried Pasta

The many hundreds of different types of dried pasta are divided into categories. Long, short and flat shapes are the most common, but there are also stuffed shapes, shapes suitable for stuffing and tiny shapes for use in soup. Among these, you will find some less well-known regional shapes and the more unusual and decorative designer shapes.

Only buy dried pasta that is made using 100 per cent durum wheat. If you decant pasta shapes into storage jars, use up any remaining pasta before adding more from a new packet. Older pasta may take longer to cook than that from a fresher package, and different brands of the same shape may not necessarily have the same cooking time.

### Long Pasta / *Pasta Lunga*

Dried long pasta in the form of spaghetti is probably the best-known pasta of all time, and was certainly one of the first types to be exported from Italy. Spaghetti is still very widely used, but nowadays there are many other varieties of long pasta that look and taste just as good. There are no hard-and-fast rules when matching pasta to sauce, so experiment with alternative varieties to add interest to your cooking, always remembering that long pasta is best served with either a thin, clinging sauce or one that is smooth and thick. If too thin and watery, the sauce will simply run off the long strands; if too chunky or heavy, the sauce will fall to the bottom of the bowl and you will be left with a bowl full of chunks and no pasta to eat it with. Clinging sauces made with olive oil, butter, cream, eggs, finely grated cheese and chopped fresh herbs are good with long pasta. When ingredients such as vegetables, fish and meat are added to a smooth thick sauce, they should be very finely chopped.

Long pasta comes in different lengths, but 12 inches is about the average. In specialist food stores, you may see dried pasta that is much longer than this but think twice before buying it because extra-long pasta can be tricky to cook and eat, and often not worth the bother. The width of long pasta varies too; the strands can be flat, hollow, round or square, while other types have the pasta strands coiled up into nests.

Most long shapes are available in plain durum wheat only. The shapes made with egg (all'uovo) are very delicate, and are either packed in nests or compressed as waves. Fine long pasta, such as spaghetti, is far too delicate to be made with egg, but a short version from Emilia-Romagna, called capricciosa all'uovo, is available.

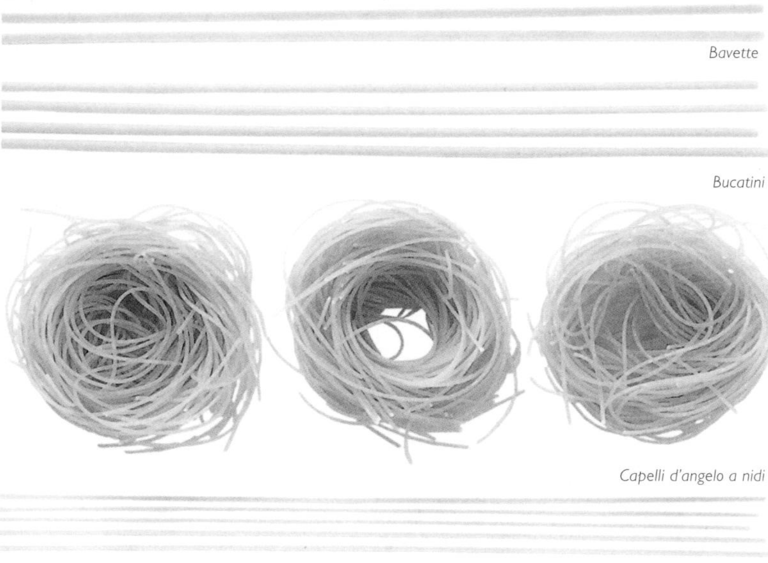

*Bavette*

*Bucatini*

*Capelli d'angelo a nidi*

*Capelli d'angelo*

*Capellini*

*Capellini a nidi*

**Bavette**

This type of long pasta is known all over Italy, but is very common in the South. The noodles are narrow and flat, like tagliatelle, only slimmer. Indeed, some southern Italians use the name bavette to describe tagliatelle. Bavettine is a narrower version. Both types can be plain or all'uovo (with egg).

**Bucatini**

This looks like spaghetti but is slightly chunkier. The strands are hollow (*buco* means hole), like hard, inflexible drinking straws. This type of pasta is best known in the Roman dish, *Bucatini all'Amatriciana*, which has a tomato, bacon and bell pepper sauce, and in Sicily it is traditionally served with a sauce of fresh sardines. Bucatoni is a fatter version, while perciatelli is bucatini by another name.

**Capelli d'angelo**

The name means angel's hair, which is an evocative description for this extremely fine pasta. It is used in broths and soups, and is popular with children. You may find it packed in nests, labeled capelli d'angelo a nidi. These nests are easy to handle and cook—one nest per person is the usual serving, so you can use as many nests as you require. Capellini and capel Venere are similar to capelli d'angelo.

**Chitarra**

Also known as spaghetti alla chitarra, this type of pasta is cut on a special wooden frame strung with wires like guitar strings (*chitarra* is Italian for guitar). It is therefore square shaped rather than round, but can be used as an alternative to spaghetti.

**Fusilli**

Spaghetti spirals that look like long opened-out corkscrews. You may see these labeled fusilli lunghi or fusilli col buco, to distinguish them from the more widely known short fusilli and eliche. Fusilli is often used with tomato sauces.

**Lasagnette**

This flat pasta resembles tagliatelle, but the noodles are slightly wider. There are several types, most of which have frilly edges. Reginette is similar. You can use lasagnette in place of any ribbon pasta.

**Linguine**

In Italian the name means little tongues and accurately describes a very thin spaghetti-like pasta that has flattened edges. You may also see linguinette and lingue di passera (sparrows' tongues), both of which are even narrower. Whole-wheat linguine is also available. All are good with the simple olive oil-based sauces and smooth tomato sauces of southern Italy.

**Maccheroni**

A very familiar form of pasta. We know a short version of it as macaroni, but in Italy the long thick tubes are widely used for all kinds of sauces—in some regions the word maccheroni is even used as a generic term for pasta and maccheroncini is simply the name given to very thin, long pasta. Maccheroni comes in different lengths and thicknesses, with straight or angled ends, in plain, egg and whole-wheat varieties. There is even a square-shaped chitarra version, which comes from Abruzzi. There they call it maccheroni alla chitarra, but it also goes by the name of tonnarelli. Maccheroni is useful because it goes with so many different sauces.

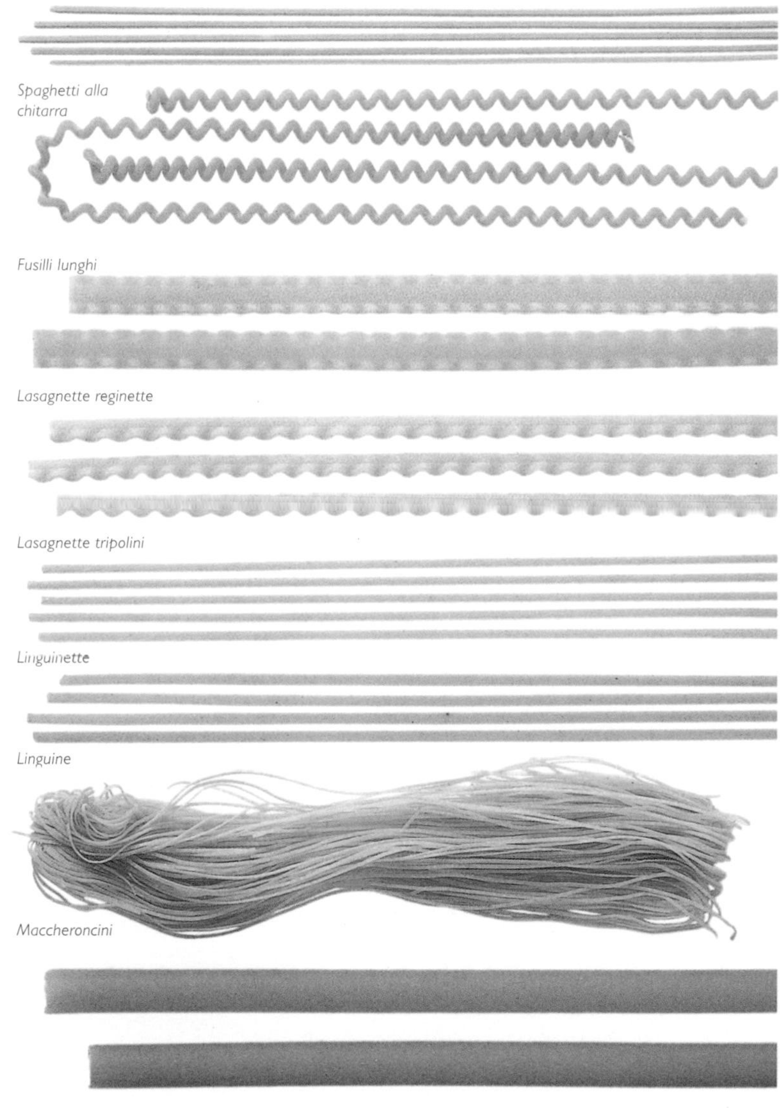

*Spaghetti alla chitarra*

*Fusilli lunghi*

*Lasagnette reginette*

*Lasagnette tripolini*

*Linguinette*

*Linguine*

*Maccheroncini*

*Maccheroni*

**Spaghetti**

This familiar type of pasta takes its name from the word *spago*, which means string. Spaghetti means little strings; spaghettini is a thinner variety, and spaghettoni is thicker. Spaghetti originally came from Naples, but today it is made in other parts of Italy too, and the length and width vary from one region to another.

Numerous different brands, flavors and colors are available, including whole-wheat (integrali), spinach (spinaci) and chile (peperoncini) so the choice is yours, but avoid the inexpensive brands. Long Italian spaghetti tends to be very good; it is graded by number according to the thickness. Good-quality spaghetti made in Italy is still one of the best forms of pasta, despite the ever-increasing range of other shapes. It goes well with many different kinds of sauces.

**Tagliatelle**

The most common form of ribbon noodles, tagliatelle derives its name from the Italian verb *tagliare* meaning to cut. The noodles are usually about 1/3–1/2-inch wide, but there are fine versions called tagliatellina, tagliarini and tagliolini, and an even finer type called tagliolini fini. Traditional tagliatelle comes from Bologna. It is made both with and without egg and with spinach (verdi), but new flavors and colors are constantly arriving in the market.

All types of tagliatelle are sold coiled in nests, which conveniently unravel during cooking when given a good stir. Paglia e fieno, which literally means straw and hay, is a mixture consisting of half plain egg and half spinach egg pasta, packed together in separate bundles of each color. The noodles are usually quite thin, either tagliarini or tagliolini. Both tagliatelle and paglia e fieno are very popular because they go well with most sauces, although strictly speaking, tagliatelle should not be served with a fish sauce. Meat sauce is the classic, as in *Tagliatelle alla Bolognese*.

The Roman version of tagliatelle is called fettuccine. These long, flat noodles are virtually the same as tagliatelle, but slightly thinner.

*Spaghetti*

*Spaghetti integrali*

*Spaghetti con spinaci*

*Spaghettoni*

*Spaghettini*

*Spaghettini con peperoncini*

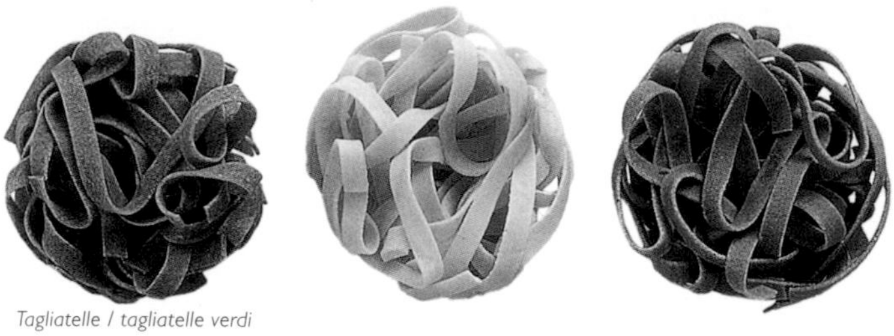

*Tagliatelle / tagliatelle verdi*

*Vermicelli*

*Ziti*

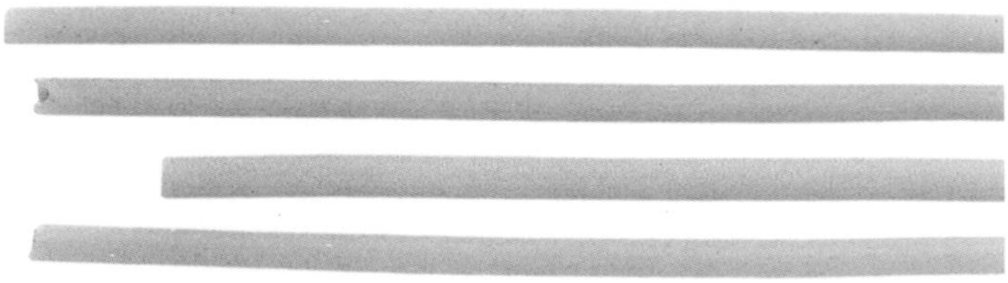

*Mezza zita*

### Vermicelli

This sounds appealing, but the name means little worms, which is rather unfortunate. It describes a very fine form of spaghetti—the original Neapolitan name for spaghetti was vermicelli, and southern Italians still sometimes refer to spaghetti as vermicelli, which can be confusing. This type of pasta comes in plain and egg (all'uovo) varieties and is very versatile, going well with most light sauces, but especially the light, fresh tomato and seafood sauces for which Naples is famous. There is an even finer version called vermicellini, and a similar noodle called fidelini.

### Ziti

This pasta takes its name from the word *zita*, meaning fiancée. In the old days it was traditional in southern Italy to serve ziti at wedding feasts and on other special occasions. Ziti is very long, thick and hollow—like maccheroni—and the custom is to break it into the length required when you cook it. Because of their size, the tubes go well with robust and chunky sauces; they are also sometimes broken into short lengths and baked in a *timballo*, which is a cup-shaped mold. The pasta is used to line the mold, which is then filled with a savory mixture such as mushrooms, ham or chicken livers combined with a sauce and topped with cheese. Zitoni are fatter than ziti; mezza zita are thinner.

*Tagliolini all'uovo*

*Paglia e fieno*

*Tagliarini all'uovo*

### Some Regional Types of Long Dried Pasta

Fettuccine comes from Lazio, and these noodles are used in classic Roman pasta dishes, such as *Fettuccine all'Alfredo*. They are flat ribbons, like tagliatelle but narrower (about 1/4-inch wide), and always sold coiled into loose nests. The three most common types are plain durum wheat, with egg (all'uovo), and with spinach (verdi), and you can use them interchangeably with tagliatelle. Fettuccelle is similar, but is straight rather than coiled. Fettuccelle integrali is the whole-wheat variety.

Frappe is a type of pasta from Emilia-Romagna. The 1–1 1/2-inch wide noodles are flat, with wavy edges, about halfway in size between tagliatelle and lasagne. Made with egg and very delicate, the noodles are packed by a special machine that presses them into waves.

Pappardelle are broad ribbon noodles (3/4–1-inch wide), with wavy edges. They come from Tuscany, where they are still made fresh with egg every day, but dried versions are now becoming more widely available, many of them with only one wavy edge or straight edges. They are good with heavy meat and game sauces. Nastroni are similar straight-sided noodles that are sold coiled into nests.

Trenette are noodles from Liguria, where they are traditionally served with pesto sauce. The Genoese dish, *Trenette alla Genovese*, combines trenette with pesto, potatoes and beans. The noodles are about 1/8-inch wide, and are made with egg. They resemble bavette and linguine, which can be substituted for them if you find trenette difficult to find.

*Fettuccine al nero*

*Pappardelle*

*Trenette*

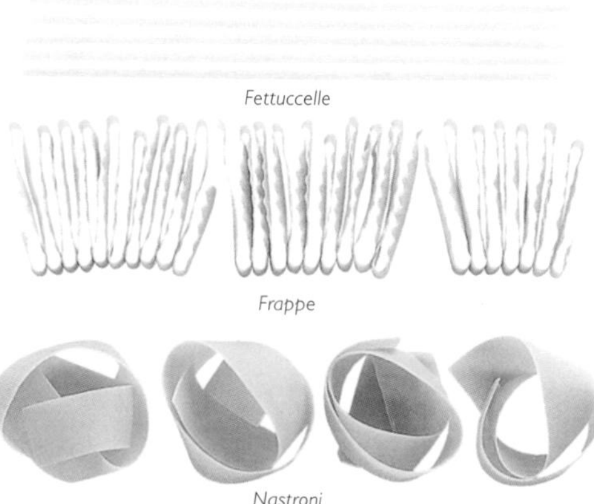

*Fettuccelle*

*Frappe*

*Nastroni*

## Short Pasta / *Pasta Corta*

There are literally hundreds of different short pasta shapes, and new ones are constantly arriving in stores. Some people prefer short pasta simply because it is easier to cook and eat than long pasta. It also goes well with many different sauces, and in most cases you can choose any shape you fancy, regardless of whether your sauce is a smooth tomato-, cream- or olive oil-based type, or is chunky with large pieces of fish, meat or vegetables. Exceptions are regional dishes that are traditionally cooked with a specific shape, such as *Penne all'Arrabbiata* from Lazio.

Short pasta is divided into two main groups. Pasta secca is factory-made, using durum wheat flour and water. This is by far the largest group, and you will find that most packages of dried pasta list only these two ingredients on the label. *Pasta all'uovo* is made with the addition of eggs. It is naturally a brighter yellow than pasta secca and has more nutritional value. Popular in the north of Italy, especially in Emilia-Romagna, *pasta all'uovo* has different properties from plain pasta and goes especially well with the rich creamy and meaty sauces associated with that part of Italy. It has an advantage over plain durum wheat pasta in that it cooks slightly more quickly and is less likely to become overcooked and soggy. Although it is more expensive than plain pasta, egg pasta is becoming more popular and therefore more widely available, so look out for it in an increasing number of shapes.

New flavors and colors in short pasta shapes are on the increase too. For many years, tomato (pomodoro) and spinach (verde) were all that was available, but today there seems to be no end to the number of different color and flavor combinations, ranging from garlic, chiles and herbs to beet, salmon, mushroom, squid ink and even chocolate. Often three colors (red, white and green) are packed together and labelled tricolore. Whole-wheat pasta, called pasta integrale, is made from durum wheat and other cereals. It is higher in fiber than plain durum wheat pasta and takes longer to cook. It has a chewy texture and nutty flavor.

*Benfatti*

**Benfatti**

The word *benfatti* means well made and originally described the little scraps of pasta left over from making other shapes, such as tagliatelle. Traditionally these were used in soups so they would not be wasted, but they proved so popular that they are now made and marketed as a shape in their own right. Benfatti are available plain and with egg, and are good in salads as well as soups.

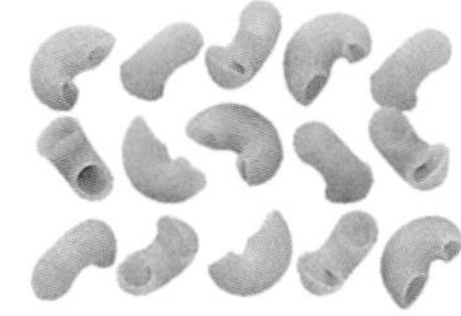

*Chifferini rigatini*

**Chifferini**

Also called chifferi, chifferoni and chifferotti, these are small curved tubes like short maccheroni that has been bent. Some versions are ridged (rigatini). The holes in the middle fill with sauce, making them an excellent shape for all types of pasta sauces and soups.

*Conchigliette rigate*

**Conchiglie**

As the name suggests, these shapes resemble small conch shells. Sometimes they are ridged, in which case they are called conchiglie rigate. They are one of the most useful small shapes because they are concave and trap virtually any sauce. For this reason they are extremely popular and are widely available in many different colors

*Conchiglie rigate*

*Conchiglioni rigati*

and flavors. Sizes vary too, from tiny conchigliette for soups to conchiglione, which are jumbo shells for stuffing.

**Eliche**

The name comes from the Italian word for screws or propellers, which is exactly what these shapes look like. They are often mislabeled as fusilli, which are similar, but when you see the two side by side there is a marked difference. Eliche are short lengths of pasta, each twisted into a spiral, like the thread of a screw. They are available in different thicknesses, colors and flavors, including whole-wheat and tricolore, and are good with most sauces, but especially those that are tomato-based. You may only be able to buy them labeled as fusilli—the two are interchangeable and their names often depend on which part of Italy they come from.

*Eliche all'uovo*

*Eliche tricolori*

*Farfalle*

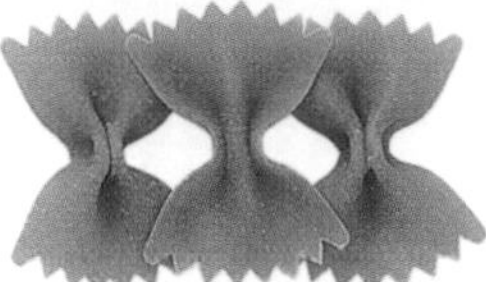

*Farfalle verde*

*Farfalle salmonseppia*

*Farfalle tricolore*

**Farfalle**

The word means butterflies, but these shapes are sometimes also described as bow-ties—the Italian word for bow-tie is *cravatta a farfalla.* They are very pretty, with crinkled edges, and are sometimes ridged. Due to their popularity, farfalle are available in a wide variety of colors and flavors, including plain, with egg and tricolore (plain, tomato and spinach flavors, which are sold together in mixed packages). Farfalle can be served with any sauce, but they are particularly good with cream and tomato sauces. Children love them. In Modena, farfalle are known as strichetti.

**Fusilli**

These spirals of thin pasta look like tight coils or springs and are formed by winding fresh dough around a thin rod. The spiral opens out, rather than remaining solid as it does in the case of eliche, for which fusilli are often mistaken. Check when buying, because most packages of fusilli are in fact eliche. Genuine fusilli is likely to be plain, neither made with egg nor colored. The shapes go well with thin sauces.

*Fusilli*

*Fusilli con spinaci*

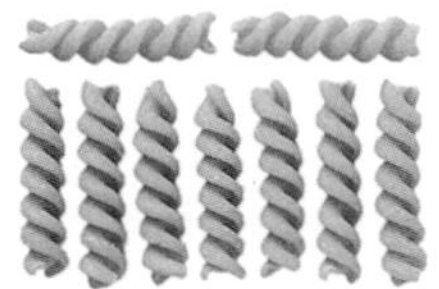

*Fusilli all'uovo*

*Lumache rigate*

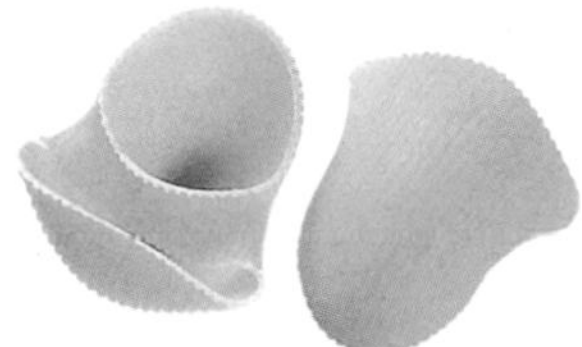

*Lumachoni rigati*

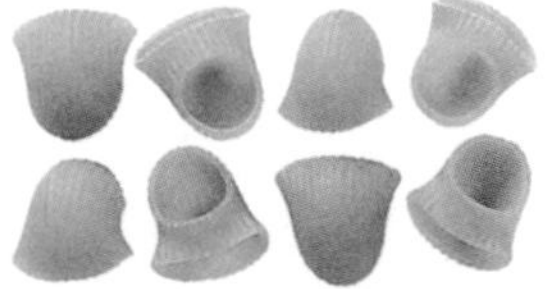

*Gomiti rigati*

*Maccheroni*

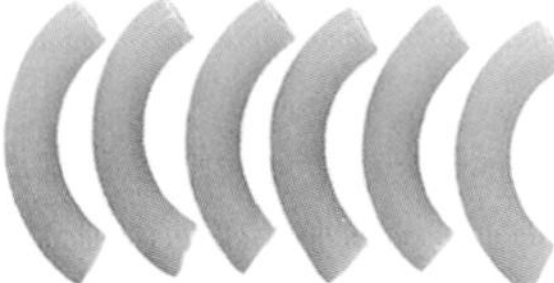

*Maccheroncelli*

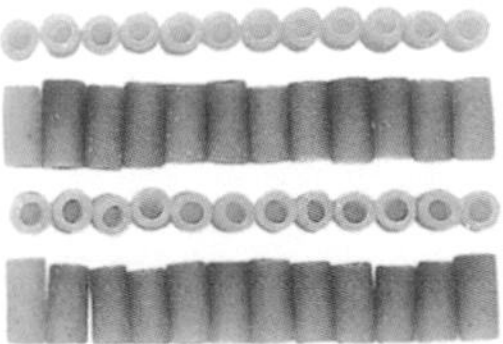

*Tubetti*

**Lumache**

Snail shells were the inspiration for this attractively shaped pasta. Unlike conchiglie, they are not shaped like conch shells, but resemble a larger version of pipe, because they are fashioned out of hollow pasta. Lumache are excellent for trapping sauces. The most common type available is lumache rigate (ridged), and there is also a large version called lumaconi. Gomiti is a similar conch shell shape.

**Maccheroni**

When cooks in the south of Italy speak of maccheroni, they usually mean long pasta, but in the north of the country they prefer it short. It is the short type that is generally exported as macaroni (sometimes labeled "elbow macaroni" although some brands are straighter than others). This used to be the most common short pasta shape outside Italy, but other more interesting shapes now rival its popularity. Being hollow, it is a good shape for most sauces and baked dishes, so will always remain popular. Both plain and egg maccheroni are available, and there are also many different sizes, including a thin, quick-cooking variety. Tubetti is the name given to a miniature version that is often used in soups.

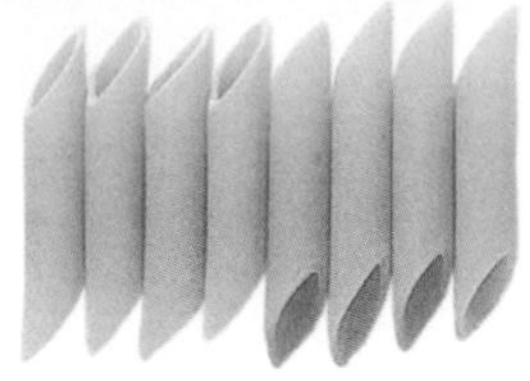

Penne lisce

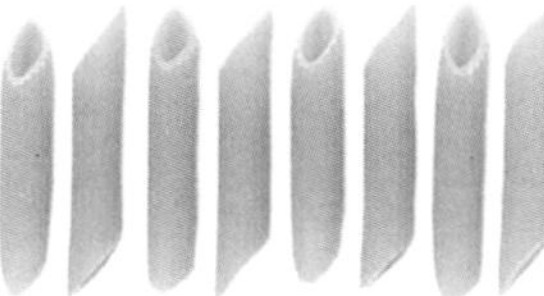

Penne rigate

Penne rigate con spinaci

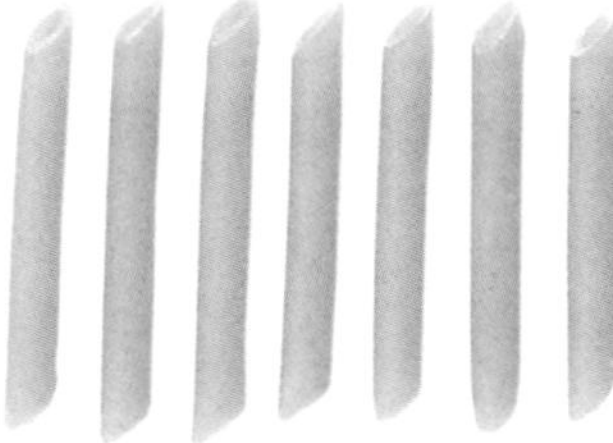

Penne mezzanine

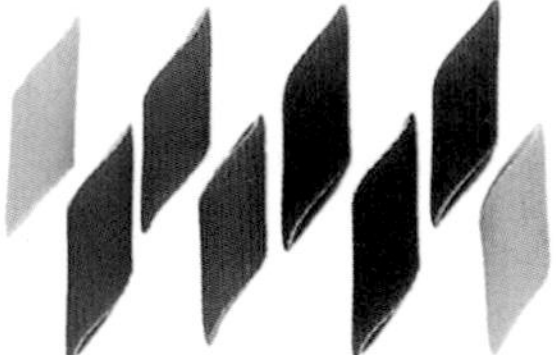

Mezze penne tricolori

Pennoni

**Penne**

Like maccheroni, penne are hollow tubes, but their ends are cut diagonally so they are pointed like quills (penne means feather or quill pen). In the popularity stakes, they seem to have taken over from maccheroni, possibly because of their more interesting shape. They go well with virtually every sauce and are particularly good with chunky sauces as their sturdiness means that they hold the weight well. Penne lisce are smooth; penne rigate are ridged. Other less common varieties include the small and thin pennette and even thinner pennini and penne mezzanine, the short and stubby mezze penne or "half penne", and the large pennoni. Penne made with egg and flavored penne are very common.

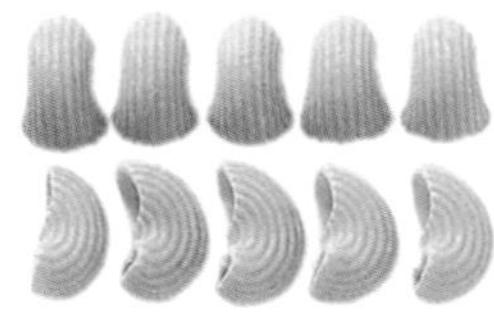

Pipe rigate

**Pipe**

These shapes look like a cross between conchiglie and lumache. They are curved and hollow (the name means pipes) and more often than not ridged (pipe rigate). As short pasta shapes go, they are quite small. They are excellent for catching sauce and make an interesting change from other more common hollow varieties. Plain and whole-wheat types are available, and there is also a smaller version called pipette.

Rigatoni

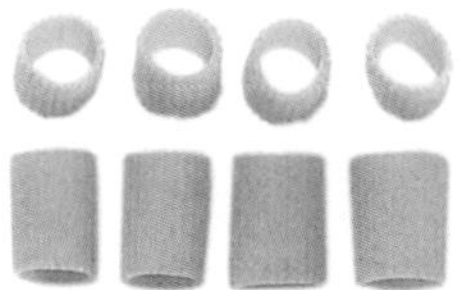

Mezzi rigatoni

Elicoidali

Elicoidali con basilico

**Rigatoni**

From the maccheroni family, these are ridged, hollow, chunky-looking shapes. They are very popular because they are sturdy enough to hold chunky sauces, and they come in many flavors. There is a short version called mezzi rigatoni and a straight, stubby version called millerighe. The texture of rigatoni always seems slightly chewier than that of other short pasta. Similar in shape but slightly narrower are elicoidali, which have curved ridges (their name means helixes). Elicoidali can be plain or flavored with ingredients such as basil.

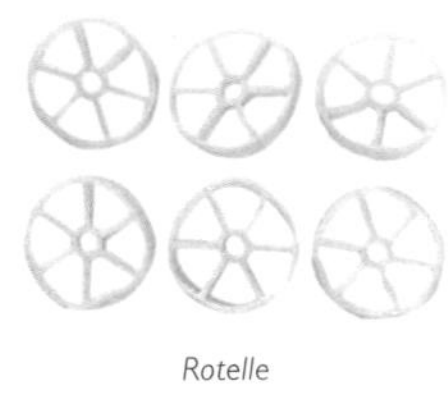

Rotelle

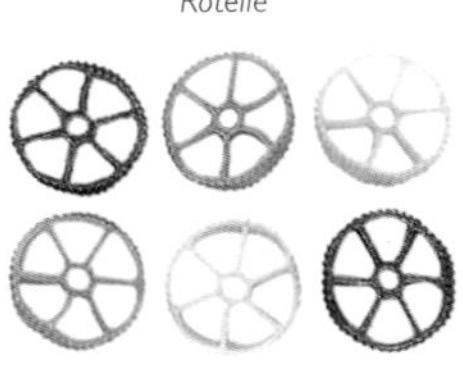

Rotelle tricolore

**Rotelle**

These are cartwheel shapes. There is a ridged variety, rotelle rigate, and sometimes this shape goes under other names such as ruote, ruote di carro and trulli. Although not a classic Italian shape, the spokes of the wheels are very good for holding chunky sauces. Children like them, and most supermarkets sell them in different colors and flavors. The plain Italian brands taste very good.

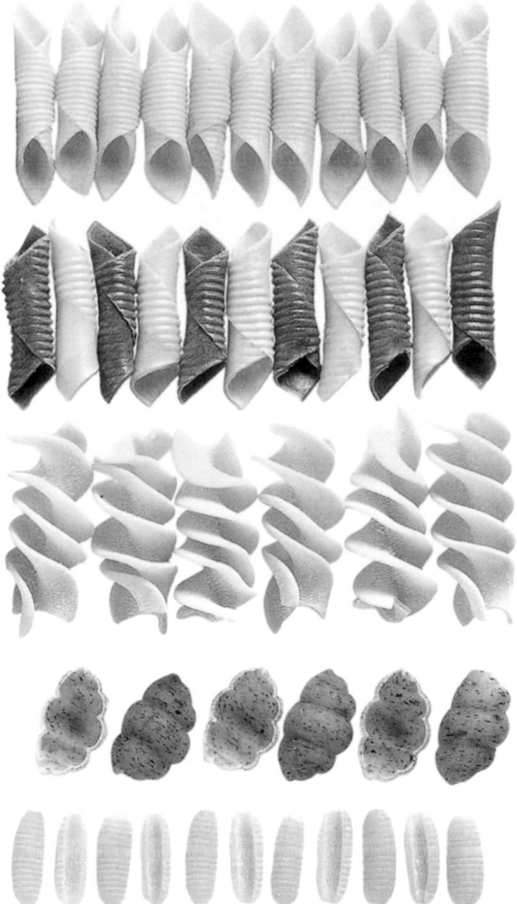

Above from the top: Garganelli all'uovo, garganelli paglia e fieno, girondole di Puglia, gnocchi sardi integrali and gnocchetti sardi

## Some Regional Types of Short Dried Pasta

Garganelli come from Emilia-Romagna. They are tubular egg pasta shapes that resemble penne, but which look more like scrolls than quills because you can clearly see how they have been rolled. This is done on a special tool, called *il pettine*, that looks like a large comb.

Gnocchi sardi are from Sardinia. They are named after the gnocchi potato dumplings, but are smaller, like little razor shells. Gnocchetti sardi are smaller still, and are mostly used for soups. Malloreddus is another Sardinian name for gnocchi. These shapes are often flavored with saffron, and served with traditional meat and vegetable sauces. They are quite chewy in texture.

Orecchiette, or little ears, are from Puglia in the south-east of Italy. Always made with durum wheat, they have a chewy texture and are served with the traditional sauces of the region, especially those made with broccoli.

Pizzoccheri are buckwheat noodles from Valtellina in Lombardy, not far from the border with Switzerland. They are thin and flat and usually sold in nests (a nidi) like fettuccine, but they are about half the length. Pizzoccheri are also sometimes cut to make short noodles. Their flavor is nutty, and they go well with the robust flavors of northern Italian cuisine, most famously with cabbage, potatoes and cheese in the baked dish of the same name.

Strozzapreti, which literally translated means priest stranglers, come from Modena. They are said to derive their name from the story of a priest who liked them so much he ate too many—and nearly choked to death. In fact, strozzapreti consist of two pieces of pasta twisted or "strangled" together. Other similar twisted shapes are caserecce, fileia and gemelli. The Genoese trofie, although not twisted, are similar, and can be substituted for strozzapreti.

Trofie are from the Ligurian port of Genoa, where it is traditional to serve them with pesto sauce. They are rolls of solid pasta with pointed ends, quite small and dainty. At one time you could only get home-made trofie, but now they are available dried in Italian delicatessens or specialty food stores, in which case the shapes are sometimes open along one side rather than solid. They are well worth buying if you want to make an authentic *Genoese Trofie al Pesto*.

Gnocchetti sardi

Orecchiette

Pizzocheri a nidi

Short-cut pizzocheri

Strozzapreti

Trofie

### Flat Pasta

Although there are many kinds of long flat ribbon pasta, such as fettuccine and tagliatelle, there is really only one broad, flat pasta used for baking in the oven (al forno), and that is lasagne. Thin sheets of lasagne are designed to be baked between layers of sauce in the oven, or cooked in boiling water until *al dente*, rolled around a filling to make cannelloni, then baked. All types of lasagne are designed to be used in this way, and are never served with a separate sauce.

**Plain lasagne**

Made from durum wheat and water, this type of lasagne comes flat-packed in cartons. There are three different colors—yellow (plain), green (verdi), which is made with spinach, and brown or whole-wheat (integrali). The shape varies according to the manufacturer, from narrow or broad rectangles to squares. Most sheets are completely flat, but some are wavy all over. Others have crimped or curly edges, which help to trap the sauce and look attractive too. Get to know the different brands and their sizes and choose the ones that fit your baking dish, to avoid having to cut them to fit. This makes light work of assembling the layers before baking. Check the cooking instructions on the carton because regular plain lasagne needs to be pre-cooked before being layered or rolled. The usual method is to plunge about four sheets at a time into a large pan of salted boiling water, boil for about 8 minutes until *al dente*, then carefully remove each sheet with a large slotted spoon and/or tongs and lay it flat on a damp cloth to drain. The sheets need to be drained in a single layer or they will stick to each other. This method is fairly time-consuming and messy, but once it has been completed and the lasagne has been assembled, the cooking time in the oven is usually about 30 minutes.

Lasagnette are long, narrow strips of flat pasta, which are crimped on one or two sides. They are used in the same way as lasagne, layered with sauces, then topped with grated cheese and baked in the oven. Festonelle are small squares of lasagnette,

*Lasagne verdi*

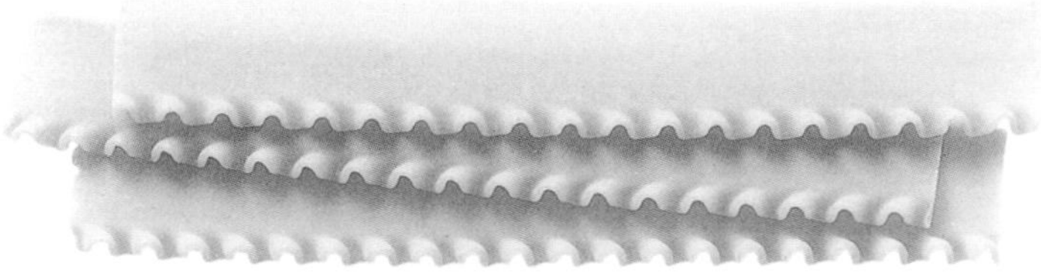

*Lasagnette*

*Lasagnette*

*Festonelle*

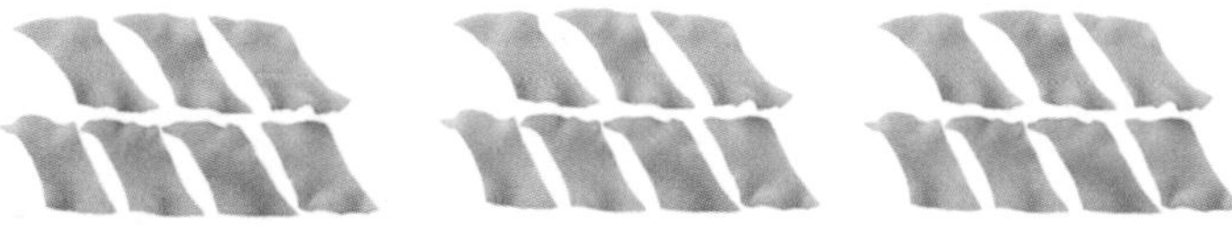

*Pantacce*

*Lasagne*

*Lasagne*

*Lasagne verdi*

*Lasagne verdi all'uovo*

which are also used in baked dishes. Pantacce are tiny diagonal pieces cut from lasagnette. They are similar to the hand-cut quadrucci and can be used in baked dishes, but are more often added to soups.

**Lasagne all'uovo**

This type of lasagne is made with durum wheat and water like plain lasagne, but with the addition of egg. This makes it a brighter yellow than plain lasagne, and richer in flavor and nutrients. It is available as plain egg (lasagne all'uovo) and egg and spinach (lasagne verdi all'uovo). Like the plain lasagne, it comes in different shapes and sizes with a variety of different edgings.

*Lasagne*

*Lasagne all'uovo*

**Easy-cook Lasagne**

Although a relatively recent innovation, easy-cook lasagne is fast becoming the number one favorite. Sometimes labeled "no pre-cooking required," it does not need to be boiled first, but is layered in the baking dish straight from the package, so saving lots of time and mess. As with the plain and egg lasagne, it comes in all sorts of different shapes, sizes and colors, with straight or fancy edges. It is easiest to use if it is the right shape to fit neatly into your baking dish, although it can be broken to fit. Baking time is slightly longer than with the pre-boiled varieties, so allow at least 40 minutes. Make sure that the sauce you use is runnier than usual because this type of lasagne absorbs liquid during baking and needs extra sauce to keep it moist.

*Tortellini all'uovo*

*Tortellini verdi*

*Ravioli all'uovo*

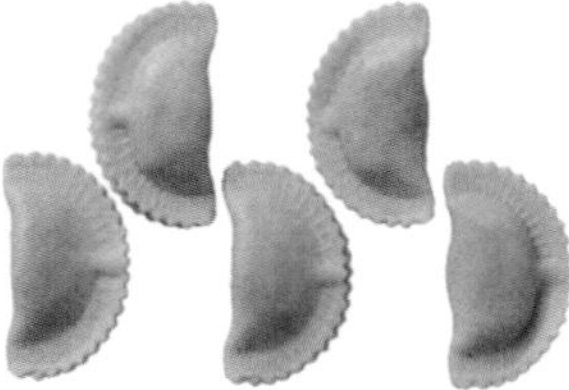

*Agnolotti all'uovo*

### Dried Stuffed Pasta / *Pasta Ripiena*

The most common dried stuffed pasta shapes are tortellini (little pies), a speciality of Bologna said to be modeled on the shape of Venus's navel. They are made from rounds or circles of pasta, so they look like little plump rings; another name for them is anolini. Some Italian delicatessens and specialty food stores also sell dried cappelletti (little hats), which resemble tortellini but are made from squares of pasta so have little peaks. Cappelletti are more likely to be sold fresh than dried. The same goes for ravioli and agnolotti, although you may find them in larger supermarkets. Tortellini are popular dried because they are traditionally used *in brodo*—simmered in a clear beef or chicken stock until they swell and plump up to make a satisfying soup. Most Italian cooks keep a package or two of tortellini in the store cupboard for just this purpose, and *Tortellini in Brodo* is often served for an evening meal when the main meal of the day has been at lunchtime. You can also be sure that *Tortellini in Brodo* will be served as a pick-me-up if ever a member of the family is unwell. They are also traditionally served on New Year's Eve in Bologna, perhaps as an antidote to the excesses of Christmas.

Dried tortellini are generally available with a choice of fillings—with meat (*alla carne*) or cheese (*ai formaggi*). The pasta is made with egg and may be plain and yellow in color, green if flavored with spinach, or red if flavored with tomato. All types of tortellini need to be cooked for at least 15 minutes to allow time for the pasta to swell and the ingredients in the filling to develop their flavor. Meat fillings are a mixture of pork sausage and beef with bread crumbs, Parmesan cheese and spices. Cheese fillings usually consist of a minimum of 35 per cent cheese mixed with bread crumbs and spices.

Dried tortellini are a useful store-cupboard item as they will keep for up to 12 months (but always check the use-by date on the package). For a soup, only a handful of the filled shapes are needed and the package can be resealed. Tortellini are also good boiled, then drained and tossed in melted butter and herbs or a cream, tomato or meat sauce, and served with grated Parmesan. Children like their shape, and they provide a good way of persuading them to eat meat and cheese. A 9-ounce package will serve four people.

### Dried Pasta for Stuffing / *Pasta da Ripieno*

Large pasta shapes are made commercially for stuffing and baking in the oven. Fillings vary, from meat and poultry to spinach, mushrooms and cheese, and the pasta can be baked in either a béchamel or a tomato sauce. Keep the filling moist and the sauce runny to ensure that the finished dish will not be dry. Dried shapes make an interesting change from lasagne, especially for children's meals, and they are attractive as a first course for a dinner party. They do not need to be boiled before being stuffed.

*Cannelloni*

**Cannelloni**

These large pasta tubes (their name means large reeds) are about 4 inches long. Plain, spinach and whole-wheat versions are available. In Italy, cannelloni is traditionally made from fresh sheets of lasagne rolled around a filling, but the ready-made dried tubes are convenient and less time-consuming to use. They are easy to stuff, using either a teaspoon or a pastry bag.

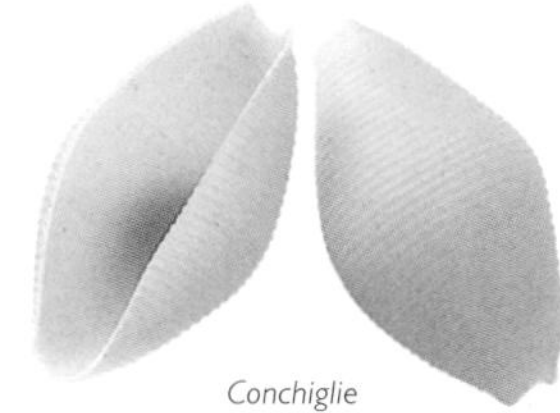

*Conchiglie*

**Conchiglie**

Sometimes also called conchiglioni, these jumbo conch shells are available in plain, spinach and tomato flavors, both smooth and ridged. There are often two sizes—medium and large—both of which are suitable for stuffing, although you will probably find the larger ones less fiddly.

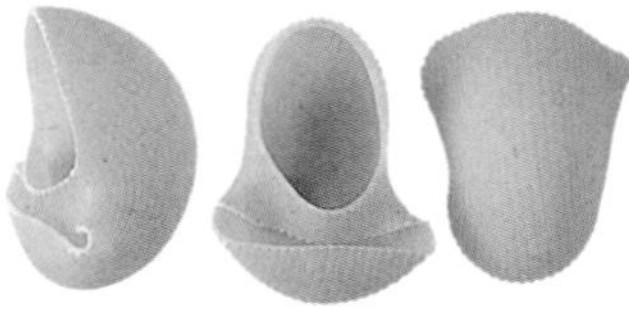

*Lumaconi*

**Lumaconi**

These are like conchiglie, but are elbow-shaped—like large snail shells—with an opening at either end. The ones most commonly available are plain and ridged, but you may find different colors in specialty food stores. You may also come across similar shapes called chioccioloni, gorzettoni, manicotti and tuffolini.

*Alfabetini* 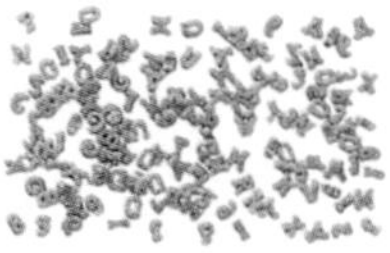 | *Alfabetini integrali*  | *Risoni*  | *Risoni all'uovo*

*Tubettini*  | *Quadretti*  | *Anellini* 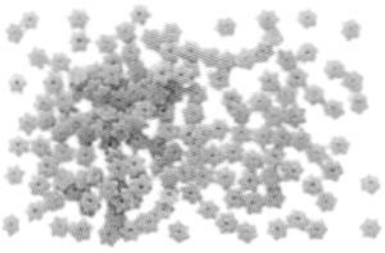 | *Stelline*

*Farfalline all'uovo* 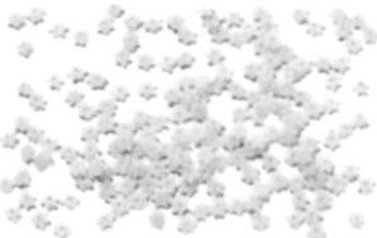 | *Stellette*  | *Ditalini rigati*  | *Conchigliette*

*Tubetti*  | *Occhi di lupo*  | *Mezzi tubetti*  | *Funghetti all'uovo*

**Dried Pasta for Soup / *Pastina***

Extremely small pasta shapes are called pastina in Italian, and there are literally hundreds of different ones to choose from. They are mostly made from plain durum wheat, although you may find them with egg and even flavored with carrot or spinach. In Italy they are always served in broths and clear soups, and are regarded almost as nursery food because they are so often served for children's meals (many Italian babies are weaned on them) or as a pick-me-up for adults who are not feeling well. If you stay in an Italian hospital, you are likely to be served *Pastina in Brodo*.

Shapes of pastina vary enormously, and seem to get more and more fanciful as the market demands.

The smallest and most plain pasta per minestre (pasta for soups) are like tiny grains. Some look like rice and are in fact called risi or risoni, while others are more like barley and are called orzi. Fregola, from Sardinia, look like couscous, and have a similar nutty texture and flavor. Semi di melone are like melon seeds, as their name suggests, while acini de pepe or peperini are named after peppercorns, which they resemble in shape and size if not in color. Coralline, grattini and occhi are three more very popular tiny shapes.

The next size up are the ones that are most popular with children. These include alfabeti and alfabetini (alphabet shapes), stelline and stellette (stars), rotellini (tiny wagon wheels) and anellini, which can be tiny rings, sometimes with ridges that make them look very pretty, or larger hoops. Ditali are similar to anellini but slightly thicker, while tubettini are thicker still.

Another category of pasta per minestre consists of slightly larger shapes, more like miniature versions of familiar types of short pasta. Their names end in "ine", "ette" or "etti", denoting that they are the diminutive forms. These include conchigliette (little shells), farfalline and farfallette (little bows), funghetti (little mushrooms), lumachine

*Peperini*

(little snails), quadretti and quadrettini (little squares), orecchiettini (little ears), renette (like baby penne) and tubetti (little tubes). The size of these varies: the smaller ones are for use in clear broths, while the larger ones are more often used in thicker soups, such as minestrone.

# Designer Pasta

Relative newcomers to the market are the pasta shapes that bear little or no resemblance to the traditional or regional Italian varieties. Many of these are made outside Italy in any case, while the ones made in Italy are often for export only. It seems that the majority of Italians are happy enough with the pasta they know and love.

Supermarkets, gourmet specialty stores, and specialty delicatessens are the best places to find these new shapes. Quality varies enormously, and some of them are nothing more than a gimmick, with very disappointing textures and flavors. Others are more successful, especially the ones made by long-established Italian firms. They make a change from the more usual shapes and are often an interesting talking point, especially when you are entertaining. As a general rule, flavored pasta is best served with very simple sauces based on olive oil or butter, otherwise the flavors of the pasta and sauce tend to fight one another.

### Long Shapes and Noodles

Spaghetti and tagliatelle are often flavored and colored. These shapes are either dramatically long or coiled in nests (*a nidi*), and you can even buy a type of pasta called spagliatelle, which is like a cross between the two. You can choose from a single flavor in one package, or up to five different flavors mixed together, and they can be either plain durum wheat pasta or made with the addition of egg and labeled "all'uovo." Spinach, tomato, mushroom, beet, saffron and smoked salmon are all popular flavors, but there are also other stronger flavors, such as chile and garlic (singly and together) and black squid ink (*nero di seppia*).

*Tagliatelle flavored with red and green chiles*

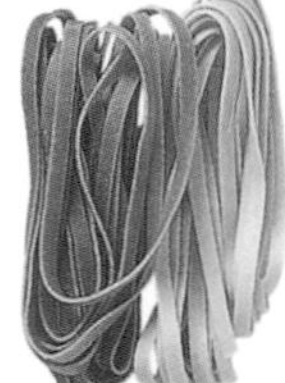

*Egg and smoked salmon-flavored tagliatelle*

*Three-color tagliatelle*

*Garlic- and chile-flavored spaghetti*

*Porcini-flavored tagliatelle*

*Tagliatelle flavored with squid ink and bottarga (mullet roe)*

*Porcini-flavored tagliatelle*

*Poppy seed tagliatelle*

*Porcini-flavored bavette*

*Five-color spagliatelle*

*Multi-colored arlecchino*

*Basil-flavored strangozzi*

One of the most fanciful combinations comes from Venice. Called arlecchino (harlequin), it is a mixture of black (squid ink), green (spinach and herbs), red (tomato and beet) and blue (blueberry and blue Curaçao liqueur). More common and perhaps most successful is tagliatelle speckled with herbs or seeds or, if it comes from Tuscany, flavored with wild mushrooms (porcini). A broad variety of tagliatelle called bavette from Puglia is also flavored with porcini. Strangozzi is an unusual thin noodle from Umbria. It comes plain and flavored with spinach, basil or tomato. It is sometimes sold twisted into a long, thick plait, which looks pretty in the package, but is best broken into short lengths to cook.

### Short Shapes

The most inventive and unusual designer shapes fall into this category. Short pasta is the easiest pasta to eat and so it's the most popular. Manufacturers, ever on the lookout to make and sell more, quickly realised that new short shapes had the most appeal and so developed this sector of the market more than any other. Ever since the 19th century competition in the pasta industry has thrived on the "design" of different short shapes, with some more successful at holding sauces than others. Among these are the frilly ballerine, fiorelli, gigli del gargano, rocchetti rigati and spaccatella, all of which trap sauces quite well but somehow give a strange sensation in the mouth. Shapes such as banane, coralli rigati, creste di gallo, radiatori and riccioli are perhaps too gimmicky for their own good; so too are the mixed bags of highly colored pasta shapes, such as the seven-color orecchiette (little ears) and five-color chiocciolоni (snails), which includes chocolate-flavored pasta along with the more run-of-the-mill plain, tomato, squid ink and wild mushroom (porcini) varieties.

These colored designer pasta shapes are often labeled *lavorazione artigianale* or *prodotto artigianale*, to indicate that they are made by artisans or local craftsmen, but they are too often disappointing, and they rarely match up to the more traditional shapes that have been tried and tested over very many years.

*Five-color chiocciolоni are made from plain pasta and pasta flavored with squid ink, chocolate, tomato and porcini*

*Spinach, plain and tomato conchiglie (hand-crafted shells)*

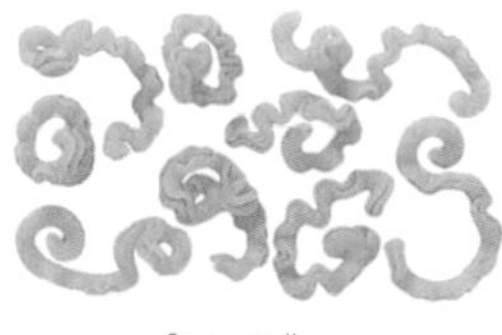

*Spaccatella*

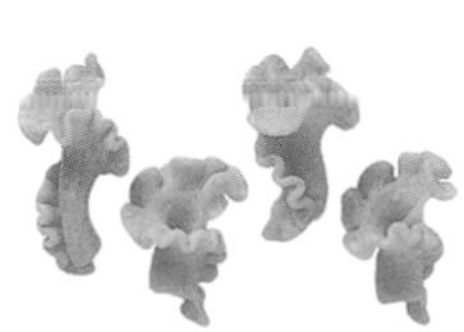

*Gigli del gargano*

*Seven-color orecchiette are made from plain pasta and pasta flavored with spinach, tomato, saffron, squid ink, beet and porcini*

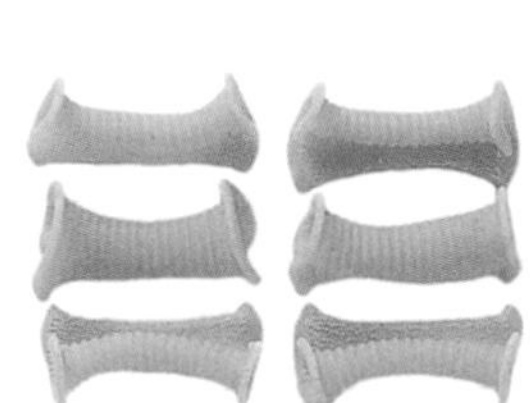

*Rocchetti rigati*

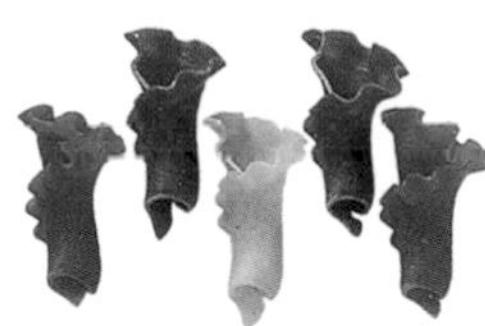

*Fiorelli tricolori*

*Three-color pennoti rigati*

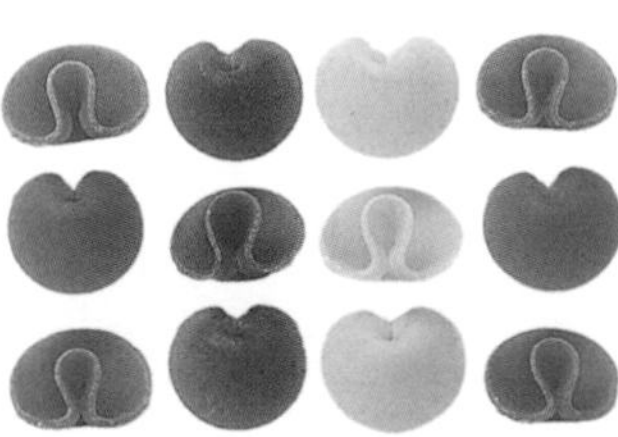

*Three-color cappelletti*

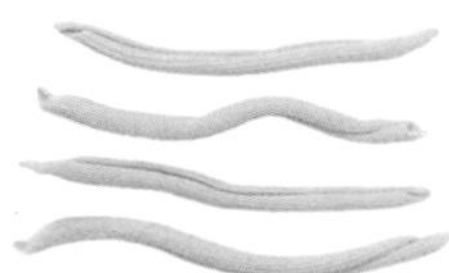

*Coralli rigati*

# Fresh Pasta

In Italy there has long been a tradition for buying fresh pasta, and now the custom has caught on in other countries too. Italians buy from their local *pastificio* or baker, where the beautiful window displays are such a tempting feast for the eye, while we have to content ourselves with delicatessens, supermarkets and gourmet specialty stores. Yet here too, creative talent is running wild when it comes to making fresh pasta, and the choice of different shapes, flavors and fillings is continually increasing—by popular demand. It seems that everybody loves fresh pasta, and we simply can't get enough of it. Quality is excellent, especially with the loose kinds sold in Italian food stores. Pre-packaged brands, although labeled fresh, are obviously not as "just-made" and silky-textured as the pasta made on a daily basis, but they are quite good nevertheless. Flavors vary, but the usual ingredients are spinach, tomato, chestnut, mushroom, beet juice, saffron, herbs, garlic, chiles and squid ink.

Buy freshly made pasta on the day you need it or you defeat the object of buying it; otherwise keep it in its wrapping and use it within 1–2 days of purchase (or according to the storage time given on the package). If you buy fresh pasta loose from an Italian specialty store, ask the storekeeper for advice on storage. Fresh pasta is made with egg, which shortens its storage time, but on the plus side this increases its nutritional value and flavor, and gives the plain varieties a lovely sunshine yellow color.

Fresh pasta takes far less time to cook than dried pasta, but the cooking technique is generally the same for each type. Most plain shapes will be *al dente* in 2–4 minutes, while stuffed shapes take 5–7 minutes, but always ask advice in the store where it is made (or check the label).

The same rules apply for matching sauces to shapes as with dried pasta—long shapes are best with smooth sauces, while chunky sauces go better with short shapes.

### Long and Flat Shapes

These were the first forms of fresh pasta to be available commercially, and were generally made in the local Italian delicatessen by the proprietor or his wife. The choice used to be between plain egg tagliatelle and fettuccine, possibly flavored with spinach, but now there are far more exciting varieties. Pre-packaged long fresh pasta comes in standard shapes and sizes, but Italian specialty stores sometimes have weekend specials when they offer different flavors and colors according to the seasonal availability of ingredients. This is often the case when a delicatessen supplies a local restaurant with fresh pasta. If a special order is made for a restaurant, the delicatessen may make extra to sell to customers in the shop. These occasional treats are well worth looking out for, as are regional specialities. If the owners of your local Italian store are from Lazio you may find fresh home-made fettuccine on sale. Ligurians are more likely to make trenette, whereas pappardelle indicates that the owners of the store probably have family ties with Tuscany or Bologna.

**Fettuccine**

These long, flat ribbon noodles are the narrow Roman version of tagliatelle, traditionally made about 1/4-inch wide. Fettuccine are readily available, made with egg and flavored with spinach. You may also see similar noodles called fettuccelle. The two are interchangeable, and are at their best served very simply with butter and cream.

*Fettuccine all'uovo*

*Fettuccine al nero*

*Chile-flavored fettuccine*

*Fettuccine verdi*

*Spaghetti all'uovo*

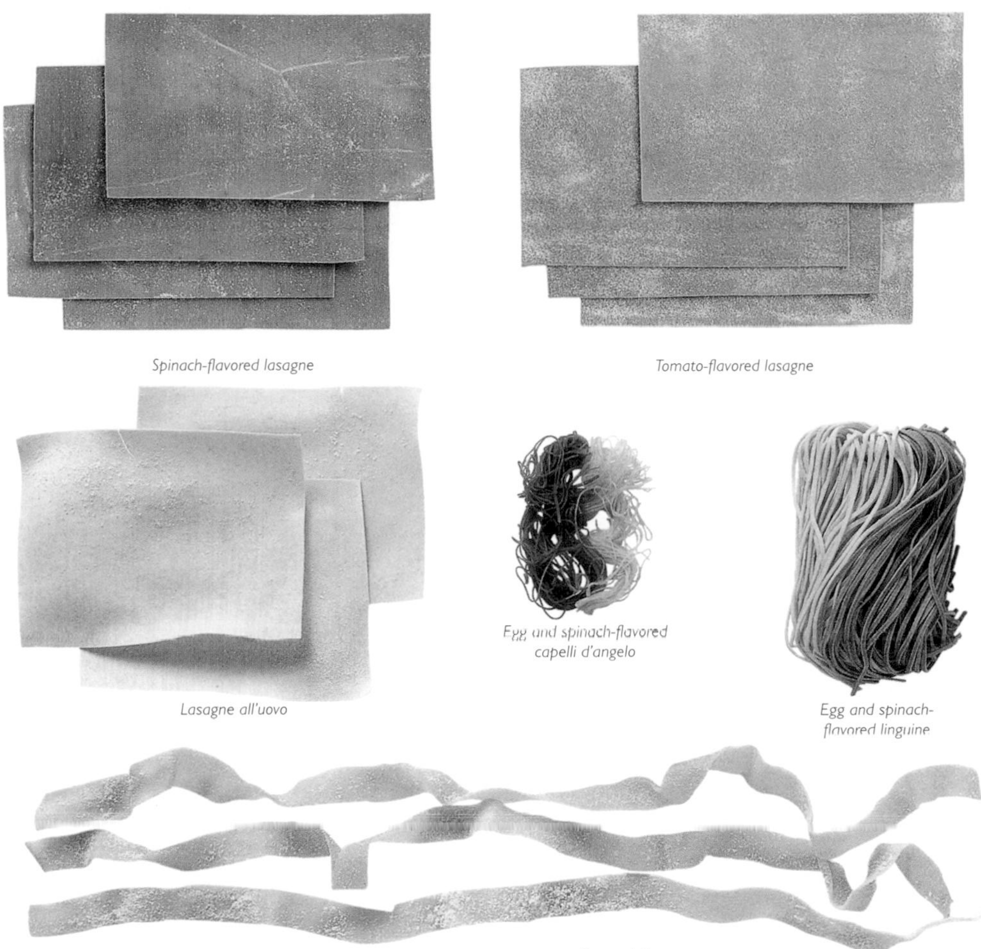

Spinach-flavored lasagne

Tomato-flavored lasagne

Lasagne all'uovo

Egg and spinach-flavored capelli d'angelo

Egg and spinach-flavored linguine

Pappardelle

**Spaghetti**

This pasta is widely available, in various widths. A narrow version, spaghettini, is popular, and can be found in some specialty stores. Serve fresh spaghetti or spaghettini Neapolitan style with sauces based on olive oil and tomatoes. Both spaghetti and spaghettini are also good with fish and shellfish, as long as the pieces are cut small. Capelli d'angelo, plain or flavored with spinach, is also available.

**Lasagne**

Sheets of lasagne can be found plain, with egg, and flavored with spinach or tomato. Depending on the manufacturer, they may be rectangles, squares or strips with plain or frilly edges. Lasagne al forno (baked lasagne) made with fresh sheets of pasta tastes much better than that made with dried pasta, so the fresh sheets are well worth buying.

**Linguine**

These look like strands of flattened spaghetti and are very narrow and thin. They are made with egg (all'uovo), and go well with a simple dressing of olive oil and flavorings such as finely chopped garlic, chiles or freshly ground black pepper. Linguine are also good with fish and shellfish sauces.

**Pappardelle**

Flat egg noodles, these vary in width from ¾–1-inch wide. Traditional pappardelle have wavy edges, but you may see them with plain edges—the main thing is that they are wider than any of the other ribbon noodles. They originated in Tuscany, but are also popular in the city of Bologna in Emilia-Romagna. In both these regions, pasta is often served with a rich meat or game sauce, and pappardelle are the perfect choice because the noodles are wide and strong enough to support the chunkiest mixtures. Pappardelle are available plain and flavored, sometimes with sun-dried tomatoes or porcini.

*Squid ink tagliolini*

*Tagliolini all'uovo*

*Salmon-flavored tagliolini*

*Spinach-flavored tagliolini*

*Tagliatelle all'uovo*

*Spinach-flavored tagliatelle*

**Tagliatelle**

This is probably the best-known form of fresh pasta. The noodles are long and straight, about 1/2-inch wide. They are available everywhere, in a wide variety of flavors and colors. After plain egg tagliatelle, spinach is the most popular, but it is often flecked and flavored with fresh herbs, garlic, porcini, sun-dried tomatoes, pepper, chiles and other spices, or beautifully colored with saffron or tomato. When made with squid ink, it is black and dramatic. Tagliatelle comes from Bologna, where it is always served with Bolognese sauce, but it goes well with any meat sauce. Tagliarini and tagliolini are very thin versions of tagliatelle, about 1/8-inch wide, sold either as plain egg (all'uovo) or as paglia e fieno—half white and half green. Mixed packages are versatile and attractive because you can cook the different colors together or keep them separate, depending on the visual effect required. They go well with tomato and cream sauces.

**Short Shapes**

Supermarkets and other large outlets sell fresh short shapes, but the range is limited. Italian stores sometimes sell a few simple home-made shapes, but because many short shapes need special machines for cutting and shaping there is seldom a wide range in small outlets, and making them by hand would be too time-consuming to be commercially viable. Short shapes tend to stick together, so in supermarkets they are kept in plastic bags in the chilled cabinets; these packages are useful in that they can be stored in the freezer. In some small stores excess moisture is removed by briefly fan-drying the shapes straight after they are made. These are then described as semi-dried and must be sold within 24–48 hours. Shapes vary widely, depending on whether they come from large manufacturers or individual stores. Conchiglie, fusilli and penne are easy to find, while other shapes, such as garganelli and ballerine, are less widely available.

**Conchiglie**

These shell shapes come in different sizes and colors, and conchiglie tricolore (red, white and green) are popular. They are one of the best shapes for trapping chunky sauces. If they are ridged, so much the better. Conchiglie are also good in salads because they hold dressings well.

**Fusilli**

Resembling the threads of screws, these should correctly be called eliche, but they are almost always labeled fusilli. Plain, spinach and tomato flavors, either sold separately or mixed together, are easy to obtain. Squid ink fusilli are made in some shops. The versatile shape of this type of pasta means that it goes well with most sauces and is also good in salads.

**Garganelli**

Sold in some specialty stores, these are made from a very special type of egg pasta from Emilia-Romagna, and look like ridged scrolls. Garganelli need to be made

*Ballerine*

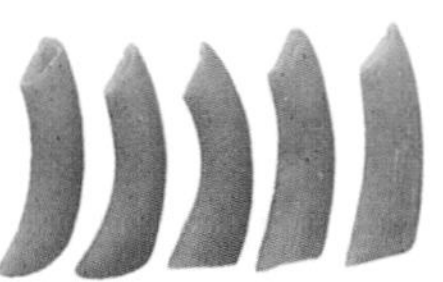

*Penne rigate*

*Eliche all'uovo*

*Conchiglie*

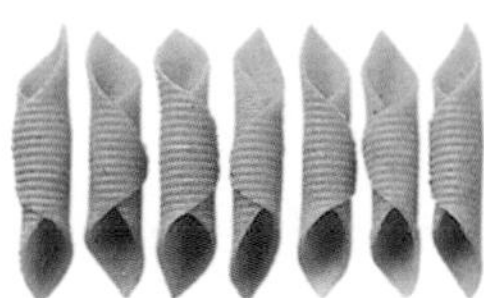

*Semi-dried garganelli*

with a special tool, called *il pettine* in Italian. Squares of fresh dough are rolled around a rod and against the *pettine*, which has teeth like a comb. The teeth produce the characteristic fine ridges on the outside of the pasta. Plain and spinach flavors are available, either sold separately or mixed together. In Emilia-Romagna, garganelli are traditionally served with a rich meat sauce, but you can use them in any recipe that calls for short maccheroni or penne. They are especially good with rich, creamy sauces.

**Penne**

Sometimes called quills, these come in a variety of sizes and colors, both smooth and ribbed, just like their dried counterpart. In Rome, fresh penne are served with the chile-hot arrabbiata sauce, but they go with just about any sauce.

**Stuffed Shapes**

Until recent years, the only stuffed fresh pasta shapes available were the classic ones traditionally associated with specific regions of Italy. Ravioli was the best known shape, followed by tortellini. These regional specialties are still popular, but nowadays the traditional shapes and fillings are often varied, whether they are being made by a large-scale manufacturer or a single cook working for a local delicatessen. Individual interpretations on the basic shapes, a wide variety of fresh seasonal ingredients for the fillings, plus eye-catching color combinations for both the pasta and the fillings make variations on the theme seemingly endless. New ideas are being developed all of the time, some more successful than others, so experiment with different kinds of stuffed shapes to find the ones you like the best. Listed here are the most popular and widely available shapes, following the regional tradition.

**Agnolotti**

These filled pasta shapes come from northern Italy and are a speciality of Piedmont in particular. Traditionally they were shaped like plump little half moons and stuffed with meat, but this is no longer the case: nowadays you will see round and square shapes with vegetable fillings labelled as agnolotti. Square agnolotti with a pleat in the center are called *dal plin* (with a pleat). One characteristic that all agnolotti should share is a crinkled edge, made by cutting the dough around the filling with a fluted pasta wheel.

**Cappelletti**

These take their name from the Italian word for little hats. In Emilia-Romagna, small squares of dough are filled and folded to make triangular shapes, then two of the ends are wrapped around

*Semi-dried agnolotti all'uovo*

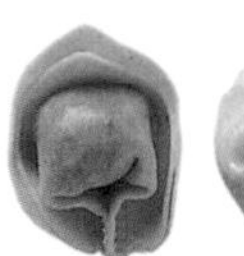

*Semi-dried cappelletti all'uovo*

*Cappelletti all'uovo stuffed with mushroom filling*

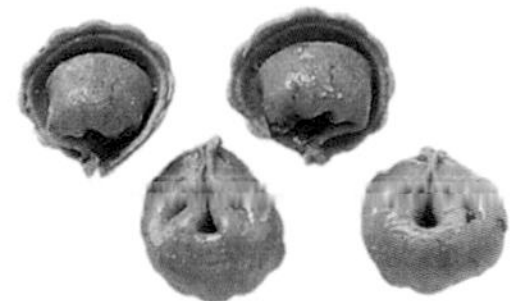

*Semi-dried tomato-flavored cappelletti stuffed with sun-dried tomato filling*

and the bottom edge turned up to make a party hat shape with a brim. In some central regions of Italy, however, cappelletti are made with either plain or fluted circles of dough instead of squares. The dough for cappelletti can be plain or egg (all'uovo), or flavored with tomato or spinach. Cappelletti are traditionally filled with ground meat and cheese and are eaten in northern and central regions of Italy at Christmas and New Year, especially in clear broth—*Cappelletti in Brodo*. You can use them in this way or serve them as a pasta course with a little melted butter and freshly grated Parmesan cheese or, alternatively, toss the cappelletti in a tomato or cream sauce.

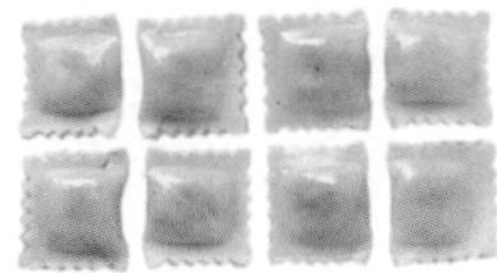

*Semi-dried raviolini all'uovo (mini egg ravioli) with a simple ground meat filling*

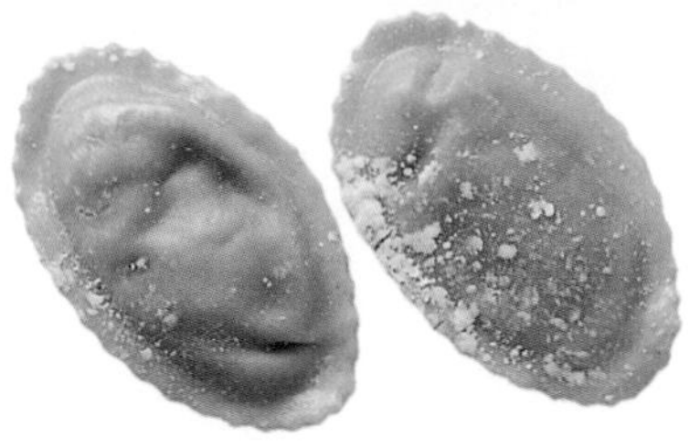

*Oval ravioli, which are sometimes called rotondi, stuffed with artichoke filling*

*Ravioli all'uovo with ground chicken filling*

*Large rectangular ravioli stuffed with Roquefort cheese*

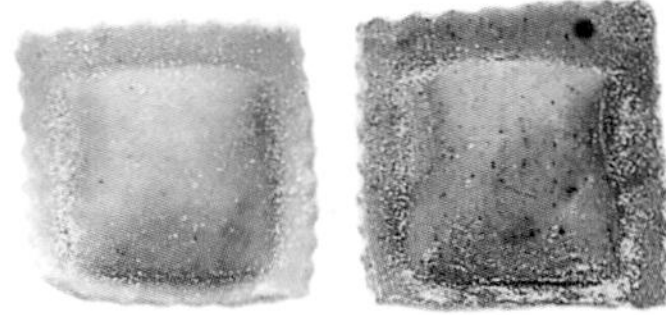

*Hand-made plain and spinach-flavored ravioli*

*Large ravioli stuffed with ground chicken and asparagus*

*Plain ravioli stuffed with asparagus filling (left), squid ink-flavored ravioli stuffed with a herb filling and saffron-flavored ravioli stuffed with smoked salmon and mascarpone cheese*

**Pansotti**

Sometimes spelled pansoti, these stuffed pasta shapes are Ligurian. The word means chubby, and they are triangular in shape with little pot bellies of filling in the center. It is traditional to fill pansotti with chopped cooked spinach, chopped hard-cooked eggs and grated Pecorino cheese, then serve them with a walnut sauce. Pansotti are made with small squares of pasta dough and may have straight or fluted edges.

**Ravioli**

These are usually square with fluted edges, but size and shape vary enormously. Along with tortellini, they are the most widely made of the fresh stuffed pasta shapes, and everyone seems to have their own favorite way of making them. Plain, spinach and tomato doughs are used for the pasta (although other flavors, such as squid ink and saffron, are becoming increasingly available), and the fillings can be anything from vegetables, such as spinach, artichoke and mushroom, to fish and shellfish, and minced veal and chicken. Very tiny ravioli are called raviolini, while the name for ravioli with a pumpkin filling is cappellacci. Tiny round ravioli are sometimes called medaglioni. Large round, oval and rectangular ravioli, stuffed with cheese or vegetable fillings, are occasionally available at Italian specialty stores. Oval ravioli are sometimes called rotondi, while the large rectangular shapes may be called cannelloni rather than ravioli.

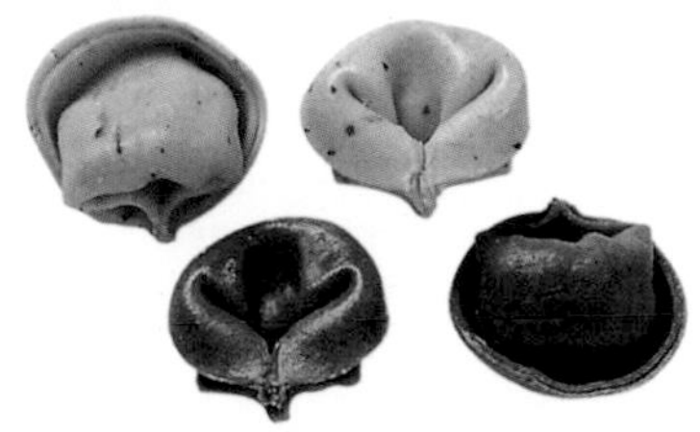

Plain and spinach-flavored tortellini

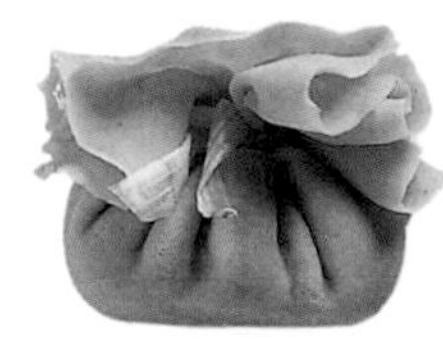

Sacchetti filled with a spinach and ricotta filling and tied with thin strips of spring onion

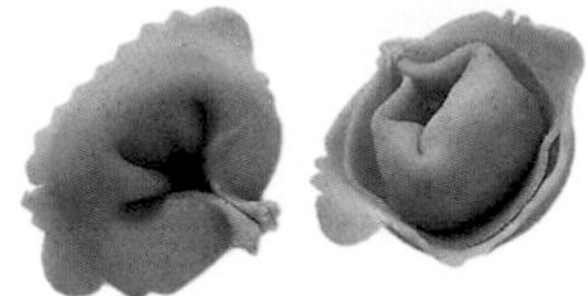

Tortelloni stuffed with an artichoke and truffle oil filling

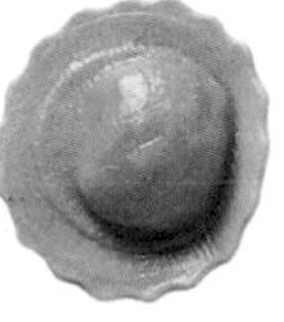

Cappelli all'uovo stuffed with minced salmon

Tomato-flavored medaglioni all'uovo stuffed with a prawn and trout filling

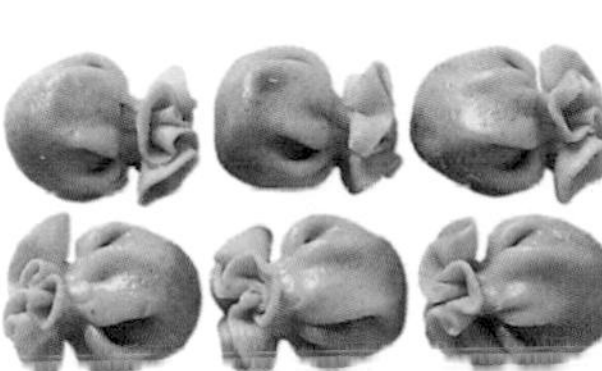

Sacchettini

Sweet-shaped caramelle all'uovo stuffed with spinach and ricotta cheese

Spinach cannelloni stuffed with a herb and cream cheese filling

**Tortellini**

Hugely popular, these look more or less the same as cappelletti, but are made from circles of dough rather than squares so do not have peaks. They are usually slightly larger than cappelletti, while tortelloni and tortelli are larger still. Tortellini are a speciality from the city of Bologna in Emilia-Romagna, where the traditional filling is ground meats and prosciutto. At Christmas it is the local custom to eat *Tortellini in Brodo* as a first course soup before the main course of roast capon or turkey.

Nowadays, tortellini are available everywhere and are eaten all year round. There is a wide variety of color combinations and fanciful fillings. Black squid ink, garlic, herbs, green olive, spinach and sun-dried tomatoes are among the many ingredients used to flavor the dough, while for the filling you can choose from such delicacies as white crabmeat, pumpkin, ricotta, asparagus, cream cheese, caramelized onions, mushrooms, marinated tuna, red bell peppers, artichokes and even truffles. A mixture of four cheeses is a popular filling.

**Other stuffed pasta shapes**

Creative cooks have started a trend for making shapes that are not based on regional traditions, so check out your local Italian store or supermarket for the latest shapes to arrive—you will find new ones appearing all the time. Two very popular pasta shapes are caramelle and sacchetti. Caramelle means "caramel," and this pasta shape takes its name from the familiar shape of caramels or toffees with their wrappings twisted at both ends. The filling is encased in the lozenge-shaped center and is often ricotta-cheese based, while the pasta itself is made with egg and may be plain, spinach or tomato flavored. Sacchetti are little purses or money bags with scrunched tops. The pasta may be plain or flavored and the fillings based on cheese or meat. Sacchettini are a tiny version, most often served in soups but also good with smooth, creamy sauces.

# Equipment

Pasta demands little in the way of specialist equipment. You are bound to have a large saucepan for cooking the pasta and a colander for draining, while for making sauces you need only a sharp knife and a cutting board for chopping ingredients, a skillet or saucepan for cooking, and a large bowl plus spoons and forks for tossing and serving. There are a few items that will make cooking and serving easier, however, and if you eat pasta frequently you will find them a wise investment. They are all available at good kitchenware stores and department stores.

### General Cooking Equipment

You may already have some of these basic items in your kitchen.

**Pasta cooking pot**

Made of stainless steel, this pan has straight sides with two short handles and an inner perforated draining basket, which also has two short handles. Different sizes are available, so choose the one that suits your needs best. One that will comfortably hold at least 5 pints water is adequate if you usually cook for two to three people, whereas an 8 pint pan is the one you will need if you often have to cook enough pasta for 6–8 servings. Pasta pots are quite expensive as pans go, but they are so practical that if you buy one you will wonder how you ever managed without it. The pasta is boiled in the inner basket, which is lifted out of the water once the pasta is *al dente*, making draining very easy and safe. This kind of pan is also quite versatile: you can use it with the draining basket for cooking or steaming vegetables and desserts, or use the outer pan on its own for cooking stocks, soups, stews —and even preserves. When buying a pasta cooking pot, choose one that is not too heavy or you will find it difficult to manage once it is filled with water.

**Skillet**

A skillet was originally a cooking pot that stood on three or four legs in the hearth. In the United States, the term came to mean a frying pan. Nowadays, it is used on both sides of the Atlantic to describe a wide, deep pan—like a cross between a wok and a frying pan—with a long handle and a lid. This is the perfect pan for making sauces. Look for one that is at least 9 inches in diameter (10–12-inches is ideal) and 2–3-inches deep. If you often cook for a crowd or for varying numbers of people, it is worth buying two of these pans, in different sizes. Choose the best quality you can afford. Some skillets have non-stick surfaces, which is fine as long as they are of good quality.

*Left: This purpose-made pasta pan comes complete with an inner perforated basket for draining the pasta.*

*Above: A wide, deep skillet or frying pan is the ideal pan for making sauces, while a large, deep saucepan will double as a pasta pan if you don't have a purpose-made one.*

*Left: A large, deep-bowled ladle is extremely useful. It can be used for serving broths and soups as well as for spooning sauces over pasta.*

*A large perforated ladle (left) or a flatter scoop (right) are ideal for lifting short pasta shapes out of boiling water.*

*Right: This odd-looking tool is useful for measuring spaghetti—each hole holds a different amount of pasta.*

*Above: These simply designed tongs can be used for lifting long strands of pasta out of boiling water.*

*Left: A long-handled wooden fork is the best tool to use for stirring pasta to separate the strands during cooking.*

**Pasta measurer**

Spaghetti is difficult to put on the scales, and measuring by the handful is not always accurate. This wooden gadget has four or five holes, each of which holds enough pasta for a given number of people.

**Long-handled fork**

This is useful for stirring pasta during cooking to help keep the strands or pieces from sticking together. A wooden fork is better for separating pasta than a solid wooden spoon. There are also wooden pasta rakes or hooks, which look like flat wooden spoons with prongs attached to one side. They do a good job because the pasta does not slip off when it is lifted, but sometimes the teeth come unglued in the boiling water.

**Tongs**

Nothing is more effective for picking strands of spaghetti and long noodles out of hot water than a good pair of tongs. Sturdy stainless steel tongs are the best, preferably with long handles for safety, but the most important thing is that they feel comfortable in your hand, so check this before buying. Some tongs have awkward mechanisms, springs and hinges—the simpler the design the better. Tongs can be used for lifting out individual strands to check for doneness and for serving.

**Scoop or draining spoon**

A large, deep perforated, slotted or mesh spoon is the perfect utensil for lifting short pasta shapes out of boiling water. Stainless steel is best.

**Ladle**

For spooning sauce over pasta and for serving soups, a deep-bowled ladle is the most effective utensil. Sizes vary from small and pointed with a lip for easy pouring, to very large, functional-looking types. Stainless steel is the best material, and it's a good idea to have several ladles in different sizes.

**Parmesan knife**

This is a short, quite stubby little knife with a shaped handle and a small and sturdy, double-sided blade. It is by no means an essential item, but is quite effective for scraping off shavings of Parmesan cheese from a block. It also looks good if you are serving Parmesan on a cheese board.

*Below: The choice of Parmesan graters available includes a small, rotary grater with a storage space for a piece of Parmesan; a standard, stainless steel box grater; and the traditional small, hand-held Parmesan grater, which is ideal for using at the table.*

### Parmesan graters

There is a huge choice of graters, ranging from the very simple hand grater to electrically operated machines. A simple stainless steel box grater will grate Parmesan and other hard cheeses, such as Pecorino, but it can be cumbersome to use with its choice of different-size teeth. It is possible to buy a small grater especially for Parmesan. This consists of a single rectangular grating plate that is designed specifically for grating hard cheese finely, and has a small handle, which can be grasped firmly. The grater is small and unobtrusive, ideal for using at the table. Mechanical Parmesan mills are also good, as are small, hand-cranked rotary graters, and there are special Parmesan graters available with a box and a lid so that the cheese can be stored after grating. Electric Parmesan cheese graters are only worth buying if you frequently grate a lot of cheese; a less expensive alternative is to use a small electrical chopper, the kind used for chopping herbs.

*Above: The traditional Italian pasta rolling pin is very long, slightly wide in the centre and narrow at both ends.*

## Equipment for Making Pasta at Home

You can make pasta at home with nothing more sophisticated than a set of scales, some measuring spoons, a work surface and an ordinary rolling pin, but there are a few items of special equipment that will make the job easier. They are all available at specialty kitchenware stores and good department stores.

### Tapered rolling pin

The traditional pin used in Italy for rolling out pasta dough is very long—it measures almost 32 inches in length. It is about 1 1/2 inches wide in the center and tapers almost to a point at either end. This type of rolling pin is very easy to use and is well worth buying if you enjoy making pasta by hand and don't intend to buy a special machine. A conventional, straight rolling pin can be used instead, but try to get one that is quite slim—no more than 2 inches in diameter.

### Mechanical pasta machine

The same type of hand-cranked pasta machine has been used in Italian kitchens for many, many years. It has stood the test of time well, because it is still manufactured and used today, with very little modification. Made of stainless steel, it has rollers to press out the dough as thinly as possible and cutters for creating different shapes. The standard cutters usually allow you to make tagliatelle and tagliarini, but you can get attachments and accessories for other shapes including pappardelle, ravioli and cannelloni. The machine is clamped to the edge of a work surface or table and worked by turning the handle. If you make pasta frequently, it is a good buy because it is inexpensive, easy and fun to use, and makes excellent pasta in a very short time. It takes all of the hard work out of making pasta by hand, and you can even get an electric motor attachment so you don't have to turn the handle.

*Left: The traditional hand-cranked pasta machine with rollers to press out the dough and cutters for tagliatelle and tagliarini is still one of the best ways of making pasta.*

**Electric Pasta Machines**

Tabletop electric pasta machines mix the dough, knead it and then extrude it through cutters, so all you have to do is put the ingredients in the machine and turn it on. You can make more shapes with this type of machine than the mechanical one, but you have less control over the dough because you don't actually handle it at all. Electric pasta machines are only sold in some specialty kitchenware stores. They are expensive to buy, but are a worthwhile investment if you frequently make a lot of pasta—they can make up to 2¼-pounds at a time—and have the space to house the machine in a convenient spot.

*Left: A stainless steel pasta wheel makes light work of cutting noodles and ravioli.*

**Pasta wheel**

This is a useful gadget for cutting lasagne and noodles such as tagliatelle when you don't have a pasta machine, and for cutting out small stuffed shapes such as ravioli. The wheel can be straight or fluted, and there are some types that will cut several lengths of noodle at a time. A sharp knife can be used instead, but a pasta wheel is easier and gives a neater finish. With a pasta wheel, the pasta edges are less likely to be dragged out of shape or torn.

**Ravioli cutter**

This is virtually the same as a fluted cookie cutter except that it has a wooden handle and can be square or round. If you want to make square ravioli and cappelletti, you can use a pasta wheel instead of this cutter, so it isn't a vital piece of equipment. For round ravioli, tortellini and anolini you can use a cookie cutter if you have one. The most useful sizes are 2 inches and 3 inches.

**Ravioli tray**

You can buy a special metal tray for making ravioli. A sheet of rolled-out dough is laid over the tray, then pressed into the indentations. The filling is then spooned into the indentations and another sheet of dough placed on top. The ravioli squares are cut out by rolling a rolling pin over the serrated top. This is good for making very small ravioli, which are fiddly and time-consuming to make individually. Sometimes the tray is sold as a set with its own small rolling pin, or as an accessory for a pasta machine.

*Above: This special metal tray is used for making mini ravioli.*

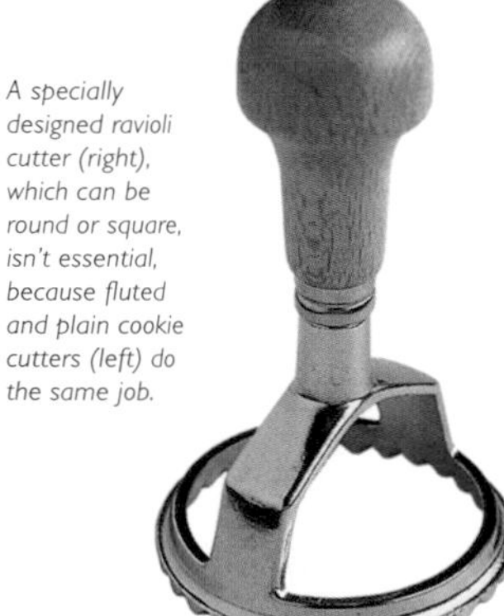

*A specially designed ravioli cutter (right), which can be round or square, isn't essential, because fluted and plain cookie cutters (left) do the same job.*

# How to Cook and Serve Pasta

It is very easy to cook pasta properly, but without care and attention it is equally easy to cook it badly. A few simple guidelines need to be observed if pasta is to be at its best. Once you have mastered these, you will be able to cook pasta successfully every time, no matter whether it is dried, homemade or bought fresh.

**Cooking Pasta in the Microwave**

Because of the large amount of water needed to boil pasta, you will not save any time by cooking it in the microwave, but for short shapes and quantities under 8-ounces, you may find it more convenient than cooking the pasta on top of the stove. The results can be quite successful. Large and long shapes, such as lasagne sheets and spaghetti, need to be cooked in batches, so there seems hardly any point. Where the microwave comes into its own is in reheating pasta sauces, and for reheating previously baked pasta dishes, such as lasagne and cannelloni, especially individual portions of these. The microwave is also useful for thawing and reheating sauces and baked dishes that have been stored in the freezer.

**How to microwave short pasta shapes**

Put the pasta in a large heatproof bowl with salt to taste and pour over boiling water to cover by 1 inch. Carefully transfer the bowl to the microwave and cook on High (100 per cent power) for 3–4 minutes for fresh pasta and 8–10 minutes for dried, then let stand for 5 minutes before draining.

1 **Synchronize sauce and pasta**
Before starting to cook either sauce or pasta, read through the recipe carefully. It is important to know which needs to be cooked for the longest time—sometimes it is the pasta and sometimes the sauce, so don't always assume one or the other. The sauce can often be made ahead of time and reheated, and it is quite unusual for the timing of a sauce to be crucial, but pasta is almost like a hot soufflé—it waits for no one. This is especially true if you are cooking fresh pasta, for which timing is often only a few minutes, so the sauce needs to be ready and waiting before the pasta hits the water.

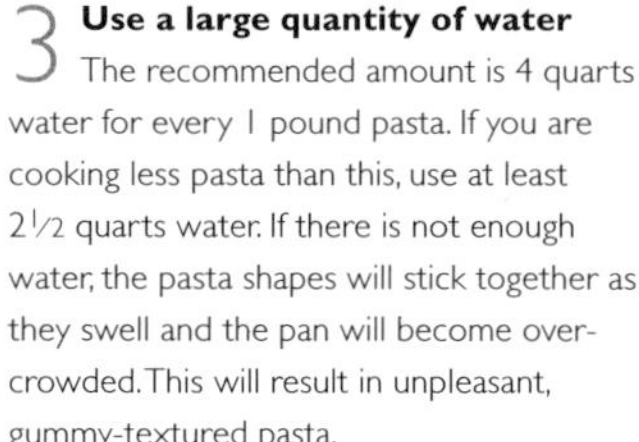

3 **Use a large quantity of water**
The recommended amount is 4 quarts water for every 1 pound pasta. If you are cooking less pasta than this, use at least 2½ quarts water. If there is not enough water, the pasta shapes will stick together as they swell and the pan will become over-crowded. This will result in unpleasant, gummy-textured pasta.

**Watchpoint**

*It is best not to cook more than 1½ pounds pasta at a time, even if you have a very large saucepan, because of the danger in handling such a large amount of water. If you are using the microwave to cook pasta it is best not to cook more than 8 ounces pasta at a time. Use a large heatproof bowl, don't overfill the bowl and transfer it carefully to and from the microwave using oven mitts.*

2 **Use a big pan**
There needs to be plenty of room for the pasta to move around in the large amount of water it requires, so a big pan is essential. The best type of pan is a tall, lightweight, straight-sided, stainless steel pasta cooking pot with its own in-built draining pan. Both outer and inner pans have two handles each, which ensure easy and safe lifting and draining. If you cook pasta a lot, it is well worth investing in one of these special pans; otherwise use the largest saucepan you have for cooking the pasta and a large stainless steel colander, preferably one with feet for stability, for draining it.

4 **Get the water boiling**
Before adding the pasta, the water should be at a fast rolling boil. The quickest way to do this is to boil water in the kettle, then pour it into the pasta pan, which should be set over a high heat. You may need as much as 2–3 kettlefuls, so keep the water in the pan simmering, covered by the lid, while you boil the kettle again.

5 **Add enough salt**
Pasta cooked without salt is more or less tasteless, and with insufficient salt it is hardly any better. The recommended amount is 1 1/2–2 tablespoons salt for every 1 pound pasta. There is no need to use sea or rock salt; cooking salt is perfectly acceptable. Add the salt when the water is boiling and just before you are ready to add the pasta. The water will bubble furiously just as the salt is added, which is your cue to shoot in the pasta.

6 **Add the pasta all at once**
Try to get all of the pasta into the boiling water at the same time so that it will cook evenly and be ready at the same time. The quickest and easiest way is literally to shake it out of the packet or the bowl of the scales, covering the surface of the water as much as possible.

7 **Return the water quickly to a boil**
Once the pasta is submerged in the water, give it a brisk stir with a long-handled fork or spoon and then cover the pan tightly with the lid—this will help to bring the water back to a boil as quickly as possible. Once the water is boiling, lift off the lid, turn down the heat slightly and let the water simmer over medium to high heat for the required cooking time.

8 **Stir the pasta frequently during cooking**
To prevent the pasta strands or shapes from sticking together, stir them frequently during cooking so they are kept constantly on the move. Use a long-handled wooden fork or spoon so you can stir right down to the bottom of the pan.

9 **Drain carefully and thoroughly**
If you have a pasta pot with an inner drainer, lift the draining pan up and out of the water. Shake the draining pan vigorously and stir the pasta well so that any water trapped in pasta shapes can drain out as quickly as possible. It is a good idea to reserve a few ladlefuls of the pasta cooking water in case the pasta needs a little extra moistening when it is tossed with the sauce before serving.

**Accurate Timing is Essential for Cooking Pasta**
Start timing the pasta from the moment the water returns to a boil after adding the pasta. Always go by the time given on the package or, in the case of fresh homemade pasta, by the time given in the recipe. For the greatest accuracy, use a kitchen timer with a bell or buzzer because even half a minute of overcooking can ruin pasta, especially if it is freshly made. Dried egg pasta is more difficult to spoil, so if you are new to pasta cooking and nervous about getting it right, start with this type.

**For fresh pasta**
As a general guide, thin fresh noodles will take only 2–3 minutes, thicker fresh noodles and pasta shapes 3–4 minutes, and stuffed fresh pasta 5–7 minutes.

**For dried pasta**
The cooking time for dried pasta will vary from 8–20 minutes depending on the type and the manufacturer. Always check the time on the label.

## Cooking Fresh Pasta

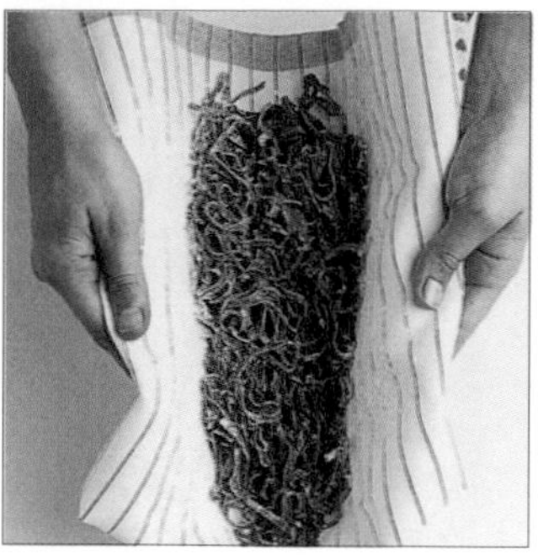

1 For freshly made pasta that has been drying on a dish towel, gather the cloth up around the pasta in a loose cylindrical shape and hold it firmly at both ends.

2 Hold the towel over the water, then let go of the end nearest to the water so that the pasta shoots in.

## Cooking Long Dried Pasta

1 For spaghetti you need to coil the pasta into the water as it softens. Take a handful at a time and dip it in the boiling water so that it touches the bottom of the pan.

2 As the spaghetti strands soften, coil them round using a wooden spoon or fork until they are all submerged.

## Cooking Stuffed Pasta

1 Stuffed shapes require more gentle handling or they may break open and release their filling into the water, so stir them gently during cooking.

2 The best method of draining stuffed shapes after cooking is to lift them carefully out of the water with a large pasta scoop or slotted spoon (left).

### When is it cooked?

The Italian term *al dente* is used to describe pasta that is cooked to perfection. Literally translated this means "to the tooth," meaning that it should be firm to the bite, which is how Italians like their pasta, and therefore how it should be served. Dried pasta, which is made from durum wheat, is always served *al dente*, whereas fresh pasta is made from a softer wheat and so is never as firm as dried, but it should still have some resistance to it. Overcooked pasta is limp and unpalatable and an Italian cook would not serve it.

To check that the pasta is ready, test pasta frequently towards the end of the recommended cooking time by lifting out a piece with tongs, a pasta scoop or a slotted spoon and biting into it. When you are satisfied that it is done to your liking, it is time to stop the cooking.

### At-a-glance Quantities

Amounts of pasta given here are intended only as a guide to the number of people they will serve. If you are cooking fresh pasta, you may need a little more than if you are using dried, but the difference is really negligible. What is more significant is whether you are serving a light or substantial sauce with the pasta.

**For an Italian-style first course (primo piatto) for 4–6 people, or a main course for 2–3 people:**

*2½ quarts water*
*1 tablespoon salt*
*9–12 ounces fresh or dried pasta*

**For a first course for 6–8 people, or a main course for 4–6 people:**

*4 quarts water*
*1½–2 tablespoons salt*
*11 ounces–1 pound fresh or dried pasta*

### Cook's Tip

*If you are using an ordinary saucepan and a colander for cooking and draining pasta, have the colander ready in the sink. Carefully pour the contents of the pan into the colander, then shake the colander vigorously over the sink and stir the pasta to release any trapped water.*

### Combining the Pasta and Sauce

Recipes vary in the way they combine sauce and pasta. The majority add the sauce to the pasta, but with some it is the other way around. There are no hard-and-fast rules. If you are going to add the sauce to the drained pasta, the most important thing is to have a warmed bowl ready. The larger the bowl the better, because this will allow room for the sauce and pasta to be tossed together easily so that every piece of pasta can be thoroughly coated in sauce.

1 After draining, immediately turn the pasta into the warmed bowl, then pour the sauce over the pasta and quickly toss the two together.

2 If the pasta is not moist enough, add a little of the pasta cooking water. Some recipes call for extra butter or oil to be added at this stage, others have grated Parmesan or Pecorino cheese tossed with the pasta and sauce.

3 Use two large spoons or forks for tossing, or a large spoon and a fork. Lift the pasta and swirl it around, making sure you have scooped it up from the base of the bowl. The idea is to coat every piece of pasta evenly in sauce, so keep tossing until you are satisfied that this is done.

4 Occasionally, recipes call for the pasta to be returned to the cooking pan, to be combined with oil or butter and seasonings and tossed over heat until coated. A sauce may be added at this stage too, but care should be taken not to cook the pasta too much in the first place or it may overcook when it is reheated.

### Serving and Presentation

Most important of all is to have your family and friends waiting at the table for the pasta, not the other way round. With the exception of baked dishes, all pasta should be eaten as soon as it is cooked and tossed with the sauce, so invite everyone to sit down just before you are ready to drain the pasta.

In most cases, pasta and sauce are tossed together in a large serving bowl in the kitchen, and the bowl is then brought straight to the table. Each person is served straight from the bowl—or the bowl is passed around the table for everyone to help themselves.

To give the pasta a finishing touch, a little Parmesan or Pecorino cheese can be grated on top, or a few chopped fresh herbs, such as parsley or basil, can be sprinkled over. The choice of garnish depends on the dish and the cook, but as a general rule, grated cheese is never served with fish and shellfish sauces. For guidance, follow the garnishing instructions in individual recipes.

Occasionally, the pasta and sauce are divided among individual plates or bowls before serving—as is the practice in restaurants. This is not the traditional custom in Italian homes, but it sometimes helps to get the pasta served quickly. It is an especially good idea when you are entertaining, because each individual serving can have its own attractive garnish.

## Matching Sauces to Recipes

Some regional dishes are always made with the same pasta shape. *Bucatini all'Amatriciana*, *Penne all'Arrabbiata* and *Fettuccine all'Alfredo* are all classic Roman recipes, for example, and it is rare to see them served with anything other than the named pasta. The same applies to *Tagliatelle alla Bolognese* from Emilia-Romagna and *Trenette con Pesto* from Genoa. These classics are few and far between, however, and with the ever-increasing number of different shapes on the market it may seem difficult to know which sauces and shapes go well together. Happily, there are no rigid rules, and common sense usually prevails. Heavy sauces with large chunks of meat are unlikely to go well with thin spaghettini or tagliolini, simply because the chunks will slide off, so these sauces and others like them are always served with wide noodles, such as pappardelle, maccheroni and tagliatelle, or with short tubular shapes, such as penne, fusilli, conchiglie and rigatoni.

In the south of Italy, olive oil is used for cooking rather than butter, so sauces tend to be made with olive oil and they are usually served with the dried plain durum wheat pasta such as spaghetti and vermicelli that is also popular in the south. These long, thin shapes are traditionally served with tomato and seafood sauces, most of which are made with olive oil, and with light vegetable sauces. Spaghetti and vermicelli are also ideal vehicles for minimalist sauces such as *Aglio e Olio* (garlic and olive oil) from Rome. Grated cheese is not normally used in these sauces.

*Classic dishes, such as Bucatini all'Amatriciana (left), Penne all'Arrabbiata (below) and Fettuccine all'Alfredo (above), are almost always served with the named pasta.*

Grated cheese is often tossed with pasta and sauce at the last moment, as well as being sprinkled over individual servings at the table.

In the North, butter and cream are used in sauces, and not surprisingly these go well with the egg pasta that is made there, especially fresh home-made egg pasta, which absorbs butter and cream and makes the sauce cling to it. Butter and cream also go well with tomato sauces when these are served with short shapes, especially penne, rigatoni, farfalle and fusilli.

## Eating Pasta

Opinions vary as to whether pasta should be eaten from a plate or a bowl. There are no rules, so you can serve it on either. Large, shallow soup plates seem the ideal compromise, and setting each warmed soup plate on a large, cold underplate makes for easy carrying from kitchen to table.

If the recipe recommends extra Parmesan or Pecorino for serving, grate the cheese just before the meal and hand it round in a bowl with a small spoon so that people can help themselves. Salt and pepper mills should also be on the table for those who like to adjust the seasoning.

Pasta is traditionally eaten with a single fork. Spaghetti and other long shapes should not be difficult to manage if they have been well tossed with the sauce. The trick is to twizzle only a small amount around the fork at a time.

# Wines to Serve with Pasta

It is impossible to recommend a particular wine to go with every pasta dish, but there are a few guidelines you can follow. If you know where the dish comes from, choose a wine from the same region. If a red or a white wine is used in the cooking of the sauce, select a good-quality wine for cooking and serve the rest with the meal. Otherwise, look at the main ingredient of the sauce and choose a wine that is recommended for that. Many pasta sauces are strong-tasting, flavored with garlic or spiced with chiles, and some are served with mature Parmesan or Pecorino cheese; for these you will need to choose a robust, full-flavored wine.

**Barbaresco**
A great red wine from Piedmont. Full-bodied and complex in flavor. Good with poultry and meat sauces.

**Barbera**
A medium-bodied red from Piedmont, which varies from young and slightly sparkling to rich and concentrated in flavor. Good with meat lasagne.

**Bardolino**
This fresh-tasting, light and fruity red from Veneto is very good to serve with poultry sauces.

**Barolo**
A full-bodied red made in Piedmont from Nebbiolo grapes. Good with red meat and game sauces.

**Castel del Monte**
Full-bodied smooth red and rosé wines from Puglia. Good with poultry and meat.

**Chianti**
Famous, uncomplicated red from Tuscany. Look for Chianti Classico to serve with red meat, poultry and game sauces.

**Cirò**
Fresh, zingy white and full-bodied red from Calabria. Drink the white with fish and shellfish sauces, the red with red meat and game sauces.

**Est! Est!! Est!!!**
A clean tasting, dry white from the Lazio region. It is good with fish and shellfish sauces.

**Frascati**
A crisp and fruity dry white from the town of Frascati, which is near Rome in the Lazio region. Good with the very spicy Amatriciana sauce.

**Lambrusco**
This effervescent red from Emilia-Romagna is good with pork and rich meat sauces.

**Orvieto Secco**
Dry white, from the town of the same name in Umbria. Serve with fish, shellfish and poultry sauces.

**Pinot Grigio**
A fresh, fruity dry white from Friuli-Venezia. It is good with any sauce or pasta dish.

**Soave**
Light, dry white from Veneto made from Garganega grapes. It is good with any sauce or pasta dish, and is reasonably priced.

**Valpolicella**
Fruity red, sometimes with a bitter aftertaste, from Veneto. The name means valley of many cellars. It is good with red meat sauces.

**Valtellina**
This perfumed red from Lombardy is made from Nebbiolo grapes. Look for Grumello, Inferno, Sassella and Valgella. It is good with rich meat, poultry and game sauces.

**Verdicchio**
Crisp, dry white with character from Marche in central Italy. It comes in a carved bottle shaped like a Roman amphora. Good with all kinds of fish and shellfish sauces.

**Vernaccia**
Rich, nutty red from the island of Sardinia that goes well with fish and shellfish sauces.

# How to Make Pasta

Homemade pasta has a wonderfully light, almost silky texture—quite different from the so-called fresh pasta that you buy pre-packaged in some supermarkets. If you use egg in the mixture, which is recommended if you are making pasta at home, the dough is easy to make, either by hand or machine, and the initial process is not that different from making bread. Kneading, rolling and cutting require some patience and practice, but if you invest in an inexpensive mechanical pasta machine, this part of the process will become quick and easy—and great fun too.

*Pasta all'Uovo*

## Pasta with Eggs

The best place to make, knead and roll out pasta dough is on a wooden kitchen table, the larger the better. The surface should be warm, so marble is not suitable.

**INGREDIENTS**

*2¾ cups flour*
*3 eggs*
*1 teaspoon salt*

**Ingredients for Pasta with Eggs**
Only three inexpensive ingredients are used for making pasta with eggs: flour, eggs and salt. However, ultimate success depends as much on their quality as on the technique used for making the dough. Olive oil is added to the mixture by some cooks, especially in Tuscany, but it is by no means essential. It gives the pasta a softer texture and a slightly different flavor, and some say it helps make the dough easier to work with, especially if you don't have a pasta machine. For a 3-egg quantity of dough, use 1 tablespoon olive oil and add it with the eggs.

**The best flour** is called Farina Bianca 00 or Tipo 00, available from Italian specialty stores. Imported from Italy, this is a very fine, soft white wheat flour. If you use ordinary all-purose flour, you will find the dough quite difficult to knead and roll, especially if you are doing this by hand. If you can't get 00 flour, use a strong stone-ground bread flour.

**Very fresh eggs** are essential, and the deeper the yellow of the yolks the better the color of the pasta. Buy the eggs fresh and use them at room temperature. If they have been stored in the fridge, take them out for about 1 hour before using.

**Salt** is important for flavor.

1 Mound the flour on a clean work surface and make a large, deep well in the center with your hands. Keep the sides of the well quite high so that when the eggs are added they will not run out of the well.

2 Crack the eggs into the well, then add the salt. With a table knife or fork, mix the eggs and salt together, then gradually start incorporating the flour from the sides of the well. Try not to break the sides of the well or the runny mixture will escape and quickly spread over the work surface.

3 As soon as the egg mixture is no longer liquid, dip your fingers in the flour and use them to work the ingredients together until they form a rough and sticky dough. Scrape up any dough that sticks to the countertop with a knife, then scrape this off the knife with your fingers. If the dough is too dry, add a few drops of cold water; if it is too moist, sprinkle a little flour over it.

5 Give the dough a quarter turn counter-clockwise, then continue kneading, folding and turning for 5 minutes if you intend using a pasta machine, or for 10 minutes if you will be rolling it out by hand. The dough should be very smooth and elastic. If you are going to roll it out and cut it by hand, thorough kneading is essential.

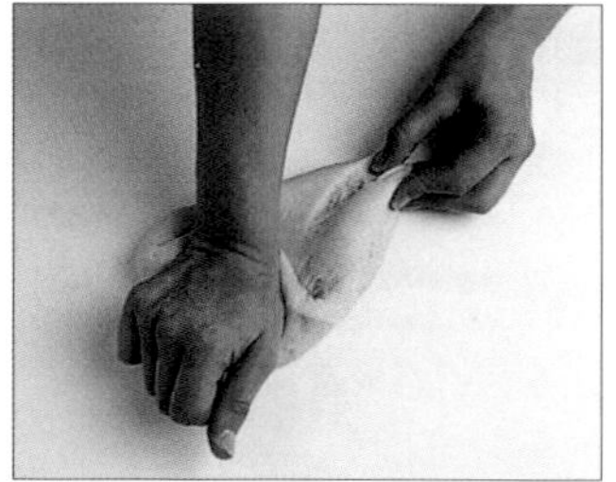

4 Press the dough into a rough ball and knead it as you would bread. Push it away from you with the heel of your hand, then fold the end of the dough back on itself so that it faces towards you and push it out again. Continue folding the dough back a little further each time and pushing it out until you have folded it back all the way towards you and all the dough has been kneaded.

6 Wrap the dough in plastic wrap and let rest for 15–20 minutes at room temperature. It will then be ready to roll out.

**COOK'S TIP**

*Don't skimp on the kneading time or the finished pasta will not be light and silky.*

### Making Pasta Dough in a Food Processor

If you have a food processor, you can save a little time and effort by using it for making pasta dough. It will not knead the dough adequately, however, so you may find it just as quick and easy to make it by hand, especially if you take into account the washing and drying of the bowl and blade. The ingredients are the same as when making pasta by hand.

1 Put the flour and salt in the bowl of a food processor fitted with the metal blade.

2 Add 1 whole egg and then pulse-blend until the ingredients are mixed.

3 Turn the food processor on to full speed and add the remaining whole eggs through the feeder tube. Keep the machine running for just long enough to allow a dough to be formed.

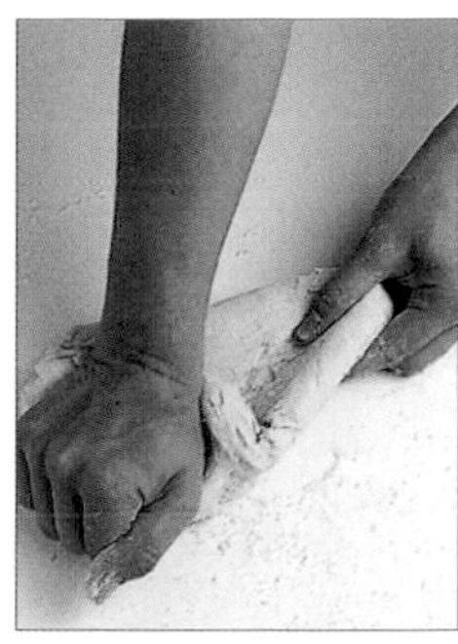

4 Turn the dough out on to a clean countertop. Knead as when making pasta by hand, then wrap in plastic wrap and let rest at room temperature for 15–20 minutes.

# Making Pasta Shapes by Hand

Once you have made your pasta dough and let it rest, it is ready to be rolled out and cut into various shapes. If you don't have a pasta machine, the following steps show how to do it by hand. The technique is quite hard work and the pasta may not be quite as thin as that made in a machine, but it is equally good nevertheless. If you enjoy making your own pasta and think you would like to make it regularly, it is well worth buying a mechanical pasta machine to save you both time and effort.

1 Unwrap the ball of dough and cut it in half. Roll and cut one half at a time, keeping the other half wrapped in plastic wrap as before.

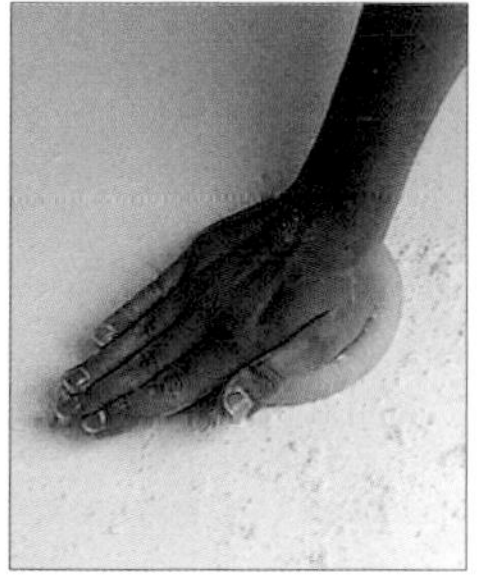

2 Sprinkle a very large, clean countertop lightly with flour. Put the unwrapped dough on the surface, sprinkle it with a little flour and flatten it with the heel of your hand. Turn the dough over and repeat the process to form the dough into a 5-inch disk.

3 Using a lightly floured rolling pin, start to roll the dough out. Always roll the dough away from you, stretching it outwards from the center and moving the dough round a quarter turn after each rolling. If the dough gets sticky, sprinkle the rolling pin, dough and countertop lightly with flour.

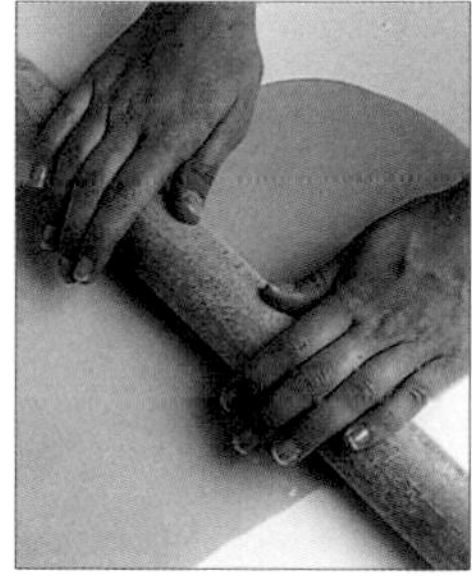

4 Continue rolling, turning and stretching the dough until it is a large oval, as thin as you can possibly get it. Ideally it should be about 1/8-inch thick. Try to get it even all over or the shapes will not cook in the same length of time. Don't worry if the edges are not neat; this is not important.

### Cutting Ribbon Noodles

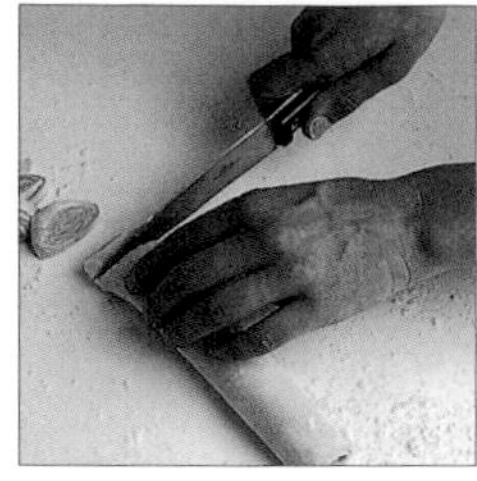

1 Before you begin, have ready plenty of clean dish towels lightly dusted with flour; you will need to spread the shapes out on them after cutting. Dust the sheet of pasta (called *la sfoglia* in Italian) lightly with flour. Starting from one long edge, roll up the sheet into a loose cylinder.

2 With a large sharp knife, cut cleanly across the pasta roll. Cut at ½-inch intervals for tagliatelle, slightly narrower (about ¼-inch) for fettuccine, and as narrow as you can possibly get for tagliarini or capelli d'angelo. Take care not to drag the knife or the edges of the ribbons will be ragged.

3 With floured fingers, unravel the rolls on the work surface, then toss the noodles lightly together on the floured dish towels, sprinkling them with more flour.

4 Repeat the rolling and cutting with the remaining pasta. Let the strips dry on the dish towels for at least 15 minutes before cooking, tossing them from time to time and sprinkling them with a little flour if they become sticky.

### Cutting Pappardelle

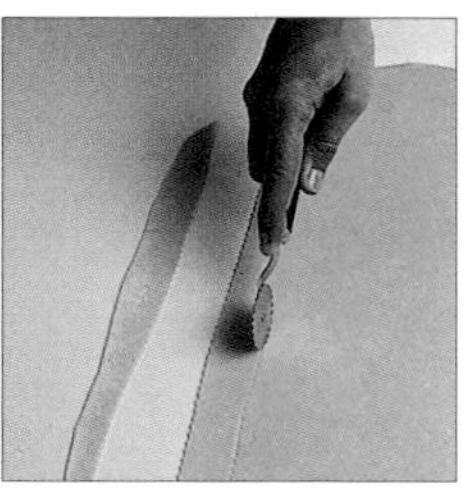

1 Using a fluted pasta wheel, cut the pasta sheet into long strips about ¾–1-inch wide. Try to keep the strips the same width or they will not cook evenly.

2 Spread the pappardelle strips out in a single layer on floured dish towels and sprinkle them with a little more flour. Let the pappardelle dry on the towels for at least 15 minutes before cooking.

### Cutting Lasagne and Cannelloni

1 With a large sharp knife, cut the pasta sheets into 5–6 x 3–4-inch rectangles or whatever size fits your baking dish best.

2 Spread the rectangles out in a single layer on floured dish towels, sprinkle them with more flour and let dry for at least 15 minutes before cooking. They can be used for both lasagne and cannelloni.

### Cook's Tip

*Don't throw away the trimmings when making pasta shapes, such as tagliatelle and lasagne—cut the trimmings into small pieces and pop them into soup at the last minute. You can cut leftover scraps into any rough shape you like, but there are two shapes that are made especially for soups: quadrucci and maltagliati.*

### Cutting Quadrucci (for Soups)

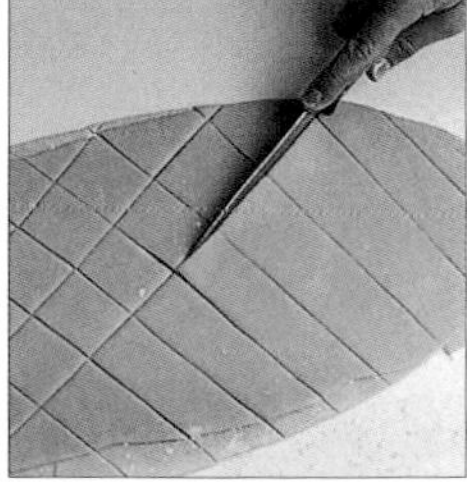

1 Stack two pasta sheets on top of each other, with a light sprinkling of flour in between. With a large sharp knife, cut the pasta diagonally into 1½-inch wide strips, then cut across the strips in the opposite direction to make 1½-inch squares.

2 Spread the squares out on floured dish towels and sprinkle with more flour. Let dry for at least 15 minutes before cooking.

### Cutting Maltagliati (for Soups)

1 Dust one pasta sheet lightly with flour. Starting from one long edge, roll the sheet up into a cylinder. Lightly flatten the cylinder, then, with a sharp knife, slice off the corners at one end, making two diagonal cuts to form two sides of a triangle. Cut straight across to complete the triangle. Repeat all the way along the cylinder, then unfold the maltagliati.

2 Spread out the maltagliati on floured dish towels. Sprinkle the shapes with a little more flour and let them dry for at least 15 minutes before cooking.

**Cook's Tip**

*Maltagliati means badly cut, so don't worry if the pasta is misshapen—it is meant to be. Quadrucci and maltagliati can also be cut from fresh lasagne rectangles, but this will take slightly longer.*

# Making Short Pasta Shapes

Most small pasta shapes are best left to the professionals, because they either take too long to make in any quantity or require special equipment. There are a couple of shapes that are an exception: garganelli and farfalle. Garganelli are traditionally made with a special tool called *il pettine*, but you can improvise with an old-fashioned butter paddle and a round pencil.

### Making Garganelli

1 Cut the pasta sheets into 2-inch squares. Lay the butter paddle ridges horizontally on the work surface, with the ridges facing towards you. Angle the square so that it is diamond-shaped and place it over the ridges. Put a pencil diagonally across the corner of the square that is closest to you.

2 Roll the pasta square up around the pencil, pressing down hard on the ends of the pencil as you go. The ridges of the butter paddle will imprint themselves on the pasta.

3 Stand the pencil upright on the work surface and tap the end so that the tube of pasta slides off.

4 Spread the garganelli out in a single layer on floured dish towels, sprinkle them with more flour and let them dry for at least 15 minutes before cooking.

### Making Farfalle

1 With a fluted pasta wheel, cut the pasta sheets into rectangles measuring 1¼ x 1 inch. Pinch the long sides of each rectangle between your index finger and thumb and squeeze hard to make a bow-tie shape. If the pasta will not hold the shape, moisten your fingers with water and squeeze again.

2 Spread the farfalle out in a single layer on floured dish towels, sprinkle them with a little more flour and let dry for at least 15 minutes before cooking.

# Making Pasta Shapes Using a Machine

### Rolling the Dough

A machine makes light work of rolling pasta dough. It makes thinner, smoother pasta than you can make by hand, and the thickness is always even. Some shapes, such as lasagne, are cut by hand, but for cutting noodles, a machine is invaluable.

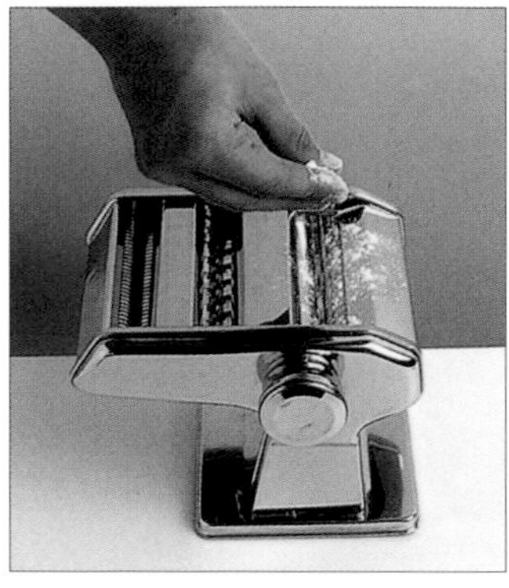

1 Clamp the machine securely to your work surface and insert the handle in the roller slot. Set the rollers at their widest setting and sprinkle them lightly with flour. Unwrap the ball of pasta and cut it into quarters. Work with one quarter at a time, wrapping the other three pieces of pasta dough in plastic wrap.

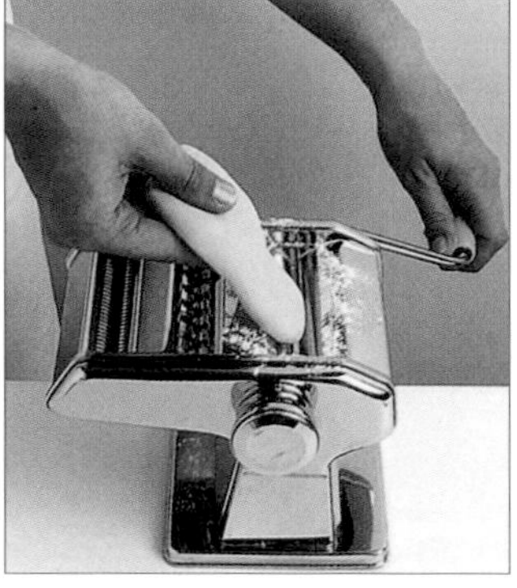

2 Flatten the quarter of dough with lightly floured hands and make it into a rough rectangle, just a little narrower in width than the rollers of the machine. Feed this through the rollers of the machine.

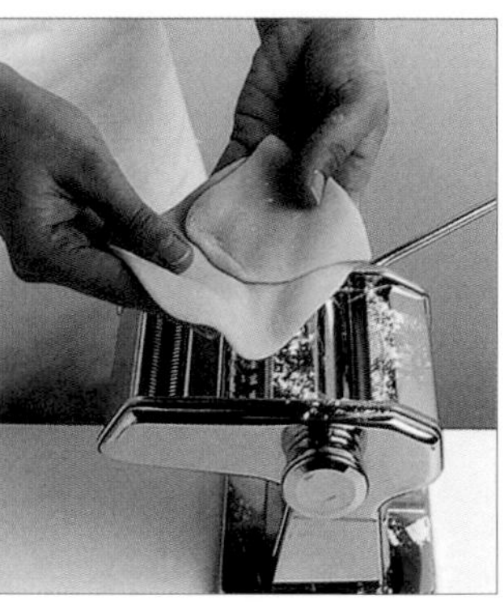

3 Fold the dough into thirds, then feed it lengthwise through the rollers. Repeat the folding and rolling five times.

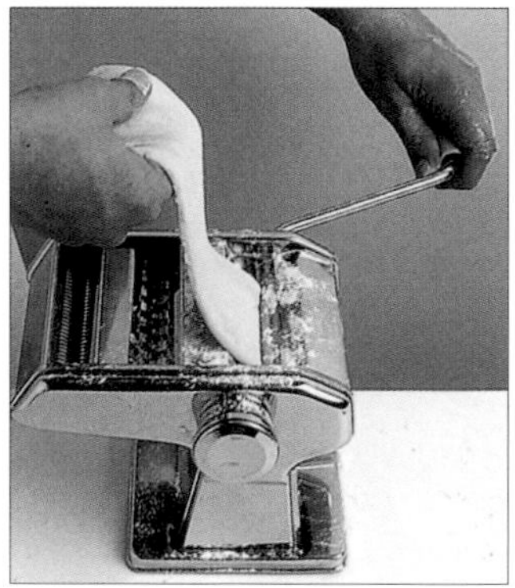

4 Turn the roller setting one notch. Sprinkle the pasta lightly with flour and feed it through the rollers again, only this time unfolded.

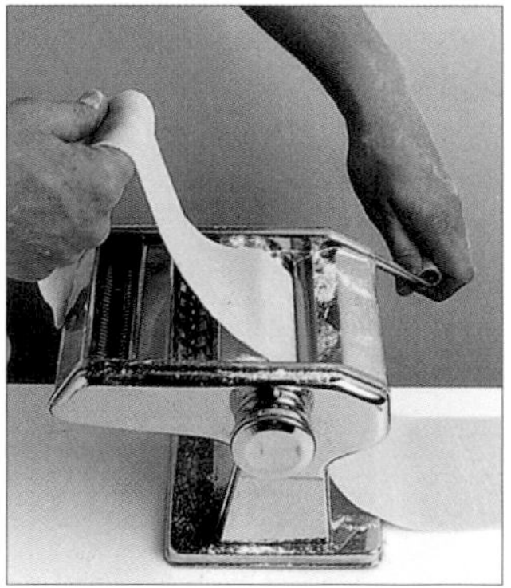

5 Turn the roller setting another notch and repeat the rolling, then continue in this way without folding the dough until you get to the last setting, turning the roller setting another notch after each rolling and sprinkling it lightly with flour if it becomes sticky. The dough will get longer and thinner with every rolling until it reaches 3 feet in length. Once the dough has been rolled, it is ready for cutting into the required shape.

#### Cook's Tips

- *About halfway through the rolling process, you may find that the pasta strip becomes too unwieldy and difficult to handle because it is so long. In this case, cut the strip in half or into thirds and work with one piece at a time. Remember to return the notch on the roller to the setting where you left off when you start with the next piece of dough.*
- *You may find that the dough is thin enough on the penultimate setting, in which case you can stop there. This will definitely be the case if you are going to make tonnarelli or spaghetti alla chitarra.*
- *Keep sprinkling the pasta dough lightly with flour if it becomes sticky, and keep the rollers lightly floured to prevent the pasta sticking to the machine.*
- *Any trimmings and leftover pieces of pasta dough can be re-rolled and more shapes cut from them.*
- *Once they are dry, noodles and pasta shapes can be stored in a paper bag for 3–4 days, or frozen in plastic bags for up to 1 month.*

### Cutting Lasagne and Cannelloni

1 Using a sharp knife, cut the rolled pasta strip into 5–6 x 3–4-inch rectangles, or whatever size fits your baking dish best.

2 Spread out the rectangles in a single layer on floured dish towels and sprinkle with flour.

**Cook's Tip**

*•Leave the lasagne sheets to dry on the dish towels while rolling and cutting the remaining three pieces of dough.*

*•Stack each successive batch of lasagne sheets on top of the previous one, with a floured dish towel in between.*

### Cutting Tagliatelle and Fettuccine

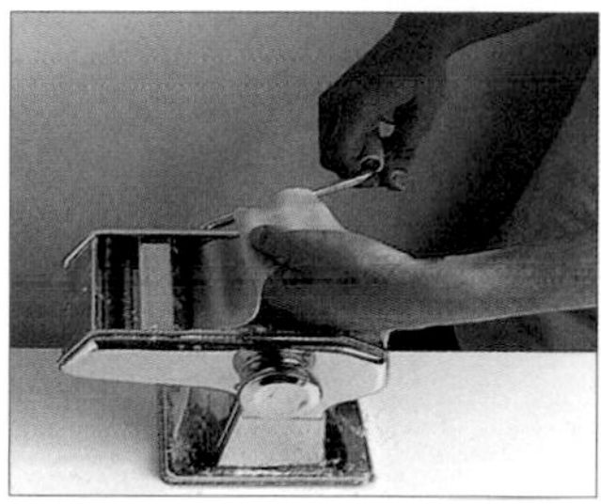

1 Insert the handle in the slot for the widest cutters and sprinkle these cutters lightly with flour. Cut the pasta strip to about 12 inches long if you haven't done so already, and sprinkle it lightly with flour. Feed the pasta through the widest cutters.

2 Continue turning the handle of the pasta machine slowly and steadily, guiding the strands with your other hand.

3 Toss the tagliatelle or fettuccine in flour and spread the noodles out on a floured dish towel. Let dry while rolling and cutting the remaining dough.

### Cutting Tonnarelli and Spaghetti alla Chitarra

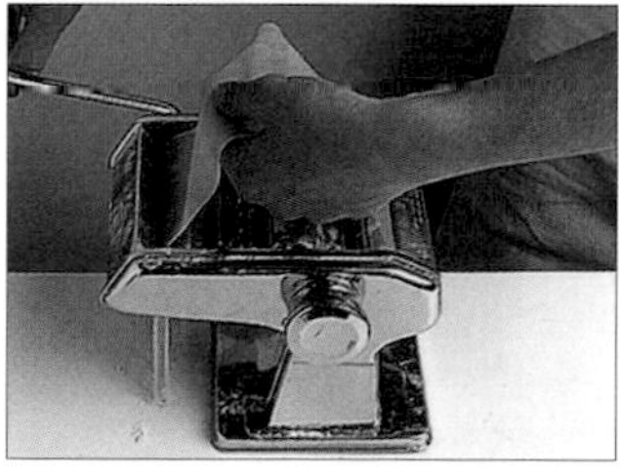

1 Stop rolling the pasta strip after the last but two or last but one setting, then insert the handle in the slot for the narrowest cutters and feed the pasta through the machine.

2 Proceed as for tagliatelle or fettuccine, turning the handle and guiding the long strands with your other hand. Toss the tonnarelli or spaghetti in flour and spread out on floured dish towels.

**Cook's Tip**

*When making spaghetti alla chitarra, the thickness and width of the pasta should be equal so the noodles come out square. You may need to experiment with this shape a few times until you get it just the right thickness.*

**Variations**

*To make tagliarini or spaghettini, insert the pasta machine handle in the slot for the narrowest cutters and proceed as for tonnarelli and spaghetti alla chitarra.*

1 Using a large sharp knife, cut the rolled pasta strip into two 18–20-inch lengths, if this has not been done already.

2 Using a teaspoon, put 10–12 little mounds of your chosen filling along one side of one of the pasta strips, spacing them evenly.

3 Using a pastry brush, carefully brush a little water on to the pasta strip around each mound of filling.

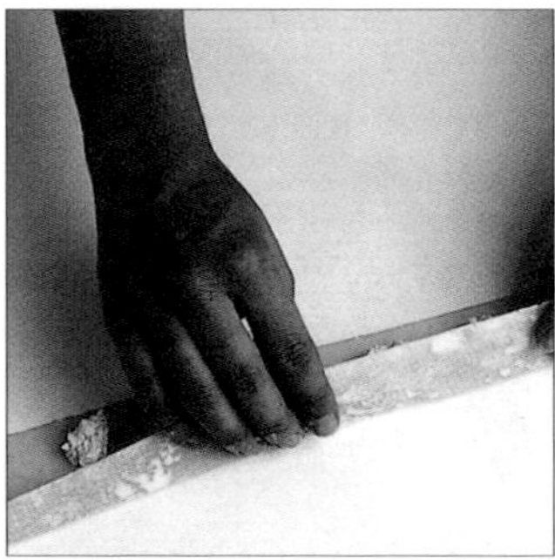

4 Fold the plain side of the pasta strip over the filling.

5 Starting from the folded edge, press down gently with your fingertips around each mound, pushing the air out at the unfolded edge. Sprinkle lightly with flour.

6 With a fluted pasta wheel, cut along each long side, then in between each mound to make small square shapes.

7 Put the ravioli on floured dish towels, sprinkle lightly with more flour and let dry while repeating the process with the remaining dough. For a 3-egg dough, you should get 80–96 ravioli, more if you re-roll the trimmings.

### Cook's Tips

*•Ravioli made in this way are not perfectly square, but they look charmingly homemade. If you prefer a more precise finish, you should use a ravioli tray, which you can buy from a specialty kitchenware store. The ravioli tray can be bought on its own or as an extra accessory to a pasta machine. Another alternative is to use a hand-held ravioli cutter or a round, plain or fluted biscuit cutter.*

*•Have ready 3 or 4 floured dish towels before you begin cutting the pasta shapes. Arrange the stuffed shapes on the towels, well-spaced and in one layer, because if you overlap them, they may stick together.*

*•Once they are dry, stuffed pasta shapes can be frozen for up to 1 month, layered between sheets of plastic wrap in plastic bags.*

**Fillings for Stuffed Pasta**

These vary from one or two simple ingredients to special traditional recipes. The ingredients are mixed together and often bound with beaten egg. Seasoning is added to taste.

**Simple ideas**

*•spinach, Parmesan, ricotta and nutmeg*
*•crab, mascarpone, lemon, parsley and chiles*
*•taleggio cheese and fresh marjoram*

**Regional specialities**

*•ground pork and turkey with fresh herbs, ricotta and Parmesan*
*•fresh herbs, ricotta, Parmesan and garlic*
*•puréed cooked pumpkin, prosciutto, mozzarella and parsley*

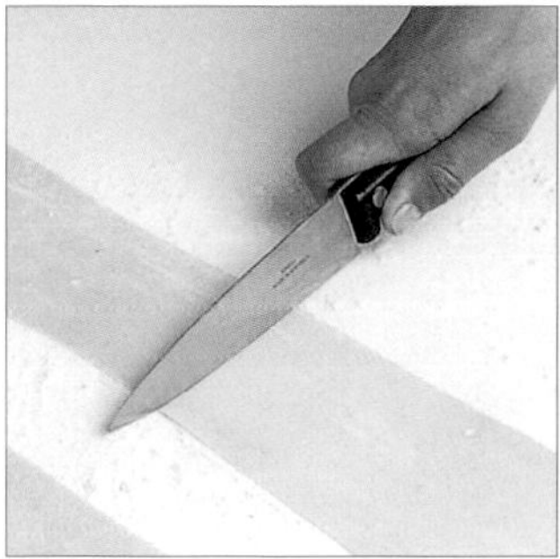

1 Using a sharp knife, cut the rolled strip of pasta dough by hand into two 18–20-inch lengths, if this has not been done already.

2 Using a teaspoon, put 8–10 little mounds of your chosen filling along one side of one of the pasta strips, spacing them evenly.

3 Using a pastry brush, carefully brush a little water onto the pasta strip around each mound of filling.

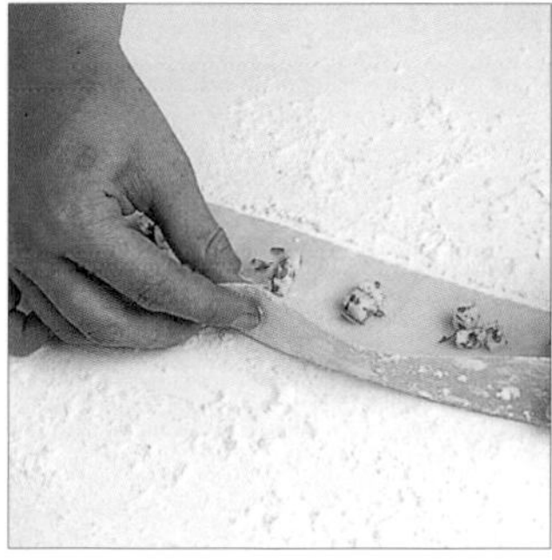

4 Fold the plain side of the pasta strip over the filling.

5 Starting from the folded edge, press down gently with your fingertips around each mound, pushing the air out at the unfolded edge. Sprinkle lightly with flour.

6 Using only half of a 2-inch fluted round ravioli or biscuit cutter, cut around each mound of filling to make a half-moon shape.

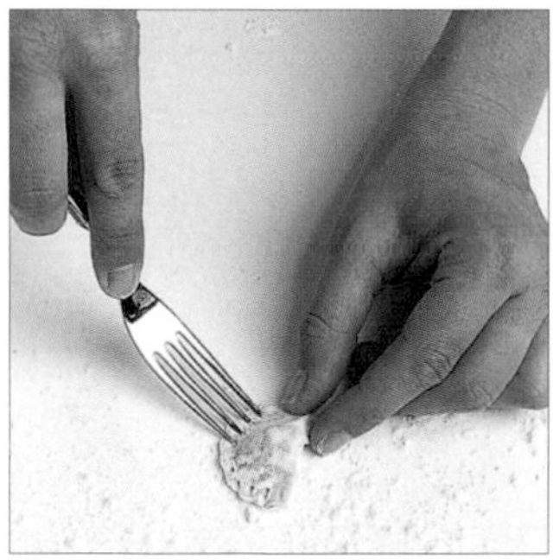

7 If you like, press the cut edges of the agnolotti with the tines of a fork to give a decorative effect.

8 Put the agnolotti on floured dish towels, sprinkle lightly with more flour and let dry while repeating the process with the remaining dough. For a 3-egg dough, you should get 64–80 agnolotti, more if you re-roll the trimmings.

### Cook's Tips

- *When cutting out the agnolotti, make sure that the folded edge is the straight edge.*
- *Don't re-roll the trimmings after cutting each pasta strip, but wait until you have done them all. If there is no filling left for the rolled pasta trimmings, you can use them to make noodles or small shapes for soup.*

## Making Tortellini / Tortelloni

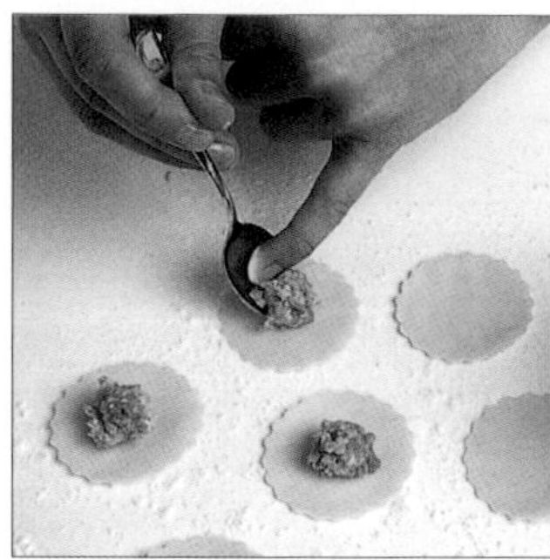

1 Using a sharp knife, cut the rolled strip of pasta dough by hand into two 18–20-inch lengths, if this has not been done already.

2 To make tortellini: with a 2-inch fluted ravioli or biscuit cutter, cut out 8–10 discs from one of the pasta strips. For tortelloni use a $2^1/2$-inch cutter.

3 Using a teaspoon and a fingertip, put a little mound of your chosen filling in the center of each disc.

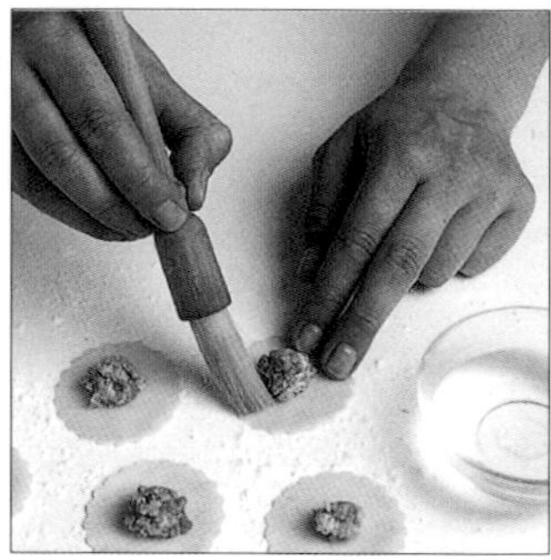

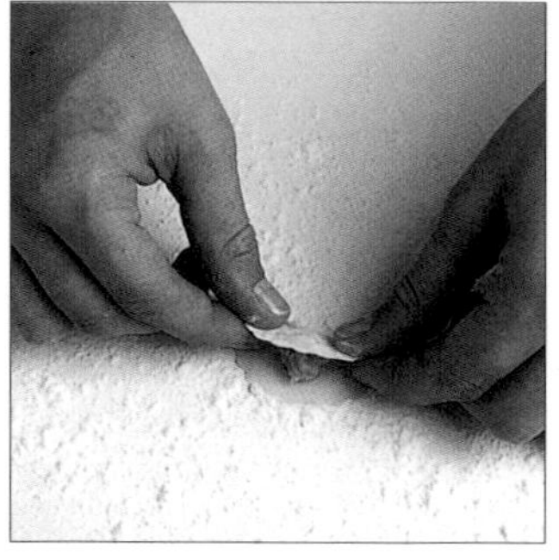

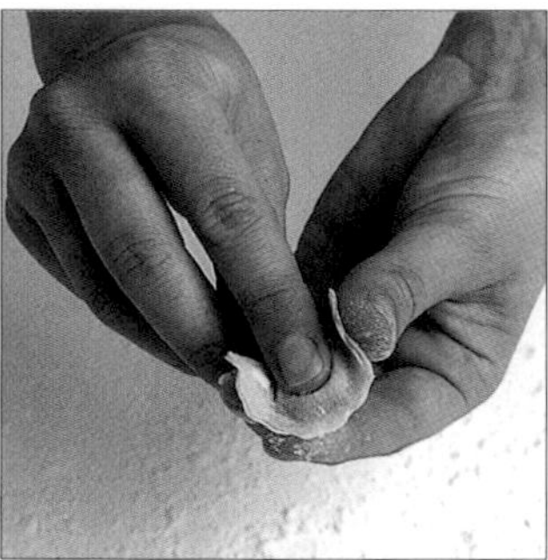

4 Brush a little water around the edge of each disc.

5 Fold the disc in half over the filling so that the top and bottom edges do not quite meet. Press to seal.

6 Wrap the half-moon shape around an index finger and pinch the ends together to seal.

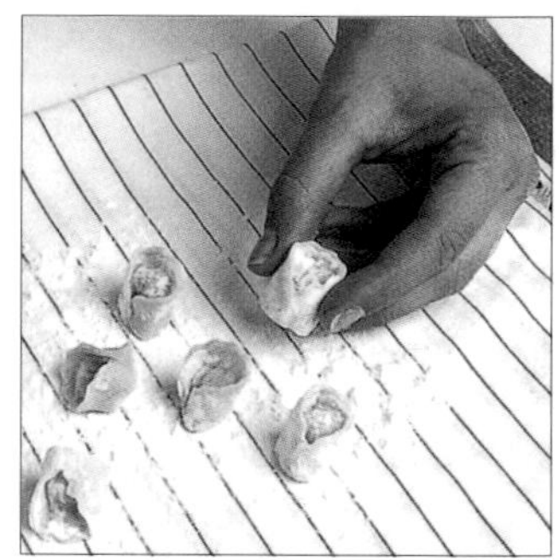

7 Put the tortellini or tortelloni on floured dish towels, sprinkle with flour and let dry while repeating the process with the remaining dough. For a 3-egg dough, you should get 64–80 tortellini, more if you re-roll the trimmings.

## Making Pansotti and Cappelletti / Cappellacci

Pansotti are made from 2-inch squares of pasta that are folded in half over the filling to make triangles. Moisten the edges of the triangles and press to seal in the filling.

Cappelletti and cappellacci are made in the same way as tortellini, using squares of pasta rather than discs. The edges are turned up so they look like little hats.

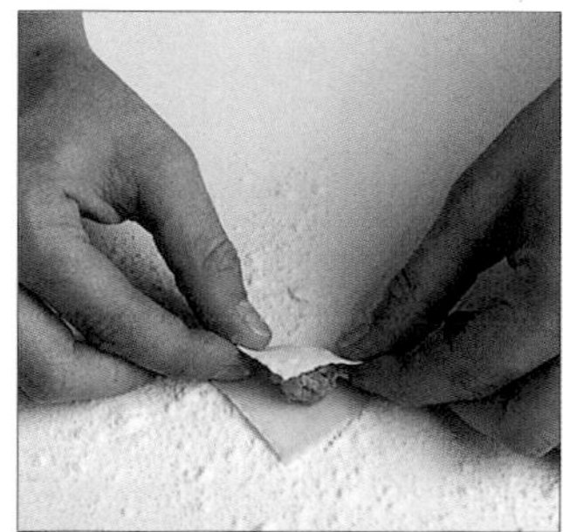

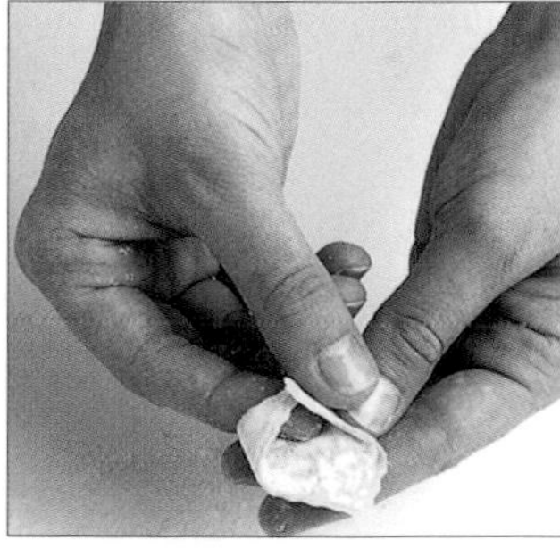

# Making Flavored and Colored Pasta

There are many different ingredients you can use to change the flavor and color of pasta, whether you are making the dough by hand or machine, although you will find it easier to get a more even color with a machine. Some flavors are more trouble than they are worth, so it is best to restrict your choice to the tried and tested ones. The following flavorings are the most successful, and the amounts of ingredients given are for a 3-egg quantity of pasta all'uovo (pasta dough with eggs).

*Black pepper*

*Chile*

*Porcini*

*Tomato*

**Black pepper**
Put 2 tablespoons black peppercorns or mixed peppercorns in a mortar and crush them coarsely with a pestle. Add to the eggs in the well before you start to incorporate the flour.

**Chile**
Add 1–2 teaspoons crushed dried red chiles to the eggs in the well before you start to incorporate the flour.

**Porcini**
Soak 1/2 ounce porcini (dried wild mushrooms) in 3/4 cup warm water. Drain the porcini and squeeze to remove as much water as possible. Dry the mushrooms thoroughly on paper towels, then chop them finely and add them to the eggs in the well before you start to incorporate the flour. The dough will be stickier than usual, so you will need to add more flour during kneading, rolling and cutting. If you like, you can add the porcini soaking water to the water for boiling the pasta. This will intensify the mushroom flavor of the pasta.

**Tomato**
Add 2 tablespoons tomato paste to the eggs in the well before you start to incorporate the flour. The pasta dough will be stickier than usual, so you will need to add more flour during kneading, rolling and cutting.

**Spinach**
Wash 5 ounces fresh spinach leaves and place them in a large saucepan with only the water that clings to the leaves. Add a pinch of salt, then cover the pan and cook over medium heat for about 8 minutes or until the spinach is wilted and tender. Drain the spinach, leave for a few minutes until cool enough to handle, then squeeze it hard in your hands to remove as much water as possible. Dry the spinach thoroughly on several sheets of paper towel, then finely chop it using a large sharp knife or a food processor and add it to the eggs in the well before you start to incorporate the flour. The pasta dough will be much stickier than usual, so you will need to add a little extra flour during kneading and when rolling and cutting the dough.

**Squid ink**
Add two 1/8-ounce envelopes of squid ink to the eggs in the well before you start to incorporate the flour. The dough will be stickier than usual, so you will need to add more flour during kneading, rolling and cutting.

**Herb**
Wash and dry three small handfuls of fresh herbs. Basil, Italian parsley, sage and thyme are all good choices, either singly or together. Finely chop the herbs and add them to the eggs in the well before you start to incorporate the flour. The dough may be a little more sticky than usual, in which case you may need to add a little extra flour during kneading and when rolling and cutting it.

**Saffron**
Sift 3 or 4 envelopes of saffron powder with the flour before starting to make the pasta dough.

*Spinach*

*Squid ink*

*Herb*

*Saffron*

# Making Striped Pasta

You can use different colors to make striped dough that can be cut into rectangles for lasagne and cannelloni. It is quite fiddly, and the rolling out is best done with a pasta machine.

Plain or saffron yellow and spinach doughs look very good together, and another excellent combination is plain or saffron yellow dough contrasted with dough colored with tomato or squid ink. To make pasta tricolore (three-colored pasta), mix stripes of tomato dough, squid ink or spinach dough and plain dough. Some creative chefs make check and tartan patterns with colored pasta, but this is very time-consuming for the home cook.

1 Roll out two different colored pieces of dough on a pasta machine, keeping them separate and taking them up to and including the last setting but two.

2 With a fluted pasta wheel, cut one strip of each color lengthwise into three or four narrower strips. Select three strips of one color and two of the other, setting the rest aside for the next batch of striped pasta.

3 The aim is to join the pasta strips together, using water as glue. Brush one long edge of one pasta strip with a little water, then join a pasta of a different color to it, placing it over the moistened edge and pressing it firmly to seal the join. Repeat this process, alternating the pasta colors until you have a length of pasta that resembles a scarf, with three stripes of one color and two stripes of the other.

4 Sprinkle the pasta liberally with flour, lift it very carefully and put it through the pasta machine, which should be set to the last but one setting.

5 Cut the dough into rectangles or squares for cannelloni or lasagne and spread these out in a single layer on floured dish towels. Sprinkle them with flour and let dry for at least 15 minutes before cooking.

### Cook's Tips

- *When cutting flavored tagliatelle or tagliarini on a pasta machine, sprinkle the cutters liberally with flour before putting the dough through. The noodles tend to stick together as they come through the machine, so you may need to separate them gently with floured hands before putting them on dish towels and tossing them in more flour.*
- *When cooking flavored pasta, start testing for doneness earlier than usual. The ingredients added for some flavors make the pasta more moist and soft than usual, and this means that it cooks a little more quickly.*
- *You can use striped pasta for making ravioli: keep the strips fairly narrow and make sure that they are well sealed, otherwise the ravioli may split open during cooking.*

# Making Silhouette Pasta

Fresh herbs can be rolled between sheets of pasta to give a very pretty decorative effect. The pasta needs to be very thin, so it is best to roll it out on a pasta machine. Use only soft, leafy herbs such as Italian parsley, chervil, green or purple basil or sage. Silhouette pasta can be boiled and served with melted butter and grated Parmesan, or cooked in a clear soup (*in brodo*).

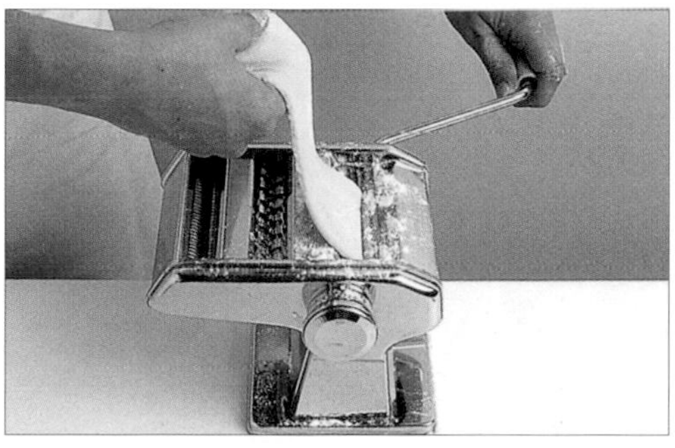

1 Roll out a piece of dough on a pasta machine, taking it up to and including the last setting. Moisten one side of the strip of dough lightly with water. A mister or spray gun is ideal for this.

*Above: Fresh herbs, such as basil (top left), Italian parsley (left) and sage (right), can be rolled between sheets of dough to make pretty silhouette pasta.*

2 Arrange individual fresh herb leaves on the moistened half of the dough, placing them at regular intervals. Fold the dry half of the dough over the herbs and press the edges firmly to seal.

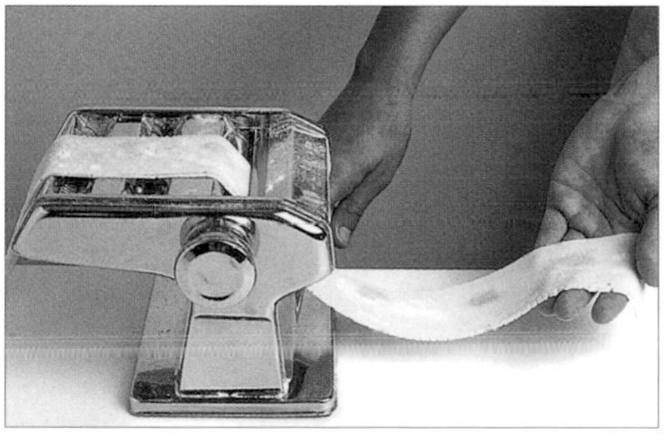

3 Sprinkle the pasta liberally with flour and put it through the machine, on the penultimate setting.

4 With a floured pasta wheel, cut around each herb leaf to make square ravioli shapes. Spread the shapes out in a single layer on floured dish towels. Sprinkle them with more flour and let dry for at least 15 minutes before cooking.

As an alternative to using a pasta wheel for cutting out rectangular shapes, use a small, fluted cookie cutter and stamp out round shapes.

# The Pasta Pantry

Certain ingredients crop up time and time again in sauces for pasta. Some can be kept in the storecupboard, while fresh ones must either be bought just before use, or kept in the fridge. Fresh herbs and leaves, spices, oils, vinegars and other less well-known ingredients add flavor. Canned and dried fish and shellfish are useful additions to your storecupboard, while fresh vegetables, such as eggplant, tomatoes and bell peppers, along with garlic and sun-dried vegetables, play an important part in many pasta dishes. Cheese and cream are used in sauces, in fillings and for baked pasta dishes.

## Fresh Herbs and Leaves

These are used extensively for flavoring sauces for pasta, and for presentation and garnishing. Italian cooks keep pots of fresh herbs growing on the windowsill or in the garden, and think nothing of tossing in a handful of this or that herb to freshen up the flavor of their cooking. Herbs are added according to the individual cook's taste, and are seldom measured.

*Basil*

**Basil**
***Basilico***
The variety known as sweet basil is used in Italian cooking, and this is the one you are most likely to find in the supermarkets. It is used all over Italy, but most of all in Liguria, where it grows prolifically and is used in large quantities for pesto. Basil has a special affinity with tomatoes, and is frequently used with them in sauces for pasta. It is best torn or shredded and added at the last moment. Fine chopping and long cooking spoil its pungent flavor.

*Bay leaves*

**Bay**
***Alloro/lauro***
Both fresh and dried bay leaves are used all over Italy for flavoring soups and broths and long-cooking sauces, especially those made with meat, poultry and game. The leaves are removed before serving.

*Marjoram*

**Marjoram and Oregano**
***Maggiorana e Origano***
These two herbs are closely related, but their flavors are quite different. Marjoram is sweet and delicate, while oregano, a wild variety of marjoram, is a pungent herb that should be used sparingly. They are both used in sauces for pasta, especially tomato-based ones, but marjoram is used more in Liguria and the north of Italy and oregano in the south, where it is perhaps best known for being sprinkled over pizza. Both marjoram and oregano are best chopped quite finely. They are sometimes used dried in the winter.

*Oregano*

*Mint*

**Mint**
***Mentuccia***
Mint is not usually associated with Italian cooking, but it is frequently used in Roman dishes, in the cooking of central Italy, and even as far south as Calabria. Mentuccia is a particular kind of wild mint with small leaves grown in Rome, and there is also another variety called nepitella. You may come across the flavor of fresh mint in pasta soups, and occasionally in sauces for pasta.

**Parsley**
***Prezzemolo***
Italians use the Italian variety of parsley, which is sometimes sold here as continental parsley. It looks very similar to cilantro, and has a stronger flavor than curly parsley. It is used frequently in sauces for pasta, in fairly large quantities, and is often coarsely chopped and fried in olive oil with a *battuto* of onion and garlic at the beginning of sauce making. It is popular all over Italy, and is only ever used fresh.

*Italian parsley*

Radicchio di Treviso

Radicchio di Verona

**Radicchio**

***Radicchio***

This ruby red and white salad leaf is a member of the chicory family. The most common variety, *radicchio di Verona*, is small and round with very tightly furled leaves, but there is another type called *radicchio di Treviso*, which is streaked creamy white and red with looser, long and tapering leaves. Both have a bitter flavor, which is much appreciated in small quantities in pasta sauces. Shredded leaves should be added at the last moment, to preserve their color.

Arugula

**Arugula**

***Rucola***

Peppery hot *rucola* loses its pungency when cooked, so it is added to pasta sauces at the last minute, or strewn liberally over the top of pasta dishes just before serving. Bunches of large-leaved *rucola* are best; the small packets sold in supermarkets are very expensive and seem to lack flavor. Use *rucola* as soon as possible after purchase because the leaves can quickly go limp and yellow, especially in warm weather.

Rosemary

**Rosemary**

***Rosmarino***

This most fragrant and pungent herb is very popular all over Italy. Rosemary is used sparingly in meat and tomato sauces, either very finely chopped or on the sprig, which is then removed from the sauce before serving. Dried rosemary is sometimes used in the winter months.

**Sage**

***Salvia***

Along with parsley, basil and rosemary, sage is one of Italy's favorite herbs. It is frequently used by Roman cooks who sizzle fresh sage in butter to create a classic sauce to serve with ravioli. Fresh sage leaves are also used with meat, sausage, poultry and game sauces, either finely shredded or chopped or as whole leaves, which are removed before serving. Fresh sage is preferred to dried, but dried sage is occasionally used in the winter, in sauces that are cooked for a long time.

Sage

**Thyme**

***Timo***

This aromatic and distinctively flavored herb is used both fresh and dried. It is a Mediterranean herb that goes well with tomato-based sauces and with meat and poultry, and it is also good mixed with rosemary and bay.

Thyme

SPICES AND SALT

Spicy, highly seasoned foods are not normally associated with Italian cooking, but the use of spices in cooking dates back to Roman—and even Etruscan—times, when spices were used freely, often to excess. Nowadays, spices tend to be used more sparingly and the range tends to be limited to a few favorites.

Dried chiles

Fresh chiles

Chile flakes

### Chile

***Peperoncino***

Small red chiles are immensely popular in the south of Italy and Sardinia, and they are frequently used in sauces for pasta. Sometimes the sauce is a classic that depends on chiles for its essential flavor—the hot and spicy *Penne all'Arrabbiata* from Rome being perhaps the most famous. Most often, however, chiles are added more sparingly with the aim of livening up a sauce and intensifying its flavor rather than giving it a fiery flavor.

Fresh chiles tend to be fried with a *soffritto* of olive oil, onion, garlic and parsley at the beginning of sauce making, whereas dried chiles are popped into the sauce when it is bubbling. Both fresh and dried chiles are often added whole to sauces in order to impart a subtle flavor. They are later lifted out and either discarded or chopped or crumbled, then returned to the sauce. The seeds may be included or left out, depending on the degree of heat required (the seeds contain most of the heat). Crushed dried red chiles or chile flakes (sold in little jars) are very handy when just a pinch or two of chile is required in a recipe.

### Cinnamon

***Cannella***

Ground cinnamon is used in stuffings for pasta, both with meat and cheese. It gives a fragrant aroma and subtle sweetness, and is always used sparingly.

### Nutmeg

***Noce moscata***

Whole nutmeg is grated fresh when needed. It is used for flavoring *la beschiamella* (béchamel sauce) and is often used in combination with spinach and ricotta cheese. In Emilia-Romagna, it is traditionally used for flavoring meat sauces and stuffings for pasta.

### Pepper

***Pepe***

Black peppercorns are ground fresh from a pepper mill as and when they are needed, both in cooking and at the table. Black pepper is used in just about every pasta sauce that is made, and it is also used to speckle and flavor homemade pasta. If coarsely crushed peppercorns are required, they are ground with a mortar and pestle.

### Saffron

***Zafferano***

The most expensive spice in the world, saffron comes in two different forms. Threads of saffron, the actual dried stigmas of the crocus, are usually wrapped in cellophane and sold in envelopes. They can be sprinkled into a sauce, but are more often soaked in warm water for 20–30 minutes, so that the water can be strained off and used for coloring and flavoring. Saffron powder is sold in envelopes and can be sprinkled directly into sauces. It is less expensive than the threads and considered by many to be inferior, but it is more convenient to use. Saffron has a delicate but distinctive flavor, which is good with both cream and butter-based sauces as well as with fish and shellfish. The spice is also used to color homemade pasta.

Saffron

### Salt

***Sale***

Coarse sea salt and rock salt are ground in a salt mill and used both as a seasoning in cooking and at the table. It is essential that salt is added to the water when boiling pasta to give it flavor, but for this you can use refined cooking salt rather than the more expensive sea or rock salt. Just about every pasta sauce will have salt as a seasoning, except perhaps those containing salty anchovies or bottarga (air-dried mullet or tuna roe).

Peppercorns (left) and sea salt

OILS AND VINEGARS

Oil and vinegar are essential store-cupboard items for the Italian cook. Don't buy cheap brands; it will be false economy. Good olive oil and wine or balsamic vinegar will lift the flavor of a sauce or salad and enhance the other ingredients in it.

### Olive oil

***Olio d'oliva***

Extra virgin olive oil is the best and most expensive of the olive oils. This is literally the oil that is secreted when the olives are crushed mechanically by cold presses.

No other processing nor any heat is involved in the making of extra virgin olive oil. It should have an acidity level of one per cent or less, but as this information is seldom on the label of the bottle, this is difficult to check.

Extra virgin is the oil to use for salads, since heating may spoil its natural olive flavor. It is also the one to use for sprinkling over warm food or for tossing with pasta in dishes, such as *Spaghetti Aglio e Olio*, that rely on olive oil for their predominant flavor.

Fruity, often peppery, Tuscan oil is reputed to be among the best of the extra virgin olive oils, although some cooks prefer oil from Umbria, or from Veneto or Liguria, which are more delicate. Oils from the South are stronger and more intensely flavored, and these may be more to your taste. Brands vary enormously, so experiment to find what suits you best.

For cooking and heating, virgin olive oil is the one to use. This is less expensive than extra virgin because it has a higher acidity level (up to four per cent), but it is cold pressed and not refined in any way so it still has a good, full flavor. Many pasta sauces start with the frying of flavoring ingredients, such as onion, garlic, celery, parsley, chiles and carrot. If these are fried in an oil with a good flavor, the sauce will have a strong base (*soffritto*), the flavor of which will then permeate through the other ingredients during cooking.

*Virgin olive oil (left), extra virgin olive oil (center) and balsamic vinegar (right)*

## Vinegar

*Aceto*

Occasionally a splash of red or white wine vinegar may be added to a pasta sauce, but wine vinegar is more often used in salad dressings. Flavorwise, red and white vinegars are interchangeable, but the color of the salad ingredients may dictate whether you use red or white.

Balsamic vinegar (aceto balsamico) from Modena in Emilia-Romagna is a different thing altogether. It is a dark, syrupy vinegar which is aged in wooden casks for many years. The best and most authentic *aceto balsamico* will have been aged in casks or barrels of different woods for 40–50 years. Labelled *tradizionale di Modena*, this vinegar is only used a drop at a time, usually at the moment of serving on fish or meat, salads and even fresh strawberries. For flavoring a pasta sauce or salad, use the much less expensive balsamic vinegar that has been aged between five and ten

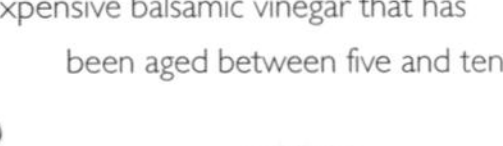

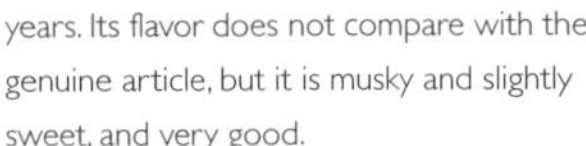

years. Its flavor does not compare with the genuine article, but it is musky and slightly sweet, and very good.

## Flavorings

Some special ingredients are used in different regions of Italy, and you may need to buy them for a particular sauce.

*Salted capers*

*Capers bottled in brine*

### Capers

*Capperi*

Capers are the fruit of a flowering shrub that grows in the Mediterranean. They are sold in various ways. The best are the large, salted capers sold in small jars in Italian delicatessens. Check before buying that the salt is white and has not discolored at all. Yellow salt is a sign that the capers are past their best and may have a rancid taste. Before use, salted capers need to be soaked in several changes of water for 10–15 minutes, then drained, rinsed in fresh water and dried, but after this initial preparation they taste very fresh and good. They can be chopped and used to add piquancy to sauces—you will often find them in recipes from the south of Italy and Sicily and Sardinia.

It is also possible to buy tiny capers sold in small bottles of brine or vinegar. These have a strong flavor and should be rinsed well before use. They almost always taste sharp and vinegary, so use them sparingly.

### Olives
*Olive*

Both black and green olives are used in making sauces and salads, although black olives are more highly favored. The best type for pasta sauces are the small, shiny, very black *gaeta* olives from Liguria. Buy the plain ones for cooking, not those with additional flavorings, such as herbs, garlic, chiles and other spices, which are intended for antipasto. Olives are best added to a sauce towards the end of cooking. They need no cooking, only heating through, and if added too early they can impart a bitter flavor. When using olives in a pasta sauce or salad, pit them first, because the stones are awkward to manage when you are eating pasta.

*Olives*

### Pancetta
*Pancetta*

This is cured belly of pork, the Italian equivalent of bacon, which has a spicy, sweet flavor and aroma. Unsmoked pancetta is sold in a roll in Italian specialty stores, and is called pancetta arrotolata or pancetta coppata. A machine is used to slice it very thinly to order and it can be eaten as it is for an antipasto, or cut into strips or diced for use in cooking. Pancetta affumicata is smoked and comes in strips, which look like lean bacon complete with rind. There is a version called pancetta stesa, which is long and flat. Smoked pancetta is cut into strips or dice and used as the base for ragù and many other pasta sauces, the most famous of which is carbonara. Some supermarkets sell packages of ready-diced pancetta. The quality and flavor are generally good, so these are well worth buying for convenience. If you are unable to get pancetta, lean bacon can be used instead, and you can buy smoked or unsmoked, whichever flavor you prefer.

*Smoked (left) and unsmoked pancetta*

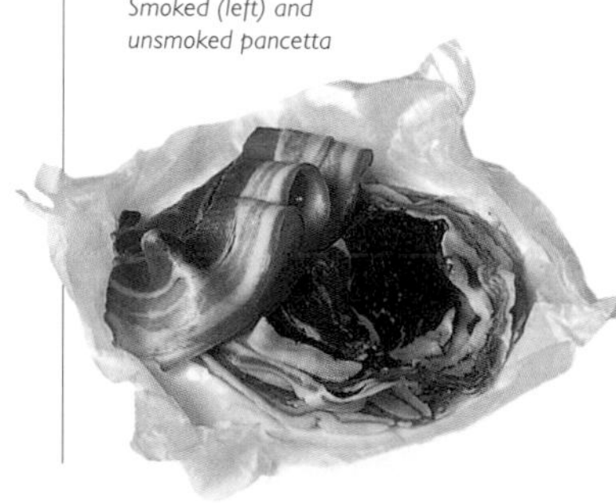

### Pine nuts
*Pinoli*

Best known for their inclusion in pesto, these small, creamy white nuts have an unusual waxy texture and resinous flavor. They look and taste good sprinkled over pasta salads, and they add a welcome crunchy bite. To enhance their flavor, they are often toasted before use. Only buy the quantity of pine nuts you need because they do not keep well and quickly go rancid. They are sold ready-shelled in small packages, in supermarkets.

*Pine nuts*

## Fish and Shellfish

Pasta sauces made with fish or shellfish are quick and delicious. Fresh seafood is often the main ingredient, but there are a few other fishy staples that are used over and over again.

### Anchovies
*Acciughe*

The best anchovies are the salted ones that are packed in large cans. You see them on the counters of Italian specialty stores, where they are sold loose by the pound. They must be rinsed, skinned and filleted before use, but are plumper and more flavorsome than the fillets sold in jars and cans, so repay the effort. Anchovies are used in sauces for pasta all over Italy, but particularly in the hot South and in Sicily and Sardinia where strong and salty flavors are so popular. When chopped and heated gently with a little olive oil, they melt down to a creamy paste that is packed with flavor, so you only need to use a small quantity at a time. If you can't get salted anchovies, try to locate anchovy fillets that are bottled in olive oil. These taste better than the ones canned in vegetable oil.

*Anchovies in brine (left) and salt*

### Bottarga
*Bottarga*

This is the salted and air-dried roe of mullet or tuna. The best is the mullet, bottarga di muggine. It is a great delicacy in Sardinia, Sicily and the Veneto, where they like it grated over pasta or very thinly sliced as an antipasto with lemon juice and olive oil. You can buy bottarga quite easily in Italian specialty stores, where it is kept in vacuum packs in the fridge. Mullet bottarga is delicate, moist and golden, like a pale, thin version of smoked cod's roe, and bears little resemblance to tuna bottarga, which

*Tuna bottarga*

Ready-grated bottarga

Mullet bottarga

comes in a thick, dark block. For grating over pasta you need only a small quantity and it can be kept in the fridge for a long time (check the use-by date). You can also buy ready-grated bottarga in small jars, but this product has a dry texture and the flavor does not compare with that of freshly grated bottarga.

Clams

*Vongole*

In Italy, small fresh clams are frequently used in pasta sauces on the coast and in Sicily and Sardinia, but they are not always easy to get in other parts of the country or further afield. Names vary from one region and one country to another, but the name is not important; it is the size that counts.

Fresh clams (left) and canned clams

Small *vongole* cook quickly and have a tender texture and sweet flavor, which make them ideal for pasta sauces. Don't be tempted to buy the large ones. Some fishmarkets sell frozen small clams, which are a good substitute for fresh; otherwise you should buy the bottled shelled clams in natural juice. Check labels carefully and don't buy the ones in vinegar or brine—these are intended for antipasto; their sharp flavor will spoil a pasta sauce. You can also buy bottled clams in their shells. These are packed in oil and, although intended primarily for antipasto, they also make an attractive garnish for a clam sauce.

Squid ink

*Nero di seppia*

If you want to color homemade pasta black, you can buy handy little envelopes of squid ink at fishmarkets and Italian specialty stores. There is usually about $\frac{1}{8}$ ounce of ink in each envelope and the envelopes are sold in pairs. Two envelopes are enough to color a 3-egg quantity of *pasta all'uovo*.

Tuna

*Tonno*

For pasta sauces, use only best-quality canned tuna in olive oil, not the kind packed in vegetable oil, water or brine. Some supermarkets sell it; otherwise you will have to go to an Italian specialty store. The flesh of good-quality canned tuna is moist and meaty. The cost of a good can of tuna is generally less than that of fresh fish, so no matter how much you spend on it, pasta with a tuna sauce will still be an inexpensive meal.

Canned tuna

VEGETABLES

Tomatoes are not the only vegetable to be used in sauces for pasta. Many others play an important part, either as a main ingredient or in a more minor role. Dried vegetables such as porcini mushrooms, bell peppers and tomatoes are used almost as often as fresh; valued for the intense flavor they impart to pasta sauces and soups.

Dried chargrilled eggplant

Eggplant

*Melanzane*

Fresh eggplant are used as a main ingredient in many pasta sauces, especially in southern Italy, Sicily and Sardinia. Dried eggplant are not used as a substitute for fresh, but are added to fresh vegetables for their characteristic earthy flavor and meaty texture. Sold in packages, they are thin slices of eggplant that have been dried in the sun, and are a good storecupboard item in that you can use as few or as many as you like. They need to be rehydrated in boiling water with a splash of white wine vinegar for 2 minutes before use, then drained and dried. They can then be snipped into strips and either added immediately to a simmering pasta sauce or fried first in olive oil.

**Garlic**

***Aglio***

Crushed, sliced and chopped garlic is used in many pasta sauces, but especially in those from the south of Italy, and whole garlic cloves are sometimes fried in olive oil at the beginning of cooking, then removed to leave behind a subtly flavored base for a sauce. One famous Roman pasta dish, *Spaghetti Aglio e Olio*, holds garlic in such high esteem that the sauce contains only two ingredients—garlic and olive oil—and in Rome they maintain it is the best cure for a hangover. The best Italian garlic is pink or purple tinged, with plump juicy cloves. In spring and early summer you can buy it fresh at some markets. This is the newly picked garlic that is sweet, moist and mild. As it dries out it becomes more pungent, so you need to adjust quantities accordingly. Buy garlic little and often so it neither sprouts green shoots nor becomes papery and dry.

*Garlic*

**Porcini mushrooms**

***Funghi porcini***

Dried porcini (*boletus edulis*) are invaluable for the intense, musky aroma and flavor they impart to pasta sauces and soups. Italians use them all year round, not as a substitute for fresh porcini, but as a valued ingredient in its own right. A few dried porcini added to ordinary fresh mushrooms, for example, will give them the flavor of wild mushrooms. Don't buy cheap porcini, but look for packages containing large pale-colored pieces. Although they will seem expensive, a little goes a long way, and ½–1 ounce is the most you will need in a recipe that serves 4–6 people. Before use, dried porcini must be reconstituted in warm water for 15–20 minutes. Drain, rinse and squeeze dry, then slice or chop as required. Don't throw the soaking liquid away. Strain it to remove any grit and use it in soups and stocks, or add it to the water when cooking pasta to impart a mushroomy flavor—this is especially effective with fresh pasta.

*Dried porcini mushrooms*

*Dried bell peppers*

**Bell peppers**

***Peperoni***

Sun-dried red bell peppers are sold in packages. They resemble sun-dried tomatoes, but their flavor is more peppery and piquant. They are used in the same way as tomatoes, to add a firm meaty bite to sauces and soups, especially those made with vegetables. Before use they should be rinsed under the cold tap, then dried and cut into thin strips or chopped.

Roasted bell peppers can be bought loose or in jars, packed in olive oil or brine. Although you can easily roast fresh bell peppers yourself when you need them, it is handy to keep a jar of commercially roasted bell peppers in the fridge. Just one piece of roasted bell pepper, sliced or chopped, will add a wonderful smoky flavor to pasta sauces, salads and soups. The best ones come from Italian specialty stores, who chargrill the bell peppers themselves and sell them loose in extra virgin olive oil.

*Bottled roasted bell peppers*

**Tomatoes**

***Pomodori***

In summer, when fresh Italian plum tomatoes are ripe and full of flavor, it is wonderful to use these for sauce making, but at other times of the year you will get a far better flavor and color by using preserved tomatoes.

There are plenty of excellent tomato products to choose from, most of which come from southern Italy, where the hot sun ripens the tomatoes on the vine to an incomparable flavor.

Canned peeled plum tomatoes (*pomodori pelati*) come whole and chopped. Don't buy cheap brands; instead, opt for the top-quality Italian brands,

*Chopped canned plum tomatoes*

*Filetti di pomodoro (plum tomatoes in water and salt)*

especially those that identify the tomatoes as San Marzano on the label. If you ask at your local Italian specialty store, they will give you good advice. Plain chopped tomatoes are a good buy because they save you having to chop them yourself, but they are slightly more expensive. If they are labelled polpa di pomodoro, they are likely to be very finely chopped or even crushed. Flavorings, such as garlic and herbs, should be added fresh, so don't buy chopped canned tomatoes containing these.

*Filetti di pomodoro* are sold in jars at good Italian specialty stores. These are plum tomatoes that have been halved or quartered and bottled *al naturale* in water and salt. They are about the nearest thing you can get to bottling tomatoes yourself at home, which Italians do in summer to preserve surplus tomatoes for winter use.

Crushed tomatoes come in many guises, and are a real boon for sauce making because they take all the hard work out of peeling, seeding and chopping. They are plum tomatoes that have been mechanically peeled and crushed, then sieved to remove the seeds. You can choose from passata, which is quite smooth, to polpa and sugocasa, which are quite chunky.

Bottles and jars of these products are good in that they allow you to see what you are buying. Cartons of very smooth passata take up less room and are lighter to carry; they are very popular with Italian cooks for making almost instant sauces.

Sun-dried tomatoes (*pomodori secchi*) are sold in two different forms—as dry pieces and in oil. Both types are piquant in flavor, but the dry pieces have a chewier texture than those in oil. Dried tomatoes are sold in packages and can be snipped directly into a long-cooking pasta sauce to intensify its tomato flavor, but generally they are best if softened in hot water for 2–3 hours before use. Sun-dried tomatoes in oil are sold in jars and can also be bought loose at some specialty stores. For the best flavor, buy the ones in olive oil. They are soft and juicy and can be used as they are, either sliced or chopped, in sauces and salads.

Sun-dried tomato paste is a thick mixture of sun-dried tomatoes and olive oil. It can be used on its own as a quick sauce for pasta or added by the spoonful to tomato sauces to color and enrich them.

Although thick in texture, the flavor of sun-dried tomato paste is sweet and mild compared with tomato paste, and the color is paler.

*Sun-dried tomato paste (left) and tomato paste*

*Sun-dried tomatoes bottled in oil (top), and dry pieces*

Tomato paste or concentrate (*concentrato di pomodoro*) is a very strong, thick paste made commercially from tomatoes, salt and citric acid. You can buy it in tubes, jars or cans, and its strength varies according to the manufacturer.

*Clockwise from left, sugocasa, polpa and passata*

Get to know the brand you like because some are quite bitter and sharp, and can overwhelm other flavors in a sauce. Only use tomato paste in small quantities or it may make a dish too acidic. A way to counteract acidity is to add a pinch or two or a lump of sugar.

## Cheese and Cream

Italy's magnificent cheeses are famous all over the world, both as table cheeses and for their use in cooking. Many of them are used in sauces for pasta, in fillings for stuffed pasta and baked dishes.

*Fontina*

### Fontina

A mountain cheese from the Val d'Aosta in the northwest of Italy, fontina is used in baked pasta dishes, such as lasagne. It has superb melting qualities and a wonderful nutty, slightly sweet flavor. Some large supermarkets sell it; otherwise you can get it at specialty cheese stores.

### Gorgonzola

This blue-veined cheese comes from Lombardy. Although it is a table cheese, it melts quickly and well, so it is good in sauces and stuffed pasta, and its sharp flavor tastes very good combined with cream and leafy greens, such as spinach, sorrel and herbs. Gorgonzola piccante is the very strong version, while dolcelatte is milder and sweeter, almost buttery.

*Gorgonzola*

### Mascarpone

This is a fullfat cream cheese with a smooth silky texture, often used in pasta sauces instead of cream. It melts without curdling and has a slightly tangy flavor. It is widely available in tubs in supermarkets.

*Mascarpone*

### Mozzarella

A soft white cheese, which is used in both salads and cooking, mozzarella melts quickly in hot sauces to serve with pasta, but must not be overcooked or it may become stringy. The whey should be drained off and discarded before the cheese is used. By tradition mozzarella should be made with buffalo milk, but today it is often made with cow or sheep milk. Buy only the type that is swimming in whey in little bags—blocks of mozzarella are rubbery and tasteless. Mozzarella di bufala has the best texture and the most flavor, but it is more expensive than cow or sheep milk mozzarella and not so easy to find.

*Mozzarella*

### Parmesan

Grated Parmesan is most often used for sprinkling over pasta at the table, although it is also tossed with pasta after draining or added to sauces at the end of cooking. Genuine Parmigiano Reggiano has its name stamped on the rind and comes only from the area between Parma, Modena, Reggio-Emilia, Bologna and Mantua. It must be aged for a minimum of 2 years, which is one of the reasons why it is so costly. Grana Padano is a similar, less expensive, cheese, which is used in the same way as Parmigiano Reggiano. Both are excellent melting cheeses, but Reggiano has a milder, less salty flavor and its texture is more flaky. Never buy these cheeses ready grated. Buy them in the piece and grate them as and when you need them, or shave into curls with a vegetable peeler.

*Pecorino (left) and Parmigiano Reggiano*

### Pecorino

This salty, hard sheep milk cheese is called Pecorino Romano if it comes from Lazio and Pecorino Sardo if it is Sardinian. It is used for grating in the same way as Parmesan, but because its flavor is sharper, it is used with the strong-tasting and spicy sauces associated with southern Italian and Sardinian cooking.

*Ricotta salata (right) and ricotta*

## Dressing up Commercial Sauces

There are lots of bottled sauces for serving with pasta, ranging from chopped tomato sugocasa to classics, such as vongole, arrabbiata and carbonara, as well as unusual combinations of ingredients created by individual manufacturers. Generally speaking it is best to stick to the Italian brands that are sold in specialty stores and supermarkets, because these are the ones that Italians keep in their own store cupboards for times when they want to serve pasta at a moment's notice. You can use these sauces just as they are, but they will taste more homemade if you liven them up by adding something fresh.

**Pesto**

Both classic basil pesto and red pesto—made using sun-dried tomatoes—are available in jars, and are useful store cupboard standbys. Grate a little fresh Parmesan cheese over the pasta before tossing with the pesto, and add a spoonful or two of extra virgin olive oil for a more fruity flavor. For a richer pesto sauce, add a spoonful or two of mascarpone cheese or cream (*below left*). Just before serving, sprinkle the pasta with more freshly grated Parmesan or with toasted pine nuts or shredded basil leaves.

**Sugocasa/Chopped tomatoes**

Add a little sun-dried tomato paste and/or a splash of red or white wine when heating up sugocasa, and season well with salt and ground black pepper. If you like a creamy tomato sauce, add up to ⅔ cup *panna da cucina*, heavy cream or crème fraîche. For a spicy kick, add a sprinkling of crushed dried red chiles. Finish the sauce off with a small handful of shredded fresh basil or arugula, or use 1–2 tablespoons chopped fresh marjoram or oregano.

**Arrabbiata**

Strew a generous handful of finely shredded arugula leaves on top of the tossed pasta and sauce just before serving.

**Carbonara**

Stir a few spoonfuls of fresh cream into the sauce while it is heating up, then top with thin shavings of Parmesan cheese once the sauce and pasta have been tossed together.

**Vongole**

Add a splash of wine, some chopped fresh parsley and garlic. You can add all of these ingredients or just one or two of them. A few pitted and sliced black olives also look and taste good with a vongole sauce.

### Ricotta

Fresh ricotta is a very soft white cheese, sold loose by the pound in Italian specialty stores. It has superb melting qualities and is used in fillings for stuffed and baked pasta dishes, and for tossing with fresh raw vegetables, such as tomatoes, spinach and arugula for uncooked sauces. Ricotta is low in fat and has a bland flavor, so it goes well with flavorsome ingredients, such as herbs and garlic. Fresh ricotta does not keep well, so check before buying and only buy it if it is snowy white in color. If not, it is better to buy the ricotta sold in tubs—these are widely available at supermarkets. Ricotta salata is a hard, salted version of ricotta, cut from the block in Italian specialty stores. It too is very white and low in fat. Ricotta salata is used for grating or crumbling over soups and pasta, especially in the south of Italy. You will find it saltier than Parmesan, Grana Padano or Pecorino, so will need less.

### Cream

***Panna da cucina***

For creamy pasta sauces, Italians use a type of cream called panna da cucina (cream for cooking). It is sold in little tubs, often joined together in pairs. Each tub contains scant ½ cup, which is enough to make a pasta sauce to serve 4 people. Panna da cucina is a long-life product, so it is well worth buying to keep in the store cupboard for making impromptu sauces. It is widely available in Italian specialty stores.

*Panna da cucina*

# Pasta Recipes

Pasta proves its enormous versatility in this section. There are complete recipes, plus many variations, and since there are very few hard-and-fast rules with sauces for pasta you can personalize them to your heart's content—and make even more. The recipes in the Broths and Soups chapter range from clear light liquids supporting delicate pieces of pasta to substantial soups that make meals in themselves. Tomato Sauces can be smooth and subtle, fiery or chunky, while Cream Sauces are deliciously rich and luxurious, and unbelievably quick to make. The Fish and Shellfish recipes have fabulous flavors, some of which are surprisingly spicy and strong. They make good first courses and after-work suppers, as do the recipes in Meat and Poultry, many of which you will recognize as traditional and regional favorites. In Vegetables and Vegetarian, some of the recipes are classic, but most are new. They're quick and easy, colorful and light, and they look and taste absolutely stunning. There's a choice of both family favorites and dinner party dishes in Baked Pasta, while in the Stuffed Pasta chapter you can have fun making your own dough. You'll be amazed how easy it is, and delighted with the results too. The chapter devoted to Fresh and Healthy recipes proves the point that pasta not only looks and tastes good, but it's nutritionally sound too, something that can also be said of delicious Pasta Salads. And finally, there is a section on Noodles, the Chinese equivalent of pasta, to prove just how versatile this food really is.

# Broths and Soups

Soups made with pasta range from clear broths with just a surface sprinkling of *pastina* to filling and substantial *minestre* or *zuppe*, which include chunkier pieces of pasta and vegetables, fish or meat. Broth, called *brodo* in Italian, is generally served as a first course or *primo piatto*, especially for evening meals. It also makes a marvelous pick-me-up if you are tired, unwell or simply under the weather. The chunkier pasta soups are more likely to make a meal in themselves, especially when served with bread.

This chapter explores the full range of pasta soups. Some, such as Genoese Minestrone *and* Pasta, Bean and Vegetable Soup are regional classics, others are less well known yet equally delicious, but all are gloriously adaptable: use a different shape or size of pasta if you prefer, and don't worry too much about exact quantities.

# Genoese Minestrone

In Genoa they often make minestrone like this, with pesto stirred in toward the end of cooking. It is packed full of vegetables and has a good strong flavor, making it an excellent vegetarian supper dish when served with bread. There is Parmesan cheese in the pesto, so there is no need to serve extra with the soup.

**INGREDIENTS**

*1 onion*
*2 celery stalks*
*1 large carrot*
*3 tablespoons olive oil*
*5 ounces green beans, cut into 2-inch pieces*
*1 zucchini, thinly sliced*
*1 potato, cut into ½-inch cubes*
*¼ Savoy cabbage, shredded*
*small eggplant, cut into ½-inch cubes*
*7 ounces canned cannellini beans, drained and rinsed*
*2 Italian plum tomatoes, chopped*
*5 cups vegetable stock*
*3½ ounces dried spaghetti or vermicelli*
*salt and ground black pepper*

***For the pesto***
*about 20 fresh basil leaves*
*1 garlic clove*
*2 teaspoons pine nuts*
*1 tablespoon freshly grated Parmesan cheese*
*1 tablespoon freshly grated Pecorino cheese*
*2 tablespoons olive oil*

**Serves 4–6**

1 Chop the onion, celery and carrot finely, either in a food processor or by hand. Heat the oil in a large saucepan, add the chopped mixture and cook over low heat, stirring frequently, for 5–7 minutes.

2 Mix in the green beans, zucchini, potato and cabbage. Stir-fry over medium heat for about 3 minutes. Add the eggplant, cannellini beans and tomatoes, and stir-fry for 2–3 minutes more. Pour in the stock with salt and pepper to taste. Bring to a boil. Stir well, cover and lower the heat. Simmer for 40 minutes, stirring occasionally.

3 Meanwhile, process all the pesto ingredients in a food processor until the mixture forms a smooth sauce, adding 1–3 tablespoons water through the feeder tube if necessary.

4 Break the pasta into small pieces and add it to the soup. Simmer, stirring frequently, for 5 minutes. Add the pesto sauce and stir it in well, then simmer for 2–3 minutes more, or until the pasta is *al dente*. Taste for seasoning. Serve hot, in warmed soup plates or bowls.

**Cook's Tip**

*If you don't want to go to the trouble of making your own pesto, use the bottled variety—the traditional green basil pesto rather than the red sun-dried tomato pesto. You will need about 3 tablespoons.*

# Rich Minestrone

THIS IS A SPECIAL minestrone made with chicken. Served with crusty Italian bread, it makes a hearty meal.

**INGREDIENTS**

*1 tablespoon olive oil*
*2 chicken thighs*
*3 rindless lean bacon strips, chopped*
*1 onion, finely chopped*
*a few fresh basil leaves, shredded*
*a few fresh rosemary leaves, finely chopped*
*1 tablespoon chopped fresh Italian parsley*
*2 potatoes, cut into ½-inch cubes*
*1 large carrot, cut into ½-inch cubes*
*2 small zucchini, cut into ½-inch cubes*
*1–2 celery stalks, cut into ½-inch cubes*
*4 cups chicken stock*
*1¾ cups frozen peas*
*scant 1 cup stellette or other dried tiny soup pasta*
*salt and ground black pepper*
*fresh basil leaves, to garnish*
*coarsely shaved Parmesan cheese, to serve*

**Serves 4–6**

1 Heat the oil in a large frying pan, add the chicken thighs and fry for about 5 minutes on each side. Remove with a slotted spoon and set aside.

2 Lower the heat, add the bacon, onion and herbs to the pan and stir well. Cook gently, stirring constantly, for about 5 minutes. Add all the vegetables, except the frozen peas, and cook for 5–7 minutes more, stirring frequently.

3 Return the chicken thighs to the pan, add the stock and bring to a boil. Cover and cook over low heat for 35–40 minutes, stirring the soup occasionally.

4 Remove the chicken thighs with a slotted spoon and place them on a board. Stir the peas and pasta into the soup and bring back to a boil. Simmer, stirring frequently until the pasta is *al dente*: 7–8 minutes or according to the instructions on the package.

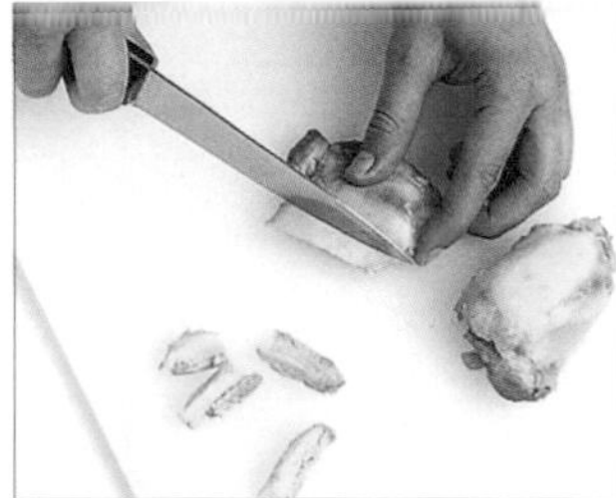

5 Meanwhile, remove and discard the chicken skin, then remove the meat from the bones and cut it into ½-inch pieces. Return the meat to the soup and heat through. Taste for seasoning. Ladle into soup bowls; scatter over Parmesan shavings and garnish with one or two basil leaves.

**COOK'S TIP**

*For extra flavour, add any Parmesan rind to the simmering soup.*

# Red Onion and Beet Soup

THIS BEAUTIFUL, VIVID ruby-red soup will look stunning at any dinner-party table.

**INGREDIENTS**

*1 tablespoon olive oil*
*12 ounces red onions, sliced*
*2 garlic cloves, crushed*
*scant 1 cup dried small pasta shapes*
*10 ounces cooked beets, cut into sticks*
*5 cups vegetable stock or water*
*2 tablespoons raspberry vinegar*
*salt and ground black pepper*
*lowfat plain yogurt or fromage blanc, to garnish*
*chopped chives, to garnish*

**Serves 4–6**

1 Heat the olive oil in a flameproof casserole and add the red onions and garlic.

2 Cook gently for 20 minutes or until soft and tender.

3 Cook the pasta in salted boiling water according to the instructions on the package. Drain.

4 Add the beet, stock or water, cooked pasta and vinegar, and heat through. Season to taste with salt and pepper.

5 Ladle into warmed soup bowls. Top each one with a spoonful of lowfat yogurt or fromage blanc and sprinkle with chives.

# Parmesan and Cauliflower Soup

A SILKY SMOOTH, mild cheese flavored soup which isn't overpowered by the cauliflower. It makes an elegant dinner-party soup served with crisp Melba toast.

**INGREDIENTS**

*1 large cauliflower*
*5 cups chicken or vegetable stock*
*1 ½ cups dried farfalle*
*⅔ cup light cream or half-and-half*
*freshly grated nutmeg*
*pinch of cayenne pepper*
*4 tablespoons freshly grated Parmesan cheese*
*salt and ground black pepper*

**For the Melba toast**

*3–4 slices day-old white bread*
*freshly grated Parmesan cheese, for sprinkling*
*¼ teaspoon paprika*
**Serves 6**

1 Cut the leaves and central stem away from the cauliflower and discard. Divide the cauliflower into similar-size flowerets.

2 Bring the stock to a boil and add the cauliflower. Simmer for about 10 minutes or until very soft. Remove the cauliflower with a slotted spoon and place in a blender or food processor.

3 Add the pasta to the stock and simmer for 10 minutes until tender. Drain, reserve the pasta, and pour the liquid over the cauliflower. Add the cream or half-and-half, nutmeg and cayenne to the cauliflower. Blend until smooth, then press through a strainer.

4 Stir in the cooked pasta. Reheat the soup and then stir in the Parmesan. Taste and adjust the seasoning if necessary.

5 Meanwhile make the Melba toast. Preheat the oven to 350°F. Toast the bread lightly on both sides. Quickly cut off the crusts and split each slice in half horizontally. Scrape off any doughy bits and sprinkle with Parmesan and paprika. Place on a baking sheet and bake in the oven for about 10–15 minutes or until uniformly golden. Serve with the soup.

# Little Stuffed Hats in Broth

THIS SOUP IS SERVED in northern Italy on Santo Stefano (St Stephen's Day—26 December) and on New Year's Day. It makes a welcome light change from all the special celebration food the day before. In Italy, the stock is traditionally made with the Christmas capon carcass.

**INGREDIENTS**

*5 cups chicken stock*
*1 cup fresh or dried cappelletti*
*2 tablespoons dry white wine (optional)*
*about 1 tablespoon finely chopped fresh Italian parsley (optional)*
*salt and ground black pepper*
*about 2 tablespoons freshly grated Parmesan cheese, to serve*
*shredded Italian parsley, to garnish*
**Serves 4**

1 Pour the chicken stock into a large saucepan and bring to a boil. Add a little salt and pepper to taste, then drop in the pasta.

2 Stir well and bring back to a boil. Lower the heat to a simmer and cook according to the instructions on the package, until the pasta is *al dente*. Stir frequently during cooking to ensure the pasta cooks evenly.

3 Swirl in the wine and parsley, if using, then taste for seasoning. Ladle into four warmed soup plates, then sprinkle with grated Parmesan and Italian parsley. Serve immediately.

**COOK'S TIP**

*Cappelletti is just another name for tortellini, which come from Romagna. You can buy them or make your own.*

# Tiny Pasta in Broth

IN ITALY THIS SOUP is often served with bread for a light evening supper.

**INGREDIENTS**

*5 cups beef stock*
*¾ cup dried tiny soup pasta, e.g. funghetti*
*2 pieces bottled roasted red bell pepper, about 2 ounces*
*salt and ground black pepper*
*coarsely shaved Parmesan cheese, to serve*
**Serves 4**

**COOK'S TIP**

*Stock cubes are not really suitable for a recipe like this in which the flavor of the broth is so important. If you don't have time to make your own stock, use 6 cups diluted canned consommé.*

1 Bring the beef stock to a boil in a large saucepan. Add salt and pepper to taste, then drop in the dried soup pasta. Stir well and bring the stock back to a boil.

2 Lower the heat to a simmer and cook until the pasta is *al dente*: 7–8 minutes or according to the package instructions. Stir frequently during cooking to prevent the pasta shapes from sticking together.

3 Drain the pieces of roasted pepper and dice them finely. Place them in the base of four warmed soup plates. Taste the soup for seasoning. Ladle into the soup plates and serve immediately, with shavings of Parmesan handed separately.

**VARIATION**

*You can use other dried tiny soup pastas in place of the funghetti.*

# Pasta, Bean and Vegetable Soup

THIS IS A CALABRIAN specialty. The Italian name for it, *millecosedde*, comes from the word *millecose*, meaning "a thousand things." Literally anything edible can go in this soup. In Calabria they include a bean called *cicerchia* that is peculiar to the region.

**INGREDIENTS**

*scant ½ cup brown lentils*
*½ ounce dried mushrooms*
*4 tablespoons olive oil*
*1 carrot, diced*
*1 celery stalk, diced*
*1 onion, finely chopped*
*1 garlic clove, finely chopped*
*a little chopped fresh Italian parsley*
*a good pinch of crushed red chiles (optional)*
*6¼ cups vegetable stock*
*scant 1 cup each canned red kidney beans, cannellini beans and chickpeas, rinsed and drained*
*1 cup dried small pasta shapes, such as. rigatoni, penne or penne rigate*
*salt and ground black pepper*
*freshly grated Pecorino cheese, to serve*
*chopped Italian parsley, to garnish*

**Serves 4–6**

1 Put the lentils in a medium saucepan, add 2 cups water and bring to a boil over high heat. Lower the heat to a gentle simmer and cook, stirring occasionally, for 15–20 minutes or until the lentils are just tender. Meanwhile, soak the dried mushrooms in ¾ cup warm water for 15–20 minutes.

2 Tip the lentils into a strainer to drain, then rinse under the cold tap. Drain the soaked mushrooms and reserve the soaking liquid. Finely chop the mushrooms and set aside.

3 Heat the oil in a large saucepan and add the carrot, celery, onion, garlic, parsley and chiles, if using. Cook over low heat, stirring constantly, for 5–7 minutes.

4 Add the stock, then the mushrooms and their soaking liquid. Bring to a boil, then add the beans, chickpeas and lentils, with salt and pepper to taste. Cover, and simmer gently for 20 minutes.

5 Add the pasta and bring the soup back to a boil, stirring. Simmer, stirring frequently, until the pasta is *al dente*: 7–8 minutes or according to the instructions on the package. Season, then serve hot in soup bowls, with grated Pecorino and chopped parsley.

**COOK'S TIP**

*If you like, you can freeze the soup at the end of Step 4. To serve, thaw and bring to a boil, then add the pasta and simmer until it is just tender.*

# Clam and Pasta Soup

SUBTLY SWEET AND SPICY, this soup is substantial enough to be served on its own for lunch or supper. A crusty Italian loaf such as *pugliese* is the ideal accompaniment.

**INGREDIENTS**

*2 tablespoons olive oil*
*1 onion, finely chopped*
*leaves from 1 fresh or dried thyme sprig, chopped, plus extra to garnish*
*2 garlic cloves, crushed*
*5–6 fresh basil leaves, plus extra to garnish*
*1/4–1/2 teaspoon crushed red chiles, to taste*
*4 cups fish stock*
*1 1/2 cups tomato sauce*
*1 teaspoon sugar*
*scant 1 cup frozen peas*
*2/3 cup dried small pasta shapes, e.g. chifferini*
*8 ounces frozen shelled clams*
*salt and ground black pepper*
**Serves 4–6**

1 Heat the oil in a large saucepan, add the onion and cook gently for about 5 minutes until softened, but not colored. Add the thyme, then stir in the garlic, basil leaves and chiles.

2 Add the stock, tomato sauce and sugar to the saucepan, with salt and pepper to taste. Bring to a boil, then lower the heat and simmer gently, stirring occasionally, for 15 minutes. Add the frozen peas and cook for another 5 minutes.

3 Add the pasta to the stock mixture and bring to a boil, stirring. Lower the heat and simmer, stirring frequently, until the pasta is only just *al dente*: about 5 minutes or according to the package instructions.

4 Turn the heat down to low, add the frozen clams and heat through for 2–3 minutes. Taste for seasoning. Serve hot in warmed bowls, garnished with basil and thyme.

**COOK'S TIP**

*Frozen shelled clams are available at good fishmarkets and supermarkets; if you can't get them, use bottled or canned clams in natural juice (not vinegar). These both look and taste delicious and they are not too expensive. For a special occasion, stir some into the soup.*

# Bean and Pasta Soup

THIS HEARTY MAIN MEAL soup sometimes goes by the name of *Pasta e Fagioli*, while some Italians refer to it as *Minestrone di Pasta e Fagioli*. Traditional country recipes use dried beans and a ham bone, and require the soup to be cooked for a long time.

**INGREDIENTS**

*1 onion*
*1 carrot*
*1 celery stalk*
*2 tablespoons olive oil*
*4 ounces pancetta or smoked lean bacon, diced*
*$7\frac{1}{2}$ cups beef stock*
*1 cinnamon stick or a good pinch of ground cinnamon*
*scant 1 cup dried pasta shapes, such as conchiglie or corallini*
*14 ounces canned borlotti beans, rinsed and drained*
*1 thick slice cooked ham, about 8 ounces, diced*
*salt and ground black pepper*
*coarsely shaved Parmesan cheese, to serve*

**Serves 4–6**

1 Chop the vegetables. Heat the oil in a large saucepan, add the pancetta or bacon and cook, stirring, until lightly colored. Add the chopped vegetable mixture to the pan and cook for about 10 minutes, stirring frequently, until lightly colored. Pour in the stock, add the cinnamon with salt and pepper to taste, and bring to a boil. Cover and simmer gently for 15–20 minutes.

2 Add the pasta. Bring back to a boil, stirring constantly. Lower the heat and simmer, stirring frequently, for 5 minutes. Add the beans and diced ham and simmer until the pasta is *al dente*: 2–3 minutes or according to the instructions on the package.

3 Taste the soup for seasoning. Serve hot in warmed bowls, sprinkled with shavings of Parmesan.

**VARIATIONS**

- *Use spaghetti or tagliatelle instead of the small pasta shapes, breaking it into small pieces over the pan.*
- *Use cannellini or navy beans instead of the borlotti. Alternatively, use dried beans that have been soaked, drained and boiled for 1 hour or until tender. Add them to the pan after the stock in Step 1.*
- *If you like, add 1 tablespoon tomato paste, or 1 large ripe tomato, skinned and chopped, with the beans and diced ham.*

# Pasta and Chickpea Soup

A SIMPLE, COUNTRY-STYLE soup. The shape of the pasta and the beans complement one another beautifully.

**INGREDIENTS**

*1 onion*
*2 carrots*
*2 celery stalks*
*4 tablespoons olive oil*
*14 ounces canned chickpeas, rinsed and drained*
*7 ounces canned cannellini beans, rinsed and drained*
*⅔ cup tomato juice*
*½ cup water*
*6¼ cups vegetable or chicken stock*
*2 fresh or dried rosemary sprigs*
*scant 2 cups dried conchiglie*
*salt and ground black pepper*
*freshly grated Parmesan cheese, to serve*

**Serves 4–6**

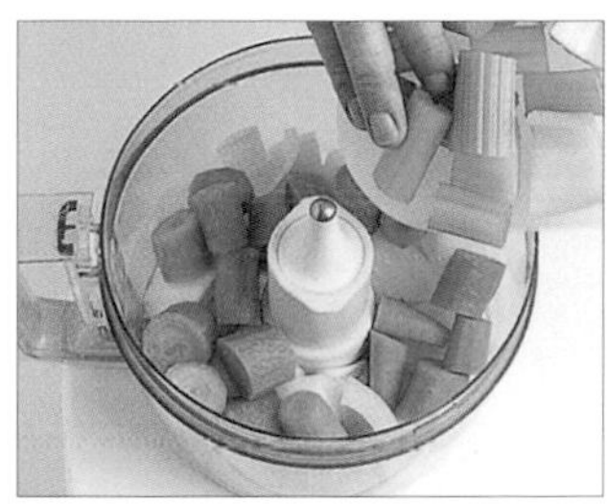

1 Chop the onion, carrots and celery finely, either in a food processor or by hand.

2 Heat the oil in a large saucepan, add the chopped vegetable mixture and cook over low heat, stirring frequently, for 5–7 minutes.

3 Add the chickpeas and cannellini beans, stir to mix, then cook for 5 minutes. Stir in the tomato juice and water. Cook, stirring, for 2–3 minutes.

4 Add 2 cups of the stock, one of the rosemary sprigs and salt and pepper to taste. Bring to a boil, cover, then simmer gently, stirring occasionally, for 1 hour.

5 Pour in the remaining stock, add the pasta and bring to a boil, stirring. Lower the heat and simmer, stirring frequently, until the pasta is *al dente*: 7–8 minutes or according to the instructions on the package. Taste for seasoning. Remove the rosemary sprig and serve the soup, in warmed bowls, topped with grated Parmesan and a few rosemary leaves.

**VARIATIONS**

- *You can use other pasta shapes, but conchiglie are ideal because they scoop up the chickpeas and beans.*
- *If you like, crush 1–2 garlic cloves and fry them with the vegetables.*

# Zucchini Soup with Conchigliette

A PRETTY, FRESH-TASTING soup which could be made using cucumber instead of zucchini.

**INGREDIENTS**

*4 tablespoons olive or sunflower oil*
*2 onions, finely chopped*
*6¼ cups chicken stock*
*2 pounds zucchini*
*1 cup diced conchigliette*
*freshly squeezed lemon juice*
*2 tablespoons chopped fresh chervil*
*salt and ground black pepper*
*sour cream, to serve*
**Serves 4–6**

1 Heat the oil in a large saucepan and add the finely chopped onions. Cover and cook gently for about 20 minutes until very soft but not colored, stirring occasionally.

2 Add the chicken stock to the saucepan and bring the mixture to a boil.

3 Meanwhile shred the zucchini and stir into a boiling stock with the pasta. Reduce the heat and simmer for 15 minutes until the pasta is tender. Season to taste with lemon juice, salt and pepper.

4 Stir in the chopped fresh chervil and add a swirl of sour cream before serving.

# Provençal Fish Soup with Pasta

THIS COLORFUL SOUP has all the flavors of the Mediterranean. Serve it as a main course for a deliciously filling lunch.

**INGREDIENTS**

*2 tablespoons olive oil*
*1 onion, sliced*
*1 garlic clove, crushed*
*1 leek, sliced*
*4 cups water*
*8 ounces canned chopped tomatoes*
*pinch of Mediterranean herbs*
*¼ teaspoon saffron strands (optional)*
*1 cup dried small pasta shapes*
*about 8 live mussels in the shell*
*1 pound filleted and skinned firm white fish, such as cod, flounder or monkfish*
*salt and ground black pepper*

**For the rouille**

*2 garlic cloves, crushed*
*1 canned pimiento, drained and chopped*
*1 tablespoon fresh white bread crumbs*
*4 tablespoons mayonnaise*
*toasted French bread, to serve*

**Serves 4**

1 Heat the oil in a large saucepan and add the onion, garlic and leek. Cover and cook gently for 5 minutes, stirring until the vegetables are soft.

2 Pour in the water, the tomatoes, herbs, saffron, if using, and pasta. Season with salt and ground black pepper and cook for 15–20 minutes.

3 Scrub the mussels and pull off the "beards." Discard any that will not close when sharply tapped.

4 Cut the fish into bite-size chunks and add to the soup in the saucepan, placing the mussels on top. Then simmer with the lid on for 5-10 minutes until the mussels open and the fish is just cooked. Discard any unopened mussels.

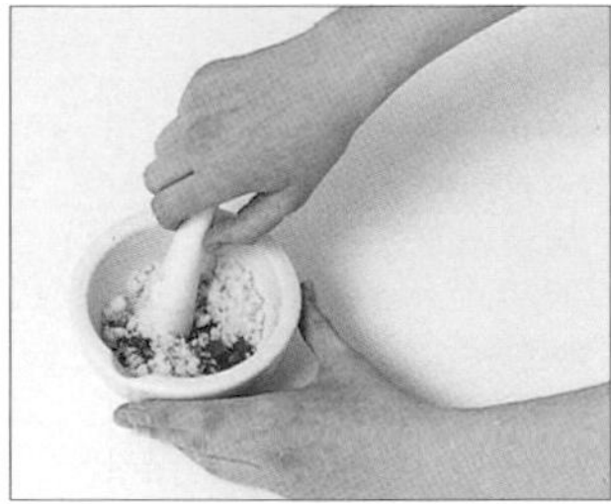

5 To make the rouille, pound the garlic, canned pimiento and bread crumbs together in a pestle and mortar (or in a blender or food processor). Then stir in the mayonnaise and season the mixture well.

6 Spread the toasted French bread with the rouille and serve the slices with the soup.

# Farmhouse Soup

Root vegetables form the base of this chunky, minestrone-style main meal soup. You can vary the vegetables according to what you have to hand.

**INGREDIENTS**

*2 tablespoons olive oil*
*1 onion, coarsely chopped*
*3 carrots, cut into large chunks*
*6–7 ounces turnips, cut into large chunks*
*about 6 ounces yellow turnip, cut into large chunks*
*1 can (14 ounces) chopped Italian tomatoes*
*1 tablespoon tomato paste*
*1 teaspoon mixed dried herbs*
*1 teaspoon dried oregano*
*½ cup dried Italian peppers, washed and thinly sliced (optional)*
*6¼ cups vegetable stock or water*
*½ cup dried small macaroni or conchiglie*
*1 can (14 ounces) red kidney beans, rinsed and drained*
*2 tablespoons chopped fresh Italian parsley*
*salt and ground black pepper*
*freshly grated Parmesan cheese, to serve*

**Serves 4**

1 Heat the oil in a large saucepan, add the onion and cook over low heat for about 5 minutes until softened. Add the fresh vegetables, canned tomatoes, tomato paste, dried herbs and dried peppers, if using. Stir in salt and pepper to taste. Pour in the stock or water and bring to a boil. Stir well, cover, lower the heat and simmer for 30 minutes, stirring occasionally.

**Cook's Tip**

*Packets of dried Italian peppers are sold in many supermarkets. They are piquant and firm with a "meaty" bite to them, which makes them ideal for adding substance to vegetarian soups.*

2 Add the pasta and bring to a boil, stirring. Lower the heat and simmer, uncovered, until the pasta is only just *al dente*: about 5 minutes or according to the instructions on the package. Stir frequently.

3 Stir in the beans. Heat through for 2–3 minutes, then remove from the heat and stir in the parsley. Taste the soup for seasoning. Serve hot in warmed soup bowls, with grated Parmesan handed separately.

# Roasted Tomato and Pasta Soup

WHEN THE ONLY TOMATOES you can buy are not particularly flavorsome, make this soup. The roasting compensates for any lack of flavor in the tomatoes, and the soup has a wonderful smoky taste.

**INGREDIENTS**

*1 pound ripe Italian plum tomatoes, halved lengthwise*
*1 large red bell pepper, quartered lengthwise and seeded*
*1 large red onion, quartered lengthwise*
*2 garlic cloves, unpeeled*
*1 tablespoon olive oil*
*5 cups vegetable stock or water*
*good pinch of granulated sugar*
*scant 1 cup dried small pasta shapes, such as tubetti or small macaroni*
*salt and ground black pepper*
*fresh basil leaves, to garnish*

**Serves 4**

1 Preheat the oven to 375°F. Spread out the tomatoes, red pepper, onion and garlic in a roasting pan and drizzle with the olive oil. Roast for 30–40 minutes until the vegetables are soft and charred, stirring and turning them halfway.

2 Put the vegetables into a food processor, add about 1 cup of the stock or water and process until puréed. Scrape the mixture into a strainer placed over a large saucepan and press the purée through into the pan.

3 Add the remaining stock or water to the pan, then the sugar and salt and pepper to taste. Bring to a boil, stirring constantly.

4 Add the pasta and simmer, stirring frequently, until *al dente*: 7–8 minutes or according to the instructions on the package. Taste for seasoning. Serve hot in warmed bowls, garnished with the fresh basil.

**COOK'S TIPS**

- *You can roast the vegetables in advance, allow them to cool, then leave them in a covered bowl in the refrigerator overnight before puréeing.*
- *The soup can be frozen without the pasta. Thaw and bring to a boil before adding the pasta.*

# Pasta Soup with Chicken Livers

A SOUP THAT CAN BE served as either a first or main course. The fried *fegatini* are so delicious that even if you do not normally like chicken livers you will find yourself loving them in this soup.

**INGREDIENTS**

*1 tablespoon olive oil*
*knob of butter*
*4 garlic cloves, crushed*
*3 sprigs each fresh parsley, marjoram and sage, chopped*
*leaves from 1 fresh thyme sprig, chopped*
*5–6 fresh basil leaves*
*⅔ cup chicken livers, thawed if frozen*
*1–2 tablespoons dry white wine*
*2 cans (11-ounce) condensed chicken consommé*
*2 cups frozen peas*
*½ cup dried pasta shapes, such as farfalle*
*2–3 scallions, diagonally sliced*
*salt and ground black pepper*

**Serves 4–6**

1 Heat the oil and butter in a frying pan, add the garlic and herbs, with salt and pepper to taste, and fry gently for a few minutes. Add the livers, increase the heat to high and stir-fry for a few minutes until they change color and become dry. Pour the wine over the livers, cook until the wine evaporates, then remove the livers from the heat and taste for seasoning.

2 Pour both cans of condensed chicken consommé into a large saucepan and add water to the condensed soup as directed on the labels. Add an extra can of water, then stir in a little salt and pepper to taste and bring to a boil.

3 Add the frozen peas to the pan and simmer for about 5 minutes, then add the small pasta shapes and bring the soup back to a boil, stirring. Allow to simmer, stirring frequently, until the pasta is only just *al dente*: about 5 minutes or according to the instructions on the package.

4 Add the fried chicken livers and scallions and heat through for 2–3 minutes. Taste for seasoning. Serve hot, in warmed bowls.

# Meatball and Pasta Soup

EVEN THOUGH THIS SOUP comes from sunny Sicily, it is substantial enough for a hearty supper on a winter's day.

**INGREDIENTS**

*2 cans (11-ounce) condensed beef consommé*
*¾ cup dried very thin pasta, such as fidelini or spaghettini*
*fresh Italian parsley, to garnish*
*freshly grated Parmesan cheese, to serve*

***For the meatballs***

*1 very thick slice of white bread, crusts removed*
*2 tablespoons milk*
*1 cup ground beef*
*1 garlic clove, crushed*
*2 tablespoons freshly grated Parmesan cheese*
*2–3 tablespoons fresh Italian parsley leaves, coarsely chopped*
*1 egg*
*nutmeg*
*salt and ground black pepper*

**Serves 4**

1 Make the meatballs. Break the bread into a small bowl, add the milk and set aside to soak. Meanwhile, put the ground beef, garlic, Parmesan, parsley and egg in another large bowl. Grate fresh nutmeg liberally over the top and add salt and pepper to taste.

2 Squeeze the bread with your hands to remove as much milk as possible, then add the bread to the meatball mixture and mix everything together well with your hands. Wash your hands, rinse them under the cold tap, then form the mixture into tiny balls about the size of small marbles.

3 Pour both cans of consommé into a large saucepan, add water as directed on the labels, then add an extra can of water. Stir in salt and pepper to taste and bring to a boil.

4 Drop in the meatballs, then break the pasta into small pieces and add it to the soup. Bring the soup to a boil, stirring gently. Simmer, stirring frequently, until the pasta is *al dente*: 7–8 minutes or according to the instructions on the package. Taste for seasoning. Serve hot in warmed bowls, sprinkled with parsley and freshly grated Parmesan cheese.

# Pea and Ham Soup

FROZEN PEAS PROVIDE flavor, freshness and color in this delicious winter soup, which is filling enough to make a light main course.

**INGREDIENTS**

*1 cup dried small pasta shapes, such as tubetti*
*2 tablespoons vegetable oil*
*1 small bunch scallions, chopped*
*3 cups frozen peas*
*5 cups chicken stock*
*8 ounces raw unsmoked ham*
*4 tablespoons heavy cream*
*salt and ground black pepper*
*warm crusty bread, to serve*

**Serves 4**

1 Cook the small pasta shapes in plenty of boiling salted water according to the package instructions. Drain through a colander, place in the pan again, cover with cold water and set aside until required.

2 Heat the vegetable oil in a large heavy saucepan and cook the scallions gently, stirring until soft but not browned. Add the frozen peas and chicken stock to the saucepan, then simmer gently over low heat for about 10 minutes.

3 Process the soup in a blender or food processor then return to the saucepan. Cut the ham into short fingers and add, with the pasta, to the saucepan. Simmer for 2–3 minutes and season to taste.

4 Stir in the heavy cream and serve the soup immediately with the warm crusty bread.

# Consommé with Agnolotti

A DELICIOUS AND SATISFYING consommé with wonderful flavors.

**INGREDIENTS**

*3 ounces cooked shelled shrimp*
*3 ounces canned crab meat, drained*
*1 teaspoon fresh ginger root, peeled and finely shredded*
*1 tablespoon fresh white bread crumbs*
*1 teaspoon light soy sauce*
*1 scallion, finely chopped*
*1 garlic clove, crushed*
*1 recipe Pasta with Eggs*
*flour, for dusting*
*egg white, beaten*
*14 ounces canned chicken or fish consommé*
*2 tablespoons sherry or vermouth*
*salt and ground black pepper*
*2 ounces cooked, shelled shrimp and fresh cilantro leaves, to garnish*

**Serves 4–6**

1 To make the filling, put the shrimp, crab meat, ginger, bread crumbs, soy sauce, onion, garlic and seasoning into a food processor or blender and process until smooth.

2 Roll the pasta into thin sheets and dust lightly with flour. Stamp out 32 rounds 2 inches in diameter, with a fluted cookie cutter.

3 Place a small teaspoon of the filling in the center of half the pasta rounds. Brush the edges of each round with egg white and sandwich together with a second round on top. Pinch the edges together firmly to stop the filling seeping out.

4 Cook the pasta in a large pan of boiling salted water for 5 minutes (cook in batches to stop them sticking together). Remove and drop into a bowl of cold water for 5 seconds before placing on a tray. (You can make these pasta shapes a day in advance. Cover with plastic wrap and store in the refrigerator until required.)

5 Heat the chicken or fish consommé in a pan with the sherry or vermouth. When piping hot, add the pasta shapes and simmer for 1–2 minutes.

6 Serve in a shallow soup bowl covered with hot consommé. Garnish with extra shelled shrimp and fresh cilantro leaves.

# Broccoli, Anchovy and Pasta Soup

THIS SOUP IS FROM PUGLIA in the south of Italy, where anchovies and broccoli are often used together.

**INGREDIENTS**

*2 tablespoons olive oil*
*1 small onion, finely chopped*
*1 garlic clove, finely chopped*
*1/4–1/3 fresh red chile, seeded and finely chopped*
*2 drained canned anchovies*
*scant 1 cup tomato sauce*
*3 tablespoons dry white wine*
*5 cups vegetable stock*
*2 cups broccoli flowerets*
*1 3/4 cups dried orecchiette*
*salt and ground black pepper*
*freshly grated Pecorino cheese, to serve*

**Serves 4**

1 Heat the oil in a large saucepan. Add the onion, garlic, chile and anchovies and cook over low heat, stirring constantly, for 5–6 minutes.

2 Add the tomato sauce and wine, with salt and pepper to taste. Bring to a boil, cover the pan, then cook over low heat, stirring occasionally, for 12–15 minutes.

3 Pour in the stock. Bring to a boil, then add the broccoli and simmer for about 5 minutes. Add the pasta and bring back to a boil, stirring. Simmer, stirring frequently, until the pasta is *al dente*: 7–8 minutes or according to the instructions on the package. Taste for seasoning. Serve hot, in warmed bowls. Hand around grated Pecorino separately.

# Pasta Squares and Peas in Broth

THIS THICK SOUP IS FROM LAZIO, where it is traditionally made with fresh home-made pasta and peas. In this modern version, ready-made pasta is used with frozen peas, to save time.

**INGREDIENTS**

*2 tablespoons butter*
*2 ounces pancetta or rindless lean bacon, coarsely chopped*
*1 small onion, finely chopped*
*1 celery stalk, finely chopped*
*3 1/2 cups frozen peas*
*1 teaspoon tomato paste*
*1–2 teaspoons finely chopped fresh Italian parsley*
*4 cups chicken stock*
*11 ounces fresh lasagne sheets*
*about 2 ounces prosciutto crudo, cut into cubes*
*salt and ground black pepper*
*freshly grated Parmesan cheese, to serve*

**Serves 4–6**

1 Melt the butter in a large saucepan and add the pancetta or bacon, with the onion and celery. Cook over low heat, stirring constantly, for 5 minutes.

2 Add the peas and cook, stirring, for 3–4 minutes. Stir in the tomato paste and parsley, then add the chicken stock, with salt and pepper to taste. Bring to a boil. Cover, lower the heat and simmer for 10 minutes. Meanwhile, cut the lasagne sheets into 3/4-inch squares.

3 Taste the stock for seasoning. Drop in the pasta, stir and bring to a boil. Simmer for 2–3 minutes or until the pasta is *al dente*, then stir in the prosciutto. Serve hot in warmed bowls, with grated Parmesan handed around separately.

**COOK'S TIP**

*Take care when adding salt, because of the saltiness of the pancetta and the prosciutto.*

# Puglia-style Minestrone

THIS IS A TASTY SOUP for a Monday supper, because it can be made with the leftover carcass of Sunday's roast chicken. The sprinkling of salty ricotta salata at the finish is typical of Puglian cooking.

**INGREDIENTS**

*1 roast chicken carcass*
*1 onion, quartered lengthwise*
*1 carrot, coarsely chopped*
*1 celery stalk, coarsely chopped*
*a few black peppercorns*
*1 small handful mixed fresh herbs*
*1 chicken stock cube*
*½ cup small dried pasta shapes, such as tubetti, chifferini or pennette*
*2 tablespoons fresh mint leaves, to garnish*
*2 ounces ricotta salata, coarsely grated or crumbled, to serve*
*salt and ground black pepper*

**Serves 4**

1 Break the chicken carcass into pieces and place these in a large saucepan. Add the onion, carrot, celery, peppercorns and herbs, then crumble in the stock cube and add a good pinch of salt. Cover the chicken generously with cold water (you will need about 6¼ cups) and bring to a boil over high heat.

2 Lower the heat, half cover the pan and simmer gently for about 1 hour. Remove the pan from the heat and leave to cool, then strain the liquid through a colander or strainer into a clean large saucepan.

3 Remove any meat from the chicken bones, cut it into bite-size pieces and set aside. Discard the carcass and flavoring ingredients.

4 Bring the stock in the pan to a boil, add the pasta and simmer, stirring frequently, until only just *al dente*: 5–6 minutes or according to the instructions on the package.

5 Add the pieces of chicken and heat through for a few minutes, by which time the pasta will be ready. Taste for seasoning. Serve hot in warmed bowls, sprinkled with the mint leaves and ricotta salata.

**COOK'S TIP**

- *Use other small, hollow pasta shapes, such as chifferini or pennette, for this soup, if you like.*
- *Ricotta salata is a salted and dried version of ricotta cheese. It is firmer than the traditional soft white ricotta, and can be easily diced, crumbled and even grated. It is available from some delicatessens, good cheese shops and large supermarkets. If you can't locate it, use feta cheese instead.*

# Lentil and Pasta Soup

THIS RUSTIC VEGETARIAN soup makes a warming winter meal and goes well with whole-wheat or crusty Italian bread.

**INGREDIENTS**

*¾ cup brown lentils*
*3 garlic cloves*
*4 cups water*
*3 tablespoons olive oil*
*2 tablespoons butter*
*1 onion, finely chopped*
*2 celery stalks, finely chopped*
*2 tablespoons sun-dried tomato paste*
*7½ cups vegetable stock*
*a few fresh marjoram leaves*
*a few fresh basil leaves*
*leaves from 1 fresh thyme sprig*
*½ cup dried small pasta shapes, such as tubetti*
*salt and ground black pepper*
*tiny fresh herb leaves, to garnish*

**Serves 4–6**

### COOK'S TIP

*Use green lentils instead of brown if you like, but the orange or red ones go mushy.*

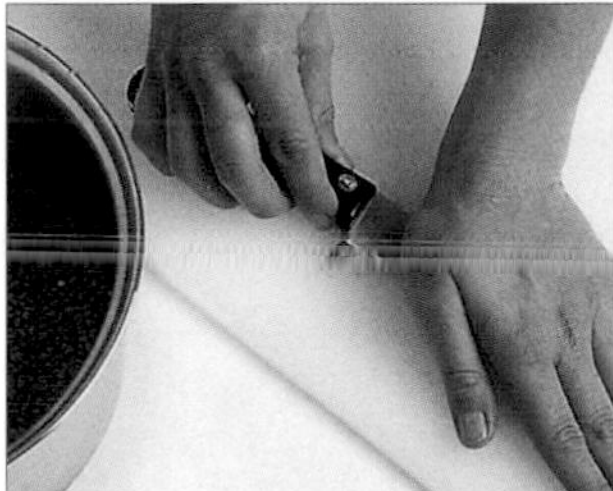

1 Put the lentils in a large saucepan. Smash 1 garlic clove (there's no need to peel it first) and add it to the lentils. Pour in the water and bring to a boil. Lower the heat to a gentle simmer and cook, stirring occasionally, for about 20 minutes or until the lentils are just tender. Turn the lentils into a strainer, remove the garlic and set it aside. Rinse the lentils under the cold tap, then leave them to drain.

2 Heat 2 tablespoons of the oil with half of the butter in a large saucepan. Add the onion and celery and cook over low heat, stirring, for 5–7 minutes until softened.

3 Crush the remaining garlic, then peel and mash the reserved garlic. Add to the vegetables with the remaining oil, the tomato paste and the lentils. Stir, then add the stock, the fresh herbs and salt and pepper to taste. Bring to a boil, stirring. Simmer for 30 minutes, stirring occasionally.

4 Add the pasta and bring the water back to a boil, stirring. Simmer, stirring frequently, until the pasta is *al dente*: 7–8 minutes or according to the package instructions. Add the remaining butter and taste for seasoning. Serve hot in warmed bowls, sprinkled with the herb leaves.

# Italian Bean and Pasta Soup

A THICK AND HEARTY soup which, followed by bread and cheese, makes a substantial lunch.

**INGREDIENTS**

*1½ cups dried navy beans, soaked overnight in cold water*
*7½ cups chicken stock or water*
*1 cup dried conchigliette*
*4 tablespoons olive oil, plus extra to serve*
*2 garlic cloves, crushed*
*4 tablespoons chopped fresh parsley*
*salt and ground black pepper*
**Serves 6**

1 Drain the beans and place in a large saucepan with the stock or water. Half-cover the pan, and simmer for 2–2½ hours or until the beans are tender.

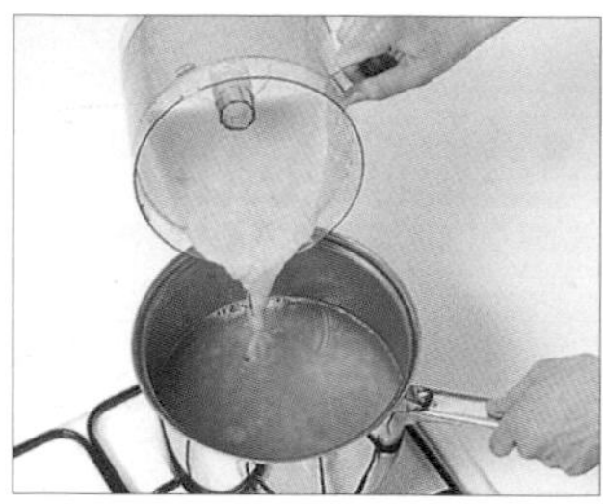

2 In a blender or food processor, process half the beans with a little of their cooking liquid to form a smooth paste. Then stir into the unprocessed beans in the pan.

3 Add the pasta and simmer gently for 15 minutes until tender. (Add extra water or stock if the soup seems too thick.)

4 Heat the oil in a small pan and fry the garlic until golden. Stir into the soup with the parsley and season well with salt and pepper. Ladle into individual bowls and drizzle each with a little extra olive oil, to serve.

# Chunky Pasta Soup

SERVE THIS filling main-meal soup with tasty, pesto-topped French bread crouton.

**INGREDIENTS**

*⅔ cup dry beans (a mixture of red kidney and navy beans), soaked in cold water overnight*
*1 tablespoon oil*
*1 onion, chopped*
*2 celery stalks, thinly sliced*
*2–3 garlic cloves, crushed*
*2 leeks, thinly sliced*
*1 vegetable stock cube*
*14 ounce can or jar of pimientos*
*3–4 tablespoons tomato paste*
*1 cup dried conchiglie*
*4 pieces French bread*
*1 tablespoon pesto sauce*
*1 cup baby corn, halved*
*2 ounces each broccoli and cauliflower flowerets*
*few drops of Tabasco sauce, to taste*
*salt and ground black pepper*
**Serves 4**

1 Drain the beans and place in a large saucepan with 5 cups water. Bring to a boil and simmer for about 1 hour, or until nearly tender.

2 When the beans are almost ready, heat the oil in a large pan and fry the vegetables for 2 minutes, stirring. Add the stock cube and the beans with 2 cups of their liquid. Cover and simmer the mixture for 10 minutes.

3 Meanwhile, purée the pimientos with a little of their liquid and add to the pan. Stir in the tomato paste, then add the pasta and cook for 15 minutes. Preheat the oven to 400°F.

4 Meanwhile, make the pesto crouton; spread the French bread with the pesto sauce and bake for 10 minutes, or until crispy.

5 When the pasta is just cooked, add the corn, broccoli and cauliflower flowerets, Tabasco sauce and seasoning to taste. Heat through for 2–3 minutes and serve at once with the crouton.

# Tomato Sauces

It was the Neapolitans who first discovered the delights of pasta and tomato sauce. Tomatoes originally came to Italy from the New World. They were yellow, which is why they were called golden apples (*pomodori*), and were originally used only as ornamental plants. They quickly took to the sunshine of southern Italy, however, and by the 18th century the red tomato was being enjoyed in salads. It wasn't long before they were partnered with pasta—and so began one of the most successful marriages in culinary history.

Tomato sauces, simple and uncooked or simmered for a longish while, are typically southern Italian. They go best with the dried, commercially produced pasta of the south, and taste divine with those other wonderful southern ingredients—basil, garlic and olive oil. Most recipes in this chapter give advice on the best type of pasta to serve with the sauce, while some go further and include cooking the pasta as part of the recipe.

Spaghetti is the pasta most often used with tomato sauces, but all the sauces work well with a wide range of pastas, so feel free to mix and match.

# Fresh Tomato Sauce

THIS IS THE FAMOUS Neapolitan sauce that is made in summer when tomatoes are very ripe and sweet. It is very simple, so that nothing detracts from the flavor of the tomatoes themselves. It is served here with spaghetti, which is the traditional choice of pasta.

**INGREDIENTS**

*1 ½ pounds ripe Italian plum tomatoes*
*4 tablespoons olive oil*
*1 onion, finely chopped*
*12 ounces fresh or dried spaghetti*
*1 small handful fresh basil leaves*
*salt and ground black pepper*
*coarsely shaved Parmesan cheese, to serve*
**Serves 4**

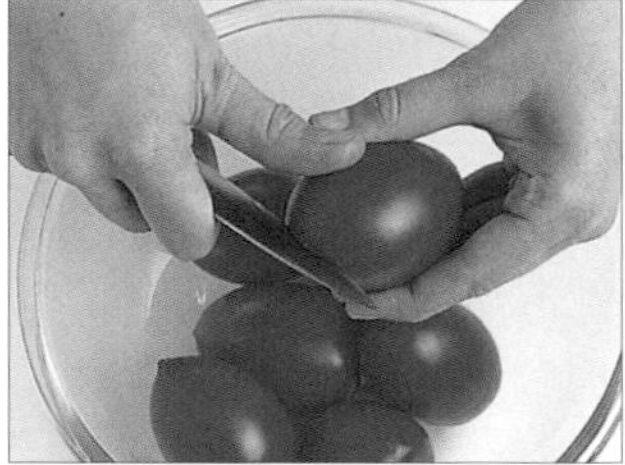

1 With a sharp knife, cut a cross in the bottom (flower) end of each tomato. Bring a medium saucepan of water to a boil and remove from the heat. Plunge a few of the tomatoes into the water, leave for 30 seconds or so, then lift them out with a slotted spoon. Repeat with the remaining tomatoes, then peel off the skin and coarsely chop the flesh.

2 Heat the oil in a large saucepan, add the onion and cook over low heat, stirring frequently, for about 5 minutes until softened and lightly colored. Add the tomatoes, with salt and pepper to taste, bring to a simmer, then turn the heat down to low and cover. Cook, stirring occasionally, for 30–40 minutes until thick.

3 Meanwhile, cook the pasta according to the instructions on the package. Shred the basil leaves finely.

4 Remove the sauce from the heat, stir in the basil and taste for seasoning. Drain the pasta, turn it into a warmed bowl, pour the sauce over and toss well. Serve immediately, with shaved Parmesan handed separately.

**COOK'S TIPS**

- *The Italian plum tomatoes called* San Marzano *are the best variety to use. When fully ripe, they have thin skins that peel off easily.*
- *In Italy, cooks often make this sauce in bulk in the summer months and freeze it for later use. Let it cool, then freeze in usable quantities in rigid containers. Thaw before reheating.*

**VARIATIONS**

*Some Neapolitan cooks add a little crushed garlic with the onion and some use chopped fresh oregano or Italian parsley with the basil; it is a matter of personal taste.*

# Rigatoni with Winter Tomato Sauce

IN WINTER, WHEN FRESH tomatoes are not at their best, this is the sauce the Italians make. Canned tomatoes combined with *soffritto* (the sautéed mixture of chopped onion, carrot, celery and garlic) and herbs give a better flavor than winter tomatoes.

**INGREDIENTS**

*1 onion*
*1 carrot*
*1 celery stalk*
*4 tablespoons olive oil*
*1 garlic clove, thinly sliced*
*a few leaves each fresh basil, thyme and oregano or marjoram*
*2 cans (14-ounce) chopped Italian plum tomatoes*
*1 tablespoon sun-dried tomato paste*
*1 teaspoon granulated sugar*
*about 6 tablespoons dry red or white wine (optional)*
*3 cups dried rigatoni*
*salt and ground black pepper*
*coarsely shaved Parmesan cheese, to serve*

**Serves 6–8**

1 Chop the onion, carrot and celery stalk finely, either in a food processor or by hand.

2 Heat the olive oil in a medium saucepan, add the garlic slices and stir over very low heat for 1–2 minutes.

3 Add the chopped vegetables and the fresh herbs. Cook over low heat, stirring frequently, for 5–7 minutes until the vegetables have softened and are lightly colored.

4 Add the canned tomatoes, tomato paste and sugar, then stir in the wine, if using. Add salt and pepper to taste. Bring to a boil, stirring, then lower the heat to a gentle simmer. Cook, uncovered, for about 45 minutes, stirring occasionally.

5 Cook the pasta according to the instructions on the package. Drain it and turn it into a warmed bowl. Taste the sauce for seasoning, pour the sauce over the pasta and toss well. Serve immediately, with shavings of Parmesan handed separately. If you like, garnish with extra chopped herbs.

# Noodles with Italian Mushrooms

PORCINI MUSHROOMS give this sauce a wonderful depth.

**INGREDIENTS**

*1 ounce dried Italian mushrooms (porcini)*
*3/4 cup warm water*
*2 pounds tomatoes, peeled, seeded and chopped or drained canned tomatoes*
*1/4 teaspoon dried hot chile flakes*
*3 tablespoons olive oil*
*4 slices pancetta or thin strips unsmoked bacon*
*1 large garlic clove, finely chopped*
*3 cups fresh or dried tagliatelle or fettuccine*
*salt and ground black pepper*
*freshly grated Parmesan cheese, to serve*

**Serves 2–4**

1 Put the mushrooms in a bowl and cover with the warm water. Let soak for 20 minutes.

2 Meanwhile, put the tomatoes in a saucepan with the chile flakes and seasoning. If using canned tomatoes, crush them coarsely with a fork or potato masher. Bring to a boil, reduce the heat and simmer for about 30–40 minutes, until reduced to 3 cups. Stir from time to time to prevent sticking.

3 When the mushrooms have finished soaking, lift them out and squeeze the remaining liquid into the bowl. Set aside while you prepare the other ingredients.

4 Carefully pour the soaking liquid into the tomatoes through a muslin-lined strainer. Simmer the tomatoes for a further 15 minutes.

5 Meanwhile, heat 2 tablespoons of the oil in a frying pan. Add the strips of pancetta or bacon and fry until golden but not crisp. Add the garlic and mushrooms and fry for 3 minutes, stirring. Set aside.

6 Cook the pasta in a large saucepan with plenty of boiling salted water until just *al dente*.

7 Add the bacon and mushroom mixture to the tomato sauce and mix well. Season with salt and ground black pepper.

8 Drain the pasta and return to the pan. Add the remaining oil and toss to coat the strands. Divide the pasta among hot plates, spoon the sauce on top and serve with freshly grated Parmesan cheese.

# Tagliatelle with Sun-dried Tomatoes

CHOOSE PLAIN sun-dried tomatoes for this sauce, instead of those preserved in oil, if you wish to reduce the fat content of the dish.

**INGREDIENTS**

*1 garlic clove, crushed*
*1 celery stalk, finely sliced*
*1 cup sun-dried tomatoes, finely chopped*
*scant ½ cup red wine*
*8 plum tomatoes*
*12 ounces dried tagliatelle*
*salt and ground black pepper*
**Serves 4**

1 Put the garlic, celery, sun-dried tomatoes and wine into a large saucepan. Gently cook for about 15 minutes.

2 Slash the bottoms of the plum tomatoes and plunge into a saucepan of boiling water for 1 minute, then transfer them into a saucepan of cold water. Slip off their skins. Halve, remove the seeds and cores and coarsely chop the flesh.

3 Add the plum tomatoes to the saucepan and simmer for a further 5 minutes. Season to taste.

4 Meanwhile, cook the tagliatelle in plenty of boiling salted water for 8–10 minutes, or until *al dente*. Drain well. Toss with half the sauce and serve on warmed plates, with the remaining sauce spooned over.

# Spaghetti with Tomatoes, Anchovies, Olives and Capers

FROM CAMPANIA IN THE SOUTH, this classic sauce has a strong flavor from the anchovies and olives.

**INGREDIENTS**

*2 tablespoons olive oil*
*1 small onion, finely chopped*
*1 garlic clove, finely chopped*
*4 drained canned anchovies*
*½ cup pitted black olives, sliced*
*1 tablespoon capers*
*1 can (14 ounces) chopped Italian plum tomatoes*
*3 tablespoons water*
*1 tablespoon chopped fresh Italian parsley*
*12 ounces fresh or dried spaghetti*
*salt and ground black pepper*

**Serves 4**

1 Heat the oil in a medium saucepan and add the onion, garlic and drained anchovies. Cook over low heat, stirring constantly, for 5–7 minutes or until the anchovies break down to form a very soft pulp. Add the black olives and capers and stir-fry for a minute or so.

2 Add the tomatoes, water, half the parsley and salt and pepper to taste. Stir well and bring to a boil, then lower the heat and cover the pan. Simmer gently for 30 minutes, stirring occasionally. Meanwhile, cook the pasta according to the package instructions.

3 Drain the pasta and turn it into a warmed bowl. Taste the sauce for seasoning, pour it over the pasta and toss well. Serve immediately, with the remaining parsley sprinkled on top.

**COOK'S TIP**

*Use good-quality, shiny black olives—Gaeta olives from Liguria are very good.*

# Bucatini with Tomato and Chile Sauce

THIS CLASSIC TOMATO sauce is called *Amatriciana* after the town of Amatrice in the Sabine hills, Lazio. If you visit Rome, you will see it on many restaurant menus served with either bucatini or spaghetti.

**INGREDIENTS**

*1 tablespoon olive oil*
*1 small onion, finely sliced*
*4 ounces smoked pancetta or rindless lean bacon, diced*
*1 fresh red chile, seeded and cut into thin strips*
*1 can (14 ounces) chopped Italian plum tomatoes*
*2–3 tablespoons dry white wine or water*
*12 ounces dried bucatini*
*2–3 tablespoons freshly grated Pecorino cheese, plus extra to serve (optional)*
*salt and ground black pepper*

**Serves 4**

1 Heat the oil in a medium saucepan and cook the onion, pancetta and chile over low heat for 5–7 minutes, stirring. Add the tomatoes and wine or water, with salt and pepper to taste. Bring to a boil, stirring, then cover and simmer for 15–20 minutes, stirring occasionally. If the sauce is too dry, stir in a little of the pasta water.

2 Meanwhile, cook the pasta in a pan of salted boiling water according to the package instructions.

3 Drain the pasta and turn it into a warmed bowl. Taste the sauce for seasoning, pour it over the pasta and add the grated Pecorino. Toss well. Serve immediately, with more grated Pecorino handed separately if liked.

**COOK'S TIP**

*Always take care when dealing with chiles. They contain a substance called capsaicin, which will irritate delicate skin, so it's a good idea to wear rubber gloves.*

# Fusilli with Tomato and Balsamic Vinegar Sauce

THIS IS A MODERN CAL-ITAL recipe (Californian/Italian). The intense, sweet-sour flavor of balsamic vinegar gives a pleasant kick to a sauce made with canned tomatoes.

**INGREDIENTS**

*2 cans (14-ounce) chopped Italian plum tomatoes*
*2 pieces of drained sun-dried tomato in olive oil, thinly sliced*
*2 garlic cloves, crushed*
*3 tablespoons olive oil*
*1 teaspoon granulated sugar*
*3 cups fresh or dried fusilli*
*3 tablespoons balsamic vinegar*
*salt and ground black pepper*
*coarsely shaved Pecorino cheese and arugula salad, to serve*

**Serves 6–8**

1 Put the canned and sun-dried tomatoes in a medium saucepan with the garlic, olive oil and sugar. Add salt and pepper to taste. Bring to a boil, stirring. Lower the heat and simmer for about 30 minutes until reduced.

2 Meanwhile, cook the pasta in salted boiling water according to the instructions on the package.

3 Add the balsamic vinegar to the sauce and stir to mix evenly. Cook for 1–2 minutes, then remove from the heat and taste for seasoning.

4 Drain the pasta and turn it into a warmed bowl. Pour the sauce over the pasta and toss well. Serve immediately, with arugula salad and the shaved Pecorino handed separately.

# Linguine with Sun-dried Tomato Pesto

TOMATO PESTO WAS ONCE a rarity, but is becoming increasingly popular. To make it, sun-dried tomatoes are used instead of basil. The result is absolutely delicious.

**INGREDIENTS**

*1/3 cup pine nuts*
*1/3 cup freshly grated Parmesan cheese*
*1/2 cup sun-dried tomatoes in olive oil*
*1 garlic clove, coarsely chopped*
*4 tablespoons olive oil*
*12 ounces fresh or dried linguine*
*ground black pepper*
*basil leaves, to garnish*
*coarsely shaved Parmesan cheese, to serve*

**Serves 4**

1 Put the pine nuts in a small non-stick frying pan and toss over low to medium heat for 1–2 minutes or until the nuts are lightly toasted and golden.

2 Turn the nuts into a food processor. Add the Parmesan, sun-dried tomatoes and garlic, with pepper to taste. Process until finely chopped.

### COOK'S TIP

*You can make this pesto up to 2 days in advance and keep it in a bowl in the refrigerator until ready to use. Pour a thin film of olive oil over the pesto in the bowl, then cover the bowl tightly with plastic wrap to prevent the pesto from tainting other foods in the refrigerator.*

3 Gradually add the olive oil to the mixture in the food processor through the feeder tube, with the machine running, until it has all been incorporated evenly and all the ingredients have formed a smooth-looking paste.

4 Cook the pasta according to the package instructions. Drain well, reserving a little of the cooking water. Turn the pasta into a warmed bowl, add the pesto and a few spoonfuls of the hot water and toss well. Serve immediately garnished with basil leaves. Hand shavings of Parmesan separately.

# Curly Lasagne with Classic Tomato Sauce

A CLASSIC SAUCE that is simply delicious just served by itself.

**INGREDIENTS**

*2 tablespoons olive oil*
*1 onion, chopped*
*2 tablespoons tomato paste*
*1 teaspoon paprika*
*2 cans (14-ounce) chopped tomatoes, drained*
*pinch of dried oregano*
*1¼ cups dry red wine*
*large pinch of superfine sugar*
*12 ounces fresh or dried curly lasagne sheets*
*salt and ground black pepper*
*chopped fresh Italian parsley, to garnish*
*Parmesan cheese shavings, to serve*

**Serves 4**

1 Heat the oil in a large frying pan and fry the onion for 10 minutes, stirring occasionally, until softened but not brown. Add the tomato paste and paprika and cook for a further 3 minutes.

2 Add the tomatoes, oregano, wine and sugar to the pan and season the mixture to taste, then bring to a boil.

3 Simmer for 20 minutes until the sauce has reduced and thickened, stirring occasionally.

4 Meanwhile, cook the pasta in plenty of boiling salted water according to the instructions on the package. Drain thoroughly and turn into a large serving dish. Pour over the sauce and toss to coat. Serve sprinkled with Parmesan cheese shavings and the chopped fresh Italian parsley.

**COOK'S TIP**

*If you cannot find curly lasagne in the supermarket use plain lasagne snipped in half lengthwise.*

# Linguine with Clam and Tomato Sauce

THERE ARE TWO TYPES of traditional Italian clam sauce for pasta: one with tomatoes, as here, and another version without.

**INGREDIENTS**

*2 pounds fresh clams in the shell, or 12 ounces bottled clams, with their liquid*
*6 tablespoons olive oil*
*1 garlic clove, crushed*
*1 can (14 ounces) tomatoes, very finely chopped*
*12 ounces linguine*
*4 tablespoons chopped fresh parsley*
*salt and ground black pepper*

**Serves 4**

1 Scrub and rinse the clams well under cold running water discarding any that are already open. Place them in a large saucepan with a cupful of water, and heat until the clams begin to open. Lift each clam out as soon as it opens, and scoop it out of its shell using a small spoon. Place them in a separate bowl.

2 If the clams are large, you may prefer to chop them up into 2 or 3 pieces. Reserve any liquid from the shells in a separate bowl. When all the clams have opened (discard any that do not open), pour the cooking liquid into the juices from the clams, and strain them through a piece of paper towel to remove any sand. If using bottled clams, use the liquid from the jar.

3 Place the olive oil in a medium saucepan with the garlic. Cook, stirring, over moderate heat until golden but not brown.

4 Remove the garlic from the pan and discard. Add the chopped tomatoes to the oil, and pour in the reserved clam liquid. Mix together well and cook over low to moderate heat until the sauce begins to dry out and thickens slightly.

5 Cook the pasta in a large saucepan with plenty of boiling salted water until just *al dente*, following the instructions on the package.

6 A minute or two before the pasta is cooked, stir the parsley and the clams into the tomato sauce, and increase the heat. Add pepper and taste for seasoning, adding salt if necessary. Drain the pasta and turn into a warmed serving dish. Pour on the hot sauce and mix well before serving immediately.

# Cappelletti with Tomatoes and Cream

TOMATOES, CREAM AND FRESH BASIL are a winning combination. In this very quick and easy recipe, the sauce coats little pasta purses filled with soft cheeses to make a substantial supper dish for vegetarians. If you prefer a lighter dish, you can use the sauce to coat plain, unstuffed pasta. Small shapes such as penne, farfalle or conchiglie are best.

**INGREDIENTS**

*1 ⅔ cups passata or tomato sauce*
*6 tablespoons dry white wine*
*⅔ cup heavy cream*
*2½ cups fresh cappelletti*
*1 small handful of fresh basil leaves*
*4 tablespoons freshly grated Parmesan cheese*
*salt and ground black pepper*
**Serves 4–6**

1 Pour the passata or tomato sauce and wine into a medium saucepan and stir to mix. Bring to a boil over medium heat, then add the cream and stir until evenly mixed and bubbling. Turn the heat down to low and let simmer.

2 Cook the pasta until *al dente*: 5–7 minutes or according to the instructions on the package. Meanwhile, finely shred most of the basil leaves.

3 Drain the pasta well, return it to the pan and toss it with the grated Parmesan. Taste the sauce for seasoning, pour it over the pasta and toss well. Serve immediately, sprinkled with the shredded basil and whole basil leaves.

**COOK'S TIP**

- *Cappelletti with a variety of fillings are available at supermarkets and Italian delicatessens.*
- *Other stuffed pasta shapes, such as tortelloni, ravioli, or the more unusual sacchettini (little purses), can be used with this sauce.*
- *The tomato sauce can be made up to a day ahead, then chilled until ready to use. Reheat gently in a heavy-based saucepan while the pasta is cooking.*

# Raw Tomato Sauce

THIS IS A WONDERFULLY simple uncooked tomato sauce that goes well with many different kinds of pasta, both long strands and short shapes. It is always made in summer when plum tomatoes have ripened on the vine in the sun and have their fullest flavor.

**INGREDIENTS**

*1¾ pounds ripe Italian plum tomatoes*
*1 large handful fresh basil leaves*
*5 tablespoons extra virgin olive oil*
*4 ounces ricotta salata cheese, diced*
*1 garlic clove, crushed*
*salt and ground black pepper*
*coarsely shaved Pecorino cheese, to serve*
**Serves 4**

1 Coarsely chop the plum tomatoes, removing the cores and as many of the seeds as you can. Tear the basil leaves into shreds with your fingers.

2 Put all the ingredients in a bowl, adding salt and pepper to taste, and stir well to mix. Cover and let stand at room temperature for 1–2 hours to let the flavors mingle.

3 Taste the sauce to check the seasoning then pour it over hot, freshly cooked pasta of your choice and toss well. Serve immediately with shavings of Pecorino handed separately.

**COOK'S TIPS**

- *Ricotta salata is a salted and dried version of ricotta cheese. It is firmer than the traditional soft white ricotta, and can be easily diced, crumbled and even grated. It is available from some specialty stores. If you can't locate it, use feta cheese instead.*
- *Long pasta goes well with this sauce, especially spaghetti or bucatini, or you could serve it with short shapes, such as fusilli or orecchiette.*

# Meaty Tomato Sauce

THIS ROMAN SAUCE came into being during the days when meat was scarce and expensive, so cooks would put a little meat fat in with the basic tomato sauce to make it taste of meat. Sometimes meat stock was used for the same purpose.

**INGREDIENTS**

*1 small onion*
*1 small carrot*
*2 celery stalks*
*2 garlic cloves*
*1 small handful fresh Italian parsley*
*2 ounces bacon fat, finely chopped*
*4–6 tablespoons dry white wine, or more to taste*
*1 1/4 pounds ripe Italian plum tomatoes, chopped*
*salt and ground black pepper*
**Serves 4**

1 Chop the onion, carrot and celery finely in a food processor. Add the garlic cloves and parsley and process until finely chopped. Alternatively, chop everything by hand.

2 Put the chopped vegetable mixture in a medium shallow saucepan or skillet with the bacon fat and cook, stirring, over low heat for about 5 minutes. Add the wine, with salt and pepper to taste and simmer for 5 minutes, then stir in the tomatoes. Simmer for 40 minutes, stirring occasionally and adding a little hot water if the sauce seems too dry.

3 Have ready a large strainer placed over a large bowl. Carefully pour in the sauce and press it through the strainer with the back of a metal spoon, leaving behind the tomato skins and any tough pieces of vegetable that won't go through.

4 Return the sauce to the clean pan and heat it through, adding a little more wine or hot water if it is too thick. Taste the sauce for seasoning, then toss with hot, freshly cooked pasta of your choice.

**COOK'S TIPS**

- *Capelli d'angelo, preferably made without egg, is the traditional pasta to serve with this sauce, but you can use tagliolini or tagliarini if you prefer.*
- *If you like, you can add about 1/4 ounce dried porcini mushrooms, soaked, drained and squeezed dry, when first cooking the other vegetables.*

# Farfalle with Tomatoes and Peas

THIS PRETTY SAUCE should be served with plain white pasta so that the red, green and white make it *tricolore*, the three colors of the Italian flag. Here farfalle (bow-tie shaped pasta) are used, but other pasta shapes will work just as well.

**INGREDIENTS**

*1 tablespoon olive oil*
*5–6 rindless lean bacon, cut into strips*
*1 can (14 ounces) chopped Italian plum tomatoes*
*4 tablespoons water*
*3 cups dried farfalle*
*2 cups frozen peas*
*4 tablespoons mascarpone cheese*
*a few fresh basil leaves, shredded*
*salt and ground black pepper*
*basil leaves, to garnish*
*freshly grated Parmesan cheese, to serve*

**Serves 4**

1 Heat the oil in a medium saucepan and add the bacon. Cook over low heat, stirring frequently, for 5–7 minutes.

2 Add the tomatoes and water, with salt and pepper to taste. Bring to a boil. Lower the heat, cover and simmer gently for about 15 minutes, stirring from time to time.

3 Meanwhile, cook the pasta in salted boiling water according to the instructions on the package.

4 Add the peas to the tomato sauce, stir well to mix and bring to a boil. Cover the pan and cook for 5–8 minutes until the peas are cooked and the sauce is quite thick. Taste the sauce for seasoning.

5 Turn off the heat under the pan and add the mascarpone and shredded basil. Mix well, cover the pan and let stand for 1–2 minutes. Drain the pasta and turn it into a warmed bowl. Pour the sauce over the pasta and toss well. Serve immediately, garnished with basil, and hand round some grated Parmesan separately.

# Spaghetti with Tomatoes and Pancetta

THIS SAUCE comes from Spoleto in Umbria. It is a fresh, light sauce in which the tomatoes are cooked for a short time, so it should only be made in summer when tomatoes have a good flavor.

**INGREDIENTS**

*12 ounces ripe Italian plum tomatoes*
*5 ounces pancetta or rindless lean bacon, diced*
*2 tablespoons olive oil*
*1 onion, finely chopped*
*12 ounces fresh or dried spaghetti*
*2–3 fresh marjoram sprigs, leaves stripped*
*salt and ground black pepper*
*shredded fresh basil, to garnish*
*freshly grated Pecorino cheese, to serve*

**Serves 4**

1 With a sharp knife, cut a cross in the bottom (flower) end of each plum tomato. Bring a medium saucepan of water to a boil and remove from the heat. Plunge a few of the tomatoes into the water, leave for 30 seconds or so, then lift them out with a slotted spoon and set aside. Repeat with the remaining tomatoes, then peel off the skin and finely chop the flesh.

**COOK'S TIP**

*Do try to find pancetta—bacon can be substituted but the sauce will not taste precisely the same. You can buy ready diced pancetta in packets in supermarkets. Alternatively, you can buy it thinly sliced, sometimes cut from a roll (arrotolata), and dice it yourself.*

2 Put the pancetta or bacon in a medium saucepan with the oil. Stir over low heat until the fat runs. Add the onion and stir to mix. Cook gently for about 10 minutes, stirring.

3 Add the tomatoes, with salt and pepper to taste. Stir well and cook, uncovered, for about 10 minutes. Meanwhile, cook the pasta according to the instructions on the package.

4 Remove the sauce from the heat, stir in the marjoram and taste for seasoning. Drain the pasta and turn it into a warmed bowl. Pour the sauce over the pasta and toss well. Serve immediately, sprinkled with shredded basil. Hand around grated Pecorino.

# Penne with Tomato and Chile Sauce

THIS IS ONE OF ROME'S most famous pasta dishes—called *Penne all'Arrabbiata* in Italy. Literally translated, *arrabbiata* means "enraged" or "furious" but in this context it should be translated as "fiery." Make the sauce as hot as you like by adding more chiles to taste.

**INGREDIENTS**

*1 ounce dried porcini mushrooms*
*7 tablespoons butter*
*5 ounces pancetta or rindless smoked lean bacon, diced*
*1–2 dried red chiles, to taste*
*2 garlic cloves, crushed*
*8 ripe Italian plum tomatoes, peeled and chopped*
*a few fresh basil leaves, torn, plus extra to garnish*
*3 cups fresh or dried penne*
*2/3 cup freshly grated Parmesan cheese*
*1/3 cup freshly grated Pecorino cheese*
*salt*

**Serves 4**

1 Soak the dried mushrooms in warm water to cover for 15–20 minutes. Drain, then squeeze dry with your hands. Finely chop the mushrooms.

2 Melt 4 tablespoons of the butter in a medium saucepan or skillet. Add the pancetta or bacon and stir-fry over medium heat until golden and slightly crispy. Remove the pancetta with a slotted spoon and set it aside.

3 Add the chopped mushrooms to the pan and cook in the same way. Remove and set aside with the pancetta or bacon. Crumble 1 chile into the pan, add the garlic and cook, stirring, for a few minutes until the garlic turns golden.

4 Add the tomatoes and basil and season with salt. Cook gently, stirring occasionally, for 10–15 minutes. Meanwhile, cook the penne in a pan of salted boiling water, according to the instructions on the package.

5 Add the pancetta or bacon and the mushrooms to the tomato sauce. Taste for seasoning, adding more chiles if you prefer a hotter flavor. If the sauce is too dry, stir in a little of the pasta water.

6 Drain the pasta and turn it into a warmed bowl. Dice the remaining butter, add it to the pasta with the cheeses, then toss until well coated. Pour the tomato sauce over the pasta, toss well and serve immediately, with a few basil leaves sprinkled on top.

# Linguine with Scallops and Tomatoes

FRESH BASIL gives this sauce a distinctive flavor.

**INGREDIENTS**

*1 pound fresh or dried linguine*
*2 tablespoons olive oil*
*2 garlic cloves, crushed*
*1 pound sea scallops, halved horizontally*
*salt and ground black pepper*
*2 tablespoons chopped fresh basil*

***For the sauce***

*2 tablespoons olive oil*
*½ onion, finely chopped*
*1 garlic clove, crushed*
*½ teaspoon salt*
*2 cans (14-ounce) plum tomatoes*

**Serves 4**

1 To make the tomato sauce, heat the oil in a non-stick frying pan. Add the onion, garlic and a little salt, and cook over medium heat for about 5 minutes until just softened, stirring occasionally.

2 Add the tomatoes to the pan, with their juice, and crush with a fork. Bring to a boil, then reduce the heat and simmer gently for 15 minutes. Remove from the heat and set aside.

3 Cook the pasta in a large saucepan with plenty of boiling salted water, according to the instructions on the package, until the pasta is *al dente*.

4 Meanwhile, heat the oil in another non-stick frying pan and cook the garlic until just sizzling, for about 30 seconds.

5 Add the scallops and ½ teaspoon salt and cook over high heat, tossing until the scallops are cooked through, about 3 minutes.

6 Add the scallops to the tomato sauce. Season with salt and pepper, stir and keep warm.

7 Drain the pasta, rinse under hot water and drain again. Place in a large serving dish. Add the sauce and the basil and toss thoroughly. Serve the pasta immediately.

# Fusilli with Tomato and Smoky Bacon

PREPARE THIS SAUCE using tomatoes that are perfectly ripe and sweet.

**INGREDIENTS**

*2 pounds ripe tomatoes*
*6 strips smoked lean bacon*
*4 tablespoons butter*
*1 onion, chopped*
*1 tablespoon chopped fresh oregano or 1 teaspoon dried*
*1 pound fresh or dried pasta, such as fusilli col buco*
*salt and ground black pepper*
*freshly grated Parmesan cheese, to serve*
**Serves 4**

1 Plunge the tomatoes into boiling water for 1 minute, then transfer them into a bowl of cold water. Slip off the skins. Halve the tomatoes, remove the seeds and cores and coarsely chop the flesh.

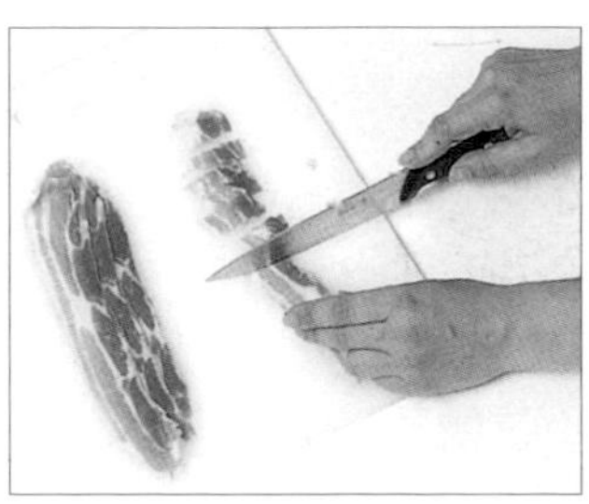

2 Remove the rind from the lean bacon and coarsely chop the meat.

3 Melt the butter in a saucepan and add the chopped bacon. Fry until lightly browned on all sides, then add the onion and cook gently, stirring, for 5 minutes until softened.

4 Add the tomatoes, salt, pepper and oregano to the other ingredients in the pan. Simmer gently for 10 minutes.

5 Cook the pasta in plenty of boiling salted water according to the instructions on the package. Drain well and toss with the tomato sauce. Serve with plenty of freshly grated Parmesan cheese.

P

# Cream Sauces

The northern Italians love cream sauce with pasta. Its unctuous texture goes well with *pasta all'uovo*—pasta made with egg. The pasta in the north is often fresh rather than dried, and cream sauces complement it perfectly. The cream used in Italy is different from our fresh cream. Called *panna da cucina* (cream for cooking), it has a thin, almost runny, consistency and a slight tang. You can buy it fresh in Italy, but beyond its borders you are more likely to see long-life *panna da cucina* in specialty stores.

Oddly enough, the most famous cream sauce of all does not come from northern Italy, but from Rome. *Fettuccine all'Alfredo*—a simple dish of fresh fettuccine tossed in nothing more than cream, butter and grated Parmesan—is one of the best pasta dishes of all time, and very hard to beat. You will find the recipe in this chapter, plus many other simple sauces based on cream to rival Alfredo's creation. From classic favorites, such as Spaghetti Carbonara and Vermicelli with Lemon to recipes using seasonal vegetables, such as asparagus and wild mushrooms, or more unusual ingredients, such as radicchio, there is plenty of choice.

Pasta with a cream sauce is always special and makes a good dinner party first course, but keep portions small, because flavors are rich.

# Spaghetti Carbonara

AN ALL-TIME FAVORITE that needs no introducing. This version has plenty of pancetta or bacon and is not too creamy, but you can vary the amounts as you please.

**INGREDIENTS**

*2 tablespoons olive oil*
*1 small onion, finely chopped*
*8 pancetta or rindless smoked lean bacon, cut into ½-inch strips*
*12 ounces fresh or dried spaghetti*
*4 eggs*
*4 tablespoons crème fraîche*
*4 tablespoons freshly grated Parmesan cheese, plus extra to serve*
*salt and ground black pepper*
**Serves 4**

1 Heat the oil in a large saucepan or skillet, add the finely chopped onion and cook over low heat, stirring frequently, for about 5 minutes until softened but not colored.

2 Add the strips of pancetta or bacon to the onion in the pan and cook for about 10 minutes, stirring almost all of the time. Meanwhile, cook the pasta in a pan of salted boiling water according to the instructions on the package until *al dente*.

3 Put the eggs, crème fraîche and grated Parmesan in a bowl. Grind in plenty of pepper, then beat everything together well.

4 Drain the pasta, turn it into the pan with the pancetta or bacon and toss well to mix. Turn the heat off under the pan. Immediately add the egg mixture and toss vigorously so that it cooks lightly and coats the pasta.

5 Quickly taste for seasoning, then divide among four warmed bowls and sprinkle with black pepper. Serve immediately, with extra grated Parmesan handed separately.

# Fusilli with Wild Mushrooms

A VERY RICH DISH WITH AN earthy flavor and lots of garlic, this makes an ideal main course for vegetarians, especially if it is followed by a crisp green salad.

**INGREDIENTS**

*½ x 10-ounce jar wild mushrooms in olive oil*
*2 tablespoons butter*
*2 cups fresh wild mushrooms, thinly sliced*
*1 teaspoon finely chopped fresh thyme*
*1 teaspoon finely chopped fresh marjoram or oregano, plus extra to serve*
*4 garlic cloves, crushed*
*3 cups fresh or dried fusilli*
*scant 1 cup* panna da cucina *or heavy cream*
*salt and ground black pepper*
**Serves 4**

1 Drain about 1 tablespoon of the oil from the mushrooms into a medium saucepan. Slice or chop the bottled mushrooms into bite-size pieces, if they are large.

2 Add the butter to the oil in the pan and place over low heat until sizzling. Add the bottled and the fresh mushrooms, the chopped herbs and the garlic, with salt and pepper to taste. Simmer over medium heat, stirring frequently, for about 10 minutes or until the fresh mushrooms are soft and tender. Meanwhile, cook the pasta in salted boiling water according to the instructions on the package.

3 As soon as the mushrooms are cooked, increase the heat to high and toss the mixture with a wooden spoon to drive off any excess liquid. Pour in the cream and bring to a boil, stirring, then taste and add more salt and pepper if needed.

4 Drain the pasta and turn it into a warmed bowl. Pour the sauce over the pasta and toss well. Serve immediately, sprinkled with finely chopped fresh herbs.

# Fusilli with Walnuts

A CLASSIC ITALIAN DISH with a strong, nutty flavor, this should be served with a delicately flavored salad.

**INGREDIENTS**

*3 cups dried fusilli col buco*
*½ cup walnut pieces*
*2 tablespoons butter*
*1¼ cups milk*
*1 cup fresh bread crumbs*
*2 tablespoons freshly grated Parmesan cheese*
*pinch of freshly grated nutmeg*
*salt and ground black pepper*
*fresh rosemary sprigs, to garnish*

**Serves 4**

1 Cook the pasta in plenty of boiling salted water according to the instructions on the package. Meanwhile, preheat the broiler.

2 Spread the walnuts evenly over the broiler pan. Cook for about 5 minutes, turning occasionally until evenly toasted.

3 Remove the walnuts from the heat, place in a clean dish towel and rub away the skins. Coarsely chop the nuts.

4 Heat the butter and milk in a saucepan until the butter is completely melted.

5 Stir in the bread crumbs and nuts and heat gently for 2 minutes, stirring constantly until the mixture has thickened.

6 Add the Parmesan cheese, nutmeg and seasoning to taste.

7 Drain the pasta thoroughly through a colander then pour over the sauce and combine thoroughly. Serve immediately, garnished with fresh sprigs of rosemary.

# Farfalle with Mushrooms and Cheese

FRESH WILD MUSHROOMS are very good in this sauce, but they are expensive. To cut the cost, use half wild and half cultivated, or as many wild as you can afford—even a small handful will intensify the mushroom flavor of the sauce.

**INGREDIENTS**

*1/4 cup dried porcini mushrooms*
*1 cup warm water*
*2 tablespoons butter*
*1 small onion, finely chopped*
*1 garlic clove, crushed*
*3 cups fresh mushrooms, thinly sliced*
*a few fresh sage leaves, very finely chopped, plus a few whole leaves, to garnish*
*2/3 cup dry white wine*
*2 cups dried farfalle*
*1/2 cup mascarpone cheese*
*1 cup Gorgonzola or torta di Gorgonzola cheese, crumbled*
*salt and ground black pepper*

**Serves 4**

1 Put the dried porcini in a small bowl with the warm water and leave to soak for 20–30 minutes. Remove the porcini from the liquid with a slotted spoon and squeeze over the bowl to extract as much liquid as possible. Strain the liquid and set it aside. Finely chop the porcini.

2 Melt the butter in a large saucepan, add the onion and chopped porcini and cook gently, stirring for about 3 minutes until the onion is soft. Add the garlic and fresh mushrooms, chopped sage, salt and plenty of black pepper. Cook over medium heat, stirring frequently, for about 5 minutes or until the mushrooms are soft and juicy. Stir in the soaking liquid and the wine and simmer gently.

3 Cook the farfalle in a large saucepan of rapidly boiling salted water, for about 10 minutes or until it is *al dente*.

4 Meanwhile, stir the mascarpone and Gorgonzola into the mushroom sauce. Heat through, stirring, until melted. Taste for seasoning and adjust if necessary. Drain the pasta thoroughly, add to the sauce and toss to mix. Serve at once, with black pepper ground liberally on top. Garnish with sage leaves.

**VARIATION**

*For a lighter sauce, use crème fraîche instead of mascarpone.*

# Pink and Green Farfalle

IN THIS MODERN RECIPE, pink shrimp and green zucchini combine prettily with cream and pasta bows to make a substantial main course. Serve with crusty Italian rolls or chunks of warm ciabatta bread.

**INGREDIENTS**

*¼ cup butter*
*2–3 scallions, very thinly sliced on the diagonal*
*12 ounces zucchini, thinly sliced on the diagonal*
*4 tablespoons dry white wine*
*2⅔ cups dried farfalle*
*5 tablespoons crème fraîche*
*1⅓ cups shelled cooked shrimp, thawed and thoroughly dried if frozen*
*1 tablespoon finely chopped fresh marjoram or Italian parsley, or a mixture*
*salt and ground black pepper*

**Serves 4**

1 Melt the butter in a large saucepan, add the scallions and cook over low heat, stirring frequently, for about 5 minutes until softened. Add the zucchini, with salt and pepper to taste, and stir-fry for 5 minutes. Pour over the wine and let it bubble, then cover and simmer for 10 minutes.

**VARIATION**

*Use penne instead of the farfalle, and asparagus tips instead of the zucchini.*

2 Cook the pasta in a saucepan of salted boiling water according to the instructions on the package. Meanwhile, add the crème fraîche to the zucchini mixture and simmer for about 10 minutes until well reduced.

3 Add the shrimp to the zucchini mixture, heat through gently and taste for seasoning. Drain the pasta and turn it into a warmed bowl. Add the sauce and chopped herbs and toss well. Serve immediately.

# Penne with Shrimp and Pernod

THIS IS A MODERN RECIPE, typical of those found on menus in the most innovative Italian restaurants. The Pernod and dill weed go well together, but you could use white wine and basil.

**INGREDIENTS**

*scant 1 cup* panna da cucina *or heavy cream*
*1 cup fish stock*
*3 cups dried penne*
*2–3 tablespoons Pernod*
*1⅓ cups shelled cooked shrimp, thawed and thoroughly dried if frozen*
*2 tablespoons chopped fresh dill weed, plus extra to garnish*
*salt and ground black pepper*

**Serves 4**

1 Put the cream and the fish stock in a medium saucepan and bring to a boil. Lower the heat and simmer, stirring occasionally, for 10–15 minutes until reduced by about half. Meanwhile, cook the dried pasta in a saucepan of salted boiling water according to the instructions on the package.

2 Add the Pernod and shrimp to the cream sauce, with salt and pepper to taste, if necessary. Heat the shrimp through very gently. Drain the pasta and turn it into a warmed bowl. Pour the sauce over the pasta, add the dill weed and toss well. Serve immediately, sprinkled with chopped dill weed.

# Pipe Rigate with Peas and Ham

PRETTILY FLECKED WITH PINK and green, this is a lovely dish for a spring or summer supper party.

**INGREDIENTS**

*2 tablespoons butter*
*1 tablespoon olive oil*
*1¼–1½ cups frozen peas, thawed*
*1 garlic clove, crushed*
*⅔ cup chicken stock, dry white wine or water*
*2 tablespoons chopped fresh Italian parsley*
*¾ cup* panna da cucina *or heavy cream*
*4 ounces prosciutto crudo, shredded*
*3 cups dried pipe rigate*
*salt and ground black pepper*
*chopped fresh herbs, to garnish*
**Serves 4**

1 Melt half the butter with the olive oil in a medium saucepan until foaming. Add the thawed frozen peas and the crushed garlic to the pan, followed by the chicken stock, wine or water.

2 Sprinkle in the chopped parsley and add salt and pepper to taste. Cook over medium heat, stirring frequently, for 5–8 minutes or until most of the liquid has been absorbed.

3 Add about half the cream, increase the heat to high and let the cream bubble, stirring constantly, until it thickens and coats the peas. Remove from the heat, stir in the prosciutto and taste for seasoning.

4 Cook the pasta according to the instructions on the package. Turn into a colander and drain well.

5 Immediately melt the remaining butter with the cream in the pan in which the pasta was cooked. Add the pasta and toss over medium heat until it is evenly coated. Pour in the sauce, toss lightly to mix with the pasta and heat through. Serve immediately, sprinkled with fresh herbs.

**COOK'S TIPS**

- *Prosciutto is quite expensive, but it tastes very good in this dish. To cut the cost you could use ordinary cooked ham or pancetta.*
- *If you can't get pipe rigate, use conchiglie or orecchiette instead, all of which trap the peas.*

# Alfredo's Fettuccine

THIS SIMPLE RECIPE WAS invented by a Roman restaurateur called Alfredo, who became famous for serving it with a gold fork and spoon.

**INGREDIENTS**

*¼ cup butter*

*scant 1 cup* panna da cucina *or heavy cream*

*⅔ cup freshly grated Parmesan cheese, plus extra to serve*

*12 ounces fresh fettuccine*

*salt and ground black pepper*

**Serves 4**

1 Melt the butter in a large saucepan or skillet. Add the cream and bring it to a boil. Simmer for 5 minutes, stirring, then add the Parmesan, with salt and pepper to taste, and turn off the heat under the pan.

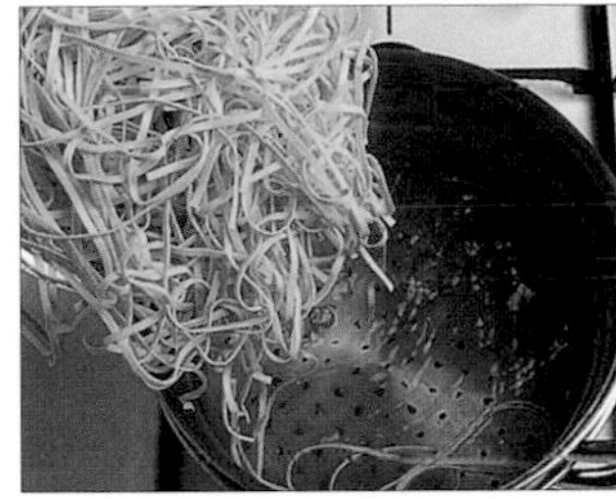

2 Bring a large saucepan of salted water to a boil. Drop in the pasta all at once and quickly bring back to a boil, stirring occasionally. Cook until *al dente*: 2–3 minutes, or according to the instructions on the package. Drain well.

3 Turn on the heat under the pan of cream to low, add the pasta all at once and toss until it is coated in the sauce. Taste for seasoning. Serve immediately, with extra grated Parmesan handed around separately.

**COOK'S TIPS**

- *With so few ingredients, it is particularly important to use only the best-quality ones for this dish to be a success. Use good unsalted butter and top-quality Parmesan cheese. The best is Parmigiano-Reggiano, which has its name stamped on the rind. Grate it only just before using.*
- *Fresh fettuccine is traditional, so either make it yourself or buy it from an Italian market. If you cannot get fettuccine, you can use tagliatelle instead.*

# Vermicelli with Lemon

FRESH AND TANGY, this makes an excellent first course for a dinner party. It doesn't rely on fresh seasonal ingredients, so it is good at any time of year. It is also a recipe to remember when you're pushed for time, because the sauce can easily be made in the time it takes to cook the pasta.

**INGREDIENTS**

*12 ounces dried vermicelli*
*juice of 2 large lemons*
*¼ cup butter*
*scant 1 cup* panna da cucina *or heavy cream*
*1⅓ cups freshly grated Parmesan cheese*
*salt and ground black pepper*

**Serves 4**

1 Cook the pasta in salted boiling water according to the instructions on the package.

2 Meanwhile, pour the lemon juice into a medium saucepan. Add the butter and cream, then salt and pepper to taste.

3 Bring to a boil, then lower the heat and simmer for about 5 minutes, stirring occasionally, until the cream reduces slightly.

4 Drain the pasta and return it to the pan. Add the grated Parmesan, then taste the sauce for seasoning and pour it over the pasta. Toss quickly over medium heat until the pasta is evenly coated with the sauce, then divide among four warmed bowls and serve immediately.

## COOK'S TIP

*Lemons vary in the amount of juice they yield. On average, a large fresh lemon will yield 4–6 tablespoons. The lemony flavor of this dish is supposed to be quite sharp—you can use less juice if you prefer.*

## VARIATIONS

- *Use spaghettini or spaghetti, or even small pasta shapes, such as fusilli, farfalle or orecchiette.*
- *For an even tangier taste, add a little grated lemon rind to the sauce when you add the butter and the cream to the pan in Step 2.*

# Spaghetti with Saffron

A QUICK AND EASY DISH THAT makes a delicious midweek supper. The ingredients are all staples that you are likely to have in the refrigerator, so this recipe is perfect for impromptu meals.

**INGREDIENTS**

*12 ounces dried spaghetti*
*a few saffron strands*
*2 tablespoons water*
*5 ounces cooked ham, cut into thin sticks*
*scant 1 cup panna da cucina or heavy cream*
*2/3 cup freshly grated Parmesan cheese, plus extra to serve*
*2 egg yolks*
*salt and ground black pepper*
**Serves 4**

1 Cook the pasta in a saucepan of salted boiling water according to the instructions on the package.

2 Meanwhile, put the saffron strands in a saucepan, add the water and bring to a boil immediately. Remove the pan from the heat and let stand for a while.

3 Add the strips of ham to the pan containing the saffron. Stir in the cream and Parmesan, with a little salt and pepper to taste. Heat gently, stirring all the time. When the cream starts to bubble around the edges, remove the sauce from the heat and add the egg yolks. Beat well to mix, then taste for seasoning.

4 Drain the pasta and turn it into a warmed bowl. Immediately pour the sauce over the pasta and toss well. Serve immediately, with extra grated Parmesan handed separately.

**COOK'S TIPS**

- *Individual envelopes of saffron powder, enough for four servings, are sold at Italian markets and some supermarkets, and one envelope can be used for this sauce instead of the saffron strands. Simply sprinkle in the powder in Step 3, when adding salt and pepper.*
- *Use a heavy pan for heating the cream so that it does not catch on the bottom. Make sure you beat the sauce immediately the eggs are added.*

# Fettuccine with Ham and Cream

PROSCIUTTO IS PERFECT for this rich and delicious dish, which makes a very elegant appetizer.

**INGREDIENTS**

*4 ounces prosciutto crudo or other unsmoked ham (raw or cooked)*
*¼ cup butter*
*2 shallots, very finely chopped*
*⅔ cup heavy cream*
*12 ounces fresh or dried fettucine*
*½ cup grated Parmesan cheese*
*salt and ground black pepper*
*fresh parsley sprig, to garnish*
**Serves 4**

1 Cut the fat from the ham and chop both lean and fat parts separately into small squares.

2 Melt the butter in a medium frying pan and add the shallots and the squares of ham fat. Cook, stirring, until golden. Add the lean ham, and cook for a further 2 minutes. Season with black pepper. Stir the cream into the cooked ham, and keep the sauce warm over low heat while the pasta is cooking.

3 Cook the pasta in plenty of boiling salted water until *al dente*. Drain, turn into a warmed serving dish and toss with the sauce. Stir in the cheese and serve immediately, garnished with a sprig of parsley.

# Tagliatelle with Smoked Salmon

IN ITALY SMOKED SALMON is imported and quite expensive. This elegant creamy sauce makes a little go a long way. Use a mixture of green and white pasta if you wish.

**INGREDIENTS**

*6 ounces smoked salmon slices or ends, fresh or frozen*
*1¼ cups light cream*
*pinch of ground mace or grated nutmeg*
*12 ounces fresh or dried green and white tagliatelle*
*salt and ground black pepper*
*3 tablespoons chopped fresh chives, to garnish*
**Serves 4–5**

1 Cut the salmon into thin strips, each about 2 inches long. Place the strips in a bowl and add the cream and the mace or nutmeg. Stir to combine, cover and let stand for at least 2 hours in a cool place.

2 Cook the pasta in a large saucepan with plenty of boiling salted water according to the instructions on the package, or until it is just *al dente*.

3 Meanwhile, gently warm the cream and salmon mixture in a small saucepan, without boiling.

4 Drain the pasta, pour the sauce over and mix well. Season to taste and garnish with the chives.

# Fusilli with Mascarpone and Spinach

THIS CREAMY, GREEN SAUCE tossed in lightly cooked pasta is best served with plenty of sun-dried tomato ciabatta bread.

**INGREDIENTS**

*3 cups fresh or dried fusilli*
*¼ cup butter*
*1 onion, chopped*
*1 garlic clove, chopped*
*2 tablespoons fresh thyme leaves*
*8 ounces frozen spinach leaves, thawed*
*1 cup mascarpone cheese*
*salt and ground black pepper*
*fresh thyme sprigs, to garnish*
**Serves 4**

1 Cook the pasta in plenty of boiling salted water according to the instructions on the package.

2 Melt the butter in a large saucepan and fry the onion for 10 minutes until softened.

3 Stir in the garlic, fresh thyme, spinach and seasoning and heat gently for about 5 minutes, stirring occasionally, until heated through.

4 Stir in the mascarpone cheese and cook gently until heated through. Do not boil.

5 Drain the pasta thoroughly and stir into the sauce. Toss until well coated. Serve immediately, garnished with fresh thyme.

**COOK'S TIP**

*Mascarpone is a rich Italian cream cheese. If you cannot find any, use ordinary full-fat cream cheese instead.*

# Ravioli with Four-cheese Sauce

THIS IS A SMOOTH, cheese flavored sauce that coats the pasta very evenly.

**INGREDIENTS**

*12 ounces fresh or dried ravioli*
*1/4 cup butter*
*1/4 cup all-purpose flour*
*1 3/4 cups milk*
*2 ounces freshly grated Parmesan cheese*
*2 ounces freshly grated Edam cheese*
*2 ounces freshly grated Gruyère cheese*
*2 ounces freshly grated fontina cheese*
*salt and ground black pepper*
*chopped fresh Italian parsley, to garnish*

**Serves 4**

1 Cook the pasta in plenty of boiling salted water according to the instructions on the package.

2 Melt the butter in a saucepan, stir in the flour and cook for 2 minutes, stirring occasionally.

3 Gradually stir in the milk until completely blended.

4 Bring the milk slowly to a boil, stirring constantly until the sauce is thickened.

5 Stir the grated cheeses into the sauce. Mix together until they are just beginning to melt. Remove from the heat and season.

6 Drain the pasta thoroughly and turn into a large serving dish. Pour over the sauce and toss to coat. Serve immediately, garnished with the chopped fresh parsley.

# Linguine with Ham and Mascarpone

MASCARPONE CHEESE masquerades as cream in this recipe. Its thick, unctuous consistency makes it perfect for sauces. Have the water boiling, ready for the pasta, before you start making the sauce, because everything cooks so quickly.

**INGREDIENTS**

*2 tablespoons butter*
*3½ ounces cooked ham, cut into short thin sticks*
*¾ cup mascarpone cheese*
*2 tablespoons milk*
*3 tablespoons freshly grated Parmesan cheese, plus extra to serve*
*1¼ pounds fresh linguine*
*salt and ground black pepper*
**Serves 6**

1 Melt the butter in a medium saucepan, add the ham, mascarpone and milk and stir well over low heat until the mascarpone has melted. Add 1 tablespoon of the grated Parmesan and plenty of pepper and stir well.

2 Cook the pasta in a large saucepan of salted boiling water for 2–3 minutes until *al dente*.

3 Drain the cooked pasta well and turn it into a warmed bowl. Pour the sauce over the pasta, add the remaining Parmesan and toss well until thoroughly combined.

4 Taste for seasoning and serve the pasta immediately, with more ground black pepper and extra grated Parmesan handed separately.

# Farfalle with Gorgonzola Cream

SWEET AND SIMPLE, this sauce has a nutty tang from the blue cheese. It is also good with long pasta, such as spaghetti or trenette.

**INGREDIENTS**

*3 cups dried farfalle*
*6 ounces Gorgonzola cheese, any rind removed, diced*
*⅔ cup* panna da cucina *or heavy cream*
*pinch of granulated sugar*
*2 teaspoons finely chopped fresh sage, plus fresh sage leaves (some whole, some shredded) to garnish*
*salt and ground black pepper*
**Serves 4**

1 Cook the pasta until *al dente*: 8–10 minutes or according to the instructions on the package.

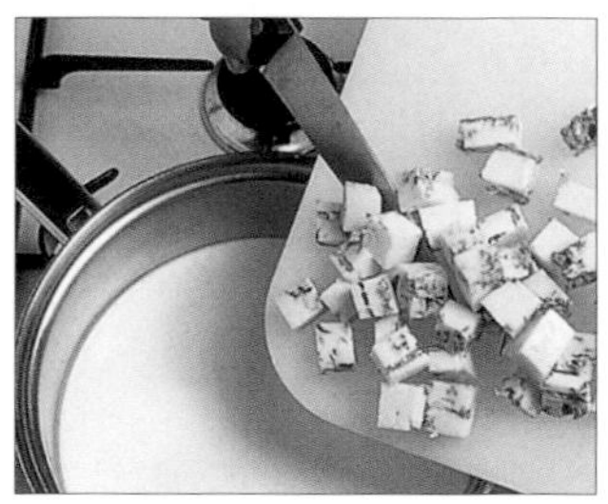

2 Meanwhile, put the Gorgonzola and cream in a medium saucepan. Add the sugar and plenty of ground black pepper and heat gently, stirring frequently, until the cheese has melted. Remove the pan from the heat.

3 Drain the cooked pasta well and return it to the pan in which it was cooked. Pour the sauce into the pan with the pasta.

4 Add the chopped sage to the pasta and toss over medium heat until the pasta is evenly coated. Taste for seasoning, adding salt if necessary, then divide among four warmed bowls. Garnish each portion with sage and serve immediately.

# Garganelli with Asparagus and Cream

A LOVELY RECIPE FOR LATE SPRING when bunches of fresh young asparagus are found on sale in stores and markets everywhere.

**INGREDIENTS**

*1 bunch fresh young asparagus, 9–11 ounces*
*3 cups dried garganelli*
*2 tablespoons butter*
*scant 1 cup* panna da cucina *or heavy cream*
*2 tablespoons dry white wine*
*1–1 1/3 cups freshly grated Parmesan cheese*
*2 tablespoons chopped mixed fresh herbs, such as basil, Italian parsley, chervil, marjoram and oregano*
*salt and ground black pepper*
**Serves 4**

1 Trim off and throw away the woody ends of the asparagus—after trimming, you should have about 7 ounces asparagus spears. Cut the spears diagonally into pieces that are about the same length and shape as the garganelli.

2 Blanch the asparagus spears in salted boiling water for 2 minutes, the tips for 1 minute. Immediately after blanching drain the asparagus spears and tips, rinse in cold water and set aside.

3 Cook the pasta according to the instructions on the package. Meanwhile, put the butter and cream in a medium saucepan, add salt and pepper to taste and bring to a boil. Simmer for a few minutes until the cream reduces and thickens, then add the asparagus, wine and about half the grated Parmesan. Taste for seasoning and keep on low heat.

4 Drain the pasta when cooked and turn it into a warmed bowl. Pour the sauce over the pasta, sprinkle with the fresh herbs and toss well. Serve immediately, topped with the remaining grated Parmesan.

### COOK'S TIPS

- *When buying asparagus look for thin stalks, which will be sweet and tender. Don't buy asparagus with thick or woody stalks, which will be tough.*
- *Garganelli all'uovo (with egg) are just perfect for this dish. You can buy packages of this pasta in Italian markets.*
- *Penne (quills) or penne rigate (ridged quills) are an alternative pasta for this recipe. They are similar in shape and size to garganelli.*

# Tagliatelle with Radicchio and Cream

THIS IS A MODERN RECIPE that is very quick and easy to make. It is deliciously rich, and makes a good dinner party first course.

**INGREDIENTS**

*8 ounces dried tagliatelle*
*3–3½ ounces pancetta or rindless lean bacon, diced*
*2 tablespoons butter*
*1 onion, finely chopped*
*1 garlic clove, crushed*
*1 head of radicchio, about 4–6 ounces, finely shredded*
*⅔ cup panna da cucina or heavy cream*
*⅔ cup freshly grated Parmesan cheese*
*salt and ground black pepper*
**Serves 4**

1 Cook the pasta according to the instructions on the package.

2 Meanwhile, put the pancetta or bacon in a medium saucepan and heat gently until the fat begins to run. Increase the heat slightly and stir-fry the pancetta or bacon for a further 5 minutes until crisp and golden.

3 Add the butter, onion and garlic to the pan and stir-fry for 5 minutes more. Add the radicchio and toss for 1–2 minutes until wilted.

4 Pour in the cream and add the grated Parmesan, with salt and pepper to taste. Stir for 1–2 minutes until the cream is bubbling and the ingredients are evenly mixed. Taste for seasoning.

5 Drain the pasta and turn it into a warmed bowl. Pour the sauce over and toss well. Serve immediately.

### COOK'S TIP

*In Italy, cooks use a type of radicchio called radicchio di Treviso. It is very striking to look at, having long leaves that are dramatically striped in dark red and white. Radicchio di Treviso is available in some supermarkets, but if you cannot get it you can use the round radicchio instead, which is easier to obtain.*

# Tagliatelle with Gorgonzola Sauce

GORGONZOLA IS A creamy Italian blue cheese. As an alternative you could use Danablue cheese.

**INGREDIENTS**

*2 tablespoons butter, plus extra for tossing the pasta*
*8 ounces Gorgonzola cheese*
*⅔ cup heavy or whipping cream*
*2 tablespoons dry vermouth*
*1 teaspoon cornstarch*
*1 tablespoon chopped fresh sage*
*1 pound tagliatelle*
*salt and ground black pepper*
**Serves 4**

1 Melt 2 tablespoons butter in a heavy saucepan (it needs to have a thick base to prevent the cheese from burning). Stir in 6 ounces crumbled Gorgonzola cheese and stir over gentle heat for about 2–3 minutes until melted.

2 Whisk in the cream, vermouth and cornstarch. Add the sage; season. Cook, whisking, until the sauce boils and thickens. Set aside.

3 Boil the pasta in a large saucepan with plenty of salted water according to the instructions on the package. Drain well and toss with a little butter.

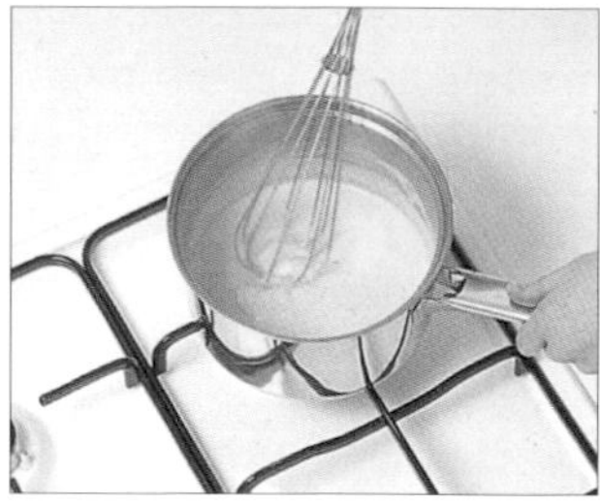

4 Reheat the sauce gently, whisking well. Divide the pasta among four serving bowls, top with the sauce and sprinkle over the remaining crumbled cheese. Serve immediately.

# Lima Bean and Pesto Elicho

BUY GOOD QUALITY, ready-made pesto, rather than making your own, if you prefer. Pesto forms the basis of many very tasty sauces, and is especially good with lima beans.

**INGREDIENTS**

*2 cups dried elicho*
*freshly grated nutmeg*
*2 tablespoons extra virgin olive oil*
*1 can (14 ounces) lima beans, drained*
*3 tablespoons pesto sauce*
*⅔ cup light cream*
*salt and ground black pepper*
*3 tablespoons pine nuts*
*fresh basil sprigs, to garnish*

**Serves 4**

1 Cook the pasta in plenty of salted boiling water until *al dente*, then drain, leaving it a little wet. Return the pasta to the pan, season, and stir in the nutmeg and extra virgin olive oil.

2 Heat the beans in a saucepan with the pesto and cream, stirring until the mixture begins to simmer. Toss the beans and pesto into the pasta and mix well.

3 Serve immediately in warmed bowls topped with pine nuts, and some fresh basil sprigs, if wished.

# Fish and Shellfish

It is not surprising that seafood sauces are often served with pasta along the Italian coastline, and on the islands of Sicily and Sardinia, but they're very popular inland, too. Clams, mussels, tuna, shrimp, anchovies, salmon, scallops and squid are the most common fish and shellfish used, but cooks in coastal areas also create unique pasta dishes using the local catch. These are hard to replicate elsewhere. Sometimes seafood is cooked with tomatoes, sometimes with a cream-based sauce, so the look and taste of seafood pasta can vary considerably from one dish to another. Intense flavors are found in Sicilian recipes, such as Spaghetti with Anchovies and Olives and Spaghetti with Bottarga, while the popular modern classic Penne with Cream and Smoked Salmon is mild and creamy. Linguine with Clams, Leeks and Tomatoes offers a fresh and light alternative. When partnered with seafood, pasta really proves its versatility. Spaghetti is the traditional pasta to serve with seafood sauces, since so many of them are based on olive oil and tomatoes, and it remains the all-time favorite, but other shapes work equally well.

# Vermicelli with Clam Sauce

THIS RECIPE COMES from the city of Naples, where both fresh tomato sauce and seafood are traditionally served with vermicelli. Here the two are combined to make a very tasty dish.

**INGREDIENTS**

*2¼ pounds fresh clams*
*1 cup dry white wine*
*2 garlic cloves, bruised*
*1 large handful fresh Italian parsley*
*2 tablespoons olive oil*
*1 small onion, finely chopped*
*8 ripe Italian plum tomatoes, peeled, seeded and finely chopped*
*½–1 fresh red chile, seeded and finely chopped*
*12 ounces dried vermicelli*
*salt and ground black pepper*
**Serves 4**

1 Scrub the clams thoroughly under cold running water and discard any that are open or that do not close when sharply tapped against the counter.

2 Pour the wine into a large saucepan, add the garlic cloves and half the parsley, then the clams. Cover tightly with the lid and bring to a boil over high heat. Cook for about 5 minutes, shaking the pan frequently, until the clams have opened.

3 Turn the clams into a large colander set over a bowl and let the liquid drain through. Leave the clams until cool enough to handle, then remove about two-thirds of them from their shells, pouring the clam liquor into the bowl of cooking liquid. Discard any clams that have failed to open. Set both shelled and unshelled clams aside, keeping the unshelled clams warm in a bowl covered with a lid.

4 Heat the oil in a saucepan, add the onion and cook gently, stirring frequently, for about 5 minutes until softened and lightly colored. Add the tomatoes, then strain in the clam cooking liquid. Add the chile and salt and pepper to taste.

5 Bring to a boil, half cover and simmer gently for 15–20 minutes. Meanwhile, cook the pasta according to the instructions on the package. Chop the remaining parsley finely.

6 Add the shelled clams to the tomato sauce, stir well and heat through very gently for 2–3 minutes.

7 Drain the cooked pasta well and turn it into a warmed bowl. Taste the sauce for seasoning, then pour the sauce over the pasta and toss everything together well. Garnish with the reserved clams, sprinkle the parsley over the pasta and serve immediately.

# Seafood Conchiglie

THIS IS A VERY SPECIAL MODERN dish, a warm salad composed of scallops, pasta and fresh arugula flavored with roasted bell pepper, chile and balsamic vinegar. It makes a substantial and impressive dinner party starter, or a main course for a light lunch.

**INGREDIENTS**

*8 large fresh sea scallops*
*2¾ cups dried conchiglie*
*1 tablespoon olive oil*
*1 tablespoon butter*
*½ cup dry white wine*
*3½ ounces arugula leaves, stalks trimmed*
*salt and ground black pepper*

***For the vinaigrette***

*4 tablespoons extra virgin olive oil*
*1 tablespoon balsamic vinegar*
*1 piece bottled roasted bell pepper, drained and finely chopped*
*1–2 fresh red chiles, seeded and chopped*
*1 garlic clove, crushed*
*1–2 teaspoons honey, to taste*

**Serves 4**

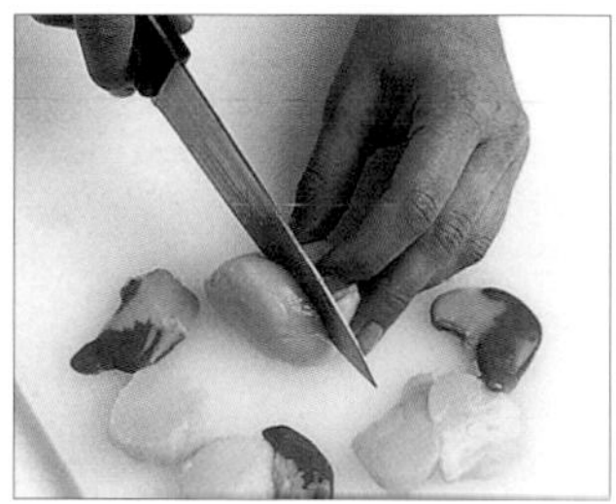

1 Cut each scallop into 2–3 pieces. If the corals are attached, pull them off and cut each piece in half. Season the scallops and corals with salt and pepper.

2 To make the vinaigrette, put the oil, vinegar, chopped bell pepper and chiles in a measuring cup with the garlic and honey and whisk well.

3 Cook the pasta according to the instructions on the package.

4 Meanwhile, heat the oil and butter in a non-stick frying pan until sizzling. Add half the scallops and toss over high heat for 2 minutes. Remove with a slotted spoon and keep warm. Cook the remaining scallops in the same way.

5 Add the wine to the liquid remaining in the pan and stir over high heat until the mixture has reduced to a few tablespoons. Remove from the heat and keep warm.

6 Drain the pasta and turn it into a warmed bowl. Add the arugula, scallops, the reduced cooking juices and the vinaigrette and toss well to combine. Serve immediately.

**COOK'S TIPS**

*• Use only fresh scallops for this dish—they are available all year round in most fishmarkets and supermarkets. Frozen scallops tend to be watery and tasteless, and often prove to be rubbery when cooked.*

*• For a more formal presentation, arrange the arugula leaves in a circle on each of four individual serving plates. Toss the pasta, scallops, reduced cooking juices and vinaigrette together and spoon into the center of the arugula leaves.*

# Salmon Rigatoni with Parsley Sauce

THIS DISH IS SO QUICK and easy to make—and delicious.

**INGREDIENTS**

*1 pound salmon fillet, skinned*
*2 cups dried rigatoni*
*6 ounces cherry tomatoes, halved*
*⅔ cup lowfat crème fraîche*
*3 tablespoons finely chopped parsley*
*finely grated rind of ½ orange*
*salt and ground black pepper*

**Serves 4**

1 Cut the salmon into bite-size pieces, arrange on a heatproof plate and cover with foil.

2 Bring a large pan of salted water to a boil, add the pasta and return to a boil. Place the plate of salmon on top of the pan and simmer for 10–12 minutes, until the pasta and salmon are cooked.

3 Drain the pasta and toss with the tomatoes and salmon. In a separate bowl mix together the crème fraîche, parsley, orange rind and pepper to taste. Spoon this mixture over the salmon and pasta, toss well and serve hot or cold.

# Tagliatelle with Saffron Mussels

MUSSELS IN A SAFFRON and cream sauce are served with tagliatelle in this recipe, but you can use any other pasta if you prefer.

**INGREDIENTS**

*4½ pounds live mussels in the shell*
*⅔ cup dry white wine*
*2 shallots, chopped*
*12 ounces dried tagliatelle*
*2 tablespoons butter*
*2 garlic cloves, crushed*
*1 cup heavy cream*
*generous pinch of saffron strands*
*1 egg yolk*
*salt and ground black pepper*
*2 tablespoons chopped fresh parsley, to garnish*

**Serves 4**

1 Scrub the mussels well under cold running water. Remove the "beards" and discard any mussels that are open.

2 Place the mussels in a large pan with the shallots and pour over the wine. Cover and cook over high heat, shaking the pan occasionally, for 5–8 minutes until the mussels have opened. Drain the mussels, reserving the liquid. Discard any that remain closed. Shell all but a few of the mussels and keep warm.

3 Bring the reserved cooking liquid to a boil in the pan, then reduce by half. Strain the liquid into a measuring cup to remove any grit.

4 Cook the tagliatelle in plenty of boiling salted water for about 10 minutes, until *al dente*.

5 Meanwhile, melt the butter and fry the garlic for 1 minute. Pour in the mussel liquid, cream and saffron strands. Heat gently until the sauce thickens slightly. Off the heat, stir in the egg yolk and shelled mussels and season the sauce to taste.

6 Drain the tagliatelle and transfer to warmed serving dishes. Spoon the sauce over and sprinkle with chopped parsley. Garnish with the mussels in shells and serve immediately.

# Orecchiette with Anchovies and Broccoli

WITH ITS ROBUST FLAVORS, this pasta dish is typical of southern Italian and Sicilian cooking. Anchovies, pine nuts, garlic and Pecorino cheese are all very popular ingredients. Serve with crusty Italian bread for a light lunch or supper.

**INGREDIENTS**

*2 cups broccoli flowerets*
*½ cup pine nuts*
*3 cups dried orecchiette*
*4 tablespoons olive oil*
*1 small red onion, thinly sliced*
*2-ounce jar anchovies in olive oil*
*1 garlic clove, crushed*
*⅔ cup freshly grated Pecorino cheese*
*salt and ground black pepper*

**Serves 4**

### COOK'S TIP

*Orecchiette (little ears) from Puglia are a special type of pasta with a chewy texture. You can get them in Italian markets, or use conchiglie instead.*

1 Break the broccoli flowerets into small pieces and cut off the stalks. If the stalks are large, chop or slice them. Cook the broccoli flowerets and stalks in a saucepan of boiling salted water for 2 minutes, then drain and refresh under cold running water. Leave to drain on paper towels.

2 Put the pine nuts in a dry non-stick frying pan and toss over low to medium heat for 1–2 minutes or until the nuts are lightly toasted and golden. Remove and set aside.

3 Cook the pasta according to the instructions on the package.

4 Meanwhile, heat the oil in a skillet, add the red onion and fry gently, stirring frequently, for about 5 minutes until softened. Add the anchovies with their oil, then add the garlic and fry over medium heat, stirring frequently, for 1–2 minutes until the anchovies break down to form a paste. Add the broccoli and plenty of pepper and toss over the heat for a minute or two until the broccoli is hot. Taste for seasoning.

5 Drain the pasta and turn it into a warmed bowl. Add the broccoli mixture and grated Pecorino and toss well to combine. Sprinkle the pine nuts over the top and serve immediately.

# Trenette with Shellfish

Colorful and delicious, this typical Genoese dish is ideal for a dinner party. The sauce is quite runny, so serve it with crusty bread and spoons as well as forks.

**INGREDIENTS**

*3 tablespoons olive oil*
*1 small onion, finely chopped*
*1 garlic clove, crushed*
*½ fresh red chile, seeded and chopped*
*7 ounces canned chopped Italian plum tomatoes*
*2 tablespoons chopped fresh Italian parsley*
*14 ounces fresh clams*
*14 ounces fresh mussels*
*4 tablespoons dry white wine*
*3½ cups dried trenette*
*a few fresh basil leaves*
*⅔ cup shelled cooked shrimp, thawed and thoroughly dried if frozen*
*salt and ground black pepper*
*chopped fresh herbs, to garnish*

**Serves 4**

1 Heat 2 tablespoons of the oil in a skillet or medium saucepan. Add the onion, garlic and chile and cook over a medium heat for 1–2 minutes, stirring constantly. Stir in the tomatoes, half the parsley and pepper to taste. Bring to a boil, lower the heat, cover and simmer for 15 minutes.

2 Meanwhile, scrub the clams and mussels under cold running water. Discard any that are open or that do not close when sharply tapped against the work surface.

3 In a large saucepan, heat the remaining oil. Add the clams and mussels, with the rest of the parsley and toss over high heat for a few seconds. Pour in the wine, then cover tightly. Cook for about 5 minutes, shaking the pan frequently, until the clams and mussels have opened.

4 Remove the pan from the heat and transfer the clams and mussels to a bowl with a slotted spoon, discarding any shellfish that have failed to open.

5 Strain the cooking liquid into a measuring cup and set aside. Reserve eight clams and four mussels in their shells for the garnish, then remove the rest from their shells.

6 Cook the pasta according to the instructions on the package. Meanwhile, add ½ cup of the reserved seafood liquid to the tomato sauce. Bring to a boil over high heat, stirring. Lower the heat, tear in the basil leaves and add the shrimp with the shelled clams and mussels. Stir well, then taste for seasoning.

7 Drain the pasta and turn it into a warmed bowl. Add the seafood sauce and toss well to combine. Serve in individual bowls, sprinkle with herbs and garnish each portion with two reserved clams and one mussel in their shells.

# Seafood Conchiglie with Spinach Sauce

YOU'LL NEED VERY LARGE pasta shells, measuring about 1 1/2-inch long for this dish; don't try stuffing smaller shells—they will be much too fiddly!

**INGREDIENTS**

*1 tablespoon margarine*
*8 scallions, finely sliced*
*6 tomatoes*
*32 large dried conchiglie*
*1 cup lowfat soft cheese*
*6 tablespoons skimmed milk*
*pinch of freshly grated nutmeg*
*2 cups shrimp*
*6 ounces can white crabmeat, drained and flaked*
*4 ounces frozen chopped spinach, thawed and drained*
*salt and ground black pepper*

**Serves 4**

1 Preheat the oven to 300°F. Melt the margarine in a small saucepan and gently cook the scallions for 3–4 minutes, or until softened but not brown.

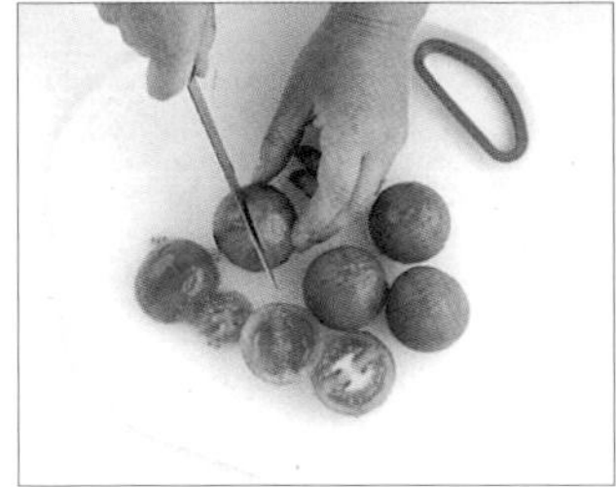

2 With a sharp knife, slash the bottoms of the tomatoes, plunge into a saucepan of boiling water for 45 seconds, then into a bowl of cold water. Slip off the skins. Halve the tomatoes, remove and discard the seeds and cores and coarsely chop the flesh.

3 Cook the conchiglie in plenty of boiling salted water for about 10 minutes, or until *al dente*. Drain well and set aside.

4 Heat the soft cheese and milk in a saucepan, stirring until blended. Season with salt, pepper and nutmeg. Measure 2 tablespoons of the sauce into a large bowl.

5 Add the scallions, chopped tomatoes, shrimp and crabmeat to the bowl. Mix well. When the shells are cool enough to handle, spoon the filling into them and place in a single layer in a shallow ovenproof dish. Cover with foil and cook in the preheated oven for 10 minutes.

6 Stir the spinach into the remaining sauce in the pan. Bring to a boil and simmer gently for 1 minute, stirring all the time.

7 Transfer the pasta onto plates and drizzle the spinach sauce over. Serve hot.

# Spaghetti with Tomato and Clam Sauce

SMALL SWEET CLAMS make this a delicately succulent sauce. Cockles would make a good substitute, but don't be tempted to use seafood pickled in vinegar.

**INGREDIENTS**

*2 pounds live small clams in the shell, or 2 cans (14-ounce) clams in brine, drained*
*6 tablespoons olive oil*
*2 garlic cloves, crushed*
*1 ¼ pounds canned chopped tomatoes*
*3 tablespoons chopped fresh parsley*
*1 pound dried spaghetti*
*salt and ground black pepper*

**Serves 4**

1 If using live clams, place them in a bowl of cold water and rinse several times to remove any grit or sand, then drain well.

2 Heat the oil in a saucepan and add the clams. Stir over high heat until the clams open. Discard any that do not open. Transfer the clams to a bowl with a slotted spoon and set the bowl aside.

3 Reduce the clam juice left in the pan to almost nothing by boiling fast. Add the garlic and fry until golden. Pour in the tomatoes, bring to a boil and cook for 3–4 minutes until reduced. Stir in the clam mixture or canned clams and half the parsley and heat through. Season to taste.

4 Cook the pasta in plenty of boiling salted water according to the instructions on the package. Drain well and turn into a warm serving dish. Pour the sauce over and sprinkle with the remaining chopped parsley.

# Rigatoni with Tuna and Anchovies

THIS PIQUANT SAUCE could be made without the addition of tomatoes—just heat the oil, add the other ingredients and heat through gently before tossing with the pasta.

**INGREDIENTS**

*1 can (14 ounces) tuna fish in oil*
*2 tablespoons olive oil*
*2 garlic cloves, crushed*
*1¾ pounds canned chopped tomatoes*
*6 canned anchovy fillets, drained*
*2 tablespoons capers in vinegar, drained*
*2 tablespoons chopped fresh basil*
*3½ cups dried rigatoni*
*salt and ground black pepper*
*fresh basil sprigs, to garnish*

**Serves 4**

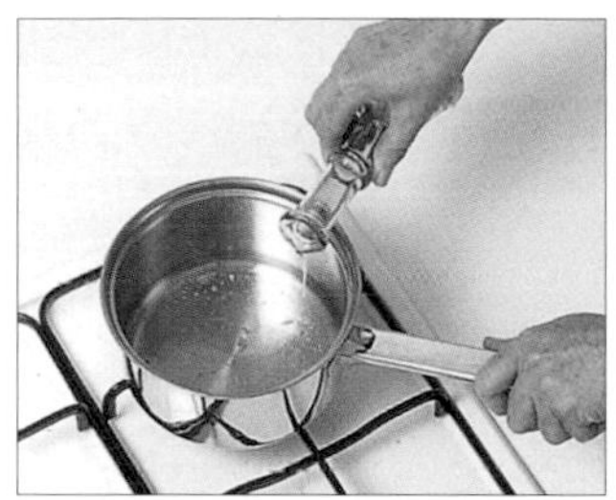

1 Drain the oil from the can of tuna fish into a large saucepan, add the olive oil and heat gently until the oil mixture stops spitting.

2 Add the garlic and fry until golden. Stir in the tomatoes and simmer for about 25 minutes until the sauce has thickened.

3 Flake the tuna and cut the anchovies in half. Stir into the sauce with the capers and chopped basil. Season well.

4 Cook the pasta in plenty of boiling salted water according to the instructions on the package. Drain well and toss with the sauce. Garnish with fresh basil sprigs and serve.

# Fish with Fregola

THIS SARDINIAN SPECIALTY is a cross between a soup and a stew. Serve it with crusty Italian country bread to mop up the juices.

**INGREDIENTS**

*5 tablespoons olive oil*
*4 garlic cloves, finely chopped*
*½ small fresh red chile, seeded and finely chopped*
*1 large handful fresh Italian parsley, coarsely chopped*
*1 red snapper, about 1 pound, cleaned, with head and tail removed*
*1 red mullet, about 1¼ pounds, cleaned, with head and tail removed*
*12 ounces–1 pound thick cod fillet or monkfish*
*1 can (14 ounces) chopped Italian plum tomatoes*
*1½ cups dried fregola*
*salt and ground black pepper*
**Serves 4–6**

1 Heat 2 tablespoons of the olive oil in a large flameproof casserole. Add the chopped garlic and chile, with about half the chopped parsley. Fry over medium heat, stirring occasionally, for about 5 minutes.

2 Cut all of the fish into large chunks—including the skin and the bones in the case of the snapper and mullet—and add the pieces to the casserole as you cut them. Sprinkle the pieces with a further 2 tablespoons of the olive oil and fry for a few minutes more.

3 Add the tomatoes, then fill the empty can with water and pour this into the pan. Bring to a boil. Stir in salt and pepper to taste, lower the heat and cook for 10 minutes, stirring occasionally.

4 Add the fregola and simmer for 5 minutes, then add 1 cup water and the remaining oil. Simmer for 15 minutes until the fregola is *al dente*.

5 If the sauce becomes too thick, add more water, then taste for seasoning. Serve hot, in warmed bowls, sprinkled with the remaining parsley.

**COOK'S TIPS**

- *You can make the basic fish sauce several hours in advance or even the day before, bringing it to a boil and adding the fregola just before serving.*
- *Fregola is a tiny pasta shape from Sardinia. If you can't get it, use a tiny soup pasta* (pastina)*, such as corallini or semi de melone.*

# Farfalle with Tuna

A QUICK AND SIMPLE DISH that makes a good weekday supper if you have canned tomatoes and tuna in the storecupboard.

**INGREDIENTS**

*2 tablespoons olive oil*
*1 small onion, finely chopped*
*1 garlic clove, finely chopped*
*1 can (14 ounces) chopped Italian plum tomatoes*
*3 tablespoons dry white wine*
*8–10 pitted black olives, cut into rings*
*2 teaspoons chopped fresh oregano or 1 teaspoon dried oregano, plus extra fresh oregano to garnish*
*3½ cups dried farfalle*
*1 can (6 ounces) tuna in olive oil*
*salt and ground black pepper*

**Serves 4**

1 Heat the olive oil in a medium skillet or saucepan, add the onion and garlic and fry gently for 2–3 minutes until the onion is soft and golden.

2 Add the plum tomatoes to the pan and bring to a boil, then pour over the white wine and simmer the mixture for a minute or so. Stir in the olives and oregano, with salt and pepper to taste, then cover and cook for 20–25 minutes, stirring from time to time.

3 Meanwhile, cook the pasta in a large saucepan of salted boiling water according to the instructions on the package.

4 Drain the canned tuna and flake it with a fork. Add the tuna to the sauce with about 4 tablespoons of the water used for cooking the pasta. Taste and adjust the seasoning.

5 Drain the cooked pasta well and turn it into a warmed large serving bowl. Pour the tuna sauce over the top and toss to mix. Serve immediately, garnished with sprigs of oregano.

# Capelli d'Angelo with Spinach Sauce

DELICIOUSLY EARTHY, this would make a good appetizer or light supper dish. Add some golden raisins to the sauce to ring the changes.

**INGREDIENTS**

*2 pounds fresh spinach or 1 ¼ pounds frozen leaf spinach, thawed*
*1 pound fresh capelli d'angelo*
*salt, to taste*
*4 tablespoons olive oil*
*3 tablespoons pine nuts*
*2 garlic cloves*
*6 canned anchovy fillets, drained and chopped, or whole salted anchovies, rinsed, boned and chopped*
*butter, for tossing the pasta*
*salt*

**Serves 4**

1 If using fresh spinach, wash it well and remove any tough stalks before cooking. Drain thoroughly. Place in a large saucepan with only the water that clings to the leaves. Cover with a lid and cook over high heat, shaking the pan occasionally, until the spinach is just wilted and still bright green. Drain well.

2 Cook the pasta in plenty of boiling salted water according to the instructions on the package.

3 Heat the oil in a saucepan and fry the pine nuts until golden. Remove with a slotted spoon and set aside. Add the garlic to the oil in the pan and fry until golden. Add the chopped anchovies to the pan.

4 Stir in the spinach and cook for 2–3 minutes or until heated through. Stir in the reserved pine nuts.

5 Drain the pasta, toss in a little butter and turn into a warmed serving dish. Top with the hot sauce and toss together before serving.

# Tagliatelle with Haddock and Avocado

YOU WILL NEED to start this recipe the day before because the haddock should be left to marinate overnight.

**INGREDIENTS**

*12 ounces fresh haddock or cod fillets, skinned*
*½ teaspoon each ground cumin, ground coriander and turmeric*
*⅔ cup ricotta cheese or mascarpone*
*⅔ cup heavy cream*
*1 tablespoon lemon juice*
*2 tablespoons butter*
*1 onion, chopped*
*1 tablespoon all-purpose flour*
*⅔ cup fish stock*
*12 ounces fresh or dried tagliatelle*
*1 avocado, peeled, pitted and sliced*
*2 tomatoes, seeded and chopped*
*salt and ground black pepper*
*fresh rosemary sprigs, to garnish*

**Serves 4**

1 Carefully cut the haddock into bite-size pieces.

2 Mix together all the spices, seasoning, ricotta cheese, cream and lemon juice.

3 Stir in the haddock to coat. Cover the dish and leave to marinate overnight in the refrigerator.

4 Heat the butter in a frying pan and fry the onion for about 10 minutes until softened but not brown. Stir in the flour, cook for a minute, then blend in the stock until the sauce is smooth.

5 Carefully stir in the haddock mixture until well blended. Bring to a boil, stirring, cover and simmer for about 30 seconds. Remove from the heat.

6 Meanwhile, cook the pasta in plenty of boiling salted water according to the instructions on the package until *al dente*.

7 Stir the avocado and tomatoes into the haddock mixture.

8 Drain the pasta thoroughly and divide among four serving plates. Spoon the sauce over and serve immediately, garnished with fresh rosemary sprigs.

# Tagliatelle with Scallops

SCALLOPS AND BRANDY make this a relatively expensive dish, but it is so delicious that you will find it well worth the cost. Serve it for a dinner party first course.

**INGREDIENTS**

*7 ounces sea scallops, sliced*
*2 tablespoons all-purpose flour*
*3 tablespoons butter*
*2 scallions, cut into thin rings*
*½–1 small fresh red chille seeded and very finely chopped*
*2 tablespoons finely chopped fresh Italian parsley*
*4 tablespoons brandy*
*7 tablespoons fish stock*
*10 ounces fresh spinach-flavored tagliatelle*
*salt and ground black pepper*
**Serves 4**

1 Toss the scallops in the flour, then shake off the excess. Bring a saucepan of salted water to a boil, ready for cooking the pasta.

2 Meanwhile, melt the butter in a skillet or large saucepan. Add the scallions, finely chopped chille and half the parsley and fry, stirring frequently, for 1–2 minutes over medium heat. Add the scallops and toss over the heat for 1–2 minutes.

3 Pour the brandy over the scallops, then set it alight with a match. As soon as the flames have died down, stir in the fish stock and salt and pepper to taste. Mix well. Simmer for 2–3 minutes, then cover the pan and remove it from the heat.

4 Add the pasta to a boiling water and cook it according to the instructions on the package. Drain, add to the sauce and toss over medium heat until mixed. Serve at once, in warmed bowls sprinkled with the remaining parsley.

**COOK'S TIP**

*Buy fresh scallops, with their corals if possible. Fresh scallops always have a better texture and flavor than frozen scallops, which tend to be watery.*

# Spaghetti with Squid and Peas

IN TUSCANY, SQUID IS OFTEN cooked with peas in a tomato sauce. This recipe is a variation on the theme, and it works very well.

**INGREDIENTS**

*1 pound prepared squid*
*2 tablespoons olive oil*
*1 small onion, finely chopped*
*1 can (14 ounces) chopped Italian plum tomatoes*
*1 garlic clove, finely chopped*
*1 tablespoon red wine vinegar*
*1 teaspoon granulated sugar*
*2 teaspoons finely chopped fresh rosemary*
*1 cup frozen peas*
*12 ounces fresh or dried spaghetti*
*1 tablespoon chopped fresh Italian parsley*
*salt and ground black pepper*
**Serves 4**

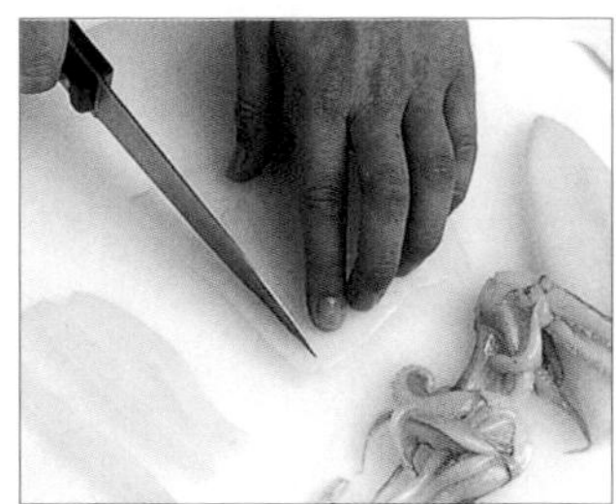

1 Cut the prepared squid into strips about ¼ inch wide. Finely chop any tentacles.

2 Heat the oil in a skillet or medium saucepan, add the finely chopped onion and cook gently, stirring, for about 5 minutes until softened. Add the squid, tomatoes, garlic, red wine vinegar and sugar.

3 Add the rosemary, with salt and pepper to taste. Bring to a boil, stirring, then cover and simmer gently for 20 minutes. Uncover the pan, add the peas and cook for 10 minutes. Meanwhile, cook the pasta according to the instructions on the package, then drain and turn it into a warmed bowl. Pour the sauce over the pasta, add the parsley, then toss well and serve.

# Capelli d'Angelo with Lobster

THIS IS A SOPHISTICATED, stylish dish for a special occasion. Some cooks make the sauce with champagne rather than sparkling white wine, especially when they are planning to serve champagne with the meal.

**INGREDIENTS**

*meat from the body, tail and claws of 1 cooked lobster*
*juice of ½ lemon*
*3 tablespoons butter*
*4 fresh tarragon sprigs, leaves stripped and chopped*
*4 tablespoons heavy cream*
*6 tablespoons sparkling dry white wine*
*4 tablespoons fish stock*
*11 ounces fresh capelli d'angelo*
*salt and ground black pepper*
*about 2 teaspoons lumpfish roe, to garnish (optional)*

**Serves 4**

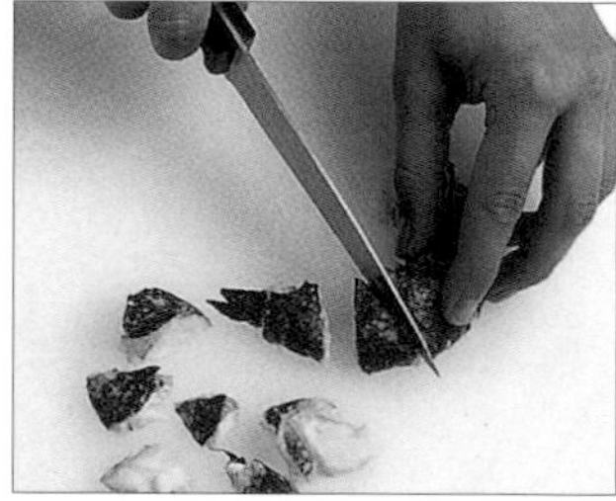

1 Cut the lobster meat into small pieces and put it in a bowl. Sprinkle with the lemon juice. Melt the butter in a skillet or large saucepan, add the lobster meat and tarragon and stir over the heat for a few seconds. Add the cream and stir for a few seconds more, then pour in the wine and stock, with salt and pepper to taste. Simmer for 2 minutes, then remove from the heat and cover.

2 Cook the pasta according to the instructions on the package. Drain well, reserving a few spoonfuls of the cooking water.

3 Place the pan of lobster sauce over medium to high heat, add the pasta and toss for just long enough to combine and heat through; moisten with a little of the reserved water from the pasta. Serve immediately in warmed bowls, sprinkled with lumpfish roe if you like.

### COOK'S TIP

*To remove the meat from a lobster, place the lobster on a board with its underbelly facing uppermost. With a large sharp knife, cut the lobster in half lengthwise. Spoon out the green liver and any pink roe (coral) and reserve these, then remove and discard the gravel sac (stomach). Pull the white tail meat out from either side of the shell and discard the black intestinal vein. Crack the claws with a nutcracker just below the pincers and remove the meat from the base. Pull away the small pincer, taking the white membrane with it, then remove the meat from this part of the shell. Pull the meat from the large pincer shell.*

# Linguine with Crab

THIS RECIPE COMES FROM Rome. It makes a very rich and tasty first course on its own, or can be served for a lunch or supper with crusty Italian bread. Some cooks like a finer sauce, and work the crabmeat through a strainer after pounding. If you fancy following their example, be warned—it's hard work.

**INGREDIENTS**

*about 9 ounces shelled crabmeat*
*3 tablespoons olive oil*
*1 small handful fresh Italian parsley, coarsely chopped, plus extra to garnish*
*1 garlic clove, crushed*
*12 ounces ripe Italian plum tomatoes, skinned and chopped*
*4–6 tablespoons dry white wine*
*12 ounces fresh or dried linguine*
*salt and ground black pepper*

**Serves 4**

1 Put the crabmeat in a mortar and pound to a coarse pulp with a pestle. If you do not have a pestle and mortar, use a sturdy bowl and the end of a rolling pin. Set aside.

2 Heat 2 tablespoons of the oil in a large saucepan. Add the parsley and garlic, with salt and pepper to taste, and fry for a few minutes until the garlic begins to brown.

3 Add the tomatoes, pounded crabmeat and wine, cover the pan and simmer gently for 15 minutes, stirring occasionally.

4 Meanwhile, cook the pasta according to the instructions on the package, draining it the moment it is *al dente*, and reserving a little of the cooking water.

5 Return the pasta to the clean pan, add the remaining oil and toss quickly over medium heat until the oil coats the strands.

6 Add the tomato and crab mixture to the pasta and toss again, adding a little of the reserved cooking water if you think it necessary. Adjust the seasoning to taste. Serve hot, in warmed bowls, sprinkled with parsley.

**COOK'S TIP**

*The best way to obtain crabmeat is to buy dressed crab from the supermarket or fishmarket. For this recipe you will need one large crab, and you should use both the white and dark meat.*

# Spaghetti with Salmon and Shrimp

THIS IS A LOVELY FRESH-TASTING pasta dish, perfect for an *al fresco* meal in summer. Serve it as a main course lunch with warm ciabatta or focaccia and a dry white wine.

**INGREDIENTS**

*11 ounces salmon fillet*
*scant 1 cup dry white wine*
*a few fresh basil sprigs, plus extra basil leaves, to garnish*
*6 ripe Italian plum tomatoes, peeled and finely chopped*
*⅔ cup heavy cream*
*3 cups fresh or dried spaghetti*
*⅔ cup shelled cooked shrimp, thawed and thoroughly dried if frozen*
*salt and ground black pepper*

**Serves 4**

1 Put the salmon skin-side up in a wide shallow pan. Pour the wine over, then add the basil sprigs to the pan and sprinkle the fish with salt and pepper. Bring the wine to a boil, cover the pan and simmer gently for no more than 5 minutes. Using a fish slice, lift the fish out of the pan and set aside to cool a little.

2 Add the tomatoes and cream to the liquid remaining in the pan and bring to a boil. Stir well, then lower the heat and simmer, uncovered, for 10–15 minutes. Meanwhile, cook the pasta according to the instructions on the package.

3 When cool enough to handle, flake the fish into large chunks, discarding the skin and any bones. Add the fish to the sauce with the shrimp, shaking the pan until the fish and shellfish are well coated. Taste for seasoning.

4 Drain the pasta and turn it into a warmed bowl. Pour the sauce over the pasta and toss to combine. Serve immediately, garnished with fresh basil leaves.

**COOK'S TIP**

*Check the salmon fillet carefully for small bones when you are flaking the flesh. Although the salmon is already filleted, you will always find a few stray "pin" bones. Pick them out carefully using tweezers or your fingertips.*

# Tagliolini with Clams and Mussels

SERVED ON WHITE CHINA, this makes a stunning looking dish for a dinner party first course. The sauce can be prepared a few hours ahead of time, then the pasta cooked and the dish assembled at the last minute.

**INGREDIENTS**

*1 pound fresh mussels*
*1 pound fresh clams*
*4 tablespoons olive oil*
*1 small onion, finely chopped*
*2 garlic cloves, finely chopped*
*1 large handful fresh Italian parsley, plus extra chopped parsley to garnish*
*¾ cup dry white wine*
*1 cup fish stock*
*1 small fresh red chile, seeded and chopped*
*12 ounces squid ink tagliolini or tagliatelle*
*salt and ground black pepper*

**Serves 4**

1 Scrub the mussels and clams under cold running water and discard any that are open or damaged, or that do not close when sharply tapped against the counter.

2 Heat half the oil in a large saucepan, add the onion and cook gently for about 5 minutes until softened. Sprinkle in the garlic, then add about half the parsley sprigs, with salt and pepper to taste. Add the mussels and clams and pour in the wine. Cover with the lid and bring to a boil over high heat. Cook for about 5 minutes, shaking the pan frequently, until the shellfish have opened.

3 Turn the mussels and clams into a fine strainer set over a bowl and let the liquid drain through. Discard the aromatics in the strainer, together with any mussels or clams that have failed to open. Return the liquid to the clean pan and add the fish stock. Chop the remaining parsley finely and add it to the liquid with the chopped chile. Bring to a boil, then lower the heat and simmer, stirring, for a few minutes until slightly reduced. Turn off the heat.

4 Remove and discard the top shells from about half the mussels and clams. Put all the mussels and clams in the pan of liquid and seasonings, then cover the pan tightly and set aside.

5 Cook the pasta according to the instructions on the package.

6 Drain well, then return to the clean pan; toss with the remaining olive oil. Put the pan of shellfish over high heat and toss to heat the shellfish through quickly and combine with the liquid and seasonings.

7 Divide the pasta among four warmed plates, spoon the shellfish mixture over and around, then serve immediately, sprinkled with parsley.

# Spaghetti with Anchovies and Olives

THE STRONG FLAVORS of this dish are typical of Sicilian cuisine.

**INGREDIENTS**

*3 tablespoons olive oil*
*1 large red bell pepper, seeded and chopped*
*1 small eggplant, finely chopped*
*1 onion, finely chopped*
*8 ripe Italian plum tomatoes, peeled, seeded and finely chopped*
*2 garlic cloves, finely chopped*
*½ cup dry red or white wine*
*½ cup water*
*1 handful fresh herbs, such as basil, Italian parsley and rosemary*
*11 ounces dried spaghetti*
*2 ounces canned anchovies, chopped, plus extra whole anchovies to garnish*
*12 pitted black olives*
*1–2 tablespoons capers, to taste*
*salt and ground black pepper*

**Serves 4**

1 Heat the oil in a saucepan and add all the finely chopped vegetables and garlic. Cook gently, stirring frequently, for 10–15 minutes until the vegetables are soft. Pour in the wine and water, add the fresh herbs and pepper to taste and bring to a boil. Lower the heat and simmer, stirring occasionally, for 10–15 minutes. Meanwhile, cook the pasta in a large saucepan of salted boiling water according to the instructions on the package.

2 Add the chopped anchovies, olives and capers to the sauce, heat through for a few minutes and taste for seasoning. Drain the pasta and turn it into a warmed bowl. Pour the sauce over the pasta, toss well and serve immediately.

**COOK'S TIP**

*If the anchovies are omitted, this makes a good sauce for vegetarians.*

# Spaghetti with Tuna, Anchovies, Olives and Mozzarella

THIS RECIPE FROM CAPRI is fresh, light and full of flavor, so serve it as soon as it is cooked to enjoy it at its best.

**INGREDIENTS**

*11 ounces dried spaghetti*
*2 tablespoons olive oil*
*6 ripe Italian plum tomatoes, chopped*
*1 teaspoon granulated sugar*
*2-ounce jar anchovies in olive oil, drained*
*about 4 tablespoons dry white wine*
*½ cup pitted black olives, quartered lengthwise*
*1 can (7 ounces) tuna in olive oil, drained*
*4½ ounces package Italian-style mozzarella cheese, drained and diced*
*salt and ground black pepper*
*fresh basil leaves, to garnish*

**Serves 4**

1 Cook the pasta according to the instructions on the package. Meanwhile, heat the oil in a medium saucepan. Add the tomatoes, sugar and pepper to taste, and toss over medium heat for a few minutes until the tomatoes soften and the juices run. Snip a few anchovies at a time into the pan of tomatoes with kitchen scissors.

2 Add the wine, tuna and olives and stir once or twice until they are just evenly mixed into the sauce. Add the mozzarella and heat through without stirring. Taste and add salt if necessary. Drain the pasta and turn it into a warmed bowl. Pour the sauce over, toss gently and sprinkle with basil leaves. Serve immediately.

# Mixed Summer Pasta

A PRETTY AND COLORFUL sauce with bags of flavor makes this a popular dish for the summer.

**INGREDIENTS**

*4 ounces French beans, cut into 1-inch pieces*
*12 ounces fresh or dried fusilli col buco*
*2 tablespoons olive oil*
*½ fennel bulb, sliced*
*1 bunch scallions, sliced diagonally*
*4 ounces yellow cherry tomatoes*
*4 ounces red cherry tomatoes*
*2 tablespoons chopped fresh dill weed*
*2 cups peeled shrimp*
*1 tablespoon lemon juice*
*1 tablespoon whole-grain mustard*
*4 tablespoons sour cream*
*salt and ground black pepper*
*fresh dill weed sprigs, to garnish*

**Serves 4**

1 Cook the beans in a saucepan of boiling salted water for about 5 minutes until tender. Drain through a colander.

2 Cook the pasta in plenty of boiling salted water, according to the instructions on the package, until *al dente*.

3 Heat the oil in a frying pan and fry the sliced fennel and scallions for about 5 minutes.

4 Stir in all the cherry tomatoes and fry for a further 5 minutes, stirring the pan occasionally.

5 Add the dill weed and shrimp and cook for a further minute.

6 Stir in the lemon juice, whole-grain mustard, sour cream, seasoning and beans and simmer for 1 minute.

7 Drain the pasta and toss with the sauce. Serve immediately, garnished with fresh dill weed.

# Spaghetti with Seafood Sauce

THE ITALIAN NAME for this popular tomato-based seafood sauce is *marinara.*

**INGREDIENTS**

*3 tablespoons olive oil*
*1 onion, chopped*
*1 garlic clove, finely chopped*
*8 ounces fresh or dried spaghetti*
*2½ cups passata or tomato sauce*
*1 tablespoon tomato paste*
*1 teaspoon dried oregano*
*1 bay leaf*
*1 teaspoon sugar*
*1 cup cooked miniature shelled shrimp, rinsed well if canned*
*1 cup cooked medium shelled shrimp*
*1½ cups cooked clam or cockle meat, rinsed well if canned or bottled*
*1 tablespoon lemon juice*
*3 tablespoons chopped fresh parsley*
*2 tablespoons butter*
*salt and ground black pepper*
*4 whole cooked shrimp, to garnish*

**Serves 4**

1 Heat the oil in a pan and add the onion and garlic. Fry over a moderate heat for 6–7 minutes, until the onions have softened.

2 Meanwhile, cook the spaghetti in a large saucepan of boiling salted water for 10–12 minutes until *al dente.*

3 Stir the passata, tomato paste, oregano, bay leaf and sugar into the cooked onions and season well. Bring to a boil, then simmer for 2–3 minutes.

4 Add all the shellfish, lemon juice and 2 tablespoons of the parsley. Stir well, then cover and cook for 6–7 minutes.

5 Meanwhile, drain the spaghetti when it is ready and add the butter to the pan. Return the drained spaghetti to the pan and toss in the butter. Season well.

6 Divide the spaghetti among four warmed plates and top with the seafood sauce. Sprinkle with the remaining chopped parsley, garnish each plate with whole shrimp and serve immediately.

# Farfalle with Smoked Salmon and Dill

IN ITALY, pasta cooked with smoked salmon is very fashionable. This is a quick and luxurious sauce.

**INGREDIENTS**

*6 scallions*
*4 tablespoons butter*
*6 tablespoons dry white wine or vermouth*
*1¾ cups heavy cream*
*freshly grated nutmeg*
*8 ounces smoked salmon*
*2 tablespoons chopped fresh dill weed or 1 tablespoon dried*
*freshly squeezed lemon juice*
*4 cups dried farfalle*
*salt and ground black pepper*
**Serves 4**

1 Slice the scallions finely making diagonal cuts along the length. Melt the butter in a saucepan and gently fry the scallions for 1 minute until softened.

2 Add the wine or vermouth and boil hard to reduce to about 2 tablespoons. Stir in the cream and add salt, pepper and nutmeg to taste. Bring to a boil and simmer for 2–3 minutes until the sauce is slightly thickened.

3 On a board, cut the smoked salmon into 1-inch squares. Transfer into the prepared sauce with the dill weed and stir to combine thoroughly. Taste and add a little lemon juice. Keep the sauce warm while you cook the pasta.

4 Cook the pasta in plenty of boiling salted water according to the instructions on the package. Drain well. Then add the pasta to the sauce in the pan and toss thoroughly. Transfer the pasta to warmed plates and serve immediately.

# Spaghetti with Mixed Shellfish Sauce

A SPECIAL OCCASION sauce for an evening of entertaining is just what this is, so serve it in bountiful portions to your guests.

**INGREDIENTS**

*4 tablespoons butter*
*2 shallots, chopped*
*2 garlic cloves, chopped*
*12 ounces fresh or dried spaghetti*
*2 tablespoons finely chopped fresh basil*
*1 ¼ cups dry white wine*
*1 pound mussels, scrubbed*
*4 ounces squid, washed*
*1 teaspoon chili powder*
*12 ounces raw peeled shrimp*
*1 ¼ cups sour cream*
*⅓ cup freshly grated Parmesan cheese*
*salt and ground black pepper*
*chopped fresh Italian parsley, to garnish*

**Serves 4**

1 Melt half the butter in a frying pan and fry 1 shallot and 1 garlic clove for about 5 minutes until softened.

2 Cook the pasta in plenty of boiling salted water according to the instructions on the package.

3 Add half the basil and pour over the wine. Stir the ingredients together and bring to a boil.

4 Discard any mussels that are open and do not shut when tapped on the counter. Quickly add the remaining mussels to the pan, cover and simmer for about 5 minutes until all the shells have opened. Discard any mussels that do not open. Using a slotted spoon, transfer the mussels to a plate, remove them from their shells and return to the pan. Reserve a few mussels in the shells for garnishing.

5 Meanwhile, slice the squid into thin circles. Melt the remaining butter in a frying pan and fry the remaining shallot and garlic for about 5 minutes until softened.

6 Add the remaining basil, the squid, chili powder and shrimp to the pan and stir-fry for 5 minutes until the shrimp have turned pink and tender.

7 Turn the mussel mixture into the shrimp mixture and bring to a boil. Stir in the sour cream and season to taste. Bring almost to a boil and simmer for 1 minute.

8 Drain the pasta thoroughly and stir it into the sauce with the Parmesan cheese until well coated. Serve immediately, garnished with chopped Italian parsley and the reserved mussels in their shells.

# Zite with Fresh Sardine Sauce

IN THIS CLASSIC Sicilian dish, fresh sardines are combined with raisins and pine nuts.

**INGREDIENTS**

*3 tablespoons golden raisins*
*1 pound fresh sardines*
*6 tablespoons bread crumbs*
*1 small fennel bulb*
*6 tablespoons olive oil*
*1 onion, very thinly sliced*
*3 tablespoons pine nuts*
*½ teaspoon fennel seeds*
*14 ounces fresh or dried zite*
*salt and ground black pepper*

**Serves 4**

1 Soak the golden raisins in warm water for 15 minutes. Drain and pat dry.

2 Clean the sardines. Open each one out flat and remove the central bones and head. Wash well and shake dry. Sprinkle evenly with the bread crumbs.

3 Coarsely chop the top greenery of the fennel and reserve. Pull off a few outer leaves and wash. Fill a large saucepan with enough water to cook the pasta. Add the fennel leaves and bring to a boil.

4 Heat the oil in a large frying pan and sauté the onion lightly until soft but not brown. Remove to a side dish. Add the sardines, a few at a time, and cook over moderate heat until golden on both sides, turning once. When all the sardines have been cooked, gently return them to the pan. Add the onion, and the golden raisins, pine nuts and fennel seeds. Season with salt and pepper.

5 Take about 4 tablespoons of a boiling water for the pasta, and add it to the sauce. Add salt to a boiling water, and cook the pasta until *al dente*. Drain, and remove the fennel leaves. Toss the pasta with the sauce to combine. Divide among four individual serving plates, arranging several sardines on each. Sprinkle with the reserved chopped fennel tops and serve immediately.

# Spaghetti with Olives and Capers

THIS SPICY SAUCE originated in the Naples area. It can be quickly assembled using a few store-cupboard ingredients.

**INGREDIENTS**

*4 tablespoons olive oil*
*2 garlic cloves, finely chopped*
*small piece of dried red chile, crumbled*
*1 can (2 ounces) anchovy fillets, chopped*
*12 ounces tomatoes, fresh or canned, chopped*
*1 cup pitted black olives*
*2 tablespoons capers, rinsed*
*1 tablespoon tomato paste*
*14 ounces fresh or dried spaghetti*
*2 tablespoons chopped fresh parsley*

**Serves 4**

1 Heat the oil in a large frying pan. Add the garlic and the dried red chile, and cook for 2–3 minutes over moderate heat until the garlic has just turned golden.

2 Add the chopped anchovies to the pan, and mash them into the garlic with the back of a fork so that they form a paste-like consistency.

3 Add the fresh or canned tomatoes, olives, capers and tomato paste to the ingredients in the pan. Stir well and continue to cook over moderate heat.

4 Cook the spaghetti in a large saucepan with plenty of boiling salted water until *al dente*. Drain well.

5 Turn the spaghetti into the sauce. Increase the heat and cook for 3–4 minutes, turning the pasta constantly. Divide between four plates, sprinkle with parsley and serve at once.

# Paglia e Fieno with Shrimp and Vodka

THE COMBINATION OF SHRIMP, vodka and pasta may seem unusual, but it has become something of a modern classic in Italy. Here it is stylishly presented with two-colored pasta, but the sauce goes equally well with short shapes such as penne, rigatoni and farfalle.

**INGREDIENTS**

*2 tablespoons olive oil*
*1/4 large onion, finely chopped*
*1 garlic clove, crushed*
*1–2 tablespoons sun-dried tomato paste*
*scant 1 cup* panna da cucina *or heavy cream*
*12 ounces fresh or dried* paglia e fieno
*12 raw shrimp, shelled and chopped*
*2 tablespoons vodka*
*salt and ground black pepper*
**Serves 4**

1 Heat the oil in a medium saucepan, add the onion and garlic and cook gently, stirring frequently, for about 5 minutes until softened.

2 Add the tomato paste and stir for 1–2 minutes, then add the cream and bring to a boil, stirring. Season with salt and pepper to taste and let the sauce bubble until it starts to thicken slightly. Remove from the heat.

3 Cook the pasta according to the instructions on the package. When it is almost ready, add the shrimp and vodka to the sauce; toss quickly over a medium heat for 2–3 minutes until the shrimp turn pink.

4 Drain the pasta thoroughly and turn it into a warmed bowl. Pour the sauce over and toss well. Divide among warmed bowls and serve immediately.

**COOK'S TIP**

*This sauce is best served as soon as it is ready, otherwise the shrimp will overcook and become tough. Make sure that the pasta has only a minute or two of cooking time left before adding the shrimp to the sauce.*

# Penne with Cream and Smoked Salmon

THIS MODERN WAY OF serving pasta is popular all over Italy. The three essential ingredients combine together beautifully, and the dish is very quick and easy to make.

**INGREDIENTS**

*3 cups dried penne*
*4 ounces thinly sliced smoked salmon*
*2–3 fresh thyme sprigs*
*2 tablespoons butter*
*2/3 cup light cream*
*salt and ground black pepper*
**Serves 4**

1 Cook the pasta in a saucepan of salted boiling water according to the instructions on the package.

2 Meanwhile, using kitchen scissors, cut the smoked salmon into thin strips, about 1/4-inch wide. Strip the leaves from the thyme sprigs.

3 Melt the butter in a large saucepan. Add the cream and three-quarters of the salmon and thyme leaves, then season with pepper. Heat gently for 3–4 minutes, stirring continuously. Do not allow the sauce to boil. Taste for seasoning.

4 Drain the pasta, return to the pan, and toss in the cream and salmon sauce. Divide among four warmed bowls and top with the remaining salmon and thyme leaves. Serve hot.

**VARIATION**

*Although penne is traditional with this sauce, it also goes very well with fresh ravioli stuffed with spinach and ricotta.*

# Fusilli with Vegetable and Shrimp Sauce

YOU WILL NEED to start this recipe the day before because the shrimp should be left to marinate overnight.

**INGREDIENTS**

*4 cups shelled shrimp*
*4 tablespoons soy sauce*
*3 tablespoons olive oil*
*12 ounces fusilli col buco*
*1 yellow bell pepper, cored, seeded and cut into strips*
*8 ounces broccoli flowerets*
*1 bunch scallions, shredded*
*1-inch piece fresh ginger root, peeled and shredded*
*1 tablespoon chopped fresh oregano*
*2 tablespoons dry sherry*
*1 tablespoon cornstarch*
*1 1/4 cups fish stock*
*salt and ground black pepper*

**Serves 4**

1 Place the shrimp in a mixing bowl. Stir in half the soy sauce and 2 tablespoons of the olive oil. Cover and marinate overnight in the refrigerator.

2 Cook the pasta in plenty of boiling salted water according to the instructions on the package.

3 Meanwhile, heat the remaining oil in a wok or frying pan and fry the shrimp for 1 minute.

4 Add the pepper, broccoli, scallions, ginger and oregano and stir-fry for about 1–2 minutes.

5 Drain the pasta thoroughly, set aside and keep warm. Meanwhile, in a bowl, blend together the sherry and cornstarch until smooth. Stir in the stock and remaining soy sauce until well blended.

6 Pour the stock mixture into the wok or pan, bring to a boil and stir-fry for 2 minutes until thickened. Pour over the pasta and serve.

# Rigatoni with Tuna and Olive Sauce

THIS COLORFUL SAUCE combines well with a thicker and shorter pasta.

**INGREDIENTS**

*3 cups dried rigatoni*
*2 tablespoons olive oil*
*1 onion, chopped*
*2 garlic cloves, chopped*
*1 can (14 ounces) chopped tomatoes*
*4 tablespoons tomato paste*
*½ cup pitted black olives, quartered*
*1 tablespoon chopped fresh oregano*
*1 can (8 ounces) tuna in oil, drained and flaked*
*½ teaspoon anchovy paste*
*1 tablespoon capers, rinsed*
*1 cup grated Cheddar cheese or Monterey Jack*
*3 tablespoons fresh white bread crumbs*
*salt and ground black pepper*
*Italian parsley sprigs, to garnish*

**Serves 4**

1 Cook the pasta in plenty of boiling salted water according to the instructions on the package.

2 Meanwhile, heat the oil in a frying pan and fry the onion and garlic for about 10 minutes until softened.

3 Add the tomatoes, tomato paste, and salt and pepper, and bring to a boil. Simmer gently for 5 minutes, stirring occasionally.

4 Stir the olives, oregano, tuna, anchovy paste and capers into the pan. Spoon the mixture into a separate mixing bowl.

5 Drain the pasta, toss well in the sauce and spoon into flameproof serving dishes.

6 Preheat the broiler and sprinkle the cheese and bread crumbs evenly over the pasta. Place under the broiler for about 10 minutes until the pasta is heated through and the cheese topping has melted. Serve immediately, garnished with Italian parsley.

# Spaghetti with Bottarga

Although this may seem an unusual recipe, with bottarga (salted and air-dried mullet or tuna roe) as the principal ingredient, it is very well known in Sardinia—and also in Sicily and parts of southern Italy. It is simplicity itself to make and tastes very, very good.

**INGREDIENTS**

*12 ounces fresh or dried spaghetti*
*about 4 tablespoons olive oil*
*2–3 garlic cloves, peeled*
*ground black pepper*
*4–6 tablespoons grated bottarga, to taste*
**Serves 4**

1 Cook the pasta according to the instructions on the package.

2 Meanwhile, heat half the olive oil in a large saucepan. Add the garlic and cook gently, stirring, for a few minutes. Remove the pan from the heat, scoop out the garlic with a slotted spoon and discard, leaving the garlic-flavored oil in the bottom.

3 Drain the pasta very well. Return the pan of oil to the heat and add the pasta. Toss well, season with pepper and moisten with the remaining oil, or more to taste. Divide the pasta among four warmed bowls, sprinkle the grated bottarga over the top and serve immediately.

**Cook's Tip**

*You can buy bottarga in Italian markets. Small jars of ready-grated bottarga are convenient, but the best flavor comes from vacuum-packed slices of mullet bottarga. This is very easy to grate on a box grater. Keep any leftover bottarga in the refrigerator, tightly wrapped so that it does not taint other foods.*

# Spaghetti with Tuna, Mushrooms and Bacon

THE ITALIAN TERM for this dish, *alla carrettiera*, means "cart-driver's style." The Romans lay claim to the recipe, as do the Neapolitans and Sicilians, so there are lots of versions.

**INGREDIENTS**

*½ ounce dried porcini mushrooms*
*¾ cup warm water*
*2 tablespoons olive oil*
*1 garlic clove*
*3 ounces pancetta or rindless lean bacon, cut into ¼-inch strips*
*3 cups button mushrooms, chopped*
*14 ounces fresh or dried spaghetti*
*1 can (7 ounces) tuna in olive oil, drained*
*salt and ground black pepper*
*freshly grated Parmesan cheese, to serve*

**Serves 4**

1 Put the porcini in a small bowl. Pour the warm water over and let soak for 15–20 minutes.

2 Heat the oil in a large saucepan, add the garlic clove and cook gently for about 2 minutes, crushing it with a wooden spoon to release the flavor. Remove the garlic and discard. Add the pancetta or bacon to the oil remaining in the pan and cook for 3–4 minutes, stirring occasionally.

3 Meanwhile, drain the dried mushrooms, reserving the soaking liquid, and chop them finely.

4 Add both types of mushroom to the pan and cook, stirring, for 1–2 minutes, then add 6 tablespoons of the reserved liquid from soaking the dried mushrooms, with salt and pepper to taste. Simmer for 10 minutes, stirring occasionally. Meanwhile, cook the pasta according to the instructions on the package, adding the remaining soaking liquid from the mushrooms to the pasta cooking water.

5 Add the drained canned tuna to the mushroom sauce and fold it in gently. Taste for seasoning.

6 Drain the cooked pasta well and turn it into a warmed serving bowl. Pour the sauce over the top, toss well and sprinkle liberally with some freshly grated Parmesan. Serve immediately, with more Parmesan handed around separately.

# Penne with Shrimp and Feta Cheese

THIS DISH COMBINES the richness of fresh shrimp with the tartness of feta cheese. If you find feta cheese a little too salty, soak it in fresh, cold water or milk for a few minutes, to make it less salty.

**INGREDIENTS**

*1 pound raw shrimp in the shell*
*6 scallions*
*8 ounces feta cheese*
*4 tablespoons butter*
*small bunch fresh chives*
*1 pound penne, garganelle or rigatoni*
*salt and ground black pepper*
**Serves 4**

### COOK'S TIP

*If fresh shrimp are not available, use well-thawed frozen, and add to the sauce at the last minute together with the scallions.*

### VARIATION

*Another cheese that works well with this dish is goat cheese.*

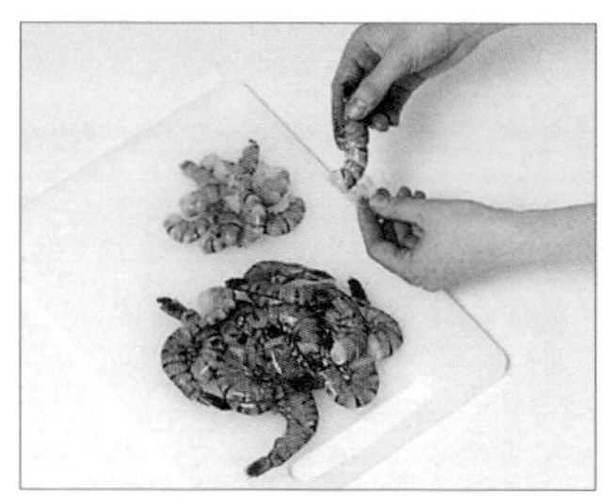

1 Remove the heads from the shrimp by twisting gently and pulling off. Shell the body of the shrimp and discard the shells.

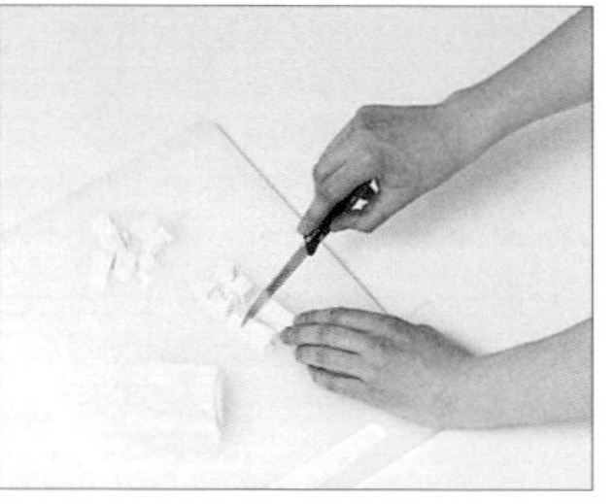

2 On a nylon cutting board, chop the scallions and the feta cheese using a sharp knife. Put them to one side.

3 Melt the butter in a large saucepan and stir in the peeled shrimp. When they turn pink, add the chopped scallions and cook gently over low heat for about 1 minute, stirring.

4 Stir the chopped feta cheese into the shrimp mixture in the saucepan and season with ground black pepper.

5 Cut the chives into 1-inch lengths on a plate. Turn half of them into the shrimp mixture and toss well to combine.

6 Cook the pasta in plenty of boiling salted water according to the instructions on the package.

7 Drain well and spoon into warmed serving dishes. Top with the sauce. Sprinkle with the remaining chives and serve immediately.

# Black Tagliatelle with Scallops

A STUNNING PASTA DISH using black tagliatelle with a contrasting white fish sauce.

**INGREDIENTS**

*½ cup lowfat crème fraîche*
*2 teaspoons whole-grain mustard*
*2 garlic cloves, crushed*
*2–3 tablespoons fresh lime juice*
*4 tablespoons chopped fresh parsley*
*2 tablespoons chopped chives*
*12 ounces fresh or dried black tagliatelle*
*12 large sea scallops*
*4 tablespoons white wine*
*⅔ cup fish stock*
*salt and ground black pepper*
*lime wedges and parsley sprigs, to garnish*
**Serves 4**

1 To make the tartare sauce, mix the crème fraîche, mustard, garlic, lime juice, herbs and seasoning together in a bowl.

2 Cook the pasta in a large pan of boiling, salted water until *al dente*: 8–10 minutes, or according to the instructions on the package. Drain the pasta thoroughly.

3 Slice each of the scallops in half horizontally. Keep any coral whole. Put the white wine and fish stock into a medium saucepan and heat until the mixture reaches simmering point. Add the scallops to the pan and cook very gently for 3–4 minutes (do not be tempted to cook them for any longer or they will become tough).

4 Remove the scallops from the pan with a slotted spoon. Boil the wine and stock to reduce by half and add the tartare sauce to the pan.

5 Heat the combined mixture gently to warm, replace the scallops and cook gently for 1 minute. Spoon over the pasta and garnish with lime wedges and sprigs of parsley.

# Tagliatelle with Smoked Salmon

THIS IS A PRETTY PASTA DISH with the light texture of the cucumber complementing the fish perfectly.

**INGREDIENTS**

*12 ounces fresh or dried tagliatelle*
*½ cucumber*
*6 tablespoons butter*
*grated rind of 1 orange*
*2 tablespoons chopped fresh dill weed*
*1 ¼ cups light cream*
*1 tablespoon orange juice*
*4 ounces smoked salmon, skinned*
*salt and ground black pepper*

**Serves 4**

1 Cook the pasta in plenty of boiling salted water according to the instructions on the package.

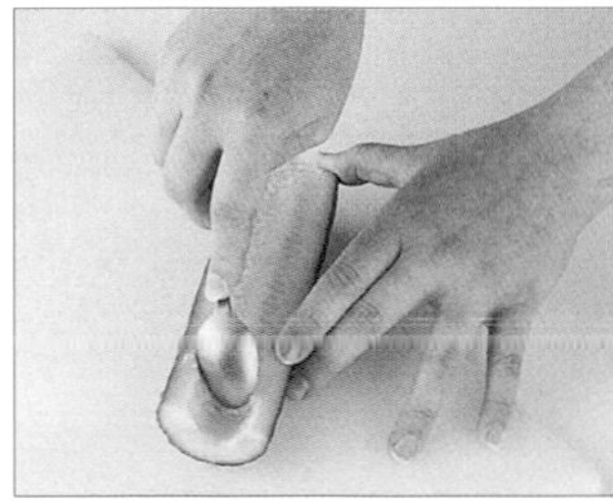

2 Using a sharp knife, cut the cucumber in half lengthwise then, using a small spoon, scoop out the seeds and discard.

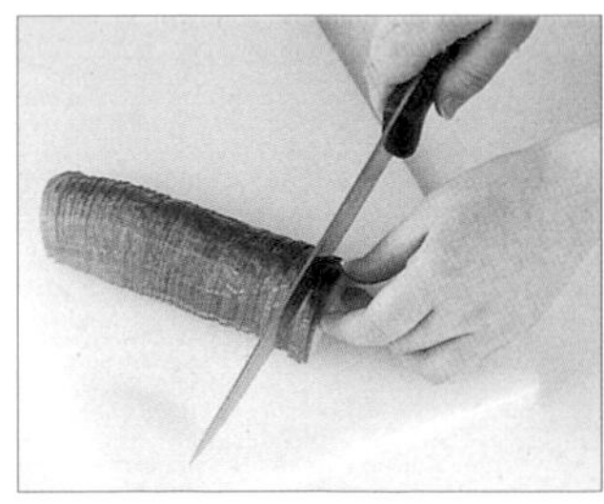

3 Turn the cucumber over onto the flat side and slice thinly along the length.

4 Melt the butter in a large saucepan, add the orange rind and dill weed and stir well. Add the sliced cucumber and cook gently for 2 minutes, stirring occasionally.

5 Add the cream and orange juice, and season to taste. Then simmer for 1 minute.

6 Meanwhile, cut the salmon into thin strips. Stir into the sauce and heat through.

7 Drain the pasta thoroughly and toss in the sauce until well coated. Serve immediately.

# Spaghetti with Clam Sauce

THIS IS ONE OF ITALY'S most famous pasta dishes, sometimes known as "white clam sauce" to distinguish it from that other classic, clams in tomato sauce. It is how they serve clams with pasta in Venice.

**INGREDIENTS**

*2¼ pounds fresh clams*
*4 tablespoons olive oil*
*3 tablespoons chopped fresh Italian parsley*
*½ cup dry white wine*
*12 ounces dried spaghetti*
*2 garlic cloves*
*salt and ground black pepper*
**Serves 4**

1 Scrub the clams under cold running water, discarding any that are open or that do not close when sharply tapped against the counter.

2 Heat half the oil in a large saucepan, add the clams and 1 tablespoon of the parsley and cook over high heat for a few seconds. Pour in the wine, then cover tightly. Cook for about 5 minutes, shaking the pan frequently, until the clams have opened. Meanwhile, cook the pasta in salted boiling water according to the instructions on the package.

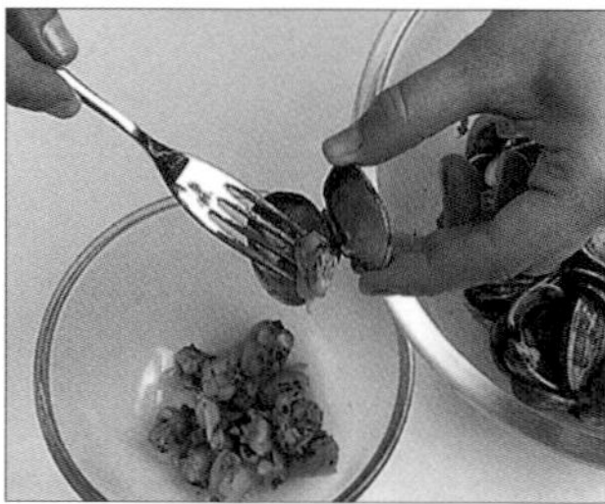

3 Using a slotted spoon, transfer the clams to a bowl, discarding any that have failed to open. Strain the liquid and set it aside. Put eight clams in their shells to one side for the garnish, then remove the rest from their shells.

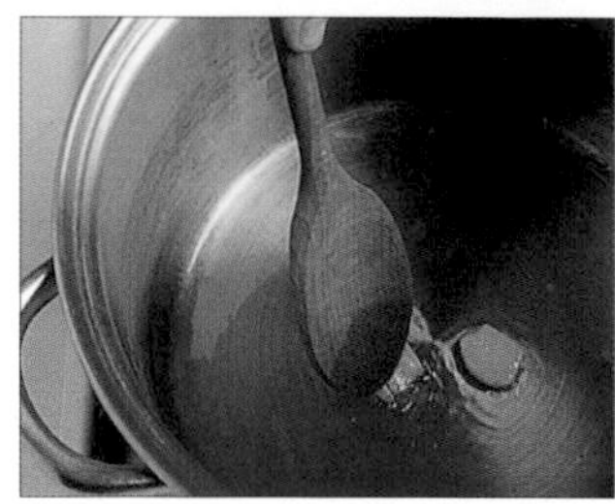

4 Heat the remaining oil in the clean pan. Fry the whole garlic cloves over medium heat until golden, crushing them with the back of a spoon. Remove the garlic with a slotted spoon and discard.

5 Add the shelled clams to the oil remaining in the pan, gradually add some of the strained liquid from the clams, then add plenty of pepper. Cook for 1–2 minutes, gradually adding more liquid as the sauce reduces. Add the remaining parsley and cook for 1–2 minutes.

6 Drain the pasta, add it to the pan and toss well. Serve in individual dishes, scooping the shelled clams from the bottom of the pan and placing some of them on top of each serving. Garnish with the reserved clams in their shells and serve immediately.

# Penne with Shrimp and Artichokes

THIS IS A GOOD DISH TO MAKE in late spring or early summer, when greeny-purple baby artichokes appear in stores and markets.

**INGREDIENTS**

*juice of ½ lemon*
*4 baby globe artichokes*
*6 tablespoons olive oil*
*2 garlic cloves, crushed*
*2 tablespoons chopped fresh mint*
*2 tablespoons chopped fresh Italian parsley*
*3 cups dried penne*
*8–12 peeled cooked jumbo shrimp, each cut into 2–3 pieces*
*2 tablespoons butter*
*salt and ground black pepper*

**Serves 4**

1 Have ready a bowl of cold water to which you have added the lemon juice. To prepare the artichokes, cut off the artichoke stalks, if any, and cut across the tops of the leaves. Peel off and discard any tough or discolored outer leaves.

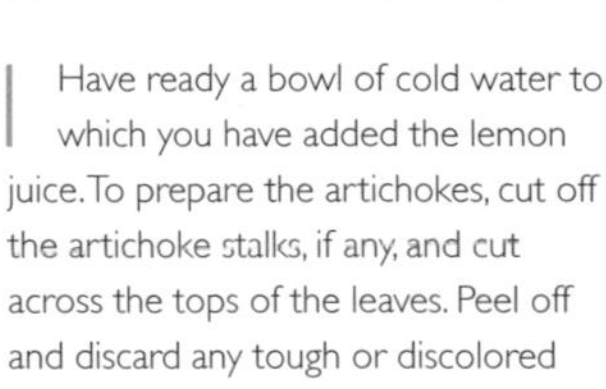

2 Cut the artichokes lengthwise into quarters and remove any hairy chokes from their centers. Finally, cut the pieces of artichoke lengthwise into ¼-inch slices and put these in the bowl of acidulated water.

3 Drain the slices of artichoke and pat them dry. Heat the olive oil in a non-stick frying pan and add the artichokes, the crushed garlic and half the mint and parsley to the pan.

4 Season with plenty of salt and pepper. Cook over low heat, stirring frequently, for about 10 minutes or until the artichokes feel tender when pierced with a sharp knife.

5 Meanwhile, cook the pasta in a large saucepan of salted boiling water according to the instructions on the package.

6 Add the shrimp to the artichokes, stir well to mix, then heat through gently for 1–2 minutes.

7 Drain the pasta and turn it into a warmed bowl. Add the butter and toss until it has melted. Spoon the artichoke mixture over the pasta and toss to combine. Serve immediately, sprinkled with the remaining herbs.

# Spaghetti with Mussels

MUSSELS ARE POPULAR in all the coastal regions of Italy, and are delicious with pasta. This simple dish is greatly improved by using the freshest mussels available.

**INGREDIENTS**

*2 pounds fresh mussels, in the shell*
*5 tablespoons olive oil*
*3 garlic cloves, finely chopped*
*4 tablespoons chopped fresh parsley*
*4 tablespoons white wine*
*14 ounces fresh or dried spaghetti*
*salt and ground black pepper*
**Serves 4**

1 Scrub the mussels well under cold running water, carefully cutting off the "beards" with a small sharp knife. Discard any that do not close when tapped sharply on the counter.

**COOK'S TIP**

*Mussels should be firmly closed when fresh. If a mussel is slightly open, pinch it closed. If it remains closed on its own, it is alive. If it remains open, discard it. Fresh mussels should be consumed as soon as possible after being purchased. They may be kept in a bowl of cold, salted water in the refrigerator.*

2 Place the mussels with a cupful of water in a large saucepan over moderate heat. As soon as they open, lift them out one by one with a slotted spoon and set aside.

3 When all the mussels have opened (discard any that do not), strain the cooking liquid in the saucepan through a layer of paper towel to remove any grit, and reserve until needed.

4 Heat the oil in a large frying pan. Add the garlic and parsley, and cook for 2–3 minutes. Add the mussels, their cooking liquid and the wine. Cook the sauce over moderate heat until heated through.

5 Add a generous amount of pepper to the sauce. Taste for seasoning; add salt if necessary.

6 Cook the pasta in plenty of boiling salted water until *al dente*. Drain, then turn it into the frying pan with the sauce, and stir well over a moderate heat for 3–4 minutes. Serve immediately on individual plates.

# Spaghetti with Hot-and-Sour Fish

A TRULY CHINESE spicy taste is what makes this sauce so different.

**INGREDIENTS**

*12 ounces fresh or dried spaghetti*
*1 pound monkfish, skinned*
*8 ounces zucchini*
*1 green chile, cored and seeded (optional)*
*1 tablespoon olive oil*
*1 large onion, chopped*
*1 teaspoon turmeric*
*1 cup shelled peas, thawed if frozen*
*2 teaspoons lemon juice*
*5 tablespoons hoisin sauce*
*⅔ cup water*
*salt and ground black pepper*
*fresh dill weed sprig, to garnish*

**Serves 4**

1 Cook the pasta in plenty of boiling salted water according to the instructions on the package.

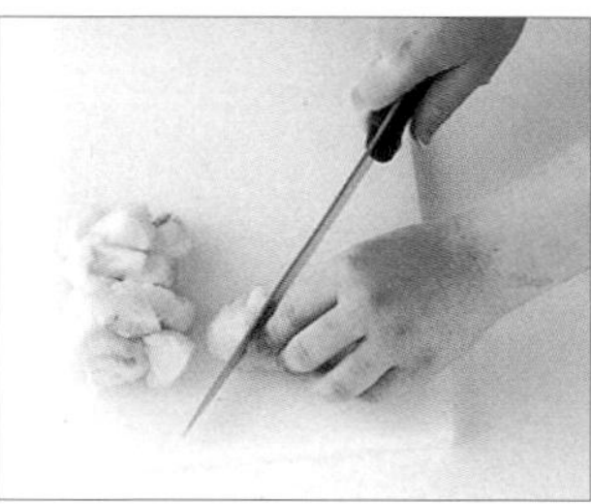

2 Cut the monkfish into bite-size pieces. Thinly slice the zucchini, then finely chop the chile, if using.

3 Heat the oil in a large frying pan and fry the onion for 5 minutes until softened. Add the turmeric.

4 Add the chile, if using, zucchini and peas, and fry over medium heat for 5 minutes until the vegetables have softened.

5 Stir in the fish, lemon juice, hoisin sauce and water. Bring the mixture to a boil, then simmer, uncovered, for about 5 minutes or until the fish is tender. Season.

6 Drain the pasta thoroughly and turn into a serving dish. Toss in the sauce to coat. Serve immediately, garnished with fresh dill weed.

# Saffron Pappardelle

A WONDERFUL DISH with a delicious shellfish sauce.

**INGREDIENTS**

*large pinch of saffron strands*
*4 sun-dried tomatoes, chopped*
*1 teaspoon fresh thyme*
*4 tablespoons hot water*
*12 jumbo shrimp in their shells*
*8 ounces baby squid*
*8 ounces monkfish fillet*
*2–3 garlic cloves*
*2 small onions, quartered*
*1 small bulb fennel, trimmed and sliced*
*⅔ cup white wine*
*8 ounces fresh or dried pappardelle*
*salt and ground black pepper*
*chopped fresh parsley, to garnish*
**Serves 4**

1 Put the saffron strands, sun-dried tomatoes and thyme into a bowl and pour over the hot water. Mix together and then let soak for at least 30 minutes.

2 Wash the shrimp and carefully remove the shells, leaving the heads and tails intact.

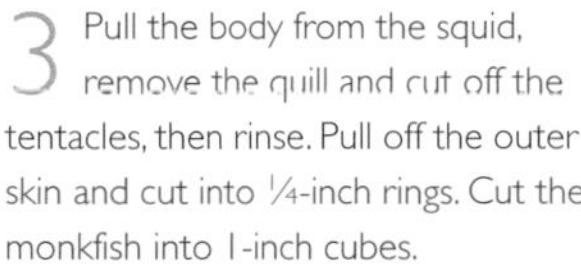

3 Pull the body from the squid, remove the quill and cut off the tentacles, then rinse. Pull off the outer skin and cut into ¼-inch rings. Cut the monkfish into 1-inch cubes.

4 Put the garlic, onions and fennel into a pan and pour over the wine. Cover and simmer for 5 minutes until tender.

5 Add the monkfish, saffron, tomatoes and thyme in their liquid. Cover and cook for 3 minutes. Then add the shrimp and squid. Cover and cook gently for a further 1–2 minutes (do not overcook or the squid will become tough).

6 Meanwhile, cook the pasta in a large pan of boiling, salted water until *al dente*. Drain the pasta thoroughly in the colander.

7 Divide the pasta among four serving dishes and top each one with the fish and shellfish sauce. Sprinkle with chopped fresh parsley and serve immediately.

# Linguine with Clams, Leeks and Tomatoes

CANNED CLAMS make this a speedy dish for those in a real hurry.

**INGREDIENTS**

*12 ounces fresh or dried linguine*
*2 tablespoons butter*
*2 leeks, thinly sliced*
*⅔ cup dry white wine*
*4 tomatoes, skinned, seeded and chopped*
*pinch of turmeric (optional)*
*9 ounces canned clams, drained*
*2 tablespoons chopped fresh basil*
*4 tablespoons crème fraîche*
*salt and ground black pepper*

**Serves 4**

1 Cook the pasta in plenty of boiling salted water according to the instructions on the package.

2 Meanwhile, melt the butter in a small saucepan and fry the sliced leeks for about 5 minutes until softened but not colored.

3 Add the wine, tomatoes and turmeric, bring to a boil and boil until reduced by half.

4 Stir in the clams, basil, crème fraîche and seasoning and heat through gently without boiling the sauce.

5 Drain the pasta thoroughly and toss in the clam and leek sauce. Serve immediately.

# Macaroni with Jumbo Shrimp and Ham

COOKED RADICCHIO makes a novel addition to this sauce. The bitter flavor of this salad vegetable mellows on cooking and perfectly complements the rich shrimp.

**INGREDIENTS**

*12 ounces dried short macaroni*
*3 tablespoons olive oil*
*12 shelled raw jumbo shrimp*
*1 garlic clove, chopped*
*generous 1 cup diced smoked ham*
*⅔ cup red wine*
*½ small radicchio, shredded*
*2 egg yolks, beaten*
*2 tablespoons chopped fresh Italian parsley*
*⅔ cup heavy cream*
*salt and ground black pepper*
*shredded fresh basil, to garnish*

**Serves 4**

1 Cook the pasta in plenty of boiling salted water, according to the instructions on the package.

2 Meanwhile, heat the oil in a frying pan and cook the shrimp, garlic and ham for about 5 minutes, stirring occasionally until the shrimp are just opaque and tender. Be careful not to overcook.

3 Add the wine and radicchio, bring to a boil and boil rapidly until the juices are reduced by about half.

4 Add the egg yolks to the sauce and stir.

5 Now add the parsley and cream and bring almost to a boil, stirring constantly, then simmer until the sauce thickens slightly. Check the seasoning and adjust if necessary.

6 Drain the pasta thoroughly once it is cooked and toss in the sauce to coat. Serve immediately, garnished with some shredded fresh basil.

# Rigatoni with Scallop Sauce

A JEWEL FROM THE SEA, the scallop is what makes this sauce so special. Serve with a green salad, if liked.

**INGREDIENTS**

*12 ounces fresh or dried rigatoni*
*12 ounces Bay scallops*
*3 tablespoons olive oil*
*1 garlic clove, chopped*
*1 onion, chopped*
*2 carrots, cut into short thin sticks*
*2 tablespoons chopped fresh parsley*
*2 tablespoons dry white wine*
*2 tablespoons Pernod*
*⅔ cup heavy cream*
*salt and ground black pepper*

**Serves 4**

1 Cook the pasta in plenty of boiling salted water according to the instructions on the package.

2 Trim the scallops, separating the corals from the white eye part of the meat.

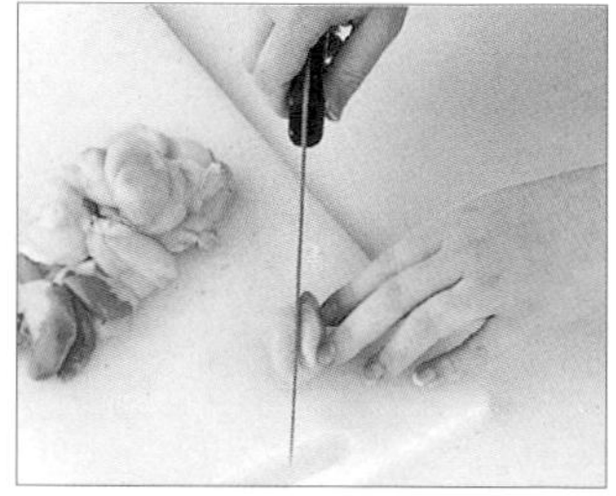

3 Using a sharp knife on a board, cut the white eye sections in half lengthwise.

4 Heat the oil in a frying pan and fry the garlic, onion and carrots for 5–10 minutes, stirring occasionally, until the carrots are softened.

5 Stir in the scallops, parsley, wine and Pernod and bring to a boil. Cover and simmer for about 1 minute. Using a slotted spoon, transfer the scallops and vegetables to a plate and keep them warm until required.

6 Bring the pan juices back to a boil and boil rapidly until reduced by half. Stir in the cream and heat the sauce through.

7 Return the scallops and cooked vegetables to the sauce in the pan and heat them through. Season the mixture to taste.

8 Drain the pasta thoroughly and toss with the sauce until thoroughly combined. Serve the rigatoni immediately.

# Spaghetti with Mussels and Saffron

IN THIS RECIPE the pasta is tossed with a delicious pale yellow mussel sauce, streaked with yellow strands of saffron. Powdered saffron will do just as well, but don't use turmeric—the flavor will be too strong.

**INGREDIENTS**

*2 pounds live mussels, in the shell*
*⅔ cup dry white wine*
*2 shallots, finely chopped*
*2 tablespoons butter*
*2 garlic cloves, crushed*
*2 teaspoons cornstarch*
*1¼ cups heavy cream*
*pinch of saffron strands*
*juice of ½ lemon*
*1 egg yolk*
*1 pound fresh or dried spaghetti*
*salt and ground black pepper*
*chopped fresh parsley, to garnish*

**Serves 4**

1 Scrub the mussels and rinse well. Pull off any "beards" and leave the mussels to soak in cold water for 30 minutes. Tap each mussel sharply after this time. Discard any that do not close immediately.

2 Drain the mussels and place them in a large saucepan. Pour over the wine and add the finely chopped shallots.

3 Cover and cook the mussels, shaking frequently, over a high heat for 5–10 minutes until they are all open. Discard any that do not open.

4 Drain the mussels through a strainer, reserving the liquid. Remove most of the mussels from their shells, reserving some in the shell to use as a garnish. Boil the reserved liquid rapidly until reduced by half.

5 Melt the butter in another saucepan, add the garlic and cook until golden. Stir in the cornstarch and gradually stir in the cooking liquid and the cream. Add the saffron and seasoning and simmer until slightly thickened.

6 Stir in lemon juice to taste, then the egg yolk and mussels. Keep warm, but do not boil.

7 Cook the pasta according to the instructions on the package. Drain well. Toss the mussels with the spaghetti, spoon into individual bowls, top with the reserved mussels and sprinkle with the parsley. Serve with crusty bread, if you like.

# Meat and Poultry

When we think of a meat sauce to serve with pasta, our minds automatically turn to Bolognese sauce, or *ragù alla Bolognese*, as it is correctly called in Italian. Thanks to Italian emigrés, Bolognese sauce has become one of the most famous pasta sauces outside Italy, especially in Great Britain and the United States. Beef, pork and pancetta simmered with wine and tomatoes until rich, intensely meaty and satisfying, is very hard to beat. Unfortunately, this superb sauce is almost always served with spaghetti outside Italy, which is incorrect. It should be teamed with tagliatelle.

Many meat sauces hail from the north of Italy, especially from the region of Emilia-Romagna, where both fresh meat and the famous hams, salami and sausages are enjoyed in abundance. The actual quantity of meat in the sauce is never very large, however, and the size of the pieces must be small or the sauce will simply slide off the pasta. The egg-enriched pasta of the northern regions is good with meat sauces because it holds the sauce well, but it is by no means the only possibility. Long, thin types of pasta like spaghetti and vermicelli, find favor precisely because they do not hold a great deal of sauce with each forkful, a point worth considering when a meat sauce is very rich.

# Tagliatelle with Bolognese Sauce

THIS RECIPE IS an authentic meat sauce—ragù—from the city of Bologna in Emilia-Romagna. It is very rich, and is always served with tagliatelle, never with spaghetti.

**INGREDIENTS**

*1 pound fresh or dried tagliatelle*
*salt and ground black pepper*
*freshly grated Parmesan cheese, to serve*

***For the Bolognese meat sauce***

*2 tablespoons butter*
*1 tablespoon olive oil*
*1 onion, finely chopped*
*2 carrots, finely chopped*
*2 celery stalks, finely chopped*
*2 garlic cloves, finely chopped*
*4½ ounces pancetta or rindless lean bacon, diced*
*9 ounces lean ground beef*
*9 ounces lean ground pork*
*½ cup dry white wine*
*2 cans (14-ounce) crushed Italian plum tomatoes*
*2–3 cups beef stock*
*scant ½ cup* panna da cucina *or heavy cream*

**Serves 6–8**

1 Make the meat sauce first. Heat the butter and oil in a large skillet or saucepan until sizzling. Add the garlic, vegetables and the pancetta or bacon and cook over medium heat, stirring frequently, for 10 minutes or until the vegetables have softened.

2 Add the ground beef and pork, lower the heat and cook gently for 10 minutes, stirring frequently and breaking up any lumps in the meat with a wooden spoon. Stir in salt and pepper to taste, then add the wine and stir again. Simmer for about 5 minutes, or until reduced.

3 Add the canned tomatoes and 1 cup of the beef stock and bring to a boil. Stir the sauce well, then lower the heat. Half cover the pan with a lid and let simmer very gently for 2 hours. Stir occasionally during this time and add more stock as it becomes absorbed.

4 Pour the cream into the sauce, stir well to mix, then simmer, without a lid, for another 30 minutes, stirring frequently. Meanwhile, cook the pasta according to the package instructions. Taste the sauce to check the seasoning. Drain the cooked pasta and turn it into a warmed bowl. Pour the sauce over the pasta and toss well. Serve immediately, sprinkled with grated Parmesan.

**VARIATION**

*Some cooks add a few chopped chicken livers when frying the meat at the beginning of Step 2. This gives the sauce a stronger, almost gamey, flavor.*

# Spaghetti with Meatballs

TINY MEATBALLS SIMMERED in a sweet and spicy tomato sauce are truly delicious with spaghetti. Children love them and you can easily leave out the chiles.

**INGREDIENTS**

*12 ounces ground beef*
*1 egg*
*4 tablespoons coarsely chopped fresh Italian parsley*
*½ teaspoon crushed dried red chiles*
*1 thick slice white bread, crusts removed*
*2 tablespoons milk*
*about 2 tablespoons olive oil*
*1¼ cups passata or tomato sauce*
*1¾ cups vegetable stock*
*1 teaspoon granulated sugar*
*12 ounces–1 pound fresh or dried spaghetti*
*salt and ground black pepper*
*freshly grated Parmesan cheese, to serve*

**Serves 6–8**

1 Put the ground beef in a large bowl. Add the egg, and half the parsley and crushed chiles. Season with plenty of salt and pepper.

2 Tear the bread into small pieces and place in a small bowl. Moisten with the milk. Let soak for a few minutes, then squeeze out the excess milk and crumble the bread over the meat mixture. Mix everything together with a wooden spoon, then use your hands to squeeze and knead the mixture so that it becomes smooth and quite sticky.

3 Wash your hands, rinse them under the cold tap, then pick up small pieces of the mixture and roll them between your palms to make about 60 very small balls. Place the meatballs on a tray and chill in the refrigerator for about 30 minutes.

4 Heat the oil in a large, deep non-stick frying pan. Cook the meatballs in batches until browned on all sides. Pour the passata or tomato sauce and stock into the pan. Heat gently, then add the remaining chiles and the sugar, with salt and pepper to taste. Return all the meatballs to the pan. Bring to a boil, lower the heat and cover. Simmer for 20 minutes.

5 Cook the pasta according to the package instructions. When it is *al dente*, drain and turn it into a warmed large bowl. Pour the sauce over the pasta and toss gently. Sprinkle with the remaining parsley and serve with grated Parmesan handed separately.

# Lamb and Sweet Pepper Sauce

THIS SIMPLE SAUCE is a specialty of the Abruzzo-Molise region, east of Rome, where it is traditionally served with *maccheroni alla chitarra* —square-shaped long macaroni.

**INGREDIENTS**

*4 tablespoons olive oil*
*9 ounces boneless lamb neck tenderloin, diced quite small*
*2 garlic cloves, finely chopped*
*2 bay leaves, torn*
*1 cup dry white wine*
*4 ripe Italian plum tomatoes, peeled and chopped*
*2 large red bell peppers, seeded and diced*
*salt and ground black pepper*

**Serves 4–6**

1 Heat half the olive oil in a medium skillet or saucepan, add the small pieces of lamb and sprinkle with a little salt and pepper. Cook the meat over medium to high heat for about 10 minutes, stirring often, until it is browned on all sides.

2 Sprinkle in the garlic and add the bay leaves, then pour in the wine and let it bubble until reduced.

3 Add the remaining oil, the tomatoes and the bell peppers; stir to mix with the lamb. Season again. Cover with the lid and simmer over low heat for 45–55 minutes or until the lamb is very tender. Stir occasionally during cooking and moisten with water if the sauce becomes too dry. Remove the bay leaves from the sauce before serving it with pasta.

**COOK'S TIPS**

• *The bell peppers don't have to be red. Use yellow, orange or green if you prefer; either one color or a mixture.*
• *If you need to add water to the sauce towards the end of cooking, take it from the pan used for cooking the pasta.*
• *You can make your own fresh* maccheroni alla chitarra *or buy the dried pasta. Alternatively, this sauce is just as good with ordinary long or short macaroni. You will need 12–15 ounces.*

# Fusilli with Sausage

SPICY HOT SAUSAGE and tomato sauce combine with spirals of pasta to make this really tasty dish from southern Italy. Pecorino cheese, with its strong and salty flavor, is the perfect accompaniment. Serve for an informal supper party with a full-bodied red wine and crusty country bread.

**INGREDIENTS**

*14 ounces spicy pork sausages*
*2 tablespoons olive oil*
*1 small onion, finely chopped*
*2 garlic cloves, crushed*
*1 large yellow bell pepper, seeded and cut into strips*
*1 teaspoon paprika*
*1 teaspoon mixed dried herbs*
*1–2 teaspoons chilli sauce*
*1 can (14 ounces) Italian plum tomatoes*
*1–1¼ cups vegetable stock*
*2¾ cups fresh or dried fusilli*
*salt and ground black pepper*
*freshly grated Pecorino cheese, to serve*

**Serves 4**

1 Broil the sausages for 10–12 minutes until they are browned on all sides, then drain them on paper towels.

2 Heat the oil in a large skillet or saucepan, add the onion and garlic and cook over low heat, stirring frequently, for 5–7 minutes until soft. Add the yellow bell pepper, paprika, herbs and chile sauce to taste. Cook gently for 5–7 minutes, stirring occasionally.

3 Pour in the canned tomatoes, breaking them up with a wooden spoon, then add salt and pepper to taste and stir well. Cook over medium heat for 10–12 minutes, adding the vegetable stock gradually as the sauce reduces.

4 While the tomato sauce is cooking, cut the cooked sausages diagonally into ½-inch pieces.

5 Add the sausage pieces to the sauce, reduce the heat to low and cook for 10 minutes. Meanwhile, cook the pasta according to the instructions on the package.

6 Taste the sauce for seasoning. Drain the pasta and add it to the pan of sauce. Toss well, then divide among four warmed bowls. Sprinkle each serving with a little grated Pecorino and serve immediately, with more Pecorino handed separately.

# Rigatoni with Garlic Crumbs

A HOT AND SPICY DISH—halve the quantity of chile if you like a milder flavor. The bacon is an optional addition; you can leave it out if you are cooking for vegetarians.

**INGREDIENTS**

*3 tablespoons olive oil*
*2 shallots, chopped*
*8 strips lean bacon, chopped (optional)*
*2 teaspoons crushed dried red chiles*
*1 can (14 ounces) chopped tomatoes with garlic and herbs*
*6 slices white bread*
*½ cup butter*
*2 garlic cloves, chopped*
*4 cups fresh or dried rigatoni*
*salt and ground black pepper*

**Serves 4–6**

**COOK'S TIP**

*To keep the bread crumbs crisp and dry after frying, drain them on paper towels and place in a low oven until ready to use.*

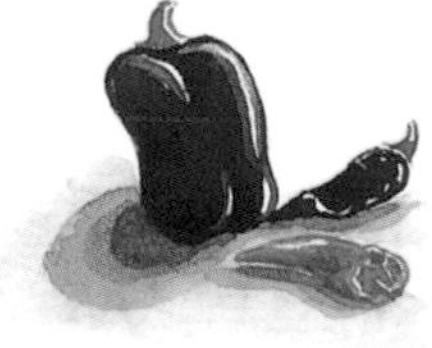

1 Heat the oil in a medium saucepan and fry the shallots and bacon, if using, gently for about 6–8 minutes, stirring continuously until golden. Add the dried chiles and chopped tomatoes, half-cover the pan and simmer for 20 minutes.

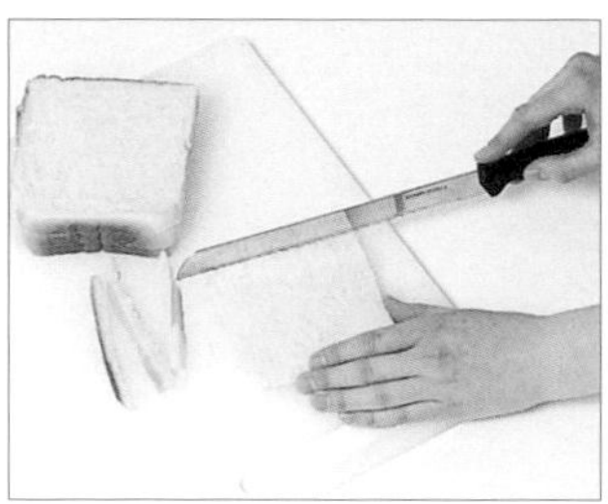

2 Meanwhile, cut the crusts off the bread and discard them. Reduce the bread to crumbs in a blender or food processor.

3 Heat the butter in a frying pan, add the garlic and bread crumbs and stir-fry until golden and crisp. (Keep stirring and don't let the crumbs catch and burn or the final result will be ruined.)

4 Cook the pasta in plenty of boiling salted water according to the instructions on the package, until *al dente*. Drain well.

5 Toss the pasta with the tomato sauce and divide among four or six warmed serving plates.

6 Sprinkle the pasta with the golden bread crumbs and serve immediately.

# Spaghetti with Eggs and Bacon

ONE OF THE CLASSIC pasta sauces, about which a debate still remains: whether or not it should contain cream. Pasta purists believe that it should not.

**INGREDIENTS**

*2 tablespoons olive oil*
*5 ounces bacon, cut into short thin sticks*
*1 garlic clove, crushed*
*14 ounces fresh or dried spaghetti*
*3 eggs, at room temperature*
*¾ cup freshly grated Parmesan cheese*
*salt and ground black pepper*

**Serves 4**

1 In a medium frying pan, heat the oil and sauté the bacon and the garlic until the bacon renders its fat and starts to brown. Remove and discard the garlic. Keep the bacon and its fat hot, until needed.

2 Cook the spaghetti in a large saucepan in plenty of rapidly boiling salted water according to the instructions on the package or until *al dente*.

3 Meanwhile, warm a large serving bowl and break the eggs into it. Beat in the Parmesan cheese with a fork, and season with salt and pepper.

4 As soon as the pasta is done, drain it quickly, and mix it into the egg mixture. Pour on the hot bacon and its fat. Stir well. The heat from the pasta and bacon fat will lightly cook the beaten eggs. Serve immediately.

# Piquant Chicken with Spaghetti

THE ADDITION of cucumber and tomatoes adds a deliciously fresh flavor to this unusual dish.

**INGREDIENTS**

*1 onion, finely chopped*
*1 carrot, diced*
*1 garlic clove, crushed*
*1 1/4 cups vegetable stock*
*4 chicken breasts, boned and skinned*
*1 bouquet garni*
*4 ounces white mushrooms, thinly sliced*
*1 teaspoon wine vinegar or lemon juice*
*12 ounces fresh or dried spaghetti*
*1/2 cucumber, peeled and cut into fingers*
*2 tomatoes, skinned, seeded and chopped*
*2 tablespoons crème fraîche*
*1 tablespoon chopped fresh parsley*
*1 tablespoon chopped chives*
*salt and ground black pepper*

**Serves 4**

1 Put the onion, carrot, garlic, vegetable stock, chicken and bouquet garni into a saucepan.

2 Bring to a boil, cover and simmer for 15–20 minutes or until the chicken is tender. Transfer the chicken to a plate with a slotted spoon and cover with foil.

3 Strain the remaining cooking liquid in the pan. Discard the vegetables and return the liquid to the pan. Add the sliced mushrooms, wine vinegar or lemon juice, then stir and simmer for 2–3 minutes.

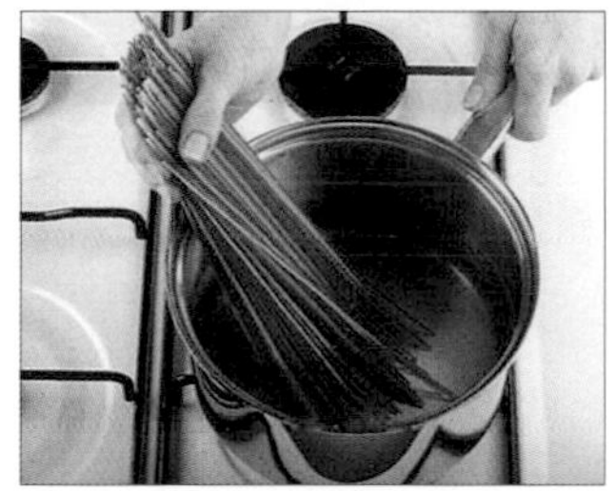

4 Cook the spaghetti in plenty of boiling salted water according to the instructions on the package or until *al dente*. Drain thoroughly.

5 Blanch the cucumber in boiling water for 10 seconds. Drain and rinse under cold water.

6 Cut the chicken breasts into bite-size pieces. Boil the stock to reduce by half, then add the chicken, tomatoes, crème fraîche, cucumber and herbs. Season with salt and pepper to taste.

7 Transfer the spaghetti to a warmed serving dish and spoon over the piquant chicken and tomato sauce. Serve immediately.

# Eliche with Sausage and Radicchio

SAUSAGE AND RADICCHIO may seem odd companions, but the combined flavor of these ingredients is really delicious. This robust and hearty dish makes a good main course.

**INGREDIENTS**

*2 tablespoons olive oil*
*1 onion, finely chopped*
*7 ounces Italian pure pork sausage*
*¾ cup passata or tomato sauce*
*6 tablespoons dry white wine*
*2¾ cups dried eliche*
*2 ounces radicchio leaves*
*salt and ground black pepper*
**Serves 4**

1 Heat the olive oil in a large, deep skillet or saucepan. Add the finely chopped onion and cook over low heat, stirring frequently, for about 5 minutes until softened.

2 Snip the end off the sausage casing and squeeze the sausage meat into the pan. With a wooden spoon, stir the sausage meat to mix it with the oil and onion and break it up into small pieces.

3 Continue to fry the mixture, increasing the heat if necessary, until the sausage meat is brown all over and looks crumbly. Stir in the passata, then sprinkle in the wine, with salt and pepper to taste. Simmer over low heat, stirring occasionally, for 10–12 minutes.

4 Meanwhile, cook the pasta according to the instructions on the package. Just before draining the pasta, add a ladleful or two of the cooking water to the sausage sauce and stir it in well. Taste the sauce to check the seasoning.

5 Finely shred the radicchio leaves. Drain the cooked pasta and tip it into the pan of sausage sauce. Add the shredded radicchio and toss well to combine. Serve immediately.

**COOK'S TIPS**

• *The best Italian sausage to use is called* salsiccia puro suino. *It is made from 100 percent pure pork plus flavorings and seasonings.*
• *If you can get it, use the long, tapering* radicchio di Treviso *for this dish; otherwise the tightly furled, round radicchio can be used.*

# Spaghetti with Ground Beef Sauce

SPAGHETTI BOLOGNESE is not an authentic Italian dish. It was "invented" by Italian emigrés in America in the sixties in response to popular demand for a spaghetti dish with meat sauce. This is a rich, spicy version.

**INGREDIENTS**

*2 tablespoons olive oil*
*1 onion, finely chopped*
*1 garlic clove, crushed*
*1 teaspoon dried mixed herbs*
*¼ teaspoon cayenne pepper*
*12 ounces–1 pound ground beef*
*1 can (14 ounces) chopped Italian plum tomatoes*
*3 tablespoons tomato ketchup*
*1 tablespoon sun-dried tomato paste*
*1 teaspoon Worcestershire sauce*
*1 teaspoon dried oregano*
*1¾ cups beef or vegetable stock*
*45ml/3 tablespoons red wine*
*14 ounces–1 pound dried spaghetti*
*salt and ground black pepper*
*freshly grated Parmesan cheese, to serve*

**Serves 4–6**

1 Heat the oil in a medium saucepan, add the onion and garlic and cook over low heat, stirring frequently, for about 5 minutes until softened. Stir in the mixed herbs and cayenne and cook for 2–3 minutes more. Add the ground beef and cook gently for about 5 minutes, stirring frequently and breaking up any lumps in the meat with a wooden spoon.

2 Stir in the canned tomatoes, ketchup, sun-dried tomato paste, Worcestershire sauce, oregano and plenty of black pepper. Pour in the stock and red wine and bring to a boil, stirring. Cover the pan, lower the heat and let the sauce simmer for 30 minutes, stirring occasionally.

3 Cook the pasta according to the instructions on the package. Drain well and divide among warmed bowls. Taste the sauce and add a little salt if necessary, then spoon it on top of the pasta and sprinkle with a little grated Parmesan. Serve immediately, with grated Parmesan handed separately.

# Tortellini with Ham

THIS IS A VERY EASY RECIPE that can be made quickly from storecupboard ingredients. It is therefore ideal for an after-work supper.

**INGREDIENTS**

*9 ounces package* tortellini alla carne *(meat-filled tortellini)*
*2 tablespoons olive oil*
*¼ large onion, finely chopped*
*4 ounces cooked ham, diced*
*⅔ cup strained crushed Italian plum tomatoes*
*scant ½ cup* panna da cucina *or heavy cream*
*generous 1 cup freshly grated Parmesan cheese*
*salt and ground black pepper*
**Serves 4**

1 Cook the pasta according to the instructions on the package.

2 Meanwhile, heat the oil in a large skillet or saucepan, add the onion and cook over low heat, stirring frequently, for about 5 minutes until softened. Add the ham and cook, stirring occasionally, until it darkens.

3 Add the strained crushed tomatoes. Fill the empty cup with water and pour it into the pan. Stir well, then add salt and pepper to taste. Bring to a boil, lower the heat and simmer the sauce for a few minutes, stirring occasionally, until it has reduced slightly. Stir in the cream. Drain the pasta well and add it to the sauce.

4 Add a handful of grated Parmesan to the pan. Stir, toss well and taste for seasoning. Serve in warmed bowls, topped with the remaining Parmesan.

**COOK'S TIP**

*Cartons of strained crushed tomatoes are handy for making quick sauces.*

# Bolognese Sauce with Red Wine

THIS IS A VERSATILE meat sauce. You can toss it with freshly cooked pasta—the quantity here is enough for 1 pound tagliatelle, spaghetti or a short pasta shape such as penne or fusilli—or alternatively you can layer it in a baked dish like lasagne.

**INGREDIENTS**

*1 medium onion*
*1 small carrot*
*1 celery stalk*
*2 garlic cloves*
*3 tablespoons olive oil*
*4 ounces ground beef*
*½ cup red wine*
*scant 1 cup passata or tomato sauce*
*1 tablespoon tomato paste*
*1 teaspoon dried oregano*
*1 tablespoon chopped fresh Italian parsley*
*about 1½ cups beef stock*
*8 baby Italian tomatoes (optional)*
*salt and ground black pepper*
**Serves 4–6**

1 Chop all the vegetables finely, either in a food processor or by hand. Heat the oil in a large saucepan, add the chopped vegetable mixture and cook over a low heat, stirring frequently, for 5–7 minutes.

2 Add the ground beef and cook for 5 minutes, stirring frequently and breaking up any lumps in the meat with a wooden spoon. Stir in the wine and mix well.

3 Cook for 1–2 minutes, then add the passata, tomato paste, herbs and 4 tablespoons of the stock. Season with salt and pepper to taste. Stir well and bring to a boil.

4 Cover the pan and cook on a gentle heat for 30 minutes, stirring occasionally and adding more stock as necessary. Add the tomatoes if using, and simmer for 5—10 minutes more. Taste for seasoning and toss with hot, freshly cooked pasta, or use in baked pasta dishes.

# Tagliatelle with Prosciutto and Asparagus

A STUNNING SAUCE, this is worth every effort to serve at a dinner party or as a special treat.

**INGREDIENTS**

*12 ounces fresh or dried tagliatelle*
*2 tablespoons butter*
*1 tablespoon olive oil*
*8 ounces asparagus tips*
*1 garlic clove, chopped*
*4 ounces prosciutto di Parma, sliced into strips*
*2 tablespoons chopped fresh sage*
*⅔ cup light cream*
*1 cup grated double Gloucester cheese*
*1 cup grated Gruyère cheese*
*salt and ground black pepper*
*fresh sage sprigs, to garnish*

**Serves 4**

1 Cook the pasta in plenty of boiling salted water according to the instructions on the package.

2 Melt the butter and oil in a frying pan and gently fry the asparagus tips for about 5 minutes, stirring occasionally, until they are almost tender.

3 Stir the garlic and prosciutto into the pan with the asparagus and fry everything for 1 minute.

4 Stir in the chopped sage and fry for a further 1 minute.

5 Pour in the cream and bring the mixture to a boil.

6 Add the cheeses and simmer gently, stirring occasionally, until thoroughly melted. Season.

7 Drain the pasta thoroughly and toss with the sauce to coat. Serve immediately in four warmed plates, garnished with fresh sage sprigs.

# Tagliatelle with Chicken and Herb Sauce

SERVE THIS DELICIOUS dish with its wine-flavored sauce and a fresh green salad.

**INGREDIENTS**

*2 tablespoons olive oil*
*1 red onion, cut into wedges*
*12 ounces fresh or dried tagliatelle*
*1 garlic clove, chopped*
*12 ounces chicken, diced*
*1 1/4 cups dry vermouth*
*3 tablespoons chopped fresh mixed herbs*
*2/3 cup ricotta cheese*
*salt and ground black pepper*
*shredded fresh mint, to garnish*

**Serves 4**

1 Heat the oil in a large frying pan and fry the red onion for 10 minutes until softened but not colored and the layers have separated.

2 Cook the pasta in plenty of boiling salted water according to the instructions on the package.

3 Add the garlic and chicken to the frying pan and fry for 10 minutes, stirring occasionally, until the chicken is browned all over and cooked through.

4 Pour in the vermouth, bring to boiling point and boil rapidly until reduced by about half.

5 Stir in the herbs, ricotta cheese and seasoning and heat through gently, but do not boil.

6 Drain the pasta thoroughly and spoon the sauce over. Toss the mixture to coat the pasta. Serve immediately, garnished with shredded fresh mint.

# Farfalle with Chicken and Cherry Tomatoes

QUICK TO PREPARE and easy to cook, this colorful dish is full of flavor. Serve it for a midweek supper, with a green salad to follow.

**INGREDIENTS**

*12 ounces skinless chicken breast fillets, cut into bite-size pieces*
*4 tablespoons Italian dry vermouth*
*2 teaspoons chopped fresh rosemary, plus 4 fresh rosemary sprigs, to garnish*
*1 tablespoon olive oil*
*1 onion, finely chopped*
*$3\frac{1}{2}$ ounces piece Italian salami, diced*
*$2\frac{1}{2}$ cups dried farfalle*
*1 tablespoon balsamic vinegar*
*1 can (14 ounces) Italian cherry tomatoes*
*good pinch of crushed dried red chiles*
*salt and ground black pepper*

**Serves 4**

1 Put the pieces of chicken in a large bowl, pour in the dry vermouth and sprinkle with half the chopped rosemary and salt and pepper to taste. Stir well and set aside.

2 Heat the oil in a large skillet or saucepan, add the onion and salami and fry over medium heat for about 5 minutes, stirring frequently.

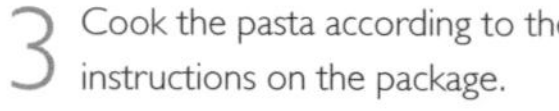

3 Cook the pasta according to the instructions on the package.

4 Add the chicken and vermouth to the onion and salami, increase the heat to high and fry for 3 minutes or until the chicken is white on all sides. Sprinkle the vinegar over the chicken.

5 Add the cherry tomatoes and dried chiles. Stir well and simmer for a few minutes more. Taste the sauce for seasoning.

6 Drain the pasta and turn it into the skillet or saucepan. Add the remaining chopped rosemary and toss to mix the pasta and sauce together. Serve immediately in warmed bowls, garnished with the rosemary sprigs.

**COOK'S TIP**

*The tomatoes look good left whole, but if you prefer you can crush them with the back of a wooden spoon while they are simmering in the pan.*

# Penne with Chicken, Broccoli and Cheese

THE COMBINATION OF BROCCOLI, garlic and Gorgonzola is very good, and goes especially well with chicken.

**INGREDIENTS**

*scant 1 cup broccoli flowerets, divided into tiny sprigs*
*1/4 cup butter*
*2 skinless chicken breast fillets, cut into thin strips*
*2 garlic cloves, crushed*
*3 1/2 cups dried penne*
*1/2 cup dry white wine*
*scant 1 cup* panna da cucina *or heavy cream*
*3 1/2 ounces Gorgonzola cheese, rind removed and diced small*
*salt and ground black pepper*
*freshly grated Parmesan cheese, to serve*

**Serves 4**

1 Plunge the broccoli into a saucepan of boiling salted water. Bring back to a boil and boil for 2 minutes, then drain in a colander and refresh under cold running water. Shake well to remove the surplus water and set aside to drain completely.

2 Melt the butter in a large skillet or saucepan, add the chicken and garlic, with salt and pepper to taste, and stir well. Fry over medium heat for 3 minutes or until the chicken becomes white. Meanwhile, start cooking the pasta according to the instructions on the package.

3 Pour the wine and cream over the chicken mixture in the pan, stir to mix, then simmer, stirring occasionally, for about 5 minutes until the sauce has reduced and thickened. Add the broccoli, increase the heat and toss to heat it through and mix it with the chicken. Taste for seasoning.

4 Drain the pasta and turn it into the sauce. Add the Gorgonzola and toss well. Serve with grated Parmesan.

**VARIATION**

*Use leeks instead of broccoli if you prefer. Fry them with the chicken.*

# Penne with Sausage and Parmesan Sauce

Spicy sausage tossed in a cheese flavored tomato sauce is delicious served on a bed of cooked pasta.

**INGREDIENTS**

*3 cups dried penne*
*1 pound ripe tomatoes*
*2 tablespoons olive oil*
*8 ounces chorizo sausage, diagonally sliced*
*1 garlic clove, chopped*
*2 tablespoons chopped fresh Italian parsley*
*grated rind of 1 lemon*
*½ cup freshly grated Parmesan cheese*
*salt and ground black pepper*
*finely chopped fresh Italian parsley, to garnish*

**Serves 4**

1 Cook the pasta in plenty of boiling salted water according to the instructions on the package.

2 Slash the bottoms of the tomatoes with a knife, making a cross. Place in a large bowl, cover with boiling water and let stand for 45 seconds. Plunge into cold water for 30 seconds, then peel off the skins and coarsely chop the flesh.

3 Heat the oil in a frying pan and fry the sliced chorizo sausage for 5 minutes, stirring occasionally, until browned.

4 Add the chopped tomatoes, garlic, parsley and grated lemon rind. Heat through gently, stirring, for 1 minute.

5 Finally, add the grated Parmesan cheese to the sauce, stir to combine and season to taste.

6 Drain the pasta well through a colander and toss it with the sauce to coat. Serve immediately, garnished with finely chopped fresh Italian parsley.

# Fusilli with Chicken and Tomato

A RECIPE FOR a speedy supper—serve this dish with a mixed bean salad.

**INGREDIENTS**

*1 tablespoon olive oil*
*1 onion, chopped*
*1 carrot, chopped*
*2 ounces sun-dried tomatoes in olive oil, drained weight*
*1 garlic clove, chopped*
*1 can (14 ounces) chopped tomatoes, drained*
*1 tablespoon tomato paste*
*⅔ cup chicken stock*
*3 cups dried fusilli*
*8 ounces chicken, diagonally sliced*
*salt and ground black pepper*
*fresh mint sprigs, to garnish*

**Serves 4**

1 Heat the oil in a large frying pan and fry the chopped onion and carrot for 5 minutes, stirring the vegetables occasionally.

2 Chop the sun-dried tomatoes and set aside until needed.

3 Stir the garlic, tomatoes, tomato paste and stock into the onions and carrots in the frying pan and bring to a boil. Simmer for 10 minutes, stirring occasionally.

4 Cook the pasta in plenty of boiling salted water according to the instructions on the package.

5 Pour the sauce into a blender or food processor and process until smooth and well blended.

6 Return the sauce to the pan and stir in the sun-dried tomatoes and chicken. Bring back to a boil and then simmer for 10 minutes until the chicken is cooked. Adjust the seasoning, if necessary.

7 Drain the pasta thoroughly and toss in the sauce. Serve immediately, garnished with sprigs of fresh mint.

# Sardinian Sausage and Pasta

IN SARDINIA THEY CALL this dish simply "malloreddus," which is the local name for the type of pasta traditionally used to make it.

**INGREDIENTS**

*2 tablespoons olive oil*
*6 garlic cloves*
*7 ounces Italian pure pork sausage, diced small*
*2 small handfuls fresh basil leaves*
*1 can (14 ounces) chopped Italian plum tomatoes*
*a good pinch of saffron strands*
*1 tablespoon granulated sugar*
*3 cups dried* malloreddus *(gnocchi sardi)*
*1 cup freshly grated* Pecorino sardo *cheese*
*salt and ground black pepper*

**Serves 4–6**

1 Heat the oil in a medium skillet or saucepan. Add the garlic, sausage and half the basil leaves. Fry, stirring frequently, until the sausage is browned all over. Remove and discard the garlic Add the tomatoes. Fill the empty can with water, pour it into the pan, then stir in the saffron, sugar, 1 teaspoon salt and pepper to taste. Bring to a boil, lower the heat and simmer for 20–30 minutes, stirring occasionally.

2 Meanwhile, cook the pasta in a pan of salted boiling water according to the package instructions.

3 Drain the pasta and turn it into a warmed bowl. Taste the sauce for seasoning, pour it over the pasta and toss well. Add about one-third of the grated Pecorino and the remaining basil and toss well to mix again. Serve immediately, with the remaining Pecorino sprinkled on top.

**COOKS TIP**

*In Sardinia, a special type of sausage is used for* malloreddus. *It is flavored with aniseed and black pepper and is called* sartizzu sardo. *A good alternative to* sartizzu sardo *would be the piquant* salsiccia piccante. *If, however, you prefer a slightly milder flavor, try* luganega, *which is much more widely available. Some butchers make their own Italian-style sausage on the premises, in which case you can always ask the butcher if he will season it for you with aniseed and black pepper if you want to try and create the authentic taste for yourself.*

# Rigatoni with Bresaola and Bell Peppers

*BRESAOLA*—CURED RAW BEEF—is usually served thinly sliced as an antipasto. Here its strong, almost gamey, flavor is used to good effect.

**INGREDIENTS**

*2 tablespoons olive oil*
*1 small onion, finely chopped*
*5 ounces* bresaola, *cut into thin strips*
*1 small handful fresh basil leaves*
*4 bell peppers (red and orange or yellow), diced*
*½ cup dry white wine*
*1 can (14 ounces) chopped plum tomatoes*
*4 cups dried rigatoni*
*⅔ cup freshly grated Parmesan cheese*
*1 small handful fresh basil leaves*
*salt and ground black pepper*

**Serves 6**

1 Heat the oil in a medium saucepan, add the onion and *bresaola.* Cover the pan and cook over low heat for 5–8 minutes until the onion has softened. Stir in the basil leaves, then add the bell peppers, wine, 1 teaspoon salt and plenty of pepper. Stir well, then simmer for 10–15 minutes.

2 Add the canned tomatoes to the pan and increase the heat to high. Bring to a boil, stirring, then lower the heat and replace the lid again. Simmer gently, stirring occasionally, for 20 minutes or until the bell peppers are very soft and quite creamy. Meanwhile, cook the pasta in a pan of salted boiling water according to the instructions on the package.

3 Drain the cooked pasta and turn it into a warmed bowl. Taste the sauce for seasoning, then pour over the pasta and add about half the Parmesan. Toss well and serve immediately, with the basil leaves and the remaining Parmesan sprinkled on top.

# Pappardelle with Chicken and Mushrooms

RICH AND CREAMY, this is a good supper party dish.

**INGREDIENTS**

*½ ounce dried porcini mushrooms*
*¾ cup warm water*
*2 tablespoons butter*
*1 small leek or 4 scallions, chopped*
*1 garlic clove, crushed*
*1 small handful fresh Italian parsley, coarsely chopped*
*½ cup dry white wine*
*1 cup chicken stock*
*14 ounces fresh or dried pappardelle*
*2 skinless chicken breast fillets, cut into thin strips*
*7 tablespoons mascarpone cheese*
*salt and ground black pepper*
*fresh basil leaves, shredded, to garnish*

**Serves 4**

1 Put the dried mushrooms in a bowl. Pour in the warm water and let soak for 15–20 minutes. Turn into a fine strainer set over a bowl and squeeze the mushrooms with your hands to release as much liquid as possible.

2 Chop the mushrooms finely and set aside the strained soaking liquid until required.

3 Melt the butter in a medium skillet or saucepan, add the chopped mushrooms, leek or scallions, garlic and parsley, with salt and pepper to taste. Cook over low heat, stirring frequently, for about 5 minutes, then pour in the wine and stock and bring to a boil. Lower the heat and simmer for about 5 minutes or until the liquid has reduced and is thickened.

4 Meanwhile, start cooking the pasta in salted boiling water according to the package instructions, adding the reserved soaking liquid from the mushrooms to the water.

5 Add the chicken strips to the sauce and simmer for 5 minutes or until just tender. Add the mascarpone a spoonful at a time, stirring well after each addition, then add one or two spoonfuls of the water used for cooking the pasta. Taste for seasoning.

6 Drain the pasta and turn it into a warmed large bowl. Add the chicken and sauce and toss well. Serve immediately, topped with the shredded basil leaves.

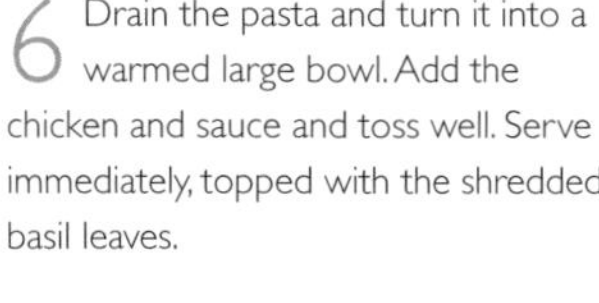

**VARIATIONS**

- *Add 1 cup sliced white or brown mushrooms with the chicken.*
- *Add blanched sprigs of broccoli before the mascarpone in Step 5.*

# Conchiglie with Chicken Livers and Herbs

FRESH HERBS AND CHICKEN livers are a good combination, often used together on crostini in Tuscany. Here they are tossed with pasta shells to make a very tasty supper dish.

**INGREDIENTS**

*¼ cup butter*
*4 ounces pancetta or rindless lean bacon, diced*
*9 ounces frozen chicken livers, thawed, drained and diced*
*2 garlic cloves, crushed*
*2 teaspoons chopped fresh sage*
*2¾ cups dried conchiglie*
*⅔ cup dry white wine*
*4 ripe Italian plum tomatoes, peeled and diced*
*1 tablespoon chopped fresh Italian parsley*
*salt and ground black pepper*

**Serves 4**

1 Melt half the butter in a medium skillet or saucepan, add the pancetta or bacon and fry over medium heat for a few minutes until it is lightly colored but not crisp.

2 Add the chicken livers, garlic, half the sage and plenty of pepper. Increase the heat and toss the livers for about 5 minutes, until they change color all over. Meanwhile, start cooking the pasta according to the instructions on the package.

3 Pour the wine over the chicken livers in the pan and let it sizzle, then lower the heat and simmer gently for 5 minutes. Add the remaining butter to the pan. As soon as it has melted, add the diced tomatoes, toss to mix, then add the remaining sage and the parsley. Stir well. Taste and add salt if needed.

4 Drain the pasta and turn it into a warmed bowl. Pour the sauce over and toss well. Serve immediately.

# Twin Cities Meatballs

SERVE THESE meatballs without gravy as drinks party nibbles.

**INGREDIENTS**

*2 tablespoons butter or margarine*
*½ small onion, very finely chopped*
*2¼ cups ground beef*
*1 cup ground veal*
*2 cups ground pork*
*1 egg*
*½ cup mashed potatoes*
*2 tablespoons finely chopped fresh dill weed or parsley*
*1 garlic clove, crushed*
*1 teaspoon salt*
*½ teaspoon black pepper*
*½ teaspoon ground allspice*
*¼ teaspoon grated nutmeg*
*¾ cup fresh bread crumbs*
*¾ cup milk*
*¼ cup all-purpose flour plus 1 tablespoon extra*
*2 tablespoons olive oil*
*12 ounces fresh or dried fettucini*
*¾ cup evaporated milk*

**Serves 6**

1 Melt the butter or margarine in a large frying pan. Add the onion and cook, stirring, over low heat until softened but not brown, about 8–10 minutes. Remove the pan from the heat. Using a slotted spoon, transfer the cooked onion to a large mixing bowl.

2 Add the beef, veal and pork, the egg, mashed potatoes, dill weed or parsley, garlic, salt, pepper, allspice and nutmeg to the bowl.

3 Put the bread crumbs in a separate small bowl and add the milk. Stir until well moistened, then add to the other ingredients in the large mixing bowl. Mix well.

4 Shape the mixture into balls about 1-inch in diameter.

5 Place ¼ cup of the flour on a plate and roll the meatballs in the flour until coated all over. Shake off the excess flour.

6 Add the olive oil to the frying pan and heat over medium heat. Add the meatballs to the pan and brown on all sides for 8–10 minutes. Shake the pan occasionally to roll the balls so that they color and cook evenly. With a slotted spoon, remove the meatballs to a serving dish. Cover with foil and keep warm.

7 Cook the pasta in salted boiling water until *al dente*.

8 Meanwhile, stir the 1 tablespoon of flour into the fat in the frying pan. Add the evaporated milk and mix in thoroughly with a small whisk. Simmer for 3–4 minutes.

9 Drain the pasta and serve hot with the meatballs and gravy poured over.

# Peasant Bolognese

A SPICY VERSION of a popular dish. Worcestershire sauce and chorizo sausages add an extra element to this perfect family standby.

**INGREDIENTS**

*1 tablespoon oil*
*2 cups ground beef*
*1 onion, chopped*
*1 teaspoon chili powder*
*1 tablespoon Worcestershire sauce*
*2 tablespoons all-purpose flour*
*⅔ cup beef stock*
*4 chorizo sausages*
*2 ounces baby corn*
*7 ounces canned chopped tomatoes*
*1 tablespoon chopped fresh basil*
*salt and ground black pepper*
*fresh basil, to garnish*
*1 pound cooked spaghetti, to serve*
**Serves 4**

1 Heat the oil in a large pan and fry the ground beef for 5 minutes. Add the onion and chili powder to the pan and cook for a further 3 minutes.

2 Stir the Worcestershire sauce and flour into the pan, making sure it is well combined.

3 Continue to cook for 1 minute then pour in the stock.

4 Slice the chirozo sausages and halve the corn lengthwise.

5 Stir the sliced sausages, tomatoes, corn and chopped basil into the pan. Season and bring the sauce to a boil. Reduce the heat and simmer for 30 minutes.

6 Serve hot, with spaghetti, garnished with fresh basil leaves.

### Cook's Tip

*Make the Bolognese sauce and freeze in conveniently sized portions for up to two months.*

# Fettuccine with Ham and Peas

THIS SIMPLE DISH MAKES a very good first course for six people, or a main course for three to four. The ingredients are all easily available from the supermarket, so the recipe makes an ideal impromptu supper.

**INGREDIENTS**

*1/4 cup butter*
*1 small onion, finely chopped*
*1 3/4 cups fresh or frozen peas*
*scant 1/2 cup chicken stock*
*1/2 teaspoon granulated sugar*
*2/3 cup dry white wine*
*12 ounces fresh fettuccine*
*3-ounce piece cooked ham, cut into bite-size chunks*
*1 1/3 cups freshly grated Parmesan cheese*
*salt and ground black pepper*

**Serves 3–6**

1 Melt the butter in a medium skillet or saucepan, add the onion and cook over low heat for about 5 minutes until softened but not colored. Add the peas, stock and sugar, with salt and pepper to taste.

2 Bring to a boil, then lower the heat and simmer for 3–5 minutes or until the peas are tender. Add the wine, increase the heat and boil until the wine has reduced.

3 Cook the pasta according to the instructions on the package. When it is almost ready, add the ham to the sauce, with about a third of the grated Parmesan. Heat through, stirring, then taste for seasoning.

4 Drain the pasta and turn it into a warmed large bowl. Pour the sauce over the pasta and toss well. Serve immediately, sprinkled with the remaining grated Parmesan.

# Pappardelle with Rabbit Sauce

THIS RICH-TASTING DISH comes from the north of Italy, where rabbit sauces for pasta are very popular.

**INGREDIENTS**

*½ ounce dried porcini mushrooms*
*¾ cup warm water*
*1 small onion*
*½ carrot*
*½ celery stalk*
*2 bay leaves*
*2 tablespoons butter*
*1 tablespoon olive oil*
*1½ ounces pancetta or rindless lean bacon, chopped*
*1 tablespoon coarsely chopped fresh Italian parsley, plus extra to garnish*
*9 ounces boneless rabbit meat*
*6 tablespoons dry white wine*
*7 ounces canned chopped Italian plum tomatoes or scant 1 cup tomato sauce*
*11 ounces fresh or dried pappardelle*
*salt and ground black pepper*

**Serves 4**

1 Put the dried mushrooms in a bowl, pour over the warm water and leave to soak for 15–20 minutes. Finely chop the vegetables, either in a food processor or by hand. Make a tear in each bay leaf, so that they will release their flavor when added to the sauce.

2 Heat the butter and oil in a skillet or medium saucepan until just sizzling. Add the chopped vegetables, pancetta or bacon and the parsley and cook for about 5 minutes.

3 Add the pieces of rabbit and fry on both sides for 3–4 minutes. Pour the wine over and let it reduce for a few minutes, then add the tomatoes or tom ato sauce. Drain the mushrooms and pour the soaking liquid into the pan. Chop the mushrooms and add them to the mixture, with the bay leaves and salt and pepper to taste. Stir well, cover and simmer for 35–40 minutes until the rabbit is tender, stirring occasionally.

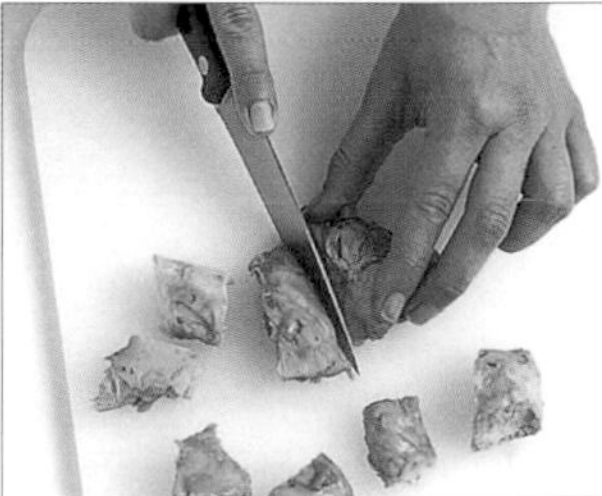

4 Remove the pan from the heat and lift out the pieces of rabbit with a slotted spoon. Cut them into bite-size chunks and stir them into the sauce. Remove and discard the bay leaves. Taste the sauce and add more salt and pepper, if needed. Cook the pasta according to the instructions on the package. Meanwhile, reheat the sauce. Drain the pasta and toss with the sauce in a warmed bowl. Serve immediately, sprinkled with parsley.

# Tagliatelle with Deviled Kidneys

ASK YOUR BUTCHER to prepare the kidneys for you if you prefer.

**INGREDIENTS**

*8–10 lambs' kidneys*
*1 tablespoon sunflower oil*
*2 tablespoons butter*
*2 teaspoons paprika*
*1–2 teaspoons mild grainy mustard*
*salt*
*8 ounces fresh tagliatelle*
*chopped fresh parsley, to garnish*

**Serves 4**

1 Cut the kidneys in half and neatly cut out the white cores with scissors. Cut the kidneys in half again if very large.

2 Heat the oil and butter together. Add the kidneys and cook, turning frequently, for about 2 minutes. Blend the paprika and mustard together with a little salt and stir into the pan.

3 Continue cooking the kidneys, basting frequently, for a further 3–4 minutes.

4 Cook the pasta for about 10–12 minutes, or according to the instructions on the package. Serve the kidneys and their sauce, topped with the chopped fresh parsley, and accompanied by the pasta.

# Golden-topped Eliche

WHEN IT COMES TO the children helping you to plan the menus, this is the sort of dish that always wins hands down. It is also perfect for "padding out" if you have to feed eight instead of four people.

**INGREDIENTS**

*2 cups dried eliche*
*⅔ cup chopped cooked ham, beef or turkey*
*12 ounces par-cooked mixed vegetables, such as carrots, cauliflower, beans, etc*
*1–2 teaspoons oil*

***For the cheese sauce***

*2 tablespoons butter*
*2 tablespoons all-purpose flour*
*1¼ cups milk*
*1½ cups grated Cheddar cheese*
*1–2 teaspoons mustard*
*salt and ground black pepper*

**Serves 4–6**

1 Cook the pasta according to the instructions on the package. Drain and place in a flameproof dish with the chopped meat, the mixed vegetables and oil.

2 Melt the butter in a saucepan, stir in the flour and cook for 1 minute, stirring. Remove from the heat and gradually stir in the milk. Return to the heat, bring to a boil, stirring and cook for 2 minutes. Add half the cheese, the mustard and seasoning to taste.

3 Spoon the sauce over the meat and vegetables. Sprinkle with the rest of the cheese and cook under the broiler until golden and bubbling. Let stand for a few minutes before serving.

**VARIATION**

*Any mature hard cheese is suitable for the topping. Try Monterey Jack as an alternative, or Red Leicester which will give the sauce a deep golden color.*

# Fusilli Col Buco with Pepperoni

A WARMING SUPPER DISH, perfect for a cold winter's night. All types of sausage are suitable, but if using raw sausages, add them with the onion to cook thoroughly.

**INGREDIENTS**

*1 onion*
*1 red bell pepper*
*1 green bell pepper*
*2 tablespoons olive oil, plus extra for tossing the pasta*
*1¾ pounds canned chopped tomatoes*
*2 tablespoons tomato paste*
*2 teaspoons paprika*
*6 ounces pepperoni or chorizo sausage*
*3 tablespoons chopped fresh parsley*
*1 pound dried fusilli col buco*
*salt and ground black pepper*
**Serves 4**

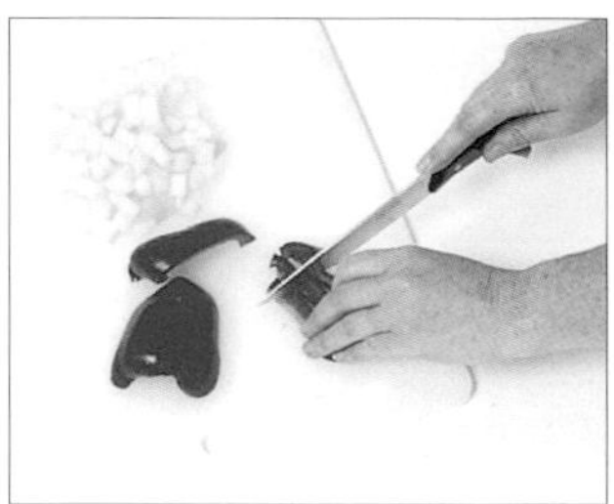

1 Chop the onion. Halve, core and seed the bell peppers. Cut the flesh into dice.

2 Heat the oil in a medium saucepan, add the onion and cook for 2–3 minutes until beginning to color and soften, but before they go brown.

3 Add the bell peppers, tomatoes, tomato paste and paprika to the pan and bring to a boil. Simmer uncovered for about 15–20 minutes until reduced and thickened.

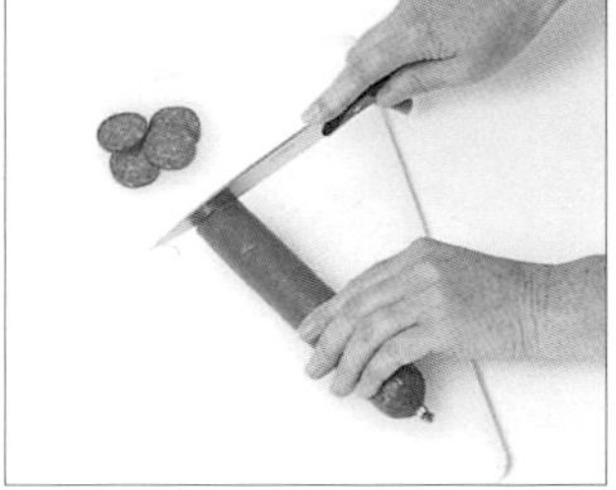

4 Slice the pepperoni or chorizo and stir into the sauce with 2 tablespoons of the chopped parsley. Season to taste with salt and pepper.

5 While the sauce is simmering, cook the pasta in plenty of boiling salted water according to the instructions on the package. Drain well. Toss the pasta with the remaining parsley in a little extra olive oil. Divide among four warmed bowls and top with the prepared sauce.

# Tagliatelle with Prosciutto and Parmesan

THIS IS A REALLY SIMPLE DISH, prepared in minutes from the best ingredients.

**INGREDIENTS**

*4 ounces prosciutto*
*1 pound fresh or dried tagliatelle*
*6 tablespoons butter*
*½ cup freshly grated Parmesan cheese*
*salt and ground black pepper*
*a few fresh sage leaves, to garnish*

**Serves 4**

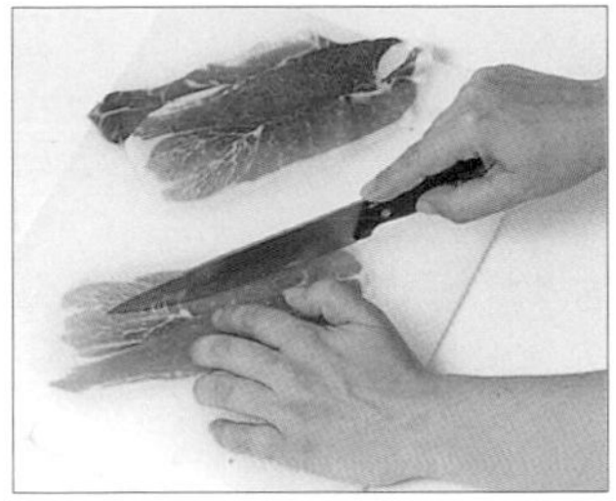

1 Cut the prosciutto into strips the same width as the tagliatelle. Cook the pasta in plenty of boiling salted water according to the instructions on the package.

2 Meanwhile, melt the butter gently in a saucepan, stir in the prosciutto strips and heat through over very gentle heat, being careful not to let them color.

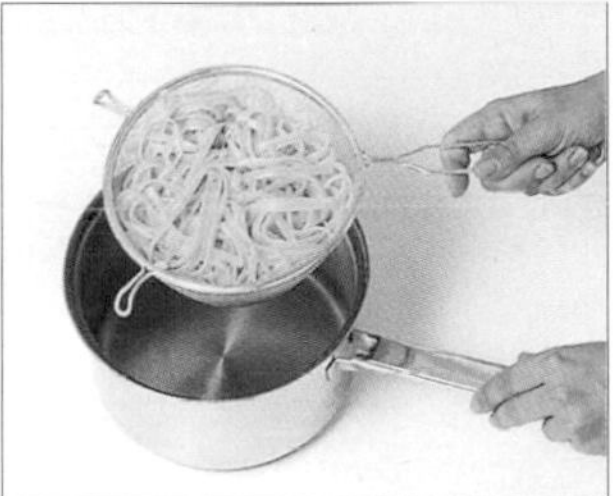

3 Drain the tagliatelle through a colander and pile into a warmed serving dish.

4 Sprinkle the Parmesan cheese over and pour the buttery prosciutto on the top. Season well with black pepper and garnish with the sage leaves.

# Bucatini with Sausage and Pancetta

THIS IS A VERY RICH and satisfying main course dish. It hardly needs grated Parmesan cheese as an accompaniment, but you can hand some round in a separate bowl if you wish.

**INGREDIENTS**

*4 ounces pork sausage*
*1 can (14 ounces) Italian plum tomatoes*
*1 tablespoon olive oil*
*1 garlic clove, crushed*
*4 ounces pancetta or rindless lean bacon, coarsely chopped*
*2 tablespoons chopped fresh Italian parsley*
*14 ounces dried bucatini*
*4–5 tablespoons* panna da cucina *or heavy cream*
*2 egg yolks*
*salt and ground black pepper*
**Serves 4**

1 Remove any casing from the sausage and break the meat up with a knife. Purée the tomatoes in a food processor or blender.

2 Heat the oil in a medium skillet or saucepan, add the garlic and fry over low heat for 1–2 minutes. Remove the garlic with a slotted spoon and discard it.

3 Add the pancetta or bacon and the pork sausage and cook over medium heat for 3–4 minutes. Stir constantly with a wooden spoon to break up the sausage—it will become brown and look crumbly.

4 Add the puréed tomatoes to the pan with half the parsley and salt and pepper to taste. Stir well and bring to a boil, scraping up any sediment from the sausage that has stuck to the bottom of the pan.

5 Lower the heat, cover and simmer for 30 minutes, stirring occasionally. Taste the sauce for seasoning.

6 Meanwhile, cook the pasta according to the instructions on the package. Put the cream and egg yolks in a warmed large bowl and mix with a fork. As soon as the pasta is *al dente*, drain it well and add it to the bowl of cream mixture. Toss until the pasta is coated, then pour the sausage sauce over the pasta and toss again. Serve immediately, sprinkled with the remaining parsley.

**COOK'S TIPS**

- *To save time puréeing the tomatoes, use passata or tomato sauce.*
- *For authenticity, buy* salsiccia a metro, *a pure pork sausage sold in lengths at Italian specialty stores.*
- *Bucatini is a long hollow pasta that looks like hard drinking straws; spaghetti works equally well.*

# Rigatoni with Pork

THIS IS AN EXCELLENT meat sauce using ground pork rather than the more usual ground beef. Here it is served with rigatoni, a short tubular pasta shape, but you could serve it with tagliatelle or spaghetti to make a pork version of Bolognese.

**INGREDIENTS**

*1 small onion*
*½ carrot*
*½ celery stalk*
*2 garlic cloves*
*2 tablespoons butter*
*2 tablespoons olive oil*
*5 ounces ground pork*
*4 tablespoons dry white wine*
*1 can (14 ounces) chopped Italian plum tomatoes*
*a few fresh basil leaves, plus extra basil leaves, to garnish*
*3½ cups dried rigatoni*
*salt and ground black pepper*
*freshly shaved Parmesan cheese, to serve*

**Serves 4**

1 Chop all the fresh vegetables finely, either in a food processor or by hand. Heat the butter and oil in a large skillet or saucepan until just sizzling, add the chopped vegetables and cook over medium heat, stirring frequently, for 3–4 minutes.

2 Add the ground pork and cook gently for 2–3 minutes, breaking up any lumps in the meat with a wooden spoon.

3 Lower the heat and fry for a further 2–3 minutes, stirring frequently, then stir in the wine. Mix in the tomatoes, whole basil leaves, salt to taste and plenty of pepper. Bring to a boil, then lower the heat, cover and simmer for 40 minutes, stirring occasionally.

4 Cook the pasta according to the instructions on the package. Just before draining it, add a ladleful or two of the cooking water to the sauce. Stir well, then taste the sauce for seasoning.

5 Drain the pasta, add it to the pan of sauce and toss well. Serve immediately, sprinkled with the shredded basil and shaved Parmesan.

**VARIATION**

*To give the sauce a more intense flavor, soak ½ ounce dried porcini mushrooms in ¾ cup warm water for 15–20 minutes, then drain, chop and add with the meat.*

# Cavatappi with Mushroom and Chorizo

THE DELICIOUS COMBINATION of wild mushrooms and spicy sausage make this a tempting supper dish.

**INGREDIENTS**

*12 ounces dried cavatappi*
*4 tablespoons olive oil*
*1 garlic clove, chopped*
*1 celery stalk, chopped*
*8 ounces chorizo sausage, sliced*
*8 ounces mixed mushrooms, such as oyster, brown cap and shiitake*
*1 tablespoon lemon juice*
*2 tablespoons chopped fresh oregano*
*salt and ground black pepper*
*finely chopped fresh parsley, to garnish*

**Serves 4**

1 Cook the pasta in plenty of boiling salted water according to the instructions on the package.

2 Heat the oil in a frying pan and cook the garlic and celery for 5 minutes until the celery is softened but not browned.

**COOK'S TIP**

*Use any combination of mushrooms for this full-bodied sauce, but take care not to overcook them or they will lose their robust, earthy flavor.*

3 Add the chorizo and cook for 5 minutes, stirring occasionally, until browned.

4 Next add the mushrooms, either chopped or whole, depending on their size, and cook for a further 4 minutes, stirring occasionally, until they are slightly softened.

5 Stir in the remaining ingredients, and heat through.

6 Drain the pasta well through a colander and turn into a large serving dish. Add the sauce to the pasta and toss to coat. Serve immediately, garnished with finely chopped fresh parsley.

# Penne with Chicken and Ham Sauce

A MEAL IN ITSELF, this colorful pasta sauce is perfect for lunch or supper.

**INGREDIENTS**

*3 cups dried penne*
*2 tablespoons butter*
*1 onion, chopped*
*1 garlic clove, chopped*
*1 bay leaf*
*1¾ cups dry white wine*
*⅔ cup crème fraîche*
*8 ounces cooked chicken, skinned, boned and diced*
*4 ounces cooked lean ham, diced*
*4 ounces Gouda cheese, grated*
*1 tablespoon chopped fresh mint*
*salt and ground black pepper*
*finely shredded fresh mint, to garnish*

**Serves 4**

1 Cook the pasta in plenty of boiling salted water according to the instructions on the package.

2 Heat the butter in a large frying pan and fry the onion for about 10 minutes, or until softened.

3 Add the garlic, bay leaf and wine and bring to a boil. Boil rapidly until reduced by about half. Remove the bay leaf, then stir in the crème fraîche and return to a boil.

4 Add the chicken, ham and grated Gouda cheese and simmer for 5 minutes, stirring occasionally until heated through.

5 Add the chopped fresh mint and season to taste.

6 Drain the pasta thoroughly and turn it into a large serving dish. Toss the pasta with the sauce, garnish with finely shredded fresh mint and serve immediately.

# Spaghetti with Bacon and Tomato Sauce

THIS SUBSTANTIAL SAUCE is a meal in itself, so serve it up as a warming winter supper.

**INGREDIENTS**

*1 tablespoon olive oil*
*8 ounces lean bacon, rinded and coarsely chopped*
*9 ounces fresh or dried spaghetti*
*1 teaspoon chili powder*
*1 quantity Classic Tomato Sauce (see Curly Lasagne with Classic Tomato Sauce)*
*salt and ground black pepper*
*coarsely chopped fresh Italian parsley, to garnish*
**Serves 4**

1 Heat the oil in large frying pan and fry the bacon for about 10 minutes, stirring occasionally until crisp and golden.

2 Cook the pasta following the instructions on the package, until *al dente.*

3 Add the chili powder to the bacon and cook for 2 minutes. Stir in the tomato sauce and bring to a boil. Cover and simmer for 10 minutes. Season with salt and pepper to taste.

4 Drain the pasta thoroughly and toss it together with the sauce. Serve garnished with the coarsely chopped fresh parsley.

# Tagliatelle with Pea and Ham Sauce

A COLORFUL SAUCE, this is ideal served with crusty Italian or French bread.

**INGREDIENTS**

*12 ounces fresh or dried tagliatelle*
*1½ cups fresh shelled peas*
*1¼ cups light cream*
*⅓ cup freshly grated fontina cheese*
*3 ounces prosciutto crudo, sliced into strips*
*salt and ground black pepper*
**Serves 4**

1 Cook the pasta following the instructions on the package until *al dente.*

2 Plunge the peas into a pan of boiling salted water and cook for about 7 minutes or until tender. Drain.

3 Place the cream and half the fontina cheese in a small saucepan and heat gently, stirring continuously until heated through.

4 Drain the pasta thoroughly and turn it into a large serving bowl. Toss together the pasta, ham and peas and pour on the sauce. Add the remaining cheese and season with salt and pepper to taste.

# Two-way Chicken and Vegetables

THIS TENDER slow-cooked chicken makes a tasty lunch or supper, with the stock and remaining vegetables providing a nourishing soup as a second meal.

**INGREDIENTS**

*3½ pounds chicken*
*2 onions, quartered*
*3 carrots, thickly sliced*
*2 celery stalks, chopped*
*1 parsnip or turnip, thickly sliced*
*½ cup white mushrooms, with stalks, coarsely chopped*
*1–2 fresh thyme sprigs or 1 teaspoon dried thyme*
*4 bay leaves*
*large bunch of fresh parsley*
*pasta, snow peas or green beans, to serve with the chicken*
*1 cup dried whole wheat pasta shapes, for the soup*
*sea salt and ground black pepper*

**Serves 6**

1 Trim the chicken of any extra fat. Put it in a flameproof casserole and add the vegetables and herbs. Pour in water to cover. Bring to a boil over medium heat, skimming off any scum. When the water boils, lower the heat and simmer for 2–3 hours.

2 Carve the meat neatly, discarding the skin and bones, but returning any small pieces of chicken to the pan. Serve the chicken with some of the vegetables from the pan, plus the pasta of your choice and snow peas or green beans, if you like.

3 Remove any large pieces of parsley and thyme from the pan, let the remaining mixture cool, then chill it overnight. Next day, lift off the fat that has solidified on the surface. Reheat the soup gently.

4 When the soup comes to a boil, add the pasta shapes, with salt, if required, and cook for 10–12 minutes or until the pasta is tender. Season the soup with salt and plenty of ground black pepper and garnish with sprigs of fresh parsley.

# Pork Meatballs with Spaghetti

SERVE THESE TASTY MEATBALLS on a bed of freshly cooked corn spaghetti, which is gluten-free.

**INGREDIENTS**

*1 pound lean ground pork*
*1 leek, finely chopped*
*1 ½ cups mushrooms, finely chopped*
*1 tablespoon chopped fresh thyme*
*1 tablespoon tomato paste*
*1 egg, beaten*
*2 tablespoons potato flour*
*1 tablespoon sunflower oil*
*12 ounces–1 ¼ pounds fresh or dried corn spaghetti*
*fresh thyme sprigs, to garnish*

***For the tomato sauce***

*1 onion, finely chopped*
*1 carrot, finely chopped*
*1 celery stalk, finely chopped*
*1 garlic clove, crushed*
*1 ½ pounds ripe tomatoes, skinned, seeded and chopped*
*⅔ cup dry white wine*
*⅔ cup well-flavored vegetable stock*
*1 tablespoon tomato paste*
*1 tablespoon chopped fresh basil*
*salt and ground black pepper*

**Serves 6**

1 Preheat the oven to 350°F. Put the pork, leek, mushrooms, chopped thyme, tomato paste, egg and potato flour in a bowl and mix together. Shape into small balls, place on a plate, cover and chill.

2 Place all the sauce ingredients in a small saucepan, season to taste, then bring to a boil. Boil, uncovered, for 10 minutes until thickened.

3 Heat the oil in a frying pan, add the meatballs and cook in batches until lightly browned.

4 Place the meatballs in a shallow, ovenproof dish and pour the sauce over. Cover and bake for 1 hour.

5 Meanwhile, cook the pasta in a pan of lightly salted, boiling water for 8–12 minutes, or according to the package instructions, until *al dente*. Rinse under boiling water and drain. Divide the pasta into warmed bowls, spoon the meatballs and sauce over the top and serve garnished with fresh thyme.

# Rigatoni with Meat and Cheese Sauce

THE TWO SAUCES complement each other perfectly in this wonderfully flavorsome dish.

**INGREDIENTS**

*3 cups dried rigatoni*
*salt and ground black pepper*
*fresh basil sprigs, to garnish*

***For the meat sauce***

*1 tablespoon olive oil*
*3 cups ground beef*
*1 onion, chopped*
*1 garlic clove, chopped*
*1 can (14 ounces) chopped tomatoes*
*1 tablespoon mixed dried herbs*
*2 tablespoons tomato paste*

***For the cheese sauce***

*¼ cup butter*
*½ cup all-purpose flour*
*1¾ cups milk*
*2 egg yolks*
*½ cup freshly grated Parmesan cheese*

**Serves 4**

1 To make the meat sauce, heat the oil in a large frying pan and fry the beef for 10 minutes, stirring occasionally until browned all over. Add the onion to the pan and cook for 5 minutes, stirring occasionally.

2 Stir in the garlic, tomatoes, herbs and tomato paste. Bring to a boil, cover, and simmer for about 30 minutes.

3 Meanwhile, to make the cheese sauce, melt the butter in a small saucepan, then add in the flour and cook for 2 minutes, stirring constantly.

4 Remove the pan from the heat and gradually pour in the milk, stirring constantly. Return the pan to the heat and bring to a boil, stirring the mixture occasionally, until creamy and thickened.

5 Add the egg yolks, cheese and seasoning and stir until the sauce is well blended.

6 Preheat the broiler. Meanwhile, cook the pasta in plenty of salted boiling water according to the instructions on the package. Drain thoroughly and turn into a large mixing bowl. Pour the meat sauce over and toss to coat.

7 Divide the pasta among four flameproof dishes. Spoon over the cheese sauce and place under the grill until brown. Serve immediately, garnished with fresh basil.

# Spaghetti in a Cream and Bacon Sauce

THIS IS A LIGHT and creamy sauce flavored with bacon and lightly cooked eggs.

**INGREDIENTS**

*12 ounces fresh or dried spaghetti*
*1 tablespoon olive oil*
*1 onion, chopped*
*4 ounces rindless lean bacon or pancetta, diced*
*1 garlic clove, chopped*
*3 eggs*
*1 ¼ cups heavy cream*
*2 ounces freshly grated Parmesan cheese*
*chopped fresh basil, to garnish*
**Serves 4**

1 Cook the pasta in plenty of boiling salted water according to the instructions on the package.

2 Heat the oil in a frying pan and fry the onion and bacon or pancetta for 10 minutes, until softened. Stir in the garlic and fry for a further 2 minutes, stirring occasionally.

3 Meanwhile, beat the eggs in a bowl, then stir in the cream and seasoning. Add the Parmesan cheese and stir into the egg and cream mixture.

4 Stir the cream mixture into the onion and bacon or pancetta and cook over low heat for a few minutes, stirring continuously, until heated through. Season to taste.

5 Drain the pasta thoroughly and turn into a large serving dish. Pour the sauce over and toss to coat. Serve immediately, garnished with chopped fresh basil.

# Classic Meat Sauce

THIS IS A RICH meat sauce which is ideal to serve with all types of pasta. The sauce definitely improves if kept overnight in the refrigerator. This allows the flavors time to mature.

**INGREDIENTS**

*4 cups ground beef*
*4 ounces lean bacon, rinded and chopped*
*1 onion, chopped*
*2 celery stalks, chopped*
*1 tablespoon all-purpose flour*
*⅔ cup chicken stock or water*
*3 tablespoons tomato paste*
*1 garlic clove, chopped*
*3 tablespoons chopped mixed fresh herbs, such as oregano, parsley, marjoram and chives or 1 tablespoon mixed dried herbs*
*1 tablespoon red currant jelly*
*12 ounces dried pasta shapes, such as fusilli*
*salt and ground black pepper*
*chopped oregano, to garnish*
**Serves 4**

1 Heat a large saucepan and fry the beef and bacon for about 10 minutes, stirring occasionally until lightly browned.

2 Add the chopped onion and celery and cook for 2 minutes, stirring occasionally.

**COOK'S TIP**

*The red currant jelly helps to draw out the flavor of the tomato paste. You can use cranberry sauce or a sweet chutney instead, if you like.*

3 Stir in the flour and cook for 2 minutes, stirring continuously.

4 Pour in the stock or water and bring to a boil.

5 Stir in the tomato paste, garlic, herbs, red currant jelly and seasoning. Bring to a boil, cover and simmer for about 30 minutes.

6 Cook the pasta in plenty of boiling salted water according to the instructions on the package until *al dente*. Drain thoroughly and turn into a large serving dish. Pour the sauce over and toss to coat. Serve the pasta immediately, garnished with chopped fresh oregano.

# Penne with Pancetta and Cream

THIS MAKES a gloriously rich supper dish. Follow it with a simple salad.

**INGREDIENTS**

*2¾ cups dried penne*
*2 tablespoons olive oil*
*1 small onion, finely chopped*
*6 ounces pancetta, any rinds removed, cut into bite-size strips*
*1–2 garlic cloves, crushed*
*5 egg yolks*
*¾ cup heavy cream*
*1⅓ cups grated Parmesan cheese, plus extra to serve*
*salt and freshly ground black pepper*
**Serves 3–4**

### COOK'S TIP

*Serve this dish the moment it is ready or it will not be hot enough. Having added the egg yolks, don't return the pan to the heat or attempt to reheat the pasta and cream sauce together or the egg yolks will scramble and give the pasta a curdled appearance.*

1 Cook the penne in a large pan of rapidly boiling salted water for about 10 minutes or until *al dente*.

2 Meanwhile, heat the oil in a large flameproof casserole. Add the onion and cook gently for about 5 minutes, stirring, until softened. Add the pancetta and garlic. Cook over medium heat until the pancetta is cooked but not crisp. Remove the pan from the heat and set aside.

3 Put the egg yolks in a jug and add the cream and Parmesan cheese. Grind in plenty of black pepper. Beat well to mix.

4 Drain the penne thoroughly, turn into the casserole and toss over medium to high heat until the pancetta mixture is evenly mixed with the pasta.

5 Remove from the heat, pour in the egg yolk mixture and toss well to combine. Spoon into a large shallow serving dish, grind a little black pepper over and sprinkle with some of the extra Parmesan. Serve the rest of the Parmesan separately.

# Cannelloni Stuffed with Meat

CANNELLONI ARE RECTANGLES of home-made egg pasta which are spread with a filling, rolled up and baked in a sauce. In this recipe, they are baked in a béchamel sauce.

**INGREDIENTS**

*2 tablespoons olive oil*
*1 onion, very finely chopped*
*1 ½ cups very lean ground beef*
*½ cup finely chopped cooked ham*
*1 tablespoon chopped fresh parsley*
*2 tablespoons tomato paste, softened in 1 tablespoon warm water*
*1 egg*
*1 quantity Pasta with Eggs*
*3 cups béchamel sauce*
*½ cup freshly grated Parmesan cheese*
*3 tablespoons butter*
*salt and ground black pepper*

**Serves 6–8**

1 Prepare the meat filling by heating the oil in a medium saucepan. Add the onion and sauté gently until translucent. Stir in the beef, crumbling it with a fork, and stirring constantly until it has lost its raw red color. Cook for about 3–4 minutes.

2 Remove from the heat and turn the beef mixture into a large bowl with the ham and parsley. Add the tomato paste mixture and the egg, and mix well to combine. Season with salt and pepper. Set aside.

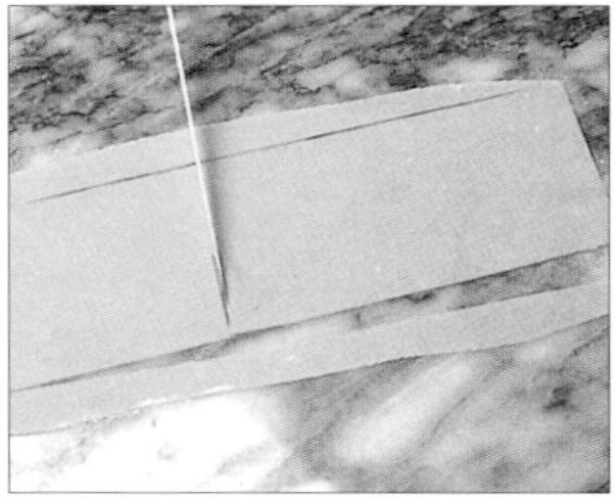

3 If you are making the pasta yourself, do not let it dry before cutting it into rectangles, about 5–6 inches long and as wide as they come from the machine (3 inches if you are not using a pasta machine).

4 Bring a very large pan of water to a boil. Place a large bowl of cold water near the stove. Cover a large counter with a tablecloth. Add salt to the rapidly boiling water. Drop in three or four of the egg pasta rectangles. Cook very briefly, for about 30 seconds. Remove them from the pan and plunge them into the cold water, shake off the excess and lay them out flat on the tablecloth. Continue until all the pasta has been cooked in this way.

5 Preheat the oven to 425°F. Select a shallow baking dish large enough to take all the cannelloni in one layer. Butter the base and sides of the dish and smear about 2–3 tablespoons of béchamel sauce over the base.

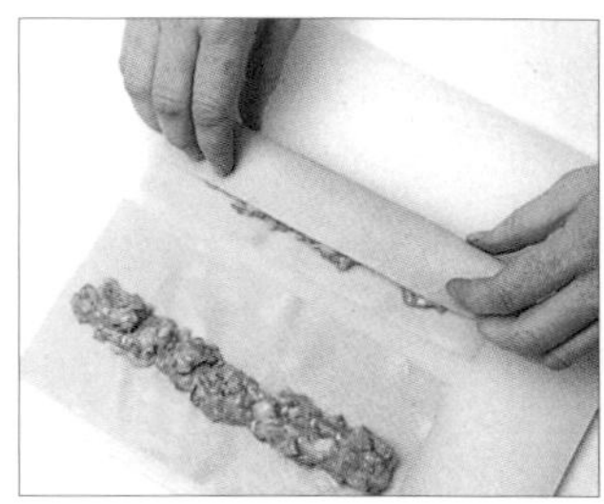

6 Stir about one-third of the remaining sauce into the meat filling. Spread a thin layer of filling on each pasta rectangle. Roll the rectangles up loosely starting from a long side, jelly roll style. Place the filled cannelloni in the baking dish with their open edges underneath.

7 Spoon the rest of the sauce over the cannelloni, pushing a little down between each pasta roll. Sprinkle the top with the grated Parmesan and dot with butter. Bake in the oven for about 20 minutes. Let rest for 5–8 minutes before serving on warmed plates.

# Vegetables and Vegetarian

Pasta really comes into its own when it is served with a vegetable sauce. After all, when pasta was first "invented" it was a food for the poor, and vegetables were often all they could afford.

Vegetable sauces are invariably simple, in fact the simpler the better. Modern recipes often consist of nothing more elaborate than chopped or sliced raw vegetables "cooked" by the heat of freshly drained pasta. Color, crunch and flavor are all retained, along with maximum nutritive value.

Almost all the recipes in this chapter can be cooked in a very short time, making them perfect for quick after-work suppers. Not all of them contain vegetables; some simply consist of butter and herbs, cheese and pepper, garlic and oil. These are the easiest of all pasta sauces to make, and some of the best.

Traditional vegetable sauces come from the south of Italy, where commercially dried pasta is favored more than fresh. Generally speaking, dried pasta does seem to be the best choice for serving with vegetables, but for extra nutritional value there is no reason why fresh, egg-enriched pasta cannot be used.

# Trenette with Pesto, Green Beans and Potatoes

In Liguria, it is traditional to serve pesto with trenette, green beans and diced potatoes. The ingredients for making fresh pesto are quite expensive, so the green beans and potatoes are added to help make the pesto go further.

**INGREDIENTS**

*about 40 fresh basil leaves*
*2 garlic cloves, thinly sliced*
*1½ tablespoons pine nuts*
*3 tablespoons freshly grated Parmesan cheese, plus extra to serve*
*2 tablespoons freshly grated Pecorino cheese, plus extra to serve*
*4 tablespoons extra virgin olive oil*
*2 potatoes, total weight about 9 ounces*
*3½ ounces green beans*
*12 ounces dried trenette*
*salt and ground black pepper*
**Serves 4**

1 Put the basil leaves, garlic, pine nuts and cheeses in a blender or food processor and process for about 5 seconds. Add half the olive oil and a pinch of salt and process for 5 seconds more. Stop the machine, remove the lid and scrape down the side of the bowl. Add the remaining oil and process for 5–10 seconds.

2 Cut the potatoes in half lengthwise. Slice each half crosswise into ¼-inch thick slices. Top and tail the beans, then cut them into ¾-inch pieces. Plunge the potatoes and beans into a large saucepan of salted boiling water and boil, uncovered, for 5 minutes.

3 Add the pasta, bring the water back to a boil, stir well, then cook for 5–7 minutes or until the pasta is *al dente*.

4 Meanwhile, put the pesto in a large bowl and add 3–4 tablespoons of the water used for cooking the pasta. Mix well.

5 Drain the pasta and vegetables, add them to the pesto and toss well. Serve immediately on warmed plates, with extra grated Parmesan and Pecorino handed separately.

**Cook's Tips**

*• Don't worry if the potatoes break up during cooking—this will add to the creaminess of the finished dish.*
*• The pesto can be made up to 2–3 days in advance and kept in a bowl in the refrigerator until needed. Pour a thin film of olive oil over the surface of the pesto and cover the bowl tightly with plastic wrap before refrigerating.*
*• Trenette is the traditional Ligurian pasta that is served with pesto, but if you find it difficult to obtain you can use bavette or linguine instead. The two-colored paglia e fieno would be another good choice.*

# Paglia e Fieno with Sun-dried Tomatoes and Radicchio

THIS IS A LIGHT, MODERN PASTA dish of the kind served in fashionable restaurants. It is the presentation that sets it apart, not the preparation, which is very quick and easy.

**INGREDIENTS**

*3 tablespoons pine nuts*
*12 ounces dried paglia e fieno*
*3 tablespoons extra virgin olive oil*
*2 tablespoons sun-dried tomato paste*
*2 pieces drained sun-dried tomatoes in olive oil, cut into very thin slivers*
*1½ ounces radicchio leaves, finely shredded*
*4–6 scallions, thinly sliced into rings*
*salt and ground black pepper*
**Serves 4**

1 Put the pine nuts in a non-stick frying pan and toss over low to medium heat for 1–2 minutes or until they are lightly toasted and golden. Remove and set aside.

2 Cook the pasta according to the package instructions, keeping the colors separate by using two pans.

3 While the pasta is cooking, heat 1 tablespoon of the oil in a medium skillet or saucepan. Add the sun-dried tomato paste and the sun-dried tomatoes, then stir in 2 ladlefuls of the water used for cooking the pasta. Simmer until the sauce is slightly reduced, stirring constantly.

4 Mix in the shredded radicchio, then taste and season if necessary. Keep on low heat. Drain the paglia e fieno, keeping the colors separate, and return the noodles to the pans in which they were cooked. Add about 1 tablespoon oil to each pan and toss over medium to high heat until the pasta is glistening with the oil.

5 Arrange a portion of green and white pasta in each of four warmed bowls, then spoon the sun-dried tomato and radicchio mixture in the center. Sprinkle the scallions and toasted pine nuts decoratively over the top and serve immediately. Before eating, each diner should toss the sauce ingredients with the pasta to mix well.

**COOK'S TIP**

*If you find the presentation too fiddly, you can toss the sun-dried tomato and radicchio mixture with the pasta in one large warmed bowl before serving, then serve it sprinkled with the scallions and toasted pine nuts.*

# Penne with Artichokes

ARTICHOKES ARE A VERY popular vegetable in Italy, and are often used in sauces for pasta. This sauce is garlicky and richly flavored, the perfect dinner party first course during the globe artichoke season.

**INGREDIENTS**

*juice of ½–1 lemon*
*2 globe artichokes*
*2 tablespoons olive oil*
*1 small fennel bulb, thinly sliced, with feathery tops reserved*
*1 onion, finely chopped*
*4 garlic cloves, finely chopped*
*1 handful fresh Italian parsley, coarsely chopped*
*1 can (14 ounce) chopped Italian plum tomatoes*
*⅔ cup dry white wine*
*3 cups dried penne*
*2 teaspoons capers, chopped*
*salt and ground black pepper*
*freshly grated Parmesan cheese, to serve*
**Serves 6**

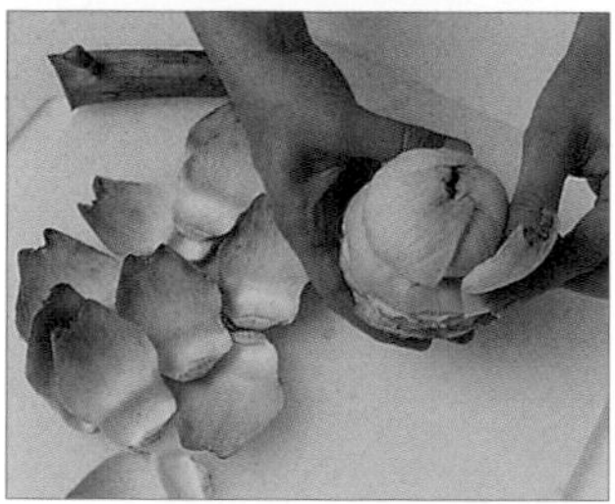

1 Have ready a bowl of cold water to which you have added the juice of half a lemon. Cut off the artichoke stalks, then discard the outer leaves until the pale inner leaves that are almost white at the base remain.

2 Cut off the tops of these leaves so that the base remains. Cut the base in half lengthwise, then prise the hairy choke out of the center with the tip of the knife and discard. Cut the artichokes lengthwise into ¼-inch slices, adding them immediately to the bowl of acidulated water.

3 Bring a large saucepan of water to a boil. Add a good pinch of salt, then drain the artichokes and add them immediately to the water. Boil for 5 minutes, drain and set aside.

4 Heat the oil in a large skillet or saucepan and add the fennel, onion, garlic and parsley. Cook over low to medium heat, stirring frequently, for about 10 minutes until the fennel has softened and is lightly colored.

5 Add the tomatoes and wine, with salt and pepper to taste. Bring to a boil, stirring, then lower the heat, cover the pan and simmer for 10–15 minutes. Stir in the artichokes, replace the lid and simmer for 10 minutes more. Meanwhile, cook the pasta in salted boiling water according to the instructions on the package.

6 Drain the pasta, reserving a little of the cooking water. Stir the capers into the sauce, then taste for seasoning and add the remaining lemon juice if you like.

7 Turn the pasta into a warmed large bowl, pour the sauce over and toss well to mix, adding a little of the reserved cooking water if you like a runnier sauce. Serve immediately, garnished with the reserved fennel fronds. Hand around a bowl of grated Parmesan separately.

# Spaghetti with Eggplant

THIS COMBINATION of ingredients is very popular in Italy, where it is known as *Spaghetti alla Norma*, after Bellini's opera.

**INGREDIENTS**

*4 tablespoons olive oil*
*1 garlic clove, roughly chopped*
*1 pound ripe Italian plum tomatoes, peeled and chopped*
*vegetable oil for shallow-frying*
*12 ounces eggplant, diced small*
*14 ounces fresh or dried spaghetti*
*1 handful fresh basil leaves, shredded*
*4 ounces ricotta salata cheese, coarsely grated*
*salt and ground black pepper*

**Serves 4–6**

1 Heat the olive oil, add the garlic and cook over low heat, stirring constantly, for 1–2 minutes. Stir in the tomatoes, then add salt and pepper to taste. Cover and simmer for 20 minutes.

2 Meanwhile, pour oil into a deep frying pan to a depth of about 1/2 inch. Heat the oil until hot but not smoking, then fry the eggplant cubes in batches for 4–5 minutes until tender and lightly browned. Remove the eggplant with a slotted spoon and drain on paper towels.

3 Cook the pasta according to the instructions on the package. Meanwhile, stir the fried eggplant into the tomato sauce and warm through. Taste for seasoning.

4 Drain the pasta and turn it into a warmed bowl. Add the sauce, with the shredded basil and a generous handful of the grated ricotta salata. Toss well and serve immediately, with the remaining ricotta sprinkled on top.

**COOK'S TIP**

*Some cooks sprinkle eggplant with salt and leave them for 20–30 minutes. This is said to help remove any bitterness, but it is not necessary if the eggplant are young and fresh.*

# Farfalle with Fennel and Walnut

A SCRUMPTIOUS BLEND of walnuts and crisp steamed fennel.

**INGREDIENTS**

*½ cup walnuts, roughly chopped*
*1 garlic clove, chopped*
*1 ounce fresh Italian parsley, picked from the stalks*
*½ cup ricotta cheese*
*4 cups dried farfalle*
*1 pound fennel bulbs*
*chopped walnuts, to garnish*

**Serves 4**

1 Place the chopped walnuts, garlic and parsley in a food processor. Process until coarsely chopped. Transfer the mixture to a bowl and stir in the ricotta cheese.

2 Cook the pasta in a large saucepan of salted boiling water following the instructions on the package until *al dente*. Drain thoroughly through a colander.

3 Slice the fennel thinly and steam for 4–5 minutes until just tender but still crisp.

4 Return the pasta to the pan and add the walnut mixture and the fennel. Toss well and sprinkle with the chopped walnuts to garnish. Serve the pasta immediately.

# Pappardelle with Grilled Vegetables

A HEARTY DISH to be eaten with crusty bread and washed down with a robust red wine. Try barbecuing the vegetables for a really smoky flavor.

**INGREDIENTS**

*1 eggplant*
*2 zucchini*
*1 red bell pepper*
*3 garlic cloves, unpeeled*
*about ⅔ cup extra virgin olive oil*
*1 pound fresh or dried pappardelle*
*salt and ground black pepper*
*a few sprigs fresh thyme, to garnish*
**Serves 4**

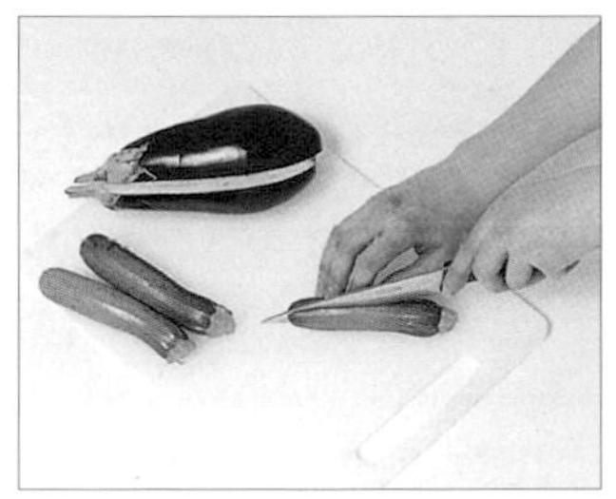

1 Preheat the broiler. With a sharp knife, trim then slice the eggplant and zucchini lengthwise.

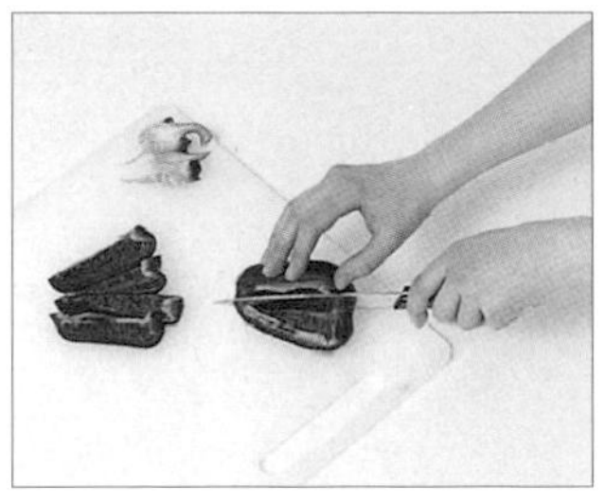

2 Halve the bell pepper, cut out the stalk and white pith and scrape out the seeds. Slice the bell pepper lengthwise into eight pieces.

3 Line a broiler pan with foil and arrange the vegetables and unpeeled garlic in a single layer over the foil. Brush liberally with olive oil and season with salt and ground black pepper.

4 Cook the vegetables until they are slightly charred on the surface, turning once. If you can't fit all the vegetables on the broiler pan at once, cook them in two batches.

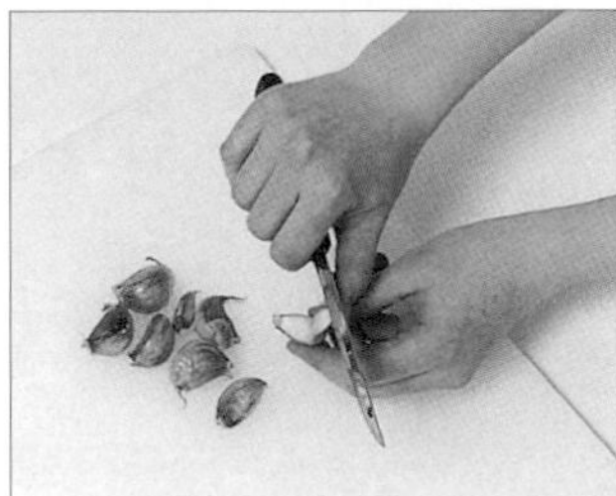

5 Once the garlic is cool enough to handle, remove the charred skins and halve. Toss all of the vegetables with the remaining olive oil and keep warm in a low oven.

6 Meanwhile cook the pasta in plenty of salted boiling water according to the instructions on the package. Drain well and toss with the cooked vegetables. Serve immediately garnished with sprigs of fresh thyme.

# Buckwheat Noodles with Cabbage, Potatoes and Cheese

THIS IS A VERY UNUSUAL PASTA dish from Valtellina in the Italian Alps. The buckwheat noodles are unique to this area, and have a slightly nutty flavor.

**INGREDIENTS**

*14 ounces Savoy cabbage, cut into ½-inch strips*
*2 potatoes, total weight about 7 ounces, cut into ¼-inch slices*
*14 ounces dried pizzoccheri*
*6 tablespoons butter*
*1 generous bunch fresh sage leaves, shredded*
*2 garlic cloves*
*7 ounces Fontina cheese, rind removed and thinly sliced*
*2–3 tablespoons freshly grated Parmesan cheese, plus extra to serve*
*salt and ground black pepper*

**Serves 6**

1 Bring a very large saucepan of salted water to a boil. Add the cabbage and potatoes and boil for 5 minutes.

2 Add the pasta, stir well and let the water return to a boil. Lower the heat and simmer for 15 minutes, or according to the instructions on the package, until the pasta is *al dente*.

3 A few minutes before the pasta is ready, melt the butter in a small saucepan. Add the sage and whole garlic cloves and fry over low to medium heat until the garlic is golden and sizzling. Lift the garlic out of the pan and discard it. Set the sage and garlic butter aside.

4 Drain the pasta and vegetables. Pour a quarter of the mixture into a warmed large bowl and arrange about a third of the Fontina slices on top. Repeat these layers until all the ingredients have been used, then sprinkle with the grated Parmesan. Pour the sage and garlic butter over the top and serve immediately, with extra Parmesan handed separately.

**COOK'S TIPS**

- *Look for packages of dried pizzoccheri pasta in Italian markets.*
- *Fontina is a mountain cheese with a sweet, nutty taste that is quite widely available, but if you cannot get it, look for Taleggio, Gruyère or Emmental—they are all similar cheeses. Cooks in the mountain regions of northern Italy would probably use either* bitto *or* casera *cheese, but these are not so easy to obtain outside the region.*
- *When in season, chard is used instead of cabbage, as is spinach.*

# Fettuccine with Butter and Parmesan

VERY FEW INGREDIENTS are needed to make up this incredibly simple dish. It comes from northern Italy, where butter and cheese are the most popular ingredients for serving with pasta. Children love it.

**INGREDIENTS**

*14 ounces fresh or dried fettuccine*
*¼ cup unsalted butter, cubed*
*1⅓ cups freshly grated Parmesan cheese*
*salt and ground black pepper*

**Serves 4**

1 Cook the pasta in a pan of salted boiling water according to the instructions on the package. Drain thoroughly, then turn into a warmed bowl.

2 Add the butter and Parmesan a third at a time, tossing the pasta after each addition until it is evenly coated. Season to taste and serve.

# Linguine with Sweet Pepper and Cream

**INGREDIENTS**

*1 orange bell pepper, quartered, cored and seeded*
*1 yellow bell pepper, quartered, cored and seeded*
*1 red bell pepper, quartered, cored and seeded*
*12 ounces fresh or dried linguine*
*2 tablespoons olive oil*
*1 red onion, sliced*
*1 garlic clove, chopped*
*2 tablespoons chopped fresh rosemary*
*⅔ cup heavy cream*
*salt and ground black pepper*
*fresh rosemary sprigs, to garnish*

**Serves 4**

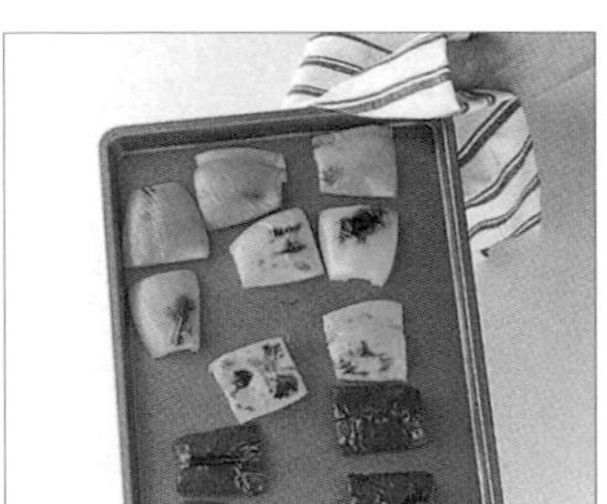

1 Preheat the broiler to hot. Place the bell peppers, skin-side up, on a broiler rack. Broil for 5–10 minutes until the skins begin to blister and char, turning occasionally.

2 Remove the bell peppers from the heat, cover with a clean dish towel and let stand for about 5 minutes.

3 Carefully peel away the skins from the bell peppers and discard. Slice the bell peppers into thin strips.

4 Cook the pasta in plenty of salted boiling water according to the instructions on the package.

5 Heat the oil in a frying pan and fry the onion and garlic for about 5 minutes until softened.

6 Stir in the sliced bell peppers and chopped rosemary and fry gently for about 5 minutes until heated through stirring occasionally.

7 Stir in the cream and heat through gently. Season to taste with salt and pepper.

8 Drain the pasta thoroughly and toss in the sauce. Serve immediately in warmed bowls, garnished with sprigs of fresh rosemary.

# Macaroni Cheese with Mushrooms

MACARONI CHEESE is an all-time classic from the mid-week menu. Here it is served in a light creamy sauce with mushrooms and topped with pine nuts.

**INGREDIENTS**

*4 cups quick-cooking elbow macaroni*
*3 tablespoons olive oil*
*8 ounces white mushrooms, sliced*
*2 fresh thyme sprigs*
*4 tablespoons all-purpose flour*
*1 vegetable stock cube*
*2½ cups milk*
*½ teaspoon celery salt*
*1 teaspoon Dijon mustard*
*1½ cups grated Cheddar cheese*
*¼ cup freshly grated Parmesan cheese*
*2 tablespoons pine nuts*
*salt and ground black pepper*
**Serves 4**

1 Cook the macaroni in plenty of salted boiling water according to the instructions on the package until *al dente*.

2 Heat the oil in a heavy saucepan. Add the mushrooms and thyme, cover and cook over gentle heat for 2–3 minutes.

3 Stir in the flour and remove from the heat, add the stock cube and stir continuously until evenly blended. Pour over the milk, a little at a time, stirring after each addition. Add the celery salt, Dijon mustard and grated Cheddar cheese and season. Stir and simmer for 1–2 minutes until the sauce is thickened.

4 Preheat a broiler. Drain the macaroni; toss into the sauce. Turn into four individual dishes or one large flameproof gratin dish. Scatter with grated Parmesan cheese and pine nuts; cook under a moderate heat until brown and bubbly.

**COOK'S TIP**

*Closed white mushrooms are best for white cream sauces. Open varieties can darken a pale sauce to an unattractive sludgy gray.*

# Rigatoni with Wild Mushrooms

THIS IS A GOOD SAUCE to make from storecupboard ingredients because it doesn't rely on anything fresh, apart from the fresh herbs.

**INGREDIENTS**

*1 ounce dried porcini mushrooms*
*¾ cup warm water*
*2 tablespoons olive oil*
*2 shallots, finely chopped*
*2 garlic cloves, crushed*
*a few sprigs of fresh marjoram, leaves stripped and finely chopped, plus extra to garnish*
*1 handful fresh Italian parsley, chopped*
*2 tablespoons butter, diced*
*1 can (14 ounces) chopped Italian plum tomatoes*
*3½ cups dried rigatoni*
*⅓ cup freshly grated Parmesan cheese, plus extra to serve*
*salt and ground black pepper*
**Serves 4–6**

1 Put the dried mushrooms in a bowl, pour the warm water over and soak for 15–20 minutes. Turn into a fine strainer set over a bowl and squeeze the mushrooms to release as much liquid as possible. Reserve the mushrooms and the strained liquid.

2 Heat the oil in a medium skillet and fry the shallots, garlic and herbs over low heat, stirring frequently, for about 5 minutes. Add the mushrooms and butter and stir until the butter has melted. Season well.

3 Stir in the tomatoes and the reserved liquid from the soaked mushrooms. Bring to a boil, then cover, lower the heat and simmer for about 20 minutes, stirring occasionally. Meanwhile, cook the pasta according to the instructions on the package.

4 Taste the sauce for seasoning. Drain the pasta, reserving some of the cooking water, and turn it into a warmed large bowl. Add the sauce and the grated Parmesan and toss to mix. Add a little cooking water if you prefer a runnier sauce. Serve immediately, garnished with marjoram and with more Parmesan handed separately.

**VARIATIONS**

- *If you have a bottle of wine open, add a splash with the canned tomatoes.*
- *For a richer sauce, add a few spoonfuls of* panna da cucina*, cream or mascarpone to the sauce just before serving.*

# Eliche with Pesto

Bottled pesto is a useful stand-by, but if you have a food processor, it is very easy to make your own.

**INGREDIENTS**

*1⅓ cups fresh basil leaves, plus fresh basil sprigs, to garnish*
*2–4 garlic cloves*
*4 tablespoons pine nuts*
*½ cup extra virgin olive oil*
*1⅓ cups freshly grated Parmesan cheese, plus extra to serve*
*⅓ cup freshly grated Pecorino cheese*
*3½ cups dried eliche*
*salt and ground black pepper*
**Serves 4**

1 Put the basil leaves, garlic and pine nuts in a blender or food processor. Add 4 tablespoons of the olive oil. Process until the ingredients are finely chopped, then stop the machine, remove the lid and scrape down the sides of the bowl.

2 Turn the machine on again and slowly pour the remaining oil in a thin, steady stream through the feeder tube. You may need to stop the machine and scrape down the sides of the bowl once or twice to make sure everything is evenly mixed.

3 Scrape the mixture into a large bowl and beat in the cheeses with a wooden spoon. Taste and add salt and pepper if necessary.

4 Cook the pasta according to the instructions on the package. Drain it well, then add it to the bowl of pesto and toss to mix. Serve immediately, garnished with the fresh basil leaves. Hand grated Parmesan separately.

**Cook's Tip**

*Pesto can be made up to 2–3 days in advance. To store pesto, transfer it to a small bowl and pour a thin film of olive oil over the surface. Cover the bowl tightly with plastic wrap and keep it in the refrigerator.*

# Spaghetti with Garlic, Oil and Chile

In Rome this is called *Spaghetti Aglio e Olio*. Sometimes it is given its full name of *Spaghetti Aglio, Olio e Peperoncino* because chile—*peperoncino*—is always used to give the dish some bite.

**INGREDIENTS**

*14 ounces fresh or dried spaghetti*
*6 tablespoons extra virgin olive oil*
*2–4 garlic cloves, crushed*
*1 dried red chile*
*1 small handful fresh Italian parsley, roughly chopped*
*salt*

**Serves 4**

1 Cook the pasta according to the package instructions, adding plenty of salt to the water. (See Cook's Tips.)

2 Meanwhile, heat the oil very gently in a small frying pan or saucepan. Add the crushed garlic and whole dried chile and stir over low heat until the garlic is just beginning to brown. Remove the chile and discard.

3 Drain the pasta and turn it into a warmed large bowl. Pour on the oil and garlic mixture, add the parsley and toss vigorously until the pasta glistens. Serve immediately.

### Cook's Tips

- *Since the oil is such an important ingredient here, only use the very best cold-pressed extra virgin olive oil.*
- *Don't use salt in the oil and garlic mixture, because it will not dissolve sufficiently. This is why plenty of salt is recommended for cooking the pasta.*
- *In Rome, grated Parmesan is never served with* Spaghetti Aglio e Olio, *nor is the dish seasoned with pepper.*
- *In summer, Romans use fresh chiles, which they grow in pots on their terraces and window ledges.*

# Ruote with Mushrooms

THESE FUN PASTA SHAPES will appeal to the little people in your household—and that doesn't mean the Italians.

**INGREDIENTS**

*½ ounce dried porcini mushrooms*
*¾ cup warm water*
*3 tablespoons olive oil*
*2 garlic cloves, finely chopped*
*1 handful fresh Italian parsley, coarsely chopped*
*2 large pieces drained sun-dried tomato in olive oil, sliced into thin strips*
*½ cup dry white wine*
*2 cups brown mushrooms, thinly sliced*
*2 cups vegetable stock*
*4 cups dried ruote or other pasta shapes, such as penne, fusilli or eliche*
*salt and ground black pepper*
*arugula and/or fresh Italian parsley, to garnish*

**Serves 4**

1 Put the dried porcini mushrooms in a bowl, pour the warm water over and leave to soak for 15–20 minutes. Turn into a fine strainer set over a bowl and squeeze the porcini with your hands to release as much liquid as possible. Reserve the strained soaking liquid. Chop the porcini finely.

2 Heat the oil and cook the garlic, parsley, sun-dried tomato strips and porcini over low heat, stirring frequently, for about 5 minutes.

3 Stir in the wine, simmer for a few minutes until reduced, then stir in the mushrooms. Pour in the stock and simmer, uncovered, for 15–20 minutes more until the liquid has reduced and the sauce is quite thick and rich.

4 Cook the pasta according to the instructions on the package.

5 Taste the mushroom sauce for seasoning. Drain the pasta, reserving a little of the cooking liquid, and turn it into a warmed large bowl. Add the mushroom sauce and toss well, thinning the sauce if necessary with some of the pasta cooking water. Serve immediately, sprinkled liberally with chopped arugula and/or parsley.

**VARIATION**

*Fresh wild mushrooms can be used instead of brown mushrooms, but they are seasonal and often expensive. A cheaper alternative is to use a box of mixed wild mushrooms. These are sold in many supermarkets.*

# Tagliatelle with Walnut Sauce

AN UNUSUAL SAUCE which would make this a spectacular dinner party starter or satisfying supper.

**INGREDIENTS**

*2 thick slices whole wheatl bread*
*1¼ cups milk*
*2½ cups walnut pieces*
*1 garlic clove, crushed*
*½ cup freshly grated Parmesan cheese*
*6 tablespoons olive oil, plus extra for tossing the pasta*
*⅔ cup heavy cream (optional)*
*1 pound tagliatelle*
*salt and ground black pepper*
*2 tablespoons chopped fresh parsley, to garnish*
**Serves 4–6**

1 Cut the crusts off the bread and soak in the milk until all of the milk is absorbed.

2 Preheat the oven to 375°F. Spread the walnuts on a baking sheet and toast in the oven for 5 minutes. Let cool.

3 Place the bread, walnuts, garlic, Parmesan cheese and olive oil in a blender or food processor and blend until smooth. Season to taste with salt and pepper. Stir in the cream, if using.

4 Cook the pasta in plenty of salted boiling water according to the instructions on the package, drain and toss with a little olive oil. Divide the pasta equally among four or six bowls and place a dollop of sauce on each portion. Sprinkle with parsley and serve immediately.

**VARIATION**

*Replace the walnuts with pecans or hazelnuts if you prefer, and prepare as above.*

# Eliche with Zucchini and Walnuts

THE VEGETABLES are softened slowly to release their flavors.

**INGREDIENTS**

*5 tablespoons butter*
*1 large Spanish onion, halved and thinly sliced*
*1 pound zucchini, very thinly sliced*
*3 cups dried eliche*
*½ cup walnuts, coarsely chopped*
*3 tablespoons chopped fresh parsley*
*2 tablespoons light cream*
*salt and ground black pepper*
*freshly grated Parmesan cheese, to serve*

**Serves 4**

1 Melt the butter in a frying pan. Add the sliced onion, cover and sweat for 5 minutes until translucent, then add the zucchini.

2 Stir well, cover again and sweat until the vegetables are very soft, stirring occasionally.

3 Meanwhile, cook the pasta in plenty of salted boiling water, according to the instructions on the package, until *al dente*.

4 While the pasta is cooking, add the walnuts, parsley and cream to the zucchini mixture and stir well. Season with salt and pepper.

5 Drain the pasta and return to the pan. Add the zucchini sauce and mix together well. Serve immediately in a warmed bowl, with freshly grated Parmesan handed separately.

# Pappardelle with Beans and Mushrooms

A MIXTURE OF WILD and cultivated mushrooms help to give this dish a rich and nutty flavor.

**INGREDIENTS**

*2 tablespoons olive oil*
*4 tablespoons butter*
*2 shallots, chopped*
*2–3 garlic cloves, crushed*
*1 ½ pounds mixed mushrooms, thickly sliced*
*4 sun-dried tomatoes in oil, drained and chopped*
*6 tablespoons dry white wine*
*1 can (14 ounces) borlotti beans, drained*
*3 cups fresh or dried pappardelle*
*3 tablespoons grated Parmesan cheese*
*salt and ground black pepper*
*chopped fresh parsley, to garnish*

**Serves 4**

1 Heat the oil and butter in a frying pan and fry the shallots until they are soft but not colored.

2 Add the garlic and mushrooms and fry for 3–4 minutes. Stir in the sun-dried tomatoes, wine and add seasoning to taste.

3 Stir in the borlotti beans and cook for 5–6 minutes, until most of the liquid has evaporated from the pan and the beans are warmed through.

4 Meanwhile, cook the pasta in a saucepan of salted boiling water according to the instructions on the package.

5 Stir the grated Parmesan cheese. into the sauce.

6 As soon as the pasta is *al dente*, drain it through a colander and serve immediately with the sauce and a sprinkling of parsley.

# Mushroom and Chile Carbonara

FOR A RICHER mushroom flavor, use a small package of dried Italian porcini mushrooms in this quick, eggy sauce as they have a really good, meaty taste. For an extra spicy zing, toss in some chile flakes too.

**INGREDIENTS**

*½-ounce pack dried porcini mushrooms*
*1¼ cups hot water*
*8 ounces dried spaghetti*
*2 tablespoons butter*
*1 garlic clove, crushed*
*8 ounces white or brown mushrooms, thinly sliced*
*1 teaspoon dried red chile flakes*
*2 eggs*
*1¼ cups light cream*
*salt and ground black pepper*
*freshly grated Parmesan cheese and chopped fresh parsley, to serve*

**Serves 4**

1 Soak the dried mushrooms in the hot water for 15 minutes; drain and reserve the liquid.

2 Cook the spaghetti according to the instructions in plenty of salted boiling water. Drain and rinse in cold water.

3 In a large saucepan, heat the butter and oil together and lightly sauté the garlic for half a minute.

4 Add the mushrooms, including the soaked porcini, and the chile flakes to the pan of garlic, and stir well. Cook for about 2 minutes.

5 Pour in the reserved soaking liquid from the mushrooms, give the mixture a good stir and then boil to reduce slightly.

6 Beat the eggs with the cream and season well. Turn the cooked spaghetti into the mushroom sauce in the pan and then toss in the eggs and cream. Reheat the mixture, without boiling, and serve hot, sprinkled with freshly grated Parmesan cheese and chopped parsley.

**VARIATION**

*If you don't want to use mushrooms, try replacing them with finely sliced and sautéed leeks or perhaps coarsely shredded lettuce with peas. If chile flakes are too hot and spicy for you, then try the delicious alternative of skinned and chopped tomatoes with torn, fresh basil leaves as a garnish.*

# Chitarra Spaghetti with Butter and Herbs

THIS IS A VERSATILE RECIPE. You can use just one favorite herb or several—basil, Italian parsley, rosemary, thyme, marjoram or sage would all work well. Square-shaped spaghetti is traditional for this type of sauce, but you can use ordinary spaghetti or spaghettini, or even linguine.

**INGREDIENTS**

*14 ounces fresh or dried spaghetti alla chitarra*
*2 good handfuls mixed fresh herbs, plus extra herb leaves and flowers, to garnish*
*½ cup butter*
*salt and ground black pepper*
*freshly grated Parmesan cheese, to serve*
**Serves 4**

**VARIATION**

*If you like the flavor of garlic with herbs, add 1–2 crushed garlic cloves when melting the butter.*

1 Cook the pasta according to the instructions on the package.

2 Chop the herbs coarsely or finely, whichever you prefer.

3 When the pasta is almost *al dente*, melt the butter in a large skillet or saucepan. As soon as it sizzles, drain the pasta and add it to the pan, then sprinkle in the herbs and salt and pepper to taste.

4 Toss over medium heat until the pasta is coated in the oil and herbs. Serve immediately in warmed bowls, sprinkled with extra herb leaves and flowers. Hand around freshly grated Parmesan separately.

# Spaghetti with Cheese and Pepper

THIS IS A ROMAN DISH, always made with spaghetti. It is remarkably easy to cook, and tastes wonderful.

**INGREDIENTS**

*14 ounces fresh or dried spaghetti*
*1⅓ cup freshly grated Pecorino (preferably Pecorino Romano) cheese*
*1 teaspoon coarsely ground black pepper*
*extra virgin olive oil, to taste*
*salt*
**Serves 4**

1 Cook the pasta according to the instructions on the package.

2 As soon as the pasta is *al dente*, drain it through a colander, but leave it a little more moist than is usual, before turning it into a large warmed bowl.

3 Add the cheese, pepper and salt to taste. Toss well to mix, then moisten with as much olive oil as you like. Serve immediately.

# Chile and Eggplant Pasta

FULL OF FLAVOR, THIS EXCELLENT vegetarian sauce goes well with any short pasta shape. It can also be layered with sheets of pasta and béchamel or cheese sauce to make a delicious vegetarian lasagne.

**INGREDIENTS**

*2 tablespoons olive oil*
*1 small fresh red chile*
*2 garlic cloves*
*2 handfuls fresh Italian parsley, roughly chopped*
*1 pound eggplant, coarsely chopped*
*1 handful fresh basil leaves*
*scant 1 cup water*
*1 vegetable stock cube*
*8 ripe Italian plum tomatoes, peeled and finely chopped*
*4 tablespoons red wine*
*1 teaspoon granulated sugar*
*1 envelope saffron powder*
*½ teaspoon ground paprika*
*salt and ground black pepper*

**Serves 4–6**

1 Heat the oil in a large skillet or saucepan and add the whole chile, whole garlic cloves and half the chopped parsley. Smash the garlic cloves with a wooden spoon to release their juice, then cover the pan and cook the mixture over low to medium heat for about 10 minutes, stirring occasionally.

2 Remove and discard the chile. Add the eggplant to the pan with the rest of the parsley and all the basil. Pour in half the water. Crumble in the stock cube and stir until it is dissolved, then cover and cook, stirring frequently, for about 10 minutes.

3 Add the tomatoes, wine, sugar, saffron and paprika, with salt and pepper to taste, then pour in the remaining water. Stir well, replace the lid and cook for 30–40 minutes more, stirring occasionally. Taste for seasoning and serve with pasta or use as suggested in a baked dish. If you like, garnish with extra chopped parsley.

**COOK'S TIP**

*Italian cooks often sprinkle a little "all-purpose seasoning" into sauces like this one. It is very good for accentuating savory flavors, and is well worth keeping in the storecupboard.*

# Orecchiette with Arugula

THIS HEARTY DISH IS FROM PUGLIA in the south-east of Italy. Serve it as a main course with country bread. Some supermarkets sell a farmhouse-style Italian loaf called *pugliese*, which would be most appropriate.

**INGREDIENTS**

*3 tablespoons olive oil*
*1 small onion, finely chopped*
*11 ounces canned chopped Italian plum tomatoes*
*½ teaspoon dried oregano*
*pinch of chile powder or cayenne pepper*
*about 2 tablespoons red or white wine (optional)*
*2 potatoes, total weight about 7 ounces, diced*
*2¾ cups dried orecchiette*
*2 garlic cloves, finely chopped*
*5 ounces arugula leaves, stems removed, shredded*
*scant ½ cup ricotta cheese*
*salt and ground black pepper*
*freshly grated Pecorino cheese, to serve*

**Serves 4–6**

1 Heat 1 tablespoon of the olive oil in a medium saucepan, add half the finely chopped onion and cook gently, stirring frequently, for about 5 minutes until softened. Add the canned tomatoes, oregano and chile powder or cayenne pepper to the onion. Pour the wine over, if using, and add a little salt and pepper to taste. Cover the pan and simmer for about 15 minutes, stirring occasionally.

2 Bring a large saucepan of salted water to a boil. Add the potatoes and pasta. Stir well and let the water return to a boil. Lower the heat and simmer for 15 minutes, or according to the instructions on the package, until the pasta is cooked.

3 Heat the remaining oil in a large skillet or saucepan, add the rest of the onion and the garlic and fry for 2–3 minutes, stirring occasionally. Add the arugula, toss over the heat for about 2 minutes until wilted, then stir in the tomato sauce and the ricotta. Mix well.

4 Drain the pasta and potatoes, add both to the pan of sauce and toss to mix. Taste for seasoning and serve immediately in warmed bowls, with grated Pecorino handed separately.

**COOK'S TIP**

*Orecchiette are always slightly chewy. When making this dish it is traditional to cook them in the same pan as the potatoes, but if you are unsure of getting the timing right, cook them separately.*

# Tagliolini with Asparagus

TAGLIOLINI ARE VERY THIN egg noodles, more delicate in texture than spaghetti. They go well with this subtle cream sauce, flavored with fresh asparagus.

**INGREDIENTS**

*1 pound fresh asparagus*
*egg pasta sheets made with 2 eggs, or 12 ounces fresh tagliolini or other egg noodles*
*¼ cup butter*
*3 scallions, finely chopped*
*3–4 fresh mint or basil leaves, finely chopped*
*⅔ cup heavy cream*
*½ cup freshly grated Parmesan cheese*
*salt and ground black pepper*
**Serves 4**

1 Peel the asparagus by inserting a small sharp knife at the base of the stalks and pulling upwards towards the tips. Drop them into a pan of boiling water and boil until just tender, about 4–6 minutes.

2 Remove from the pan, reserving the cooking water. Cut the tips off, and then cut the stalks into 1½-inch pieces. Set aside.

3 Make the egg pasta sheets, if using, and fold and cut into thin noodles, or feed through the narrowest setting of a pasta-making machine. Open them out and dry for 5–10 minutes.

4 Melt the butter in a large frying pan. Add the scallions and herbs, and cook for 3–4 minutes. Stir in the cream and asparagus, and heat gently, but do not boil. Season to taste.

5 Bring the asparagus cooking water back to a boil. Add salt. Drop the noodles in all at once. Cook until just tender (freshly made noodles will cook in about 30–60 seconds). Drain thoroughly through a colander.

6 Turn the pasta into the pan with the sauce, increase the heat slightly and mix well. Stir in the Parmesan cheese. Mix well and serve immediately.

# Magnificent Squash

BOTH SUMMER AND WINTER squash, with their wonderful colored skins, look so attractive and tempting. They make delicious, inexpensive main courses, just right for a satisfying family meal.

**INGREDIENTS**

*$2\frac{1}{4}$ cups dried conchiglie*
*3–$4\frac{1}{2}$ pounds large winter squash, or large zucchini*
*3 tablespoons sunflower oil*
*1 onion, chopped*
*1 bell pepper, seeded and chopped*
*1 tablespoon fresh ginger root, grated*
*2 garlic cloves, crushed*
*4 large tomatoes, skinned and chopped*
*$\frac{1}{2}$ cup pine nuts*
*1 tablespoon chopped fresh basil*
*salt and ground black pepper*
*grated cheese, to serve (optional)*

**Serves 4–6**

1 Preheat the oven to 375°F. Cook the pasta in a large saucepan containing plenty of salted boiling water according to the instructions on the package, slightly overcooking it so it is just a little soft. Drain well and reserve.

2 Cut the squash in half lengthwise, and scoop out and discard the seeds. Use a small sharp knife and tablespoon to scoop out the squash flesh. Chop the flesh coarsely.

3 Heat the oil in a large saucepan and gently fry the onion, bell pepper, ginger and garlic for 5 minutes then add the squash flesh, tomatoes and seasoning. Cover and cook for 10–12 minutes until the vegetables are soft.

4 Add the pasta, pine nuts and basil to the pan, stir well and set aside until required.

5 Meanwhile, place the squash halves in a roasting pan, season lightly and pour a little water around the squash, taking care it does not spill inside. Cover with foil and bake for 15 minutes.

6 Remove the foil, discard the water and fill the shells with the vegetable mixture. Cover with foil and return to the hot oven for a further 20–25 minutes.

7 Top with cheese, if using. To serve, scoop the filling out of the "shell" or cut the squash into sections.

# Pasta with Caponata

THE SICILIANS have an excellent sweet-and-sour vegetable dish, called *caponata*, which goes wonderfully well with pasta.

**INGREDIENTS**

*1 eggplant, cut into sticks*
*2 zucchini, cut into sticks*
*4 tablespoons extra virgin olive oil*
*8 baby onions, peeled or 1 large onion, sliced*
*2 garlic cloves, crushed*
*1 large red bell pepper, cored, seeded and sliced*
*1¾ cups tomato juice*
*⅔ cup water*
*2 tablespoons balsamic vinegar*
*juice of 1 lemon*
*1 tablespoon sugar*
*2 tablespoons sliced black olives*
*2 tablespoons capers*
*14 ounces fresh or dried tagliatelle or other ribbon pasta*
*salt and ground black pepper*
**Serves 4**

1 Lightly salt the eggplant and zucchini and leave them to drain in a colander for 30 minutes. Rinse and pat dry thoroughly with paper towels.

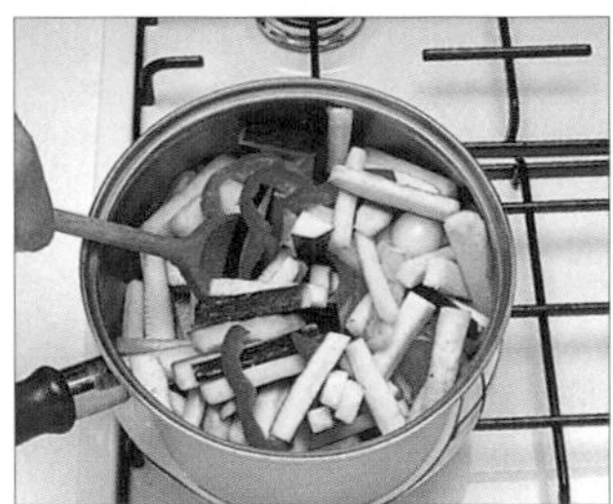

2 Heat the olive oil in a large saucepan, and lightly fry the onions, garlic and pepper for 5 minutes, then stir in the eggplant and zucchini and fry for a further 5 minutes.

3 Stir in the tomato juice and the water. Stir well, bring the mixture to a boil, then add all the rest of the ingredients except the pasta. Season to taste and simmer for 10 minutes.

4 Meanwhile, cook the pasta according to the instructions on the package, then drain. Serve the caponata with the pasta.

**VARIATION**

*Caponata is often made with the addition of anchovies and pine nuts. It also makes a delicious salad or side dish when served at room temperature.*

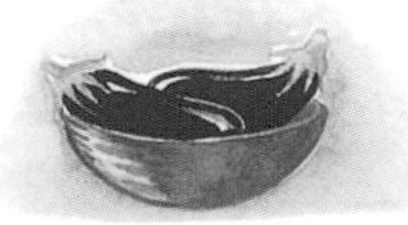

# Fusilli with Lentils and Cheese

THIS SURPRISING combination works extremely well.

**INGREDIENTS**

*1 tablespoon olive oil*
*1 onion, chopped*
*1 garlic clove, chopped*
*1 carrot, cut into short thin sticks*
*3 cups dried fusilli*
*½ cup green lentils, boiled for 25 minutes*
*1 tablespoon tomato paste*
*1 tablespoon chopped fresh oregano*
*⅔ cup vegetable stock*
*2 cups grated Cheddar cheese*
*salt and ground black pepper*
*freshly grated Cheddar cheese, to serve*
**Serves 4**

1 Heat the oil in a large frying pan and fry the onion and garlic for 3 minutes. Add the carrot and cook for a further 5 minutes.

**COOK'S TIP**

*Tomato paste is sold in small cans and tubes. If you use a can for this small amount, you can keep the remainder fresh by transferring it to a bowl, covering it with a thin layer of olive oil and then putting it in the refrigerator until needed.*

2 Cook the pasta in plenty of salted boiling water according to the instructions on the package.

3 Add the lentils, tomato paste and oregano to the frying pan, stirring to mix thoroughly, then cover and cook for 3 minutes.

4 Add the stock and salt and pepper to the pan. Cover and simmer for 10 minutes. Stir in the grated Cheddar cheese.

5 Drain the pasta thoroughly and stir into the sauce to coat. Serve in warmed bowls with plenty of extra grated cheese handed separately.

# Spaghettini with Roasted Garlic

ROASTED GARLIC TASTES sweet and is milder than you would expect.

**INGREDIENTS**

*1 whole head of garlic*
*14 ounces fresh or dried spaghettini*
*½ cup extra virgin olive oil*
*salt and ground black pepper*
*coarsely shaved Parmesan cheese, to serve*
**Serves 4**

1 Preheat the oven to 350°F. Place the garlic in an oiled baking pan and roast it for 30 minutes.

2 Cook the pasta in a saucepan of salted boiling water according to the instructions on the package.

3 Let the garlic cool, then lay it on its side and slice off the top third with a sharp knife.

4 Hold the garlic over a bowl and dig out the flesh from each clove with the point of the knife. When all the flesh has been added to the bowl, pour in the oil and add plenty of black pepper. Mix well.

5 Drain the pasta and return it to the clean pan. Pour in the oil and garlic mixture and toss the pasta vigorously over medium heat until all the strands are thoroughly coated. Serve immediately, with shavings of Parmesan handed separately.

**VARIATION**

*For a fiery finish, sprinkle crushed, dried red chiles over the pasta when tossing it with the oil and garlic.*

**COOK'S TIP**

*Although you can now buy roasted garlic in supermarkets, it is best to roast it yourself for this simple recipe, so that it melts into the olive oil and coats the strands of pasta beautifully.*

# Elicoidali with Cheese and Cream

ALTHOUGH THE INGREDIENTS for this dish are quite plain, the combination is very appetizing. It is very quick, so if you have a tub of ricotta in the refrigerator it makes a swift and simple evening meal.

**INGREDIENTS**

*3½ cups dried elicoidali*
*3 egg yolks*
*7 tablespoons freshly grated Parmesan cheese*
*scant 1 cup ricotta cheese*
*4 tablespoons* panna da cucina *or heavy cream*
*nutmeg*
*3 tablespoons butter*
*salt and ground black pepper*

**Serves 4**

1 Cook the pasta according to the instructions on the package.

2 Meanwhile, mix the egg yolks, grated Parmesan and ricotta together in a bowl. Add the cream and mix with a fork.

3 Grate in nutmeg to taste, then season with plenty of black pepper and a little salt. Drain the pasta thoroughly when cooked. Return the clean pan to the heat. Melt the butter, add the drained pasta and toss vigorously over medium heat.

4 Turn off the heat under the pan and add the ricotta mixture. Stir well with a large spoon for 10–15 seconds until all the pasta is coated in sauce. Serve immediately, in warmed individual bowls.

**COOK'S TIP**

*Elicoidali are a short tubular pasta with curved ridges. If you can't get them, use rigatoni, which have straight ridges.*

# Tagliatelle with "Hit-the-Pan" Salsa

IT IS POSSIBLE to make a hot, filling meal within just 15 minutes with this quick-cook salsa sauce. If you have no time don't peel the tomatoes.

**INGREDIENTS**

*4 ounces fresh or dried tagliatelle*
*3 tablespoons extra virgin olive oil*
*3 large tomatoes*
*1 garlic clove, crushed*
*4 scallions, sliced*
*1 green chile, halved, seeded and sliced*
*juice of 1 orange (optional)*
*2 tablespoons chopped fresh parsley*
*salt and ground black pepper*
*grated cheese, to serve (optional)*
**Serves 2**

1 Cook the tagliatelle in plenty of salted boiling water until *al dente*. Drain and toss in a little of the oil. Season well.

2 Skin the tomatoes by dipping them in a bowl of boiling water for about 45 seconds and then into cold water. The skins should slip off easily. Coarsely chop the flesh.

3 Heat the remaining oil until quite hot and stir-fry the garlic, onions and chile for 1 minute.

4 Add the tomatoes, orange juice, if using, and parsley. Season well and stir in the tagliatelle to reheat. Serve with grated cheese, if desired.

### COOK'S TIPS

*• You could use any pasta shape for this recipe. It would be particularly good with large rigatoni or linguini, or as a sauce for fresh ravioli or tortellini.*

*• This sauce is so easy to prepare, you could save yourself some later later by preparing double the quantity and freezing the excess. Prepare for freezing as above, but omit the parsley. Add fresh parsley when you prepare to serve from frozen.*

# Campanelle with Yellow Bell Pepper Sauce

ROASTED YELLOW BELL PEPPERS make a deliciously sweet and creamy sauce to serve with pasta.

**INGREDIENTS**

*2 yellow bell peppers*
*¼ cup soft goat cheese*
*½ cup lowfat fromage blanc*
*1 pound dried campanelle*
*salt and ground black pepper*
*½ cup toasted sliced almonds, to serve*

**Serves 4**

1 After deseeding the bell peppers, place them under a preheated broiler and turn them frequently until charred and blistered. Place in a plastic bag, seal and let cool. Then peel and remove all the pith and seeds.

2 Place the bell pepper flesh in a blender or food processor with the goat cheese and fromage blanc. Process until well mixed and smooth. Season with salt and plenty of ground black pepper.

3 Cook the pasta in plenty of salted boiling water, according to the instructions on the package, until *al dente*. Drain well.

4 Toss the pasta with the sauce and serve in warmed bowls sprinkled with the toasted sliced almonds.

# Black Pasta with Ricotta

THIS IS DESIGNER PASTA at its most dramatic, the kind of dish you are most likely to see at a fashionable Italian restaurant. Serve it for a smart dinner party first course—it will be a great talking point.

**INGREDIENTS**

*11 ounces dried black pasta*
*4 tablespoons ricotta cheese, as fresh as possible*
*4 tablespoons extra virgin olive oil*
*1 small fresh red chile, seeded and finely chopped*
*1 small handful fresh basil leaves*
*salt and ground black pepper*
**Serves 4**

1 Cook the pasta in salted boiling water according to the instructions on the package. Meanwhile, put the ricotta in a bowl, add salt and pepper to taste and use a little of the hot water from the pasta pan to mix it to a smooth, creamy consistency. Taste for seasoning.

2 Drain the pasta. Heat the oil gently in the clean pan and add the pasta with the chile and salt and pepper to taste. Toss quickly over high heat to combine.

3 Divide the pasta equally among four warmed bowls, then top with the ricotta. Sprinkle with the basil leaves and serve immediately. Each diner tosses their own portion of pasta and cheese.

**COOK'S TIP**

*Black pasta is made with squid ink. If you prefer, use green spinach-flavored pasta or red tomato-flavored pasta.*

# Paglia e Fieno with Walnuts and Gorgonzola

CHEESE AND NUTS ARE popular ingredients for pasta sauces. The combination is very rich, so reserve this dish for a dinner party appetizer. It needs no accompaniment other than wine—a dry white would be good.

**INGREDIENTS**

*10 ounces dried paglia e fieno*
*2 tablespoons butter*
*1 teaspoon finely chopped fresh sage or ½ teaspoon dried sage, plus fresh sage leaves, to garnish*
*4 ounces torta di Gorgonzola cheese, diced*
*3 tablespoons mascarpone cheese*
*5 tablespoons milk*
*½ cup walnut halves, ground*
*2 tablespoons freshly grated Parmesan cheese*
*freshly ground black pepper*
**Serves 4**

1 Cook the pasta in a large saucepan of salted boiling water, according to the instructions on the package. Meanwhile, melt the butter in a large skillet or saucepan over low heat, add the sage and stir it around. Sprinkle in the diced *torta di Gorgonzola* and then add the mascarpone. Stir the ingredients with a wooden spoon until the cheeses start to melt. Pour in the milk and keep stirring.

2 Sprinkle in the walnuts and grated Parmesan and add plenty of black pepper. Continue to stir over low heat until the mixture forms a creamy sauce. Do not allow it to boil or the nuts will taste bitter, and do not cook the sauce for longer than a few minutes or the nuts will discolor it.

3 Drain the pasta, add it to the pan of sauce and toss well. Serve immediately, with more black pepper ground liberally on top. Garnish with the sage leaves.

**COOK'S TIP**

*Ready-ground nuts are sold in packages in supermarkets, but you will get a better flavor if you buy walnut halves and grind them yourself in a food processor.*

# Tagliatelle with Peas, Asparagus and Beans

A CREAMY PEA SAUCE makes a wonderful combination with crunchy young vegetables.

**INGREDIENTS**

*1 tablespoon olive oil*
*1 garlic clove, crushed*
*6 scallions, sliced*
*2 cups frozen peas, thawed*
*12 ounces fresh young asparagus*
*2 tablespoons chopped fresh sage, plus extra leaves to garnish*
*finely grated rind of 2 lemons*
*1¾ cups vegetable stock or water*
*2 cups frozen fava beans, thawed*
*1 pound fresh egg tagliatelle*
*4 tablespoons lowfat natural yogurt*

**Serves 4**

1 Heat the oil in a pan. Add the garlic and scallions and cook gently for 2–3 minutes.

2 Add the peas and 4 ounces of the asparagus, together with the sage, lemon rind and stock or water. Bring the mixture to a boil, reduce the heat and simmer for 10 minutes until tender. Purée in a blender or food processor until smooth.

3 Meanwhile remove the outer skins from the thawed fava beans and discard.

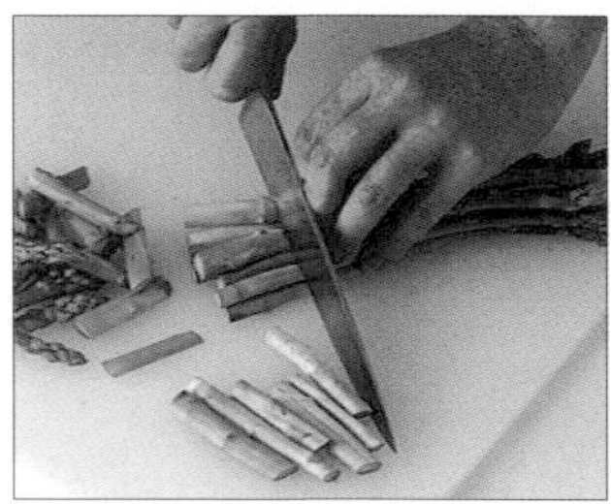

4 Cut the remaining asparagus into 2-inch lengths, trimming off any fibrous stems, and blanch in boiling water for 2 minutes.

5 Cook the tagliatelle in plenty of salted boiling water according to the instructions on the package until *al dente*. Drain well.

6 Add the cooked asparagus and shelled beans to the sauce and reheat. Stir in the yogurt and toss into the tagliatelle. Garnish with sage leaves and serve immediately.

# Conchiglie with Roasted Bell Peppers

ADD OTHER VEGETABLES such as green beans or zucchini or even chickpeas if you like.

**INGREDIENTS**

*2 red bell peppers*
*2 yellow bell peppers*
*3 tablespoons olive oil*
*1 onion, sliced*
*2 garlic cloves, crushed*
*½ teaspoon mild chili powder*
*1 can (14 ounces) chopped tomatoes*
*4 cups dried conchiglie or other pasta shapes, such as eliche or fusilli*
*salt and ground black pepper*
*freshly grated Parmesan cheese, to serve*

**Serves 4**

1 Preheat the oven to 400°F. Place the bell peppers on a baking sheet or in a roasting pan and bake for about 20 minutes or until they are beginning to char. Alternatively you could cook the peppers under a preheated broiler, turning frequently until evenly blistered.

2 Rub the skins off the bell peppers under cold water. Halve, seed and coarsely chop the flesh.

3 Heat the oil in a medium saucepan and add the onion and garlic. Cook gently for 5 minutes until soft and golden.

4 Stir in the chili powder, cook for 2 minutes, then add the tomatoes and bell peppers. Bring to a boil and simmer for 10–15 minutes until the sauce is slightly thickened and reduced. Season to taste.

5 Cook the pasta in plenty of salted boiling water according to the instructions on the package. Drain well through a colander and toss with the sauce. Serve piping hot with plenty of grated Parmesan cheese.

**VARIATION**

*If you like, increase the strength of the chili flavor by using a hotter blend of chilli powder.*

# Conchiglie with Roasted Vegetables

NOTHING COULD BE SIMPLER—or more delicious—than tossing freshly cooked pasta with roasted vegetables. The flavor is superb.

**INGREDIENTS**

*1 red bell pepper, seeded and cut into ½-inch squares*
*1 yellow or orange bell pepper, seeded and cut into ½-inch squares*
*1 small eggplant, coarsely diced*
*2 zucchini, coarsely diced*
*5 tablespoons extra virgin olive oil*
*1 tablespoon chopped fresh Italian parsley*
*1 teaspoon dried oregano or marjoram*
*9 ounces baby Italian plum tomatoes, hulled and halved lengthwise*
*2 garlic cloves, coarsely chopped*
*3–3½ cups dried conchiglie*
*salt and ground black pepper*
*4–6 fresh marjoram or oregano sprigs, to garnish*

**Serves 4–6**

1 Preheat the oven to 375°F. Rinse the prepared bell peppers, eggplant and zucchini in a strainer or colander under cold running water, drain, then put the vegetables into a large roasting pan.

2 Pour 3 tablespoons of the olive oil over the vegetables and sprinkle with the fresh and dried herbs. Add salt and pepper to taste and stir well. Roast for about 30 minutes, stirring two or three times.

3 Stir the halved tomatoes and chopped garlic into the vegetable mixture, then roast for 20 minutes more, stirring once or twice. Meanwhile, cook the pasta according to the instructions on the package.

4 Drain the pasta and turn it into a warmed bowl. Add the roasted vegetables and the remaining oil and toss well. Serve the pasta and vegetables hot in warmed bowls, garnishing each portion with a herb sprig.

### COOK'S TIP

*Pasta and roasted vegetables are very good served cold, so if you have any of this dish left over, cover it tightly with plastic wrap, chill in the refrigerator overnight and serve it the next day as a salad. It would also make a particularly good salad to take on a picnic.*

# Green Vegetable Sauce

ALTHOUGH DESCRIBED AS *SUGO* in Italian, this is not a true "sauce," because it does not have any liquid apart from the oil and melted butter. It is more a medley of vegetables. Tossed with freshly cooked pasta, it is ideal for a fresh and light lunch or supper. Allow about 1 pound dried pasta for this amount of sauce.

**INGREDIENTS**

*2 carrots*
*1 zucchini*
*3 ounces green beans*
*1 small leek*
*2 ripe Italian plum tomatoes*
*1 handful fresh Italian parsley*
*2 tablespoons butter*
*3 tablespoons extra virgin olive oil*
*1/2 teaspoon granulated sugar*
*1 cup frozen peas*
*salt and ground black pepper*
*freshly cooked pasta, to serve*

**Serves 4**

1 Dice the carrots and the zucchini finely. Top and tail the green beans, then cut them into 3/4-inch lengths. Slice the leek thinly. Peel and dice the tomatoes. Chop the Italian parsley and set aside.

2 Melt the butter in the oil in a medium skillet or saucepan. When the mixture sizzles, add the prepared leek and carrots. Sprinkle the sugar over and fry, stirring frequently, for about 5 minutes.

3 Stir in the zucchini, green beans, peas and plenty of salt and pepper. Cover and cook over low to medium heat for 5–8 minutes until the vegetables are tender, stirring occasionally.

4 Stir in the parsley and chopped plum tomatoes and adjust the seasoning to taste. Serve immediately, tossed with freshly cooked pasta of your choice.

# Penne with Eggplant and Mint Pesto

THIS SPLENDID VARIATION on the classic Italian pesto uses fresh mint rather than basil for a deliciously different flavor.

**INGREDIENTS**

*2 large eggplant*
*4 cups dried penne*
*½ cup walnut halves*
*salt and ground black pepper*

***For the pesto***

*1 ounce fresh mint*
*½ ounce Italian parsley*
*scant ½ cup walnuts*
*1½ ounces finely grated Parmesan cheese*
*2 garlic cloves*
*6 tablespoons olive oil*

**Serves 4**

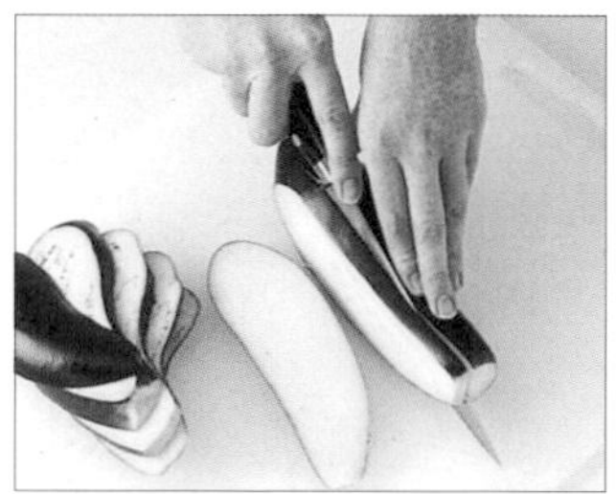

1 Cut the eggplant lengthwise into ½-inch slices.

2 Cut the slices again crosswise to give short strips.

3 Layer the strips in a colander with salt and let stand for 30 minutes over a plate to catch any juices. Rinse well in cool water and then drain thoroughly.

4 Place all the pesto ingredients, except the oil, in a blender or food processor. Blend until very smooth, then gradually add the oil in a thin stream until the mixture amalgamates. Season to taste.

5 Cook the penne in plenty of boiling salted water according to the instructions on the package for about 8 minutes or until *al dente*. Add the eggplant and cook for a further 3 minutes.

6 Drain the pasta well and mix in the mint pesto and walnut halves. Serve immediately.

# Macaroni with Hazelnut and Cilantro Sauce

THIS IS A VARIATION on pesto sauce, giving a smooth, herbed flavor of cilantro.

**INGREDIENTS**

*3 cups dried macaroni*
*1/3 cup hazelnuts*
*2 garlic cloves*
*1 bunch fresh cilantro*
*1 teaspoon salt*
*6 tablespoons olive oil*
*fresh cilantro sprigs, to garnish*

**Serves 4**

1 Cook the pasta following the instructions on the package, until *al dente*.

2 Meanwhile, finely chop the hazelnuts.

**COOK'S TIP**

*To remove the skins from the hazelnuts, place them in a 350°F oven for 20 minutes, then rub off the skins with a clean dish towel.*

**VARIATION**

*If you like the crunchy texture of the nuts, only process the nut and herb mixture briefly.*

3 Place the nuts, garlic, cilantro, salt and 5 tablespoons of the olive oil in a food processor, or use a pestle and mortar and grind together to create the sauce.

4 Heat the remaining oil in a saucepan and add the sauce. Fry very gently for about 1 minute until heated through.

5 Drain the pasta thoroughly and stir it into the sauce. Toss well to coat. Serve immediately, garnished with fresh cilantro.

# Tagliatelle with Spinach and Garlic Cheese

IT'S FUN TO MIX ingredients from different cuisines and produce a delicious dish as a result. Italian colored pasta and spinach combine with Chinese soy sauce and French garlic-and-herb cream cheese to create this mouthwatering and wonderfully rich dish.

**INGREDIENTS**

*8 ounces fresh egg tagliatelle*
*8 ounces fresh leaf spinach*
*2 tablespoons light soy sauce*
*3 ounces garlic-and-herb cheese*
*3 tablespoons milk*
*salt and ground black pepper*
**Serves 4**

1 Cook the tagliatelle in plenty of salted boiling water according to the instructions on the package. Drain and return to the pan.

2 Blanch the spinach in a tiny amount of water until just wilted, then drain well, squeezing dry with the back of a wooden spoon. Chop coarsely with scissors.

3 Return the spinach to its pan and stir in the soy sauce, garlic-and-herb cheese and the milk. Bring slowly to a boil, stirring until smooth. Season to taste.

4 When the sauce is ready, pour over the pasta. Toss the pasta and sauce together and serve hot in warmed plates.

# Tagliatelle with Greek Avocado Sauce

THIS IS AN UNUSUAL sauce with a pale green color, studded with red tomato. It has a luxurious, velvety texture. The sauce is rather rich, so you don't need too much of it.

**INGREDIENTS**

*3 ripe tomatoes*
*2 large ripe avocados*
*2 tablespoons butter, plus extra for tossing the pasta*
*1 garlic clove, crushed*
*1 ½ cups heavy cream*
*dash of Tabasco sauce*
*1 pound fresh egg tagliatelle*
*salt and ground black pepper*
*freshly grated Parmesan cheese, to garnish*
*4 tablespoons sour cream, to garnish*
**Serves 6**

1 Halve the tomatoes and remove the cores. Squeeze out the seeds and dice the flesh. Set the flesh aside until required.

2 Halve the avocados, remove the pits and peel. Coarsely chop the flesh. If hard-skinned, scoop out the flesh with a spoon.

3 Melt the butter in a saucepan and add the garlic. Cook for 1 minute, then add the cream and chopped avocados. Increase the heat, stirring constantly and breaking up the avocado flesh with a spoon.

4 Add the diced tomatoes and season to taste with salt, pepper and a little Tabasco sauce. Keep the mixture warm.

5 Cook the pasta in plenty of salted boiling water according to the instructions on the package. Drain well through a colander and toss with a pat of butter.

6 Divide the pasta among four warmed bowls and spoon the sauce on top. Sprinkle with grated Parmesan cheese and top with a spoonful of sour cream.

# Fusilli with Bell Peppers and Onions

BELL PEPPERS ARE characteristic of southern Italy. When grilled and peeled they have a delicious smoky flavor, and are easier to digest.

**INGREDIENTS**

*1 pound red and yellow bell peppers*
*6 tablespoons olive oil*
*1 large red onion, thinly sliced*
*2 garlic cloves, minced*
*3½ cups fresh or dried fusilli*
*3 tablespoons finely chopped fresh parsley*
*salt and ground black pepper*
*freshly grated Parmesan cheese, to serve*

**Serves 4**

1 Place the bell peppers under a hot broiler and turn occasionally until they are blackened and blistered on all sides. Remove from the heat, place in a plastic bag, seal and put to one side for 5 minutes or so.

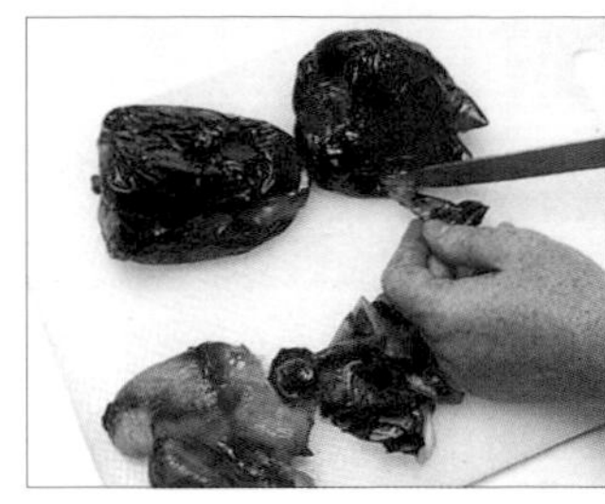

2 Peel the bell peppers. Cut them into quarters, remove the stems and seeds, and slice into thin strips.

3 Heat the oil in a large frying pan. Add the onion, and cook over a moderate heat until softened but not brown, about 5–8 minutes. Stir in the garlic, and cook for a further 2 minutes, stirring continuously.

4 Cook the pasta in a large saucepan with plenty of salted boiling water until just *al dente*. Do not drain yet.

5 Meanwhile, add the bell peppers to the onion, and mix together gently. Stir in about 3 tablespoons of the pasta cooking water. Season with salt and pepper. Stir in the finely chopped fresh parsley.

6 Drain the pasta well through a colander. Turn it into the pan with the vegetables, and cook over a moderate heat for 3–4 minutes, stirring continuously to mix the pasta into the sauce. Serve immediately in warmed plates with the grated Parmesan cheese handed separately.

# Fusilli with Cream and Cheese

Sour cream and two cheeses make a lovely rich sauce.

**INGREDIENTS**

*12 ounces dried fusilli col buco*
*2 tablespoons butter*
*1 onion, chopped*
*1 garlic clove, chopped*
*1 tablespoon chopped fresh oregano*
*1 ¼ cups sour cream*
*¾ cup grated mozzarella cheese*
*¾ cup grated Bel Paese cheese*
*5 sun-dried tomatoes in oil, drained and sliced*
*salt and ground black pepper*

**Serves 4**

1 Cook the pasta in plenty of salted boiling water according to the instructions on the package.

2 Melt the butter in a large frying pan and fry the onion for about 10 minutes until softened. Add the garlic and cook for 1 minute.

3 Stir in the oregano and cream and heat gently until almost boiling. Stir in the mozzarella and Bel Paese cheese and heat gently, stirring occasionally, until melted. Add the sun-dried tomatoes and season to taste.

4 Drain the pasta twists well and turn into a serving dish. Pour over the sauce and toss well to coat. Serve immediately.

# Mezze with Cheese and Coriander

A speedy supper dish, this is best served with a simple tomato and fresh basil salad.

**INGREDIENTS**

*4 cups dried mezze rigatoni*
*4 ounces full-fat garlic-and-herb cheese*
*2 tablespoons fresh cilantro, very finely chopped*
*1 ¼ cups light cream*
*1 cup shelled fresh peas or frozen, cooked*
*salt and ground black pepper*

**Serves 4**

1 Cook the pasta in a large saucepan with plenty of salted boiling water according to the instructions on the package.

2 Melt the cheese in a small pan over low heat until smooth.

3 Stir in the cilantro, cream and salt and pepper. Bring slowly to a boil, stirring occasionally, until well blended. Stir in the peas and continue cooking until heated through.

4 Drain the pasta and turn into a large serving dish. Pour over the sauce and toss well to coat thoroughly. Serve immediately.

**Cook's Tip**

*If you do not like the pronounced flavor of fresh cilantro, substitute another fresh herb, such as basil leaves or Italian parsley.*

# Spaghetti with Pesto Sauce

DON'T STINT on the fresh basil—this is the most wonderful sauce in the world—and it tastes completely different from the ready-made pesto sold in jars.

**INGREDIENTS**

*2 garlic cloves*
*½ cup pine nuts*
*1 cup fresh basil leaves*
*⅔ cup olive oil*
*4 tablespoons unsalted butter, softened*
*4 tablespoons freshly grated Parmesan cheese*
*1 pound fresh or dried spaghetti*
*salt and ground black pepper*

**Serves 4**

1 Peel the garlic and place it in a blender or food processor. Add a little salt and the pine nuts and process the ingredients until broken up. Add the basil leaves to the mixture and continue to process until you have formed a thick paste.

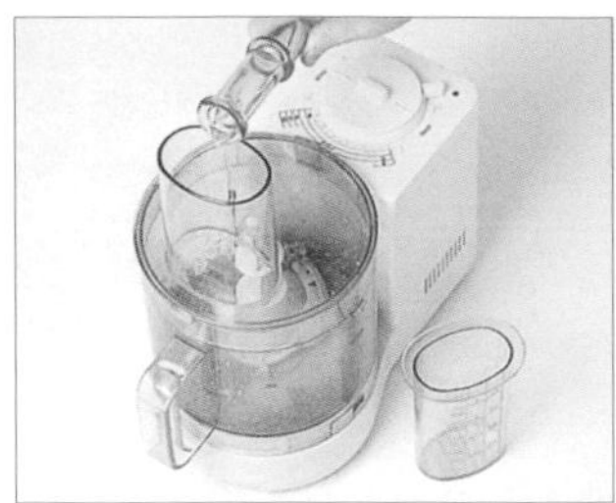

2 Gradually add the olive oil, little by little, until the mixture is creamy, smooth and thick.

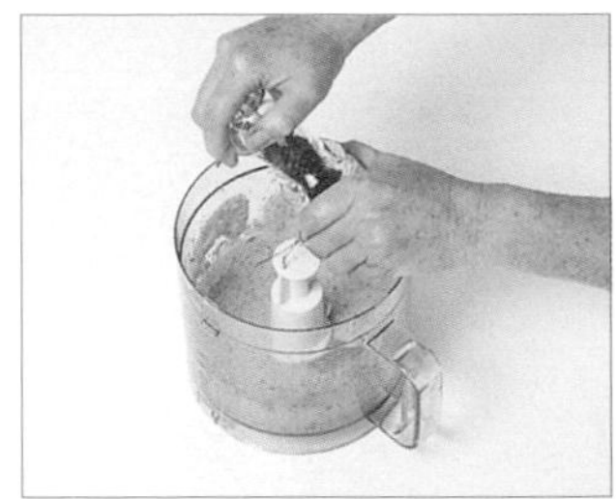

3 Beat in the butter and season with ground black pepper. Beat in the cheese. Alternatively, you can make the pesto by hand using a pestle and mortar to blend the ingredients.

4 Store the pesto sauce in a jar, with a layer of olive oil on top to exclude the air, in the refrigerator until you are ready to use it.

5 Cook the pasta in plenty of salted boiling water according to the instructions on the package, until *al dente*. Drain well.

6 Toss the pasta with half the pesto and serve in warm bowls, with the remaining pesto sauce spooned over the top.

# Spaghetti with Fresh Tomato Sauce

THE HEAT FROM the pasta will release the delicious flavors of this sauce. Only use the really red and soft tomatoes—large ripe beefsteak tomatoes are ideal. Don't be tempted to use small hard tomatoes: they have very little flavor.

**INGREDIENTS**

*4 large ripe tomatoes*
*2 garlic cloves, finely chopped*
*4 tablespoons chopped fresh herbs, such as basil, marjoram, oregano or parsley*
*⅔ cup olive oil*
*1 pound dried spaghetti*
*salt and ground black pepper*
**Serves 4**

1 Skin the tomatoes by placing them in a saucepan of boiling water for 1 minute. Lift out with a slotted spoon and plunge immediately into a bowl of cold water. You will then find that the skins peel off easily. Dry the tomatoes on paper towels.

2 Halve the peeled tomatoes and squeeze out the seeds. Chop into ¼-inch cubes and mix with the garlic, herbs, olive oil and seasoning in a non-metallic bowl. Cover and set aside to let the flavors mellow for at least 30 minutes.

3 Cook the pasta in plenty of salted boiling water, according to the instructions on the package.

4 Drain the pasta and mix with the sauce. Cover with a lid and leave for 2–3 minutes, then toss again and serve immediately.

**VARIATION**

*Mix 1 cup pitted and chopped black Greek olives into the sauce just before serving.*

# Spaghetti with Eggplant and Tomato

A GREAT SUPPER RECIPE—serve this eggplant and tomato dish with freshly cooked snow peas.

**INGREDIENTS**

*3 small eggplant*
*olive oil, for frying*
*1 pound dried spaghetti*
*1 quantity Classic Tomato Sauce (see Curly Lasagne with Classic Tomato Sauce)*
*8 ounces freshly grated Fontina cheese*
*salt and ground black pepper*

**Serves 4**

1 Top and tail the eggplant and cut into thin, even slices. Arrange in a colander, sprinkling with plenty of salt between each layer. Let stand for about 30 minutes.

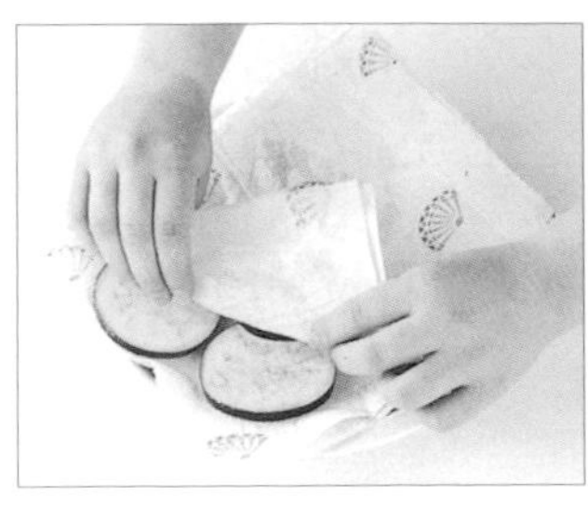

2 Rinse the eggplant slices under cold running water. Drain and pat dry on paper towels.

3 Heat plenty of oil in a large frying pan and fry the eggplant slices in batches for about 5 minutes, turning them once during the cooking time, until evenly browned.

4 Meanwhile, cook the pasta in a large saucepan with plenty of salted boiling water according to the instructions on the package, until *al dente*.

5 Stir the tomato sauce into the pan with the eggplant and bring to a boil. Cover and then simmer for 5 minutes.

6 Stir in the Fontina cheese and salt and pepper. Continue stirring over medium heat until the cheese melts.

7 Drain the pasta and stir into the sauce, tossing well to coat. Serve immediately on warmed plates.

# Pasta Pumpkin Surprise

GLORIOUS PUMPKIN SHELLS summon up the delights of fall and seem too good simply to throw away. Use one instead of a serving dish. Pumpkin and pasta make marvellous partners, especially as a main course served from the baked shell.

**INGREDIENTS**

*4–4$\frac{1}{2}$ pounds pumpkin*
*1 onion, sliced*
*1 inch piece fresh ginger root*
*3 tablespoons extra virgin olive oil*
*1 zucchini, sliced*
*4 ounces mushrooms, sliced*
*1 can (14 ounces) chopped tomatoes*
*$\frac{3}{4}$ cup dried conchiglie*
*1$\frac{3}{4}$ cups stock*
*4 tablespoons ricotta cheese*
*2 tablespoons chopped fresh basil*
*salt and ground black pepper*

**Serves 4**

1 Preheat the oven to 350°F. Cut the top off the pumpkin with a large, sharp knife and scoop out and discard all of the pumpkin seeds.

2 Using a small sharp knife and a sturdy tablespoon, cut and scrape out as much flesh from the pumpkin shell as possible, then chop the flesh into coarse chunks.

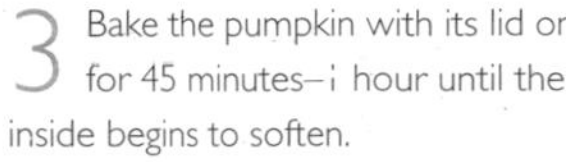

3 Bake the pumpkin with its lid on for 45 minutes–1 hour until the inside begins to soften.

4 Meanwhile, make the filling. Heat the olive oil in a pan and gently fry the onion, ginger and pumpkin flesh for about 10 minutes, stirring the mixture occasionally.

5 Add the sliced zucchini and mushrooms and cook for a further 3 minutes, then stir in the tomatoes, pasta and stock. Season well, bring to a boil, then cover the pan and simmer gently for about 10 minutes.

6 Stir the ricotta cheese and basil into the pasta and spoon the mixture into the pumpkin. It may not be possible to fit all the filling into the pumpkin shell, so serve the rest separately if necessary.

# Baked Pasta

Like Bolognese sauce, lasagne, macaroni cheese and cannelloni have become so popular outside Italy that we seldom stop to consider the origins of these delicious pasta dishes. A kind of layered pasta pie was mentioned by the Roman gastronome Apicius in the first century AD, so we know that lasagne, at least, has a very long history. In the Renaissance, sumptuous layered pasta dishes, often molded into fanciful shapes, were popular with the wealthy. Nowadays, *pasta al forno*, as baked pasta dishes are called in Italy, are more often eaten at family meals, especially on occasions when large numbers must be catered for. Baked dishes can be prepared in advance and are easy to serve.

This chapter introduces classic dishes and regional favorites with modern adaptations. In calculating serving quantities, it is assumed that the dish will be a main course, but smaller portions can be served as a first course, which in more traditional in Italy.

# Chicken Cannelloni al Forno

A LIGHTER ALTERNATIVE to the usual beef-filled, béchamel-coated version. Fill with ricotta cheese, onion and mushroom for a vegetarian version.

**INGREDIENTS**

*1 pound skinless, boneless chicken breast, cooked*
*8 ounces mushrooms*
*2 garlic cloves, crushed*
*2 tablespoons chopped fresh parsley*
*1 tablespoon chopped fresh tarragon*
*1 egg, beaten*
*freshly squeezed lemon juice*
*12–18 fresh or dried cannelloni tubes*
*1 quantity fresh tomato sauce (see Curly Lasagne with Classic Tomato Sauce)*
*1½ cup freshly grated Parmesan cheese*
*salt and ground black pepper*
*fresh parsley sprig, to garnish*

**Serves 4–6**

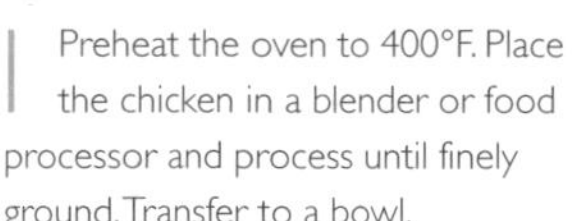

1 Preheat the oven to 400°F. Place the chicken in a blender or food processor and process until finely ground. Transfer to a bowl.

2 Place the mushrooms, garlic, parsley and tarragon in the blender or food processor and process until finely ground.

3 Beat the mushroom mixture into the chicken with the egg, salt and ground black pepper and lemon juice to taste.

4 If necessary, cook the cannelloni in plenty of salted boiling water according to the instructions on the package. Drain well and pat dry on a clean dish towel.

5 Place the filling in a pastry bag fitted with a large plain nozzle. Use to fill each tube of cannelloni

6 Lay the filled cannelloni tightly together in a single layer in a buttered shallow ovenproof dish. Spoon the tomato sauce over and sprinkle with Parmesan cheese. Bake in the oven for 30 minutes or until brown and bubbling. Serve the cannelloni garnished with a sprig of parsley.

# Eggplant Lasagne

THIS DELICIOUS LASAGNE is also suitable for home freezing.

**INGREDIENTS**

*3 eggplant, sliced*
*5 tablespoons olive oil*
*2 large onions, finely chopped*
*2 cans (14-ounce) chopped tomatoes*
*1 teaspoon dried mixed herbs*
*2–3 garlic cloves, crushed*
*6 sheets "no-need-to-pre-cook" dried lasagne sheets*
*salt and ground black pepper*

***For the cheese sauce***
*2 tablespoons butter*
*2 tablespoons all-purpose flour*
*1¼ cups milk*
*½ teaspoon hot mustard*
*8 tablespoons grated mature Cheddar*
*1 tablespoon grated Parmesan cheese*

**Serves 4**

1 Layer the sliced eggplant in a colander, sprinkling lightly with salt between each layer. Let stand for 1 hour, then rinse and pat dry with paper towel.

2 Heat 4 tablespoons of the oil in a large pan, fry the eggplant and drain on paper towels. Add the remaining oil to the pan, cook the onions for 5 minutes, then stir in the tomatoes, herbs, garlic and seasoning. Bring to a boil and simmer, covered, for 30 minutes.

3 To make the sauce, melt the butter in a pan, stir in the flour and cook gently for 1 minute, stirring. Gradually stir in the milk. Bring to a boil, stirring, and cook for 2 minutes. Remove from the heat and stir in the mustard, cheeses and seasoning.

4 Preheat the oven to 400°F. Arrange half the eggplant in the base of an ovenproof dish, spoon half the tomato sauce over. Arrange three sheets of lasagne on top. Repeat.

5 Spoon the cheese sauce over, cover and bake for 30 minutes until lightly browned.

**COOK'S TIP**

*To save time, this recipe uses lasagne that does not need pre-cooking. Look in the supermarket, or ask at your delicatessen, for lasagne sheets marked "no need to pre-cook."*

# Mushroom and Zucchini Lasagne

THIS IS THE PERFECT main-course lasagne for vegetarians. Adding dried porcini to fresh chestnut mushrooms intensifies the "mushroomy" flavor and gives the whole dish more substance. Serve with crusty Italian bread.

**INGREDIENTS**

*1/2 ounce dried porcini mushrooms*
*3/4 cup warm water*
*2 tablespoons olive oil*
*6 tablespoons butter*
*1 pound zucchini, thinly sliced*
*1 onion, finely chopped*
*6 cups brown mushrooms, thinly sliced*
*2 garlic cloves, crushed*
*1 quantity Winter Tomato Sauce*
*2 teaspoons chopped fresh marjoram or 1 teaspoon dried marjoram, plus extra fresh leaves, to garnish*
*6–8 "no-need-to-pre-cook" dried lasagne sheets*
*2/3 cup freshly grated Parmesan cheese*
*salt and ground black pepper*

***For the white sauce***
*3 tablespoons butter*
*1/3 cup all-purpose flour*
*3 3/4 cups hot milk*
*nutmeg*
**Serves 6**

1 Put the dried porcini mushrooms in a bowl. Pour over the warm water and leave to soak for 15–20 minutes. Pour the porcini and liquid into a fine strainer set over a bowl and squeeze the mushrooms with your hands to release as much liquid as possible. Chop the mushrooms finely and set aside. Strain the soaking liquid through a fine sieve and reserve half for the sauce.

2 Preheat the oven to 375°F. Heat the olive oil with 2 tablespoons of the butter in a large skillet or saucepan.

3 Add about half the zucchini slices to the pan and season with salt and pepper to taste. Cook the zucchini over medium heat, turning the slices frequently, for 5–8 minutes until they are lightly colored on both sides. Remove the zucchini from the pan with a slotted spoon and allow to drain on paper towels. Repeat with the remaining zucchini.

4 Melt half the remaining butter in the fat remaining in the pan, then cook the finely chopped onion, stirring, for 1–2 minutes. Add half of the fresh mushrooms and the crushed garlic to the pan and sprinkle with a little salt and pepper to taste.

5 Toss the mushrooms over high heat for 5 minutes or so until the mushrooms are juicy and tender. Transfer to a bowl with a slotted spoon, then repeat with the remaining butter and mushrooms.

6 Make the white sauce. Melt the butter in a large saucepan, add the flour and cook, stirring, over medium heat for 1–2 minutes.

7 Add the hot milk a little at a time, whisking well after each addition. Bring to a boil and cook, stirring, until the sauce is smooth and thick. Grate in fresh nutmeg to taste and season with a little salt and pepper. Whisk well, then remove the sauce from the heat.

8 Place the tomato sauce in a blender or food processor with the reserved porcini soaking liquid and blend to a pureé. Add the zucchini to the bowl of fried mushrooms, then stir in the porcini and marjoram.

9 Adjust the seasoning to taste, then spread a third of the tomato sauce in a baking dish. Add half the vegetable mixture, spreading it evenly.

10 Top with about a third of the white sauce, then about half the lasagne sheets. Repeat these layers, then top with the remaining tomato sauce and white sauce and sprinkle with the grated Parmesan cheese.

11 Bake the lasagne for 35–40 minutes, or until the pasta feels tender when pierced with a skewer. Let stand for about 10 minutes before serving. If you like, sprinkle each serving with marjoram leaves.

### Cook's Tips

- *The amount of pasta will depend on the size and shape of the pasta sheets and your baking dish; you may need to break the pasta to fit.*
- *This dish is time-consuming to prepare, but well worth the effort. You can make the tomato sauce in advance and chill it for up to 2 days until you are ready to assemble the lasagne, or you can freeze it. Make sure that you leave it to thaw completely before using.*

# Baked Tortellini with Three Cheeses

SERVE THIS STRAIGHT out of the oven while the cheese is still runny. If smoked mozzarella cheese is not available, try using a smoked German cheese or even grated smoked Cheddar as an alternative.

**INGREDIENTS**

*1 pound fresh tortellini*
*2 eggs*
*1 ½ cups ricotta or curd cheese*
*2 tablespoons butter*
*1 ounce fresh basil leaves*
*4 ounces smoked mozzarella cheese*
*4 tablespoons freshly grated Parmesan cheese*
*salt and ground black pepper*

**Serves 4–6**

1 Preheat the oven to 375°F. Cook the fresh tortellini in plenty of salted boiling water according to the instructions on the package. Drain well.

2 Beat the eggs with the ricotta or curd cheese and season well with salt and pepper.

3 Use the butter to grease an ovenproof dish. Spoon in half the tortellini, pour half the cheese mixture over and cover with half the basil leaves.

4 Cover with the mozzarella and remaining basil. Top with the rest of the tortellini and spread the remaining ricotta or curd cheese mixture over.

5 Sprinkle evenly with the Parmesan cheese. Bake in the oven for 35–45 minutes or until golden brown and bubbling.

# Cannelloni with Mixed Vegetables

THIS VERSION of a classic Italian dish introduces a variety of vegetables topped with cheese sauce.

**INGREDIENTS**

*8 dried cannelloni tubes*
*4 ounces spinach*
*tomatoes and green salad, to serve*

***For the filling***

*1 tablespoon oil*
*1½ cups ground beef*
*2 garlic cloves, crushed*
*2 tablespoons all-purpose flour*
*½ cup beef stock*
*1 small carrot, finely chopped*
*1 small yellow zucchini, chopped*
*salt and ground black pepper*

***For the sauce***

*2 tablespoons butter*
*2 tablespoons all-purpose flour*
*1 cup milk*
*½ cup freshly grated Parmesan cheese*

**Serves 4**

1 Preheat the oven to 350°F. For the filling, heat the oil in a large pan. Add the ground beef and garlic. Cook for 5 minutes.

2 Add the flour and cook for a further 1 minute. Slowly stir in the stock and bring to a boil.

3 Add the carrot and zucchini and season. Cook for 10 minutes.

4 Spoon the beef mixture into the cannelloni tubes and place in an ovenproof dish.

5 Blanch the spinach in boiling water for 3 minutes. Drain well and place on top of the cannelloni tubes in the dish.

6 For the sauce melt the butter in a pan. Add the flour and cook for 1 minute. Pour in the milk, add the grated cheese and season well. Bring to a boil, stirring continuously. Pour over the cannelloni and spinach and bake for 30 minutes. Serve with tomatoes and a crisp green salad, if liked.

# Vermicelli Omelet

A FRITTATA IS A FLAT BAKED omelet. Here it is made with vegetables and herbs, but you can put anything you fancy in it. Ham, sausage, salami, chicken, mushrooms, zucchini and eggplant are just a few suggestions, or you could simply add mixed herbs. Frittata is absolutely delicious cold. Cut into wedges, it is excellent food for picnics.

**INGREDIENTS**

*2 ounces dried vermicelli*
*6 eggs*
*4 tablespoons* panna da cucina *or heavy cream*
*1 handful fresh basil leaves, shredded*
*1 handful fresh Italian parsley, chopped*
*1 cup freshly grated Parmesan cheese*
*25g/1 ounces /2 tablespoons butter*
*1 tablespoon olive oil*
*1 onion, finely sliced*
*3 large pieces bottled roasted red bell pepper, drained, rinsed, dried and cut into strips*
*1 garlic clove, crushed*
*salt and ground black pepper*
*arugula leaves, to serve*

**Serves 4–6**

1 Preheat the oven to 375°F. Cook the pasta in a saucepan of salted boiling water for 8 minutes.

2 Meanwhile, break the eggs into a bowl and add the cream and herbs. Whisk in about two-thirds of the grated Parmesan and add salt and pepper to taste.

3 Drain the pasta well and allow to cool; snip it into short lengths with scissors. Add to the egg mixture and whisk again. Set aside.

4 Melt the butter in the oil in a large, ovenproof non-stick frying pan. Add the onion and cook gently, stirring frequently, for 5 minutes until softened. Add the bell peppers and garlic.

5 Pour the egg and pasta mixture into the pan and stir well. Cook over low to medium heat, without stirring, for 3–5 minutes or until the frittata is just set underneath. Sprinkle the remaining Parmesan over and bake in the oven for 5 minutes or until set. Before serving, let stand for at least 5 minutes. Cut into wedges and serve warm or cold, with arugula.

# Lasagne "Bolognese"

THIS IS THE CLASSIC *lasagne al forno*. It is based on a rich, meaty filling, as you would expect from an authentic Bolognese recipe.

**INGREDIENTS**

*1 quantity Bolognese sauce (see* Tagliatelle with Bolognese Sauce*)*
*2/3–1 cup hot beef stock*
*12 "no-need-to-pre-cook" dried lasagne sheets*
*2/3 cup freshly grated Parmesan cheese*

***For the white sauce***
*1/4 cup butter*
*1/2 cup all-purpose flour*
*3 3/4 cups hot milk*
*salt and ground black pepper*
**Serves 6**

1 Preheat the oven to 375°F. If the Bolognese sauce is cold, reheat it. Once it is hot, stir in enough stock to make it quite runny.

2 Make the white sauce. Melt the butter in a medium saucepan, add the flour and cook, stirring, for 1–2 minutes. Add the milk a little at a time, whisking vigorously after each addition. Bring to a boil and cook, stirring, until the sauce is smooth and thick. Add salt and pepper to taste, whisk well, then remove from the heat.

3 Spread about a third of the Bolognese sauce over the bottom of a baking dish.

4 Cover the Bolognese sauce in the base of the dish with about a quarter of the white sauce, followed by four sheets of lasagne. Repeat the layers twice more, then cover the top layer of lasagne with the remaining white sauce and sprinkle the grated Parmesan evenly over the top.

5 Bake for 40–45 minutes or until the pasta feels tender when pierced with a skewer. Let stand for about 10 minutes before serving.

**COOK'S TIPS**

- *The Bolognese sauce can be made up to 3 days in advance and kept in a covered container in the refrigerator.*
- *The lasagne is best baked straight after layering or the pasta will begin to absorb the sauces and dry out.*
- *To reheat leftover lasagne, prick it all over with a skewer, then slowly pour a little milk over to moisten. Cover with foil and reheat in a 375°F oven for 20 minutes, or until bubbling.*

# Baked Lasagne with Béchamel Sauce

THIS LASAGNE made from egg pasta uses a béchamel sauce flavored with bay and mace to give it a lift.

**INGREDIENTS**

*2 quantities Bolognese sauce (see Tagliatelle with Bolognese Sauce)*
*12–16 fresh egg lasagne sheets or 14 ounces dried lasagne*
*1 cup grated Parmesan cheese*
*3 tablespoons butter*

***For the béchamel sauce***
*3 cups milk*
*1 bay leaf*
*3 mace blades*
*½ cup butter*
*¾ cup all-purpose flour*
*salt and ground black pepper*
**Serves 8–10**

1 Prepare the meat sauce and set aside. Butter a large shallow baking dish, preferably rectangular or square.

**COOK'S TIP**

*If you are using dried or bought pasta, follow step 4, but boil the lasagne in just two batches, and stop the cooking about 4 minutes before the recommended cooking time on the package has elapsed. Rinse in cold water and lay the pasta out the same way as for the egg pasta.*

2 Make the béchamel sauce by gently heating the milk with the bay leaf and mace in a small saucepan. Melt the butter in a medium heavy saucepan. Add the flour, and mix well with a wire whisk. Cook for 2–3 minutes, whisking constantly. Strain the hot milk into the flour and butter, and mix smoothly with the whisk. Bring the sauce to a boil, stirring constantly, and cook for a further 4–5 minutes. Season with salt and pepper and set aside.

3 If making your own fresh pasta, make sure it does not dry out. Cut it into rectangles measuring about 4½ inches wide and the same length as the baking dish (this will make it easier to assemble the dish later). Preheat the oven to 400°F.

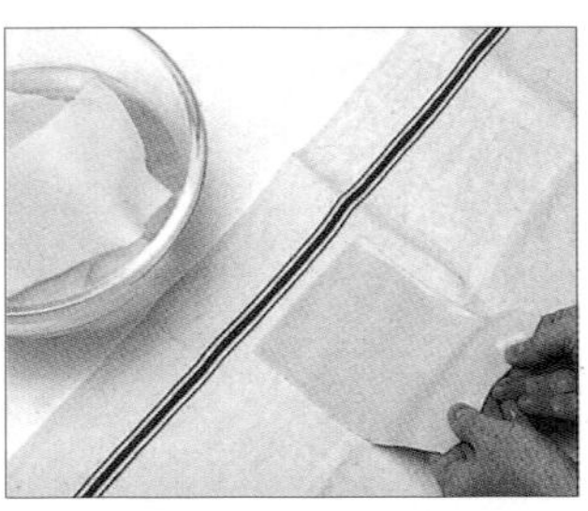

4 Bring a very large pan of water to a boil. Place a large bowl of cold water near the stove. Cover a large counter with a tablecloth. Add salt to the rapidly boiling water. Drop in 3 or 4 of the egg pasta rectangles. Cook very briefly, about 30 seconds. Remove the pasta from the pan, using a slotted spoon, and drop into the cold water for about 30 seconds. Pull them out of the water, shaking off the excess water. Lay them out flat without overlapping on the tablecloth. Repeat until all the pasta rectangles and the trimmings have been thoroughly drained on the tablecloth.

5 To assemble the lasagne, spread one large spoonful of the meat sauce over the base of the dish. Arrange a layer of pasta in the dish, cutting it with a sharp knife so that it covers the meat sauce.

6 Cover with another thin layer of meat sauce, then one of béchamel. Sprinkle with a little cheese. Repeat the layers in the same order, and ending with a layer of pasta coated with béchamel. Do not make more than about 6 layers of pasta. Use the pasta trimmings to patch any gaps in the pasta. Sprinkle the top with grated Parmesan cheese, and dot with butter.

7 Bake in the preheated oven for 20 minutes, or until brown on top. Remove from the oven and let stand for about 5 minutes before serving. Serve directly from the baking dish, cutting out rectangular or square sections for each helping.

# Pasta Timbales

An alternative way to serve pasta for a special occasion is to mix it with ground beef and tomato and bake it in a lettuce parcel.

**INGREDIENTS**

*8 cos lettuce leaves*
*fresh basil leaves, to garnish*

***For the filling***

*1 tablespoon oil*
*1½ cups ground beef*
*1 tablespoon tomato paste*
*1 garlic clove, crushed*
*1 cup fresh or dried macaroni*
*salt and ground black pepper*

***For the sauce***

*2 tablespoons butter*
*2 tablespoons all-purpose flour*
*1 cup heavy cream*
*2 tablespoons chopped fresh basil*

**Serves 4**

1 Preheat the oven to 350°F. For the filling, heat the oil in a large pan and fry the ground beef for 7 minutes. Add the tomato paste and garlic and cook for a further 5 minutes.

2 Cook the macaroni in salted boiling water for 8–10 minutes or until *al dente*. Drain.

3 Mix together the pasta and ground beef mixture.

4 Line four ⅔ cup ramekin dishes with the cos lettuce leaves. Season the mince and spoon into the lettuce-lined ramekins.

5 Fold the lettuce leaves over the filling and place the ramekins in a roasting pan. Carefully pour boiling water to come halfway up the sides of the ramekins. Cover and cook for 20 minutes.

6 For the sauce, melt the butter in a pan. Add the flour and cook for 1 minute. Stir in the cream and fresh basil. Season and bring to a boil, stirring constantly. Turn out the timbales and serve on warmed plates with the creamy basil sauce, and garnish with fresh basil leaves.

# Broccoli and Ricotta Cannelloni

A DELICIOUS AND FILLING dish for a meat-free dinner.

**INGREDIENTS**

*12 dried cannelloni tubes, 3 inches long*
*4 cups broccoli flowerets*
*1 ½ cups fresh bread crumbs*
*⅔ cup milk*
*4 tablespoons olive oil, plus extra for brushing*
*1 cup ricotta cheese*
*pinch of grated nutmeg*
*6 tablespoons grated Parmesan or Pecorino cheese*
*salt and ground black pepper*
*2 tablespoons pine nuts, for sprinkling*

***For the tomato sauce***
*2 tablespoons olive oil*
*1 onion, finely chopped*
*1 garlic clove, crushed*
*2 cans (14-ounce) chopped tomatoes*
*1 tablespoon tomato paste*
*4 black olives, pitted and chopped*
*1 teaspoon dried thyme*

**Serves 4**

1 Preheat the oven to 375°F and lightly grease an ovenproof dish with olive oil. Bring a large saucepan of water to a boil, add a little olive oil and simmer the cannelloni tubes, uncovered, for about 6–7 minutes, or until nearly cooked.

2 Meanwhile, steam or boil the broccoli for 10 minutes, until tender. Drain the pasta, rinse under cold water and reserve. Drain the broccoli and let cool, then place in a blender or food processor and process until smooth. Set aside.

3 Place the bread crumbs in a bowl, add the milk and oil and stir until softened. Add the ricotta, broccoli purée, nutmeg, 4 tablespoons of the Parmesan cheese and seasoning, then set aside.

4 To make the sauce, heat the oil in a frying pan; add the onion and garlic. Fry for 5–6 minutes, until softened but not brown.

5 Stir the tomatoes, tomato paste, black olives, thyme and seasoning into the sauce. Boil rapidly for 2–3 minutes, then pour into the base of the dish.

6 Spoon the cheese mixture into a pastry bag fitted with a ½-inch nozzle. Carefully open the cannelloni tubes. Standing each one upright on a board, pipe the filling into each tube. Lay them in rows in the tomato sauce.

7 Brush the tops of the cannelloni with a little olive oil and sprinkle over the remaining Parmesan cheese and pine nuts. Bake for about 25–30 minutes, until golden on top.

# Cannelloni al Forno

THIS IS A RICH AND SUBSTANTIAL dish, which takes quite a long time to prepare. Serve it for a party—it can be made a day ahead up to the baking stage. Your guests are bound to appreciate your efforts, because the cannelloni tastes so good.

**INGREDIENTS**

*1 tablespoon olive oil*
*1 small onion, finely chopped*
*1 pound ground beef*
*1 garlic clove, finely chopped*
*1 teaspoon mixed dried herbs*
*½ cup beef stock*
*1 egg*
*3 ounces cooked ham or mortadella sausage, finely chopped*
*3 tablespoons fine fresh white bread crumbs*
*1⅔ cups freshly grated Parmesan cheese*
*18 "no-need-to-pre-cook" cannelloni tubes*
*salt and ground black pepper*

***For the tomato sauce***

*2 tablespoons olive oil*
*1 small onion, finely chopped*
*½ carrot, finely chopped*
*1 celery stalk, finely chopped*
*1 garlic clove, crushed*
*1 can (14 ounces) chopped Italian plum tomatoes*
*a few sprigs of fresh basil*
*½ teaspoon dried oregano*

***For the white sauce***

*¼ cup butter*
*½ cup all-purpose flour*
*3¾ cups milk*
*nutmeg*

**Serves 6**

1 Heat the olive oil in a medium skillet or saucepan and cook the finely chopped onion over gentle heat, stirring occasionally, for about 5 minutes until softened.

2 Add the ground beef and garlic and cook gently for 10 minutes, stirring and breaking up any lumps with a wooden spoon. Add the dried herbs, and salt and pepper to taste, then moisten with half the stock. Cover the pan and simmer for 25 minutes, stirring occasionally and adding more stock as the mixture reduces. Spoon into a bowl and let cool.

3 Meanwhile, make the tomato sauce. Heat the olive oil in a medium saucepan, add the vegetables and garlic and cook over medium heat, stirring frequently, for about 10 minutes. Add the canned tomatoes. Fill the empty can with water, pour it into the pan, then stir in the herbs, with salt and pepper to taste. Bring to a boil, lower the heat, cover and simmer for 25–30 minutes, stirring occasionally. Purée the tomato sauce in a blender or food processor.

4 Add the egg, ham or mortadella, bread crumbs and 6 tablespoons of the grated Parmesan to the meat and stir well to mix. Taste for seasoning.

5 Spread a little of the tomato sauce over the base of a baking dish. Using a teaspoon, fill the cannelloni tubes with the meat mixture and place them in a single layer in the dish on top of the tomato sauce. Pour the remaining tomato sauce over the top.

6 Preheat the oven to 375°F. Make the white sauce. Melt the butter in a medium saucepan, add the flour and cook, stirring, for 1–2 minutes. Add the milk a little at a time, whisking vigorously after each addition.

7 Bring to a boil and cook, stirring, until the sauce is smooth and thick. Grate in fresh nutmeg to taste and season with a little salt and pepper. Whisk well, then remove from the heat.

8 Pour the white sauce over the stuffed cannelloni, then sprinkle with the remaining Parmesan. Place in the oven and bake for 40–45 minutes or until the cannelloni tubes feel tender when pierced with a skewer. Let the cannelloni stand for about 10 minutes before serving.

# Baked Macaroni with Cheese

THIS DELICIOUS DISH is perhaps less common in Italy than other pasta dishes, but has become a family favorite around the world.

**INGREDIENTS**

*2 cups milk*
*1 bay leaf*
*3 mace blades*
*4 tablespoons butter*
*⅓ cup flour*
*1½ cups grated Parmesan or Cheddar cheese, or a combination of both*
*⅓ cup bread crumbs*
*4 cups short-cut macaroni*
*salt and ground black pepper*

**Serves 6**

1 Make a béchamel sauce by gently heating the milk with the bay leaf and mace, in a small saucepan. Do not let it boil.

2 In a separate medium, heavy saucepan, melt the butter. Add the flour, and mix it in well with a wire whisk. Cook for 2–3 minutes, but do not let the butter burn.

3 Strain the hot milk into the flour and butter mixture all at once, and mix smoothly with the whisk. Bring the sauce to a boil, stirring constantly, and cook for a further 4–5 minutes.

4 Season with salt and pepper. Add all but 2 tablespoons of the cheese, and stir over low heat until melted. Place a layer of plastic wrap right on the surface of the sauce to prevent a skin forming and set aside while you prepare the pasta.

5 Preheat the oven to 400°F. Grease an ovenproof dish and sprinkle with some bread crumbs. Cook the pasta in plenty of boiling salted water until *al dente*.

6 Drain the pasta, and combine it with the sauce. Pour it into the prepared dish. Sprinkle the top with the remaining bread crumbs and grated cheese and bake in the center of the oven for 20 minutes, until golden and bubbling.

# Tagliatelle and Shrimp Parcels

A QUICK AND IMPRESSIVE dish, easy to prepare in advance and cook at the last minute. When the paper packages are opened at the table, the filling smells wonderful.

**INGREDIENTS**

*$1\frac{3}{4}$ pounds raw large shrimp in the shell*
*1 pound fresh egg tagliatelle*
*$\frac{2}{3}$ cup fresh or ready-made pesto sauce*
*4 teaspoons olive oil*
*1 garlic clove, crushed*
*$\frac{1}{2}$ cup dry white wine*
*salt and ground black pepper*
**Serves 4**

1 Preheat the oven to 400°F. Twist the heads off the shrimp, remove the legs and discard.

2 Cook the tagliatelle in plenty of rapidly boiling salted water for 2 minutes only, then drain. Mix with half the pesto.

3 Cut four 12-inch squares of waxed paper and place 1 teaspoon olive oil in the center of each. Pile equal amounts of pasta in the middle of each square.

4 Top with equal amounts of shrimp and spoon over the remaining pesto mixed with the garlic. Season with pepper; sprinkle each with the wine.

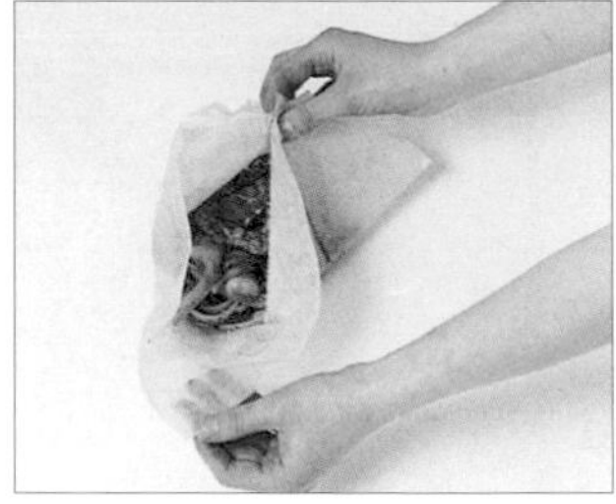

5 Brush the edges of the paper lightly with water and bring them loosely up around the filling, twisting to enclose. (The packages should look like money bags.)

6 Place the packages on a baking sheet. Bake in the oven for 10–15 minutes. Serve immediately, allowing the diners to open their own packages at the table.

**COOK'S TIP**

*Cooking in a paper package keeps the food moist and full of flavor, but care must be taken when opening the package because of the escaping steam.*

# Macaroni with Four Cheeses

RICH AND CREAMY, this is a deluxe macaroni cheese that can be served for an informal lunch or supper party. It goes well with both a tomato and basil salad or a leafy green salad.

**INGREDIENTS**

*2 1/4 cups short-cut macaroni*
*1/4 cup butter*
*1/2 cup all-purpose flour*
*2 1/2 cups milk*
*scant 1/2 cup panna da cucina or heavy cream*
*scant 1/2 cup dry white wine*
*1/2 cup grated Gruyère or Emmental cheese*
*2 ounces Fontina cheese, diced small*
*2 ounces Gorgonzola cheese, crumbled*
*1 cup freshly grated Parmesan cheese*
*salt and ground black pepper*
**Serves 4**

1 Preheat the oven to 350°F. Cook the pasta according to the instructions on the package.

2 Meanwhile, gently melt the butter in a medium saucepan, add the flour and cook, stirring, for 1–2 minutes. Add the milk a little at a time, whisking vigorously after each addition. Stir in the cream, followed by the dry white wine. Bring to a boil. Cook, stirring continuously, until the sauce thickens, then remove the sauce from the heat.

3 Add the Gruyère, Fontina, Gorgonzola and about a third of the grated Parmesan to the sauce. Stir well to mix in the cheeses, then taste for seasoning and add salt and pepper if necessary.

4 Drain the pasta well and turn it into a baking dish. Pour the sauce over the pasta and mix well, then sprinkle the remaining Parmesan over the top. Bake for 25–30 minutes or until golden brown. Serve hot.

# Sicilian Lasagne

LASAGNE IS NOT TRADITIONAL in Sicily as it is in northern Italy, but the Sicilians have their own version.

**INGREDIENTS**

*1 small onion*
*½ carrot*
*½ celery stalk*
*3 tablespoons olive oil*
*9 ounces diced boneless pork*
*4 tablespoons dry white wine*
*1 can (14 ounces) chopped Italian plum tomatoes or 1⅔ cups passata or tomato sauce*
*scant 1 cup chicken stock*
*1 tablespoon tomato paste*
*2 bay leaves*
*1 tablespoon chopped fresh Italian parsley*
*9 ounces fresh lasagne sheets, pre-cooked if necessary*
*2 hard-cooked eggs, sliced*
*4½ ounces package mozzarella cheese, drained and sliced*
*4 tablespoons freshly grated Pecorino cheese*
*salt and ground black pepper*

**Serves 6**

1 Chop the fresh vegetables finely, either in a food processor or by hand. Heat 2 tablespoons of the oil in a large skillet or saucepan, add the chopped vegetables and cook over medium heat, stirring frequently, for about 10 minutes.

2 Add the pork and fry for about 5 minutes, stirring occasionally, until well browned on all sides. Pour in the wine and let it bubble and reduce for a few minutes, then add the tomatoes or passata, the stock and the tomato paste. Make a tear in each bay leaf to release the flavor, then add to the pan with the parsley and salt and pepper to taste, mixing well. Cover and cook for 30–40 minutes until the pork is tender, stirring occasionally. Take the pan off the heat and remove and discard the bay leaves from the sauce.

3 Using a slotted spoon, lift the pieces of meat out of the sauce . Chop them coarsely, then return them to the sauce. Stir well.

4 Preheat the oven to 375°F. Bring a saucepan of salted water to a boil. Cut the lasagne sheets into 1-inch strips and add them to a boiling water. Cook for 3–4 minutes until just *al dente*. Drain well, then stir the strips into the sauce.

5 Spread out half the pasta and sauce mixture in a shallow baking dish and cover with half the egg and mozzarella slices and half the grated Pecorino. Repeat the layers, then drizzle the remaining oil over the top. Bake for 30–35 minutes until golden brown and bubbling. Let stand for about 10 minutes before serving.

# Fusilli with Ham and Cheese

WITH ITS CRISPY CRUST and moist and creamy center, this quick and easy pasta bake is both filling and nutritious. Serve it for a winter supper, with a salad on the side.

**INGREDIENTS 3**

*2¼ cups dried fusilli, eliche or other short pasta shapes*
*3 eggs*
*scant 1 cup milk*
*⅔ cup light cream*
*5 ounces Gruyère cheese*
*grated nutmeg*
*4 ounces cooked ham, cut into strips*
*2 tablespoons freshly grated Parmesan cheese*
*salt and ground black pepper*

**Serves 4**

1 Preheat the oven to 375°F. Bring a large saucepan of salted water to a boil. Add the pasta and cook for 5 minutes.

2 Meanwhile, beat the eggs in a measuring cup with the milk, cream and half the grated Gruyère. Grate in a little fresh nutmeg and season to taste.

3 Drain the pasta and turn half of it into a buttered baking dish. Arrange half the strips of ham on top, then follow with the remaining pasta and ham. Pour the egg and cream mixture into the dish, stir to mix a little, then sprinkle the remaining Gruyère and the Parmesan over the top. Bake for 30 minutes or until golden brown.

# Lasagne with Lamb

IT IS UNUSUAL TO MAKE lasagne with lamb, but the flavor is excellent.

**INGREDIENTS**

*1 tablespoon olive oil*
*1 small onion, finely chopped*
*1 pound ground lamb*
*1 garlic clove, crushed*
*3 tablespoons dry white wine*
*1 teaspoon mixed dried herbs*
*1 teaspoon dried oregano*
*scant 2 cups passata or tomato sauce*
*12–16 fresh lasagne sheets, pre-cooked if necessary*
*2 tablespoons freshly grated Parmesan cheese*
*salt and ground black pepper*

***For the white sauce***
*½ cup butter*
*½ cup all-purpose flour*
*3¾ cups hot milk*
*2 tablespoons freshly grated Parmesan cheese*
*nutmeg*

**Serves 4–6**

1 Heat the oil in a saucepan and cook the onion over gentle heat, stirring frequently, for about 5 minutes until softened. Add the ground lamb and garlic and cook gently for 10 minutes, stirring frequently. Stir in salt and pepper to taste, then add the wine and cook rapidly for about 2 minutes, stirring constantly. Stir in the herbs and passata or tomato sauce. Simmer gently for 45 minutes to 1 hour, stirring occasionally.

2 Preheat the oven to 375°F. Make the white sauce. Melt the butter in a saucepan, add the flour and cook, stirring, for 1–2 minutes. Add the milk a little at a time, whisking vigorously after each addition. Bring to a boil and cook, stirring, until the sauce is smooth and thick. Add the Parmesan, grate in fresh nutmeg to taste, season with a little salt and pepper and whisk well. Remove the pan from the heat.

3 Spread a few spoonfuls of meat sauce over the bottom of a baking dish and cover with three or four sheets of lasagne. Spread a quarter of the remaining meat sauce over the lasagne, then a quarter of the white sauce. Repeat the layers three times, finishing with white sauce.

4 Sprinkle the Parmesan over the surface and bake for 30–40 minutes or until the topping is golden brown and bubbling. Let stand for about 10 minutes before serving.

# Lasagne al Forno

The classic version of this dish is pasta layered with meat sauce and creamy béchamel sauce. You could vary it by using mozzarella cheese instead of the béchamel sauce, or by mixing ricotta cheese, Parmesan and herbs together instead of the traditional meat sauce.

**INGREDIENTS**

*12 dried lasagne sheets, pre-cooked if necessary*
*1 quantity Bolognese sauce (see Tagliatelle with Bolognese Sauce)*
*about ½ cup freshly grated Parmesan cheese*
*tomato slices and parsley sprig, to garnish*

***For the béchamel sauce***
*3¾ cups milk*
*sliced onion, carrot and celery*
*a few whole black peppercorns*
*½ cup butter*
*¾ cup all-purpose flour*
*freshly grated nutmeg*
*salt and ground black pepper*

**Serves 4–6**

1 First make the béchamel sauce. Pour the milk into a saucepan and add the vegetables and peppercorns. Bring to boiling point, remove from the heat and let infuse for at least 30 minutes for the milk to absorb the flavor.

2 Strain the milk into a measuring cup. Then melt the butter in the same saucepan and stir in the flour. Cook, stirring, for 2 minutes.

3 Remove from the heat and add the milk all at once, whisk well and return to the heat. Bring to a boil, whisking continuously, then simmer for 2–3 minutes, stirring constantly until thickened. Season to taste with nutmeg, salt and ground black pepper.

4 Preheat the oven to 350°F. If necessary, cook the sheets of lasagne in plenty of boiling salted water according to the instructions on the package. Lift out with a slotted spoon and drain on a clean dish towel. Spoon a third of the meat sauce into a buttered baking-dish.

5 Place four sheets of lasagne over the meat sauce. Spread with one-third of the béchamel sauce. Repeat twice more, finishing with a layer of béchamel sauce covering the top of the dish.

6 Sprinkle with Parmesan cheese and bake in the oven for about 45 minutes until brown and bubbling. Serve garnished with tomato slices and a sprig of parsley.

# Leek and Chèvre Lasagne

AN UNUSUAL and lighter than average lasagne using a soft French goat cheese. The pasta sheets are not so chewy if boiled briefly first, or you could use no-precook lasagne instead if you prefer.

**INGREDIENTS**

*6–8 lasagne sheets*
*1 large eggplant, sliced*
*2 tablespoons olive oil*
*3 leeks, thinly sliced*
*2 red bell peppers*
*7 ounces chèvre, broken into pieces*
*½ cup freshly grated Pecorino or Parmesan cheese*

***For the sauce***

*9 tablespoons all-purpose flour*
*5 tablespoons butter*
*3¾ cups milk*
*½ teaspoon ground bay leaves*
*freshly grated nutmeg*
*salt and ground black pepper*

**Serves 6**

1 Blanch the pasta sheets in plenty of boiling water for just 2 minutes. Drain and place on a clean dish towel.

2 Lightly salt the eggplant slices and place in a colander to drain for 30 minutes, then rinse and pat dry with paper towel.

3 Preheat the oven to 375°F. Lightly fry the leeks in the oil until softened. Cook the bell peppers under a pre-heated broiler until charred. Peel and cut into strips.

4 For the sauce, melt the butter in a saucepan and add the flour. Cook, stirring, for 2–3 minutes. Add the milk and bring to a boil, stirring constantly until thickened. Add the bay leaves, nutmeg and seasoning. Simmer for 2 minutes.

5 In a greased shallow casserole, layer the leeks, lasagne sheets, eggplant, chèvre and Pecorino or Parmesan. Trickle the sauce over the layers, ensuring that it is evenly distributed over the entire dish.

6 Finish with a layer of sauce and grated cheese. Bake in the oven for 30 minutes, or until bubbling and browned on top. Serve immediately.

# Baked Seafood Spaghetti

**IN THIS DISH, each portion is baked and served in an individual package which is then opened at the table. Use baking parchment paper or foil to make the packages.**

**INGREDIENTS**

*1 pound fresh mussels*
*½ cup dry white wine*
*4 tablespoons olive oil*
*2 garlic cloves, finely chopped*
*1 pound tomatoes, fresh or canned, peeled and finely chopped*
*14 ounces fresh or dried spaghetti*
*2 cups shelled and deveined shrimp, fresh or frozen*
*2 tablespoons chopped fresh parsley*
*salt and ground black pepper*
**Serves 4**

1 Scrub the mussels well under cold running water, cutting off the "beards" with a small sharp knife. Discard any that do not close when tapped sharply. Place the mussels and the wine in a large saucepan, cover and heat until opened.

**COOK'S TIP**

*Use mussels as soon as possible after purchasing, but if you have to keep them overnight, store them in cold water with 1 tablespoon flour and 2 ounces salt; fresh water will kill them.*

2 Lift out the mussels and remove to a side dish. Discard any that do not open. Strain the cooking liquid through a strainer lined with paper towel into a bowl and reserve until needed. Preheat the oven to 300°F.

3 In a medium saucepan, heat the oil and garlic together for 1–2 minutes. Add the tomatoes and cook over moderate to high heat until softened. Stir ¾ cup of the mussel cooking liquid into the tomato mixture in the saucepan.

4 Cook the pasta in plenty of salted boiling water until just *al dente*. Just before draining the pasta, add the shrimp and parsley to the tomato sauce. Cook for 2 minutes. Taste for seasoning, adding salt and pepper if necessary. Remove the pan from the heat.

5 Prepare four pieces of baking parchment paper or foil about 12 x 18 inches. Place each sheet in the center of a shallow bowl for ease of handling. Turn the drained pasta into a mixing bowl. Add the tomato sauce and mix together well. Stir in the mussels.

6 Divide the pasta and seafood among the four pieces of paper or foil, placing a mound in the center of each, and twisting the ends together to make a closed package. Arrange on a large baking sheet and place in the center of the oven. Bake for 8–10 minutes. Place the unopened packages on individual serving plates for each person to open on serving.

# Smoked Trout Cannelloni

SMOKED TROUT can be bought already filleted or whole. If you buy fillets, you'll need 8 ounces.

**INGREDIENTS**

*1 large onion, finely chopped*
*1 garlic clove, crushed*
*4 tablespoons vegetable stock*
*2 cans (14-ounce) chopped tomatoes*
*½ teaspoon mixed dried herbs*
*1 smoked trout, about 14 ounces*
*¾ cup frozen peas, thawed*
*1½ cups fresh bread crumbs*
*16 cannelloni tubes*
*salt and ground black pepper*
*1½ tablespoons freshly grated Parmesan cheese*
*mixed salad, to serve (optional)*

***For the cheese sauce***
*2 tablespoons margarine*
*¼ cup all-purpose flour*
*1½ cups skim milk*
*freshly grated nutmeg*

**Serves 4–6**

1 Simmer the onion, garlic and stock in a large covered saucepan for 3 minutes. Uncover and continue to cook, stirring the mixture occasionally, until the stock has reduced entirely from the other ingredients.

2 Stir the chopped tomatoes and dried herbs into the onion and garlic mixture. Simmer, uncovered, for a further 10 minutes, or until the mixture has reduced and is very thick.

3 Meanwhile, skin the smoked trout with a sharp knife. Carefully flake the flesh and discard the bones. Mix the fish together with the tomato mixture, peas, bread crumbs, salt and ground black pepper.

4 Preheat the oven to 375°F. Spoon the filling into the cannelloni tubes and arrange them side by side in a lightly greased ovenproof dish.

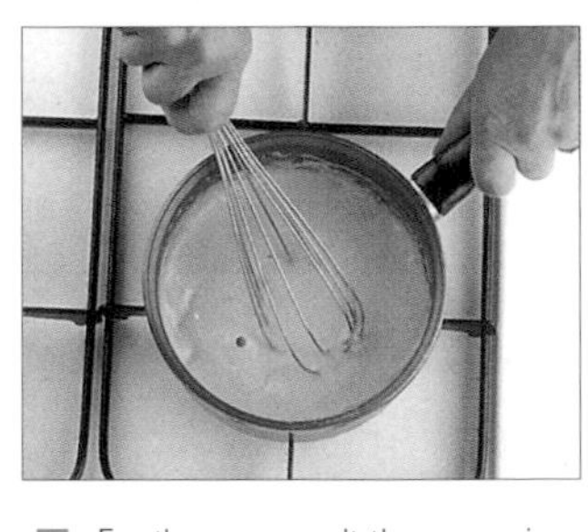

5 For the sauce, melt the margarine in a saucepan, add the flour and cook for 2–3 minutes, whisking constantly. Pour in the milk and bring to a boil, whisking, until the sauce thickens. Simmer for 2–3 minutes, stirring constantly. Season to taste with salt, pepper and nutmeg.

6 Pour the sauce over the cannelloni and sprinkle with the grated Parmesan cheese. Bake in the oven for 35–40 minutes, or until the top is golden and bubbling. Serve with a mixed salad, if desired.

# Tuna Lasagne

TUNA AND PASTA ARE always family favorites together and this version of lasagne will be no exception.

**INGREDIENTS**

*12–16 fresh or dried lasagne sheets*
*½ ounce butter*
*1 small onion, finely chopped*
*1 garlic clove, finely chopped*
*4 ounces mushrooms, thinly sliced*
*4 tablespoons dry white wine (optional)*
*2½ cups white sauce*
*⅔ cup whipping cream*
*3 tablespoons chopped parsley*
*2 cans (7-ounce) tuna, drained*
*2 canned pimientos, cut into strips*
*generous ½ cup frozen peas, thawed*
*4 ounces mozzarella cheese, grated*
*2 tablespoons freshly grated Parmesan cheese*
*salt and ground black pepper*

**Serves 6**

1 For fresh lasagne, cook in a pan of salted boiling water until *al dente*. For dried, soak in a bowl of hot water for 3–5 minutes.

2 Place the lasagne in a colander and rinse with cold water. Lay on a dish towel to drain.

3 Preheat the oven to 350°F. Melt the butter in a saucepan and cook the onion until soft.

4 Add the garlic and mushrooms, and cook until soft, stirring occasionally. Pour in the wine, if using. Boil for 1 minute. Add the white sauce, cream and parsley. Season.

5 Spoon a thin layer of sauce over the base of a 12 x 9-inch baking dish. Cover with a layer of lasagne sheets.

6 Flake the tuna. Sprinkle half the tuna, pimiento strips, peas and mozzarella over the lasagne. Spoon one-third of the remaining sauce over the top and cover with another layer of lasagne sheets.

7 Repeat the layers, ending with pasta and sauce. Sprinkle with the Parmesan. Bake for 30–40 minutes or until lightly browned.

# Spaghetti and Turkey in Cheese Sauce

AN AMERICAN-ITALIAN RECIPE, this dish makes an excellent family meal. It is quite filling and rich, so serve it with a tossed green salad.

**INGREDIENTS**

*6 tablespoons butter*
*12 ounces turkey breast fillet, cut into thin strips*
*2 pieces bottled roasted bell pepper, drained, rinsed, dried and cut into thin strips*
*6 ounces dried spaghetti*
*1/2 cup all-purpose flour*
*3 2/3 cups hot milk*
*1 1/3 cups freshly grated Parmesan cheese*
*1/4–1/2 teaspoon mustard powder*
*salt and ground black pepper*
**Serves 4–6**

1 Melt about a third of the butter in a saucepan, add the turkey and sprinkle with a little salt and plenty of pepper. Toss the turkey over medium heat for about 5 minutes until the meat turns white, then add the roasted pepper strips and toss to mix. Remove with a slotted spoon and set aside.

2 Preheat the oven to 350°F. Cook the pasta according to the instructions on the package.

3 Meanwhile, melt the remaining butter over low heat in the pan in which the turkey was cooked. Sprinkle in the flour and cook, stirring, for 1–2 minutes, then increase the heat to medium.

4 Add the hot milk a little at a time, whisking vigorously after each addition. Bring to a boil and cook, stirring, until the sauce is smooth and thick. Add two thirds of the grated Parmesan, then whisk in mustard, salt and pepper to taste. Remove the sauce from the heat.

5 Drain the pasta and return it to the clean pan. Mix in half the cheese sauce, then spoon the mixture around the edge of a baking dish. Stir the turkey mixture into the remaining cheese sauce and spoon into the center of the dish. Sprinkle the remaining Parmesan evenly over the dish and bake for 15–20 minutes until the cheese topping is just crisp. Serve hot.

# Shellfish Lasagne

THIS IS A LUXURY LASAGNE suitable for an informal supper or lunch party. It is quite expensive to make, but the flavor is superb.

**INGREDIENTS**

*4–6 fresh sea scallops*
*1 pound shelled raw large shrimp*
*1 garlic clove, crushed*
*6 tablespoons butter*
*1/2 cup all-purpose flour*
*2 1/2 cups hot milk*
*scant 1/2 cup* panna da cucina *or heavy cream*
*1/2 cup dry white wine*
*2 envelopes saffron powder*
*good pinch of cayenne pepper*
*4 1/2 ounces Fontina cheese, thinly sliced*
*1 cup freshly grated Parmesan cheese*
*6–8 fresh lasagne sheets, pre-cooked if necessary*
*salt and ground black pepper*
**Serves 4–6**

1 Preheat the oven to 375°F. Cut the scallops and shrimp into bite-size pieces and spread out in a dish. Sprinkle with the garlic and salt and pepper to taste. Melt about a third of the butter in a medium saucepan, add the scallops, corals and shrimp and toss over medium heat for 1–2 minutes or just until the shrimp turn pink. Remove the shellfish with a slotted spoon and set aside.

2 Add the remaining butter to the pan and melt over low heat. Sprinkle in the flour and cook, stirring, for 1–2 minutes, then increase the heat to medium and add the hot milk a little at a time, whisking vigorously after each addition. Bring to a boil and cook, stirring, until the sauce is smooth and very thick. Whisk in the cream, wine, saffron powder, cayenne and salt and pepper to taste, then remove the sauce from the heat.

3 Spread about a third of the sauce over the bottom of a baking dish. Arrange half the Fontina slices over the sauce and sprinkle with about a third of the grated Parmesan. Scatter about half the shellfish evenly on top, then cover with half the lasagne sheets. Repeat the layers, then cover with the remaining sauce and Parmesan.

4 Bake the lasagne for 30–40 minutes or until the topping is golden brown and bubbling. Let stand for 10 minutes before serving.

# Turkey Pastitsio

A TRADITIONAL Greek pastitsio is made with ground lamb, but this lighter version is just as tasty.

**INGREDIENTS**

*4 cups lean ground turkey*
*1 large onion, finely chopped*
*4 tablespoons tomato paste*
*1 cup red wine or stock*
*1 teaspoon ground cinnamon*
*2¾ cups dried macaroni*
*2 tablespoons sunflower margarine*
*3 tablespoons all-purpose flour*
*1¼ cups skim milk*
*1 teaspoon grated nutmeg*
*2 tomatoes, sliced*
*4 tablespoons whole wheat bread crumbs*
*salt and ground black pepper*
*green salad, to serve*

**Serves 4–6**

1 Preheat the oven to 425°F. Fry the turkey and onion in a non-stick pan without any fat, stirring until lightly browned and the turkey fat has reduced.

2 Stir in the tomato paste, red wine or stock and cinnamon. Season, then cover and simmer for about 5 minutes.

3 Cook the macaroni in plenty of salted boiling water according to the instructions on the package, until *al dente*, then drain.

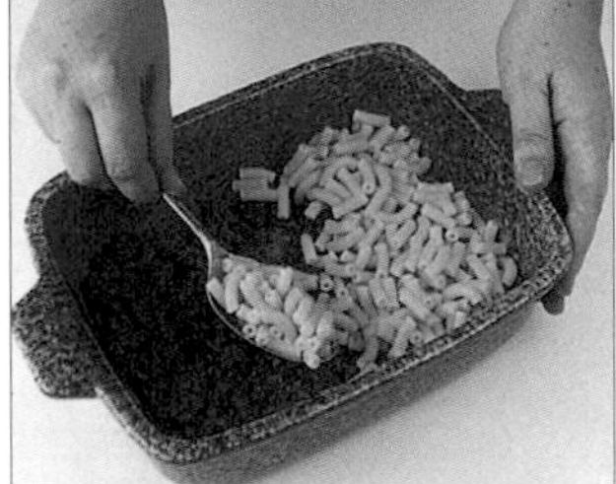

4 Layer the macaroni with the turkey mixture in a wide ovenproof dish.

5 Heat the margarine in a saucepan and add the flour, stirring. Cook for 2–3 minutes then gradually add the milk and whisk over moderate heat until thickened and smooth.

6 Whisk the nutmeg and seasoning to taste into the sauce, then pour evenly over the pasta. Arrange the tomato slices on top and sprinkle with lines of bread crumbs.

7 Bake for 30–35 minutes, or until golden brown.

# Chicken Lasagne

BASED ON THE Italian beef lasagne, this is a good dish for entertaining guests of all ages. Serve simply with a green salad.

**INGREDIENTS**

*2 tablespoons olive oil*
*8 cups ground raw chicken*
*8 ounces rindless lean bacon strips, chopped*
*2 garlic cloves, crushed*
*1 pound leeks, sliced*
*8 ounces carrots, diced*
*2 tablespoons tomato paste*
*1¾ cups chicken stock*
*12 sheets "no-need-to-pre-cook" dried lasagne sheets*

***For the cheese sauce***

*4 tablespoons butter*
*4 tablespoons all-purpose flour*
*2½ cups milk*
*1 cup grated mature Cheddar cheese*
*¼ teaspoon English mustard powder*
*salt and ground black pepper*

**Serves 8**

1 Heat the oil in a large flameproof casserole and brown the ground chicken and bacon briskly, separating the pieces with a wooden spoon. Add the crushed garlic cloves, chopped leeks and diced carrots and cook for about 5 minutes until softened. Add the tomato paste, stock and seasoning. Bring to a boil, cover and simmer for 30 minutes.

2 For the sauce, melt the butter in a saucepan, add the flour and gradually blend in the milk, stirring until smooth. Bring to a boil, stirring constantly until thickened, and simmer for several minutes. Add half the grated Cheddar cheese and the mustard and season to taste.

3 Preheat the oven to 375°F. Layer the chicken mixture, lasagne and half the cheese sauce in a 12-cup ovenproof dish, starting and finishing with the chicken mixture.

4 Pour the remaining cheese sauce over, sprinkle with the remaining cheese and bake in the preheated oven for 1 hour, or until lightly browned on top.

# Pasta Pie

THIS IS AN EXCELLENT SUPPER dish for vegetarians, and children absolutely love it. All the ingredients will probably already be in your storecupboard or refrigerator, so it makes a good "standby" meal if you have guests at short notice.

**INGREDIENTS**

*2 tablespoons olive oil*
*1 small onion, finely chopped*
*1 can (14 ounces) chopped Italian plum tomatoes*
*1 tablespoon sun-dried tomato paste*
*1 teaspoon mixed dried herbs*
*1 teaspoon dried oregano or basil*
*1 teaspoon sugar*
*1½ cups dried conchiglie or rigatoni*
*2 tablespoons freshly grated Parmesan cheese*
*2 tablespoons dried bread crumbs*
*salt and ground black pepper*

***For the white sauce***

*2 tablespoons butter*
*¼ cup all-purpose flour*
*2½ cups milk*
*1 egg*

**Serves 4**

1 Heat the olive oil in a large skillet or saucepan and cook the finely chopped onion over gentle heat, stirring frequently, for about 5 minutes until softened. Stir in the tomatoes. Fill the empty can with water and add it to the tomato mixture, with the tomato paste, herbs and sugar.

2 Add salt and pepper to taste and bring to a boil, stirring. Cover the pan, lower the heat and simmer, stirring occasionally, for 10–15 minutes.

3 Meanwhile, preheat the oven to 375°F. Cook the pasta according to the instructions on the package.

4 Meanwhile, make the white sauce. Melt the butter in a pan, add the flour and cook, stirring, for 1 minute.

5 Add the milk a little at a time, whisking well after each addition. Bring to a boil and cook, stirring, until the sauce is smooth and thick. Season, then remove the pan from the heat.

6 Drain the pasta and turn it into a baking dish. Taste the tomato sauce and add salt and pepper. Pour the sauce into the dish and stir well to mix with the pasta.

7 Beat the egg into the white sauce, then pour the sauce over the pasta mixture. With a fork, separate the pasta in several places so that the white sauce fills the gaps.

8 Level the surface, sprinkle it with grated Parmesan and bread crumbs and bake for 15–20 minutes or until the topping is golden brown and the cheese is bubbling. Let stand for about 10 minutes before serving.

**VARIATIONS**

- *If you don't have any dried bread crumbs, you can cheat by crushing a package of crisps and sprinkling them over the pie instead. Children love this crisp topping, especially if you use their favorite flavor.*
- *You could add chunks of roasted vegetables, such as zucchini, bell peppers or eggplant to the tomato sauce if you like. This will add extra flavor and make a more substantial meal.*
- *For meat eaters, Bolognese sauce can be used instead of the tomato sauce.*

# Cheesy Pasta Bolognese

MOZZARELLA GIVES the cheese sauce a particularly creamy taste.

**INGREDIENTS**

*2 tablespoons olive oil*
*1 onion, chopped*
*1 garlic clove, crushed*
*1 carrot, diced*
*2 celery stalks, chopped*
*2 strips lean bacon, finely chopped*
*5 white mushrooms, chopped*
*1 pound lean ground beef*
*½ cup red wine*
*1 tablespoon tomato paste*
*7 ounces canned chopped tomatoes*
*fresh thyme sprig*
*2 cups dried penne*
*2 tablespoons butter*
*2 tablespoons flour*
*1¼ cups milk*
*1 cup cubed mozzarella cheese*
*4 tablespoons grated Parmesan cheese*
*salt and ground black pepper*
*fresh basil sprigs, to garnish*

**Serves 4**

1 Heat the oil in a pan and fry the onion, garlic, carrot and celery for 6 minutes, until the onions have softened.

2 Add the bacon and continue frying for 3–4 minutes. Stir in the mushrooms, fry for 2 minutes, then add the beef. Fry over high heat until well browned all over.

3 Pour in the red wine, the tomato paste dissolved in 3 tablespoons water, and the tomatoes, then add the thyme and season well. Bring to a boil, cover the pan and simmer gently for about 30 minutes.

4 Preheat the oven to 400°F. Bring a pan of water to a boil, add a little oil. Cook the pasta for 10 minutes.

5 Meanwhile, melt the butter in a saucepan and add the flour. Cook, stirring for 2 minutes then gradually add the milk and whisk constantly with a balloon whisk until the mixture is thickened. Stir in the cubed mozzarella cheese, half the Parmesan and season lightly.

6 Drain the pasta and stir into the cheese sauce. Uncover the tomato sauce and boil rapidly for about 2 minutes to reduce.

7 Spoon the sauce into an ovenproof dish, top with the pasta mixture and sprinkle the remaining Parmesan cheese evenly over the top. Bake for 25 minutes until golden. Garnish with basil and serve hot.

# Rotolo di Pasta

A GIANT JELLY ROLL of pasta with a spinach filling, which is poached, sliced and baked with béchamel or tomato sauce. Use fresh homemade pasta for this recipe.

**INGREDIENTS**

*1 ½ pounds frozen chopped spinach, thawed*
*4 tablespoons butter*
*1 onion, chopped*
*4 ounces ham or bacon, diced*
*8 ounces ricotta or curd cheese*
*1 egg*
*freshly grated nutmeg*
*6 fresh spinach lasagne sheets*
*5 cups béchamel sauce, warmed (see Baked Lasagne with Béchamel Sauce)*
*½ cup freshly grated Parmesan cheese*
*salt and ground black pepper*

**Serves 6**

1 Squeeze the excess moisture from the spinach and set aside.

2 Melt the butter in a saucepan and fry the onion until golden. Add the ham and fry until beginning to brown. Take off the heat and stir in the spinach. Cool slightly, then beat in the ricotta or curd cheese and the egg. Season with salt, pepper and nutmeg.

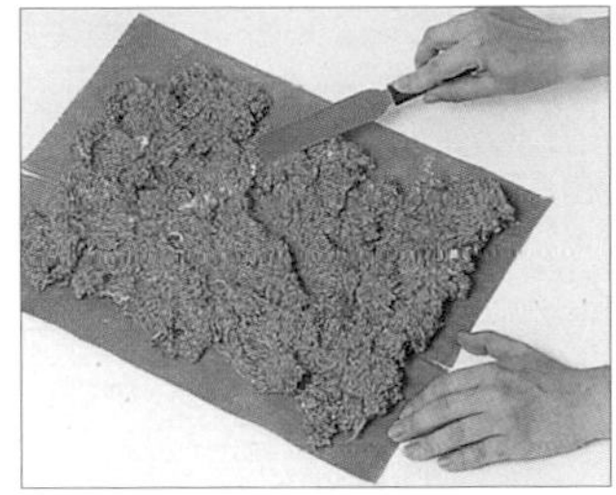

3 Roll the pasta out to a rectangle about 12 x 16 inches. Spread the filling all over, leaving a ½-inch border all round the edge of the rectangle.

4 Roll up the pasta and filling from the shorter end and wrap in cheesecloth to form a sausage shape, tying the ends securely with string.

5 Poach the pasta roll in a very large pan (or fish kettle) of simmering water for about 20 minutes or until firm. Carefully remove, drain and then unwrap. Let cool.

6 When you are ready to finish the dish, preheat the oven to 400°F. Cut the pasta roll into 1-inch slices. Spoon a little béchamel sauce over the base of a shallow baking dish and then arrange the slices on top so that they are slightly overlapping.

7 Spoon the remaining sauce over the roll slices, sprinkle with the cheese and bake for 15–20 minutes or until browned on top and bubbling. Let stand for a few minutes before serving.

# Lasagne with Meatballs

THIS IS AN UNUSUAL RECIPE for lasagne in that there is both a meat sauce and meatballs. The result is very rich and satisfying, making it an ideal dish for an informal winter lunch or supper party. It takes a long time to make, so prepare it the day before and bake it on the day.

**INGREDIENTS**

*11 ounces ground beef*
*11 ounces ground pork*
*1 large egg*
*1 cup fresh white bread crumbs*
*5 tablespoons freshly grated Parmesan cheese*
*2 tablespoons chopped fresh Italian parsley*
*2 garlic cloves, crushed*
*4 tablespoons olive oil*
*1 onion, finely chopped*
*1 carrot, finely chopped*
*1 celery stalk, finely chopped*
*2 cans (14-ounce) chopped Italian plum tomatoes*
*2 teaspoons dried oregano or basil*
*6–8 fresh lasagne sheets, pre-cooked if necessary*
*salt and ground black pepper*

***For the béchamel sauce***

*3 cups milk*
*1 bay leaf*
*1 fresh thyme sprig*
*¼ cup butter*
*½ cup all-purpose flour*
*nutmeg*

**Serves 6–8**

1 First make the meatballs. Put 6 ounces each of the ground beef and pork in a large bowl. Add the egg, bread crumbs, 2 tablespoons of the grated Parmesan, half the parsley and garlic and plenty of salt and pepper.

2 Mix everything together with a wooden spoon, then use your hands to squeeze and knead the mixture so that it becomes smooth and quite sticky.

3 Wash your hands, rinse under the cold tap, then pick up small pieces of the mixture and roll them between your palms to make about 60 very small balls. Place the balls on a tray and chill in the refrigerator for about 30 minutes.

4 Meanwhile, put the milk for the béchamel sauce in a saucepan. Make a tear in the bay leaf, then add the leaf and thyme sprig to the milk and bring it to a boil. Remove from the heat, cover and let infuse.

5 Make the meat sauce. Heat half the oil in a medium skillet or saucepan, add the onion, carrot, celery and remaining garlic and stir over low heat for about 5 minutes until softened. Add the remaining ground beef and pork and cook gently for 10 minutes, stirring frequently and breaking up any lumps in the meat.

6 Stir in salt and pepper to taste, then add the tomatoes, remaining parsley and the oregano or basil. Stir well, cover and simmer gently for 45 minutes to 1 hour, stirring occasionally.

7 Meanwhile, heat the remaining oil in a large, non-stick frying pan. When hot, cook the meatballs in batches over medium to high heat for 5–8 minutes until browned on all sides. Shake the pan from time to time so that the meatballs roll around. As they cook, transfer the meatballs to paper towels to drain.

8 Preheat the oven to 375°F. Make the béchamel sauce. Strain the milk to remove the bay leaf and thyme sprig. Melt the butter in a medium saucepan, add the flour and cook, stirring, for 1–2 minutes.

9 Add the milk a little at a time, whisking vigorously after each addition. Bring to a boil and cook, stirring constantly, until the sauce is smooth and thick. Grate in a little nutmeg to taste and season with salt and pepper. Whisk well, then remove from the heat.

10 Spread about a third of the meat sauce in the bottom of a large, shallow baking dish.

11 Add half the meatballs, spread with a third of the béchamel and cover with half the lasagne sheets. Repeat these layers, then top with the remaining meat sauce and béchamel.

12 Sprinkle the remaining grated Parmesan evenly over the surface and bake for 30–40 minutes or until golden brown and bubbling. Let the lasagne stand for 10 minutes before serving. If you like, garnish each serving with extra chopped parsley.

### Variation

*In the south of Italy, where this type of lasagne is popular, they often add salami, chopped hard-cooked eggs, mozzarella and ricotta cheese to the layers.*

### Cook's Tips

- *Home-made lasagne does not need pre-cooking, but if you have bought fresh pasta check the instructions on the package.*
- *To prevent cooked lasagne sheets from sticking together, rinse them under cold running water, then return to the pan with enough cold water to cover. Drain well on paper towels before using.*

# Macaroni Soufflé

THIS IS GENERALLY a great favorite with children, and is rather like a light and fluffy macaroni cheese. Make sure you serve the soufflé immediately after it is cooked or it will sink dramatically.

**INGREDIENTS**

*1¾ cup dried short-cut macaroni*
*melted butter, to coat*
*3 tablespoons dried bread crumbs*
*4 tablespoons butter*
*1 teaspoon ground paprika*
*⅓ cup all-purpose flour*
*1¼ cups milk*
*3 ounces Cheddar or Gruyère cheese, grated*
*2 ounces Parmesan cheese, grated*
*3 eggs, separated*
*salt and ground black pepper*

**Serves 3–4**

1 Cook the macaroni in plenty of boiling salted water according to the instructions on the package. Drain well and set aside. Preheat the oven to 300°F.

2 Brush a 5-cup soufflé dish with melted butter, then coat evenly with the bread crumbs, shaking out any excess from the dish.

3 Melt the butter in a pan and add the paprika and flour and cook, stirring for 1–2 minutes. Add the milk and bring to a boil, whisking until smooth and thick.

4 Simmer the sauce for 1 minute, then remove from the heat and stir in the cheeses until melted. Season well and mix with the cooked and drained macaroni.

5 Beat in the egg yolks. Whisk the egg whites until they form soft peaks and spoon a quarter of the beaten whites into the sauce mixture to lighten it slightly.

6 Using a large metal spoon, carefully fold the rest of the egg white into the sauce and transfer to the prepared soufflé dish.

7 Bake in the center of the oven for about 40–45 minutes until the soufflé is risen and golden brown. The middle should wobble very slightly and the soufflé should be lightly creamy inside. Serve immediately.

# Pastitsio

THIS IS A CLASSIC GREEK dish which makes an excellent main meal. The recipe is both economical and filling.

**INGREDIENTS**

*1 tablespoon oil*
*4 cups ground lamb*
*1 onion, chopped*
*2 garlic cloves, crushed*
*2 tablespoons tomato paste*
*2 tablespoons all-purpose flour*
*1¼ cups lamb stock*
*2 large tomatoes, sliced*
*1 cup dried pasta shapes, such as fusilli or conchiglie*
*1 pound strained plain yogurt*
*2 eggs, lightly beaten*
*salt and ground black pepper*
*radicchio and sliced cucumber, to serve*

**Serves 4**

1 Preheat the oven to 375°F. Heat the oil in a large pan and fry the lamb for 5 minutes, breaking up the meat with a spoon. Add the onion and garlic and continue to fry for a further 5 minutes.

2 Stir the tomato paste and flour into the pan. Cook for a further 1 minute, stirring occasionally.

3 Stir in the stock and season to taste. Bring to a boil and cook for 20 minutes.

4 Place the meat in an ovenproof dish, spreading it evenly and arrange the sliced tomatoes on top.

5 Cook the pasta shapes in salted boiling water for about 8–10 minutes or until *al dente*. Drain thoroughly through a colander.

6 Mix together the pasta, yogurt and eggs. Spoon on top of the tomatoes and then cook in the preheated oven for 1 hour. Serve with crisp radicchio leaves and slices of cucumber.

# Cannelloni Sorrentina-style

THERE'S MORE THAN ONE way of making cannelloni. For this fresh-tasting dish, sheets of cooked lasagne are rolled around a tomato filling to make a delicious main course for a summer dinner party. The ingredients are similar to those used on a Neapolitan pizza.

### INGREDIENTS

*4 tablespoons olive oil*
*1 small onion, finely chopped*
*2 pounds ripe Italian plum tomatoes, peeled and finely chopped*
*2 garlic cloves, crushed*
*1 large handful fresh basil leaves, shredded, plus extra basil leaves, to garnish*
*1 cup vegetable stock*
*1 cup dry white wine*
*2 tablespoons sun-dried tomato paste*
*½ teaspoon sugar*
*16–18 fresh or dried lasagne sheets*
*generous 1 cup ricotta cheese*
*1 package (4½ ounces) mozzarella cheese, drained and diced small*
*8 bottled anchovy fillets in olive oil, drained and halved lengthwise*
*⅔ cup freshly grated Parmesan cheese*
*salt and ground black pepper*

**Serves 4–6**

1 Heat the oil in a medium saucepan, add the onion and cook gently, stirring frequently, for about 5 minutes until softened. Stir in the tomatoes, garlic and half the basil. Season with salt and pepper to taste and toss over medium to high heat for 5 minutes.

2 Scoop about half the tomato mixture out of the pan, place in a bowl and set it aside to cool.

3 Stir the vegetable stock, white wine, tomato paste and sugar into the tomato mixture remaining in the pan and simmer for about 20 minutes, stirring occasionally.

4 Meanwhile, cook the lasagne sheets in batches in a saucepan of salted boiling water, according to the instructions on the package. Drain and separate the sheets of lasagne and lay them out flat on a clean dish towel.

### VARIATION

*For vegetarians, use 8 pitted black olives instead of the anchovies. Chop them coarsely and sprinkle them in a line along the length of the cannelloni filling.*

5 Preheat the oven to 375°F. Add the ricotta and mozzarella to the tomato mixture in the bowl. Stir in the remaining basil and season to taste with salt and pepper.

6 Spread a little of the mixture over each lasagne sheet. Place an anchovy fillet across the width of each sheet, close to one of the short ends. Starting from the end with the anchovy, roll each lasagne sheet up like a jelly roll.

7 Purée the tomato sauce in a blender or food processor. Spread a little of the tomato sauce over the bottom of a large baking dish. Arrange the cannelloni seam-side down in a single layer in the dish and spoon the remaining sauce over them.

8 Sprinkle the Parmesan over the top and bake for 20 minutes or until the topping is golden brown and bubbling. Serve hot, garnished with basil leaves.

# Macaroni and Blue Cheese

THE BLUE CHEESE gives this simple dish a new twist.

**INGREDIENTS**

*4 cups dried macaroni*
*3¾ cups milk*
*4 tablespoons butter*
*6 tablespoons all-purpose flour*
*¼ teaspoon salt*
*8 ounces blue cheese, crumbled*
*ground black pepper*
**Serves 6**

1 Preheat the oven to 350°F. Lightly grease a 12 x 9-inch baking dish.

2 Cook the macaroni in plenty of salted boiling water according to the instructions on the package, or until *al dente*. Drain and rinse under cold water. Place in a large bowl and set aside until required.

3 In another pan, bring the milk to a boil and set aside.

4 Melt the butter in a heavy saucepan over low heat. Whisk in the flour and cook for 5 minutes, whisking continuously. Be careful not to let the mixture brown.

5 Remove from the heat and whisk the hot milk into the butter and flour mixture. When smoothly blended, return to medium heat and continue cooking for about 5 minutes, whisking constantly until the sauce is smooth and thick. Add the salt.

6 Add the sauce to the macaroni. Add three-quarters of the crumbled blue cheese and stir well. Transfer the macaroni mixture to the prepared baking dish and spread in an even layer.

7 Sprinkle the remaining cheese evenly over the surface. Bake for 25 minutes, until bubbling hot.

8 If desired, lightly brown the top of the macaroni and cheese under a preheated broiler for 3–4 minutes. Serve hot, sprinkled with ground black pepper to taste.

# Tortellini with Cream, Butter and Cheese

THIS IS AN INDULGENT but quick alternative to macaroni cheese. Stir in some ham or pepperoni if you wish, though it's quite delicious as it is.

**INGREDIENTS**

*1 pound fresh tortellini*
*4 tablespoons butter*
*1 ¼ cups heavy cream*
*4 ounces Parmesan cheese*
*freshly grated nutmeg*
*salt and ground black pepper*

**Serves 4–6**

1 Cook the pasta in plenty of salted boiling water according to the instructions on the package.

2 Meanwhile melt the butter in a medium saucepan and stir in the cream. Bring to a boil and cook for 2–3 minutes until the mixture is slightly thickened, stirring frequently.

3 Grate the Parmesan cheese and stir ¾ cup of it into the sauce, stirring continuously over a moderate heat, until all of it has melted. Season to taste with salt, ground black pepper and nutmeg. Preheat the broiler.

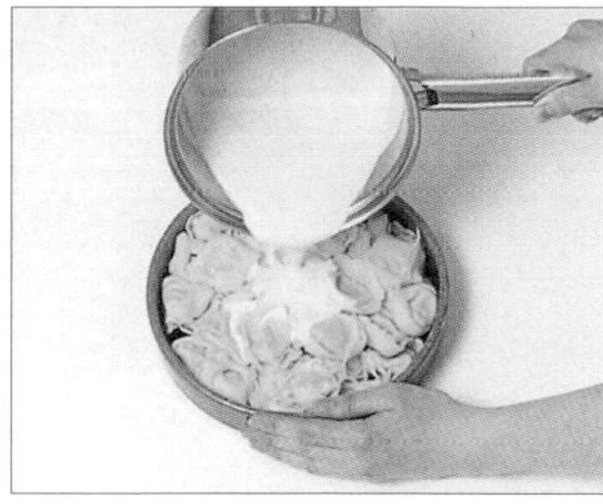

4 Drain the pasta well and spoon into a buttered heatproof serving dish. Pour the sauce over, sprinkle the remaining cheese over and place under a preheated broiler until brown and bubbling on top. Serve the tortellini and sauce immediately.

# Lasagne with Three Cheeses

RICH AND FILLING, this is the type of lasagne that is popular in America. It was invented by Italian immigrants who made full use of the abundant ingredients available to them.

### INGREDIENTS

*2 tablespoons butter*
*1 tablespoon olive oil*
*2–2¼ cups white mushrooms, quartered lengthwise*
*2 tablespoons chopped fresh Italian parsley*
*1 quantity Bolognese Sauce with Red Wine*
*1–1½ cups hot beef stock*
*9–12 fresh lasagne sheets, pre-cooked if necessary*
*2 cups ricotta cheese*
*1 large egg*
*2 packages (4½-ounce) mozzarella cheese, drained and thinly sliced*
*1⅓ cups freshly grated Parmesan cheese*
*salt and ground black pepper*

**Serves 6–8**

1 Preheat the oven to 375°F. Melt the butter in the oil in a frying pan. Add the mushrooms, with salt and pepper to taste, and toss over medium to high heat for 5–8 minutes until the mushrooms are tender and quite dry. Remove the pan from the heat and stir in the parsley.

2 Make the Bolognese sauce or, if it is cold, reheat it. Once it is hot, stir in enough hot beef stock to make the sauce quite runny.

3 Stir in the mushroom and parsley mixture, then spread about a quarter of this sauce over the base of a baking dish. Cover with three or four sheets of lasagne.

4 Beat together the ricotta and egg in a bowl, with salt and pepper to taste, then spread about a third of the mixture over the lasagne sheets. Cover with a third of the mozzarella slices, then sprinkle with about a quarter of the grated Parmesan.

5 Repeat these layers twice, using half the remaining Bolognese sauce each time, and finishing with the remaining Parmesan.

6 Bake the lasagne for 30–40 minutes or until the cheese topping is golden brown and bubbling. Let stand for about 10 minutes before serving.

### VARIATIONS

- *For a spicier alternative version of this recipe, replace the meat sauce with the sauce used for Spaghetti with Ground Beef Sauce.*
- *Grated mature Cheddar cheese is very good in lasagne. Use it instead of some, or all, of the grated Parmesan. It is a good deal less expensive than Parmesan.*

### COOK'S TIP

*If you have made the lasagne yourself, there is no need to pre-cook it, but if you have bought fresh lasagne, check whether it needs to be boiled briefly before being layered. Packages of fresh lasagne from the supermarket usually need to be boiled for 2 minutes before use.*

# Baked Conchiglie

THIS MAKES AN EXCELLENT dinner party appetizer for six, or a vegetarian main course for four, in which case you should fill 20 shells, rather than 18.

**INGREDIENTS**

*18 large pasta shells for stuffing, such as conchiglie*
*2 tablespoons butter*
*1 small onion, finely chopped*
*10 ounces fresh spinach leaves, trimmed, washed and shredded*
*1 garlic clove, crushed*
*1 envelope of saffron powder*
*nutmeg*
*generous 1 cup ricotta cheese*
*1 egg*
*1 quantity Winter Tomato Sauce (see Rigatoni with Winter Tomato Sauce)*
*about 2/3 cup dry white wine, vegetable stock or water*
*scant 1/2 cup* panna da cucina *or heavy cream*
*2/3 cup freshly grated Parmesan cheese*
*salt and ground black pepper*
**Serves 6**

1 Preheat the oven to 375°F. Bring a large saucepan of salted water to a boil. Add the pasta shells and cook for 10 minutes. Drain the shells, half fill the pan with cold water and place the shells in the water.

2 Melt the butter in a saucepan, add the onion and cook gently, stirring, for about 5 minutes until softened. Add the spinach, garlic and saffron, then grate in plenty of nutmeg and add salt and pepper to taste. Stir well, increase the heat to medium and cook for 5–8 minutes, stirring frequently, until the spinach is wilted and tender.

3 Increase the heat to high and stir until the water is driven off and the spinach is quite dry. Turn the spinach into a bowl, add the ricotta and beat well to mix. Taste for seasoning, then add the egg and beat well again.

4 Purée the tomato sauce in a blender or food processor, pour it into a measuring cup and make it up to 3 cups with wine, stock or water. Add the cream, stir well to mix and taste for seasoning.

5 Spread about half the sauce over the bottom of six individual gratin dishes. Remove the pasta shells one at a time from the water, shake them well and fill them with the spinach and ricotta mixture, using a teaspoon. Arrange three shells in the center of each dish, spoon the remaining sauce over them, then cover with the grated Parmesan. Bake in the oven for 10–12 minutes or until hot. Let stand for about 5 minutes before serving.

# Mixed Meat Cannelloni

A CREAMY, RICH FILLING and sauce make this an unusual cannelloni.

**INGREDIENTS**

*4 tablespoons olive oil*
*1 onion, finely chopped*
*1 carrot, finely chopped*
*2 garlic cloves, crushed*
*2 ripe Italian plum tomatoes, peeled and finely chopped*
*4½ ounces ground beef*
*4½ ounces ground pork*
*9 ounces ground chicken*
*2 tablespoons brandy*
*2 tablespoons butter*
*6 tablespoons* panna da cucina *or heavy cream*
*16 dried cannelloni tubes*
*1 cup freshly grated Parmesan cheese*
*salt and ground black pepper*
*green salad, to serve*

***For the white sauce***
*¼ cup butter*
*½ cup all-purpose flour*
*3¾ cups milk*
*nutmeg*
**Serves 4**

1 Heat the oil in a medium skillet, add the onion, carrot, garlic and tomatoes and cook over low heat, stirring, for about 10 minutes or until very soft.

**COOK'S TIP**

*Instead of pasta tubes you could roll fresh lasagne sheets around the filling.*

2 Add all the ground meats to the pan and cook gently for about 10 minutes, stirring frequently to break up any lumps. Add the brandy, increase the heat and stir until it has reduced, then add the butter and cream and cook gently, stirring occasionally, for about 10 minutes. Let cool.

3 Preheat the oven to 375°F. Make the white sauce. Melt the butter in a medium saucepan, add the flour and cook, stirring, for 1–2 minutes. Add the milk a little at a time, whisking vigorously after each addition. Bring to a boil and cook, stirring, until the sauce is smooth and thick. Grate in fresh nutmeg to taste, then season with salt and pepper and whisk well. Remove the pan from the heat.

4 Spoon a little of the white sauce into a baking dish. Fill the cannelloni tubes with the meat mixture and place in a single layer in the dish. Pour the remaining white sauce over them, then sprinkle with the Parmesan. Bake for 35–40 minutes or until the pasta feels tender when pierced with a skewer. Let stand for 10 minutes before serving with green salad.

# Baked Vegetable Lasagne

FOLLOWING THE PRINCIPLES of the classic meat sauce lasagne, other combinations of ingredients can be used most effectively. This vegetarian lasagne uses tomatoes and wild and cultivated mushrooms.

**INGREDIENTS**

*8 fresh lasagne sheets, pre-cooked if necessary*
*2 tablespoons olive oil*
*1 onion, very finely chopped*
*1 ¼ pounds tomatoes, fresh or canned, chopped*
*1 ½ pounds cultivated or wild mushrooms, or a combination of both*
*⅓ cup butter*
*2 garlic cloves, finely chopped*
*juice of ½ lemon*
*4 cups béchamel sauce (see Baked Lasagne with Béchamel Sauce)*
*1 ½ cups freshly grated Parmesan or Cheddar cheese, or a combination of both*
*salt and ground black pepper*
**Serves 8**

1 Butter a large shallow baking dish, rectangular or square in shape.

2 If you are making the pasta, do not let it dry out before cutting into rectangles measuring about 4½ inches wide and the same length as the baking dish (this will make it easier to assemble).

3 In a small frying pan heat the oil and sauté the onion until soft but not colored. Add the chopped tomatoes and cook for about 6–8 minutes, stirring frequently. Season with salt and pepper and set aside until required.

4 Wipe the mushrooms carefully with a damp cloth. Slice finely. Heat 3 tablespoons of the butter in a frying pan and, when it is bubbling, add the mushrooms. Cook until the mushrooms start to exude their juices. Add the garlic and lemon juice, and season with salt and pepper. Cook until the liquids have almost all evaporated and the mushrooms are starting to brown. Set aside.

5 Preheat the oven to 400°F. Bring a very large pan of water to a boil. Place a large bowl of cold water near the stove. Cover a large countertop with a tablecloth. Add salt to the rapidly boiling water. Drop in three or four of the egg pasta rectangles. Cook very briefly, about 30 seconds.

6 Once cooked, remove the pasta from the pan using a slotted spoon and then drop into the cold water for about 30 seconds. Remove and lay out to dry. Continue with the remaining pasta.

7 To assemble the lasagne, spread one large spoonful of the béchamel sauce over the base of the dish. Arrange a layer of pasta in the dish, cutting it with a sharp knife to fit. Cover with a thin layer of mushrooms, then one of béchamel sauce. Sprinkle with a little of the freshly grated Parmesan or Cheddar cheese.

8 Make another layer of pasta, spread with a thin layer of tomatoes, and then one of béchamel. Sprinkle with cheese. Repeat the layers in the same order, ending with a layer of pasta coated with béchamel. Do not make more than about six layers of pasta. Use the pasta trimmings to patch any gaps in the pasta. Sprinkle with more cheese and dot with butter.

9 Bake for 20 minutes. Remove from the oven and let stand for 5 minutes before serving.

# Spinach and Hazelnut Lasagne

A VEGETARIAN DISH which is hearty enough to satisfy meat-eaters too. Use frozen spinach—you will need 1 pound—if you're short of time.

**INGREDIENTS**

*2 pounds fresh spinach*
*1 1/4 cups vegetable or chicken stock*
*1 onion, finely chopped*
*1 garlic clove, crushed*
*3/4 cup hazelnuts*
*2 tablespoons chopped fresh basil*
*6 "no-need-to-pre-cook" dried lasagne sheets*
*1 can (14 ounces) chopped tomatoes*
*scant 1 cup lowfat ricotta cheese*
*slivered hazelnuts and chopped parsley, to garnish*

**Serves 4**

1 Preheat the oven to 400°F. Wash the fresh spinach and place in a pan with just the water that clings to the leaves. Cook the spinach over fairly high heat for 2 minutes until wilted. Drain well.

2 Heat 2 tablespoons of the stock in a large pan and simmer the onion and garlic until soft. Stir in the spinach, hazelnuts and basil.

3 In a large ovenproof dish, layer the spinach, lasagne and the tomatoes. Season well between the layers. Pour over the remaining stock. Spread the ricotta cheese over the top.

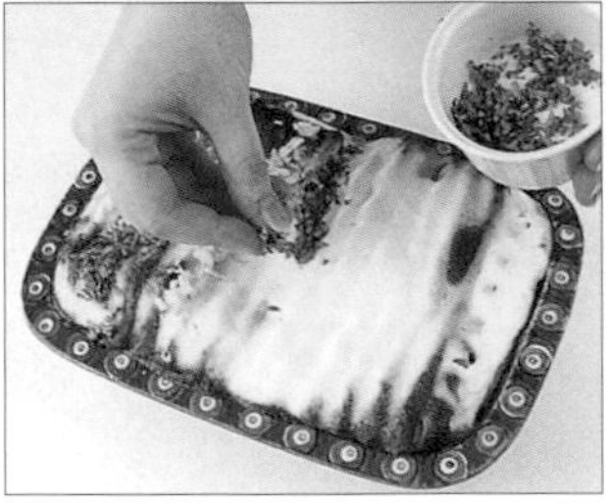

4 Bake the lasagne for about 45 minutes, or until golden brown. Serve hot, sprinkled with lines of slivered hazelnuts and chopped parsley.

# Cannelloni with Tuna

CHILDREN LOVE THIS pasta dish. Fontina cheese has a sweet, nutty flavor and good melting qualities. Look for it in large supermarkets and Italian markets.

**INGREDIENTS**

*4 tablespoons butter*
*½ cup all-purpose flour*
*about 3¾ cups hot milk*
*2 cans (7-ounce) tuna, drained*
*1 cup Fontina cheese, grated*
*¼ teaspoon grated nutmeg*
*12 "no-need-to-pre-cook" cannelloni tubes*
*⅔ cup grated Parmesan cheese*
*salt and freshly ground black pepper*
*fresh herbs, to garnish*

**Serves 4–6**

1 Melt the butter in a heavy saucepan, add the flour and stir over low heat for 1–2 minutes. Remove the pan from the heat and gradually add 1½ cups of the milk, beating vigorously after each addition. Return the pan to the heat and whisk for 1–2 minutes until the sauce is very thick and smooth. Remove from the heat.

2 Mix the drained tuna with about ½ cup of the warm white sauce in a bowl. Add salt and black pepper to taste. Preheat the oven to 350°F.

3 Gradually whisk the remaining milk into the rest of the sauce, return to the heat and simmer, whisking, until thickened. Add the grated Fontina and nutmeg, and season to taste. Simmer for a few minutes, stirring frequently. Pour one-third of the sauce into a baking dish.

4 Fill the cannelloni tubes with the tuna mixture, pushing it in with the handle of a teaspoon. Place the cannelloni in a single layer in the dish. Thin the remaining sauce with a little more milk if necessary, then pour it over the cannelloni. Sprinkle with Parmesan cheese and bake for 30 minutes or until golden. Serve hot, garnished with herbs.

# Stuffed Pasta

The recipes in this chapter are for a variety of different shapes, and the majority of them involve making your own pasta which is easier than you think, especially if you have a pasta machine. You can make pasta by hand, but the machine will save you time and effort, and make the whole process much more interesting and fun. They all use the same basic pasta dough, but the dough is always made with eggs for stuffed pasta, which strengthens it. This helps to hold the filling in during cooking. Stuffed pasta originated in the north of Italy, but now every Italian town seems to have its own specialty, often associated with a particular day in the calendar, such as a feast day or New Year. Home-made stuffed pasta is therefore a special-occasion dish, and it is usually served very simply, either drizzled with melted butter or oil, or floating in *brodo*. Practice makes perfect when it comes to making anything by hand, but the charm of home-made pasta lies in its imperfections, so don't try too hard to make every shape precisely the same size. After all, you want your guests to know you have made it yourself!

# Stuffed Pasta Half-moons

THESE STUFFED EGG PASTA half-moons are filled with a delicate mixture of cheeses. They make an elegant first course as well as a good supper.

**INGREDIENTS**

*1 quantity Pasta with Eggs*

***For the filling***

*1 1/4 cups fresh ricotta or curd cheese*
*1 1/4 cups mozzarella cheese*
*1 cup freshly grated Parmesan cheese*
*2 eggs*
*3 tablespoons finely chopped fresh basil*
*salt and ground black pepper*

***For the sauce***

*1 pound fresh tomatoes*
*2 tablespoons olive oil*
*1 small onion, very finely chopped*
*6 tablespoons cream*

**Serves 6–8**

1 Make the filling. Press the ricotta or curd cheese through a strainer. Chop the mozzarella into very small cubes. Combine all three cheeses in a bowl. Beat in the eggs and basil, season and set aside.

2 Make the sauce by dropping the tomatoes into a small pan of boiling water for 1 minute. Remove, and peel. Chop the tomatoes finely. Heat the oil in a medium saucepan. Add the onion and cook over moderate heat until softened. Add the tomatoes and cook until soft, about 15 minutes. Season with salt and pepper. Set aside.

3 Prepare the sheets of egg pasta. Roll out very thinly by hand or machine. Do not let the pasta dry out before filling.

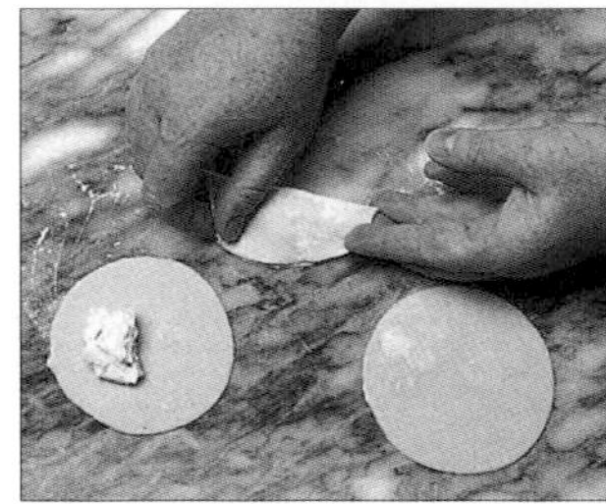

4 Using a glass or cookie cutter, cut out rounds approximately 4 inches in diameter. Spoon one large tablespoon of the cheese filling onto one half of each pasta round and fold the other pasta half over.

5 Press the edges closed with the tines of a fork. Re-roll any trimmings and use to make more rounds. Allow the half-moons to dry for at least 10–15 minutes. Turn them over so they dry evenly.

6 Bring a large pan of salted water to a boil. Meanwhile, place the tomato sauce in a small saucepan and heat gently. Stir in the cream. Do not allow to boil.

7 Gently drop the stuffed pasta into a boiling water, and stir carefully to prevent them from sticking. Cook for 5–7 minutes. Scoop them out of the water, drain carefully, and arrange in individual dishes. Spoon over some sauce and serve.

# Spinach and Dolcelatte Ravioli

THE ITALIAN DOLCELATTE cheese used in this recipe gives it a unique and strong taste so it is best served simply, with olive oil and Parmesan.

**INGREDIENTS**

*3 cups stone-ground flour*
*¾ teaspoon salt*
*2 eggs*
*1 tablespoon olive oil*

***For the filling***

*8 ounces fresh spinach*
*½ cup butter*
*1 small onion, finely chopped*
*1 ounce Parmesan cheese, grated*
*1½ ounces dolcelatte cheese, crumbled*
*1 tablespoon chopped fresh parsley*
*salt and ground black pepper*
*freshly grated Parmesan cheese, to serve*

**Serves 4**

1 To make the pasta dough, mix together the flour and salt in a large bowl or food processor. Add the eggs, olive oil and about 3 tablespoons of cold water or enough to make a pliable dough. If working by hand, mix the ingredients together and then knead the dough fo about 15 minutes until it has become very smooth. Or, process the dough for about 1 minute or so in a food processor. Place the dough in a plastic bag and chill in the refrigerator for at least 12 hours (or overnight if this is more convenient).

2 Cook the spinach in a large, covered saucepan for about 3-4 minutes, until the leaves have wilted. Strain and press out the excess liquid. Set aside to cool a little and then chop the spinach finely.

3 Melt half the butter in a small saucepan and fry the onion over gentle heat for about 5-6 minutes until soft. Place in a bowl with the chopped spinach, the Parmesan and dolcelatte cheeses and seasoning. Mix all the ingredients together well.

4 Grease a ravioli pan. Roll out half or a quarter of the pasta dough to a thickness of about 1/8 inch. Lay the dough over the ravioli pan, pressing it well into each of the squares.

5 Spoon a little spinach mixture into each cavity, then roll out a second piece of dough and lay it on top. Press a rolling pin evenly over the top of the tin to seal all the edges and then cut the ravioli into neat squares using a pastry cutter.

6 Place the ravioli in a large saucepan of boiling water and simmer for about 4-5 minutes until cooked through but *al dente*. Drain well and then toss with the remaining butter and the parsley.

7 Divide between four serving plates and serve sprinkled with shavings of Parmesan cheese.

# Meat-filled Agnolotti with Vodka Sauce

DAINTY HALF-MOON SHAPES are filled with spiced ground meat and bacon and served with a cream and blue-cheese sauce spiked with vodka. This is a very special dish for a dinner party first course.

**INGREDIENTS**

*1 quantity Pasta with Eggs*
*freshly grated Parmesan cheese, to serve*

***For the filling***

*1 tablespoon olive oil*
*3 ounces pancetta, lean bacon or ham, finely diced*
*9 ounces ground pork or veal*
*2 garlic cloves, crushed*
*good pinch of ground cinnamon*
*½ cup red wine*
*4 tablespoons chopped fresh Italian parsley*
*1 small egg*
*salt and ground black pepper*

***For the sauce***

*¼ cup butter*
*1 cup* panna da cucina *or heavy cream*
*4 ounces Gorgonzola cheese, diced*
*3 tablespoons vodka*

**Serves 6–8**

1 Make the filling. Heat the oil in a medium saucepan, add the pancetta, bacon or ham and stir-fry for a few minutes until lightly colored. Add the ground pork, the garlic, cinnamon and salt and pepper to taste and cook gently for 5–6 minutes, stirring frequently and breaking up any lumps.

2 Pour in the wine and stir well to mix, then simmer gently, stirring occasionally, for 15–20 minutes until the meat is cooked and quite dry. Transfer the meat to a bowl with a slotted spoon and let cool.

3 Add the parsley and egg to the meat mixture and stir well to mix.

4 Using a pasta machine, roll out one-quarter of the pasta into a 36-inch strip. Cut the strip with a sharp knife into two 18-inch lengths (you can do this during rolling if the strip gets too long to manage).

5 Using a teaspoon, put 8–10 little mounds of the filling along one side of one of the pasta strips, spacing them evenly. Brush a little water around each mound, then fold the plain side of the pasta strip over the filling.

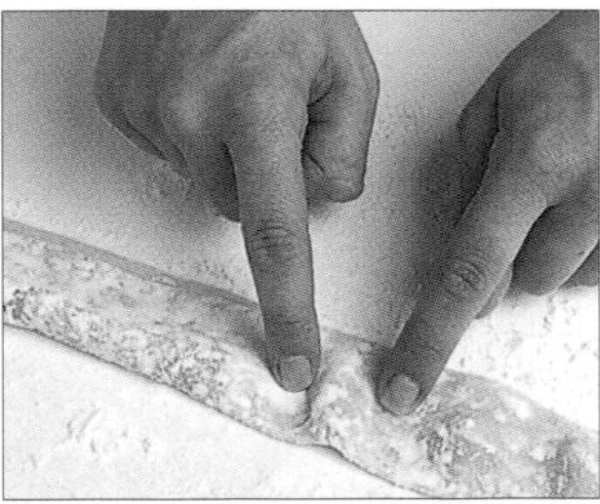

6 Starting from the folded edge, press down gently with your fingertips around each mound, pushing the air out at the unfolded edge.

7 Using only half of a 2-inch fluted round ravioli or cookie cutter, cut around each mound of filling to make a half-moon shape. The folded edge should be the straight edge. If you like, press the cut edges of the agnolotti with the tines of a fork to give a decorative effect.

8 Put the agnolotti on floured dish towels, spreading them out in a single layer, so that they don't stick together. Sprinkle them lightly with flour and let dry while repeating the process with the remaining pasta to get 64–80 agnolotti altogether.

9 Drop the agnolotti into a large pan of salted boiling water, bring back to a boil and boil for 4–5 minutes.

10 Meanwhile, make the sauce. Melt the butter in a medium saucepan, add the cream and cheese and heat through, stirring, until the cheese has melted. Add the vodka, season to taste with pepper and stir well to mix.

11 Drain the agnolotti and divide them among six or eight warmed bowls. Spoon the sauce over them and sprinkle liberally with grated Parmesan. Serve immediately.

### Variation

- *Instead of the pancetta, bacon or ham, you could use a spicy salami for the agnolotti filling. Buy the salami in one very thick piece, peel off the skin, and then chop it finely.*
- *Agnolotti are also often made with prosciutto crudo, which gives them a more delicate flavor than the streaky pancetta.*

### Cook's Tip

*Gorgonzola is a sharp-tasting blue Italian cheese with a soft and creamy consistency. Gorgonzola* piccante *is a particularly strong variety, while gorgonzola* dolce*—better known as dolcelatte—is creamier and less sharp in flavor. Supermarkets, specialty cheese shops and delicatessens usually sell both types of Gorgonzola.*

# Ravioli with Pumpkin

THIS IS A VERY SIMPLE VERSION of a Christmas Eve specialty from Lombardy. In traditional recipes the pumpkin filling is flavored with *mostarda di frutta* (a kind of sweet fruit pickle), crushed amaretti biscuits and sugar. Here the pumpkin is seasoned with Parmesan and nutmeg. It is quite sweet enough for most tastes.

**INGREDIENTS**

*1 quantity Pasta with Eggs*
*½ cup butter*
*freshly grated Parmesan cheese, to serve*

***For the filling***
*1 pound piece of pumpkin*
*1 tablespoon olive oil*
*scant ¼ cup freshly grated Parmesan cheese*
*nutmeg*
*salt and ground black pepper*
**Serves 8**

1 Make the filling. Preheat the oven to 425°F. Cut the piece of pumpkin into chunks and remove the seeds and fibers. Put the chunks, skin side down, in a roasting pan and drizzle the oil over the pumpkin flesh. Roast in the oven for 30 minutes, turning the pieces over once or twice.

2 Leave the roasted pumpkin until it is cool enough to handle, then scrape the flesh out into a bowl and discard the pumpkin skin.

3 Mash the roasted pumpkin flesh with a fork, then add the grated Parmesan and freshly grated nutmeg and salt and pepper to taste. Stir well to mix, then set aside until cold.

4 Using a pasta machine, roll out one-quarter of the pasta into a 36-inch strip. Cut the strip with a sharp knife into two 18-inch lengths (you can do this during rolling if the strip gets too long to manage).

5 Using a teaspoon, put 10–12 little mounds of the filling along one side of one of the pasta strips, spacing them evenly.

6 Brush a little water around each mound, then fold the plain side of the pasta strip over the mounds of filling. Starting from the folded edge, press down gently with your fingertips around each mound, pushing the air out at the unfolded edge. Sprinkle lightly with flour.

7 With a fluted pasta wheel, cut along each long side, then in between each mound to make small square shapes. Put the ravioli on floured dish towels, sprinkle lightly with flour and let dry, while repeating the process with the remaining pasta to get 80–96 ravioli altogether.

8 Drop the ravioli into a large pan of salted boiling water, bring back to a boil and boil for 4–5 minutes. Meanwhile, melt the butter in a small saucepan until it is sizzling.

9 Drain the ravioli and divide them equally among eight warmed dinner plates or large bowls. Drizzle the sizzling butter over the ravioli and serve immediately, sprinkled with grated Parmesan. Hand more grated Parmesan separately.

**VARIATION**

*You can buy* mostarda di frutta *at Italian markets, especially at Christmas time. If you would like to try some in the filling, add about 3 tablespoons, together with a few crushed amaretti.*

# Spinach and Ricotta Ravioli

THE ITALIAN NAME FOR this dish is *ravioli di magro* which means lean ravioli. It is used to describe meat-less ravioli, usually those with a spinach and ricotta filling. *Ravioli di magro* are served on Christmas Eve, a time when meat-filled pasta should not be eaten.

**INGREDIENTS**

*1 quantity Pasta with Eggs*
*freshly grated Parmesan cheese, to serve*

**For the filling**

*3 tablespoons butter*
*6 ounces fresh spinach leaves, trimmed, washed and shredded*
*scant 1 cup ricotta cheese*
*⅓ cup freshly grated Parmesan cheese*
*nutmeg*
*1 small egg*
*salt and ground black pepper*

**For the sauce**

*¼ cup butter*
*1 cup panna da cucina or heavy cream*
*⅔ cup freshly grated Parmesan cheese*

**Serves 8**

1 Make the filling. Melt the butter in a medium saucepan, add the spinach and salt and pepper to taste and cook over medium heat for 5–8 minutes, stirring frequently, until the spinach is wilted and tender. Increase the heat to high and stir until the water is driven off and the spinach is quite dry.

2 Turn the spinach into a bowl and leave until cold, then add the ricotta, grated Parmesan and freshly grated nutmeg to taste. Beat well to mix, taste for seasoning, then add the egg and beat well again.

3 Using a pasta machine, roll out one-quarter of the pasta into a 36-inch strip. Cut the strip with a sharp knife into two 18-inch lengths (you can do this during rolling if the strip gets too long to manage).

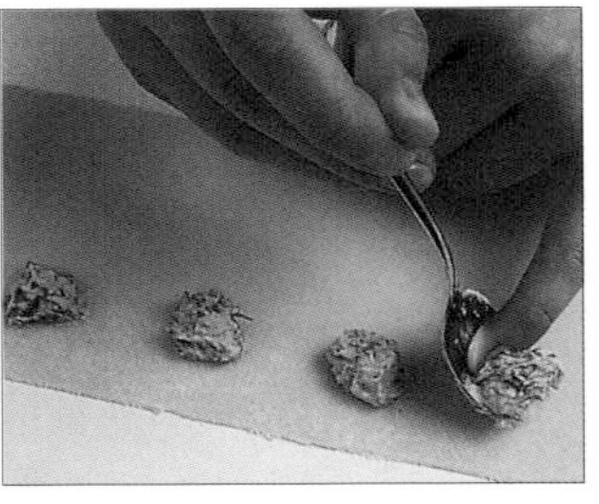

4 Using a teaspoon, put 10–12 little mounds of the filling along one side of one of the pasta strips, spacing them evenly. Brush a little water around each mound, then fold the plain side of the pasta strip over the filling.

5 Starting from the folded edge, press down gently with your fingertips around each mound of filling, pushing the air out at the unfolded edge. Sprinkle lightly with flour.

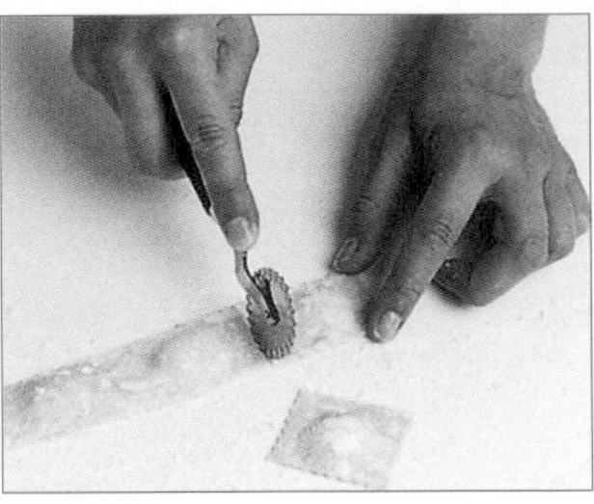

6 With a fluted pasta wheel, cut along each long side, then in between each mound to make small square shapes.

7 Put the ravioli on floured dish towels, sprinkle lightly with flour and leave to dry while repeating the process with the remaining pasta to get 80–96 ravioli altogether.

8 Drop the ravioli into a large pan of salted boiling water, bring back to a boil and boil for 4–5 minutes.

9 Meanwhile, make the sauce. Gently heat the butter, cream and Parmesan in a medium saucepan until the butter and Parmesan have melted.

10 Increase the heat and simmer for a minute or two until the sauce is slightly reduced, then add salt and pepper to taste.

11 Drain the ravioli and divide them equally among 8 warmed large bowls. Drizzle the sauce over them and serve immediately, sprinkled with grated Parmesan.

### Variation

*If you prefer, serve the ravioli with sizzling sage butter. Melt 1/4 cup butter in a small pan, add a handful of fresh sage leaves and stir constantly over medium to high heat until sizzling. This will be slightly less rich than the cream sauce suggested here.*

### Cook's Tip

*To prevent the pasta sticking when working with it, lightly flour the work surface and your cutting tools and use more flour as necessary.*

# Cilantro Ravioli with Pumpkin Filling

THIS STUNNING HERB PASTA is served with a superb creamy pumpkin and roast garlic filling.

**INGREDIENTS**

*scant 1 cup stone-ground flour*
*2 eggs*
*pinch of salt*
*3 tablespoons chopped fresh cilantro*
*cilantro sprigs, to garnish*

***For the filling***

*4 garlic cloves, unpeeled*
*1 pound pumpkin, peeled and seeded*
*½ cup ricotta cheese*
*4 sun-dried tomatoes in olive oil, drained and finely chopped, and 2 tablespoons of the oil*
*ground black pepper*

**Serves 4–6**

1 Place the flour, eggs, salt and chopped fresh cilantro into a blender or food processor and process until combined.

**COOK'S TIP**

*To get the best out of your pasta machine, start rolling your pasta on the widest roller setting, then fold the pasta and roll again. Re-roll the piece three or four times, without folding, making the roller setting thinner each time.*

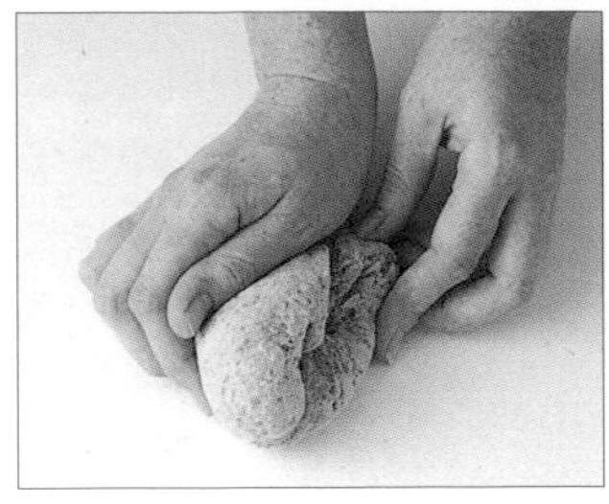

2 Place the dough on a lightly floured board and knead well for 5 minutes, until smooth. Press your finger in the dough: if it is still sticky, add a little more flour. Wrap in plastic wrap and let rest in the refrigerator for at least 20 minutes.

3 Preheat the oven to 400°F. Place the garlic cloves on a baking sheet and bake for 10 minutes until soft. Steam the pumpkin for 5–8 minutes until tender and drain well. Peel the garlic cloves and mash into the pumpkin together with the ricotta cheese and drained sun-dried tomatoes. Season with lots of ground black pepper.

4 Divide the pasta into four pieces and flatten slightly. Using a pasta machine, on its thinnest setting, roll out each piece. Leave the sheets of pasta on a lightly floured clean dish towel until they are slightly dried, about 1 hour.

5 Using a 3-inch crinkle-edged round cutter, stamp out about 36 rounds of pasta.

6 Top half of the rounds with a teaspoonful of filling, brush the edges with water and place another round of pasta on top. Press firmly around the edges to seal. Bring a large pan of water to a boil, add the ravioli and cook for 3–4 minutes. Drain well and toss into the reserved tomato oil. Serve at once garnished with fresh cilantro sprigs.

# Stuffed Pasta Roll

**This is a dinner party first course to impress. It takes quite a long time to make, but it can be made up to the baking stage the day before.**

**INGREDIENTS**

*6 tablespoons butter*
*1 small onion, finely chopped*
*5 ounces fresh spinach leaves, washed and trimmed*
*generous 1 cup ricotta cheese*
*1 egg*
*4 tablespoons freshly grated Parmesan cheese*
*4 tablespoons freshly grated Pecorino cheese*
*nutmeg*
*⅔ quantity Pasta with Eggs*
*salt and ground black pepper*

***For the tomato sauce***

*4 tablespoons olive oil*
*1 garlic clove, thinly sliced*
*1 onion, finely chopped*
*1 carrot, finely chopped*
*1 celery stalk, finely chopped*
*a few leaves each fresh basil, thyme and oregano or marjoram, plus extra basil leaves, to garnish*
*2 cans (14-ounce) chopped Italian plum tomatoes*
*1 tablespoon sun-dried tomato paste*
*1 teaspoon sugar*
*5–7 tablespoons dry white wine*

**Serves 6**

1 Melt 2 tablespoons of the butter in a medium saucepan, add the finely chopped onion and cook gently, stirring frequently, for about 5 minutes until softened.

2 Add the spinach and salt and pepper to taste and cook over a medium heat for 5–8 minutes, stirring frequently, until the spinach is wilted and tender. Increase the heat to high and stir until the water is driven off and the spinach is quite dry.

3 Finely chop the spinach mixture in a food processor or by hand. Transfer to a bowl and add the ricotta, egg and half the grated Parmesan and Pecorino. Season to taste with freshly grated nutmeg and salt, and add plenty of pepper. Beat well to mix.

4 Roll out the pasta dough to a 20 x 16-inch rectangle. Place the rectangle on a large piece of cheesecloth, with one of the short sides nearest you.

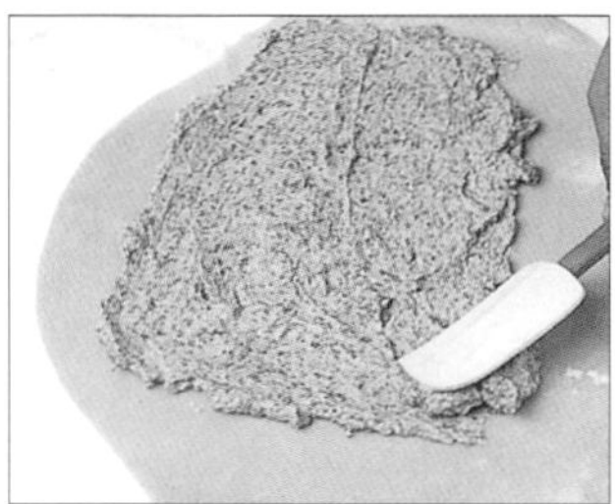

5 Spread the spinach mixture thinly over the pasta, leaving a ¾-inch margin along the two long sides and a 2-inch margin along the short side that is furthest away from you. Moisten the two long sides with water.

6 Starting from the short side that is nearest you, pick up the cheesecloth and roll the pasta away from you as you would a jelly roll. Don't press it, just let it roll until you have a 16-inch long "sausage." Press the two open ends to seal the pasta, then roll the cheesecloth around the roll a couple of times and tie the two ends tightly with string.

7 Half fill a large oval flameproof casserole with water and bring it to a boil. Add a large pinch of salt, then the pasta roll. Half cover with a lid and simmer for 45 minutes, turning the roll over twice. Remove the roll from the water and place it on a board near the sink. Prop the board up at one end to allow the excess water to drain away from the roll, then let cool.

8 Make the tomato sauce for serving with the pasta roll. Heat the oil in a saucepan, add the garlic slices and stir over very low heat for 1–2 minutes. Add the chopped vegetables and the fresh herbs. Cook over low heat, stirring continuously for 5–7 minutes until the vegetables have softened and are lightly colored but not browned.

9 Add the tomatoes, tomato paste and sugar, then add salt and pepper to taste. Bring to a boil, stirring constantly, then lower the heat and simmer gently, uncovered, for about 45 minutes, stirring occasionally.

10 Preheat the oven to 400°F. Unwrap the pasta roll and cut it into 12 thick slices. Melt the remaining butter and brush a little of it over the inside of sixindividual ovenproof dishes or a large shallow baking dish.

11 Arrange the pasta roll slices slightly overlapping in the dishes or dish and drizzle the remaining butter over them. Sprinkle with the remaining Parmesan and Pecorino and bake in the oven for 10–15 minutes or until golden brown.

12 Meanwhile, blend the tomato sauce in a food processor until smooth. Transfer to a pan and add enough wine to thin it down to a pouring consistency, then heat until bubbling. Serve the pasta roll slices on individual plates, on a pool of tomato sauce, sprinkled with basil leaves.

#### Cook's Tip

*If you have a pasta machine, roll out half the dough into a 36-inch strip. Cut the strip with a sharp knife into two 20-inch lengths (you can do this during rolling if the strip gets too long to manage). Brush the long edge of one of the strips with water, then overlap the other strip on top by about 1/2 inch. Dust lightly with flour and press together, then seal the join by rolling over it with a rolling pin. Repeat with the remaining dough, then join the two pieces of pasta together in the same way so that you have a large rectangle.*

# Cheese Cappellacci with Bolognese Sauce

IN EMILIA-ROMAGNA it is traditional to serve these *cappellacci* with a rich meat sauce, but if you prefer you can serve them with a tomato sauce, or just melted butter.

**INGREDIENTS**

*1 quantity Pasta with Eggs*
*8 cups beef stock made with stock cubes or diluted canned consommé*
*basil leaves, to garnish*
*freshly grated Parmesan cheese, to serve*

***For the filling***

*generous 1 cup ricotta cheese*
*3½ ounces taleggio cheese, rind removed, diced very small*
*4 tablespoons freshly grated Parmesan cheese*
*1 small egg*
*nutmeg*
*salt and ground black pepper*

***For the Bolognese meat sauce***

*2 tablespoons butter*
*1 tablespoon olive oil*
*1 onion, finely chopped*
*2 carrots, finely chopped*
*2 celery stalks, finely chopped*
*2 garlic cloves, finely chopped*
*4½ ounces pancetta or rindless lean bacon, diced*
*9 ounces lean ground beef*
*9 ounces lean ground pork*
*½ cup dry white wine*
*2 cans (14-ounce) crushed Italian plum tomatoes*
*2–3 cups beef stock*
*scant ½ cup* panna da cucina *or heavy cream*

**Serves 6**

1 Make the filling. Put the ricotta, taleggio and grated Parmesan in a bowl and mash together with a fork.

2 Add the egg and freshly grated nutmeg and salt and pepper to taste and stir well to mix.

3 Using a pasta machine, roll out one-quarter of the pasta into a 36-inch strip. Cut the strip with a sharp knife into two 18-inch lengths (you can do this during rolling if the strip gets too long to manage).

4 Using a 2½–3-inch square ravioli cutter, cut 6–7 squares from one of the pasta strips. Using a teaspoon, put a mound of filling in the center of each square. Brush a little water around the edge of each square, then fold the square diagonally in half over the filling to make a triangular shape. Press to seal.

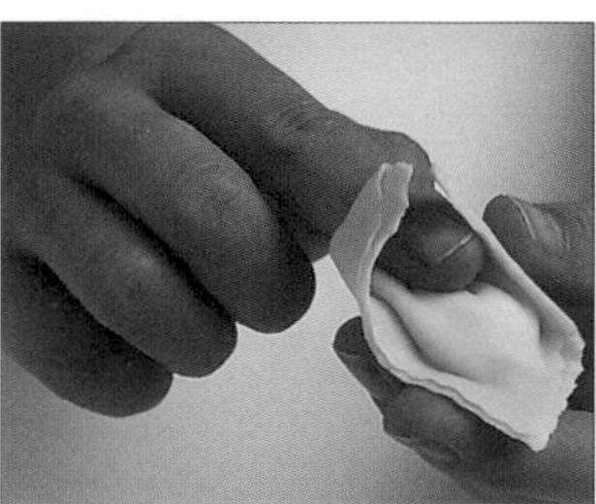

5 Wrap the triangle around one of your index fingers, bringing the bottom two corners together. Pinch the ends together to seal, then press with your fingertip around the top edge of the filling to make an indentation so that the "hat" looks like a bishop's miter.

6 Place the *cappellacci* on floured dish towels, sprinkle them lightly with flour and leave to dry while repeating the process with the remaining dough to make 48–56 *cappellacci* altogether.

7 Make the meat sauce. Heat the butter and oil in a large skillet or saucepan until sizzling. Add the vegetables, garlic, and the pancetta or bacon and cook over medium heat, stirring frequently, for 10 minutes or until the vegetables have softened.

8 Add the ground beef and pork, lower the heat and cook gently for 10 minutes, stirring frequently and breaking up any lumps in the meat with a wooden spoon. Stir in salt and pepper to taste, then add the wine and stir again. Simmer for about 5 minutes, or until reduced.

9 Add the tomatoes and 1 cup of the stock and bring to a boil. Stir well, then lower the heat, half cover the pan with a lid and let simmer very gently for 2 hours. Stir occasionally during this time and add more stock as it becomes absorbed.

10 Add the *panna da cucina* or heavy cream to the meat sauce. Stir well to mix, then simmer the sauce, without a lid, for another 30 minutes, stirring frequently.

11 Bring the stock to a boil in a large saucepan.

12 Drop the *cappellacci* into the stock, bring back to a boil and boil for 4–5 minutes; drain the *cappellacci* and divide them equally among six warmed bowls. Spoon the hot Bolognese sauce over the *cappellacci* and sprinkle with grated Parmesan and basil leaves. Serve immediately.

### Cook's Tip

*The exact shape of* cappellacci *varies from one cook to another. Some are made from discs rather than squares of pasta, although these are more often called tortellini or tortelloni. It all depends on the region in which they are made. If you prefer a party-hat shape to a bishop's miter, don't make an indentation above the filling in Step 5, but instead turn up the bottom edge of each "hat" so that they have brims.* Cappelletti *are the same shape as* cappellacci *but are made from smaller squares of pasta (about 2 inches square). Not surprisingly, because of their size,* cappelletti *are very fiddly to make.*

# Cheese and Ham Ravioli with Tomato Sauce

TYPICAL OF SOUTHERN ITALIAN cuisine, these ravioli are very tasty. They are substantial enough for a main course, served with a green or mixed salad. If you prefer them as a first course, there are enough ravioli for 8 servings.

### INGREDIENTS

*1 quantity Pasta with Eggs*
*4 tablespoons freshly grated Pecorino cheese, plus extra to serve*

***For the filling***
*¾ cup ricotta cheese*
*2 tablespoons freshly grated Parmesan cheese*
*4 ounces prosciutto crudo, finely chopped*
*1 packet (5 ounces) mozzarella cheese, drained and finely chopped*
*1 small egg*
*1 tablespoon chopped fresh Italian parsley, plus extra to garnish*

***For the tomato sauce***
*2 tablespoons olive oil*
*1 onion, finely chopped*
*1 can (14 ounces) chopped Italian plum tomatoes*
*1 tablespoon sun-dried tomato paste*
*1–2 teaspoons dried oregano, to taste*
*salt and ground black pepper*

**Serves 4–6**

1 Make the sauce. Heat the oil in a medium saucepan, add the onion and cook gently, stirring frequently, for about 5 minutes until softened.

2 Add the tomatoes. Fill the empty can with water, pour it into the pan, then stir in the tomato paste, oregano and salt and pepper to taste. Bring to a boil and stir well, then cover the pan and simmer gently for 30 minutes, stirring occasionally and adding more water if the sauce becomes too thick.

3 Meanwhile, make the filling and the ravioli. Put all the filling ingredients in a bowl with salt and pepper to taste. Mix well with a fork, breaking up any lumps in the ricotta.

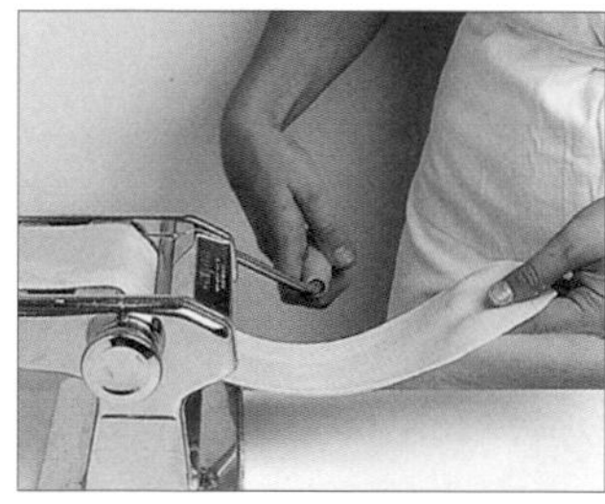

4 Using a pasta machine, roll out one-quarter of the pasta into a 36-inch strip. Cut the strip with a sharp knife into two 18-inch lengths (you can do this during rolling if the strip gets too long to manage).

5 Using 2 teaspoons, put 10–12 little mounds of the filling along one side of one of the pasta strips, spacing them evenly. The filling will be quite moist. Brush a little water around each mound, then fold the plain side of the pasta strip over the filling.

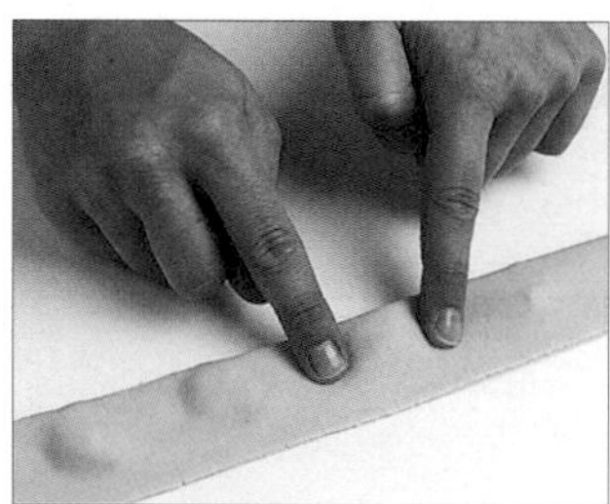

6 Starting from the folded edge, press down gently with your fingertips around each mound, pushing the air out at the unfolded edge.

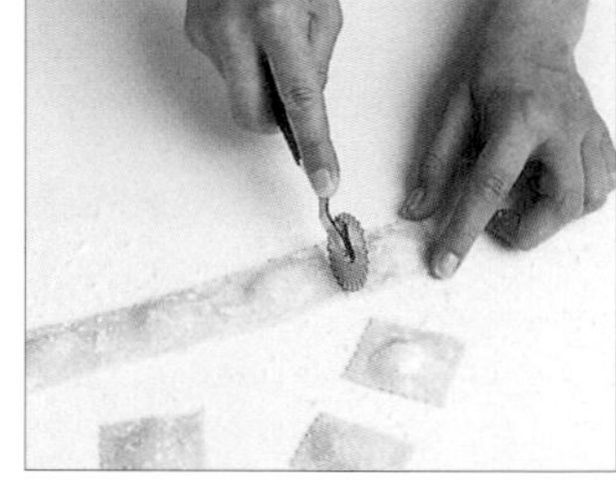

7 Sprinkle lightly with flour. With a fluted pasta wheel, cut along each long side, then in between each mound to make small square shapes.

8 Put the ravioli on floured dish towels; sprinkle lightly with flour.

9 Leave the ravioli to dry while repeating the process with the remaining pasta to get 80–96 ravioli altogether. Drop the ravioli into a large pan of salted boiling water, bring back to a boil and boil for 4–5 minutes.

10 Drain the ravioli well and pour about a third of them into a warmed bowl. Sprinkle 1 tablespoon freshly grated Pecorino over the ravioli. Pour over a third of the tomato sauce.

11 Repeat the layers twice, then top with the remaining grated Pecorino. Serve immediately, garnished with chopped parsley. Hand around more grated Pecorino separately.

**VARIATION**

*If you like the flavor of garlic with tomatoes, gently cook 1–2 crushed garlic cloves, with the onion when making the tomato sauce.*

# Agnolotti with Taleggio and Marjoram

THE FILLING FOR THESE LITTLE half-moons is very simple—only two ingredients—but the combination of flavors is absolutely delicious.

**INGREDIENTS**

*1 quantity Pasta with Eggs*
*12–14 ounces taleggio cheese*
*about 2 tablespoons finely chopped fresh marjoram, plus extra to garnish*
*½ cup butter*
*salt and ground black pepper*
*freshly grated Parmesan cheese, to serve*
**Serves 6–8**

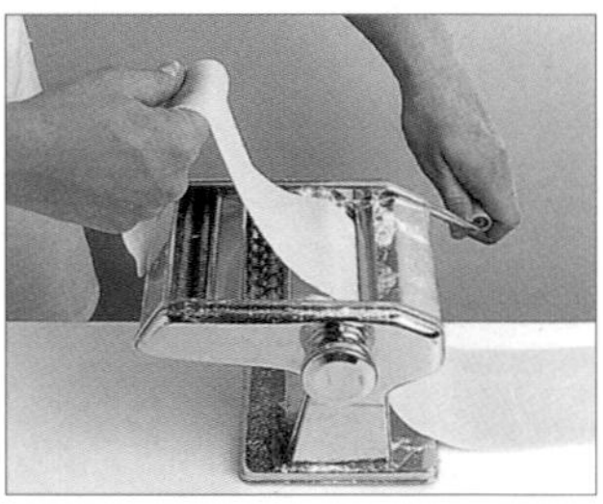

1 Using a pasta machine, roll out a quarter of the pasta into a 36-inch strip. Cut the strip with a sharp knife into two 18-inch lengths (you can do this during rolling if the strip gets too long to manage).

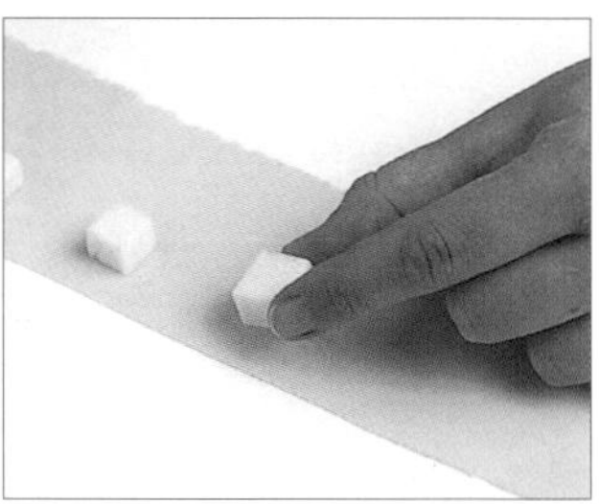

2 Cut 8–10 little cubes of taleggio and place them along one side of one of the pasta strips, spacing them evenly. Sprinkle each taleggio cube with a little chopped marjoram and pepper to taste.

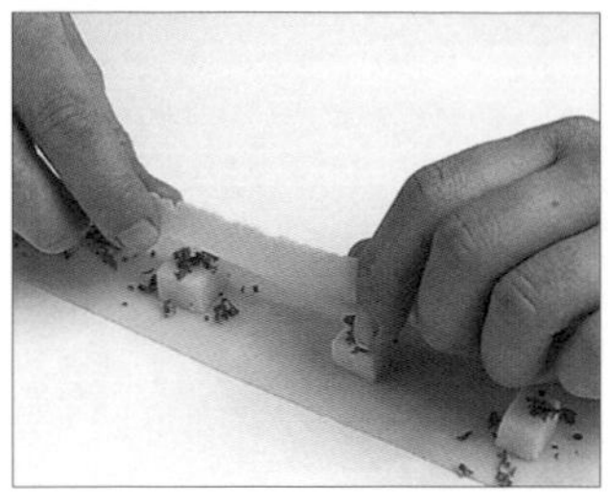

3 Brush a little water around each cube of cheese, then fold the plain side of the pasta strip over them.

4 Starting from the folded edge, press down gently with your fingertips around each cube, pushing the air out at the unfolded edge. Sprinkle lightly with flour.

5 Using only half of a 2-inch fluted round ravioli or cookie cutter, cut around each cube of cheese to make a half-moon shape. The folded edge should be the straight edge.

6 If you like, press the cut edges of the agnolotti with the tines of a fork to give a decorative effect.

7 Put the agnolotti on floured dish towels, sprinkle lightly with flour and let dry while repeating the process with the remaining pasta, cheese, marjoram and pepper to get 64–80 agnolotti altogether.

8 Drop the agnolotti into a large saucepan of salted boiling water, bring back to a boil and boil for 4–5 minutes until *al dente*.

9 Meanwhile, melt the butter in a small saucepan until it is sizzling.

10 Drain the agnolotti and divide them equally among six or eight warmed large bowls. Drizzle the sizzling butter over them and serve immediately, sprinkled with freshly grated Parmesan and chopped fresh marjoram. Hand around more grated Parmesan separately.

### COOK'S TIPS

- *Taleggio is a square-shaped, semi-soft cheese from Lombardy. It is quite easy to get in large supermarkets, or any Italian market. It has a mild, slightly nutty flavor and good melting qualities. For this recipe, make sure that you remove the rind, which tends to be quite tough and salty.*
- *If you are unable to get taleggio, use fontina cheese instead, or a strongly flavored blue cheese, such as Gorgonzola. If you use a blue cheese, substitute sage for the marjoram.*

### VARIATION

*Marjoram is traditional with the taleggio cheese in this recipe, both for the filling and the sizzling butter, but you can use other fresh herbs, such as sage, basil or Italian parsley.*

# Pansotti with Herbs and Cheese

IN LIGURIA, THE DOUGH for *pansotti* is flavored with white wine, and the stuffing is made of cheese and *preboggion*, a mixture of many different types of fresh herbs and wild leaves. The dish is traditionally served with a kind of pesto made from walnuts, making it very rich and quite complex. The recipe given here is a simple version.

**INGREDIENTS**

*1 quantity Herb-flavored Pasta with Eggs*
*1/4 cup butter*
*freshly grated Parmesan cheese, to serve*

***For the filling***

*generous 1 cup ricotta cheese*
*1 2/3 cups freshly grated Parmesan cheese*
*1 large handful fresh basil leaves, finely chopped*
*1 large handful fresh Italian parsley, finely chopped*
*a few sprigs fresh marjoram or oregano, leaves removed and finely chopped*
*1 garlic clove, crushed*
*1 small egg*
*salt and ground black pepper*

***For the sauce***

*3 1/2 ounces shelled walnuts*
*1 garlic clove*
*4 tablespoons extra virgin olive oil*
*1/2 cup* panna da cucina *or heavy cream*

**Serves 6–8**

1 First make the filling and sauce. Put the ricotta, Parmesan, herbs, garlic and egg in a bowl with salt and pepper to taste and beat well to mix.

2 To make the sauce, put the walnuts, garlic clove and oil in a food processor and process to a paste, adding up to 1/2 cup warm water through the feeder tube to slacken the consistency. Spoon the mixture into a large bowl and add the cream. Beat well to mix, then add salt and pepper to taste.

3 Using a pasta machine, roll out one-quarter of the pasta into a 36-inch strip. Cut the strip with a sharp knife into two 18-inch lengths (you can do this during rolling if the strip gets too long to manage).

4 Using a 2-inch square ravioli cutter, cut 8–10 squares from one of the pasta strips. Using a teaspoon, put a mound of filling in the center of each square.

5 Brush a little water around the edge of each square, then fold the square diagonally in half over the filling to make a triangular shape. Press gently to seal.

6 Spread out the *pansotti* on clean floured dish towels, sprinkle lightly with flour and let dry, while repeating the process with the remaining dough to make 64–80 *pansotti* altogether.

7 Cook the *pansotti* in a large saucepan of salted boiling water for 4–5 minutes. Meanwhile, put the walnut sauce in a large warmed bowl and add a ladleful of the pasta cooking water to thin it down. Melt the butter in a small saucepan until sizzling.

8 Drain the *pansotti* and turn them into the bowl of walnut sauce. Drizzle the butter over them, toss well, then sprinkle with grated Parmesan. Alternatively, toss the pansotti in the melted butter, spoon into warmed individual bowls and drizzle the sauce over. Serve immediately, with more grated Parmesan handed separately.

**COOK'S TIP**

*Try not to overfill the* pansotti, *or they will burst open during cooking.*

# Tortellini from Emilia-Romagna

THESE ARE THE TORTELLINI that are served on the day after Christmas in Emilia-Romagna. Traditionally they were made with ground leftover capon from Christmas Day, but nowadays turkey or chicken is often used.

**INGREDIENTS**

*1 quantity Pasta with Eggs*
*8 cups beef stock made with stock cubes or diluted canned consommé*
*freshly grated Parmesan cheese, to serve*

***For the filling***

*2 tablespoons butter*
*9 ounces ground turkey or chicken*
*1 teaspoon chopped fresh rosemary*
*1 teaspoon chopped fresh sage*
*nutmeg*
*1 cup chicken stock*
*4 tablespoons freshly grated Parmesan cheese*
*3½ ounces mortadella sausage, very finely chopped*
*1 small egg, lightly beaten*
*salt and ground black pepper*

**Serves 6–8**

1 Make the filling. Melt the butter in a medium skillet, then add the ground turkey or chicken and chopped herbs.

2 Grate in a little nutmeg and add salt and pepper to taste. Cook gently for 5–6 minutes, stirring frequently and breaking up any lumps in the meat with a wooden spoon.

3 Add the stock and stir well to mix, then simmer gently, uncovered, for 15–20 minutes until the meat is cooked and quite dry. Transfer the meat to a bowl with a slotted spoon and let cool. Add the grated Parmesan, mortadella and egg to the meat and stir well to mix.

4 Using a pasta machine, roll out one-quarter of the pasta into a 36-inch strip. Cut the strip with a sharp knife into two 18-inch lengths (you can do this during rolling if the strip gets too long to manage).

5 With a 2-inch fluted ravioli or cookie cutter, cut out 8–10 discs from one of the pasta strips. Using a teaspoon, put a little mound of filling in the center of each disc. Brush a little water around the edge of each disc.

6 Fold the disc in half over the filling so that the edges do not quite meet. Press to seal. Wrap the tortellini shape around your index finger and pinch the bottom corners together to seal.

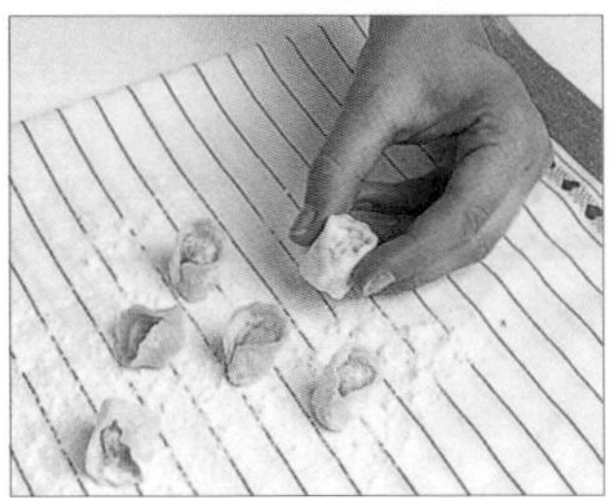

7 Put the tortellini in a single layer on floured dish towels, sprinkle lightly with flour and let dry while repeating the process with the remaining dough to make 64–80 tortellini altogether. If you have any stuffing left, re-roll the pasta trimmings and make more tortellini.

8 Bring the beef stock to a boil in a large saucepan. Drop in the tortellini, then bring back to a boil and boil for 4–5 minutes. Taste the stock and season with salt and pepper if necessary.

9 Pour the tortellini and stock into a warmed large soup tureen, sprinkle with a little grated Parmesan and serve immediately. Hand more Parmesan separately.

**COOK'S TIP**

*In Emilia-Romagna, cooked leftover meat is minced by hand for these tortellini, or raw meat is cooked in the piece and then ground. For speed and convenience in this recipe, raw minced poultry is cooked with herbs and seasonings before being used in the filling.*

# Spinach and Ricotta Conchiglioni

LARGE PASTA SHELLS are designed to hold a variety of delicious stuffings. Few are more pleasing than this mixture of spinach and ricotta.

**INGREDIENTS**

*12 ounces large fresh or dried conchiglioni*
*1¾ cups passata or tomato pulp*
*10 ounces frozen chopped spinach, thawed*
*2 ounces crustless white bread, crumbled*
*½ cup milk*
*3 tablespoons olive oil*
*9 ounces ricotta cheese*
*pinch of grated nutmeg*
*1 garlic clove, crushed*
*1 tablespoon olive oil*
*½ teaspoon black olive paste (optional)*
*Parmesan cheese, for sprinkling*
*2 tablespoons pine nuts*
*salt and ground black pepper*
**Serves 4**

1 Cook the pasta shells in plenty of salted boiling water according to the instructions on the package. Rinse under cold water, drain and reserve until needed.

2 Pour the passata or tomato pulp into a nylon strainer over a bowl and strain the liquids to thicken. Place the thawed spinach in another strainer and press out any excess liquid with the back of a spoon.

3 Place the bread, milk and oil in a blender or food processor and process to combine. Add the spinach and ricotta cheese and season with salt, pepper and grated nutmeg. Process again to combine.

4 Combine the passata or tomato pulp with the garlic, olive oil and olive paste, if using. Pour the sauce into the base of an ovenproof dish spreading it out to the corners.

5 Spoon the spinach mixture into a pastry bag fitted with a large plain nozzle and fill the pasta shells (alternatively fill with a spoon). Arrange the pasta shells over the sauce in the dish.

6 Preheat the broiler to moderate heat. Heat the pasta through in the microwave on a high power for 4 minutes. Scatter with Parmesan cheese and pine nuts, and finish under the broiler to brown the cheese until bubbling.

# Ravioli with Vegetables and Nuts

IT IS A PLEASURE to make your own fresh pasta and you might be surprised at just how easy it is to fill and shape ravioli, although it does take a little time. A blender or food processor will save you time and effort in making and kneading the dough. A pasta-making machine helps with the rolling out, but both these jobs can be done by hand if necessary.

**INGREDIENTS**

*1¾ cups stone-ground bread flour*
*½ teaspoon salt*
*1 tablespoon olive oil*
*2 eggs, beaten*

***For the filling***

*1 tablespoon olive oil*
*1 small red onion, finely chopped*
*1 small green bell pepper, finely chopped*
*1 carrot, coarsely grated*
*½ cup walnuts, chopped*
*½ cup ricotta cheese*
*2 tablespoons freshly grated Parmesan or Pecorino cheese, plus extra to serve*
*1 tablespoon chopped fresh marjoram or basil*
*salt and ground black pepper*
*extra oil or melted butter, to serve*

**Serves 6**

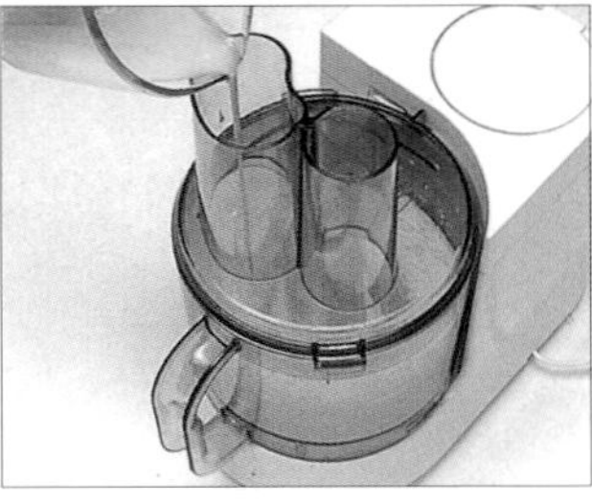

1 Sift the flour and salt together into a blender or food processor. With the machine running, trickle in the oil and eggs and blend to a stiff but smooth dough.

2 Allow the machine to run for at least 1 minute if possible, otherwise remove the dough and knead by hand for 5 minutes.

3 If you are using a pasta machine, break off small balls of dough and feed them through the rollers, several times, according to the instructions that come with the machine.

4 If rolling the pasta by hand, divide the dough into two and roll out on a lightly floured surface to a thickness of about ¼ inch.

5 Fold the pasta into three and re-roll. Repeat this up to six times until the dough is smooth and no longer sticky. Roll the pasta slightly more thinly each time.

6 Keep the rolled dough under clean, dry dish towels, to prevent it drying out, while you complete the rest and make the filling. You should aim to have an even number of pasta sheets, all the same size.

7 Heat the oil in a frying pan and cook the onion, pepper and carrot for 5 minutes, then allow to cool. Mix with the walnuts, cheeses, herbs and lots of seasoning.

8 Lay out a pasta sheet and place small scoops of the filling in neat rows about 2 inches apart. Brush between the mounds of filling with a little water.

9 Carefully place another pasta sheet of a similar size on the top, making sure that you cover all the mounds of filling.

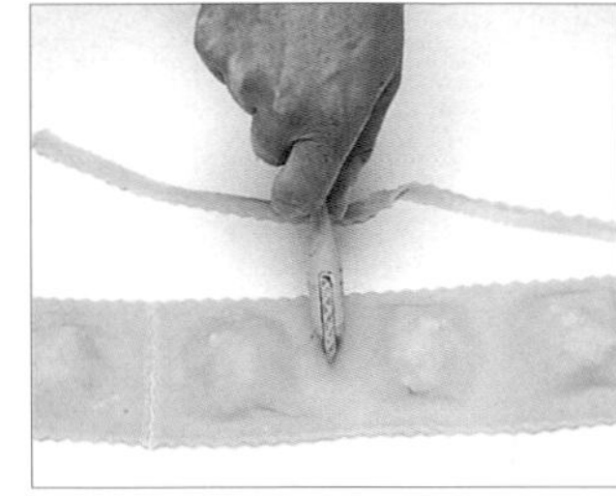

10 Press down well in between the rows then, using a ravioli or pastry cutter, cut into squares. If the edges pop open, press them back gently with your fingers or the tines of a fork.

11 Let the ravioli dry in the refrigerator, then boil in plenty of lightly salted water for just 5 minutes. Drain thoroughly.

12 Toss the cooked ravioli in a little oil or melted butter before serving with extra cheese.

# Ravioli with Pork and Turkey

THIS ROMAN-STYLE RAVIOLI stuffed with ground meat and cheese is scented with fresh herbs. It makes a substantial first course.

**INGREDIENTS**

*1 quantity Pasta with Eggs*
*¼ cup butter*
*a large bunch of fresh sage, leaves removed and roughly chopped*
*4 tablespoons freshly grated Parmesan cheese, plus extra, to serve*
*sage leaves, to garnish*

***For the filling***

*2 tablespoons butter*
*5 ounces ground pork*
*4 ounces ground turkey*
*4 fresh sage leaves, finely chopped*
*1 sprig of fresh rosemary, leaves removed and finely chopped*
*2 tablespoons dry white wine*
*generous ¼ cup ricotta cheese*
*3 tablespoons freshly grated Parmesan cheese*
*1 egg, lightly beaten*
*nutmeg*
*salt and ground black pepper*

**Serves 8**

1 Make the filling. Melt the butter in a medium saucepan, add the ground pork and turkey and the herbs and cook gently for 5–6 minutes, stirring frequently and breaking up any lumps in the meat with a wooden spoon. Add salt and pepper to taste and stir to mix.

2 Add the wine to the pan and stir again. Simmer for 1–2 minutes until reduced slightly, then cover the pan and simmer gently for about 20 minutes, stirring occasionally. With a slotted spoon, transfer the meat to a bowl and let cool.

3 Add the ricotta and Parmesan cheeses to the bowl with the egg and freshly grated nutmeg to taste. Stir well to mix the ingredients thoroughly.

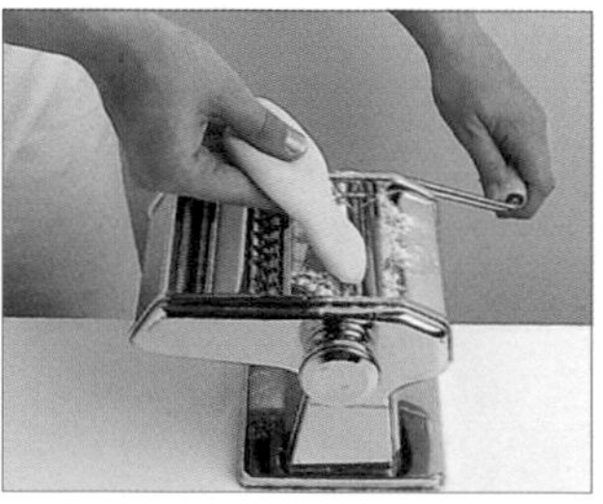

4 Using a pasta machine, roll out one-quarter of the pasta into a 36-inch strip. Cut the strip with a sharp knife into two 18-inch lengths (you can do this during rolling if the strip gets too long to manage).

5 Using a teaspoon, put 10–12 little mounds of the filling along one side of one of the pasta strips, spacing them evenly. Brush a little water on to the pasta strip around each mound, then fold the plain side of the pasta strip over the filling.

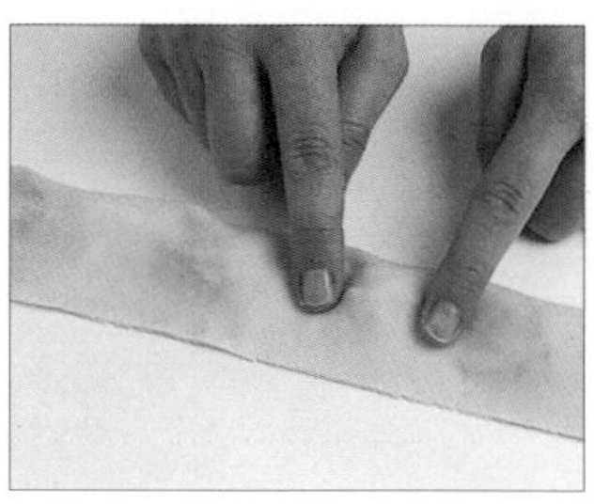

6 Starting from the folded edge, press down gently with your fingertips around each mound of filling, pushing the air out at the unfolded edge. Sprinkle lightly with flour.

7 With a fluted pasta wheel, cut along each long side, then in between each mound to make small square shapes. Dust lightly with flour.

8 Put the ravioli in a single layer on floured dish towels and leave to dry while repeating the process with the remaining pasta to make 80–96 ravioli altogether.

9 Drop the ravioli into a large pan of salted boiling water, bring back to a boil and boil for 4–5 minutes.

**COOK'S TIP**

*Ground pork and turkey are widely available at supermarkets, but if you cannot get one or the other you can use just one type of meat, or substitute ground veal, beef or lamb to use in the ravioli filling.*

10 While the ravioli are cooking, melt the butter in a small saucepan, add the fresh sage leaves and stir over medium to high heat until the sage leaves are sizzling in the butter.

11 Drain the ravioli and pour half into a warmed large bowl. Sprinkle with half the grated Parmesan, then half the sage butter. Repeat with the remaining ravioli, Parmesan and sage butter. Serve immediately, garnished with fresh sage leaves. Hand more grated Parmesan separately.

# Ravioli with Crab

This modern recipe for a dinner party starter uses chile-flavored pasta, which looks and tastes good with crab, but you can use plain pasta if you prefer.

**INGREDIENTS**

*1 quantity Chile-flavored Pasta with Eggs*
*6 tablespoons butter*
*juice of 1 lemon*

***For the filling***

*¾ cup mascarpone cheese*
*¾ cup crabmeat*
*2 tablespoons finely chopped fresh Italian parsley*
*finely grated rind of 1 lemon*
*pinch of crushed dried chillies (optional)*
*salt and ground black pepper*

**Serves 4**

**Cook's Tip**

*You can use all white crabmeat or a mixture of white and dark. If you use dark meat, the flavor will be stronger.*

1 Make the filling. Put the mascarpone in a bowl and mash it with a fork. Add the crabmeat, parsley, lemon rind, crushed dried chiles (if using) and salt and pepper to taste. Stir well.

2 Using a pasta machine, roll out one-quarter of the pasta into a 36-inch strip. Cut the strip with a sharp knife into two 18-inch lengths (you can do this during rolling if the strip gets too long to manage).

3 With a 2½-inch fluted cookie cutter, cut out 8 squares from each pasta strip.

4 Using a teaspoon, put a mound of filling in the center of half the discs. Brush a little water around the edge of the filled discs, then top with the plain discs and press the edges to seal. For a decorative finish, press the edges with the tines of a fork.

5 Put the ravioli on floured dish towels, sprinkle lightly with flour and let dry while repeating the process with the remaining dough to make 32 ravioli altogether. If you have any stuffing left, you can re-roll the pasta trimmings and make more ravioli.

6 Cook the ravioli in a large saucepan of salted boiling water for 4–5 minutes. Meanwhile, melt the butter and lemon juice in a small saucepan until sizzling.

7 Drain the ravioli and divide them equally among four warmed bowls. Drizzle the lemon butter over the ravioli and serve immediately.

# Sardinian Ravioli

THESE RAVIOLI, with their unusual mashed potato and mint filling, are from northern Sardinia. Here they are gratinéed in the oven with butter and cheese, but they are often served dressed with a tomato sauce.

**INGREDIENTS**

*1 quantity Pasta with Eggs*
*¼ cup butter*
*⅔ cup freshly grated Pecorino cheese*

***For the filling***

*2 potatoes, each about 7 ounces, diced*
*generous ⅔ cup freshly grated hard salty Pecorino cheese*
*3 ounces soft fresh Pecorino cheese*
*1 egg yolk*
*1 large bunch fresh mint, leaves removed and chopped*
*good pinch of saffron powder*
*salt and ground black pepper*

**Serves 4–6**

1 Make the filling. Cook the diced potatoes in salted boiling water for 15–20 minutes or until soft. Drain the potatoes and turn into a bowl, then mash until smooth. Leave until cold. Add the cheeses, egg yolk, mint, saffron and salt and pepper to taste and stir well to mix.

2 Using a pasta machine, roll out one-quarter of the pasta into a 36-inch strip. Cut the strip with a sharp knife into two 18-inch lengths.

3 With a fluted 4-inch cookie cutter, cut out 4–5 discs from one of the pasta strips. Using a heaped teaspoon, put a mound of filling to one side of each disc. Brush a little water around the edge of each disc, then fold the plain side of the disc over the filling to make a half-moon shape. Pleat the curved edge to seal.

4 Put the *culurgiones* on floured dish towels, sprinkle with flour and let dry. Repeat the process with the remaining dough to make 32–40 *culurgiones* altogether. If you have any stuffing left, re-roll the pasta trimmings and make more *culurgiones*.

5 Preheat the oven to 375°F. Cook the *culurgiones* in a large saucepan of salted boiling water for 4–5 minutes. Meanwhile, melt the butter in a small saucepan.

6 Drain the *culurgiones*, turn them into a large baking dish and pour the melted butter over them. Sprinkle with the grated Pecorino and bake in the oven for 10–15 minutes until golden and bubbly. Let stand for 5 minutes before serving.

**COOK'S TIP**

*There is quite an art to pleating the curved edge of* culurgiones*, but each cook has his or her own way of doing it, so don't worry about getting a precise finish. Do whatever you think looks best—some* culurgiones *look like miniature patties, others more like Chinese wontons. If you prefer, simply make square or round ravioli, or plain half-moons.*

# Fresh and Healthy

Chargrilled vegetables, designer salad leaves and pesto made with arugula are just a few of the new ingredients being introduced to pasta by today's chefs. To call these sauces is stretching the point a little: many of them consist of little more than a handful of fresh ingredients tossed with hot pasta, but the results are simply sensational.

These are not traditional pasta dishes. Many of them originated in restaurants, in response to the current taste for lighter, healthier food, but they are so quick and easy to make at home that you will find there's no need to go out to eat them.

The recipes in this chapter are tried and tested, but there are no hard-and-fast rules. Half the fun is in inventing your own combinations, using fresh vegetables and herbs according to the season. The key to success lies in the quality of these ingredients, and only the best will do. This goes for the pasta as much as anything else. Buy Italian brands of pasta to be sure of good texture and taste or, if you have the inclination and time, make your own fresh egg pasta.

Pasta is a natural, additive-free food, packed with protein, vitamins and minerals—the perfect partner for other healthy ingredients to make a high-energy meal.

# Spaghetti with Herb Sauce

HERBS MAKE a wonderfully aromatic sauce—the heat from the pasta releases their flavors.

**INGREDIENTS**

*2 ounces chopped fresh mixed herbs, such as parsley, basil and thyme*
*2 garlic cloves, crushed*
*4 tablespoons pine nuts, toasted*
*⅔ cup olive oil*
*12 ounces dried spaghetti*
*4 tablespoons freshly grated Parmesan cheese*
*salt and ground black pepper*
*basil leaves, to garnish*

**Serves 4**

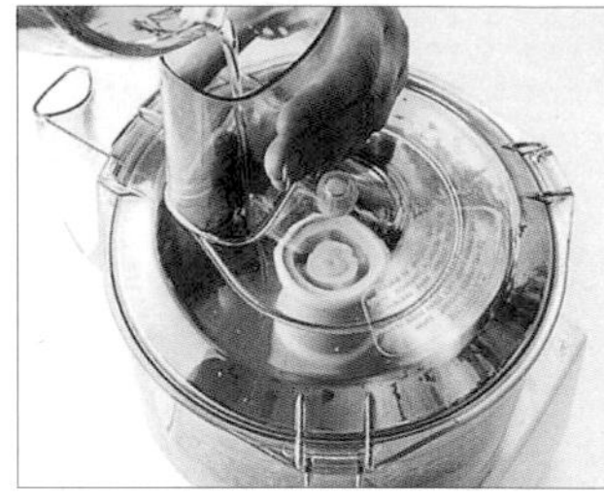

1 Put the herbs, garlic and half the pine nuts into a blender or food processor. With the machine running slowly, add the oil and process to form a thick purée.

2 Cook the spaghetti in plenty of salted boiling water for about 8 minutes until *al dente*. Drain.

3 Transfer the herb purée to a large warmed serving dish, then add the spaghetti and Parmesan. Toss well to coat the pasta with the sauce. Sprinkle the remaining pine nuts and the basil leaves over the top and serve immediately.

# Capellini with Arugula and Snow Peas

A LIGHT BUT FILLING pasta dish with the added pepperiness of fresh arugula leaves.

**INGREDIENTS**

*9 ounces dried capellini*
*8 ounces snow peas*
*3 ounces arugula leaves*
*¼ cup pine nuts, roasted*
*2 tablespoons finely grated Parmesan cheese (optional)*
*2 tablespoons olive oil (optional)*

**Serves 4**

1 Cook the capellini in a large saucepan with plenty of salted boiling water, according to the instructions on the package, until just *al dente*.

2 Meanwhile, carefully top and tail the snow peas, and discard any that are damaged.

3 As soon as the pasta is cooked, drop in the arugula and snow peas. Drain immediately.

4 Toss the pasta with the roasted pine nuts, and Parmesan and olive oil if using. Serve immediately.

# Tagliatelle with Broccoli and Spinach

THIS IS AN EXCELLENT vegetarian supper dish. It is nutritious and filling, and needs no accompaniment. If you like, you can use tagliatelle flecked with herbs.

**INGREDIENTS**

*2 heads of broccoli*
*1 pound fresh spinach, stalks removed*
*nutmeg*
*1 pound fresh or dried egg tagliatelle*
*about 3 tablespoons extra virgin olive oil*
*juice of ½ lemon, or to taste*
*salt and ground black pepper*
*freshly grated Parmesan cheese, to serve*

**Serves 4**

1 Put the broccoli in the basket of a steamer, cover and steam over boiling water for 10 minutes. Add the spinach to the broccoli, cover and steam for 4–5 minutes or until both are tender. Towards the end of the cooking time, sprinkle the vegetables with freshly grated nutmeg and salt and pepper to taste. Lift out the steamer and put to one side.

2 Add salt to the water already in the steamer and fill up with more boiling water, then add the pasta and cook according to the instructions on the package. Meanwhile, chop the broccoli and spinach in the colander.

3 Drain the pasta. Heat 3 tablespoons oil in the pasta pan, add the pasta and chopped vegetables and toss over medium heat until evenly mixed. Sprinkle in the lemon juice and plenty of black pepper, then taste and add more lemon juice, oil, salt and nutmeg if you like. Serve immediately, sprinkled liberally with freshly grated Parmesan and black pepper.

**VARIATIONS**

- *If you like, add a sprinkling of crushed dried chiles with the black pepper in Step 3.*
- *To add both texture and protein, garnish the finished dish with one or two handfuls of toasted pine nuts. They are often served with broccoli and spinach in Italy.*

# Conchiglie from Pisa

NOTHING COULD BE MORE simple than hot pasta tossed with fresh ripe tomatoes, ricotta and sweet basil. Serve it on hot summer days—it is surprisingly cool and refreshing.

**INGREDIENTS**

*3 cups dried conchiglie*
*generous ½ cup ricotta cheese*
*6 ripe Italian plum tomatoes, diced*
*2 garlic cloves, crushed*
*1 handful fresh basil leaves, shredded, plus extra basil leaves to garnish*
*4 tablespoons extra virgin olive oil*
*salt and ground black pepper*

**Serves 4–6**

1 Cook the pasta in salted boiling water according to the instructions on the package.

### COOK'S TIP

*If you like, peel the tomatoes before you dice them. It won't take long if the tomatoes are ripe.*

2 Meanwhile, put the ricotta in a large bowl and mash with a fork.

3 Add the tomatoes, garlic and basil, with salt and pepper to taste, and mix well. Add the olive oil and whisk thoroughly. Taste for seasoning.

4 Drain the cooked pasta, turn it into the ricotta mixture and toss well to mix. Garnish with basil leaves and serve immediately.

### VARIATION

- *You can use diced mozzarella instead of ricotta cheese and call the dish* Conchiglie Caprese, *after the salad of tomatoes, mozzarella and basil known as* Caprese.
- *An avocado is the ideal ingredient for adding extra color and flavor to this pasta dish. Halve, pit and peel, then dice the flesh. Toss it with the hot pasta at the last minute.*

# Conchiglie with Tomatoes and Arugula

THIS PRETTY-COLORED pasta dish relies for its success on the salad green, arugula. Available in large supermarkets, it is a leaf easily grown in the garden or a window-box and tastes slightly peppery.

**INGREDIENTS**

*1 pound conchiglie rigate*
*1 pound ripe cherry tomatoes*
*3 ounces fresh arugula leaves*
*3 tablespoons olive oil*
*salt and ground black pepper*
*Parmesan cheese shavings, to serve*
**Serves 4**

1 Cook the pasta in plenty of salted boiling water according to the instructions on the package, until *al dente*. Drain well.

2 Halve the tomatoes. Trim, wash and dry the arugula leaves.

3 Heat the oil in a large saucepan, add the tomatoes and cook for barely 1 minute. The tomatoes should only just heat through and not disintegrate or brown.

4 Add the pasta, then the arugula. Carefully stir to mix and heat through. Season well with salt and ground black pepper. Serve immediately with plenty of Parmesan cheese shavings.

# Eliche with Lowfat Pesto Sauce

TRADITIONALLY MADE with lashings of olive oil, this simple pesto sauce is still packed with flavor.

**INGREDIENTS**

*2 cups dried eliche*
*1 cup fresh basil leaves*
*½ cup parsley sprigs*
*1 garlic clove, crushed*
*¼ cup pine nuts*
*½ cup curd cheese*
*2 tablespoons freshly grated Parmesan cheese*
*salt and ground black pepper*
*fresh basil sprigs, to garnish*

**Serves 4**

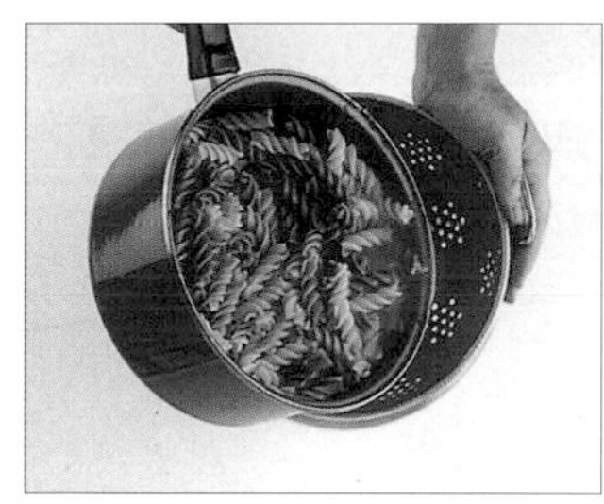

1 Cook the pasta in plenty of salted boiling water in a large saucepan for 8–10 minutes, or until *al dente*. Drain well through a colander.

2 Meanwhile put half the basil and half the parsley, the garlic clove, pine nuts and curd cheese into a blender or food processor fitted with a metal blade and process until smooth. Scrape down the sides.

3 Add the remaining basil and parsley together with the Parmesan cheese and seasoning. Continue to process until the herbs are finely chopped.

4 Toss the pasta with the pesto and serve on warmed plates. Garnish with fresh basil sprigs.

# Pipe with Ricotta, Saffron and Spinach

TOSSING PASTA IN RICOTTA is popular in Sicily and Sardinia, where this cheese is widely used in cooking. For best results, use fresh white ricotta, which is sold by weight in Italian markets. Serve this rich dish in small quantities. Omit the saffron, with its quite strong flavor, if preferred.

**INGREDIENTS**

*1 small pinch of saffron strands*
*2¾ cups dried pipe*
*11–12 ounces fresh spinach, stalks removed*
*nutmeg*
*generous 1 cup ricotta cheese*
*salt and ground black pepper*
*freshly grated Pecorino cheese, to serve*
**Serves 4–6**

1 Soak the saffron strands in 4 tablespoons warm water. Cook the pasta according to the instructions.

2 Meanwhile, wash the spinach and put the leaves in a saucepan with only the water clinging to the leaves. Season with freshly grated nutmeg, salt and pepper to taste,

3 Cover the pan and cook over medium to high heat for about 5 minutes, shaking the pan occasionally, until the spinach is wilted and tender. Turn into a colander, press to extract as much liquid as possible, then coarsely chop letting the water drain through.

4 Put the ricotta in a large bowl. Strain in the saffron water. Add the spinach, beat well to mix, then add a ladleful or two of the pasta cooking water to loosen the mixture. Season.

5 Drain the pasta, reserving some of the cooking water. Add the pasta to the ricotta mixture and toss well, adding a little of the water if necessary. Serve immediately, sprinkled with Pecorino.

# Tagliarini with White Truffle

THERE IS NOTHING QUITE like the fragrance and flavor of the Italian white truffle. It is one of the rarest and therefore most expensive of truffles, which comes from around the towns of Alba and Asti in Piedmont. This simple style of serving it is one of the best ways to enjoy it.

**INGREDIENTS**

*12 ounces fresh tagliarini*
*6 tablespoons unsalted butter, diced*
*4 tablespoons freshly grated Parmesan cheese*
*nutmeg*
*1 small white truffle, about 1–1½ ounces*
*salt and ground black pepper*
**Serves 4**

1 Cook the pasta in salted boiling water according to the instructions on the package.

2 Drain the cooked pasta thoroughly and turn it into a warmed large bowl. Add the diced butter, grated Parmesan, freshly grated nutmeg and a little salt and pepper to taste. Toss well until the pasta is coated in melted butter.

3 Divide the pasta equally among four warmed bowls and shave paper-thin slivers of the white truffle on top. Serve immediately.

**COOK'S TIPS**

- *White Italian truffles can be bought during the months of September and October from specialist food stores. They are very expensive, however, and there are some alternative ways of getting the flavor of truffles without the expense. Some Italian stores sell "truffle cheese," which is a mountain cheese with shavings of truffle in it, and this can be used instead of the Parmesan and truffle in this recipe. Another alternative is to toss hot pasta in truffle oil and serve it with freshly grated Parmesan.*
- *In Piedmont a very thin home-made egg pasta called tagliarin or tajarin is used for this dish. Tagliarini are the nearest equivalent, or you could use tagliatellini or tagliolini instead, or even fettuccine if you like.*

# Spaghetti with Arugula Pesto

THIS IS THE PESTO for real arugula lovers. It is sharp and peppery, and delicious for a summer pasta meal with a glass of chilled dry white wine.

**INGREDIENTS**

*4 garlic cloves*
*6 tablespoons pine nuts*
*2 large handfuls arugula, total weight about 5 ounces, stems removed*
*⅔ cup Parmesan cheese, freshly grated*
*⅔ cup Pecorino cheese, freshly grated*
*6 tablespoons extra virgin olive oil*
*14 ounces fresh or dried spaghetti*
*salt and ground black pepper*
*freshly grated Parmesan and Pecorino cheese, to serve*

**Serves 4**

1 Put the garlic and pine nuts in a blender or food processor and process until finely chopped.

2 Add the arugula, Parmesan and Pecorino, oil and salt and pepper to taste and process for 5 seconds. Stop and scrape down the side of the bowl. Process for 5–10 seconds more until a smooth paste is formed.

3 Cook the spaghetti in a saucepan of salted boiling water according to the package instructions.

4 Turn the pesto into a large bowl. Just before the pasta is ready, add 1–2 ladlefuls of the cooking water to the pesto and stir well to mix.

5 Drain the pasta, turn it into the bowl of pesto and toss well to mix. Serve immediately, with the grated cheeses handed separately.

**VARIATION**

*To temper the flavor of the arugula and make the pesto milder, add ½ cup ricotta or mascarpone cheese to the pesto in Step 4 and mix well before adding the water.*

# Spaghetti with Lemon

THIS IS THE DISH TO MAKE when you get home and find there's nothing to eat. If you keep spaghetti and olive oil in the storecupboard and garlic and lemons in the vegetable rack, you can prepare the most delicious meal in minutes.

**INGREDIENTS**

*12 ounces dried spaghetti*
*6 tablespoons extra virgin olive oil*
*juice of 1 large lemon*
*2 garlic cloves, cut into very thin slivers*
*salt and ground black pepper*
*freshly grated Parmesan cheese, to serve*

**Serves 4**

1 Cook the pasta in a saucepan of salted boiling water according to the instructions on the package, then drain well and return to the pan.

2 Pour the olive oil and lemon juice over the cooked pasta, sprinkle in the slivers of garlic and add salt and pepper to taste.

3 Toss the pasta over medium to high heat for 1–2 minutes. Serve immediately in four warmed bowls, with freshly grated Parmesan.

**COOK'S TIP**

*Spaghetti is the best type of pasta for this recipe, because the olive oil and lemon juice cling to its long thin strands—even more so if you serve it with freshly grated Parmesan. If you are out of spaghetti, use another dried long pasta shape instead, such as spaghettini, linguine or tagliatelle.*

# Orecchiette with Broccoli

PUGLIA, IN SOUTHERN ITALY, specializes in imaginative pasta and vegetable combinations. Using the broccoli cooking water for boiling the pasta gives it more of the vegetable's lovely fresh flavor.

**INGREDIENTS**

*$1\frac{3}{4}$ pounds broccoli*

*4 cups fresh or dried orecchiette*

*6 tablespoons olive oil*

*3 garlic cloves, finely chopped*

*6 anchovy fillets in oil*

*salt and ground black pepper*

**Serves 6**

1 Peel the stems of the broccoli, starting from the base and pulling up towards the flowerets with a knife. Discard the woody parts of the stem. Cut the flowerets and stems into 2-inch pieces.

2 Bring a large pan of water to a boil. Drop in the broccoli and boil until barely tender, about 5–8 minutes. Remove the broccoli pieces from the pan to a serving bowl. Do not discard the broccoli cooking water.

3 Add salt to the broccoli cooking water and bring back to a boil. Drop in the pasta, stir well, and cook until *al dente*.

4 While the pasta is boiling, heat the oil in a small saucepan. Add the garlic and, after 2–3 minutes, the anchovy fillets. Using a fork, mash the anchovies and garlic to a smooth paste. Then cook for a further 3–4 minutes.

5 Before draining the pasta, ladle 1–2 cupfuls of the cooking water over the broccoli. Add the drained pasta and the hot anchovy and oil mixture. Mix well, and season with salt and pepper if necessary. Serve immediately.

# Pasta Napoletana

THE SIMPLE CLASSIC cooked tomato sauce with no adornments.

**INGREDIENTS**

*2 pounds fresh ripe red tomatoes or 1¾ pounds canned plum tomatoes with their juice*
*1 onion, chopped*
*1 carrot, diced*
*1 celery stalk, diced*
*⅔ cup dry white wine (optional)*
*1 sprig fresh parsley*
*pinch of superfine sugar*
*1 tablespoon chopped fresh oregano or 1 teaspoon dried*
*1 pound pasta, any variety*
*salt and ground black pepper*
*freshly grated Parmesan cheese, to serve*

**Serves 4**

1 Coarsely chop the tomatoes and place in a medium saucepan.

2 Add the vegetables, wine if using, parsley and sugar and bring to a boil. Simmer, half-covered, for 45 minutes until thick. Strain through a strainer.

3 Stir the oregano into the sauce. Taste and adjust the seasoning if necessary.

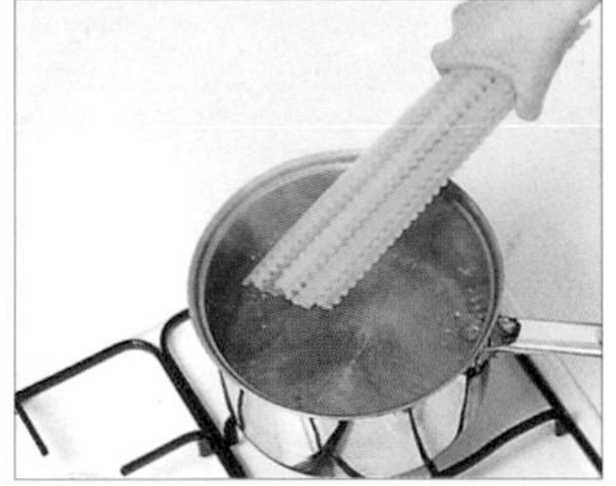

4 Cook the pasta in plenty of salted boiling water according to the instructions on the package, until *al dente*. Drain well.

5 Toss the pasta with the sauce. Serve with plenty of freshly grated Parmesan cheese.

# Spaghetti Olio e Aglio

THIS IS ANOTHER VERSION of the classic recipe from Rome. Originally the food of the poor, involving nothing more than pasta, olive oil (*olio*) and garlic (*aglio*), this is a quick and filling dish which is fast becoming fashionable the world over.

**INGREDIENTS**

*2 garlic cloves*
*¼ ounce fresh parsley*
*½ cup olive oil*
*1 pound spaghetti*
*salt and ground black pepper*
**Serves 4**

### VARIATION

*Although spaghetti is the traditional accompaniment to this sauce, this method works well with spaghettini, capellini or capellini d'angelo.*

1 Using a sharp knife, peel and chop the two cloves of garlic as finely as possible.

2 Using a nylon cutting board and a sharp knife, coarsely chop the fresh parsley.

3 Heat the olive oil in a medium saucepan and add the garlic and a pinch of salt. Cook gently, stirring constantly, until golden. If the garlic becomes too brown, it will taste bitter and spoil the dish.

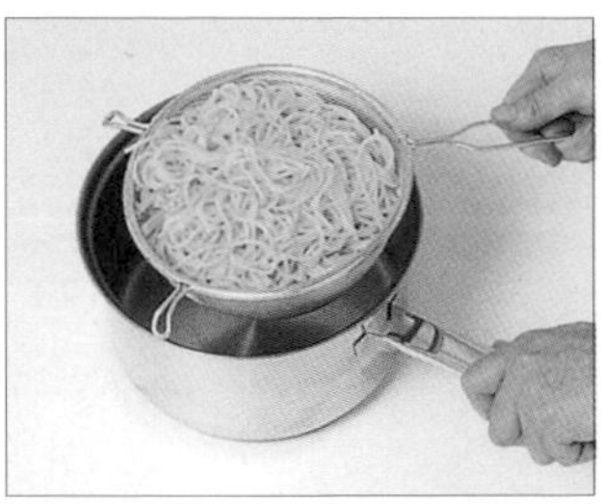

4 Meanwhile cook the spaghetti in plenty of salted boiling water according to the instructions on the package until *al dente*. Drain well through a colander.

5 Toss with the warm—not sizzling—garlic and oil and add plenty of black pepper and the parsley. Serve the dish immediately.

# Pasta Rapido with Parsley Pesto

HERE IS A FRESH and lively sauce that will appeal to even the most jaded of appetites.

**INGREDIENTS**

*1 pound dried pasta, any shape*
*1¾ cup whole almonds*
*½ cup sliced almonds*
*¼ cup freshly grated Parmesan cheese*
*pinch of salt*

***For the sauce***

*1½ ounces fresh parsley*
*2 garlic cloves, crushed*
*3 tablespoons olive oil*
*3 tablespoons lemon juice*
*1 teaspoon sugar*
*1 cup boiling water*
**Serves 4**

1 Cook the pasta in plenty of salted boiling water, according to the instructions on the package, until *al dente*. Toast the whole and sliced almonds separately under a moderate broiler until golden brown. Set the sliced almonds aside.

2 For the sauce, chop the parsley finely in a blender or food processor. Add the whole almonds; reduce to a fine consistency. Add the garlic, oil, lemon juice, sugar and water. Combine to a sauce.

3 Drain the pasta and combine with half the sauce. (The remainder of the sauce will keep in a screw-top jar in the refrigerator for up to ten days.) Top with Parmesan and sliced almonds.

# Eliche with Turkey

BROCCOLI COMBINES with the other ingredients to make a one-pan meal.

**INGREDIENTS**

*1 ½ pounds ripe, firm plum tomatoes, quartered*
*6 tablespoons olive oil*
*1 teaspoon dried oregano*
*12 ounces broccoli flowerets*
*1 small onion, sliced*
*1 teaspoon dried thyme*
*1 pound skinless, boneless turkey breast, cubed*
*3 garlic cloves, crushed*
*1 tablespoon fresh lemon juice*
*4 cups eliche*
*salt and ground black pepper*

**Serves 4**

1 Preheat the oven to 400°F. Place the plum tomatoes in a baking dish. Add 1 tablespoon of the oil, the oregano and ½ teaspoon salt and stir.

2 Bake for 30–40 minutes, until the tomatoes are just browned; do not stir.

3 Meanwhile, bring a large saucepan of salted water to a boil. Add the broccoli flowerets and cook until just tender, about 5 minutes. Drain and set aside. (Alternatively, steam the broccoli until tender.)

4 Heat 2 tablespoons of the oil in a large non-stick frying pan. Add the onion, thyme, turkey and ½ teaspoon salt. Cook over high heat, stirring often, until the meat is cooked and beginning to brown, about 5–7 minutes. Add the garlic and cook for a further 1 minute, stirring frequently.

5 Remove from the heat. Stir in the lemon juice and season with ground black pepper. Set aside and keep warm.

6 Cook the pasta in plenty of salted boiling water according to the instructions on the package until *al dente*. Drain and place in a large bowl. Toss the pasta with the remaining oil.

7 Add the broccoli to the turkey mixture, then stir into the fusilli. Add the tomatoes and stir gently to blend. Serve immediately.

# Penne with Broccoli and Chile

FOR A MILDER FLAVOR, remove the seeds from the chile. Take care, when handling chile, to wash your hands thoroughly afterwards.

**INGREDIENTS**

*3 cups fresh or dried penne*
*1 pound small broccoli flowerets*
*2 tablespoons stock*
*1 garlic clove, crushed*
*1 small red chile, sliced, or ½ teaspoon chili sauce*
*4 tablespoons plain lowfat yogurt*
*2 tablespoons toasted pine nuts or cashew nuts*
*salt and ground black pepper*

**Serves 4**

1 Add the pasta to a large pan of lightly salted boiling water and return to a boil. Then place the broccoli in a steamer basket over the top. Cover and cook for about 8–10 minutes until the penne are *al dente* and the broccoli are just tender. Drain them both through a colander once cooked.

2 Heat the stock in a large pan and add the crushed garlic and chile or chili sauce. Stir over low heat for 2–3 minutes.

3 Stir in the broccoli, pasta and yogurt. Adjust the seasoning, sprinkle with nuts and serve hot in warmed bowls.

# Spaghetti with Mixed Mushrooms

THIS COMBINATION of mixed mushrooms and freshly chopped sweet basil tossed with spaghetti would be well complemented by a simple tomato salad drizzled with extra virgin olive oil and whole fresh basil leaves.

**INGREDIENTS**

*¼ cup butter*
*1 onion, chopped*
*12 ounces spaghetti*
*12 ounces mixed mushrooms, such as brown, portobello and white, sliced*
*1 garlic clove, chopped*
*1¼ cups sour cream*
*2 tablespoons chopped fresh basil*
*½ cup freshly grated Parmesan cheese*
*salt and ground black pepper*
*torn Italian parsley, to garnish*
*freshly grated Parmesan cheese, to serve*

**Serves 4**

1 Melt the butter in a large frying pan and fry the chopped onion for 10 minutes until softened.

2 Cook the pasta in plenty of boiling salted water according to the instructions on the package.

3 Stir the mushrooms and garlic into the onion mixture and fry for 10 minutes until softened.

4 Add the sour cream, basil, grated Parmesan cheese and salt and pepper to taste. Cover and heat through over low heat.

5 Drain the pasta thoroughly and toss with the sauce. Serve immediately, garnished with torn Italian parsley, and with plenty of grated Parmesan cheese.

**VARIATION**

*For a lowfat alternative, substitute the sour cream for plain yogurt.*

# Tagliatelle with Herbs

THIS IS A LOVELY dish for summer when fresh herbs are plentiful. It is quick and ideal for vegetarians.

**INGREDIENTS**

*3 rosemary sprigs*
*1 small handful fresh Italian parsley*
*5–6 fresh mint leaves*
*5–6 fresh sage leaves*
*8–10 large fresh basil leaves*
*2 tablespoons extra virgin olive oil*
*¼ cup butter*
*1 shallot, finely chopped*
*2 garlic cloves, finely chopped*
*pinch of chili powder, to taste*
*14 ounces fresh egg tagliatelle*
*1 bay leaf*
*½ cup dry white wine*
*6–8 tablespoons vegetable stock*
*salt and ground black pepper*

**Serves 4**

1 Strip the rosemary and parsley leaves from their stems and chop them together with the fresh mint, sage and basil.

2 Heat the olive oil and half the butter in a large skillet or saucepan. Add the shallot and garlic and the chili powder, and cook over very low heat, stirring frequently, for 2–3 minutes.

3 Cook the pasta in salted boiling water according to the package instructions.

4 Add the chopped herbs and the bay leaf to the shallot mixture and stir for 2–3 minutes, then add the wine and increase the heat. Boil rapidly for 1–2 minutes until the wine reduces. Lower the heat, add the stock and simmer gently for 1–2 minutes.

5 Drain the pasta and add it to the herb mixture. Toss well to mix and remove and discard the bay leaf.

6 Put the remaining butter in a warmed large bowl, turn the dressed pasta into it and toss well to mix. Serve immediately.

# Garganelli with Spring Vegetables

YOUNG FRESH VEGETABLES both look and taste good with pasta. Butter is used to marry the two together, but you can use extra virgin olive oil if you prefer.

**INGREDIENTS**

*1 bunch asparagus, about 12 ounces*
*4 young carrots*
*1 bunch scallions*
*4½ ounces shelled fresh peas*
*3 cups dried garganelli*
*4 tablespoons dry white wine*
*6 tablespoons unsalted butter, diced*
*a few sprigs each fresh Italian parsley, mint and basil, leaves stripped and chopped*
*salt and ground black pepper*
*freshly grated Parmesan cheese, to serve*

**Serves 4**

1 Trim off and discard the woody part of each asparagus stem, then cut off the tips on the diagonal. Cut the stems on the diagonal into 1½-inch pieces. Cut the carrots and scallions on the diagonal into similar pieces.

2 Plunge the asparagus stems, carrots and peas into a saucepan of salted boiling water. Bring back to a boil and simmer for 5–8 minutes, adding the asparagus tips for the last 3 minutes.

3 Meanwhile, cook the pasta in salted boiling water according to the instructions on the package.

4 Drain the vegetables and return them to the pan. Add the wine, butter and salt and pepper to taste, then toss over medium to high heat until the wine has reduced and the vegetables glisten with melted butter.

5 Drain the pasta and turn it into a warmed large bowl. Add the vegetables, scallions and herbs and toss well. Serve immediately, with freshly grated Parmesan.

**COOK'S TIP**

*Garganelli are rolled short pasta shapes made with egg. If you can't get garganelli, use another short shape made with egg.*

# Linguine with Arugula

THIS IS A FIRST COURSE THAT you will find in many a fashionable restaurant in Italy. It is very quick and easy to make at home and is worth trying for yourself.

**INGREDIENTS**

*12 ounces fresh or dried linguine*
*½ cup extra virgin olive oil*
*1 large bunch arugula, about 5 ounces, stalks removed, leaves shredded*
*1 cup freshly grated Parmesan cheese*
*salt and ground black pepper*
**Serves 4**

1 Cook the pasta in a large saucepan of salted boiling water according to the instructions on the package, then drain thoroughly.

2 Heat about 4 tablespoons of the olive oil in the pasta pan, then add the drained pasta, followed by the arugula. Toss over medium to high heat for 1–2 minutes or until the arugula is just wilted, then remove the pan from the heat.

3 Turn the pasta and arugula into a warmed large bowl. Add half the freshly grated Parmesan and the remaining olive oil. Add a little salt and black pepper to taste.

4 Toss the mixture quickly to mix. Serve immediately, sprinkled with the remaining Parmesan.

**COOK'S TIP**

*Buy arugula by the bunch. The type sold in small cellophane packages in supermarkets is very expensive for this kind of dish. Always check when buying arugula that all the leaves are bright green. In hot weather, arugula leaves quickly turn yellow.*

# Strozzapreti with Zucchini Flowers

THIS PRETTY, SUMMERY DISH is strewn with zucchini flowers, but you can make it even if you don't have the flowers. In Italy, bunches of zucchini flowers are a common sight on vegetable stalls in summer, and are frequently used for stuffing and cooking.

**INGREDIENTS**

*¼ cup butter*
*2 tablespoons extra virgin olive oil*
*1 small onion, thinly sliced*
*7 ounces small zucchini, cut into thin julienne*
*1 garlic clove, crushed*
*2 teaspoons finely chopped fresh marjoram*
*cups dried strozzapreti*
*1 large handful zucchini flowers, thoroughly washed and dried*
*salt and ground black pepper*
*thin shavings of Parmesan cheese, to serve*

**Serves 4**

1 Heat the butter and half the olive oil in a medium skillet or saucepan, add the sliced onion and cook gently, stirring frequently, for about 5 minutes until softened. Add the zucchini to the pan and sprinkle with the crushed garlic, chopped marjoram and salt and pepper to taste. Cook for 5–8 minutes until the zucchini have softened but are not colored, turning them over occasionally.

2 Meanwhile, cook the pasta in a saucepan of salted boiling water according to the package instructions.

3 Set aside a few whole zucchini flowers for the garnish, then coarsely shred the rest and add them to the zucchini mixture. Stir to mix and taste for seasoning.

4 Drain the pasta, turn it into a warmed large bowl and add the remaining oil. Toss, add the zucchini mixture and toss again. Top with Parmesan and the reserved flowers.

**COOK'S TIP**

*Strozzapreti or "priest stranglers" are a special kind of short pasta shape from Modena. You can buy packages of them in Italian markets, or use gemelli, a similar kind of twisted pasta.*

# Paglia e Fieno

THE TITLE OF THIS DISH translates as "straw and hay" which refers to the yellow and green colors of the pasta when mixed together. Fresh peas make all the difference to this dish.

**INGREDIENTS**

*4 tablespoons butter*
*3 cups frozen baby peas or 2 pounds fresh peas, shelled*
*⅔ cup heavy cream, plus 4 tablespoons extra*
*1 pound dried tagliatelle (plain and green mixed)*
*½ cup freshly grated Parmesan cheese, plus extra to serve*
*freshly grated nutmeg*
*salt and ground black pepper*

**Serves 4**

1 Melt the butter in a heavy saucepan and add the peas. Sauté for 2–3 minutes, then add the cream, bring to a boil and simmer for 1 minute until the mixture is slightly thickened.

2 Cook the plain and green mixed tagliatelle in plenty of salted boiling water according to the instructions on the package, but for 2 minutes less time, until *al dente*.

3 Drain well and then turn the tagliatelle into the saucepan containing the cream and pea sauce.

4 Place the pan on the heat and turn the pasta in the sauce to coat. Pour in the extra cream, the cheese, salt and pepper to taste and a little grated nutmeg. Toss until well coated and heated through. Serve immediately with extra freshly grated Parmesan cheese.

**COOK'S TIP**

*Sautéed mushrooms and narrow strips of cooked ham also make good additions to this dish.*

# Spaghetti with Olives and Mushrooms

A RICH, PUNGENT SAUCE topped with sweet cherry tomatoes.

**INGREDIENTS**

*1 tablespoon olive oil*
*1 garlic clove, chopped*
*8 ounces mushrooms, chopped*
*scant 1 cup black olives, pitted*
*2 tablespoons chopped fresh parsley*
*1 red chile, seeded and chopped*
*1 pound fresh or dried spaghetti*
*8 ounces cherry tomatoes*
*Parmesan cheese shavings, to serve (optional)*

**Serves 4**

1 Heat the oil in a large pan. Add the garlic and cook for 1 minute, stirring. Add the chopped mushrooms, cover, and cook over medium heat for 5 minutes.

2 Place the mushrooms in a blender or food processor with the olives, parsley and red chile. Process the mixture until smooth.

3 Cook the pasta in plenty of salted boiling water, according to the instructions on the package, until *al dente*. Drain well and return to the pan. Add the olive mixture and toss together until the pasta is well coated. Cover and keep warm.

4 Heat an ungreased frying pan and shake the cherry tomatoes around until they start to split, about 2–3 minutes. Serve the pasta topped with the tomatoes and garnished with Parmesan cheese shavings, if desired.

# Penne with Arugula and Mozzarella

Like a warm salad, this pasta dish is very quick and easy to make—perfect for an *al fresco* summer lunch. Its success depends on the very best Italian ingredients, so make sure they are as fresh as possible and in tip-top condition.

**INGREDIENTS**

*3½ cups fresh or dried penne*
*6 ripe Italian plum tomatoes, peeled, seeded and diced*
*2 packets (5-ounce) mozzarella cheese, drained and diced*
*2 large handfuls of arugula, total weight about 5 ounces*
*5 tablespoons extra virgin olive oil*
*salt and ground black pepper*
**Serves 4**

1 Cook the pasta in a large saucepan of salted boiling water according to the package instructions.

2 Meanwhile, put the tomatoes, mozzarella, arugula and olive oil into a large bowl with a little salt and pepper to taste and toss well to mix.

3 Drain the cooked pasta and turn it into the bowl. Toss well to mix and serve immediately.

**VARIATION**

*For a less peppery taste, use basil leaves instead of arugula, or a mixture of the two.*

# Eliche with Chargrilled Bell Peppers

Chargrilled bell peppers are good with pasta because they have a soft juicy texture and a wonderful smoky flavor. This is a dish for high summer when bell peppers and tomatoes are plentiful and ripe. It is equally good cold as a salad.

**INGREDIENTS**

*3 large bell peppers (red, yellow and orange)*
*3 cups fresh or dried eliche or fusilli*
*1–2 garlic cloves, to taste, finely chopped*
*4 tablespoons extra virgin olive oil*
*4 ripe Italian plum tomatoes, peeled, seeded and diced*
*½ cup pitted black olives, halved or quartered lengthways*
*1 handful of fresh basil leaves, shredded*
*salt and ground black pepper*
**Serves 4**

1 Put the whole bell peppers under a hot broiler and cook them for about 10 minutes, turning them frequently until they are charred on all sides. Put the bell hot peppers in a plastic bag, seal the bag and set aside until the bell peppers are cold.

2 Remove the bell peppers from the bag and hold them one at a time under cold running water. Peel off the charred skins with your fingers, split the bell peppers open and pull out the cores. Rub off all the seeds under the running water, then pat the bell peppers dry on paper towels.

3 Cook the pasta in a large saucepan of salted boiling water according to the instructions on the package until *al dente*.

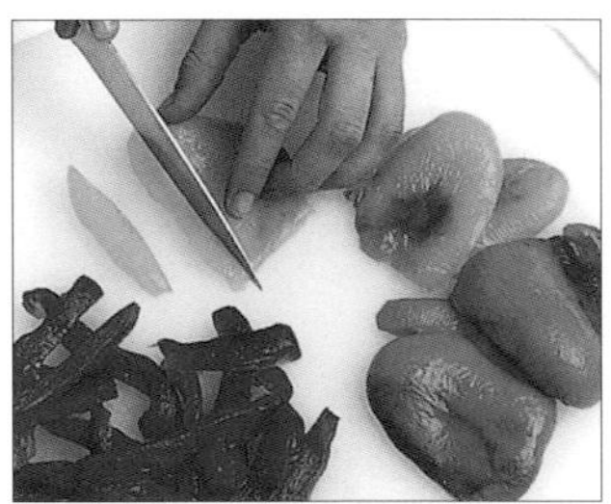

4 Meanwhile, thinly slice the bell peppers and place them in a large bowl with the remaining ingredients and salt and pepper to taste.

5 Drain the cooked pasta and turn it into the bowl. Toss well to mix and serve immediately.

**VARIATION**

*Add a few slivers of bottled or canned anchovy fillets in Step 4.*

# Penne with Spring Vegetables

DON'T BE TEMPTED to use dried herbs in this flavorsome dish.

**INGREDIENTS**

*4 ounces broccoli flowerets*
*4 ounces baby leeks*
*8 ounces asparagus*
*1 small fennel bulb*
*1 cup fresh or frozen peas*
*3 tablespoons butter*
*1 shallot, chopped*
*3 tablespoons chopped mixed fresh herbs, such as parsley, thyme and sage*
*1 1/4 cups heavy cream*
*3 cups dried penne*
*salt and ground black pepper*
*freshly grated Parmesan cheese, to serve*

**Serves 4**

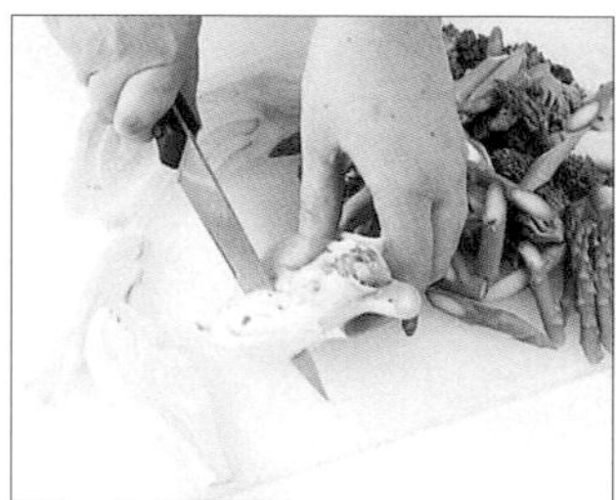

1 Divide the broccoli flowerets into tiny sprigs. Cut the leeks and asparagus diagonally into 2-inch lengths. Trim the fennel bulb and remove any tough outer leaves. Cut into wedges, leaving the layers attached at the root ends so the pieces stay intact.

2 Cook each vegetable, including the peas, separately in boiling salted water until just tender—use the same water for each vegetable. Drain well and keep warm.

3 Melt the butter in a separate pan, add the chopped shallot and cook, stirring occasionally, until softened but not browned. Stir in the herbs and cream and cook for a few minutes, until slightly thickened.

4 Meanwhile, cook the pasta in plenty of salted boiling water for 10 minutes until *al dente*. Drain well and add to the sauce with the vegetables. Toss gently and season with plenty of ground black pepper.

5 Serve the pasta immediately with a sprinkling of freshly grated Parmesan cheese on top.

# Spaghetti with Feta Cheese

WE THINK OF PASTA as being essentially Italian but, in fact, the Greeks have a great appetite for it too. It complements tangy, full-flavored feta cheese beautifully in this simple but effective dish.

**INGREDIENTS**

*4 ounces fresh or dried spaghetti*
*1 garlic clove*
*2 tablespoons extra virgin olive oil*
*8 cherry tomatoes, halved*
*a little freshly grated nutmeg*
*3 ounces feta cheese, crumbled*
*1 tablespoon chopped fresh basil*
*salt and ground black pepper*
*a few black olives, to serve (optional)*

**Serves 2–3**

1 Cook the spaghetti in plenty of salted boiling water according to the instructions on the package, then drain well.

2 In the same pan gently heat the garlic clove in the olive oil for 1–2 minutes, then add the halved cherry tomatoes.

3 Increase the heat to fry the tomatoes lightly for 1 minute, then remove the garlic and discard.

4 Toss in the spaghetti, season with the nutmeg and salt and pepper to taste, then stir in the crumbled feta cheese and basil.

5 Check the seasoning, remembering that feta can be quite salty, and serve the spaghetti hot topped with black olives, if using.

# Three-color Tagliatelle

ZUCCHINI AND CARROTS are cut into delicate ribbons so that when they are cooked and tossed with tagliatelle they look like colored pasta. Serve as a side dish, or sprinkle with freshly grated Parmesan cheese for an appetizer or vegetarian main course.

**INGREDIENTS**

*2 large zucchini*
*2 large carrots*
*9 ounces fresh egg tagliatelle*
*4 tablespoons extra virgin olive oil*
*flesh of 2 roasted garlic cloves, plus extra roasted garlic cloves, to serve (optional)*
*salt and ground black pepper*

**Serves 4**

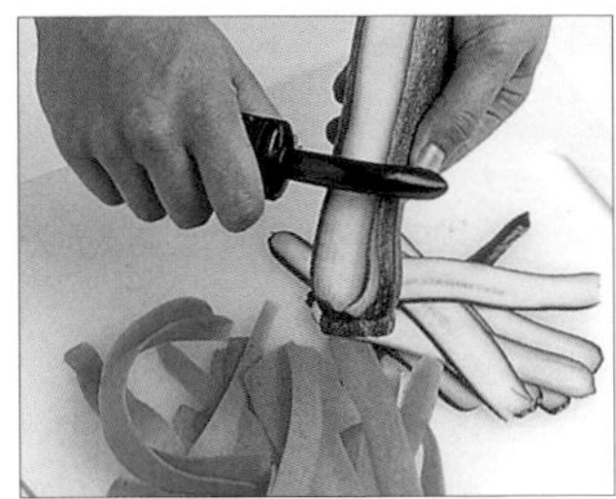

1 With a vegetable peeler, cut the zucchini and carrots into long thin ribbons. Bring a large pan of salted water to a boil, then add the zucchini and carrot ribbons. Bring the water back to a boil and boil for 30 seconds, then drain and set aside.

2 Cook the pasta according to the instructions on the package.

3 Drain the pasta and return it to the pan. Add the vegetable ribbons, oil, garlic and salt and pepper and toss over medium to high heat until the pasta and vegetables are glistening with oil. Serve immediately, with extra roasted garlic, if you like.

**COOK'S TIP**

*To roast garlic, put a whole head of garlic on a lightly oiled baking sheet. Place in a 350°F oven and roast for about 30 minutes. Remove the garlic from the oven and set aside. When cool enough to handle, dig out the flesh from the cloves with the point of a knife. If you don't want to go to the trouble of roasting garlic, you can use crushed raw garlic but the flavor will be stronger.*

# Macaroni with Broccoli and Cauliflower

THIS IS A SOUTHERN ITALIAN DISH, full of flavor. Without the anchovies, it can be served to vegetarians.

**INGREDIENTS**

*6 ounces cauliflower flowerets, cut into small sprigs*
*6 ounces broccoli flowerets, cut into small sprigs*
*3 cups short-cut macaroni*
*3 tablespoons extra virgin olive oil*
*1 onion, finely chopped*
*3 tablespoons pine nuts*
*1 envelope of saffron powder, dissolved in 1 tablespoon warm water*
*1–2 tablespoons raisins, to taste*
*2 tablespoons sun-dried tomato paste*
*4 bottled or canned anchovies in olive oil, drained and chopped, plus extra anchovies to serve (optional)*
*salt and ground black pepper*
*freshly grated Pecorino cheese, to serve*

**Serves 4**

1 Cook the cauliflower sprigs in a large saucepan of salted boiling water for 3 minutes. Add the broccoli and boil for another 2 minutes. Remove the vegetables from the pan with a large slotted spoon and set aside.

2 Add the pasta to the vegetable cooking water and bring the water back to a boil. Cook the pasta according to the instructions on the package until it is *al dente*.

3 Meanwhile, heat the olive oil in a large skillet or saucepan, add the finely chopped onion and cook over low to medium heat, stirring frequently, for 2–3 minutes or until golden. Add the pine nuts, the cooked broccoli and cauliflower, and the saffron water. Add the raisins, sun-dried tomato paste and a couple of ladlefuls of the pasta cooking water until the vegetable mixture has the consistency of a sauce. Finally, add plenty of pepper.

4 Stir well, cook for 1–2 minutes, then add the chopped anchovies. Drain the pasta and turn it into the vegetable mixture. Toss well, then taste for seasoning and add salt if necessary. Serve the pasta immediately in four warmed bowls, sprinkled with freshly grated Pecorino. If you like the flavor of anchovies, add 1–2 whole anchovies to each serving.

# Pasta Salads

Although not traditionally Italian, pasta salads have earned their place in the Italian cook's repertoire. They are extremely versatile in that they can be served as part of an antipasto, as a first course or a main course. Salads can be prepared well in advance, so make marvellous party food, and are popular for picnics, because they are so easy to transport.

Freshly cooked pasta soaks up oil, lemon juice, vinegar and seasonings so that when the pasta cools down, the shapes are separate, moist and full of flavor. Never soak pasta in cold water after cooking; this makes the pasta waterlogged and soggy, especially with shapes like shells and tubes that trap liquid. Simply cook the pasta until it is *al dente*, then drain it thoroughly and toss it in extra virgin olive oil or dressing until it glistens. This method works well for any vinaigrette-type dressing, but if you are using mayonnaise it is best to wait until the pasta has cooled down before tossing, or the mayonnaise may spoil.

Any pasta shape can be used in a salad, although shells and tubes are particularly good, because they trap the dressing so well. Many Italians prefer egg pasta to plain durum wheat pasta, because it has a good color, holds its shape well and does not stick.

# Pasta Salade Niçoise

Along the Mediterranean coast, where Italy meets France, the cuisines of both countries have many similarities. In this salad the ingredients of a classic French *salade niçoise* are given a modern Italian twist.

**INGREDIENTS**

*4 ounces green beans, topped and tailed and cut into 2-inch lengths*
*2¼ cups dried penne rigate*
*7 tablespoons extra virgin olive oil*
*2 fresh tuna steaks, total weight 12 ounces–1 pound*
*6 baby Italian plum tomatoes, quartered lengthwise*
*½ cup pitted black olives, halved lengthwise*
*6 bottled or canned anchovies in olive oil, drained and chopped*
*2–3 tablespoons chopped fresh Italian parsley, to taste*
*juice of ½–1 lemon, to taste*
*2 heads of Belgian endive, leaves separated*
*salt and ground black pepper*
*lemon wedges, to serve*

**Serves 4**

1 Cook the beans in a large pan of salted boiling water for 5–6 minutes. Remove the beans with a large slotted spoon and refresh under the cold tap.

2 Add the pasta to the pan of bean cooking water, bring back to a boil and cook according to the instructions on the package.

3 Meanwhile, heat a ridged cast-iron pan over low heat. Dip a wad of paper towel in the oil, wipe it over the surface of the pan and heat gently. Brush the tuna steaks on both sides with oil and sprinkle liberally with pepper; add to the pan and cook over medium to high heat for 1–2 minutes on each side. Remove and set aside.

4 Drain the cooked pasta well and turn into a large bowl. Add the remaining oil, the beans, tomato quarters, black olives, anchovies, parsley, lemon juice and salt and pepper to taste. Toss well to mix, then let cool.

5 Flake or slice the tuna into large pieces, discarding the skin, then fold it into the salad. Taste the salad for seasoning. Arrange the Belgian endive leaves around the insides of a large shallow bowl. Spoon the pasta salad into the center and serve with lemon wedges.

# Chargrilled Pepper Salad

THIS IS A GOOD SIDE SALAD to serve with plain broiled or barbecued chicken or fish. The ingredients are simple and few, but the overall flavor is quite intense.

**INGREDIENTS**

*2 large bell peppers (red and green)*
*2¼ cups dried fusilli tricolore*
*1 handful fresh basil leaves*
*1 handful fresh cilantro leaves*
*1 garlic clove*
*salt and ground black pepper*

***For the dressing***
*2 tablespoons bottled pesto*
*juice of ½ lemon*
*4 tablespoons extra virgin olive oil*

**Serves 4**

1 Put the bell peppers under a hot broiler and cook them for about 10 minutes, turning them frequently until they are charred on all sides. Put the hot bell peppers in a plastic bag, seal the bag and set aside until they are cool. Meanwhile, cook the pasta according to the instructions on the package.

2 Whisk all the dressing ingredients together in a large bowl. Drain the cooked pasta well and turn it into the bowl of dressing. Toss well to mix and set aside to cool.

3 Remove the bell peppers from the bag and hold them one at a time under cold running water. Peel off the charred skins with your fingers, split the bell peppers open and pull out the cores. Rub off all the seeds under the running water, then pat the bell peppers dry on paper towels.

4 Chop the bell peppers and add them to the pasta. Put the basil, cilantro and garlic on a board and chop them all together. Add to the pasta and toss to mix, then taste for seasoning and serve.

**COOK'S TIP**

*Serve the salad at room temperature or chilled, whichever you prefer.*

# Roquefort and Walnut Pasta Salad

THIS IS A SIMPLE unrefined salad, relying totally on the quality of the ingredients. There is no real substitute for Roquefort—a blue-veined ewe-milk cheese which comes from south-western France.

**INGREDIENTS**

*8 ounces pasta shapes*
*mixed salad greens, such as arugula, frisée, corn salad, baby spinach, radicchio, etc*
*2 tablespoons walnut oil*
*4 tablespoons sunflower oil*
*2 tablespoons red wine vinegar or sherry vinegar*
*8 ounces Roquefort cheese, coarsely crumbled*
*1 cup walnut halves*
*salt and ground black pepper*
**Serves 4**

1 Cook the pasta in plenty of salted boiling water according to the instructions on the package until *al dente*. Drain well and cool. Wash and dry the salad greens and place them in a large bowl.

2 Whisk together the walnut oil, sunflower oil, vinegar and salt and pepper to taste.

3 Pile the pasta in the center of the leaves, scatter the crumbled Roquefort over and pour the dressing on top.

4 Sprinkle the walnuts over the salad. Toss just before serving.

**COOK'S TIP**

*Try toasting the walnuts under the broiler for a couple of minutes to release the flavor before adding to the salad.*

# Conchiglie and Beet Salad

Color IS VITAL at a party table, and this salad is certainly eye-catching. Prepare the egg and avocado at the last moment to avoid discoloration.

**INGREDIENTS**

*2 uncooked beets, scrubbed*
*2 cups fresh or dried conchiglie*
*3 tablespoons vinaigrette dressing*
*2 celery stalks, thinly sliced*
*3 scallions, sliced*
*¾ cup walnuts or hazelnuts, coarsely chopped*
*1 eating apple, cored, halved and sliced*
*salt and ground black pepper*

***For the dressing***
*4 tablespoons mayonnaise*
*3 tablespoons natural yogurt*
*2 tablespoons milk*
*2 teaspoons creamed horseradish*

***To serve***
*curly lettuce leaves*
*3 eggs, hard-cooked and chopped*
*2 ripe avocados*
*1 box salad cress*

**Serves 8**

1 Boil the beets, without peeling, in lightly salted water until they are just tender, about 1 hour. Drain, cool, then peel and chop. Set aside.

2 Cook the pasta in plenty of salted boiling water according to the instructions on the package. Drain, toss in the vinaigrette and season well. Let cool then mix with the beet, celery, onions, nuts and apple in a bowl.

3 Stir all the dressing ingredients together and then mix into the pasta. Chill well.

4 To serve, line a salad bowl with the lettuce and spoon in the salad. Scatter the chopped egg over. Peel and slice the avocados and arrange them on top then sprinkle the cress over.

# Tuna Pasta Salad

THIS EASY PASTA SALAD uses canned beans and tuna for a quick main course dish.

**INGREDIENTS**

*1 pound short pasta, such as rotelle or farfalle*
*4 tablespoons olive oil*
*2 cans (7 ounces) tuna, drained and flaked*
*2 cans (14 ounces) cannellini or borlotti beans, rinsed and drained*
*1 small red onion, very thinly sliced*
*2 celery stalks, very thinly sliced*
*juice of 1 lemon*
*2 tablespoons chopped fresh parsley*
*salt and ground black pepper*
**Serves 6–8**

1 Cook the pasta in plenty of salted boiling water according to the package instructions until *al dente*. Drain, and rinse under cold water to stop the cooking. Drain well and turn into a large bowl. Toss with the olive oil and set aside. Let cool completely.

2 Mix the flaked tuna and the beans into the cooked pasta. Add the onion and celery slices to the pasta and toss gently to mix.

3 Combine the lemon juice with the parsley. Mix into the other ingredients. Season with salt and pepper. Let the salad stand for at least 1 hour before serving.

# Chicken Pasta Salad

THIS SALAD USES leftover chicken from a roast or a cold poached chicken breast if you prefer.

**INGREDIENTS**

*12 ounces short pasta, such as rigatoni, fusilli or penne*
*3 tablespoons olive oil*
*8 ounces cold cooked chicken*
*2 small red and yellow bell peppers, seeded and chopped*
*½ cup pitted green olives*
*4 scallions, chopped*
*3 tablespoons mayonnaise*
*1 teaspoon Worcestershire sauce*
*1 tablespoon white wine vinegar*
*salt and ground black pepper*
*a few fresh basil leaves, to garnish*
**Serves 4**

1 Cook the pasta in plenty of salted boiling water according to the package instructions until *al dente*. Drain, and rinse under cold water to stop the cooking. Drain well and turn into a large bowl. Toss with the olive oil and set aside. Let cool completely.

2 Cut the chicken into bite-size pieces, removing any bones.

3 Combine all the ingredients except the pasta in a medium bowl. Taste for seasoning, then mix into the pasta. Serve well chilled, garnished with basil leaves.

# Warm Pasta Salad with Ham and Egg

IN THE SUMMER months when the weather is hot, warm pasta salad makes a perfect supper dish. Here it is served with ham, eggs and asparagus. A mustard dressing made from the thick part of asparagus provides a rich accompaniment.

**INGREDIENTS**

*1 pound asparagus*
*1 pound dried tagliatelle*
*8 ounces sliced cooked ham, 1/4-inch thick, cut into fingers*
*2 eggs, hard-cooked and sliced*
*2 ounces Parmesan cheese, shaved*
*salt and ground black pepper*

***For the dressing***
*2 ounces cooked potato*
*5 tablespoons olive oil, preferably Sicilian*
*1 tablespoon lemon juice*
*2 teaspoons Dijon mustard*
*1/2 cup vegetable stock*
**Serves 4**

1 Bring a saucepan of salted water to a boil. Trim and discard the tough woody parts of the asparagus. Cut the asparagus in half and boil the thicker halves for 12 minutes. After 6 minutes throw in the tips. Refresh under cold water until warm, then drain.

2 Finely chop 5 ounces of the thicker section of the asparagus. Place in a blender or food processor with the dressing ingredients and process until smooth and creamy. Season to taste with salt and pepper.

3 Cook the pasta in plenty of salted boiling water according to the instructions on the package. Refresh under cold water until warm, then drain. Dress with the asparagus sauce and turn out onto four pasta plates. Top the pasta with the ham, hard-cooked eggs and asparagus tips. Finish with Parmesan cheese shavings.

# Chicken and Eliche Salad

THIS IS A DELICIOUS WAY to use up leftover cooked chicken, and makes a really filling meal.

**INGREDIENTS**

*2 cups tri-colored dried eliche*
*2 tablespoons ready-made pesto sauce*
*1 tablespoon olive oil*
*1 beefsteak tomato*
*12 stoned black olives*
*8 ounces cooked green beans, cut into 1 ½-inch lengths*
*12 ounces cooked chicken, cubed*
*salt and ground black pepper*
*fresh basil, to garnish*

**Serves 4**

1 Cook the pasta in plenty of salted boiling water according to the instructions on the package.

2 Drain the pasta and rinse in plenty of cold running water.

3 Place the cooked pasta in a large bowl and pour in the pesto sauce and olive oil. Mix well to combine.

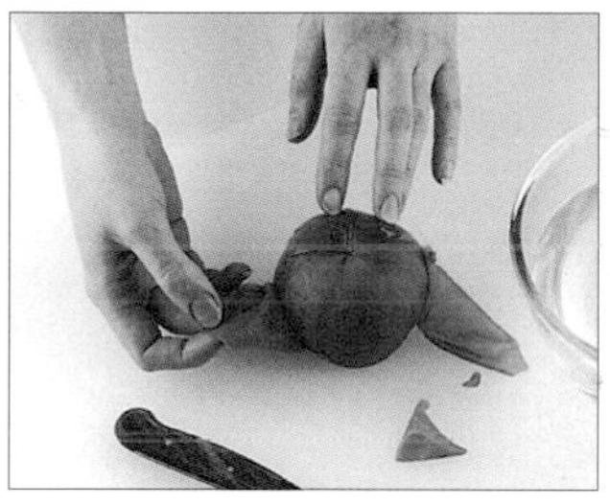

4 Skin the tomato by placing it in a pan of boiling water for about 45 seconds. Remove it with a slotted spoon and plunge it immediately into a bowl of cold water, to loosen the skin.

5 Cut the tomato into small cubes and add to the pasta mixture in the bowl with the olives, seasoning and green beans. Add the cubed chicken. Toss gently together and transfer to a serving platter or individual bowls. Garnish with fresh basil.

# Chicken and Broccoli Salad

**GORGONZOLA MAKES A tangy dressing that goes well with both chicken and broccoli. Serve for a lunch or supper dish, with crusty Italian bread.**

**INGREDIENTS**

*6 ounces broccoli flowerets, divided into small sprigs*
*2 cups dried farfalle*
*2 large cooked chicken breasts*

***For the dressing***

*3½oz Gorgonzola cheese*
*1 tablespoon white wine vinegar*
*4 tablespoons extra virgin olive oil*
*½–1 teaspoon finely chopped fresh sage, plus extra sage sprigs to garnish*
*salt and ground black pepper*

**Serves 4**

1 Cook the broccoli flowerets in a large saucepan of salted boiling water for 3 minutes. Remove with a slotted spoon and rinse under cold running water, then spread out on paper towels to drain and dry.

2 Add the pasta to the broccoli cooking water, then bring back to a boil and cook according to the package instructions. When cooked, drain the pasta into a colander, rinse under cold running water until cold, then let drain and dry, shaking the colander occasionally.

3 Remove the skin from the cooked chicken breasts and cut the meat into bite-size pieces.

4 Make the dressing. Put the cheese in a large bowl and mash with a fork, then whisk in the wine vinegar followed by the oil and sage and salt and pepper to taste.

5 Add the pasta, chicken and broccoli. Toss well, then season to taste and serve, garnished with sage.

# Pasta Salad with Salami and Olives

GARLIC AND HERB DRESSING gives a Mediterranean flavor to a handful of ingredients from the store-cupboard and refrigerator, making this an excellent salad for winter. There are many different types of Italian salami that can be used. *Salame napoletano* is coarse cut and peppery, while *salame milanese* is fine cut and mild in flavor.

**INGREDIENTS**

*2 cups dried gnocchi or conchiglie*
*½ cup pitted black olives, quartered lengthwise*
*3 ounces thinly sliced salami, any skin removed, diced*
*½ small red onion, finely chopped*
*1 large handful fresh basil leaves, shredded*

***For the dressing***

*4 tablespoons extra virgin olive oil*
*good pinch of sugar, to taste*
*juice of ½ lemon*
*1 teaspoon Dijon mustard*
*2 teaspoons dried oregano*
*1 garlic clove, crushed*
*salt and ground black pepper*

**Serves 4**

1 Cook the pasta in a pan of salted boiling water according to the package instructions.

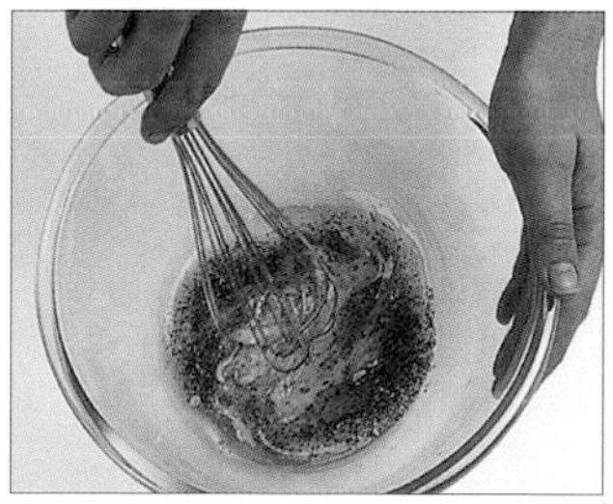

2 Meanwhile, make the dressing for the pasta. Put all the ingredients for the dressing in a large bowl with a little salt and pepper to taste, and whisk well to mix.

3 Drain the pasta thoroughly, add it to the bowl of dressing and toss well to mix. Let the dressed pasta cool, stirring occasionally.

4 When the pasta is cold, add the remaining ingredients and toss well to mix again. Taste for seasoning, then serve immediately.

# Tuna and Corn Salad

THIS IS AN EXCELLENT main course salad for a summer lunch outside. It travels very well, so it is good for picnics, too.

**INGREDIENTS**

*1 ½ cups dried conchiglie*
*1 can (6 ounces) tuna in olive oil, drained and flaked*
*1 can (6 ounces) corn, drained*
*3 ounces bottled roasted red bell pepper, rinsed, dried and finely chopped*
*1 handful of fresh basil leaves, chopped*
*salt and ground black pepper*

**For the dressing**

*4 tablespoons extra virgin olive oil*
*1 tablespoon balsamic vinegar*
*1 teaspoon red wine vinegar*
*1 teaspoon Dijon mustard*
*1–2 teaspoons honey, to taste*

**Serves 4**

1 Cook the pasta according to package instructions. Drain it into a colander, and rinse under cold running water. Let drain until cold and dry, shaking the colander occasionally.

2 Make the dressing. Put the oil in a large bowl, add the two kinds of vinegar and whisk well together until emulsified. Add the mustard, honey and salt and pepper to taste and whisk again until thick.

3 Add the pasta to the dressing and toss well to mix, then add the tuna, corn and roasted bell pepper and toss again. Mix in about half the basil and taste for seasoning. Serve at room temperature or chilled, with the remaining basil sprinkled on top.

**VARIATION**

*To save time, you could use canned corn with peppers.*

# Pink and Green Salad

SPIKED WITH A LITTLE fresh chile, this pretty salad makes a delicious light lunch served with hot ciabatta rolls and a bottle of sparkling dry Italian white wine. Shrimp and avocado are a winning combination, so it's also a good choice for a buffet party.

**INGREDIENTS**

*2 cups dried farfalle*
*juice of ½ lemon*
*1 small fresh red chile, seeded and very finely chopped*
*4 tablespoons chopped fresh basil*
*2 tablespoons chopped fresh cilantro*
*4 tablespoons extra virgin olive oil*
*1 tablespoon mayonnaise*
*1 ½ cups shelled cooked shrimp*
*1 avocado*
*salt and ground black pepper*

**Serves 4**

1 Cook the pasta in a large saucepan of salted boiling water according to the package instructions.

2 Meanwhile, put the lemon juice and chile in a bowl with half the basil and cilantro and salt and pepper to taste. Whisk well to mix, then whisk in the oil and mayonnaise until thick. Add the shrimp and gently stir to coat in the dressing.

3 Drain the pasta into a colander, and rinse under cold running water until cold. Let drain and dry, shaking the colander occasionally.

4 Halve, pit and peel the avocado, then cut the flesh into neat dice. Add to the shrimp and dressing with the pasta, toss well to mix and taste for seasoning. Serve immediately, sprinkled with the remaining basil and cilantro.

**COOK'S TIP**

*This pasta salad can be made several hours ahead of time, without the avocado. Cover the bowl with plastic wrap and chill in the refrigerator. Prepare the avocado and add it to the salad just before serving or it will discolor.*

# Smoked Trout Pasta Salad

BULB FENNEL gives this salad a lovely aniseed flavor.

**INGREDIENTS**

*1 tablespoon butter*
*4 ounces minced bulb fennel*
*6 scallions, 2 very finely chopped and 4 thinly sliced*
*8 ounces skinless smoked trout fillets, flaked*
*3 tablespoons chopped fresh dill weed*
*½ cup mayonnaise*
*2 teaspoons fresh lemon juice*
*2 tablespoons whipping cream*
*1 pound small pasta shapes, such as shells*
*salt and ground black pepper*
*fresh dill sprigs, to garnish*

**Serves 6**

1 Melt the butter in a small non-stick frying pan. Add the fennel and finely chopped scallions and season lightly with salt and black pepper. Cook over medium heat for 3–5 minutes, or until just softened. Transfer to a large bowl and let cool slightly.

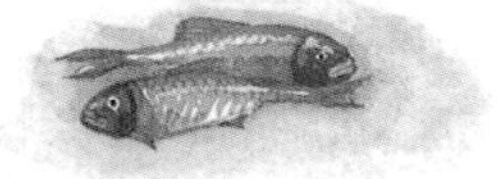

2 Add the sliced scallions, trout, dill weed, mayonnaise, lemon juice and cream to the bowl with the fennel. Mix gently until well blended.

3 Cook the pasta in plenty of boiling salted water according to the instructions on the package until *al dente*. Drain thoroughly in a colander and let cool.

4 Add the pasta to the vegetable and trout mixture and toss to coat evenly. Taste for seasoning and adjust if necessary.

5 Serve the salad lightly chilled or at room temperature, garnished with dill.

# Pasta, Asparagus and Potato Salad

A MEAL IN ITSELF, this is a real treat when made with fresh asparagus just in season.

**INGREDIENTS**

*8 ounces whole wheat pasta shapes*
*4 tablespoons extra virgin olive oil*
*12 ounces baby new potatoes*
*8 ounces fresh asparagus*
*4 ounces Parmesan cheese*
*salt and ground black pepper*

**Serves 4**

1 Cook the pasta in salted boiling water according to the instructions on the package. Drain well and toss with the olive oil and salt and pepper while still warm.

2 Wash the potatoes and cook in salted boiling water for about 12–15 minutes or until just tender. Drain the potatoes and gently toss with the pasta.

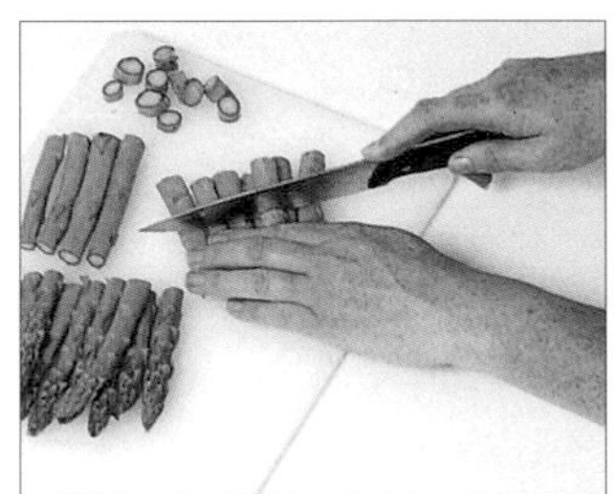

3 Trim any woody ends off the asparagus and halve the stalks if very long. Blanch in salted boiling water for 6 minutes until bright green and still crunchy. Drain, refresh in cold water and let cool. Drain well and pat dry with paper towel.

4 Toss the asparagus with the potatoes and pasta, season and transfer to a shallow bowl. Using a rotary vegetable peeler, shave the Parmesan over. Serve immediately.

# Seafood Salad

THIS IS A VERY SPECIAL SALAD which can be served as a first course or main meal. The choice of pasta shape is up to you, but one of the unusual "designer" shapes would suit it well.

**INGREDIENTS**

*1 pound mussels*
*1 cup dry white wine*
*2 garlic cloves, coarsely chopped*
*1 handful of fresh Italian parsley*
*1 cup prepared squid rings*
*1½ cups small dried pasta shapes*
*1 cup shelled cooked shrimp*

***For the dressing***

*6 tablespoons extra virgin olive oil*
*juice of 1 lemon*
*1–2 teaspoons capers, to taste, coarsely chopped*
*1 garlic clove, crushed*
*1 small handful fresh Italian parsley, finely chopped*
*salt and ground black pepper*

**Serves 4–6**

1 Scrub the mussels under cold running water to remove the beards. Discard any that are open or that do not close when sharply tapped against the countertop.

2 Pour half the wine into a large saucepan, add the garlic, parsley and mussels. Cover the pan tightly and bring to a boil over a high heat. Cook for about 5 minutes, shaking the pan frequently, until the mussels are open.

3 Turn the mussels into a large colander set over a bowl and let the cooking liquid drain through. Leave the mussels until cool enough to handle, then remove them from their shells, pouring the liquid from the mussels into the bowl of cooking liquid. Discard any closed mussels.

4 Return the mussel cooking liquid to the pan and add the remaining wine and the squid rings. Bring to a boil, cover and simmer gently, stirring occasionally, for 30 minutes or until the squid is tender. Let the squid cool in the cooking liquid.

5 Meanwhile, cook the pasta according to package instructions and whisk all the dressing ingredients in a large bowl, adding a little salt and pepper to taste.

6 Drain the cooked pasta well, add it to the bowl of dressing and toss well to mix. Let cool.

7 Turn the cooled squid into a strainer and drain well, then rinse it lightly under the cold tap. Add the squid, mussels and shrimp to the dressed pasta and toss well to mix. Cover the bowl tightly with plastic wrap and chill in the refrigerator for about 4 hours. Toss well and adjust the seasoning to taste before serving.

**COOK'S TIP**

*For a quick and easy short cut, buy ready-prepared seafood salad from an Italian delicatessen or specialty store and toss it with the pasta and dressing.*

# Roasted Cherry Tomato and Arugula Salad

THIS IS A GOOD SIDE SALAD to accompany barbecued chicken, steaks or chops. Roasted tomatoes are very juicy, with an intense, smoky-sweet flavor.

**INGREDIENTS**

*2 cups dried chifferini or pipe*
*1 pound ripe baby Italian plum tomatoes, halved lengthwise*
*5 tablespoons extra virgin olive oil*
*2 garlic cloves, cut into thin slivers*
*2 tablespoons balsamic vinegar*
*2 pieces sun-dried tomato in olive oil, drained and chopped*
*large pinch of sugar, to taste*
*1 handful arugula, about 2½ ounces*
*salt and ground black pepper*

**Serves 4**

1 Preheat the oven to 375°F. Meanwhile, cook the pasta in salted boiling water according to the instructions on the package.

2 Arrange the halved tomatoes cut side up in a roasting pan, drizzle 2 tablespoons of the oil over them and sprinkle with the slivers of garlic and salt and pepper to taste. Roast in the oven for 20 minutes, turning once.

3 Put the remaining oil in a large bowl with the vinegar, sun-dried tomatoes, sugar and a little salt and pepper to taste. Stir well to mix. Drain the pasta, add it to the bowl of dressing and toss to mix. Add the roasted tomatoes and mix gently.

4 Before serving, add the chopped arugula, toss lightly and taste for seasoning. Serve either at room temperature or chilled.

**VARIATIONS**

- *If you are in a hurry and don't have time to roast the tomatoes, you can make the salad with halved raw tomatoes instead.*
- *If you like, add 5 ounces mozzarella cheese, drained and diced, with the arugula in Step 4.*

# Summer Salad

RIPE RED TOMATOES, mozzarella and olives make a good base for a fresh and tangy salad that is perfect for a light summer lunch.

**INGREDIENTS**

*3 cups dried penne*
*3 ripe tomatoes, diced*
*1 package (5 ounce) mozzarella di bufala, drained and diced*
*10 pitted black olives, sliced*
*10 pitted green olives, sliced*
*1 scallion, thinly sliced on the diagonal*
*2 tablespoons chopped fresh Italian parsley*
*a few fresh basil leaves*

***For the dressing***
*6 tablespoons extra virgin olive oil*
*1 tablespoon balsamic vinegar or lemon juice*
*salt and ground black pepper*
**Serves 4**

1 Cook the pasta according to the instructions on the package. Turn it into a colander and rinse under cold running water, then shake the colander to remove as much water as possible. Let the pasta drain.

2 Make the dressing. Whisk the olive oil and balsamic vinegar or lemon juice in a large bowl with a little salt and pepper to taste.

3 Add the pasta, mozzarella, tomatoes, olives and scallion to the dressing and toss together well. Taste for seasoning before serving, sprinkled with basil leaves.

**VARIATION**

*Make the salad more substantial by adding other ingredients, such as sliced bell peppers, flaked tuna, bottled or canned anchovy fillets or diced ham.*

**COOK'S TIP**

*Mozzarella made from buffalo milk has more flavor than the type made with cow's milk. It is sold in most supermarkets.*

# Country Pasta Salad

COLORFUL, TASTY and nutritious, this is the ideal pasta salad for a summer picnic.

**INGREDIENTS**

*$2^3/_4$ cups dried fusilli*
*5 ounces green beans, topped and tailed and cut into 2-inch lengths*
*1 potato, about 5 ounces, diced*
*7 ounces baby tomatoes, halved*
*2 scallions, finely chopped*
*$3^1/_2$ ounces Parmesan cheese, diced or coarsely shaved*
*6–8 pitted black olives, cut into rings*
*1–2 tablespoons capers, to taste*

***For the dressing***
*6 tablespoons extra virgin olive oil*
*1 tablespoon balsamic vinegar*
*1 tablespoon chopped fresh Italian parsley*
*salt and ground black pepper*
**Serves 6**

1 Cook the pasta according to the instructions on the package. Drain it into a colander, rinse under cold running water until cold, then shake the colander to remove as much water as possible. Let drain and dry, shaking the colander occasionally.

2 Cook the beans and diced potato in a saucepan of salted boiling water for 5–6 minutes or until tender. Drain and let cool.

3 Make the dressing. Put all the ingredients in a large bowl with salt and pepper to taste and whisk well to mix.

4 Add the cherry tomatoes, scallions, Parmesan, olive rings and capers to the dressing, then the cold pasta, beans and potato. Toss together well to mix. Cover and let stand for about 30 minutes. Taste for seasoning before serving.

**COOK'S TIP**

*Buy a piece of fresh Parmesan from the delicatessen or supermarket. This is the less mature, softer type, which is sold as a table cheese, rather than the hard, mature Parmesan used for grating.*

# Pasta, Melon and Shrimp Salad

ORANGE CANTALOUPE or Charentais melon look spectacular in this salad. Or try a mixture of ogen, cantaloupe and water melon.

**INGREDIENTS**

*6 ounces pasta shapes*
*2 cups frozen shrimp, thawed and drained*
*1 large or 2 small melons*
*4 tablespoons olive oil*
*1 tablespoon tarragon vinegar*
*2 tablespoons chopped fresh chives or chopped parsley*
*herb sprigs, to garnish*
*Napa cabbage leaves, to serve*
**Serves 4–6**

1 Cook the pasta in salted boiling water according to the instructions on the package. Drain well in a colander and let cool.

2 Break the heads off the shrimp, shell them and discard the shells.

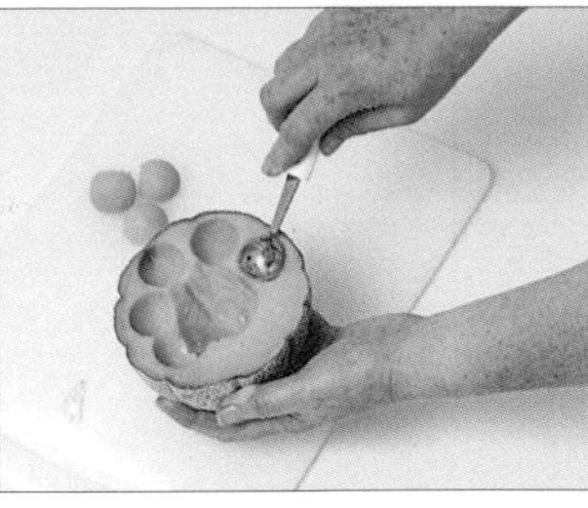

3 Halve the melon and remove the seeds with a spoon. Carefully scoop the flesh into balls with a melon baller and toss in a large bowl with the shrimp and pasta.

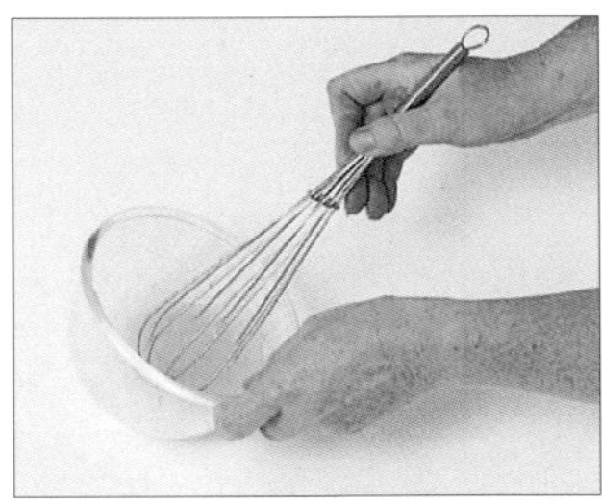

4 Whisk the oil, vinegar and chopped herbs together. Pour onto the pasta and shrimp mixture and turn to coat with the dressing. Cover and chill for at least 30 minutes.

5 Meanwhile shred the Napa cabbage leaves and use to line a shallow bowl or the empty melon halves.

6 Pile the shrimp mixture onto the Napa cabbage leaves, garnish with sprigs of herbs and serve.

# Pasta Salad with Olives

THIS DELICIOUS SALAD combines all the flavors of the Mediterranean. It is an excellent way of serving pasta and is particularly suitable for a hot summer's day.

**INGREDIENTS**

*1 pound dried short pasta, such as farfalle or penne*
*4 tablespoons extra virgin olive oil*
*10 sun-dried tomatoes, thinly sliced*
*2 tablespoons capers, in brine or salted*
*1 cup pitted black olives*
*2 garlic cloves, finely chopped*
*3 tablespoons balsamic vinegar*
*3 tablespoons chopped fresh parsley*
*salt and ground black pepper*

**Serves 6**

1 Cook the pasta in plenty of salted boiling water until *al dente*. Drain and rinse under cold water to stop the cooking. Drain well and turn into a large bowl. Toss with the olive oil and set aside until required.

2 Soak the tomatoes in a bowl of hot water for 10 minutes. Do not discard the water. Rinse the capers well. If they have been preserved in salt, soak them in a little hot water for 10 minutes. Rinse again.

3 Combine the olives, tomatoes, capers, garlic and vinegar in a small bowl. Season with salt and ground black pepper.

4 Stir the olive mixture into the cooked pasta and toss well. Add 2–3 tablespoons of the tomato soaking water if the salad seems too dry. Toss with the parsley and let stand for 15 minutes before serving.

# Whole Wheat Pasta Salad

THIS SUBSTANTIAL vegetarian salad is easily assembled from any combination of seasonal vegetables. Use raw or lightly blanched vegetables, or a mixture of both.

**INGREDIENTS**

*1 pound short whole wheat pasta, such as fusilli or penne*
*3 tablespoons olive oil*
*2 carrots*
*1 small head broccoli*
*1 ½ cups shelled peas, fresh or frozen*
*1 red or yellow bell pepper*
*2 celery stalks*
*4 scallions*
*1 large tomato*
*¾ cup pitted olives*
*1 cup diced Cheddar or mozzarella cheese or a combination of both*
*salt and ground black pepper*

***For the dressing***
*3 tablespoons white wine or balsamic vinegar*
*4 tablespoons olive oil*
*1 tablespoon Dijon mustard*
*1 tablespoon sesame seeds*
*2 teaspoons chopped mixed fresh herbs, such as parsley, thyme and basil*

**Serves 8**

1 Cook the pasta in plenty of salted boiling water until *al dente*. Drain, and rinse under cold water to stop the cooking. Drain well and turn into a large bowl. Toss with 3 tablespoons of the olive oil and set aside. Allow the pasta to cool completely.

2 Lightly blanch the carrots, broccoli and peas in a large pan of boiling water. Refresh under cold water. Drain well through a colander.

3 Chop the carrots and broccoli into bite-size pieces and add to the pasta with the peas. Slice the bell pepper, celery, scallions and tomato into small pieces. Add them to the salad with the olives.

4 To make the dressing combine the vinegar with the oil and mustard. Stir in the sesame seeds and herbs.

5 Pour the dressing into the salad and toss gently to mix. Taste for seasoning, adding salt, pepper or more olive oil and vinegar if necessary. Stir in the cheese, then let the salad stand for about 15 minutes before serving.

# Artichoke Pasta Salad

THE EXQUISITE TASTE of the artichokes adds a sweetness to this salad.

**INGREDIENTS**

*7 tablespoons olive oil*
*1 red bell pepper, quartered, seeded, and thinly sliced*
*1 onion, halved and thinly sliced*
*1 teaspoon dried thyme*
*3 tablespoons sherry vinegar*
*1 pound pasta shapes, such as penne or fusilli*
*2 jars (6-ounce) marinated artichoke hearts, drained and thinly sliced*
*5 ounces cooked broccoli, chopped*
*20–25 salt-cured black olives, pitted and chopped*
*2 tablespoons chopped fresh parsley*
*salt and ground black pepper*

**Serves 4**

1 Heat 2 tablespoons of the olive oil in a non-stick frying pan. Add the red bell pepper and onion and cook over low heat until just soft, about 10 minutes, stirring occasionally.

2 Stir in the thyme, ¼ teaspoon salt and the vinegar. Cook, stirring, for a further 30 seconds, then set aside until required.

3 Cook the pasta in plenty of salted boiling water according to the instructions on the package until *al dente*. Drain, rinse with hot water, then drain again. Transfer to a large bowl. Add 2 tablespoons of the oil and toss to coat thoroughly.

4 Add the artichokes, broccoli, olives, parsley, onion mixture and remaining oil to the pasta. Season with salt and pepper. Stir to blend. Let stand for at least 1 hour before serving or chill overnight. Serve the salad at room temperature.

# Avocado, Tomato and Mozzarella Salad

THIS SALAD is made from ingredients representing the colors of the Italian flag—a sunny cheerful dish!

**INGREDIENTS**

*1½ cups dried farfalle*
*6 ripe red tomatoes*
*8 ounces mozzarella cheese*
*1 large ripe avocado*
*2 tablespoons chopped fresh basil*
*2 tablespoons pine nuts, toasted*
*fresh basil sprig, to garnish*

***For the dressing***
*6 tablespoons olive oil*
*2 tablespoons wine vinegar*
*1 teaspoon balsamic vinegar (optional)*
*1 teaspoon whole-grain mustard*
*pinch of sugar*
*salt and ground black pepper*
**Serves 4**

1 Cook the pasta in plenty of salted boiling water according to the instructions on the package. Drain well and cool.

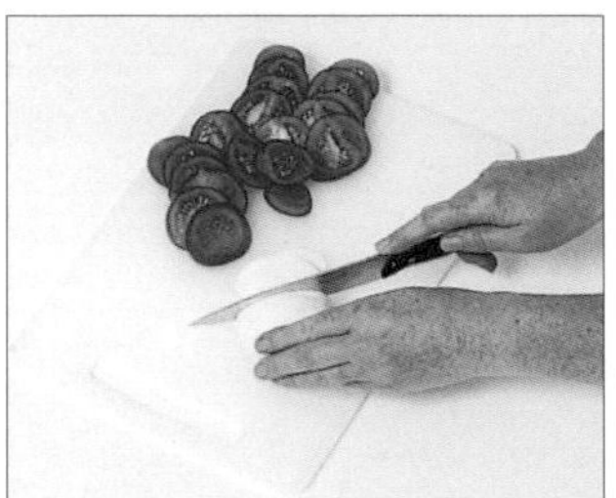

2 Using a sharp knife slice the tomatoes thinly. Repeat for the mozzarella cheese, slicing it into thin, even rounds.

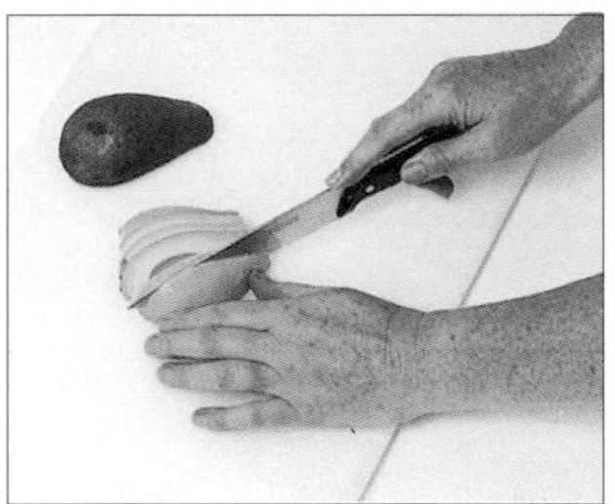

3 Halve the avocado, remove the pit and peel off the skin. Slice the flesh lengthwise.

4 Place all the dressing ingredients together in a small bowl and whisk until well blended.

5 Arrange the sliced tomato, mozzarella cheese and avocado overlapping one another around the edge of a flat serving plate.

6 Toss the pasta with half the dressing and the chopped basil. Pile into the center of the plate. Pour the remaining dressing over, sprinkle the pine nuts over and garnish with a sprig of fresh basil. Serve immediately.

# Noodles

Noodles are the original "fast food" throughout Asia and are eaten on almost every possible occasion, from weddings to funerals. There are numerous varieties and they are served both hot and cold, cooked in combination with vegetables, meat, poultry and seafood. They can be braised, deep-fried and stir-fried, as well as made into nests and cakes. Noodles may be served as a complete meal or as a side dish.

# Introduction

Noodles have universal appeal. Although thousands of words have been written on the subject, it is the Italian influence that prevails in most pasta cookbooks; scant mention is made of the ever-growing popularity of noodle dishes from China, Japan, Thailand and other Asian countries.

There has been much speculation about whether the Chinese invented noodles before the Italians discovered spaghetti. One theory is that when Marco Polo journeyed overland to China late in the thirteenth century, he brought the secret of pasta-making back to his native Italy. This seems a plausible scenario: noodles were certainly known in China before the start of the Christian era. Soon after the Chinese learned how to grind grains into flour, they discovered that by adding liquid they could make dough which could be kneaded and rolled into thin sheets. It was a short step to cutting the sheets into ribbons and cooking them in boiling water. Noodles rapidly became a staple food, in China and the entire Far East.

Noodles play an important role in many traditional festivities. In China they are a symbol of longevity and are often eaten at birthday celebrations and as "crossing of the threshold of the year" food. They are eaten at happy and sad occasions, between meals, standing up or sitting down. You could say noodles are the oldest form of fast food in the East. Asian pasta includes a wide variety of noodles, ranging from fine and thin to coarse and thick. Many are made with wheat flour, with or without egg. Most of these varieties are softer and starchier than their Italian counterparts, and are sold fresh or dried. Other varieties, such as glass noodles, are based on vegetable starch, such as that derived from mung beans. Rice flour is used for rice sticks or vermicelli and also paper-thin rice sheets. Of the many varieties of Asian pasta, the most familiar ones are the Chinese wontons and Japanese udon, soba and somen noodles. The range of noodle types is extensive, although the Asians have never felt the need to produce as many varied shapes of pasta as the Italians.

Noodles can be cooked, mixed and combined with just about every variety of meat, seafood and vegetables. Eaten hot or cold, they are used in soups, salads and stir-fries. They can also be braised, deep fried or made into cakes. In short, noodles can be served in innumerable ways, as side dishes, snacks, garnishes or complete meals.

*Left: Rice vermicelli noodles are deep fried until crisp, then tossed in a piquant sauce.*

# Equipment



No elaborate equipment is required to prepare the dishes in this book. A cleaver, cutting block, spatula and chopsticks are basic utensils that all Asian kitchens have. You would find a draining spoon useful and will certainly need a wok.

*Noodle equipment, clockwise from top left: large twisted wire draining spoon, wok and chopsticks, heavy cleaver knife and metal spider.*

### Wok

This all-purpose cooking pan, round in shape with high sides, distributes the heat evenly and allows ingredients to be stirred and tossed without spilling. Woks come in a range of sizes and are made from various metals. Traditional woks are made of thin metal and work best on gas stoves, but you can also purchase flat-bottomed woks for electric stoves. The wok's versatility is limitless. It is ideal for both stir-frying and deep frying because of its shape. It requires less oil than a flat-bottomed deep fryer and has more depth and cooking surface. It can also be used for shallow frying, poaching, boiling and, with the lid, for steaming and braising.

### Draining spoons

For deep frying you will need either a large twisted wire draining spoon with a wooden handle, or a metal spider to lift food out of the hot oil.

### Cleaver knife

This all-purpose Chinese cutting tool looks like a butcher's cleaver. There are several kinds: stainless steel looks good; carbon steel holds a better edge and is easier to sharpen, but will rust; wooden handled cleavers are also available in different sizes. Lightweight cleavers are used only for slicing. Heavier cleavers are more versatile and can also be used to chop bones. The handle is useful for pounding or mashing.

### Chopsticks

These can be used to replace spoons, forks and whisks. Wooden chopsticks are best for cooking because they can withstand high temperatures. They are also nicer to eat with than plastic ones.

#### Safety first

Oil catches fire easily when overheated and can inflict serious burns. Never fill a pan more than one-third full, keep the handle out of the way and never leave a pan of hot oil unsupervised. Oil for deep frying should cover the food by at least inch and should be heated to 375°F (or until a cube of dry bread, added to the oil, browns in 30 seconds). Food should always be fried in small batches to avoid overcrowding the pan, which causes the temperature to drop. Always lower food carefully into the fat, using a wire basket or slotted spoon. The food should be as dry as possible, as hot oil will spatter on contact with water. Never pour water on an oil fire. In the event of a fire, do not panic. Turn off the heat if it is safe to do so, and cover the pan tightly to exclude air; a fire blanket is ideal for this, but a large pan lid or a baking sheet would do. If you have not already turned off the heat, do so as soon as the flames have been smothered sufficiently. Do not move the pan.

# Types of Noodles

**Cellophane noodles**
Made from ground mung beans, these are commonly called bean thread, transparent or glass noodles. Dried noodles must be soaked in hot water before cooking.

**Egg noodles**
Egg noodles are made from wheat flour, egg and water. The dough is flattened and then shredded or extruded through a pasta machine to the chosen shape and correct thickness.

**Rice noodles**
Banh Trang are made from ground rice and water. They range in thickness from very thin to wide ribbons and sheets. Dried ribbon rice noodles, often called rice sticks, are usually sold tied up in bundles. Fresh rice noodles are also available. Rinse rice noodles in warm water and drain before use.

**Rice vermicelli**
These thin, brittle rice-flour, Chinese noodles look like white hair, and are sold in large bundles. Rice vermicelli cooks almost instantly in hot liquid, provided the noodles are first soaked in warm water. They can also be deep fried.

**Soba noodles**
Made from a mixture of buckwheat and wheat flour these noodles are very popular in Japan. They are traditionally cooked in simmering water, then drained and served hot in winter or cold in summer with a dipping sauce.

**Somen noodles**
These delicate, thin white Japanese noodles made from wheat flour come in dried form, usually tied in bundles,

**Udon noodles**
Wheat flour and water are used to make these Japanese noodles. They are usually round, but can also be flat and are available fresh, pre-cooked or dried.

## Fresh Ingredients

**Bean curd**
Bean curd is also known as tofu or dofu and is highly nutritious. The flavorless curd blends beautifully with other ingredients. Fresh, long-life and deep-fried varieties are available.

**Bean sprouts**
High in protein and very nutritious, these can be eaten raw or cooked.

**Bok choy**
This Chinese white cabbage has thick white stalks and dark green leaves.

**Chinese chives**
Better known as garlic chives, these are sometimes sold with their flowers.

**Cilantro**
Also known as Chinese parsley or coriander, this leafy green herb is often an accompaniment to meat and fish.

**Ginger**
An aromatic rhizome widely available in supermarkets. It gives a subtle piquancy to fish, meat and vegetables.

**Lemongrass**
An aromatic tropical grass that characterizes Thai and Vietnamese cuisine, lemongrass gets its name from its very distinctive scent and flavor. Crush lemongrass lightly before slicing or chopping to release more flavor.

*Fresh noodles*

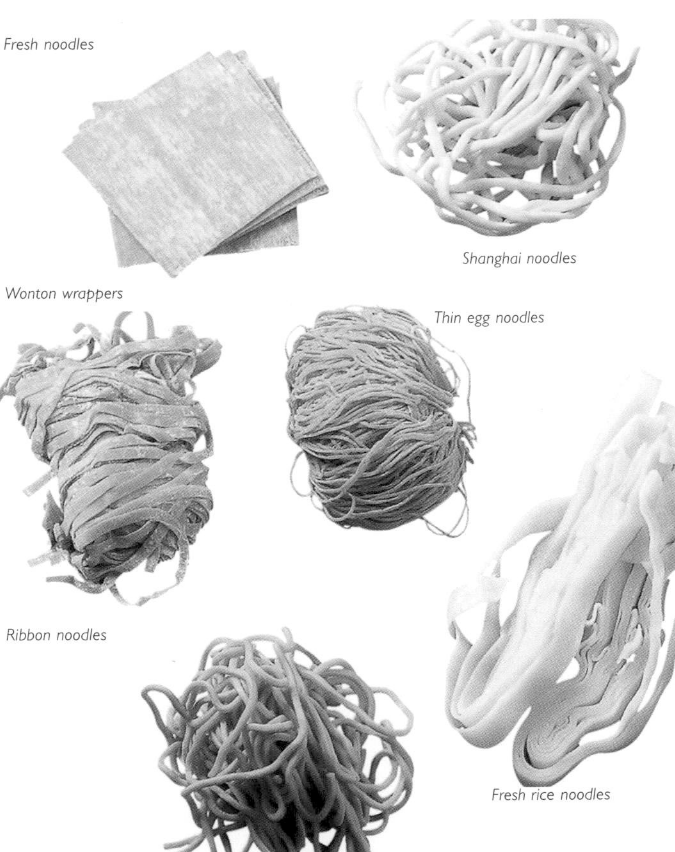

*Wonton wrappers*

*Shanghai noodles*

*Thin egg noodles*

*Ribbon noodles*

*Fresh rice noodles*

*Medium egg noodles*

### Wheat noodles

Sometimes called Shanghai noodles, these are made from wheat, water and salt. They are made in the same way as ordinary egg noodles but are whiter in color.

### Wonton skins

Small square sheets rolled from egg noodle dough, these are available in packages from Chinese food markets.

### Noodle know-how

All dried noodles should be stored in airtight containers where they can be kept for many months.

Fresh noodles can be chilled for several days in the plastic bag in which they were purchased (check use-by dates).

Allow 3–4 ounces noodles per person.

Many recipes call for noodles to be cooked twice—first parboiled and then stir-fried or simmered in a soup or sauce. Where this is the case, the preliminary cooking should be brief. Remove the noodles from the heat when they are barely tender, immediately drain them in a colander and rinse under cold running water to arrest the cooking process. Separate the noodles with a fork and add a dash of oil if not using immediately. Parboiled noodles can be prepared in advance. They will keep for several days if stored in a tightly sealed container in the refrigerator.

*Dried noodles, clockwise from top left: ribbon noodles (two bundles), somen noodles, udon noodles, soba noodles, egg ribbon noodles, medium egg noodles, cellophane noodles, rice sheets, rice vermicelli, egg noodles, and, center, rice ribbon noodles.*

## Storecupboard Ingredients

### Hoisin sauce

Also known as barbecue sauce, hoisin sauce is thick, dark-brown, savory/sweet and tangy.

### Dried mushrooms

Dried Chinese black mushrooms, cloud ears and wood ears become meaty and succulent when soaked in water.

### Oyster sauce

This thickish, slightly sweet and salty brown sauce is made from oyster extract, soy sauce, sugar and vinegar. It is used to flavor all sorts of meat, fish and vegetable dishes.

### Rice wine

Made from fermented glutinous rice, this golden wine is used for both drinking and cooking.

### Sesame oil

Extracted from toasted sesame seeds, this aromatic oil has a nutty flavor.

### Soy sauce

Essential for Chinese cooking, soy sauce enhances the flavor of meat, fish and vegetable dishes and sauces. It ranges in color from pale to dark, the light soy sauce having more flavor than the sweeter dark variety.

# Seafood Wontons

THESE TASTY WONTONS resemble tortellini. Water chestnuts add a light crunch to the filling.

**INGREDIENTS**

*8 ounces raw shrimp, peeled and deveined*
*4 ounces white crabmeat, picked over*
*4 canned water chestnuts, finely diced*
*1 scallion, finely chopped*
*1 small green chile, seeded and finely chopped*
*½ teaspoon grated fresh ginger root*
*1 egg, separated*
*20–24 wonton skins*
*salt and freshly ground black pepper*
*cilantro leaves, to garnish*

***For the cilantro dressing***
*2 tablespoons rice vinegar*
*1 tablespoon chopped pickled ginger*
*6 tablespoons olive oil*
*1 tablespoon soy sauce*
*3 tablespoons chopped cilantro*
*2 tablespoons finely diced red bell pepper*

**Serves 4**

1 Finely dice the shrimp and place them in a bowl. Add the crabmeat, water chestnuts, scallion, chile, ginger and egg white. Season with salt and pepper and stir well to combine.

2 Place a wonton skin on a board. Put about 1 teaspoon of the filling just above the center of the skin. With a pastry brush, moisten the edges of the skin with a little of the egg yolk. Bring the bottom of the skin up over the filling. Press gently to expel any air, then seal the skin neatly in a triangle.

3 For a more elaborate shape, bring the two side points up over the filling, overlap the points and pinch the ends firmly together. Space the filled wontons on a large baking sheet lined with waxed paper, so that they do not stick together.

4 Half fill a large saucepan with water. Bring to simmering point. Add the filled wontons, a few at a time, and simmer for 2–3 minutes. The wontons will float to the surface. When ready the skins will be translucent and the filling should be cooked. Remove the wontons with a large slotted spoon, drain them briefly, then spread them on trays. Keep warm while cooking the remaining wontons.

5 Make the cilantro dressing by whisking all the ingredients together in a bowl. Divide the wontons among serving dishes, drizzle with the dressing and serve garnished with a handful of cilantro leaves.

# Clay Pot of Chile Squid and Noodles

**INGREDIENTS**

*1½ pounds fresh squid*
*2 tablespoons vegetable oil*
*3 slices fresh ginger root, finely shredded*
*2 garlic cloves, finely chopped*
*1 red onion, finely sliced*
*1 carrot, finely sliced*
*1 celery stalk, diagonally sliced*
*2 ounces sugar snap peas, topped and tailed*
*1 teaspoon sugar*
*1 tablespoon chile bean paste*
*½ teaspoon chili powder*
*3 ounces dried cellophane noodles, soaked in hot water until soft*
*½ cup chicken stock or water*
*1 tablespoon soy sauce*
*1 tablespoon oyster sauce*
*1 teaspoon sesame oil*
*pinch of salt*
*cilantro leaves, to garnish*

**Serves 4**

1 Prepare the squid. Holding the body in one hand, gently pull away the head and tentacles. Discard the head; trim and reserve the tentacles. Remove the transparent "quill" from inside the body of the squid. Peel off the brown skin on the outside of the body. Rub a little salt into the squid and wash thoroughly under cold running water. Cut the body of the squid into rings or split it open lengthwise, score criss-cross patterns on the inside of the body and cut it into even 2 x 1½-inch pieces.

2 Heat the oil in a large clay pot or flameproof casserole. Add the ginger, garlic and onion, and fry for 1–2 minutes. Add the squid, carrot, celery and sugar snap peas. Fry until the squid curls up. Season with salt and sugar, and stir in the chile bean paste and chili powder. Transfer the mixture to a bowl and set aside until required.

3 Drain the soaked noodles and add them to the clay pot or casserole. Stir in the stock or water, soy sauce and oyster sauce. Cover and cook over medium heat for about 10 minutes or until the noodles are tender.

4 Return the squid and vegetables to the pot. Cover and cook for about 5–6 minutes more, until all the flavors are combined. Season to taste.

5 Just before serving, drizzle with the sesame oil and sprinkle with the cilantro leaves.

**Cook's Tip**

*These noodles have a smooth, light texture that readily absorbs the other flavors in the dish. To vary the flavor, the vegetables can be altered according to what is available.*

# Fresh Salad with Wonton Crisps

**INGREDIENTS**

*8 wonton skins*
*oil for frying*
*2 Bibb or small butterhead lettuces, separated into leaves*
*½ cucumber, halved, seeded and cut into ½-inch dice*
*2 ripe tomatoes, peeled, seeded and cut into ½-inch dice*
*1 hard-cooked egg, coarsely chopped*
*2 ounces roasted peanuts, coarsely chopped*

***For the peanut dressing***
*1 tablespoon smooth peanut butter*
*½ cup coconut milk*
*1 teaspoon sugar*
*juice of 1 lime*
*few drops of Tabasco sauce*
*salt and ground black pepper*
**Serves 4**

1 Make the peanut dressing by combining the peanut butter, coconut milk and sugar together in a small saucepan. Stir over low heat just until blended.

2 Remove the pan from the heat, stir in the lime juice and Tabasco sauce, then season with salt and pepper to taste. Set aside and let cool to room temperature before using.

3 Separate the wonton skins; restack them and cut into four.

4 Heat the oil in a deep saucepan or wok. When hot, add the wontons a few at a time and fry until browned. Lift them out of the oil using a slotted spoon and drain on paper towels. (The wontons will color very quickly; take care not to burn them.)

5 Prepare the remaining ingredients for the salad in a large bowl. Toss with the dressing and serve in bowls, topped with wonton crisps.

# Somen Noodles with Baked Cherry Tomatoes

THIS SUMMERY DISH is bursting with flavor. Baking the cherry tomatoes slowly strengthens their taste. If you can find yellow tomatoes, use half and half—the dish will look extra special.

**INGREDIENTS**

*2¼ pounds cherry tomatoes, halved*
*3 garlic cloves, finely sliced*
*1 bunch basil leaves, stripped*
*½ cup extra virgin olive oil*
*1 pound somen noodles*
*salt and ground black pepper*
*shavings of Parmesan cheese and tiny basil sprigs, to garnish (optional)*
**Serves 4–6**

1 Preheat the oven to 350°F. Arrange the tomatoes, cut side up, in a single layer in a baking dish. Season with salt and pepper and sprinkle with sliced garlic. Sprinkle half the basil leaves over the tomatoes; drizzle the olive oil over the top. Bake the tomatoes for 1–1½ hours. Set aside in a cool place until ready to serve.

2 Just before serving, cook the somen noodles in a saucepan of boiling salted water until just tender, following the directions on the package. Drain well, turn into a bowl and toss lightly with the baked tomatoes and their juices. Add the remaining basil, with more olive oil and seasoning. Serve immediately, garnished with Parmesan shavings and a few basil sprigs, if liked.

# Cheese Fritters

THESE CRISP FRITTERS owe their inspiration to Italy. A note of caution—do be careful not to burn your mouth when you take your first bite, as the soft, rich cheese filling will be very hot.

**INGREDIENTS**

*4 ounces ricotta cheese*
*2 ounces Fontina cheese, grated*
*1 ounce Parmesan cheese, finely grated*
*pinch of cayenne pepper*
*1 egg, beaten, plus a little extra to seal the wontons*
*15–16 wonton skins*
*oil for deep frying*
**Makes 15–16**

1 Line a large baking sheet with waxed paper or sprinkle it lightly with flour. Set aside. Combine the cheeses in a bowl, then add the cayenne and beaten egg and mix well.

2 Place one wonton skin at a time on a board. Brush the edges with egg. Spoon a little filling in the center; pull the top corner down to the bottom corner, to make a triangle.

3 Transfer the filled wontons to the prepared baking sheet.

4 Heat the oil in a deep-fryer or large saucepan. Slip in as many wontons at one time as can be accommodated without overcrowding. Fry them for 2–3 minutes on each side or until the fritters are golden. Remove with a slotted spoon. Drain on paper towels and serve immediately.

# Chilled Soba Noodles with Nori

THE JAPANESE INGREDIENTS used in this recipe should be available in specialist shops and in larger supermarkets.

**INGREDIENTS**

*12 ounces dried soba noodles*
*1 sheet nori seaweed*

***For the dipping sauce***
*1¼ cups bonito stock*
*½ cup dark soy sauce*
*4 tablespoons mirin*
*1 teaspoon sugar*
*¼ ounce loose bonito flakes*

***Flavorings***
*4 scallions, finely chopped*
*2 tablespoons grated daikon*
*wasabi paste*
*4 egg yolks (optional)*
**Serves 4**

1 Make the dipping sauce. Place the stock, soy sauce, mirin and sugar in a saucepan and stir to combine. Bring rapidly to a boil, add the bonito flakes, then remove from the heat. When cool, strain the sauce into a bowl and cover. (This can be done in advance and the sauce kept chilled for up to a week.)

2 Cook the soba noodles in a saucepan of lightly salted boiling water for 6–7 minutes or until just tender, following the manufacturer's directions on the package.

3 Drain and then rinse the noodles under cold running water, agitating gently to remove the excess starch. Then drain again.

4 Toast the nori over a high gas flame or under a hot broiler, then crumble into thin strips. Divide the noodles among four serving dishes and top with the nori. Serve each portion with an individual bowl of dipping sauce and offer the flavorings, handed separately.

# Shrimp Noodle Salad with Herbs

A LIGHT, REFRESHING SALAD with all the tangy flavor of the sea. Instead of shrimp, try squid or scallops.

**INGREDIENTS**

*4 ounces dried cellophane noodles, soaked in hot water until soft*
*16 cooked shrimp, shelled*
*1 small green bell pepper, seeded and cut into strips*
*½ cucumber, cut into strips*
*1 tomato, cut into strips*
*2 shallots, finely sliced*
*salt and ground black pepper*
*cilantro leaves, to garnish*

***For the dressing***
*1 tablespoon rice vinegar*
*2 tablespoons fish sauce*
*2 tablespoons fresh lime juice*
*pinch of salt*
*½ teaspoon grated fresh ginger root*
*1 lemongrass stalk, finely chopped*
*1 red chile, seeded and finely sliced*
*2 tablespoons coarsely chopped mint*
*few sprigs tarragon, roughly chopped*
*1 tablespoon chopped chives*

**Serves 4**

1 Make the dressing by placing all the ingredients in a bowl; whisk well to combine thoroughly.

2 Drain the noodles, then plunge in a saucepan of boiling water for 1 minute. Drain, rinse and drain again.

3 In a large bowl, combine the noodles with the shrimp, bell pepper, cucumber, tomato and shallots. Lightly season with salt and pepper, then toss with the dressing.

4 Spoon the noodles on to individual plates, arranging the shrimp on top. Garnish with a few cilantro leaves and serve immediately.

**COOK'S TIP**

*Shrimp are available ready-cooked and often shelled. To cook shrimp, boil them for 5 minutes. Let them cool in the cooking liquid then gently pull off the tail shell and twist off the head.*

# Smoked Trout and Noodle Salad

IT IS IMPORTANT to use ripe juicy tomatoes for this fresh salad. For a special occasion you could replace the smoked trout with smoked salmon.

**INGREDIENTS**

*8 ounces dried somen noodles*
*2 smoked trout, skinned and boned*
*2 hard-cooked eggs, coarsely chopped*
*2 tablespoons chopped chives*
*lime halves, to serve (optional)*

***For the dressing***

*6 ripe plum tomatoes*
*2 shallots, finely chopped*
*2 tablespoons tiny capers, rinsed*
*2 tablespoons chopped fresh tarragon*
*finely grated rind and juice of ½ orange*
*4 tablespoons extra virgin olive oil*
*salt and ground black pepper*

**Serves 4**

1 To make the dressing, cut the tomatoes in half, remove the cores, and cut the flesh into chunks.

2 Place in a bowl with the shallots, capers, tarragon, orange rind, orange juice and olive oil. Season with salt and pepper, and mix well to combine. Let the dressing marinate at room temperature for 1–2 hours.

3 Cook the noodles in a large saucepan of boiling water until just tender. Drain through a colander and rinse under cold running water. Drain again.

4 Toss the noodles with the dressing, then adjust the seasoning to taste. Arrange the noodles on a large serving platter or individual plates.

5 Flake the smoked trout over the noodles, then sprinkle the coarsely chopped eggs and chopped chives over the top. Serve the lime halves on the side if liked.

**COOK'S TIP**

*Choose tomatoes that are firm, bright in color and have a matt texture, avoiding any with blotched or cracked skins.*

# Spicy Szechuan Noodles

**INGREDIENTS**

*12 ounces thick, dried noodles*
*6 ounces cooked chicken, shredded*
*2 ounces roasted cashew nuts*

***For the dressing***

*4 scallions, chopped*
*2 tablespoons chopped cilantro*
*2 garlic cloves, chopped*
*2 tablespoons smooth peanut butter*
*2 tablespoons sweet chili sauce*
*1 tablespoon soy sauce*
*1 tablespoon sherry vinegar*
*1 tablespoon sesame oil*
*2 tablespoons olive oil*
*2 tablespoons chicken stock or water*
*10 toasted Szechuan peppercorns, ground*

**Serves 4**

1 Cook the noodles in a large saucepan of salted boiling water until just tender, according to the instructions on the package. Drain, rinse under cold running water and drain again.

2 While the noodles are cooking combine all the ingredients for the dressing in a large bowl and whisk together.

3 Add the noodles, shredded chicken and cashew nuts to the dressing, toss gently to coat and adjust the seasoning to taste. Serve immediately.

**COOK'S TIP**

*You could substitute cooked turkey or pork for the chicken for a change.*

# Sesame Noodles with Scallions

THIS SIMPLE BUT very tasty warm salad can be prepared and cooked in just a few minutes.

**INGREDIENTS**

*2 garlic cloves, coarsely chopped*
*2 tablespoons Chinese sesame paste*
*1 tablespoon dark sesame oil*
*2 tablespoons soy sauce*
*2 tablespoons rice wine*
*1 tablespoon honey*
*pinch of five-spice powder*
*12 ounces fresh or dried soba or buckwheat noodles*
*4 scallions, finely sliced diagonally*
*2 ounces beansprouts*
*3-inch piece of cucumber, cut into short thin sticks*
*toasted sesame seeds*
*salt and freshly ground black pepper*

**Serves 4**

1 Process the garlic, sesame paste, oil, soy sauce, rice wine, honey and five-spice powder with a pinch each of salt and pepper in a blender or food processor until they form a smooth paste.

2 Cook the noodles in a saucepan of boiling water until just tender, according to the instructions on the package. Drain the noodles immediately and turn them into a bowl.

3 Toss the hot noodles with the dressing and the scallions. Top with the bean sprouts, cucumber and sesame seeds and serve.

**COOK'S TIP**

*If you can't find Chinese sesame paste, then use either tahini paste or smooth peanut butter instead.*

# Fried Pork and Rice Vermicelli Salad

PORK CRACKLING adds a delicious crunch to this popular salad.

**INGREDIENTS**

*8 ounces lean pork*
*2 garlic cloves, finely chopped*
*2 slices fresh ginger root, finely chopped*
*2–3 tablespoons rice wine*
*3 tablespoons vegetable oil*
*2 lemongrass stalks, finely chopped*
*2 teaspoons curry powder*
*6 ounces bean sprouts*
*8 ounces dried rice vermicelli, soaked in warm water until soft*
*½ lettuce, finely shredded*
*2 tablespoons mint leaves*
*lemon juice and fish sauce, to taste*
*salt and ground black pepper*
*2 scallions, chopped, 1 ounce roasted peanuts, chopped, and pork crackling (optional), to garnish*

**Serves 4**

1 Cut the pork into thin strips. Place in a shallow dish with half the garlic and ginger. Season with salt and pepper, pour 2 tablespoons rice wine over and marinate for at least 1 hour.

2 Heat the oil in a frying pan. Add the remaining garlic and ginger and fry for a few seconds until fragrant. Stir in the pork, with the marinade, and add the lemongrass and curry powder. Fry until the pork is golden and cooked through, adding more rice wine if the mixture seems dry.

3 Place the bean sprouts in a strainer. Lower the strainer into a saucepan of boiling water for 1 minute, then drain and refresh under cold running water. Drain again. Using the same water, cook the drained rice vermicelli for 3–5 minutes until tender, drain and rinse under cold running water. Drain well and turn into a bowl.

4 Add the bean sprouts, shredded lettuce and mint leaves to the rice vermicelli. Season with the lemon juice and fish sauce. Toss lightly.

5 Divide the noodle mixture among individual serving plates, making a nest on each plate. Arrange the pork mixture on top. Garnish with scallions, roasted peanuts and pork crackles, if using.

# Potato and Cellophane Noodle Salad

**INGREDIENTS**

*2 medium potatoes, peeled and cut into eighths*
*6 ounces cellophane noodles, soaked in hot water until soft*
*4 tablespoons vegetable oil*
*1 onion, finely sliced*
*1 teaspoon ground turmeric*
*4 tablespoons besan or gram flour*
*1 teaspoon grated lemon rind*
*4–5 tablespoons lemon juice*
*3 tablespoons fish sauce*
*4 scallions, finely sliced*
*salt and ground black pepper*

**Serves 4**

1 Place the potatoes in a saucepan. Add water to cover, bring to a boil and cook for about 15 minutes until tender but firm. Drain the potatoes and set them aside to cool.

2 Meanwhile, cook the drained noodles in a saucepan of salted boiling water for 3 minutes. Drain well through a colander and rinse under cold running water. Then drain again.

3 Heat the oil in a frying pan. Add the onion and turmeric and fry for about 5 minutes until golden brown. Drain the onion, reserving the oil.

4 Heat a small frying pan. Add the gram flour and stir for about 4 minutes until it turns light golden brown in color.

5 Mix the potatoes, noodles and fried onion in a large bowl. Add the reserved oil and the toasted gram flour with the lemon rind and juice, fish sauce and scallions. Mix together well and adjust the seasoning to taste if necessary. Serve immediately.

**VARIATION**

*This healthy salad would easily convert to a vegetarian dish by substituting soy sauce for the fish sauce.*

# Noodles with Pineapple and Mango

**INGREDIENTS**

*10 ounces dried udon noodles*
*½ pineapple, peeled, cored and sliced into 1½-inch rings*
*3 tablespoons brown sugar*
*4 tablespoons fresh lime juice*
*4 tablespoons coconut milk*
*2 tablespoons fish sauce*
*2 tablespoons grated fresh ginger root*
*2 garlic cloves, finely chopped*
*1 ripe mango or 2 peaches, finely diced*
*ground black pepper*
*2 scallions, finely sliced, 2 red chiles, seeded and finely shredded, plus mint leaves, to garnish*

**Serves 4**

1 Cook the noodles in a large saucepan of boiling water until tender, following the directions on the package. Drain, refresh under cold water and drain again.

2 Place the pineapple rings on a flameproof dish, sprinkle with 2 tablespoons of the sugar and broil for about 5 minutes or until lightly golden. Cool slightly and then cut into small dice.

3 Mix the lime juice, coconut milk and fish sauce in a salad bowl. Add the remaining brown sugar, with the ginger and garlic, and whisk well to combine. Add the noodles and pineapple.

4 Add the mango or peaches and pepper to taste, and toss. Scatter over the scallions, chiles and mint leaves before serving.

# Buckwheat Noodles with Smoked Salmon

Young pea sprouts are only available for a short time. You can substitute watercress, mustard cress, young leeks or your favorite green vegetable or herb in this dish.

**INGREDIENTS**

*8 ounces fresh or dried buckwheat or soba noodles*
*1 tablespoon oyster sauce*
*juice of ½ lemon*
*2–3 tablespoons light olive oil*
*4 ounces smoked salmon, cut into fine strips*
*4 ounces young pea shoots or clau miu*
*2 ripe tomatoes, peeled, seeded and cut into strips*
*1 tablespoon chopped chives*
*ground black pepper*

**Serves 4**

1 Cook the buckwheat or soba noodles in a large saucepan of boiling water, following the directions on the package. Drain, then rinse under cold running water and drain well.

2 Turn the noodles into a large bowl. Add the oyster sauce and lemon juice and season with pepper to taste. Moisten with the olive oil.

3 Add the smoked salmon, pea sprouts, tomatoes and chives. Mix well and serve immediately.

# Egg Noodle Salad with Sesame Chicken

**INGREDIENTS**

*14 ounces fresh thin egg noodles*
*1 carrot, cut into long fine strips*
*2 ounces snow peas, topped, tailed, cut into fine strips and blanched*
*4 ounces bean sprouts, blanched*
*2 tablespoons olive oil*
*8 ounces skinless, boneless chicken breasts, finely sliced*
*2 tablespoons sesame seeds, toasted*
*salt and freshly ground black pepper*
*2 scallions, finely sliced diagonally and cilantro leaves, to garnish*

**For the dressing**

*3 tablespoons sherry vinegar*
*5 tablespoons soy sauce*
*4 tablespoons sesame oil*
*6 tablespoons light olive oil*
*1 garlic clove, finely chopped*
*1 teaspoon grated fresh ginger root*

**Serves 4–6**

1 To make the dressing. Combine all the ingredients in a small bowl with a pinch of salt and mix together well using a whisk or a fork.

2 Cook the noodles in a saucepan of boiling water. Stir them occasionally to separate. They only take a few minutes to cook: be careful not to overcook them. Drain, rinse under cold running water and drain well. Turn into a bowl.

3 Add the vegetables to the noodles. Pour in half the dressing, then toss the mixture and adjust the seasoning.

4 Heat the oil in a large frying pan. Add the chicken and stir-fry for 3 minutes, or until cooked and golden. Remove from the heat. Add the sesame seeds and drizzle in some of the remaining dressing.

5 Arrange the noodles on individual serving plates, making a nest on each plate. Spoon the chicken on top. Sprinkle with the sliced scallions and the cilantro leaves and serve any remaining dressing separately.

# Thai Noodle Salad

THE ADDITION OF coconut milk and sesame oil gives an unusual nutty flavor to the dressing for this colorful noodle salad.

**INGREDIENTS**

*12 ounces dried somen noodles*
*1 large carrot, cut into thin strips*
*1 bunch asparagus, trimmed and cut into 1½-inch lengths*
*1 red bell pepper, seeded and cut into fine strips*
*4 ounces snow peas, topped, tailed and halved*
*4 ounces baby corn, halved lengthwise*
*4 ounces bean sprouts*
*4-ounce can water chestnuts, drained and finely sliced*
*1 lime, cut into wedges, 2 ounces roasted peanuts, coarsely chopped, and cilantro leaves, to garnish*

**For the dressing**

*3 tablespoons coarsely torn basil*
*5 tablespoons coarsely chopped mint*
*1 cup coconut milk*
*2 tablespoons dark sesame oil*
*1 tablespoon grated fresh ginger root*
*2 garlic cloves, finely chopped*
*juice of 1 lime*
*2 scallions, finely chopped*
*salt and cayenne pepper*

**Serves 4–6**

### COOK'S TIP

*Shredded omelet or sliced hard-cooked eggs are also popular garnishes, and tuna noodle salad is a children's favorite.*

1 Make the dressing. Combine the basil, mint, coconut milk, sesame oil, ginger, garlic, lime juice and scallions in a bowl and mix well. Season to taste with salt and cayenne pepper.

2 Cook the noodles in a saucepan of boiling water until just tender, following the directions on the package. Drain, rinse under cold running water and drain again.

3 Cook all the vegetables in separate saucepans of boiling lightly salted water until tender but still crisp. Drain, plunge them immediately into cold water and drain again.

4 Toss the noodles, vegetables and dressing together. Arrange on individual serving plates and garnish with the lime wedges, peanuts and cilantro leaves.

# Thai Chicken Soup

THIS CLASSIC ASIAN soup now enjoys worldwide popularity.

**INGREDIENTS**

*1 tablespoon vegetable oil*
*1 garlic clove, finely chopped*
*2 boneless chicken breasts, about 6 ounces each, skinned and chopped*
*½ teaspoon ground turmeric*
*¼ teaspoon hot chili powder*
*3 ounces coconut cream*
*3¾ cups hot chicken stock*
*2 tablespoons lemon or lime juice*
*2 tablespoons crunchy peanut butter*
*2 ounces dried thread egg noodles, broken into small pieces*
*1 tablespoon scallions, finely chopped*
*1 tablespoon chopped cilantro*
*salt and ground black pepper*
*2 tablespoons dry unsweetened coconut and ½ fresh red chile, seeded and finely chopped, to garnish*

**Serves 4**

1 Heat the oil in a large pan and fry the garlic for 1 minute until lightly golden. Add the chicken and spices and stir-fry for a further 3–4 minutes.

2 Heat the chicken stock in a large saucepan. Crumble the coconut cream into the hot chicken stock and stir until dissolved. Pour onto the chicken then add the lemon or lime juice, peanut butter and egg noodles.

3 Cover the pan and simmer for about 15 minutes. Add the scallions and fresh cilantro then season well and continue to cook for a further 5 minutes.

4 Meanwhile, place the dry unsweetened coconut and chile in a small frying pan and heat for 2–3 minutes, stirring frequently, until the coconut is golden and lightly browned.

5 Serve the soup in warmed bowls sprinkled with the fried coconut and chile.

# Chinese-style Vegetable Soup

**INGREDIENTS**

*5 cups vegetable or chicken stock*
*1 garlic clove, lightly crushed*
*1-inch piece fresh ginger root, peeled and cut into fine strips*
*2 tablespoons soy sauce*
*1 tablespoon cider vinegar*
*3 ounces fresh shiitake or white mushrooms, stalks removed and thinly sliced*
*2 large scallions, thinly sliced on the diagonal*
*1½ ounces dried rice vermicelli or other fine rice noodles, soaked in warm water until soft*
*6 ounces Napa cabbage leaves, shredded*
*a few fresh cilantro leaves*

**Serves 4**

1 Pour the stock into a saucepan. Add the garlic, ginger root, soy sauce and vinegar. Bring to a boil, then cover the pan and reduce the heat to very low. Let simmer gently for 10 minutes. Remove the garlic clove from the pan and discard.

### Cook's Tip

*The flavor of a homemade chicken or vegetable stock is vastly superior to stock cubes, so prepare this soup when you have fresh stock to hand.*

2 Add the sliced mushrooms and scallions and bring the soup back to a boil. Simmer for 5 minutes, uncovered, stirring occasionally. Add the noodles and shredded Napa cabbage. Simmer for 3–4 minutes, or until the noodles and vegetables are just tender. Stir in the cilantro leaves. Simmer for a final 1 minute. Serve the soup hot.

# Seafood Wonton Soup

THIS IS A VARIATION on the popular wonton soup that is traditionally prepared using pork.

**INGREDIENTS**

*2 ounces raw jumbo shrimp*
*2 ounces bay scallops*
*3 ounces skinless cod fillet, coarsely chopped*
*1 tablespoon finely chopped chives*
*1 teaspoon dry sherry*
*1 small egg white, lightly beaten*
*½ teaspoon sesame oil*
*¼ teaspoon salt*
*large pinch of ground white pepper*
*3¾ cups fish stock*
*20 wonton skins*
*2 romaine lettuce leaves, shredded*
*fresh cilantro leaves and garlic chives, to garnish*

**Serves 4**

### COOK'S TIP

*The filled wonton skins can be made ahead, then frozen for several weeks and cooked straight from the freezer.*

1 Shell and devein the shrimp. Rinse them well, pat them dry on paper towels and cut them into small pieces.

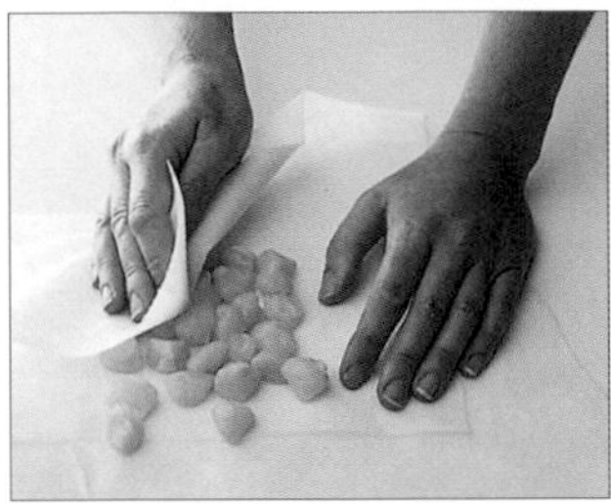

2 Rinse the scallops. Pat them dry, using paper towels. Chop them into small pieces roughly the same size as the shrimp.

3 Place the cod in a food processor and process until a paste is formed. Scrape into a bowl and stir in the shrimp, scallops, chives, sherry, egg white, sesame oil, salt and pepper. Mix thoroughly, cover and leave in a cool place to marinate for 20 minutes.

4 Heat the fish stock gently in a saucepan. Make the wontons. Place a teaspoonful of the seafood filling in the center of a wonton skin, then bring the corners together to meet at the top. Twist them together to enclose the filling. Fill the remaining wonton skins in the same way.

5 Bring a saucepan of water to a boil. Drop in the wontons. When the water returns to a boil, lower the heat and simmer for 5 minutes. Drain and divide among four bowls.

6 Add a portion of lettuce to each bowl. Bring the fish stock to a boil. Ladle it into each bowl, garnish with cilantro leaves and garlic chives.

# Noodle Soup with Pork and Pickle

USE SZECHUAN HOT pickle to give this soup a real kick.

**INGREDIENTS**

*4 cups chicken stock*
*12 ounces fresh or dried egg noodles*
*1 tablespoon dried shrimps, soaked in water*
*2 tablespoons vegetable oil*
*8 ounces lean pork, finely shredded*
*1 tablespoon yellow bean paste*
*1 tablespoon soy sauce*
*4 ounces Szechuan hot pickle, rinsed, drained and shredded*
*pinch of sugar*
*2 scallions, finely sliced, to garnish*

**Serves 4**

1 Bring the stock to a boil in a large saucepan. Add the noodles and cook until almost tender. Drain the dried shrimps, rinse them under cold water, drain again and add to the stock. Lower the heat and simmer for a further 2 minutes. Keep hot. Heat the oil in a frying pan or wok. Add the pork and stir-fry over high heat for about 3 minutes.

2 Add the bean paste and soy sauce to the pork; stir-fry for 1 minute more. Add the hot pickle with a pinch of sugar. Stir-fry for 1 minute more.

3 Divide the noodles and soup among individual serving bowls. Spoon the pork mixture on top, then sprinkle with the scallions and serve immediately.

# Snapper and Tamarind Noodle Soup

TAMARIND GIVES this light, fragrant noodle soup a slightly sour taste.

**INGREDIENTS**

*8 cups water*
*2¼ pounds red snapper (or other red fish such as mullet)*
*1 onion, sliced*
*2 ounces tamarind pods*
*1 tablespoon fish sauce*
*1 tablespoon sugar*
*2 tablespoons vegetable oil*
*2 garlic cloves, finely chopped*
*2 lemongrass stalks, very finely chopped*
*4 ripe tomatoes, coarsely chopped*
*2 tablespoons yellow bean paste*
*8 ounces dried rice vermicelli, soaked in warm water until soft*
*4 ounces bean sprouts*
*8–10 basil or mint sprigs*
*1 ounce roasted peanuts, ground*
*salt and ground black pepper*

**Serves 4**

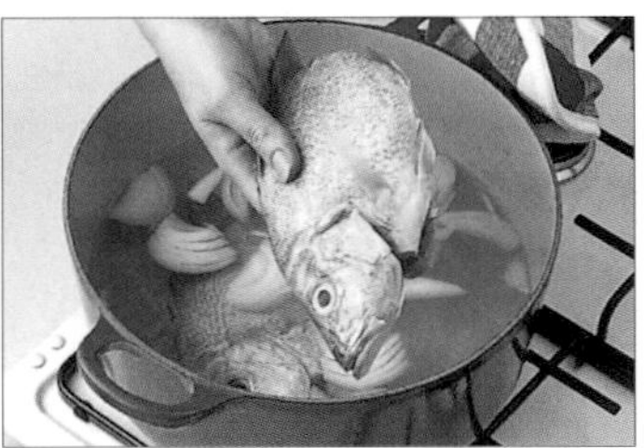

1 Bring the water to a boil in a saucepan. Lower the heat and add the fish and onion, with ½ teaspoon salt. Simmer gently until the fish is cooked through. Remove and set aside.

2 Add the tamarind, fish sauce and sugar to the stock. Cook for 5 minutes, then strain the stock into a large jug or bowl. Carefully remove all of the bones from the fish, keeping the flesh in big pieces.

3 Heat the oil in a large frying pan. Add the garlic and lemongrass and fry for a few seconds. Stir in the tomatoes and bean paste. Cook gently for 5–7 minutes, until the tomatoes are soft. Add the stock, bring back to a simmer and adjust the seasoning.

4 Drain the vermicelli. Plunge it into a saucepan of boiling water for a few minutes, drain and divide among individual serving bowls. Add the bean sprouts, fish, basil or mint, and sprinkle the ground peanuts on top. Top up each bowl with the hot soup.

# Hanoi Beef and Noodle Soup

**INGREDIENTS**

*1 onion*
*3–3½ pounds beef shank with bones*
*1-inch fresh ginger root*
*1 star anise*
*1 bay leaf*
*2 whole cloves*
*½ teaspoon fennel seeds*
*1 piece of cassia bark or cinnamon stick*
*12½ cups water*
*fish sauce, to taste*
*juice of 1 lime*
*5 ounces tenderloin steak*
*1 pound fresh flat rice noodles*

***Accompaniments***

*1 small red onion, sliced into rings*
*4 ounces bean sprouts*
*2 red chiles, seeded and sliced*
*2 scallions, finely sliced*
*handful of cilantro leaves*
*lime wedges*

**Serves 4–6**

1 Cut the onion in half. Broil under high heat, cut side up, until the exposed sides are caramelized, and deep brown. Put to one side.

2 Cut the meat into large chunks and place with the bones in a stock pot. Add the caramelized onion, ginger, star anise, bay leaf, cloves, fennel seeds and cassia bark or cinnamon stick.

3 Add the water, bring to a boil, reduce the heat and simmer gently for 2–3 hours, skimming off the fat and scum occasionally.

4 Using a slotted spoon, remove the meat from the stock; when cool enough to handle, cut into small pieces, discarding the bones. Strain the stock and return to the pan or stock pot together with the meat. Bring the mixture back to a boil and then season with the fish sauce and lime juice.

5 Slice the tenderloin steak very thinly and then chill until required. Place the accompaniments in separate bowls.

6 Cook the noodles in a large saucepan of boiling water until just tender. Drain and divide among individual serving bowls. Arrange the thinly sliced steak over the noodles, pour the hot stock on top and serve, offering the accompaniments separately so that each person may garnish their soup as they like.

# Seafood Laksa

FOR A SPECIAL OCCASION serve creamy rice noodles in a spicy coconut-flavored soup, topped with seafood. There is a fair amount of work involved in the preparation but you can make the soup base ahead.

**INGREDIENTS**

*4 red chiles, seeded and coarsely chopped*
*1 onion, coarsely chopped*
*1 piece balachan, the size of a stock cube*
*1 lemongrass stem, chopped*
*1 small piece fresh ginger root, coarsely chopped*
*6 macadamia nuts or almonds*
*4 tablespoons vegetable oil*
*1 teaspoon paprika*
*1 teaspoon ground turmeric*
*2 cups stock or water*
*2½ cups coconut milk*
*fish sauce, to taste*
*12 jumbo shrimp, shelled and deveined*
*8 scallops*
*8 ounces prepared squid, cut into rings*
*12 ounces dried rice vermicelli or rice noodles, soaked in warm water until soft*
*salt and ground black pepper*
*lime halves, to serve*

***For the garnish***

*¼ cucumber, cut into short thin sticks*
*2 red chiles, seeded and finely sliced*
*2 tablespoons mint leaves*
*2 tablespoons fried shallots or onions*

**Serves 4**

### COOK'S TIP

*Balachan is dried shrimp paste. It is sold in small blocks, powder or paste form and you will find it in Asian markets.*

1 In a blender or food processor, process the chiles, onion, blacan, lemongrass, ginger and nuts until smooth in texture.

2 Heat 3 tablespoons of the oil in a large saucepan. Add the chile paste and fry for 6 minutes. Stir in the paprika and turmeric and fry for about 2 minutes more.

3 Add the stock or water and the coconut milk to the pan. Bring to a boil, reduce the heat and simmer gently for 15–20 minutes. Season the mixture to taste with fish sauce.

4 Season the seafood. Heat the remaining oil in a frying pan, add the seafood and fry quickly for 2–3 minutes.

5 Add the drained noodles to the soup and heat through. Divide among individual serving bowls. Place the fried seafood on top, then garnish with the cucumber, chiles, mint and fried shallots or onions. Serve with the limes.

# Hot-and-Sour Soup

THIS SPICY, WARMING soup really whets the appetite and is the perfect introduction to a simple Chinese meal.

**INGREDIENTS**

*¼ ounce dried wood ear mushrooms*
*8 fresh shiitake mushrooms*
*3 ounces bean curd (tofu)*
*½ cup sliced, drained, canned bamboo shoots*
*3¾ cups vegetable stock*
*1 tablespoon sugar*
*3 tablespoons rice vinegar*
*1 tablespoon light soy sauce*
*¼ teaspoon chili oil*
*½ teaspoon salt*
*large pinch of ground white pepper*
*1 tablespoon cornstarch*
*1 tablespoon cold water*
*1 egg white*
*1 teaspoon sesame oil*
*2 scallions, cut into fine rings*
**Serves 4**

**COOK'S TIP**

*To transform this tasty soup into a nutritious light meal, add extra mushrooms, bean curd and bamboo shoots.*

1 Soak the wood ear mushrooms in hot water for 30 minutes or until soft. Drain well, trim off and discard the hard base from each and coarsely chop the wood ear mushrooms.

2 Remove and discard the stems from the shiitake mushrooms. Cut the caps into thin strips. Cut the bean curd into ½-inch cubes and shred the bamboo shoots finely.

3 Place the stock, mushrooms, bean curd, bamboo shoots and wood ears in a large saucepan. Bring the stock to a boil, lower the heat and simmer for about 5 minutes.

4 Stir in the sugar, vinegar, soy sauce, chili oil, salt and pepper. Mix the cornstarch to a paste with the water. Add the mixture to the soup, stirring constantly until it thickens slightly.

5 Lightly beat the egg white, then pour it slowly into the soup in a steady stream, stirring constantly. Cook, stirring, until the egg white changes color.

6 Add the sesame oil just before serving. Ladle into heated bowls and top each portion with scallion rings.

# Cheat's Shark's Fin Soup

SHARK'S FIN SOUP is a renowned delicacy. In this poor man's vegetarian version cellophane noodles, cut into short lengths, mimic shark's fin needles.

**INGREDIENTS**

*4 dried Chinese mushrooms*
*1½ tablespoons dried wood ear mushrooms*
*4 ounces cellophane noodles*
*2 tablespoons vegetable oil*
*2 carrots, cut into fine strips*
*4 ounces canned bamboo shoots, rinsed, drained and cut into fine strips*
*4 cups vegetable stock*
*1 tablespoon soy sauce*
*1 tablespoon arrowroot or potato flour*
*2 tablespoons water*
*1 egg white, beaten (optional)*
*1 teaspoon sesame oil*
*salt and ground black pepper*
*2 scallions, finely chopped, to garnish*
*Chinese red vinegar, to serve (optional)*

**Serves 4–6**

1 Soak the Chinese and wood ear mushrooms separately in warm water for 20 minutes. Drain well. Remove and discard stems from the mushrooms and slice the caps thinly. Cut the wood ear mushrooms into fine strips, discarding any hard bits. Soak the noodles in hot water until soft. Drain and cut into short lengths. Leave until required.

2 Heat the oil in a large saucepan. Add the mushrooms and stir-fry for 2 minutes. Add the wood ear mushrooms, stir-fry for 2 minutes, then stir in the carrots, bamboo shoots and noodles.

3 Add the stock to the pan. Bring to a boil, reduce the heat and simmer gently for 15–20 minutes. Season with salt, pepper and soy sauce.

4 Blend the arrowroot or potato flour with a little water. Pour into the soup, stirring all the time to prevent lumps from forming as the soup continues to simmer.

5 Remove the pan from the heat. Stir in the egg white if using, so that it sets to form small threads in the hot soup. Stir in the sesame oil, then pour the soup into individual serving bowls. Sprinkle each portion with chopped scallions and offer the Chinese red vinegar handed separately, if using.

# Tomato and Beef Soup

USE REALLY FRESH tomatoes and scallions to give this light beef broth a superb flavor.

**INGREDIENTS**

*3 ounces rump steak, trimmed of fat*
*3¾ cups beef stock*
*2 tablespoons tomato purée*
*6 tomatoes, halved, seeded and chopped*
*2 teaspoons sugar*
*1 tablespoon cornstarch*
*1 tablespoon cold water*
*1 egg white*
*½ teaspoon sesame oil*
*2 scallions, finely shredded*
*salt and ground black pepper*
**Serves 4**

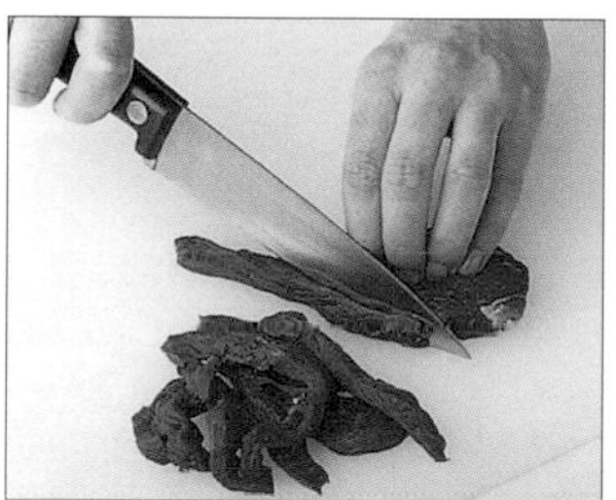

1 Cut the beef into thin strips and place it in a large saucepan. Pour over boiling water to cover. Cook for 2 minutes, then drain thoroughly and set aside.

2 Bring the stock to a boil in a clean pan. Stir in the tomato paste, tomatoes and sugar. Add the beef strips, allow the stock to boil, lower the heat and simmer for 2 minutes.

3 Mix the cornstarch to a paste with the water. Add the mixture to the soup, stirring constantly until it thickens slightly. Lightly beat the egg white in a separate cup.

**COOK'S TIP**

*Try the soup topped with thin strips of fresh basil instead of scallions for a more Mediterranean taste.*

4 Pour the egg white into the soup in a steady stream, stirring all the time. As soon as the egg white changes color, add salt and pepper, stir the soup and pour it into heated bowls. Drizzle each portion with a few drops of sesame oil, sprinkle with the scallions and serve.

# Seafood Soup Noodles

AUDIBLE SOUNDS of enjoyment are traditionally a compliment to the Chinese cook, so slurping this superb soup is not only permissible, but positively desirable.

**INGREDIENTS**

*6 ounces large shrimp, shelled and deveined*
*8 ounces monkfish fillet, cut into chunks*
*8 ounces salmon fillet, cut into chunks*
*1 teaspoon vegetable oil*
*1 tablespoon dry white wine*
*8 ounces dried egg vermicelli*
*5 cups fish stock*
*1 carrot, thinly sliced*
*8 ounces asparagus, cut into 2-inch lengths*
*2 tablespoons dark soy sauce*
*1 teaspoon sesame oil*
*salt and ground black pepper*
*2 scallions, cut into thin rings, to garnish*

**Serves 4**

**VARIATION**

*Try this simple recipe using rice vermicelli for a slightly different texture and taste.*

1 Mix the shrimp and fish in a bowl. Add the vegetable oil and wine with ¼ teaspoon salt and a little pepper. Mix lightly, cover and marinate in a cool plate for 15 minutes.

2 Bring a large saucepan of water to a boil and cook the noodles for 4 minutes until just tender, or according to the instructions on the package. Drain the noodles thoroughly through a colander and divide among four serving bowls. Keep hot.

3 Bring the fish stock to a boil in a separate pan. Add the shrimp and monkfish, cook for 1 minute, add the salmon and cook for 2 minutes.

4 Using a slotted spoon, carefully lift the fish and shrimp out of the stock, add to the noodles in the serving bowls and keep hot.

5 Strain the stock through a strainer lined with cheesecloth into a clean pan. Bring to a boil and cook the carrot and asparagus for 2 minutes, then stir in the soy sauce and sesame oil, with salt to taste. Stir well.

6 Pour the stock and vegetables over the noodles and seafood, garnish with the scallions and serve hot.

# Chicken Vermicelli Soup with Egg Shreds

THIS SOUP is very quick and easy—you can add all sorts of extra ingredients to vary the taste, using up leftovers such as scallions, mushrooms, a few shrimp or chopped salami.

**INGREDIENTS**

*3 eggs*
*2 tablespoons chopped fresh cilantro or parsley*
*6¼ cups good chicken stock or canned consommé*
*4 ounces dried rice vermicelli or angel hair pasta*
*4 ounces cooked chicken breast, sliced*
*salt and ground black pepper*

**Serves 4–6**

1 First make the egg shreds. Whisk the eggs together in a small bowl and stir in the cilantro or parsley until well combined.

2 Heat a small non-stick frying pan and pour in 2–3 tablespoons egg, swirling to cover the base evenly. Cook until set. Repeat until all the mixture is used up.

3 Roll each omelet up and slice thinly into shreds. Set aside.

4 Bring the stock or consommé to a boil and add the pasta, breaking it up into short lengths. Cook for 3–5 minutes until tender.

5 Add the chicken, and salt and pepper to taste. Heat through for about 2–3 minutes, then stir in the egg shreds. Serve immediately.

**VARIATION**

*To make a Thai variation, use Chinese rice noodles instead of pasta. Stir ½ teaspoon dried lemongrass, 2 small whole fresh chiles and 4 tablespoons coconut milk into the stock. Add 4 sliced scallions and plenty of chopped fresh cilantro.*

# Chicken and Buckwheat Noodle Soup

BUCKWHEAT OR SOBA noodles are widely enjoyed in Japan. The simplest way of serving them is in hot seasoned broth. Almost any topping can be added and the variations are endless.

**INGREDIENTS**

*8 ounces skinless, boneless chicken breasts*
*½ cup soy sauce*
*1 tablespoon sake*
*4 cups chicken stock*
*2 pieces young leek, cut into 1-inch pieces*
*6 ounces spinach leaves*
*11 ounces fresh or dried buckwheat or soba noodles*
*sesame seeds, toasted, to garnish*

**Serves 4**

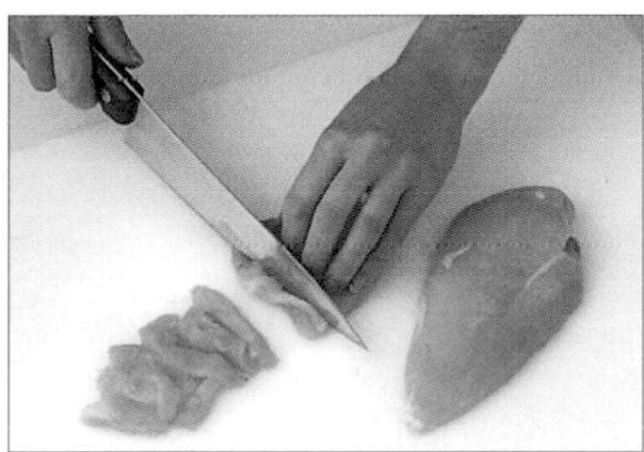

1 Slice the chicken diagonally into bite-size pieces. Combine the soy sauce and sake in a saucepan. Bring to a simmer. Then add the chicken and cook gently for about 3 minutes until it is tender. Keep hot.

2 Bring the stock to a boil in a saucepan. Add the leek and simmer for 3 minutes, then add the spinach. Remove from the heat but keep warm.

3 Cook the noodles in a large saucepan of boiling water until just tender, according to the instructions on the package.

4 Drain the noodles and divide among individual serving bowls. Ladle the hot soup into the bowls, then add a portion of chicken to each. Serve immediately, sprinkled with sesame seeds.

**COOK'S TIP**

*Home-made chicken stock makes the world of difference to noodle soup. Make a big batch of stock, use as much as you need and freeze the rest until required. Put about 3–3½ pounds meaty chicken bones into a large saucepan, add 12½ cups water and slowly bring to a boil, skimming off any foam that rises to the top. Add 2 slices fresh ginger root, 2 garlic cloves, 2 celery stalks, 4 scallions, a handful of cilantro stems and about 10 peppercorns, crushed, then reduce the heat and simmer the stock for 2–2½ hours. Remove from the heat and let cool, uncovered and undisturbed. Strain the stock into a clean bowl, leaving the last dregs behind as they tend to cloud the soup. Use as required, removing any fat that congeals on top.*

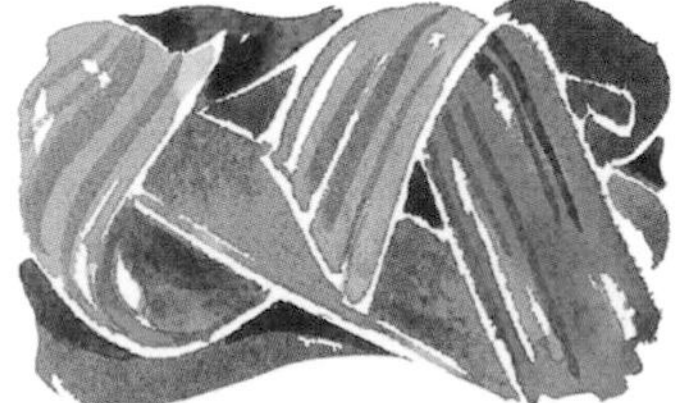

# Buckwheat Noodles with Smoked Trout

THE LIGHT, CRISP texture of the bok choy balances the earthy flavors of the mushrooms and the smokiness of the trout.

**INGREDIENTS**

*12 ounces fresh or dried buckwheat noodles*
*2 tablespoons vegetable oil*
*4 ounces fresh shiitake mushrooms, quartered*
*2 garlic cloves, finely chopped*
*1 tablespoon grated fresh ginger root*
*8 ounces bok choy, shredded*
*1 scallion, finely sliced diagonally*
*1 tablespoon dark sesame oil*
*2 tablespoons mirin*
*2 tablespoons soy sauce*
*2 smoked trout, skinned and boned*
*salt and ground black pepper*
*2 tablespoons cilantro leaves and 2 teaspoons sesame seeds, toasted, to garnish*

**Serves 4**

1 Cook the buckwheat noodles in a saucepan of boiling water until tender, according to the instructions on the package.

2 Meanwhile heat the oil in a large frying pan. Add the mushrooms and sauté over medium heat for 3 minutes. Add the garlic, ginger and bok choy, and sauté for 2 minutes.

3 Drain the noodles and add them to the mushroom mixture with the scallions, sesame oil, mirin and soy sauce. Toss and season with salt and pepper to taste.

4 Break the smoked trout in bite-size pieces. Arrange the noodle mixture on individual serving plates. Place the smoked trout on top of the noodles.

5 Garnish the noodles with cilantro leaves and sesame seeds and serve them immediately.

**COOK'S TIP**

*Mirin, or rice wine, is easily available but if you don't want to buy it specially for this dish, use sweet sherry, or omit altogether.*

# Noodles with Ginger and Cilantro

HERE IS A SIMPLE noodle dish that goes well with most Asian dishes. It can also be served as a snack for 2–3 people.

**INGREDIENTS**

*handful of cilantro sprigs*
*2 cups dried egg noodles*
*3 tablespoons groundnut oil*
*2-inch piece fresh ginger root, cut into fine shreds*
*6–8 scallions, cut into shreds*
*2 tablespoons light soy sauce*
*salt and ground black pepper*

**Serves 4–6**

1 Strip the leaves from the cilantro stalks by hand. Put them in a pile on a cutting board and coarsely chop them using a cleaver or a large sharp knife.

2 Cook the noodles according to the instructions on the package. Rinse under cold water and drain well. Toss in 1 tablespoon of the oil.

3 Heat a wok until hot, add the remaining oil and swirl it around. Add the ginger and stir-fry for a few seconds, then add the noodles and scallions. Stir-fry for 3–4 minutes until hot.

4 Sprinkle the soy sauce, cilantro and seasoning over. Toss well, then serve immediately.

**COOK'S TIP**

*Many of the dried egg noodles available are sold packed in layers. As a guide allow 1 layer of noodles per person as an average portion for a main dish.*

# Noodles with Asparagus and Saffron

A RATHER ELEGANT summery dish with fragrant saffron cream. The delicate fresh flavor of the asparagus is enhanced by the wine and lemon.

**INGREDIENTS**

*1 pound young asparagus*
*pinch of saffron strands*
*2 tablespoons hot water*
*1 ounce butter*
*2 shallots, finely chopped*
*2 tablespoons white wine*
*1 cup heavy cream*
*grated rind and juice of ½ lemon*
*4 ounces peas*
*12 ounces dried somen noodles*
*½ bunch chervil, coarsely chopped*
*salt and ground black pepper*
*grated Parmesan cheese (optional)*
**Serves 4**

1 Cut off the asparagus tips (about 2 inches in length), then slice the remaining spears into short rounds. Steep the saffron in the hot water in a cup or a small bowl.

2 Melt the butter in a saucepan, add the shallots and cook over low heat for 3 minutes until soft. Add the white wine, cream and saffron infusion. Bring to a boil, reduce the heat and simmer gently for 5 minutes or until the sauce thickens to a coating consistency. Add the grated lemon rind and juice, and season to taste.

3 Bring a saucepan of lightly salted water to a boil. Blanch the asparagus tips, scoop them out and add to the sauce, then cook the peas and short asparagus rounds in the boiling water until just tender. Scoop them out and add to the sauce.

4 Cook the somen noodles in the same water until just tender, following the directions on the package. Drain, place in a wide pan and pour the sauce over the top.

5 Toss the noodles with the sauce and vegetables, adding the chervil and more salt and pepper if needed. Finally, sprinkle with the grated Parmesan, if using, and serve hot.

# Noodles with Sun-dried Tomatoes

**INGREDIENTS**

*12 ounces dried somen noodles*
*3 tablespoons olive oil*
*20 uncooked jumbo shrimp, shelled and deveined*
*2 garlic cloves, finely chopped*
*3–4 tablespoons sun-dried tomato paste*
*salt and ground black pepper*

***For the garnish***
*handful of basil leaves*
*2 tablespoons sun-dried tomatoes in oil, drained and cut into strips*
**Serves 4**

### Cook's Tip

*Ready-made sun-dried tomato paste is readily available, however you can make your own simply by processing bottled sun-dried tomatoes with their oil. You could also add a couple of anchovy fillets and some capers if you like.*

1 Cook the noodles in a large saucepan of boiling water until tender, following the directions on the package. Drain.

2 Heat half the oil in a large frying pan. Add the shrimp and garlic and fry them over medium heat for 3–5 minutes, until the shrimp turn pink and are firm to the touch.

3 Stir in 1 tablespoon of the sun-dried tomato paste and mix well. Using a slotted spoon, transfer the shrimp to a bowl and keep hot.

4 Add the remaining oil and reheat the pan. Stir in the remaining sun-dried tomato paste. You may need to add a spoonful of water to thin the mixture.

5 When the mixture starts to sizzle, toss in the noodles. Season and mix.

6 Return the shrimp to the pan and toss to combine. Serve immediately in plates or bowls garnished with the basil and strips of sun-dried tomatoes.

# Crispy Fried Rice Vermicelli in a Garlic Sweet and Sour Sauce

THIS DISH IS USUALLY served at celebration meals. It is a crisp tangle of fried rice vermicelli, which is tossed in a piquant sauce.

**INGREDIENTS**

*4 tablespoons oil*
*1½ cups dried rice vermicelli*
*2 garlic cloves, crushed*
*4-6 dried chiles, seeded and chopped*
*2 tablespoons shallots, chopped*
*1 tablespoon dried shrimps, soaked in water and rinsed*
*4 ounces lean pork, finely shredded*
*4 ounces raw peeled shrimp, thawed if frozen, chopped*
*2 tablespoons brown bean sauce*
*2 tablespoons rice wine vinegar*
*3 tablespoons fish sauce*
*3 ounces palm sugar or jaggery*
*2 tablespoons tamarind juice or lime juice*
*2½ cups bean sprouts*

***For the garnish***
*2 scallions, shredded*
*2 tablespoons cilantro leaves*
*2-egg omelet, rolled and sliced*
*2 fresh red chiles, chopped*
**Serves 4**

1 Heat the oil in a wok. Cut or break the rice vermicelli into small handfuls about 3 inches long. Deep-fry these in the hot oil until they puff up. Lift out with a spider or slotted spoon and drain on paper towels.

2 Ladle off all but 2 tablespoons of the oil, pouring it into a pan and setting aside to cool. Reheat the oil in the wok and fry the garlic, chiles, shallots and shrimps for 1 minute.

3 Add the pork and stir-fry for 3-4 minutes, until no longer pink. Add the shrimp and fry for 2 minutes. Spoon into a bowl and set aside.

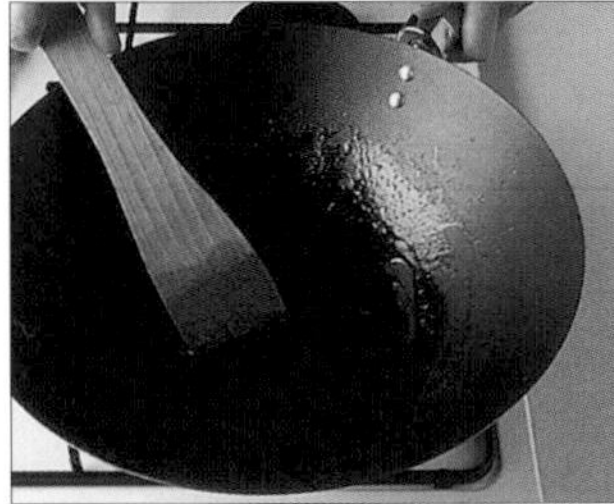

4 Add the brown bean sauce, vinegar, fish sauce and sugar. Heat gently, stirring in any sediment. Bring to a gentle boil, stir to dissolve the sugar and cook until thick and syrupy.

5 Add the tamarind or lime juice to the sauce and adjust the seasoning as necessary. The sauce should be sweet, sour and salty. Lower the heat, then return the pork and shrimp mixture to the wok. Add the bean-sprouts and stir them into the sauce.

6 Add the fried rice noodles and toss gently to coat them with the sauce without breaking them up too much. Transfer the mixture to a large serving platter. Garnish with shredded scallions, cilantro leaves, omelet strips and fresh red chiles.

**COOK'S TIP**

*Pickled garlic can also be used as a garnish. Thai garlic is smaller than European garlic; the heads are pickled whole, in sweet and sour brine.*

# Fried Singapore Noodles

THAI FISHCAKES vary in their size and their spiciness. They are available from Asian markets.

**INGREDIENTS**

*6 ounces dried rice vermicelli*
*4 tablespoons vegetable oil*
*½ teaspoon salt*
*¾ cup cooked shrimp*
*6 ounces cooked pork, cut into matchsticks*
*1 green bell pepper, seeded and cut into short thin sticks*
*½ teaspoon sugar*
*2 teaspoons curry powder*
*3 ounces Thai fishcakes*
*2 teaspoons dark soy sauce*
**Serves 4**

1 Soak the rice noodles in warm water for about 10 minutes, drain well through a colander, then pat dry with paper towels.

2 Heat a wok, then add half the oil. When the oil is hot, add the noodles and half the salt and stir-fry for 2 minutes. Transfer to a warmed serving dish and keep warm.

3 Heat the remaining oil and add the shrimp, pork, pepper, sugar, curry powder and remaining salt. Stir-fry for 1 minute.

4 Return the noodles to the pan and stir-fry with the Thai fishcakes for 2 minutes. Stir in the soy sauce and serve immediately.

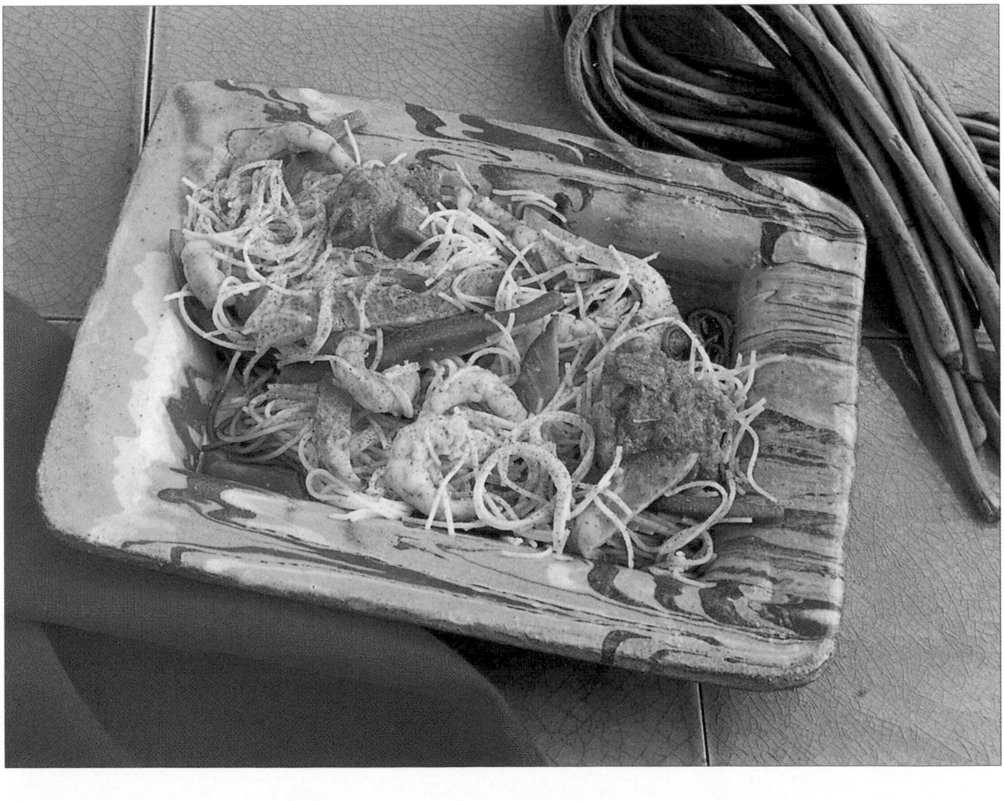

# Chow Mein

ONE OF THE MOST well-known Chinese noodle dishes.

**INGREDIENTS**

*8 ounces fresh or dried egg noodles*
*2 tablespoons oil*
*1 onion, chopped*
*½-inch piece fresh ginger root, chopped*
*2 garlic cloves, crushed*
*2 tablespoons soy sauce*
*¼ cup dry white wine*
*2 teaspoons Chinese five-spice powder*
*4 cups ground pork*
*4 scallions, sliced*
*2 ounces oyster mushrooms*
*3 ounces bamboo shoots*
*1 tablespoon sesame oil*
*shrimp crackers, to serve*
**Serves 4**

1 Cook the noodles in boiling water for 4 minutes and drain.

2 Meanwhile, heat the oil in a wok or frying pan and add the onion, ginger, garlic, soy sauce and wine. Stir-fry for 1 minute. Stir in the Chinese five-spice powder.

3 Add the ground pork and cook for 10 minutes, stirring constantly. Add the scallions, oyster mushrooms and bamboo shoots and continue to cook for a further 5 minutes still stirring.

4 Stir in the noodles and sesame oil. Mix all the ingredients together well and serve in bowls immediately with shrimp crackers.

# Spicy Fried Rice Sticks with Shrimp

THIS RECIPE IS BASED on the classic Thai noodle dish called Pad Thai. Popular all over Thailand, it is enjoyed morning, noon and night.

**INGREDIENTS**

*½ ounce dried shrimps*
*1 tablespoon tamarind pulp*
*4 tablespoons hot water*
*3 tablespoons Thai fish sauce (nam pla)*
*1 tablespoon sugar*
*2 garlic cloves, chopped*
*2 fresh red chiles, seeded and chopped*
*3 tablespoons groundnut oil*
*2 eggs, beaten*
*8 ounces dried rice sticks, soaked in warm water for 30 minutes, refreshed under cold running water and drained*
*8 ounces cooked shelled jumbo shrimp*
*3 scallions, cut into 1-inch lengths*
*scant ½ cup bean sprouts*
*2 tablespoons coarsely chopped, roasted unsalted peanuts*
*2 tablespoons chopped cilantro*
*lime slices, to garnish*
**Serves 4**

**VARIATION**

*For a vegetarian dish omit the dried shrimps and replace the jumbo shrimp with cubes of deep-fried tofu.*

1 Put the dried shrimps in a small bowl and pour over enough warm water to cover. Let soak for 30 minutes until soft; drain.

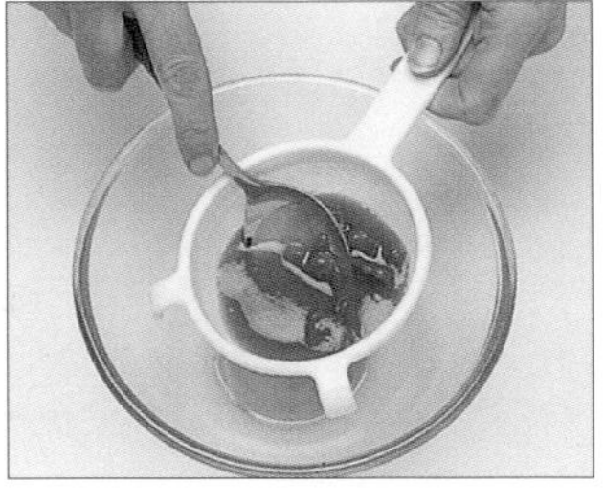

2 Put the tamarind pulp in a bowl with the hot water. Blend together, then press through a strainer to extract 2 tablespoons thick tamarind water. Mix the tamarind water with the fish sauce and sugar.

3 Using a mortar and pestle, pound the garlic and chiles to form a paste. Heat a wok over medium heat, add 1 tablespoon of the oil, then add the beaten eggs and stir for 1–2 minutes until scrambled. Remove and set aside. Wipe the wok clean.

4 Reheat the wok, until hot, add the remaining oil, then the chili paste and soaked shrimps and stir-fry for 1 minute. Add the rice sticks and tamarind mixture and continue to stir-fry for 3–4 minutes.

5 Add the scrambled eggs, shrimp, scallions, bean sprouts, peanuts and cilantro, then stir-fry for 2 minutes until well mixed. Serve immediately, garnishing each portion with lime slices.

# Stir-fried Turkey with Broccoli and Mushrooms

THIS IS A REALLY easy, tasty supper dish which works just as well if you use chicken instead of turkey.

**INGREDIENTS**

*4 ounces broccoli flowerets*
*4 scallions*
*1 teaspoon cornstarch*
*3 tablespoons oyster sauce*
*1 tablespoon dark soy sauce*
*½ cup chicken stock*
*2 teaspoons lemon juice*
*3 tablespoons groundnut oil*
*1 pound turkey steaks, cut into strips, about ¼ x 2 inches*
*1 small onion, chopped*
*2 garlic cloves, crushed*
*2 teaspoons grated fresh ginger root*
*1 cup fresh shiitake mushrooms, sliced*
*3 ounces baby corn, halved lengthwise*
*1 tablespoon sesame oil*
*salt and ground black pepper*
*egg noodles, to serve*
**Serves 4**

1 Divide the broccoli flowerets into smaller sprigs and cut the stalks into thin diagonal slices.

2 Finely chop the white parts of the scallions and slice the green parts into thin shreds.

3 In a bowl, blend together the cornstarch, oyster sauce, soy sauce, stock and lemon juice. Set aside.

4 Heat a wok until hot, add 2 tablespoons of the groundnut oil and swirl it around. Add the turkey and stir-fry for about 2 minutes until golden and crispy at the edges. Remove the turkey from the wok and keep warm while you cook the vegetables.

5 Add the remaining groundnut oil to the wok and stir-fry the chopped onion, garlic and ginger over medium heat for about 1 minute. Increase the heat to high, add the broccoli, mushrooms and corn and stir-fry for 2 minutes.

6 Return the turkey to the wok, then add the sauce with the chopped white scallion and seasoning. Cook, stirring, until the sauce has thickened. Stir in the sesame oil. Serve on a bed of egg noodles with the shredded scallion.

# Lemongrass Pork

CHILES AND LEMONGRASS flavor this simple stir-fry, while peanuts add crunch.

**INGREDIENTS**

*1½ pounds boneless loin of pork*
*2 lemongrass stems, finely chopped*
*4 scallions, thinly sliced*
*1 teaspoon salt*
*12 black peppercorns, coarsely crushed*
*2 tablespoons groundnut oil*
*2 garlic cloves, chopped*
*2 fresh red chiles, seeded and chopped*
*1 teaspoon brown sugar*
*2 tablespoons Thai fish sauce (nam pla), or to taste*
*¼ cup roasted unsalted peanuts, chopped*
*salt and ground black pepper*
*coarsely torn cilantro leaves, to garnish*
*rice noodles, to serve*

**Serves 4**

### COOK'S TIP

*If you can't get hold of lemongrass stems, use powdered, which is readily available in most supermarkets.*

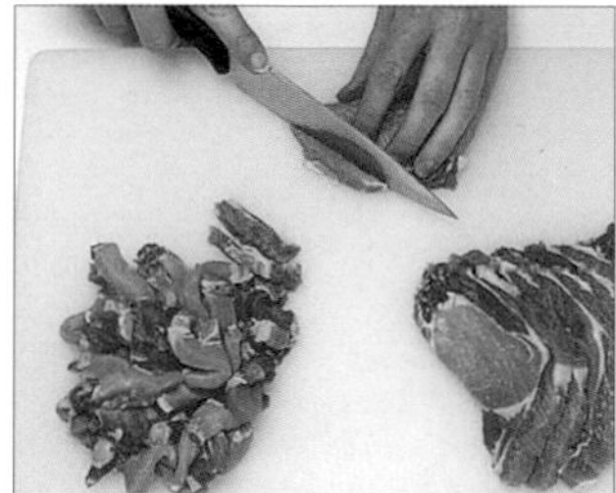

1 Trim any excess fat from the pork. Cut the meat across into ¼-inch thick slices, then cut each slice into ¼-inch strips. Put the pork into a bowl with the lemongrass, scallions, salt and crushed peppercorns; mix well. Cover and let marinate for 30 minutes.

2 Heat a wok until hot, add the oil and swirl it around. Add the pork mixture and stir-fry for 3 minutes.

3 Add the garlic and chiles and stir-fry for a further 5–8 minutes.

4 Add the sugar, fish sauce and peanuts, and toss to mix. Taste and adjust the seasoning, if necessary. Serve immediately on a bed of rice noodles, garnished with coarsely torn cilantro leaves.

# Asian Vegetable Noodles

THE SUPERIOR TASTE of balsamic vinegar makes this dish really special.

**INGREDIENTS**

*1¼ pounds thin egg noodles*
*1 red onion*
*4 ounces shiitake mushrooms*
*3 tablespoons sesame oil*
*3 tablespoons dark soy sauce*
*1 tablespoon balsamic vinegar*
*2 teaspoons sugar*
*1 teaspoon salt*
*celery leaves, to garnish*
**Serves 6**

1 Cook the noodles in plenty of salted boiling water according to the instructions on the package until

2 Cut the red onion and the shiitake mushrooms into thin slices, using a sharp knife.

3 Heat a wok, then add 1 tablespoon of the sesame oil. When the oil is hot, stir-fry the onion and mushrooms for about 2 minutes.

4 Drain the noodles, then add to the wok with the soy sauce, balsamic vinegar, sugar and salt. Stir-fry for 1 minute, then add the remaining sesame oil, and serve garnished with celery leaves.

# Rice Noodles with Vegetable Chile Sauce

**INGREDIENTS**

*1 tablespoon sunflower oil*
*1 onion, chopped*
*2 garlic cloves, crushed*
*1 fresh red chile, seeded and finely chopped*
*1 red bell pepper, seeded and diced*
*2 carrots, finely chopped*
*6 ounces baby corn, halved*
*8 ounce canned sliced bamboo shoots, rinsed and drained*
*1 can (14 ounces) red kidney beans, rinsed and drained*
*1¼ cups passata or strained tomatoes*
*1 tablespoon gluten-free soy sauce*
*1 teaspoon ground coriander*
*2¼ cups dried rice noodles*
*2 tablespoons chopped cilantro or parsley*
*salt and ground black pepper*
*fresh parsley sprigs, to garnish*

**Serves 4**

1 Heat the oil, add the onion, garlic, chile and red bell pepper and cook for 5 minutes, stirring. Stir in the carrots, corn, bamboo shoots, kidney beans, passata or strained tomatoes, soy sauce and ground coriander.

2 Bring to a boil, then cover, reduce the heat, and simmer gently for 30 minutes until the vegetables are tender, stirring occasionally. Season with salt and pepper to taste.

3 Meanwhile, place the noodles in a bowl and cover with boiling water. Stir with a fork and let stand for 3–4 minutes, or according to the instructions on the package. Rinse with boiling water and drain.

4 Stir the cilantro or parsley into the sauce. Spoon the noodles on to warmed serving plates and top with the sauce. Garnish with parsley and serve.

**COOK'S TIP**

*After handling chiles, wash your hands. Chiles contain volatile oils that can irritate and burn sensitive areas, such as the eyes, if they are touched.*

# Vegetable and Egg Noodle Ribbons

SERVE THIS ELEGANT, colorful dish with a tossed green salad as a light lunch or as an appetizer dish for six to eight people.

**INGREDIENTS**

*1 large carrot, peeled*
*2 zucchini*
*2 ounces butter*
*1 tablespoon olive oil*
*6 fresh shiitake mushrooms, finely sliced*
*2 ounces frozen peas, thawed*
*12 ounces fresh or dried broad egg ribbon noodles*
*2 teaspoons chopped mixed herbs (such as marjoram, chives and basil)*
*salt and ground black pepper*
*1 ounce Parmesan cheese, to serve (optional)*

**Serves 4**

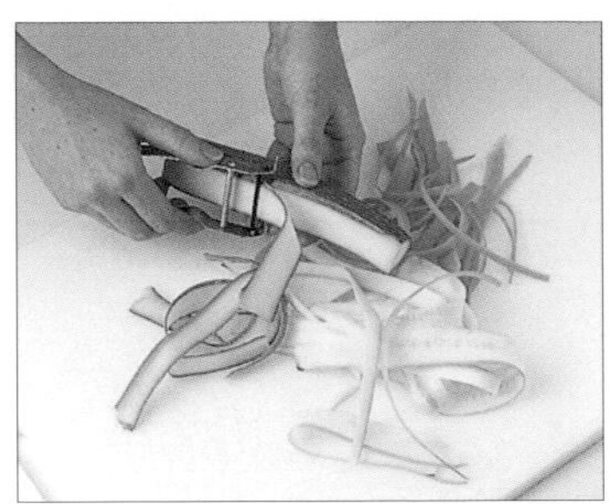

1 Using a vegetable peeler, carefully slice thin strips from the carrot and from the zucchini to form ribbons.

2 Heat the butter with the olive oil in a large frying pan. Stir in the carrots and shiitake mushrooms; fry for 2 minutes. Add the zucchini and peas and stir-fry until the zucchini are cooked, but still crisp. Season with salt and pepper.

3 Meanwhile, cook the noodles in a large saucepan of boiling water until just tender. Drain the noodles well and turn them into a bowl. Add the vegetables and toss to mix.

4 Sprinkle the fresh herbs over and season to taste. If using the Parmesan cheese, grate or shave it over the top. Toss lightly and serve.

# Buckwheat Noodles with Goat Cheese

WHEN YOU DON'T FEEL like doing a lot of cooking, try this good fast supper dish. The unrefined flavor of buckwheat goes well with the nutty, peppery taste of arugula leaves, offset by the deliciously creamy goat cheese.

**INGREDIENTS**

*12 ounces fresh or dried buckwheat noodles*
*2 ounces butter*
*2 garlic cloves, finely chopped*
*4 shallots, sliced*
*3 ounces hazelnuts, lightly roasted and roughly chopped*
*large handful arugula leaves*
*6 ounces goat cheese*
*salt and ground black pepper*

**Serves 4**

1 Cook the noodles in a large saucepan of boiling water until just tender according to the instructions on the package. Drain well.

2 Heat the butter in a large frying pan. Add the garlic and shallots and cook for 2–3 minutes, stirring all the time, until the shallots are soft.

3 Add the hazelnuts and fry for about 1 minute. Add the arugula leaves and, when they start to wilt, toss in the noodles and heat through.

4 Season with salt and pepper. Crumble in the goat cheese and serve immediately.

# Chinese Mushrooms with Noodles

RED FERMENTED bean curd adds a unique flavor to this hearty vegetarian dish. It is brick red in color, with a very strong, cheese flavor, and is made by fermenting bean curd (tofu) with salt, red rice and rice wine.

**INGREDIENTS**

*4 ounces dried Chinese mushrooms*
*1 ounce dried wood ear mushrooms*
*4 ounces dried bean curd*
*2 tablespoons vegetable oil*
*2 garlic cloves, finely chopped*
*2 slices fresh ginger root, finely chopped*
*10 Szechuan peppercorns, crushed*
*1 tablespoon red fermented bean curd*
*½ star anise*
*pinch of sugar*
*1–2 tablespoons soy sauce*
*2 ounces cellophane noodles, soaked in hot water until soft*
*salt*

**Serves 4**

1 Soak the Chinese mushrooms and wood ear mushrooms separately in bowls of hot water for about 30 minutes. Break the dried bean curd into small pieces and soak in water according to the instructions on the package.

2 Strain the mushrooms, reserving the liquid. Squeeze as much liquid from the mushrooms as possible, then discard the mushroom stems. Cut the cups in half if they are large.

3 The wood ears should swell to five times their original size. Drain them, rinse thoroughly and drain again. Cut off any gritty parts, then cut each wood ear into two or three pieces.

4 Heat the oil in a heavy pan. Add the garlic, ginger and Szechuan peppercorns. Fry for a few seconds, then add the mushrooms and red fermented bean curd. Mix lightly and fry for 5 minutes.

5 Add the reserved mushroom liquid to the pan, with sufficient water to completely cover the mushrooms. Add the star anise, sugar and soy sauce, then cover and simmer for 30 minutes.

6 Add the chopped wood ears and reconstituted bean curd pieces to the pan. Cover and cook for about 10 minutes.

7 Drain the cellophane noodles, add them to the mixture and cook for a further 10 minutes until tender, adding more liquid if necessary. Add salt to taste and serve.

**COOK'S TIP**

*If you can't find Szechuan peppercorns, then use ordinary black ones instead.*

# Toasted Noodles with Vegetables

SLIGHTLY CRISP NOODLE cakes topped with vegetables make a fabulous dinner party dish.

**INGREDIENTS**

*1½ cups dried egg vermicelli*
*1 tablespoon vegetable oil*
*2 garlic cloves, finely chopped*
*1 cup baby corn*
*1 cup fresh shiitake mushrooms, halved*
*3 celery stalks, sliced*
*1 carrot, diagonally sliced*
*1 cup snow peas*
*¾ cup sliced, drained, canned bamboo shoots*
*1 tablespoon cornstarch*
*1 tablespoon cold water*
*1 tablespoon dark soy sauce*
*1 teaspoon sugar*
*1¼ cups vegetable stock*
*salt and ground white pepper*
*scallion curls, to garnish*

**Serves 4**

1 Bring a saucepan of water to a boil. Add the egg vermicelli and cook according to instructions on the package until just tender. Drain, refresh under cold water, drain again, then dry thoroughly on paper towels.

2 Heat ½ teaspoon oil in a non-stick frying pan or wok. Fry half the noodles for 2–3 minutes until lightly toasted. Turn and fry the other side, then slide onto a heated serving plate. Repeat with the remaining noodles to make two cakes. Keep hot.

3 Heat the remaining oil in the clean pan, then fry the garlic for a few seconds. Cut the corn in half lengthwise, add to the pan with the mushrooms, then stir-fry for 3 minutes, adding a little water, if needed, to prevent the mixture burning. Then add the celery, carrot, snow peas and bamboo shoots. Stir-fry the mixture for 2 minutes or until the vegetables are tender-crisp.

4 Mix the cornstarch to a paste with the water. Add the mixture to the pan with the soy sauce, sugar and stock. Cook, stirring, until the sauce thickens. Season with salt and white pepper. Divide the vegetable mixture between the noodle cakes, garnish with the scallion curls and serve immediately. Each noodle cake serves two people.

# Tomato Noodles with Fried Egg

THIS DISH MAKES a good brunch or supper dish; if you are cooking for children, omit the chile.

**INGREDIENTS**

*12 ounces medium-thick dried noodles*
*4 tablespoons vegetable oil*
*2 garlic cloves, very finely chopped*
*4 shallots, chopped*
*½ teaspoon chili powder*
*1 teaspoon paprika*
*2 carrots, finely diced*
*4 ounces white mushrooms, quartered*
*2 ounces peas*
*1 tablespoon tomato ketchup*
*2 teaspoons tomato paste*
*butter for frying*
*4 eggs*
*salt and ground black pepper*

**Serves 4**

1 Cook the noodles in a saucepan of boiling water according to the instructions on the package until just tender. Drain, rinse under cold running water and drain well.

2 Heat the oil in a wok or large frying pan. Add the garlic, shallots, chili powder and paprika. Stir-fry for about 1 minute, then add the diced carrots, mushrooms and peas. Continue to stir-fry until the vegetables are cooked.

3 Stir the tomato ketchup and paste into the vegetable mixture in the wok. Add the noodles and cook over medium heat until the noodles are heated through and have taken on the reddish tinge of the paprika and tomato.

4 Meanwhile melt the butter in a frying pan and fry each of the eggs. Season the noodle mixture, divide it among four serving plates and top each portion with one of the fried eggs.

# Curry Fried Noodles

ON ITS OWN, bean curd (tofu) has a fairly bland flavor, but by soaking up the flavor of the curry spices it takes on a wonderful flavor.

**INGREDIENTS**

*4 tablespoons vegetable oil*
*2–3 tablespoons curry paste*
*8 ounces smoked bean curd, cut into 1-inch cubes*
*8 ounces green beans, cut into 1-inch lengths*
*1 red bell pepper, seeded and cut into fine strips*
*12 ounces dried rice vermicelli, soaked in warm water until soft*
*1 tablespoon soy sauce*
*salt and ground black pepper*
*2 scallions, finely sliced, 2 red chiles, seeded and chopped, and 1 lime, cut into wedges, to garnish*

**Serves 4**

1 Heat half the oil in a wok or large frying pan. Add the curry paste and stir-fry for a few minutes, then add the bean curd and continue to fry until golden brown. Using a slotted spoon remove the cubes from the pan and set aside until required.

2 Add the remaining oil to the wok or pan. When hot, add the green beans and red bell pepper. Stir-fry until the vegetables are cooked. You may need to moisten them with a little water.

3 Drain the noodles and add them to the wok or frying pan. Stir-fry until the noodles are heated through making sure they do not stick to the pan, then return the curried bean curd to the wok. Season with soy sauce, salt and pepper.

4 Transfer the mixture to a serving dish. Sprinkle with the scallions and chiles and serve the lime wedges on the side for squeezing over.

# Somen Noodles with Zucchini

A COLORFUL DISH with lots of flavor. Pumpkin or patty pan squashes can be used as an alternative to zucchini.

**INGREDIENTS**

*2 yellow zucchini*
*2 green zucchini*
*4 tablespoons pine nuts*
*4 tablespoons extra virgin olive oil*
*2 shallots, finely chopped*
*2 garlic cloves, finely chopped*
*2 tablespoons capers, rinsed*
*4 sun-dried tomatoes in oil, drained and cut into strips*
*11 ounces dried somen noodles*
*4 tablespoons chopped mixed herbs (such as chives, thyme and tarragon)*
*grated rind of 1 lemon*
*2 ounces Parmesan cheese, finely grated*
*salt and ground black pepper*
**Serves 4**

1 Slice the zucchini diagonally into rounds the same thickness as the noodles. Cut the zucchini slices into short thin sticks. Toast the pine nuts in an ungreased frying pan over medium heat until golden in color.

2 Heat half the oil in a large frying pan. Add the shallots and garlic and fry until fragrant. Push the shallot mixture to one side of the pan, add the remaining oil and, when hot, stir-fry the zucchini until soft.

3 Stir thoroughly to incorporate the shallot mixture and add the capers, sun-dried tomatoes and pine nuts. Remove the pan from the heat.

4 Cook the noodles in a large saucepan of salted boiling water until just tender, following the directions on the package. Drain well and toss into the zucchini mixture, adding the herbs, lemon rind and Parmesan, with salt and pepper to taste. Serve immediately.

# Noodles Primavera

**INGREDIENTS**

*8 ounces dried rice noodles*
*4 ounces broccoli flowerets*
*1 carrot, finely sliced*
*8 ounces asparagus, cut into 2-inch lengths*
*1 red or yellow bell pepper, seeded and cut into strips*
*2 ounces baby corn*
*2 ounces snow peas, topped and tailed*
*3 tablespoons olive oil*
*1 tablespoon chopped fresh ginger root*
*2 garlic cloves, chopped*
*2 scallions, finely chopped*
*1 pound tomatoes, chopped*
*1 bunch arugula leaves*
*soy sauce, to taste*
*salt and freshly ground black pepper*
**Serves 4**

1 Soak the noodles in hot water for about 30 minutes until soft. Drain.

2 Blanch the broccoli flowerets, sliced carrot, asparagus, bell pepper strips, baby corn and snow peas separately in boiling, salted water. Drain them through a colander, rinse under cold water, then drain again and set aside.

3 Heat the olive oil in a frying pan. Add the ginger, garlic and scallions. Stir-fry for 30 seconds, then add the tomatoes and stir-fry for 2–3 minutes.

4 Add the noodles and stir-fry for 3 minutes. Toss in the blanched vegetables and arugula leaves. Season with soy sauce, salt and pepper and cook until the vegetables are tender.

# Fried Wontons

THESE DELICIOUS wontons have a vegetarian filling.

**INGREDIENTS**

*30 wonton skins*
*1 egg, beaten*
*oil for deep frying*

***For the filling***

*2 teaspoons vegetable oil*
*1 tablespoon grated fresh ginger root*
*2 garlic cloves, finely chopped*
*8 ounces firm bean curd*
*6 scallions, finely chopped*
*2 teaspoons sesame oil*
*1 tablespoon soy sauce*
*salt and ground black pepper*

***For the dipping sauce***

*2 tablespoons soy sauce*
*1 tablespoon sesame oil*
*1 tablespoon rice vinegar*
*½ teaspoon chili oil*
*½ teaspoon honey*
*2 tablespoons water*

**Makes 30**

1 Line a large baking sheet with waxed paper or sprinkle lightly with flour, then set aside. To make the filling, heat the oil in a frying pan. Add the ginger root and garlic cloves and fry for 30 seconds. Crumble in the bean curd and continue to stir-fry for a few minutes.

2 Add the scallions, sesame oil and soy sauce to the pan. Stir well and taste for seasoning. Remove from the heat and set aside to cool.

3 Make the dipping sauce by combining all the ingredients in a separate bowl and mixing to combine well.

4 Place a wonton skin on a board in a diamond position. Brush the edges lightly with beaten egg. Spoon 1 teaspoon of the filling on the center of each skin.

5 Pull the top corner down to the bottom corner, folding the skin over the filling to make a triangle. Press firmly to seal. Place on the prepared baking sheet as you go. Repeat with the rest of the wonton skins.

6 Heat the oil in a deep fryer or large saucepan. Carefully drop in the wontons, a few at a time, and cook for a few minutes until golden brown all over. Drain on paper towels, then serve immediately with the dipping sauce to the side.

# Vegetarian Fried Noodles

WHEN MAKING this dish for non-vegetarians, add a piece of balachan (compressed shrimp paste). A small chunk about the size of a stock cube, mashed with the chile paste, will add a deliciously rich, aromatic flavor.

**INGREDIENTS**

*2 eggs*
*1 teaspoon chili powder*
*1 teaspoon turmeric*
*4 tablespoons vegetable oil*
*1 large onion, finely sliced*
*2 red chiles, seeded and finely sliced*
*1 tablespoon soy sauce*
*2 large cooked potatoes, cut into small cubes*
*6 pieces fried bean curd, sliced*
*8 ounces bean sprouts*
*4 ounces green beans, blanched*
*12 ounces fresh thick egg noodles*
*salt and ground black pepper*
*sliced scallions, to garnish*

**Serves 4**

1 Beat the eggs lightly, then strain them into a bowl. Heat a lightly greased omelet pan. Pour in half of the egg to cover the base of the pan thinly. When the egg is just set, turn the omelet over and fry the other side briefly. Slide on to a plate, blot with paper towel, roll up and cut into narrow strips. Make a second omelet in the same way and slice. Set the omelet strips aside for the garnish.

**COOK'S TIP**

*Always be very careful when handling chiles. Keep your hands away from your eyes as chiles will sting them. Wash your hands thoroughly after touching them.*

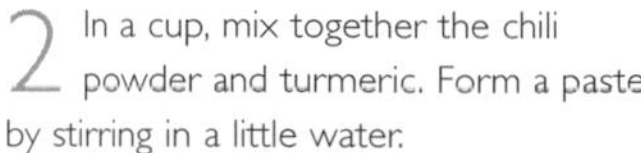

2 In a cup, mix together the chili powder and turmeric. Form a paste by stirring in a little water.

3 Heat the oil in a wok or large frying pan. Fry the onion until soft. Reduce the heat and add the chile paste, sliced chiles and soy sauce. Fry for 2–3 minutes.

4 Add the potatoes and fry for about 2 minutes, mixing well to combine. Add the bean curd, then the bean sprouts, green beans and noodles.

5 Gently stir-fry until the noodles are evenly coated and heated through. Take care not to break up the potatoes or the bean curd. Season with salt and pepper. Serve hot, garnished with the reserved omelet strips and scallion slices.

# Singapore Rice Vermicelli

SIMPLE AND SPEEDILY prepared, this lightly curried rice noodle dish is a full meal in a bowl.

**INGREDIENTS**

*2 cups dried rice vermicelli*
*1 tablespoon vegetable oil*
*1 egg, lightly beaten*
*2 garlic cloves, finely chopped*
*1 large fresh red or green chile, seeded and finely chopped*
*1 tablespoon medium curry powder*
*1 red bell pepper, seeded and thinly sliced*
*1 green bell pepper, seeded and thinly sliced*
*1 carrot, cut into short thin sticks*
*¼ teaspoon salt*
*4 tablespoons vegetable stock*
*4 ounces cooked shelled shrimp, thawed if frozen*
*3 ounces lean cooked ham, cut into ½-inch cubes*
*1 tablespoon light soy sauce*

**Serves 4**

1 Soak the rice vermicelli in a bowl of boiling water for 4 minutes, or according to the instructions on the package, then drain thoroughly and set aside until required.

2 Heat 1 teaspoon of the oil in a non-stick frying pan or wok. Add the egg and scramble until set. Remove with a slotted spoon and set aside. Clean the pan.

3 Heat the remaining oil in the clean pan. Stir-fry the garlic and chile for a few seconds, then stir in the curry powder. Cook for 1 minute, stirring, then stir in the peppers, carrot sticks, salt and stock.

4 Bring to a boil. Add the shrimp, ham, scrambled egg, rice vermicelli and soy sauce. Mix well. Cook, stirring, until all the liquid has been absorbed and the mixture is hot. Serve immediately.

# Noodles with Shrimp in Lemon Sauce

**INGREDIENTS**

*2 packages dried egg noodles*
*1 tablespoon sunflower oil*
*2 celery stalks, cut into short thin sticks*
*2 garlic cloves, crushed*
*4 scallions, sliced*
*2 carrots, cut into short thin sticks*
*3-inch piece cucumber, cut into short thin sticks*
*4 ounces shrimp in the shells*
*1 lemon*
*2 tablespoons lemon juice*
*1 teaspoon cornstarch*
*4–5 tablespoons fish stock*
*1 cup shelled shrimp*
*salt and ground black pepper*
*a few sprigs dill weed, to garnish*

**Serves 4**

1 Put the noodles in boiling water and let soak according to the instructions on the package. Meanwhile, heat the oil in a pan and stir-fry the celery, garlic, scallions and carrots for 2–3 minutes.

2 Add the cucumber and whole shrimp and cook for about 2–3 minutes. Meanwhile, peel the rind from the lemon and cut into long thin shreds. Place the rind in boiling water for 1 minute then drain.

3 Blend the lemon juice with the cornstarch and stock and add to the rest of the ingredients in the pan. Bring gently to a boil, stirring, and cook for 1 minute.

4 Stir in the shelled shrimp, the drained lemon rind and seasoning to taste. Drain the noodles and serve with the shrimp, garnished with dill.

### Cook's Tip

*These noodles can be deep-fried. Cook as above; drain on paper towels. Deep-fry in batches until golden and crisp.*

# Fried Loopy Noodles

SERVE THIS as a side dish or as a crunchy snack at any time. It will keep for 4–5 days in an airtight container.

**INGREDIENTS**

*6 ounces flat ribbon noodles*
*oil for deep frying*
**Makes 4–6 coils**

1 Cook the noodles in a large saucepan of boiling water until just tender, according to the instructions on the package. Rinse under cold water, drain and dry on paper towels.

2 Heat the oil for deep frying to hazing point. Using a spoon and fork, form the noodles into coils.

3 Carefully lower the noodle coils into the hot oil. Deep fry for about 3–4 minutes or until crisp and golden brown. Drain thoroughly on paper towels. Pile on to a dish if serving immediately or cool and store as suggested above left.

# Crisp Pork Meatballs Laced with Noodles

IT MAY SEEM time consuming to make these meatballs, but you will find it easier if you moisten your hands with water to prevent the meat sticking; do not overwork the meat or it will be dense and rubbery.

**INGREDIENTS**

*14 ounces ground pork*
*2 garlic cloves, finely chopped*
*2 tablespoons chopped cilantro or parsley*
*1 tablespoon oyster sauce*
*2 tablespoons fresh bread crumbs*
*1 egg, beaten*
*6 ounces fresh thin egg noodles*
*salt and ground black pepper*
*oil for deep frying*
*cilantro leaves, to garnish*
*spinach leaves and chile sauce or tomato sauce, to serve*
**Serves 4**

1 In a large bowl, mix together the pork, garlic, cilantro or parsley, oyster sauce, bread crumbs and egg. Season with salt and pepper.

2 Knead the pork mixture until sticky, then form it into balls, each about the size of a walnut.

3 Blanch the noodles in a saucepan of boiling water for 2–3 minutes. Drain through a colander, rinse under cold running water and drain well.

4 With a meatball in one hand and 3–5 strands of noodles in the other, wrap the noodles securely around the meatball in a criss-cross pattern. Coat the other meatballs in the same way.

5 Deep fry the meatballs in batches in hot oil until golden brown and cooked through. As each batch browns, remove with a slotted spoon and drain well on paper towels. Garnish with cilantro leaves and serve hot on a bed of spinach leaves with chile or tomato sauce.

# Stir-fried Tofu and Bean Sprouts with Noodles

THIS IS A SATISFYING DISH, which is both tasty and easy to make.

**INGREDIENTS**

*8 ounces firm tofu*
*groundnut oil, for deep frying*
*½ cup dried egg noodles*
*1 tablespoon sesame oil*
*1 teaspoon cornstarch*
*2 teaspoons dark soy sauce*
*2 tablespoons Chinese rice wine*
*1 teaspoon sugar*
*6–8 scallions, cut diagonally into 1-inch lengths*
*3 garlic cloves, sliced*
*1 fresh green chile, seeded and sliced*
*1 cup Napa cabbage leaves, coarsely shredded*
*¼ cup bean sprouts*
*½ cup cashew nuts, toasted*

**Serves 4**

1 Drain the tofu and pat dry with paper towel. Cut the tofu into 1-inch cubes. Half-fill a wok with groundnut oil and heat to hazing point. Deep-fry the tofu in batches for 1–2 minutes until golden and crisp. Drain on paper towel. Carefully pour all but 2 tablespoons of the oil from the wok.

2 Cook the noodles according to the instructions on the package. Rinse under cold water and drain. Toss in 2 teaspoons of the sesame oil and set aside. In a bowl, blend together the cornflour, soy sauce, rice wine, sugar and remaining sesame oil.

3 Reheat the groundnut oil remaining in the pan and, when hot, add the scallions, garlic, chile, Napa cabbage and bean sprouts. Stir-fry for 1–2 minutes.

4 Add the tofu, noodles and sauce. Cook, stirring, for about 1 minute. Serve with cashew nuts.

# Fried Cellophane Noodles

**INGREDIENTS**

*6 ounces dried cellophane noodles*
*3 tablespoons vegetable oil*
*3 garlic cloves, finely chopped*
*4 ounces cooked shrimp, shelled*
*2 lap cheong, rinsed, drained and finely diced*
*2 eggs*
*2 celery stalks, including leaves, diced*
*4 ounces beansprouts*
*4 ounces spinach, cut into large pieces*
*2 scallions, chopped*
*1–2 tablespoons fish sauce*
*1 teaspoon sesame oil*
*1 tablespoon sesame seeds, toasted, to garnish*

**Serves 4**

1 Soak the cellophane noodles in hot water for about 10 minutes. Drain and cut the noodles into 4-inch lengths.

2 Heat the oil in a wok, add the garlic and fry until golden brown. Add the shrimp and lap cheong; stir-fry for 2–3 minutes. Stir in the noodles and fry for 2 minutes more.

3 Make a well in the center of the shrimp mixture, break in the eggs and slowly stir them until they are creamy and just set.

**COOK'S TIP**

*This is a very versatile dish. You can vary the vegetables if you wish and substitute cooked ham, chorizo or salami for the lap cheong.*

4 Stir in the celery, bean sprouts, spinach and scallions. Season with fish sauce and stir in the sesame oil. Continue to stir-fry until all the ingredients are cooked, mixing well.

5 Transfer the ingredients to a serving dish. Sprinkle with sesame seeds to garnish and serve immediately.

# Crispy Noodles with Mixed Vegetables

In this dish, vermicelli rice noodles are deep fried until crisp, then tossed into a colorful selection of stir-fried vegetables.

**INGREDIENTS**

*2 large carrots*
*2 zucchini*
*4 scallions*
*4 ounces yard-long beans or green beans*
*1 cup dried vermicelli rice noodles or cellophane noodles, soaked in warm water until soft*
*groundnut oil, for deep frying*
*1-inch piece fresh ginger root, cut into shreds*
*1 fresh red chile, sliced*
*1 cup fresh shiitake or white mushrooms, thickly sliced*
*few Napa cabbage leaves, coarsely shredded*
*⅓ cup bean sprouts*
*2 tablespoons light soy sauce*
*2 tablespoons Chinese rice wine*
*1 teaspoon sugar*
*2 tablespoons fresh cilantro, roughly torn*

**Serves 3–4**

**VARIATION**

*You can use any selection of vegetables for this dish. Alternatives that work well include bok choy, snow peas, bell peppers and baby corn.*

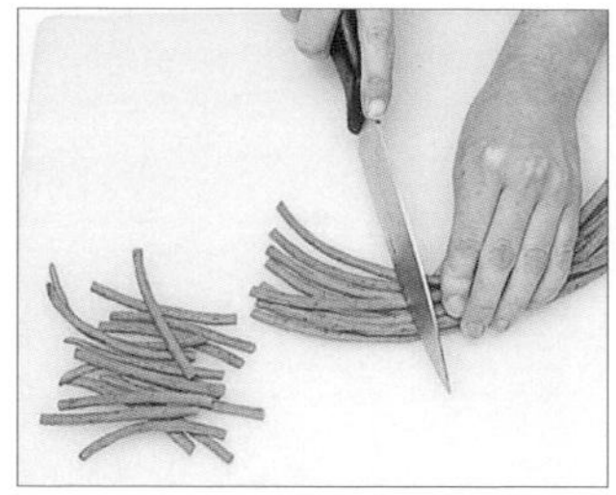

1 Cut the carrots and zucchini into fine sticks. Shred the scallions into similar-size pieces. Trim the beans. If using yard-long beans, cut them into short lengths.

2 Break the noodles into lengths of about 3 inches. Half-fill a wok with oil and heat it to hazing point. Deep fry the raw noodles, a handful at a time, for 1–2 minutes until puffed and crispy. Drain on paper towels. Carefully pour off all but 2 tablespoons of the oil.

3 Reheat the oil and add the beans and stir-fry for 2–3 minutes. Add the ginger, red chile, mushrooms, carrots and zucchini and stir-fry.

4 Add the Napa cabbage, beansprouts and scallions. Stir-fry for 1 minute, then add the soy sauce, rice wine and sugar. Cook, stirring, for about 30 seconds.

5 Add the noodles and cilantro and toss to mix, taking care not to crush the noodles too much. Serve immediately, piled up on a plate.

**COOK'S TIP**

*If a milder flavor is preferred, remove the seeds from the chile.*

# Fried Monkfish with Rice Noodles

THESE MARINATED medallions of fish are coated in rice vermicelli and deep fried—they taste as good as they look.

**INGREDIENTS**

*1 pound monkfish*
*1 teaspoon grated fresh ginger root*
*1 garlic clove, finely chopped*
*2 tablespoons soy sauce*
*6 ounces dried rice vermicelli*
*2 ounces cornstarch*
*2 eggs, beaten*
*oil for deep frying*
*salt and ground black pepper*
*banana leaves, to serve (optional)*

***For the dipping sauce***
*2 tablespoons soy sauce*
*2 tablespoons rice vinegar*
*1 tablespoon sugar*
*2 red chiles, thinly sliced*
*1 scallion, thinly sliced*
**Serves 4**

1 Trim the monkfish and cut into 1-inch thick medallions. Place in a dish and add the ginger, garlic and soy sauce. Mix lightly and let marinate for 10 minutes.

2 Meanwhile, make the dipping sauce. Combine the soy sauce, vinegar and sugar in a small saucepan. Bring to a boil. Add salt and pepper to taste. Remove from the heat, add the chiles and scallion and set aside until required.

3 Using kitchen scissors, cut the noodles into 1½-inch lengths. Spread them out in a shallow bowl.

4 Coat the fish medallions in cornstarch, dip in beaten egg and cover with noodles, pressing them onto the fish so that they stick.

5 Deep fry the coated fish in hot oil, 2–3 pieces at a time, until the noodle coating is fluffy, crisp and light golden brown. Drain and serve hot on banana leaves, if you like, accompanied by the dipping sauce.

# Rice Noodles with Beef and Black Beans

THIS IS AN EXCELLENT combination—beef with a chile sauce tossed with silky smooth rice noodles.

**INGREDIENTS**

*1 pound fresh rice noodles*
*4 tablespoons vegetable oil*
*1 onion, finely sliced*
*2 garlic cloves, finely chopped*
*2 slices fresh ginger root, finely chopped*
*8 ounces mixed bell peppers, seeded and cut into strips*
*12 ounces rump steak, finely sliced against the grain*
*3 tablespoons fermented black beans, rinsed in warm water, drained and chopped*
*2 tablespoons soy sauce*
*2 tablespoons oyster sauce*
*1 tablespoon chili black bean sauce*
*1 tablespoon cornstarch*
*½ cup stock or water*
*2 scallions, finely chopped, and 2 red chiles, seeded and finely sliced, to garnish*

**Serves 4**

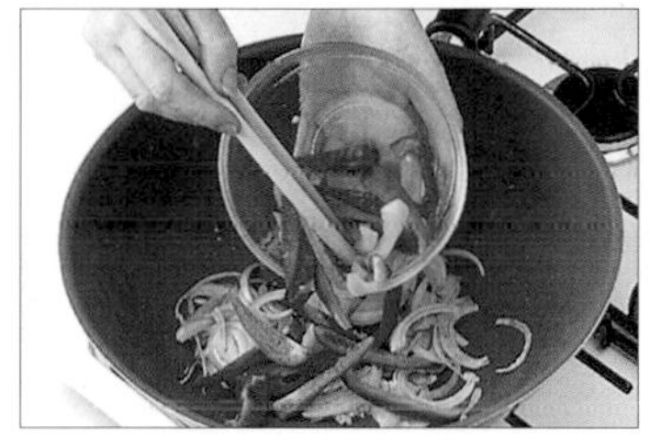

1 Rinse the noodles under hot water; drain well. Heat half the oil in a wok or large frying pan, swirling it around. Add the onion, garlic, ginger and mixed bell pepper strips. Stir-fry for 3–5 minutes, then remove with a slotted spoon and keep hot.

2 Add the remaining oil to the wok. When hot, add the sliced beef and fermented black beans and stir-fry over a high heat for 5 minutes or until cooked.

3 In a small bowl, blend the soy sauce, oyster sauce and chili black bean sauce with the cornstarch and stock or water until smooth. Add the mixture to the wok, then return the onion mixture to the wok and cook, stirring, for 1 minute.

4 Add the noodles and mix lightly. Stir over medium heat until the noodles are heated through. Adjust the seasoning if necessary. Serve immediately, garnished with the chopped scallions and chiles.

# Spicy Beef

THIS COLORFUL and healthy dish is an excellent choice for a quick and easy meal.

**INGREDIENTS**

*1 tablespoon oil*
*4 cups ground beef*
*1-inch piece fresh ginger root, sliced*
*1 teaspoon Chinese five-spice powder*
*1 red chile, sliced*
*2oz snow peas*
*1 red bell pepper, seeded and chopped*
*1 carrot, sliced*
*4 ounces bean sprouts*
*1 tablespoon sesame oil*
*cooked egg noodles, to serve*
**Serves 4**

1 Heat the oil in a wok until it is almost smoking. Add the ground beef and cook for about 3 minutes, stirring all the time.

2 Add the ginger, Chinese five-spice powder and chile. Cook for another 1 minute.

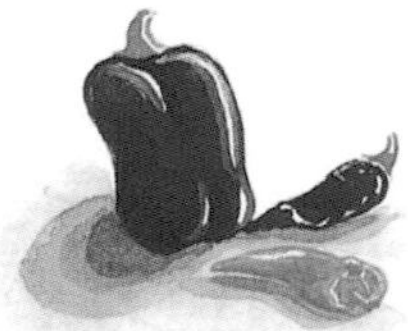

3 Add the snow peas, the seeded and chopped red bell pepper and sliced carrot and cook for a further 3 minutes, stirring the mixture continuously.

4 Add the bean sprouts and sesame oil and cook for a final 2 minutes. Serve immediately with the cooked Chinese egg noodles.

# Thai Fried Noodles

AN AMAZING ARRAY of tastes and textures make up this dish.

**INGREDIENTS**

*8 ounces dried thread egg noodles*
*4 tablespoons vegetable oil*
*2 garlic cloves, finely chopped*
*6 ounces pork tenderloin, sliced into thin strips*
*1 skinless boneless chicken breast, about 6 ounces, sliced into thin strips*
*1 cup cooked shelled shrimps (rinsed if canned)*
*3 tablespoons lime or lemon juice*
*3 tablespoons fish sauce*
*2 tablespoons brown sugar*
*2 eggs, beaten*
*½ red chile, seeded and finely chopped*
*¼ cup bean sprouts*
*4 tablespoons roasted peanuts, chopped*
*3 scallions, cut into 2-inch lengths and shredded*
*3 tablespoons chopped fresh cilantro*

**Serves 4**

1 Place the noodles in a large pan of boiling water and let stand for about 5 minutes.

2 Meanwhile, heat 3 tablespoons of the oil in a wok or large frying pan, add the garlic and cook for 30 seconds. Add the pork and chicken and stir-fry over high heat until lightly browned all over, then add the shrimp and stir-fry for a further 2 minutes.

3 Add the lime or lemon juice, fish sauce and sugar, and stir fry until the sugar has dissolved.

4 Drain the noodles and add to the pan with the remaining 1 tablespoon oil. Toss all the ingredients together to coat.

5 Pour in the beaten eggs. Stir-fry until almost set, then add the chile and bean sprouts. Divide the peanuts, scallions and cilantro leaves into two and add half to the pan. Stir-fry for 2 minutes.

6 Turn the noodle mixture onto a serving platter. Sprinkle on the remaining peanuts, scallions and cilantro and serve the noodles immediately.

# Stuffed Cabbage Parcels

SERVED WITH rice, these attractive, tied parcels make a tasty meal.

**INGREDIENTS**

*4 dried Chinese mushrooms, soaked in hot water until soft*
*2 ounces dried cellophane noodles, soaked in hot water until soft*
*1 pound ground pork*
*4 scallions, finely chopped*
*2 garlic cloves, finely chopped*
*2 tablespoons fish sauce*
*12 large outer green cabbage leaves*
*4 scallions*
*2 tablespoons vegetable oil*
*1 small onion, finely chopped*
*2 garlic cloves, crushed*
*1 can (14 ounces) plum tomatoes*
*pinch of sugar*
*salt and ground black pepper*

**Serves 4**

1 Drain the mushrooms, remove and discard the stems and coarsely chop the caps. Put them in a bowl.

2 Drain the noodles and cut them into short lengths. Add the noodles to the mushrooms with the pork, scallions and garlic. Season with the fish sauce and add pepper to taste.

3 Cut off the tough stem from each cabbage leaf. Blanch the leaves a few at a time in a saucepan of salted boiling water for about 1 minute. Remove the leaves from the pan and refresh under cold water. Drain and dry on paper towels. Add the scallions to the boiling water and blanch in the same fashion. Drain well.

4 Fill one of the cabbage leaves with a generous spoonful of the pork filling. Roll up the leaf sufficiently to enclose the filling, then tuck in the sides and continue rolling to make a tight parcel. Make more parcels in the same way.

5 Split each scallion lengthwise into three strands by cutting through the bulb and tearing upwards. Tie each cabbage parcel with a length of scallion.

6 Heat the oil in a large frying pan with lid or a flameproof casserole. Add the onion and garlic and fry for 2 minutes or until the onions are soft.

7 Pour the plum tomatoes and their juice into a bowl. Mash with a fork, then stir them into the onion mixture. Season with salt, pepper and a pinch of sugar, then bring to simmering point. Add the cabbage parcels. Cover and cook gently for 20–25 minutes or until the filling is cooked. If at any time the sauce looks a little dry, add some water or stock. Taste the sauce for seasoning and serve immediately.

# Pork Satay with Crisp Noodle Cake

SATAY ARE SKEWERS of seasoned meat or seafood, usually cooked over a charcoal fire and served with a spicy sauce.

**INGREDIENTS**

*1 pound lean pork*
*3 garlic cloves, finely chopped*
*1 tablespoon Thai curry powder*
*1 teaspoon ground cumin*
*1 teaspoon sugar*
*1 tablespoon fish sauce*
*6 tablespoons vegetable oil*
*12 ounces fresh or dried noodles*
*cilantro leaves, to garnish*

***For the satay sauce***

*2 tablespoons vegetable oil*
*2 garlic cloves, finely chopped*
*1 small onion, finely chopped*
*½ teaspoon hot chili powder*
*1 teaspoon Thai curry powder*
*8 fluid ounces coconut milk*
*1 tablespoon fish sauce*
*2 tablespoons sugar*
*juice of ½ lemon*
*5½ ounces crunchy peanut butter*

**Serves 4**

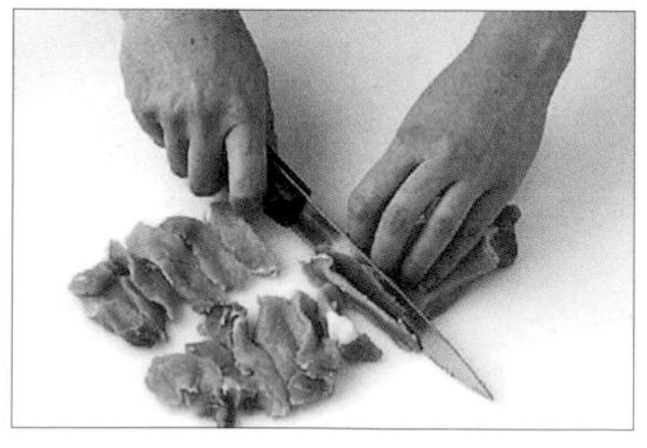

1 Soak eight 8-inch bamboo skewers in cold water to prevent them from catching fire on the barbecue. Cut the pork into thin 2-inch long strips.

2 Mix the garlic, curry powder, cumin, sugar and fish sauce in a bowl. Stir in about 2 tablespoons of the vegetable oil. Add the meat to the bowl, toss to coat and let marinate in a cool place for at least 2 hours.

3 Cook the noodles in a large saucepan of boiling water until just tender according to the instructions on the package. Drain.

4 Make the satay sauce. Heat the oil in a saucepan and fry the garlic and onion with the chili powder and curry powder for 2–3 minutes. Stir in the coconut milk, fish sauce, sugar, lemon juice and peanut butter. Mix well. Reduce the heat and cook, stirring frequently, for about 20 minutes or until the sauce thickens. Be careful not to let the sauce stick to the bottom of the pan or it will burn.

5 Heat about 1 tablespoon of the remaining vegetable oil in a frying pan. Spread the noodles evenly over the pan and fry for 4–5 minutes until crisp and golden. Turn the noodle cake over carefully and cook the other side until crisp. Keep hot.

6 Drain the meat and thread it snugly onto the drained skewers. Cook on a barbecue or under a hot broiler for about 8–10 minutes, turning occasionally and brushing with oil. Serve with wedges of noodle cake and the satay sauce.

# Mixed Rice Noodles

A DELICIOUS NOODLE DISH made extra special by adding avocado and garnishing with shrimp.

**INGREDIENTS**

*1 tablespoon sunflower oil*
*1-inch piece fresh ginger root, peeled and grated*
*2 garlic cloves, crushed*
*3 tablespoons dark soy sauce*
*⅔ cup boiling water*
*2 cups peas, thawed if frozen*
*1 pound dried rice noodles, soaked in hot water until soft*
*1 pound fresh spinach, coarse stalks removed*
*2 tablespoons smooth peanut butter*
*2 tablespoons tahini paste*
*⅔ cup milk*
*1 ripe avocado, peeled and pitted*
*roasted peanuts and shelled shrimp, to garnish*

**Serves 4**

1 Heat a wok, then add the oil. When the oil is hot, stir-fry the ginger and garlic for 30 seconds. Add 1 tablespoon of the soy sauce and the boiling water.

2 Add the peas and noodles, then cook for 3 minutes. Stir in the spinach. Remove the vegetables and noodles, drain well and keep warm.

3 Stir the smooth peanut butter, remaining soy sauce, tahini paste and milk together in the wok, and simmer for 1 minute.

4 Add the vegetables and noodles, slice in the avocado and toss together. Serve piled on individual plates. Spoon some sauce over each portion and garnish with roasted peanuts and shelled shrimp.

# Chicken Curry with Rice Vermicelli

LEMONGRASS gives this Southeast Asian curry a wonderful lemony flavor and aromatic fragrance.

**INGREDIENTS**

*1 chicken, about 3–3½ pounds*
*8 ounces sweet potatoes*
*4 tablespoons vegetable oil*
*1 onion, finely sliced*
*3 garlic cloves, crushed*
*2–3 tablespoons Thai curry powder*
*1 teaspoon sugar*
*2 teaspoons fish sauce*
*2½ cups coconut milk*
*1 lemongrass stalk, cut in half*
*12 ounces dried rice vermicelli, soaked in hot water until soft*
*1 lemon, cut into wedges, to serve*

***For the garnish***
*4 ounces bean sprouts*
*2 scallions, finely sliced diagonally*
*2 red chiles, seeded and finely sliced*
*8–10 mint leaves*
**Serves 4**

1 Skin the chicken. Cut the meat into small pieces and set aside. Peel the sweet potatoes and cut them into large chunks, the size of the chicken pieces.

2 Heat half the oil in a large heavy saucepan. Add the onion and garlic and fry until the onion softens.

3 Add the chicken pieces and stir-fry until they change color. Stir in the curry powder. Season with salt and sugar and mix thoroughly, then stir in the fish sauce.

4 Pour in the coconut milk and add the lemongrass. Stir and cook over low heat for 15 minutes.

5 Meanwhile, heat the remaining oil in a large frying pan. Fry the sweet potatoes until lightly golden. Using a slotted spoon, add them to the chicken. Cook for 10–15 minutes more, or until both the chicken and sweet potatoes are tender.

6 Drain the rice vermicelli and cook in a pan of boiling water for 3–5 minutes. Drain well. Place in shallow bowls, with the chicken curry. Garnish with bean sprouts, scallions, chiles and mint leaves and serve with lemon wedges.

# Braised Noodles with Hoisin Lamb

IN CHINA, the egg symbolizes continuity and fertility so it is an ingredient frequently included in birthday dishes.

**INGREDIENTS**

*12 ounces thick egg noodles*
*2¼ pounds lean neck of lamb*
*2 tablespoons vegetable oil*
*4 ounces fine green beans, topped and tailed, and blanched*
*salt and ground black pepper*
*2 hard-cooked eggs, halved, and 2 scallions, finely chopped, to garnish*

***For the marinade***

*2 garlic cloves, crushed*
*2 teaspoons grated fresh ginger root*
*2 tablespoons soy sauce*
*2 tablespoons rice wine*
*1–2 dried red chiles*
*2 tablespoons vegetable oil*

***For the sauce***

*1 tablespoon cornstarch*
*2 tablespoons soy sauce*
*2 tablespoons rice wine*
*grated rind and juice of ½ orange*
*1 tablespoon hoisin sauce*
*1 tablespoon wine vinegar*
*1 teaspoon brown sugar*

**Serves 4**

1 Bring a large saucepan of water to a boil. Add the noodles and cook for 2 minutes only. Drain, rinse under cold water and drain again. Set aside.

2 Cut the lamb into 2-inch thick medallions. Mix the ingredients for the marinade in a shallow dish. Add the lamb and let marinate for at least 4 hours.

3 Heat the oil in a heavy saucepan or flameproof casserole. Fry the lamb for 5 minutes until browned. Add just enough water to cover the meat. Bring to a boil, skim, then reduce the heat and simmer for 40 minutes or until the meat is tender, adding more water as necessary.

4 Make the sauce. Blend the cornstarch with the remaining ingredients in a bowl. Stir into the lamb and mix well without breaking up the meat.

5 Add the noodles to the lamb with the beans. Simmer gently until both the noodles and the beans are cooked. Add salt and pepper to taste. Divide the noodles among four large bowls, garnish each portion with half a hard-cooked egg, sprinkle with scallions and serve.

# Lemongrass Shrimp on Crisp Noodle Cake

**INGREDIENTS**

*11 ounces thin egg noodles*
*4 tablespoons vegetable oil*
*1¼ pounds medium raw jumbo shrimp, peeled and deveined*
*½ teaspoon ground coriander*
*1 tablespoon ground turmeric*
*2 garlic cloves, finely chopped*
*2 slices fresh ginger root, finely chopped*
*2 lemongrass stems, finely chopped*
*2 shallots, finely chopped*
*1 tablespoon tomato paste*
*1 cup coconut cream*
*1–2 tablespoons fresh lime juice*
*1–2 tablespoons fish sauce*
*4–6 kaffir lime leaves (optional)*
*1 cucumber, peeled, seeded and cut into 2-inch batons*
*1 tomato, seeded and cut into strips*
*2 red chiles, seeded and finely sliced*
*salt and ground black pepper*
*2 scallions, finely sliced, and a few cilantro sprigs, to garnish*

**Serves 4**

1 Cook the egg noodles in a saucepan of boiling water until just tender according to the instructions on the package. Drain, rinse under cold running water and drain well.

2 Heat 1 tablespoon of the oil in a large frying pan. Add the noodles, distributing them evenly, and fry for 4–5 minutes until crisp and golden. Turn the noodle cake over and fry the other side. Alternatively, make four individual cakes.

3 In a bowl, toss the shrimp with the ground coriander, turmeric, garlic, ginger and lemongrass. Add salt and pepper to taste.

4 Heat the remaining oil in a large frying pan. Add the shallots, fry for 1 minute, then add the shrimp and fry for 2 minutes. Remove the shrimp with a slotted spoon.

5 Stir the tomato paste and coconut cream into the mixture remaining in the pan. Stir in lime juice to taste and season with the fish sauce. Bring the sauce to a simmer, return the shrimp to the sauce, then add the kaffir lime leaves, if using, and the cucumber. Simmer gently until the shrimp are cooked and the sauce is reduced to a nice coating consistency.

6 Add the tomato, stir until just warmed through, then add the chiles. Serve on top of the crisp noodle cake(s), garnished with sliced scallions and fresh cilantro sprigs.

# Stir-fried Sweet and Sour Chicken

THERE ARE FEW cookery concepts that are better suited to today's busy lifestyle than the all-in-one stir-fry. This one has a wonderful South-east Asian influence.

**INGREDIENTS**

*10 ounces fresh or dried egg noodles*
*2 tablespoons vegetable oil*
*3 scallions, chopped*
*1 garlic clove, crushed*
*1-inch piece fresh ginger root, peeled and grated*
*1 teaspoon hot paprika*
*1 teaspoon ground coriander*
*3 boneless chicken breasts, sliced*
*1 cup snow peas, topped and tailed*
*4 ounces baby corn, halved*
*8 ounces fresh bean sprouts*
*1 tablespoon cornstarch*
*3 tablespoons soy sauce*
*3 tablespoons lemon juice*
*1 tablespoon sugar*
*3 tablespoons chopped cilantro or scallion tops, to garnish*

**Serves 4**

1 Bring a large saucepan of salted water to a boil. Add the noodles and cook according to the instructions on the package. Drain through a colander, cover and keep warm.

2 Heat the oil in a wok. Add the scallions and cook gently. Mix in the next five ingredients, then stir-fry for about 3–4 minutes. Add the next three ingredients and steam briefly. Add the noodles.

3 Combine the cornstarch, soy sauce, lemon juice and sugar in a small bowl. Add to the wok, stir and simmer briefly to thicken. Serve garnished with chopped cilantro or scallion tops.

# Beef Strips with Orange and Ginger

STIR-FRYING IS ONE of the quickest ways to cook, but you do need to choose tender meat.

**INGREDIENTS**

*1 pound lean beef rump, fillet or sirloin, cut into thin strips*
*finely grated rind and juice of 1 orange*
*1 tablespoon light soy sauce*
*1 teaspoon cornstarch*
*1-inch piece fresh ginger root, finely chopped*
*2 teaspoons sesame oil*
*1 large carrot, cut into thin strips*
*2 scallions, thinly sliced*
*cooked rice noodles*

**Serves 4**

1 Place the beef strips in a bowl and sprinkle the orange rind and juice over. Let marinate for at least 30 minutes.

2 Drain the liquid from the meat and reserve, then mix the meat with the soy sauce, cornstarch and fresh ginger root.

3 Heat the oil in a wok or large frying pan and add the beef. Stir-fry for 1 minute until lightly colored, then add the carrot and stir-fry for a further 2–3 minutes.

4 Stir in the scallions and reserved liquid, then cook, stirring, until boiling and thickened. Serve the beef hot with cooked rice noodles.

# Index